PRINCIPLES OF EUROPEAN COOPERATIVE LAW

PRINCIPLES OF EUROPEAN COOPERATIVE LAW

Principles, Commentaries and National Reports

Gemma Fajardo
Antonio Fici
Hagen Henrÿ
David Hiez
Deolinda Meira
Hans-H. Münkner
Ian Snaith

intersentia
Cambridge – Antwerp – Portland

Intersentia Ltd
Sheraton House | Castle Park
Cambridge | CB3 0AX | United Kingdom
Tel.: +44 1223 370 170 | Fax: +44 1223 370 169
Email: mail@intersentia.co.uk
www.intersentia.com | www.intersentia.co.uk

Distribution for the UK and Ireland:
NBN International
Airport Business Centre, 10 Thornbury Road
Plymouth, PL6 7 PP
United Kingdom
Tel.: +44 1752 202 301 | Fax: +44 1752 202 331
Email: orders@nbninternational.com

Distribution for Europe and all other countries:
Intersentia Publishing nv
Groenstraat 31
2640 Mortsel
Belgium
Tel.: +32 3 680 15 50 | Fax: +32 3 658 71 21
Email: mail@intersentia.be

Distribution for the USA and Canada:
International Specialized Book Services
920 NE 58th Ave. Suite 300
Portland, OR 97213
USA
Tel.: +1 800 944 6190 (toll free) | Fax: +1 503 280 8832
Email: info@isbs.com

Principles of European Cooperative Law. Principles, Commentaries and National Reports

Published with the contribution of The Autonomous Province of Trento (Italy)

Artwork on cover: Wassily Kandinsky, Im Blau © bpk / Kunstsammlung Nordrhein-Westfalen, Düsseldorf / Walter Klein

ISBN 978-1-78068-427-7
D/2017/7849/81
NUR 828

British Library Cataloguing in Publication Data. A catalogue record for this book is available from the British Library.

FOREWORD

The Principles of European Cooperative Law is, in many ways, the culmination of a line of work that started in 2009, when Euricse (the European Research Institute on Cooperative and Social Enterprises) was just established and undertook its first project on comparative analysis of cooperative law in the European Union. Since then, both the current state and the evolution of cooperative law have been key elements of Euricse's research program, which has yielded other important publications on this topic, including, most notably, the *International Handbook of Cooperative Law* in 2013. This line of research devoted particular attention to comparative analysis of the laws that regulate cooperatives in different countries, in Europe as well as in other continents. At Euricse, we are indeed convinced that the quality of the legal framework is one of the most important conditions affecting the degree of success of any institution, including cooperative and social enterprises.

These first studies, carried out by convening and working with a growing international team of legal scholars from various European universities, highlighted the high degree of fragmentation and diversity of cooperative law in different national contexts, and started to investigate the barriers that this fragmentation poses to cooperative development and growth. The research showed that not only are cooperative laws quite different from country to country, but they often also fail to take into account the specificities of cooperative enterprises. Yet, when they do, they can be one of the most powerful tools for unlocking the potential of these enterprises and maximising their contribution to social and economic development.

After the first comparative analyses of the main European countries (and some analysis of countries outside Europe), the research group realised that the difficulty of developing coherent and fairly homogeneous legislation across countries was due in part to the lack of a sufficiently general reflection on the basic tenets of a good cooperative law, regardless of national specificities. In other words, what was lacking was the construction of an ideal set of norms that would define the identity and identify the founding characteristics of cooperative enterprises without limiting their flexibility and ability to function. This was the starting point of the research that led to the results presented in this book.

The work, conducted in partnership with other European universities and research centres, was based on two premises: first, it would consider only European countries, both because they have comparable legal traditions and also in order to help the European Commission and some European countries in their effort to harmonise the different legal frameworks. Second, it would be based on the most general definition of cooperative enterprise, the one developed by the International Cooperative Alliance. The research thus follows the seven cooperative principles codified by the Alliance in 1995.

Thanks to the work of an impressive team of researchers, this book provides an important contribution towards a more unified approach to cooperative law at the European level, and will be of use not only to researchers but also to any nation that might want to update or improve its cooperative legislation. At the same time, much work remains to be done in order to develop a comprehensive framework – one that includes cooperative law as well as regulations pertaining to the other branches of law that also affect cooperatives (such as, for instance, taxation and labour law). At Euricse, we are proud of the results that the group of scholars that have carried out this research has achieved and are very grateful for their work. Moving forward, we will continue to carry out legal research as part of our multidisciplinary approach to the study of cooperative and social enterprises, and to support the analysis of the laws and regulations that define, shape and affect cooperative enterprises throughout Europe and beyond.

Carlo Borzaga
President of Euricse

CONTENTS

LIST OF ABBREVIATIONS

ACI	Alianza Cooperativa Internacional
ADG	Akademie Deutscher Genossenschaften (German Cooperative Academy)
BaFin	Bundesamt für Finanzdienstleistungsaufsicht (Federal Office for Supervision of Financial Services)
Bencom	A society registered to conduct business for the benefit of the community under CBSA 2014
BGB	Bürgerliches Gesetzbuch (German Civil Code)
BVR	Bundesverband der Volksbanken und Raiffeinsenbanken e. V. (German National Federation of Peoples Banks and Raiffeisenbanks)
C(AICE)A 2004	Companies (Audit Inspection and Community Enterprise) Act 2004
C.Com	Código de Comercio (Spanish Code of Commerce)
CA 2006	Companies Act 2006
CASES	Cooperativa António Sérgio para a Economia Social (António Sérgio Cooperative for Social Economy)
CC	Código Civil (Spanish Civil Code)
CCAA	Comunidades Autónomas (Autonomous Communities)
CCBSA	Co-operative and Community Benefit Societies Act 2014 (UK)
CE	Constitución Española (Spanish Constitution)
CIC	Community Interest Company
CLG	Company Limited by Guarantee
CONFAGR	National Confederation of Agricultural Cooperatives
CONFECOOP	Portuguese Confederation Cooperative
CRP	Constituição da República Portuguesa (Portuguese Constitution)
CSC	Código das Sociedades Comerciais (Portuguese Commercial Companies Code)
CSR	Corporate Social Responsibility
DG Bank	Deutsche Genossenschaftsbank AG (German Cooperative Bank, Ltd, Frankfurt)
DGRN	Dirección General de los Registros y del Notariado, del Ministerio de Justicia (Spanish Directorate General of Registers and Notaries, at the Ministry of Justice)

DGRV	Deutscher Genossenschafts- und Raiffeisenverband (German Cooperative and Raiffeisen Federation)
DGV	Deutscher Genossenschaftsverband (German Cooperative Federation)
DRV	Deutscher Raiffeisenverband (German Raiffeisen Federation)
eG	eingetragene Genossenschaft (registered cooperative society)
EU	European Union
EURICSE	European Research Institute on Cooperative and Social Enterprises
FCA	Financial Conduct Authority
FiCA	Finnish Law on Cooperatives (*Osuuskuntalaki*), 14.6.2013/421
FrCA	French Cooperation Act n. 47-1775 of 10 September 1947
FSA	Financial Services Authority registrar from 2001 to 2013
GCA	German Cooperative Act (1889–2006)
GenG	Genossenschaftsgesetz (German Cooperative Societies Act)
GG	Grundgesetz (German Federal Constitution)
GM	General Meeting
HGB	Handelsgesetzbuch (German Commercial Code)
IA 1986	Insolvency Act 1986
ICA	International Co-operative Alliance
ICA P	International Co-operative Alliance's Principles of 1995
ICC	Italian Civil Code of 1942
IFRS	International Financial Reporting Standards
ILO	International Labour Organization
IM	Investor/Non-user Member
IPS	Industrial and Provident Society
LAC	Law on Auditing of accounts, 22/2015 of 20 July
LBES	Lei de Bases da Economia Social (Portuguese Framework law on Social Economy)
LC	Ley de Cooperativas 27/1999 (Spanish Cooperatives Law 1999)
LESFL	Ley 49/2002, de 23 de diciembre, de Régimen fiscal de las entidades sin fines lucrativos y de los incentivos fiscales al mecenazgo (Spanish Law 49/2002 of 23 December 2002 on the fiscal system for non-profit organisations and fiscal incentives for sponsorship)
LFICA	Law 13/2013 of 2 August on Integration of agricultural cooperatives
LGC 1974	Ley General de Cooperativas 52/1974 (Spanish General Law of Cooperatives 1974)
LGC 1987	Ley General de Cooperativas 3/1987 (Spanish General Law of Cooperatives 1987)
LLP	Limited Liability Partnership

LLPA	Limited Liability Partnerships Act 2000
LOA	Ley Orgánica de Asociaciones 1/2002 (Spanish Organic Law of Associations 2002)
LOCM	Ley de Ordenación del Comercio Minorista (Spanish Ordering of Retail Trade Law)
LRFC	Ley de Régimen Fiscal de las Cooperativas 20/1990 of 19 December Spanish (Fiscal System for Cooperatives Law)
LSC	Ley de Sociedades de Capital 1/2010, of 2 July (Spanish Capital-Based Company Law)
Ltd.	private limited company
MitbestG	Mitbestimmungsgesetz (German Co-determination law)
NPO	non-profit organisation
PA	Partnership Act 1890
PCC	Código Cooperativo Português (Portuguese Cooperative Code)
PLC	public limited company
RA	Repertorio Aranzadi (Aranzadi law compendium)
RD	Real Decreto
RD Leg.	Real Decreto Legislativo
REVESCO	Revista de Estudios Cooperativos
RJCAM	Legal Framework of Mutual Agricultural Credit and Cooperative Credit Scheme
ROAC	Official Register of Auditors of Accounts
RRC	RD 136/2002 adopting the Co-operatives Register Regulations.
RRM	Reglamento del Registro Mercantil (Company Register Regulations)
RZ	Randziffer (note)
SA	Sociedad Anónima
SCA	Spanish Cooperatives Act n. 27/1999 of 16 July 1999
SCE	European Cooperative Society
SCE R	Council Regulation (EC) No. 1435/2003 of 22 July 2003 on the Statute for a European Cooperative Society (SCE)
SCEAG	SCE Ausführungsgesetz (Law on the implementation of the SCE Regulation No. 1435/2003 into German law)
SHO	self-help organisation
SN	Sistema de Normalização Contabilística (Portuguese Accounting Normalization System)
SROI	social return on investment
STS	Sentencia del Tribunal Supremo (Spanish Supreme Court Judgement)
TBL	Tripple Bottom Line Approach
TMO	taux moyen de rendement des obligations des sociétés privées

TransPuG	Transparenz- und Publizitätsgesetz (German Transparency and Public Information Law)
UmwG	Umwandlungsgesetz (German Transformation Law)
WGG	Gesetz über die Gemeinnützigkeit im Wohnungswesen (German Law on General Interest in the Field of Housing)
WGZ	Westdeutsche Genossenschafts-Zentralbank eG, Düsseldorf (West German Cooperative Central Bank)
WPO	Wirtschaftsprüferordnung (German Law Regulating the Profession of Chartered Accountant)
WSC	withdrawable share capital
ZfgG	Zeitschrift für das gesamte Genossenschaftswesen (Journal for All Cooperative Organisations)

INTRODUCTION

David Hiez

1. THE PECOL PROJECT AND ITS CONTEXT

Publishing sets of European law principles has become almost commonplace in the past twenty years, with each new set reflecting a different and new area of European private or commercial law.[1] Thus, it is no surprise that a group of European scholars, who generally focus on the law of cooperatives, decided to enter the fray. The Group (defined below) undertook, over a four-year period, the necessary research and made the necessary comparisons to compile just such a set of European principles for their distinct body of law (the 'PECOL Project').

1 From as far back as 1982, and encouraged over the years by resolutions of the European Parliament, various European legal scholars have been coming together to create sets of common European private law principles. The best-known example is the formation of the Lando Commission (initially formed in 1982) and the resulting Principles of European Contract Law (PECL), published in three parts in 1995, 1999, and 2003, respectively. Since then, a plethora of such sets of principles have appeared, for example, in European tort law, European family law, European security law, European company law, and European insolvency law.

The results of the PECOL Project have thus been published under the less-than-imaginative title 'The Principles of European Cooperative Law' or 'the PECOL' for short. Unlike some other sets of European principles published in recent years, the PECOL can rely on previous principles: the cooperative principles established by cooperators themselves.[2] This raises new questions concerning the place and function of the PECOL. But another particularity derives from research on cooperative law, and it has two typical aspects. First, there has been, to date, only scant adequate research in the field of cooperative law, as discussed below. Secondly, to the extent that such research does exist, much of it has been authored by members of cooperatives themselves, or by legal practitioners working with cooperatives, rather than by academic scholars studying this type of entity.[3] These different features give an original flavour to the PECOL compared to other sets of principles recently established. This will be explained by the presentation of the project (section 2) and its goals (section 3).

2. THE PECOL PROJECT

2.1. THE GROUP

The PECOL Project brought together a small group of European scholars who had all chosen to focus on the law of cooperatives (the 'Group') from those EU Member States with the most prominent cooperative traditions (i.e. France, Germany, Italy, Spain, Portugal, and the UK), as well as one Member State that had developed its own unique approach to cooperatives (Finland).[4] Thus, the Group[5] comprised (in alphabetical order): Gemma Fajardo (Spain);

---

2 See section 3.1.

3 These works are not easy to disseminate, since they concern national cooperative laws and are written in the corresponding languages. Nevertheless, some academic works exist, among which to be mentioned in particular are: D. Cracogna, A. Fici and H. Henrÿ (eds.), *International handbook of cooperative law*, Springer, Heidelberg, 2013; D. Hiez (ed.), *Droit comparé des cooperatives européennes*, Larcier, Brussels, 2009. A special mention should also be made of the Study on the Implementation of the Regulation 1435/2003 on the Statute for European Cooperative Society (SCE, 2010, http://ec.europa.eu/enterprise/policies/sme/files/sce_final_study_part_i.pdf.). H.-H. Münkner, *Ten Lectures on Co-operative Law*, 2nd revised edition, LIT, Zürich, 2016.

4 Finnish cooperative law is interesting in several different respects, but most notably because it is very liberal. In fact, its most recent iteration completely breaks with existing cooperative law traditions. The most convincing example is probably the possibility to create a cooperative with only one member: indeed, article 1 of Chapter 2 of Finnish Law 421/2013 does not make any reference to a minimum number of members (as did the previous law). While PECOL does not adopt any of the uniquely Finnish solutions to the various problems that cooperatives face, the opportunity to compare the broad range of possible alternatives, including the Finnish solutions, proved invaluable to the PECOL Project.

5 Although research assistance was sporadically sought from various PhD candidates and cooperative law practitioners in other countries, it was not possible to involve more academics from other jurisdictions.

Antonio Fici (Italy);[6] Hagen Henrÿ (Finland); David Hiez (France); Deolinda Meira (Portugal); Hans-H. Münkner (Germany); and Ian Snaith (the UK).[7] Ger van der Sangen joined the Group two years ago and, although he is not formally co-editor of this book, his comments have been precious and have influenced the present study.

The Group's small size facilitated its work; the PECOL Project generated its projected set of principles in just four years, after only seven meetings.[8] The Group's work was made possible by the gratefully acknowledged support of various research centres.[9]

2.2. THE PECOL PROJECT'S SCOPE

As its name implies, the PECOL Project's scope was limited to European cooperative law principles. Thus, like other sets of published European principles, PECOL is neither a set of national principles nor a set of principles inspired by the laws of non-European jurisdictions. What sets PECOL apart, however, is the existence of positive EU law – that is, actual legislation – addressing cooperatives in the form of the European Cooperative Society (SCE).[10] Thus, the field of European cooperative law is no longer just an academic field; that legislation has, to some extent, already defined the cooperative's legal construct for Europe. Nevertheless, this regulation shows some weaknesses. First, very few SCEs have been incorporated, and the European Union has apparently given up any project to amend its legislation to make the SCE more attractive. Second, the SCE regulation is not very homogeneous, since many of its provisions refer to national cooperative laws.

Moreover, that particular construct was, in fact, too specific to be the Group's only reference for PECOL because SCEs are, given their features, secondary cooperatives (i.e. cooperative entities formed by existing cooperatives), even if

6 The Group expresses its sincere thanks to Professor Fici, the PECOL Project's Secretary, for his tireless efforts to coordinate the Group's research and documents, with all the logistical headaches that the work entailed.

7 The Group also benefited from, and greatly appreciated, Professor Snaith's linguistic help, which was given unstintingly.

8 Trento (Italy), 27–31 October 2014; Valencia (Spain), 24–26 March 2014; Brussels (Belgium), 21–23 October 2013; Trento (Italy), 8–10 April 2013; Manchester (UK), 31 October 2012; Luxembourg (Grand Duchy of Luxembourg), 28–30 May 2012; Trento (Italy), 29–30 September 2011.

9 The main support was provided by Euricse, followed by the University of Luxembourg. The University of Valencia should also be mentioned for its hospitality, as well as the Italian cooperative movement for its provision of premises for the meeting in Brussels.

10 Regulation 1435/2003 on the Statute for a European Cooperative Society (SCE).

the legislation does not expressly require this secondary character.[11] Thus, the SCE Regulation could not be given any greater importance in preparing the PECOL than more comprehensive national legislation. Moreover, decisions rendered by the European Court of Justice did not play a major role in generating PECOL because it has not yet had the opportunity to directly address the SCE Regulation and its progeny. Rather, its sole decision relating to a cooperative actually addressed a State aid question;[12] the Court was asked to decide whether the application of beneficial national tax rules to cooperatives constituted prohibited State aid.[13] Thus, although the perspective from which PECOL was generated is European, that fact should not be taken to suggest that PECOL's scope is limited to legislation and case law produced by the European Union.

Therefore, the inspiration of PECOL lies mainly in national jurisdictions. National cooperative laws are characterised by the diversity of their scope. Some national cooperative laws contain constitutional provisions; one of them comprises a code, whereas in some other countries there is simply no cooperative regulation. In most countries, cooperative legal doctrine is very poor or lacking. This has several consequences. First, scholars specialised in cooperative law are very few, and this makes the establishment of European principles more difficult, as well as useful. Secondly, the input of the different national laws is unequal, and requires reliance on some major ones. Finally, the cooperative principles of the International Co-operative Alliance (ICA) are an important pillar because they provide a common orientation. A last observation concerns the opposition between common law and continental law. Whereas this is usually a major difficulty in the drafting of European principles, it was not significant in the establishment of PECOL. Even if the differences of tradition are apparent in the sources of national cooperative laws, they do not produce major differences in concepts and practical solutions.

---

11 An SCE may be created by five natural persons; but many provisions deal with questions which arise, mainly, when an SCE is composed of legal persons and, more specifically, of cooperatives.

12 See *Paint Graphos, Adige Carni, and Franchetto*, Joined Cases C-78/08, C-79/08 and C-80/08, ECLI:EU:C:2011:550. The First Chamber of the Court held: 'Tax exemptions, such as those at issue in the main proceedings, granted to … cooperative societies under national legislation … concerning rules on tax benefits constitute State aid … only in so far as all the requirements for the application of that provision are met. … [I]t is for [the national] court to determine [if the national rules were] selective and whether they may be justified … by establishing [if] cooperative societies … are in fact in a comparable situation to that of other [profit making] entities and, if [so], whether the more advantageous tax treatment enjoyed by those cooperative societies, first, forms an inherent part of the essential principles of the tax system applicable in the Member State concerned and, second, complies with the principles of consistency and proportionality.'

13 Nevertheless, the *Paint Graphos* decision is still interesting, as it acknowledged that cooperatives may be unique entities such that the application of special tax rules to them could be justified.

Although the PECOL Project's scope necessarily limited the Group's consideration of non-European legislation or case law, it was impossible, in a globalised world, to draw a strict distinction between what could or should be included within the concept of 'European' cooperative law, particularly in a scientific work. This proved especially true because the state of existing global knowledge about cooperatives is quite limited. In many jurisdictions, information on and research regarding cooperative law principles are virtually non-existent; or, if such information or research exists, it has not been widely disseminated or made particularly accessible.[14] The unfortunate consequence is a very limited understanding of cooperative law principles around the world. Moreover, US legislation, which often has a significant influence on general legal principles, is not particularly important in the area of cooperative law. Scholarly attention has been paid mainly to legislation promulgated in South America and the Canadian province of Quebec, where such legislation forms an integral part of the major developments in the field of cooperative law. Thus, despite their somewhat tangential relationship with Europe, they inform PECOL.

A last specification concerns the scope of cooperative law itself. The PECOL deals only with substantial cooperative law, which means the organisation of cooperatives. Indeed, the underlying issues related to taxation, labour law, consumer law and other questions arising from the relationship between cooperative law and other branches of law are not considered as elements of cooperative law itself. These questions are very important, but they depend so closely on national jurisdictions that it is impossible, so far, to draw general conclusions. The qualification of cooperative as company is traditional in cooperative law, but it provokes some misgivings. There is no doubt that the questions left aside are very important in practice. The most significant example is cooperative taxation. In the meantime, however, it appears that fruitful discussion on this point can be based only on a clear definition of 'cooperative' and the establishment of a precise legal regime. It is on this aspect that the PECOL has decided to concentrate. However, an important matter of cooperative debate has been neglected: determination of the relationship between the cooperative and its members as regards their cooperative transaction. In most jurisdictions, in spite of the influence of the membership on the legal nature of that transaction, it is defined in reference to the usual classification of contracts: workers in workers' cooperatives are, for example, linked to the cooperative by a labour contract. Nevertheless, in some laws, notably in Spain, the cooperative transaction is treated like an original cooperative contract. Because the PECOL concentrated on the organisation of the cooperative, it did not decide on that question. This does not make its work incomplete, but illustrates the restrictedness of its scope.

---

14 For exceptions, see n. 3 above.

2.3. THE PECOL PROJECT'S METHODOLOGY

Once formed, the Group agreed to divide the (organisational) law of cooperatives into five distinct areas, with each area intended to serve as a separate chapter of PECOL: 1. definition and objectives (first draft by Antonio Fici); 2. governance (Ian Snaith); 3. financial structure (Gemma Fajardo and Deolinda Meira); 4. external control (Hans-H. Münkner); and 5. cooperation among cooperatives (Hagen Henrÿ). Each of these five areas was then assigned to one or two Group Members (the 'Chapter Lead'), who then prepared guidelines regarding the information needed with respect to the particular area. Those guidelines gave a uniform structure to the national reports (each of them a 'National Report') that were prepared by each Group Member with respect to the development and current state of cooperative law in his or her Member State.[15]

Each Chapter Lead then drafted his, her, or their chapter on the basis of the information provided in the National Reports. Those draft chapters were then circulated amongst the Group for initial review and comment. The Group would then gather for face-to-face discussions of the various chapters and would propose revisions thereto.[16] Because changes to one chapter often instigated changes to other chapters, the Group met one final time in order collectively to review all the revised chapters and agree on the final version of PECOL. The same methodology was adopted for the introduction (first draft by David Hiez). This book is the result. But, as each principle may echo differently in the diverse Member States, they are completed with comments intended to develop their context, their possible interpretation, or the way that they are coordinated with other provisions. The comments were disseminated among the Group, and each author received and integrated the comments of other authors, but they were not redrafted by the Group itself. Therefore, the comments remain the work of their authors, and are more varied in their form.

The process was completed by an online publication of the draft principles[17] in May 2015. That publication was explicitly aimed at a first dissemination of the principles so as to receive observations from cooperative scholars, practitioners and representatives. Two events were organised specifically to receive such observations. First, during the last meeting of the Group in Trento, a discussion was organised with researchers at Euricse, and notably with Carlo Borzaga. Secondly, a public presentation of the draft principles took place in Brussels, on

---

[15] These national reports are extensive and provide a very rich account of national cooperative legislation. Like PECOL, they are structured by the five topics detailed above. Therefore, they are valuable in themselves, and form Part II of this book. Even if the goal of the Group was always the establishment of PECOL, and the collective work focused only on it, the individual work produced will facilitate the dissemination of cooperative law as well.

[16] These face-to-face discussions occurred during the meetings detailed in n. 8 above.

[17] This publication contained only the principles, but no national reports, nor the full comments.

9 June 2015, within the EU Economic and Social Committee. Representatives of cooperative movements in various countries attended the event and made stimulating comments. The project and its outcome were generally assessed positively. The most discussed point was the question of general interest cooperatives. All the observations and criticisms were discussed within the Group, and some of them led to modification of the draft. For example, whereas the first draft of PECOL stated a common definition of mutual interest cooperatives and general interest cooperatives, criticisms induced the Group to adopt a general definition that considered (only) mutual interest cooperatives. General interest cooperatives have not been set aside, however, since the Group is convinced that they are part of the future of cooperatives. But they are presented as a second model inspired by the traditional cooperatives with some adaptations.

Methodologically, one conclusion can be drawn from the experience. The final meeting devoted to the last whole-group discussion was perhaps not sufficient to eliminate all the risks of inconsistency. Regarding the most controversial points – for example, general interest cooperatives or subsidiaries – some hesitations remain, and the principles do not always provide a full regulation. Such imprecisions could have been avoided – and this is suggested to other research groups – by devoting some meetings to specific and particularly difficult points to ensure that they were fully and consistently dealt with.

The structure of the book requires some additional explanations. Its purpose is to focus on the main questions raised by cooperative law. The first chapter considers the core of any legal notion, i.e. its definition and, concerning an organisation, its objective. This enables a definition of the scope of the institution as distinct from neighbouring ones. The two following chapters deal with governance and financial structure. These are certainly the main features of cooperatives. They are distinct from, if not opposite to, those of companies, and they describe the everyday functioning of cooperatives. Aside from these features, the next two chapters are devoted to external control and cooperation among cooperatives. This latter chapter may rely on the sixth principle of the ICA. The decision to highlight the external control of cooperatives may be debated since it does not appear in the cooperative principles of the ICA. However, in various forms, external control is part of all the legislations considered and constitutes a set of rules specific to cooperatives which ensure the development of their identity. Therefore, this aspect is an important tool to legitimate the special rules applicable to cooperatives, such as taxation.

The division of these five chapters could be challenged. As such, it was not inspired by the cooperative principles of the ICA, nor by the structure of any national or European regulation. However, it did not neglect any of the ICA Principles, which inspire the five chapters. Moreover, each of the five topics is part of the national and European legislation. Lastly, the Group considered that this division is the most appropriate way to describe the cooperative law.

None of the chapters can be read separately from the others. They constitute a seamless whole, and the frequent cross-references are the consequence.

To reflect this process, the book is structured in two complementary parts: the first part includes the principles and their comments, and the second part focuses on the national reports on which the principles are based. The national reports focus on the national positive law, and do not discuss the possible influence of the hereby drafted principles. These reports provide the reader, as they did the leaders in charge of the drafting, a comprehensive picture of the national cooperative law. Given the space available, it has not been possible to include a scientific discussion of the combination of the law in force and the new principles. Even if some first discussions can be found in the comments, this is further work to be developed within each national community.

3. PECOL'S GOALS

The obvious objective of the PECOL Project was to formulate PECOL. Nevertheless, the Group's aspirations for PECOL – that is, what they firmly believe PECOL can accomplish in relation to European and international cooperative law – are the PECOL Project's ultimate objectives. Of course, the Group's aspirations for PECOL are somewhat different from those expressed by the authors of other sets of European principles in other areas of law because of the unique nature of cooperative law. For example, almost twenty years ago, Ole Lando expressed the hope that his Principles of European Contract Law (PECL), as well as other sets of European principles, would achieve several objectives. Among other things, he expected them to: promote cross-border trade; enhance the single market; provide direction to European and national legislatures and courts with respect to future legislation and legal interpretation and potentially enhance harmonisation efforts; and, finally, create a bridge between the Roman and Common law systems. He also mentioned that PECL (as opposed to other sets of principles) could act as a modern expression of *lex mercatoria* and might even be directly adopted by the parties to private contracts. Although the Group's aspirations for PECOL mirror some of these aspirations, the others are simply inapplicable in the area of cooperative law. First, the law of cooperatives already benefits from internationally-recognised cooperative principles that have existed, in various forms, for over a century. The Group's aspirations for PECOL are inevitably informed by that history, which is briefly described below. Secondly, the academic debate surrounding the 'descriptive vs. normative' use of the term 'principle' has also affected the Group's aspirations for PECOL. This debate and its effect are also briefly discussed. Thirdly, relying on the reader's understanding of these two influences, the Group's specific aspirations and objectives for PECOL are described in more detail. Finally, major justifications for the establishment of PECOL will be given.

3.1. A BRIEF HISTORY OF COOPERATIVE LAW PRINCIPLES

Very early on, in contrast to many other economic actors, cooperative entities recognised that theirs was a unique approach to economic activity. In order to better define and encourage the use of their distinctive economic approach, they created a body in which cooperative members (so-called 'cooperators') could debate, among themselves, the proper organisation and functioning of cooperative entities and promote the use and proliferation thereof. Thus, in 1895, the International Cooperative Alliance (ICA) was born. One of its main goals was to establish a common identity for cooperatives around the world.[18] After vigorous debate,[19] the ICA finally adopted and published a variety of principles generally based on those of The Rochdale Equitable Pioneers Society[20] which were intended to describe the structure and management of cooperatives on an international scale.[21]

The cooperative pattern did not, of course, stagnate over the next century; it underwent significant changes over time. The ICA Principles were, as a result, subject to a number of revisions. The latest version was adopted in 1995[22] and remains the touchstone for cooperatives around the globe. In 2015, the ICA adopted some 'Guidance notes'[23] to give guidance and advice on the practical application of the principles to cooperative enterprises and to propose some adaptations of this application at the beginning of the twentieth century. Through those different iterations, not only did the content of the ICA Principles change, but their functions changed as well. In 1937, for example, certain of the ICA Principles were obligatory or considered as defining criteria for a cooperative entity. In subsequent years, however, some of the ICA Principles became merely advisory or reflected an attempt to describe the common denominators of then-current cooperatives.[24] Certainly, such changes in content and function reflect the relative status and strength of the ICA over time, but they are also telling when one attempts to define the nature of the ICA Principles themselves as descriptive principles.

One of the most notable aspects of the ICA Principles is their international status. In fact, they have become a reference set of cooperative features for

---

18 http://www.ica.coop/en/history-ica.

19 J.-F. Draperi, *La République cooperative*, Larcier, Brussels, 2012, p. 155 f.

20 http://www.cooperativegrocer.coop/articles/2004-01-09/co-op-principles-then-and-now-part-2.

21 For example, major discussions took place on the place of salaries in cooperatives: F. Espagne, *Principes coopératifs? Lesquels? Histoire et lecture des principes coopératifs selon l'alliance coopérative internationale*, Paris, 2008, http://cediasbibli.org/opac/index.php?lvl=notice_display&id=38082.

22 Y. Macpherson, *Les principes coopératifs vers le 21e siècle*, ICA Publisher, Geneva, 1996; A. Chomel and C. Vienney, 'La continuité au risque de l'irréalité', RECMA, 1996, no. 260.

23 http://ica.coop/en/blueprint-themes/identity/guidancenotes.

24 Espagne, see n. 21 above.

the international community. In 2002, for example, the International Labour Organization (ILO) adopted Recommendation 193 on the Promotion of Cooperatives,[25] which refers to those principles.[26] Although Recommendation 193 is not legally binding, it still reflects an important contribution to the growing body of international cooperative law.[27] Moreover, regional legislation has explicitly acknowledged that the ICA Principles represent universally accepted cooperative principles.[28]

3.2. COOPERATIVE PRINCIPLES VERSUS PRINCIPLES OF COOPERATIVE LAW

Academics love to argue about the polysemic term 'principle'. Although the theoretical debate on the difference between a rule and a principle still rages, national and international legislations (see e.g. the International Court of Justice's statutes),[29] as well as model laws (see e.g. the Common European Sales Law),[30] use the term 'principle' without clearly indicating which of its possible meanings is intended.[31]

Nevertheless, for the Group, the establishment of principles by academics necessarily entails an epistemological ambiguity. The most important distinction revolves around the term's descriptive and normative meanings. Sometimes, the term 'principle' is intended to denote a general feature described by academics (i.e. descriptive principles), while at other times, the term refers to the actual source law (i.e. normative principles). Clearly, this distinction should be more fully analysed because such generalities may be the ultimate basis for legal determinations. However, such analysis would fall outside the scope of this work. Suffice it to say that, for PECOL's purposes, the important aspect of the difference between the descriptive and normative uses of the term 'principles' is

25 ILO Promotion of Co-operatives Recommendation, 2002 (No. 193), http://www.ilo.org/dyn/normlex/en/f?p=NORMLEXPUB:12100:0::NO::P12100_ILO_CODE:R193.

26 Ibid.

27 H. Henrÿ, 'The Contribution of the ILO to the Formation of Public International Cooperative Law', in S. Kott and J. Droux (eds.), *Globalizing Social Rights. The International Labour Organization and beyond*, Palgrave Macmillan, Basingstoke/New York, 2013, p. 98.

28 Acte uniforme sur les sociétés coopératives, adopté par l'Organisation pour l'harmonisation en Afrique du droit des affaires, 2010, Art. 6.

29 Statute of the International Court of Justice, art. 38 1.C., which refers to 'the general principles of law recognized by civilized nations'.

30 The word 'principle' is used in the regulation on a Common European Sales Law proposed by the Commission (COM (2011) 635), Art. 4, to designate the sources of law that must be used to fill the gaps therein.

31 Y. Adar and P. Sirena, 'Principles and rules in the emerging contract law: from the PECL to the CESL, and beyond', *European Review of Contract Law*, 2013, 1–37; B. Pozzo, 'Les principes directeurs en droit comparé', *Revue des contrats*, 2013, 400.

that it distinguishes the generally descriptive nature of the ICA Principles from the generally normative nature of the PECOL.

The PECOL, in fact, comprises meta-principles. Whereas the ICA Principles describe the actual manner in which cooperatives function, the PECOL describes cooperative law norms. In other words, the PECOL does not claim to describe the organisation or management of cooperatives, but rather the diverse regulations which govern such cooperatives, including their organisation and management. However, any such distinction is tempered by the fact that the two concepts – the descriptive and the normative – can never be completely segregated. On the one hand, the ICA Principles are based, at least in part, on the way national legislation regulates cooperatives. On the other hand, the PECOL necessarily address how cooperatives are actually organised and function. The difference, for PECOL, is that there is always intervening legislation that ensures the application of its principles to the cooperative entity.

This makes a great technical difference with respect to some projects titled 'European principles'. In particular, the PECOL do not contain any provision about their interpretation and development. Whereas some principles consider themselves good candidates to become hard law and, like many international instruments, ensure their autonomous application, there is nothing similar in the PECOL. As PECOL do not pretend to become positive law, they do not require such technical provisions.

3.3. THE PECOL PROJECT'S ULTIMATE OBJECTIVES

Like some other sets of European principles, the PECOL Project's ultimate objectives included the creation of either a set of modern principles to exist in parallel with European or national law (e.g. *lex mercatoria*) or a set of principles to be directly applied by private individuals and entities (e.g. contracting parties). Of course, the PECOL are not an alternative to existing legislation, which is mandatory, but they may set a promising pattern. However, the Group did not expect the PECOL to promote further European Union legislation in the area of cooperative law.[32] Naturally, the Group believes that the PECOL should still serve as an appropriate template for the application and/or reform of the existing SCE Regulation and associated legislation by EU institutions. But the SCE Regulation and the legislation adopted pursuant thereto are sufficient. For the Group, further EU legislation is neither desired nor desirable. Given that

32 The PECOL cannot enhance cross-border commerce or the single market because cooperatives are by their very nature typically local phenomena. However, although most of them may be local, they do at times cooperate across borders; sometimes they have members on both sides of a border. Nevertheless, they are far from the issues arising from the transfer of seats in company law.

cooperatives have always established their functioning by themselves, top-down harmonisation would be meaningless. Because written cooperative principles have been available for so long, any deviations therefrom by Member States which already have cooperative legislation can only be considered intentional (i.e. a political choice to be different). To the extent that other Member States have no such legislation on the books (typically Eastern European countries), attempts to harmonise their national laws would be of little or no value. Nevertheless, the establishment of a set of principles provides a model, which offers a toolbox. Moreover, it stands out as the most promising orientation for the future. It should also be noted that some national legislators have already used the PECOL in their legislative process to reform cooperative law. In Portugal, the Portuguese member of the PECOL Group was also a member of the 'Writing Committee for the Cooperative Law Review' (*Comissão Redatorial para a Revisão da Legislação Cooperativa*), and has been consulted by a parliamentary commission.[33] In Armenia, the reform project has been redrafted to comply more closely with the cooperative identity, drawing inspireation from the PECOL to do so.[34] These two examples are very significant, since the former concerns a country with a solid cooperative legislation, whereas the latter is about a more recent one. They show the diverse situations in which the PECOL can be used.

In this regard, the PECOL Project's objective is to provide a better understanding of cooperatives and the legal principles on which such entities rely, in order to maximise their potential. The Group recognises, however, that the existing state of cooperative law principles is not always adequate to define what cooperatives are, much less what they could be, in 21st-century Europe. Too many questions about cooperatives remain unanswered,[35] despite the various iterations of the ICA Principles. The Group recognises that a modern, coordinated approach to 21st-century cooperatives is needed. This is not to suggest, however, that the Group believes there is a need for fundamental changes to cooperative law principles. Instead, the Group expects the PECOL to function as a coherent body of cooperative law (rules and/or guiding principles) suited to present needs. In this regard, it envisions use of the PECOL as a guide for cooperative law expansion and reform throughout Europe and beyond,

---

33 D. Meira, 'The financial structure regime of cooperatives in the new Portuguese cooperative code', *Boletín de la Asociación Internacional de Derecho cooperativo*, 2016, no. 50. D. Meira, 'The Supervision of Cooperatives in the New Portuguese Cooperative Code', *CIRIEC-España, Revista Jurídica de Economía Social y Cooperativa*, 2016.

34 A. Fici and V. Urutyan, 'Current state and development prospect of cooperative legislation in Armenia', Paper presented in the ICA conference, Almeria, 24–27 May 2016.

35 Significant and important questions remain unanswered in the area of cooperative law. For example, what is the relationship between the cooperators' interests and the general interest? How should a cooperative's transactions with non-cooperators be addressed? How should cooperative transactions through subsidiaries be handled? What is the relationship between and/or what connections exist between cooperative law and company law? We do not discuss these issues in this introduction; they will be part of the PECOL and their comments.

and as a general orientation to, and a set of established best practices for, both legislatures adopting new, expanded or reformed legislation, and for courts interpreting cooperative law.

Although the PECOL Project is clearly descriptive (as any scientific work must be), it also has a normative component. To the extent that the Group reached unanimous agreement on certain cooperative law principles, it adopted them in the PECOL. When faced with alternative solutions to a particular cooperative law issue, PECOL chose those of them most suitable for modern cooperatives. And when PECOL could not rely on positive provisions about a particular question, PECOL suggested an appropriate, modern solution consistent with its general orientation. Nothing less could provide a coherent body of rules and principles for 21st-century, modern European cooperatives. Nevertheless, PECOL cannot, in the end, claim to be normative in that term's purest sense because PECOL makes no pretence of making law. Legislating is left to legislatures. At most, PECOL represents 'soft law'.

3.4. THREE REASONS TO ESTABLISH THE PECOL

3.4.1. The PECOL as a Legal Cooperative Identity

The links between principles and identity is obvious, and the wording of the ICA shows it clearly by qualifying its statements: cooperative identity, values and principles. There is consequently no doubt that the PECOL deal with cooperative identity. That proximity is not by chance, and determination of a cooperative identity is surely one of the main reasons to establish the PECOL. We have mentioned that cooperative legislations, because of their diversity and contradictions, do not provide a clear cooperative identity. Nor do the cooperative principles established by the ICA because they are too general.[36] However, it is crucial to specify that identity, since its specificity is the only reason why cooperatives should be subjected to particular regulation. It violates no secrecy to state that some cooperative practices, as well as some legislations, have weakened the differences between cooperatives and companies. This process can be described as the 'companisation' of cooperatives or, more positively, as 'hybridisation'. As legal scholars, we have no opinion about the opportuneness of these developments, but we can affirm that they provide arguments to abolish cooperative-particular legal rules.

This is exactly the motivation for the ECJ decision in 2011.[37] This case relied on the cooperative identity, and that identity implies some constraints for the

---

36 However, the ICA is aware of the problem and has appointed a 'principles committee' to create a guidance note in order to establish the pillars of identity, thus reinforcing the cooperative difference.

37 See n. 12 above.

cooperative, these latter legitimising the tax advantages. Therefore, it is very important to define a clear and updated cooperative identity. The PECOL, as the expression of the main evolutions of cooperative regulations, and drawing on comparative perspectives, may fulfil that function.

3.4.2. *The PECOL as a Pattern for Other Enterprises*

The second reason why the PECOL are useful at the present time is that cooperative law can be a model. It is already used as such, even implicitly, when some of its techniques are adopted by community interest companies. The contribution is sometimes explicit, as in the case of social cooperatives in Italy, which chose the cooperative framework to regulate social enterprises. Also the Belgian 'société à finalité sociale' aimed at favouring the pursuit of social goals in any corporation, could not avoid using the cooperative model to define the new type of organisation?

The moment is crucial from a European perspective, because the Commission, after a decade of indifference, seems to be looking again at the social economy. The Commission has begun to introduce some regulations and thereby to define, at least indirectly, the social enterprise.[38] The emphasis is increasingly placed on the specificity of the object of the enterprise, which would distinguish it from companies. But cooperatives have another purpose based on the structuration of the enterprise. In order to be able to influence the EU's choices, it is necessary to present a clear identity suited to future concerns. Once again, the PECOL could fulfil that function.

3.4.3. *The PECOL as a Tool to Enter into the Academic Debate*

Finally, the PECOL are an opportunity for cooperative law to emerge from its isolation. The international academic community has absolutely no interest in cooperative law. At the national levels, only Germany, Italy and Spain may claim a scientific tradition on this topic. To date, cooperative law has been mainly discussed among cooperators, or cooperative institutions, when it is not drafted by them. If the establishment of European principles is not considered imitative, it could highlight the fruitfulness of cooperative law and its specific mechanisms.

This is not only the interest of researchers in cooperative law. Ongoing debates on companies after the financial crisis and its consequences could

---

38 This comes about through designation of the beneficiaries of the European Fund for Social Entrepreneurship: Regulation 346/2013 of the European Parliament and of the Council of 17 April 2013 on European social entrepreneurship funds, article 3.

undoubtedly benefit from better knowledge of cooperative law.[39] This requires cooperative legal scholars to maintain some distance from cooperative institutions. Of course, discussions must be continued and developed since law has to be closely connected to the reality. Nevertheless, researchers on cooperative law cannot be the advocates of cooperatives in the academic field. Naturally, they will claim the richness of cooperative law, but this is far from pleading for cooperatives themselves.

39 It is remarkable that an attempt, by a law professor, to analyse the firm as commons, even if referring to cooperatives, makes no use of cooperative law: S. Deakin, 'The corporation as commons: rethinking property rights, governance and sustainability in the business enterprise', *Queen's Law Journal*, 2012, 339–381, 352.

PART I

PRINCIPLES OF EUROPEAN COOPERATIVE LAW AND COMMENTARIES

CHAPTER 1

DEFINITION AND OBJECTIVES OF COOPERATIVES

With Commentary by Antonio Fici

SECTION 1.1
DEFINITION AND OBJECTIVES OF COOPERATIVES

(1) Cooperatives are legal persons governed by private law that carry on any economic activity without profit as the ultimate purpose and mainly in the interest of their members, as consumers, providers or workers of the cooperative enterprise.

(2) 'Profit as the ultimate purpose' means making profits mainly for the payment of interest, dividends or bonuses on money invested or deposited with, or lent to, the cooperative or any other person.

(3) For the purpose in paragraph (1), 'cooperative enterprise' may include an enterprise carried out by a subsidiary if this is necessary to satisfy the interests of the members and the members of the cooperative maintain the ultimate control of the subsidiary.

(4) Cooperatives may also be established to carry on an economic activity mainly in the general interest of the community ('general interest cooperatives').

(5) Cooperatives shall include in their registered name the word 'cooperative', 'coop', or similar. The words 'cooperative', 'coop', or similar, may not be included in the name of entities not formed and managed as cooperatives in accordance with cooperative law and universally recognised cooperative values and principles.

COMMENTARY

The first provision of the Principles of European Cooperative Law (PECOL) is a definition of the subject matter dealt with, namely cooperatives. This is consistent with a practice common in European cooperative law. A definition of cooperatives may be found in almost all the jurisdictions considered for and within the PECOL project: see art. 2511 of the Italian Civil Code (ICC); art. 2(1) of the Portuguese Cooperative Code (PCC); art. 1(1) of French Law no. 47-1775 (FrCA); para. 1(1) of the German Cooperative Act of 1889 (GCA); art. 1(1) of Spanish Law no. 27/1999 (LC).

By contrast, European Regulation no. 1435/2003 (SCE R) does not contain a definition proper of the European Cooperative Society (SCE), although the SCE is immediately identified by certain characteristics, including member and capital variability and the objective pursued (art. 1 SCE R). A definition of a cooperative is also lacking in the Finnish Cooperative Act no. 421/2013 (FiCA).

In more complex manner, in the United Kingdom, the Cooperative and Community Benefit Societies Act of 2014 (CCBSA) lays down the conditions to be satisfied for a society to be registered as a cooperative society. It must be 'a society for carrying on any industry business or trade (including dealings of any kind with land)' (sec. 2(1) CCBSA) and show to the satisfaction of the Financial Conduct Authority (FCA) that it is a 'bona fide cooperative society' (sec. 2(2)(a)(i) CCBSA). In addition, section 2(3) CCBSA states that the expression 'cooperative society' 'does not include a society that carries on, or intends to carry on, business with the object of making profits mainly for the payment of interest, dividends or bonuses on money invested or deposited with, or lent to, the society or any other person' (sec. 2(3) CCBSA). In November 2015, the Financial Conduct Authority (FCA) published the Finalised Guidance 15/12 on the FCA's registration function under the CCBSA (FCA Guidance 2015). In the UK, therefore, the decisions of this public authority affect the essence of a genuine ('bona fide') cooperative.

The International Cooperative Alliance's Statement on the Cooperative Identity also begins with a definition ('a cooperative is an autonomous association of persons united voluntarily to meet their common economic, social, and cultural needs and aspirations through a jointly-owned and democratically-controlled enterprise'), followed by the values on which cooperatives are based ('self-help, self-responsibility, democracy, equality, equity and solidarity. In the tradition of their founders, cooperative members believe in the ethical values of honesty, openness, social responsibility and caring for others'), and finally by the International Cooperative Alliance's Principles (ICA P) proper, which are meant to be 'guidelines by which cooperatives put their values into practice'.[1]

---

1 See International Cooperative Alliance, *Guidance Notes to the Cooperative Principles*, 2015, in http://ica.coop/en/blueprint-themes/identity/guidancenotes.

A definition certainly helps to build the cooperative identity and to distinguish cooperatives from other types of entities. It is the first step towards identification of cooperatives and their distinction from business organisations of a different (legal) nature. This explains the decision to include a cooperative-defining provision in the PECOL, and to start from that provision.

Yet, the importance of a definition for the cooperative identity must not be over-emphasised.[2] In fact, the cooperative identity comprises several aspects, and results from the overall cooperative regulation, including the provisions dealing with the organisational and financial structure of a cooperative (see, respectively, PECOL sections 2 and 3). Therefore, a definition cannot be so comprehensive as to include all the distinguishing features of a cooperative; and even a definition which purports to do so should be read in conjunction with other provisions explaining the meaning and showing the contents of the features (only) mentioned therein. Moreover, different definitions may be found in European cooperative laws – some that are broader (e.g. the definitions in the PCC and in the LC), others that are less so (e.g. the one in the ICC) – and their substantial contents vary. Perhaps, the only element common to the legal definitions examined is that they all make reference to the objective of cooperatives.

Consequently, in the PECOL, the definition of a cooperative centres on its objective, leaving aside other features of the cooperative identity (capital/member variability, democracy, etc.), which are dealt with in other PECOL provisions. Indeed, the institutional purpose is (certainly not the only one, but) probably the aspect of the cooperative identity that most contributes to distinguishing cooperatives from other business organisations, notably companies (also considering the trend in company law not to attribute an explicit purpose to companies – as shown, for example, by European Regulation no. 2157/2001, which is silent on a European Company's purpose).

In the PECOL definition of a cooperative, attention is also paid to the fact that cooperatives are considered 'legal persons governed by private law' (the PECOL do not go into details on how legal or juridical personality is acquired by cooperatives, although it normally stems automatically from their registration). The legal personality stresses the autonomous legal subjectivity of cooperatives relative to their members, as well as their full legal capacity; and in some jurisdictions it also conveys (the idea or the effect of) their patrimonial autonomy (see PECOL sec. 3.5(1)). The reference to private law serves to emphasise the private nature of cooperatives and that they are one of the possible organisational types that legislatures may make available to citizens to form their businesses.

---

2 According to H. Henrÿ, Country Report (CR) Finland, p. 142, 'the definition is something that distils from the entire law'. On the other hand, a definition is a guide to many other issues, foremost, of course, a guide through the cooperative law itself'.

In PECOL cooperatives are denoted only by the title of 'cooperatives', in the same manner as in the PCC (as well as the ICA P). In other jurisdictions, reference is made to 'cooperative companies'. This is the case of the ICC, the FrCA, and the LC, where in fact the word used is 'societies', which, however, in these countries and jurisdictions has the meaning of the English term 'company'. On the other hand, cooperatives are 'societies', and not 'companies' in the CCBSA. Cooperatives are also 'societies' in the SCE R (while, at the EU level, as already mentioned, the joint-stock, investor-driven organisation provided for by European Regulation no. 2157/2001 is given the name of 'company') and in the FiCA.

Two observations are necessary in this regard. The first is that, in the PECOL, the choice of term was made to highlight the difference between cooperatives and (for-profit, commercial, joint-stock) companies. The second is that this choice, however, does not affect the possibility to apply company law to fill the gaps in cooperative law (as underlined later in this comment). This is demonstrated by the fact that cooperatives are subject to the supplemental and additional application of company law both in countries, like France and Italy, where they are referred to as 'cooperative companies', and in countries, like Portugal, where they are referred to simply as 'cooperatives'.

From a more theoretical point of view, the fact that cooperatives are considered 'companies' by legislatures does not represent a problematic issue in terms of cooperative identity once it is recognised that 'company' is a legal category that may also comprise companies without a profit purpose and with the particular characteristics of cooperatives – as it does in the Italian legal environment. The same holds true if broader notions of 'profit-making' and 'for-profit' are employed to identify the category of companies, as in the case of some Portuguese legal scholars, according to whom the notion of 'for-profit' may encompass the pursuit of economic interests (e.g. cost savings) other than capital remuneration.[3]

The definition in PECOL section 1.1(1) is a general definition conceived so as to cover all possible types of cooperatives, including those that in many jurisdictions are regulated by special laws or rules. A general definition reflects the nature of the PECOL as proposed general principles of European cooperative law covering all types of cooperatives regardless of the sector of economic activity, the type of goods and services produced, the nature of the relationship with the members, etc.

The definition in PECOL section 1.1(1) also covers secondary or higher-degree cooperatives, i.e. cooperatives composed of cooperatives, thus making an explicit provision for them unnecessary. Indeed, secondary cooperatives (or 'consortia of cooperatives', as they are referred to in Italian cooperative law, or 'unions' or 'federations', as they may be known in other countries) carry out

---

[3] Cf. D. Meira, CR Portugal, p. 417.

an enterprise in the interest of their member cooperatives as consumers/users or providers of the (enterprise run by the) secondary cooperative. This does not mean, however, that secondary (and higher-degree) cooperatives may not need a specific regulation. In fact, they will be explicitly dealt with in PECOL chapter 5.

Among the possible types of cooperatives, the PECOL make explicit reference to 'general interest cooperatives' (GICs) (sec. 1.1(4)). GICs have a specific purpose compared to the one that cooperatives in general pursue; a purpose, in fact, which makes them a 'different' type of cooperative rather than one 'particular' type of cooperatives among the others (such as cooperative banks or agricultural cooperatives). It is for this reason that, as we shall see, they have received specific consideration by the PECOL drafters and are specifically regulated throughout the PECOL.

Furthermore, the PECOL, in section 1.1(1), refer to three broad sub-types of cooperatives (consumer, producer, worker cooperatives) according to the nature of their members and their relationship with the cooperative. These sub-types cover all the existing particular types of cooperatives in all the sectors of the economy (agriculture, banking, etc.), and are particularly useful for understanding the cooperative system.

Although worker cooperatives are, in fact, a species of producer cooperatives (indeed, they are producer cooperatives where work is the input provided by the members), it has been deemed opportune to mention them separately, as some European cooperative laws do: see arts. 2512 and 2513 ICC; art. 4(1) PCC; art. 6 LC; art. 1(3) SCE R. This opportuneness also depends on the circumstance that worker cooperatives are usually subject to special laws or rules (see, among others, French Law no. 78-763; Portuguese Decree Law no. 309/81; arts. 80–87 LC; Italian Law no. 142/2001). This is the consequence of the particular nature of the mutual relationship that takes place between the worker cooperative and its worker-members, which raises specific issues of regulation in relation to labour law and its mandatory principles.

In addition, it must be underlined that there is nothing in the PECOL definition to preclude the possibility – as happens in many countries and is explicitly provided for in some cooperative laws: see art. 4(2) PCC, which names them '*cooperativas multissectoriais*'; art. 105 LC, which names them '*cooperativas integrales*'; art. 2513(2) ICC – of a cooperative being composed of, and acting in the interest of, more than one category of members, e.g. consumer-members and worker-members, thereby undertaking more than one type of cooperative transaction with its members.

The cooperative objective and its implementation

In the PECOL, the cooperative objective consists of both the ultimate purpose of acting in the interest of the members and the development of a particular activity to fulfill this purpose, namely, a cooperative enterprise with the members.

This objective substantially coincides with the one that current cooperative laws in Europe assign to cooperatives.

Cooperatives are legal entities that aim to conduct an enterprise in the interest of their members as consumers of the goods or services provided by the cooperative enterprise (consumer cooperatives), as providers of the goods or services employed in the cooperative enterprise (producer cooperatives), or as workers of the cooperative enterprise (worker cooperatives). In other words, the final objective of cooperatives is to satisfy the needs and maximise the utility of their consumer-, provider- or worker-members. Cooperatives are different from joint-stock companies, which are established (at least, mainly) to maximise the shareholder value (by distributing profits as capital remuneration and/or by increasing the shares' exchange value), not because they do not act in the interest of their members, but because they seek to satisfy interests other than the maximisation of the value of a capital investment, that is, the members' needs to obtain or provide goods (including knowledge or other immaterial things) or services or to work in the best possible conditions. This is certainly an economic purpose but it is not a lucrative one in the strict sense.

This particular purpose of cooperatives may be given a name by legislatures, as happens in Italy, where it is termed 'mutual purpose' (art. 2511 ICC). In another jurisdiction, the concept of 'member promotion' (*Förderungsauftrag*) is adopted, with the same substantial meaning.[4] A similar notion of mutuality may be found in all the other jurisdictions.[5] Owing to their purpose, cooperatives are almost everywhere seen as business organisations engaged in a 'service undertaking' aimed at the (direct) satisfaction of the members' needs, rather than a 'profit undertaking' aimed at making profits for their subsequent distribution to the capital providers.[6]

The notion of mutuality entails the ideas of 'self-help' and 'solidarity' (people unite to serve themselves, i.e. to solve their common needs in a direct

4 Cf. H.-H. Münkner, CR Germany, p. 259.

5 Cf. G. Fajardo, H. Henrÿ, D. Hiez, D. Meira and I. Snaith, Country Reports. In Finland, chapter 1, sec. 5, FiCA, allows cooperative statutes to provide for a purpose different from the stated one, which is to promote the economic or business interests of the members by way of the pursuit of economic activity whereby the members make use of the services provided by the cooperative or services that the cooperative arranges with the help of a subsidiary or otherwise.

6 This distinction goes back to G. Fauquet, *The Co-operative Sector* [a translation of the fourth French edition published in 1942], Co-operative Union Limited, Manchester, 1951, p. 88 f. On the mutual purpose of cooperatives, see, *amplius*, A. Fici, 'An Introduction to Cooperative Law', in D. Cracogna et al. (eds.), *International Handbook of Cooperative Law*, Springer, Heidelberg, 2013, p. 19 ff.; A. Fici, 'The Essential Role of Cooperative Law', *The Dovenschimdt Quarterly*, 2014, no. 4, pp. 147 ff; A. Fici, 'The Essential Role of Co-operative Law and Some Related Issues', in J. Michie et al (eds.), *Mutual, Co-operative and Co-owned Business*, OUP, Oxford, 2017, p.539 ff.

manner, by establishing a common enterprise that directly satisfies their needs). This explains the image of cooperatives as entities that 'abolish' the intermediaries in the market, since they allow people to satisfy their needs directly through 'their' cooperative enterprise.[7] Of course, this argument holds only insofar as cooperatives are organisations effectively controlled by their members, which explains why member (democratic) control is an element of the cooperative identity (see PECOL chapter 2).

The definition in PECOL section 1.1(1) does not make reference to the nature of the members' needs, whether economic, social, cultural, or ideological, as instead many European cooperative laws do: see para. 1(1) GCA; art. 1(1) LC; FCA Guidance 2015, para. 4.10;[8] art. 2(1) PCC; art. 1(3) SCE R. Indeed, the nature of the members' needs either relates to internal motivations which are not relevant to qualification of the legal entity or, if identified by the law as happens in some instances, it may show a legislature's intention to make available the cooperative form for the pursuit of a particular function that is atypical in relation to the one normally assigned to cooperatives. In particular, when national cooperative laws refer to social, cultural, ideological needs of cooperative members, they may pave the way for GICs to exist,[9] which however are explicitly contemplated in PECOL.

The mutual purpose of cooperatives does not prevent cooperatives from pursuing additional objectives that extend beyond the interests of their members and may be qualified as 'altruistic' (see explicitly para. 1(2) GCA): the use of 'mainly' in the PECOL definition of cooperatives serves also this specific function. The outward orientation of cooperatives may result, for example, from the use of part of the economic results in the interest of the cooperative movement and/or the community, thereby strengthening the 'social function' that many jurisdictions allocate, explicitly or implicitly, to cooperatives (including, at the Constitutional level, art. 45 of the Italian Constitution, art. 129 of the Spanish Constitution, and numerous provisions in the Portuguese Constitution),[10] and implementing the ICA P, notably the sixth and the seventh principle of the ICA.[11] However, cooperatives that externalise a portion of the value that they

---

7 Cf. also D. Hiez, CR France, p. 172.

8 'We generally consider something to be a bona fide co-operative society where it is an autonomous association of persons united voluntarily to meet their common economic, social and cultural needs and aspirations through a jointly owned and democratically controlled enterprise'.

9 Cf. H.-H. Münkner, CR Germany, p. 271.

10 Cf. A. Fici, 'La función social de las cooperativas: notas de derecho comparado', *Revista de estudios cooperativos* (REVESCO), 2015, no. 117, pp. 77 ff.

11 The sixth ICA Principle on 'Cooperation among Cooperatives' reads: 'Cooperatives serve their members most effectively and strengthen the cooperative movement by working together through local, national, regional and international structures'. The seventh ICA Principle on 'Concern for Community' reads: 'Cooperatives work for the sustainable development of their communities through policies approved by their members'.

are able to generate still do not coincide with GICs, in which, as will be soon pointed out, the (main) outward orientation shapes their institutional objective as opposed to that of cooperatives in general.

In the PECOL definition of a cooperative, the objective also comprises a negative element: 'without profit as the ultimate purpose', which is subsequently described, in section 1.1(2), by resorting to the same words as used in CCBSA section 2(3). Indeed, this negative statement may appear unnecessary as long as a positive statement of the objective pursued already exists, and the stated objective seems manifestly different from a for-profit purpose. However, not only is the not-for-profit purpose of cooperatives explicitly stated in some European cooperative laws (sec. 2(3) CCBSA; art. 2(1) PCC: '*sem fins lucrativos*'), but it also serves to draw even clearer boundaries between cooperatives and other business organisations, notably companies, thereby reinforcing the cooperative identity.

Indeed, according to a particular line of thought, companies are cooperatives. More precisely, they constitute a particular category of producer cooperatives or 'capital cooperatives' because shareholders are providers of capital and the service rendered by the company to shareholders is capital remuneration.[12] On this definition, the cooperative would be the genus to which also companies pertain, and the difference between cooperatives and companies would almost dissolve. This is a partial and incomplete view of cooperatives, which takes only the ownership structure into account (and not the other cooperative features) and fails to consider that a company's shareholders do not possess the double quality that a cooperative's members possess. Shareholders are not consumers/users, providers or workers of the company enterprise; they only buy and hold shares of the company capital. This also explains why in defining a cooperative it is necessary to refer to the enterprise performed (and to 'cooperative transactions with members') as a means to pursue the ultimate objective to serve the members' needs, whereas on defining companies this is not necessary (companies are 'neutral' also in this respect).

The foregoing statement requires some clarification.

---

12 In his outstanding book on the ownership of enterprises, Professor Henry Hansmann – starting from the assumptions that a firm's owners 'are those persons who share two formal rights: the right to control the firm and the right to appropriate the firm's profits, or residual earnings'; that a firm's patrons are 'all persons who transact with a firm either as purchasers of the firm's products or as sellers to the firm of supplies, labor, or other factors of production'; and that 'nearly all large firms that have owners are owned by persons who are also patrons' (H. Hansmann, *The ownership of enterprise*, Belknap HUP, Cambridge, 2000, p. 11 f.) – comes to the conclusion that 'the conventional investor-owned firm is nothing more than a special type of producer cooperative – a lenders' cooperative, or capital cooperative' (ibid., p. 11). Indeed, as in a typical producer cooperative, for example a cheese cooperative owned by farmers who supply a factory with raw milk, in a capital cooperative owners are those persons who supply a particular production factor, namely capital. In Hansmann's words, 'the members of the capital cooperative each lend the firm a given sum of money, which the firm uses to purchase the equipment and other assets it needs to operate' (ibid., p. 14).

First, the not-for-profit purpose of cooperatives regards the distribution of profits to members, and not profit-making *per se*. Section 1.1(2) of PECOL, following section 2(3) CCBSA, is clear in this regard inasmuch as it specifies 'making profits for the payment …'.

Second, in a cooperative, only certain forms of profit distribution to members (those that aim at remunerating the capital) are subject to constraints, while others, which are typical of cooperatives, may in principle occur without any limit, as we shall see when presenting and discussing the concepts of 'cooperative surplus' and 'cooperative refunds' (see in particular PECOL chapter 3).

Therefore, cooperatives are to be distinguished from both for-profit entities, like companies, and non-profit entities like associations, foundations and charities. Unlike (for-profit) companies, cooperatives face constraints in capital remuneration (as will be pointed out in PECOL chapter 3, and as already emerges from the use of 'mainly' in PECOL section 1.1(2), cooperatives are not totally, but only partially barred from remunerating the capital) as a consequence of their mutual purpose. Unlike non-profit entities in general, cooperatives may benefit their members by distributing the economic results of the business (in principle and mainly as 'cooperative refunds' rather than as 'dividends on the subscribed/invested capital').

General interest cooperatives

As already observed, the PECOL make explicit reference to, and deal specifically with, cooperatives of a particular kind denominated 'general interest cooperatives'. GICs differ from other cooperatives primarily in relation to their stated purpose, which is to satisfy not the interests of the members (through transactions with them as consumers, providers or workers of the cooperative enterprise) but 'the general interest of the community' (PECOL, sec. 1.1(4)).

While cooperatives in general pursue a 'mutual purpose' – and this purpose has been typical of cooperatives since the origins of the cooperative movement[13] – GICs perform an economic activity in the general interest of the

13 The Rochdale Society of Equitable Pioneers – which was registered on 24 October 1844 and opened its first store on 21 December of the same year in Rochdale, near Manchester, UK – is almost universally regarded as the first structured manifestation of that kind of business organisation to which the title and substance of 'cooperative' have been referred until today. The Rochdale Society began its operations by selling basic foodstuffs to and in the interest of its members. In the declaration of its objects, it was stated that the Society acted 'for the pecuniary benefit, and improvement of the social and domestic condition of its members' by performing several economic activities, beginning with 'the establishment of a store for the sale of provisions', and including the manufacture of articles for the employment of the unemployed or underemployed members, as well as the purchase or rent of estates of land to be cultivated by the members. The Rochdale Society's objectives substantially coincide with those that the PECOL and existing cooperative laws attribute to cooperatives in general, and to which we have referred as 'mutual purpose'.

community. This different purpose cannot but affect the regulation of a GIC, which ought to be as particular as the entity's identity is.

GICs find their legal basis and justification in an interesting phenomenon that has characterised several European jurisdictions over the past three decades: the provision of 'social cooperatives' as legal structures specifically designed for entrepreneurial activity of social utility or general/community interest.

This process began in 1991, when a law on social cooperatives (Law no. 381/1991) was promulgated in Italy that later became a model for many legislatures in Europe and beyond which, in the subsequent years, passed laws on social cooperatives (or cooperatives with a slightly different legal denomination but with the same substance as social cooperatives).[14]

Under Italian Law no. 381/1991, social cooperatives 'pursue the general interest of the community in the human promotion and social integration of citizens through: (a) the management of social-health and educational services; (b) the carrying out of various activities – agricultural, industrial, commercial, or service – for the work integration of disadvantaged people'. Unlike other cooperatives, therefore, social cooperatives do not act in the interest of their members as such, but in the general interest of the community. Their driving force and guiding principle is not mutuality but altruism and solidarity, as clearly emerges from their legal definition.[15] This also explains why social cooperatives are considered *ope legis* social enterprises by Italian Law no. 106/2016 on the reform of the third sector and social enterprises (whereas social enterprises established in another legal form must comply with more rigid requirements to obtain such a legal qualification).

Portugal was the first to follow the Italian example. Portuguese Law no. 78/98 regulates 'social solidarity cooperatives', whose activities are concentrated in the area of social services, and whose objective consists in assisting situations of social and economic vulnerability on the basis of a paternalistic paradigm of social intervention. Social solidarity cooperatives provide assistance to families, children, young people, seniors, disabled, unemployed and other vulnerable groups, in view of their professional integration, education, training, occupational and residential care. They base their entire activity on the notion of solidarity, and for this reason they fall within a legal framework that has distinctive features. In social solidarity cooperatives, the distribution of surplus among cooperators is not permitted, which means that all surpluses must revert, mandatorily, to reserves (art. 7). Social solidarity cooperatives

---

14 A list of these laws may be found in A. Fici, 'Recognition and Legal Forms of Social Enterprise in Europe: A Critical Analysis from a Comparative Law Perspective', *European Business Law Review*, 2016, vol. 27, no. 5, pp. 639 ff.; and more recently A. Fici, *A European Statute for Social and Solidarity-Based Enterprise*, Study for the Committee on Legal Affairs of the European Parliament, Brussels, 2017.

15 Cf. A. Fici, CR Italy, p. 363.

are eligible for the benefits granted by Decree-Law no. 119/83 (amended and republished by Decree-Law no. 172-A/2014) to the Private Institutions of Social Solidarity. Nonetheless, Portuguese legal scholarship considers social solidarity cooperatives as ordinary cooperatives that pursue a mutual purpose translated into meeting the needs of the members.[16]

The LC recognises 'social initiative cooperatives', i.e. 'non-profit cooperatives which irrespective of the class to which they belong have as their objects either the provision of welfare services through health, education, cultural or other activities of a social nature, or the conduct of any economic activity with the purpose of integrating those who suffer any kind of social exclusion into the labour market and, in general, meeting social needs that are not being attended to by the market' (art. 106(1)).

Because social initiative cooperatives are classified as non-profit, they are also subject to the following restrictions (LC, *Disposición Adicional Primera*): they may not distribute surpluses or profits to their members; they may not pay more than the legal rate of interest (currently 4%) on the capital; they must have unpaid cooperative office-holders and limitations on the salaries of the workers (members or otherwise), which may not exceed 150% of the levels set out in the applicable sector agreement (*convenio colectivo*).

Notwithstanding the above and the fact that social initiative cooperatives undertake 'public benefit' activities (according to Spanish Law no. 49/2002), these cooperatives are considered mutual in their essence. Consequently, the activity in question will be conducted mainly to attend to the needs of the members, be these consumers, users, providers or workers.[17]

The FrCA (art. 19*quinquies* ff., introduced in 2001 and last modified in 2014) allows for the establishment of 'collective interest cooperatives' whose objective is 'the production or the supply of collective interest goods and services, with a social utility character'. The law states that collective interest cooperatives may benefit third parties (art. 19*sexies*) and may not distribute cooperative refunds to their members (art. 19*nonies*(4), excluding the application of art. 15). They must have at least three categories of members, two of which are compulsory, i.e. the users/beneficiaries of the activity, and the workers or the producers (if there are no workers) (art. 19*septies*). These legal provisions may suffice to conclude that the object of French collective interest cooperatives is not (at least, mainly or essentially) mutual, and that these cooperatives are explicitly targeted on third parties. Membership is not a condition to obtain services and goods; nor are services and goods defined in consideration of the members alone. Moreover, their altruistic purpose to satisfy a wider public and not simply their

---

16 Cf. D. Meira, CR Portugal, p. 434, also with regard to the category of cooperatives that in Portuguese law take the name of 'public interest cooperatives' ('*régies cooperativas*').

17 Cf. G. Fajardo, CR Spain, p. 544.

members – as opposed to what happens within traditional cooperatives – is explicitly stated in the preamble to the law introducing them in FrCA.[18]

In the UK, a Community Interest Company (CIC, registered under the Company Act 2004 and the CIC Regulations 2005) run as a cooperative, i.e. controlled democratically by its members, provides a similar structure. The CCBSA posits an alternative between registering a society as a *bona fide* cooperative and registering it as a community benefit society ('BenCom'), but it is admitted that a society registered as a cooperative stipulates altruistic objectives in its rules and statutes and prevents any surplus distribution to members as cooperative refunds.[19]

In Germany, there are no special legal provisions for social cooperatives as in Italy, France, Portugal and Spain. However, serving the general interest may be pursued as an additional objective (*Nebenzweck*). According to para. 1(2), no. 2, GCA, besides its main objective of member-promotion, a cooperative society may also 'serve public interest goals of the cooperative society, without this being the sole or main purpose of the cooperative society'. This means that cooperatives do not operate an enterprise oriented to serving the general interest, but rather an enterprise oriented to serving the interests of its members, and the members themselves decide how this general interest-orientation shall be put into practice. Under German cooperative law, organisations pursuing only general interest are not allowed to operate in the legal form of a registered cooperative society (para. 1(1) GCA).[20]

In Finland, Law no. 1351/2003 on social enterprises allows (also) a cooperative to be qualified as a social enterprise. Furthermore, according to chapter 5, section 5, FiCA, the members of a cooperative are free to set their objectives, so that a cooperative may also be established to serve the general interest.[21]

In conclusion, social cooperatives or social enterprises in the cooperative form are a reality in most jurisdictions, although different approaches may be found as regards the relationship between this particular category of cooperatives and cooperatives in general.

As will be seen, the choice for the PECOL has been to follow the Italian and French approach: that is, to consider GICs separately from ordinary cooperatives by virtue of the diverse objective pursued. Unlike cooperatives in general, which have a mutual purpose, GICs pursue the general interest of the community. This justifies their special mention and consideration in a general text like the PECOL.

---

18 Cf. D. Hiez, CR France, p. 175.

19 Cf. I. Snaith, CR United Kingdom, p. 712.

20 In these terms H.-H. Münkner, CR Germany, p. 271.

21 Cf. H. Henrÿ, CR Finland, p. 147.

Like cooperatives in general, which shall be 'mainly' but not necessarily fully mutual, GICs are, in PECOL, section 1.1(4), 'mainly' outward oriented, which means that they may also, though not principally, act in the interest of their members.

Given that (i) (mutual) cooperatives in general serve also a social function, either indirectly by way of their system of administration, or directly due to the allocation for the community's benefit of part of the resources generated by their enterprises, and given that (ii) GICs may also (though not principally) act in the interest of their members, according to the relevant European legislation there is no sharp distinction between GICs and other cooperatives, as identified in the PECOL, but rather a sort of continuum in regard to their social dimension or role. Put otherwise, while 'concern for the community' is an additional objective for all cooperatives (also in light of the seventh ICA Principle of cooperative identity), 'concern for the community' is the main (or even exclusive) objective of GICs.

In addition, in the PECOL, to qualify a GIC no reference is made to the nature of the economic activity that it must conduct (e.g. social services, health services, etc.). In this regard, the PECOL follow the example of French law on collective interest cooperatives and UK law on CICs, whereas Italian law on social cooperatives (as well as Italian law on social enterprises) enumerates the sectors of activity in which social cooperatives (and social enterprises) must operate. Of course, support policies and tax law could provide a stricter definition of GICs in order to award particular benefits to them.

As foreseen in the PECOL, GICs are not only instruments for health, social services and work integration of disadvantaged people, as originally conceived in the European legislation. They may well be employed to organise and provide public services to a given community ('community cooperatives'), such as electricity, renewable energies, etc. This corresponds to a practice now emerging in some European countries and which is being increasingly studied by cooperative scholars.[22]

As stated, due to their particular purpose, GICs may need special legal treatment, including exceptions to general provisions. In particular, as regards PECOL chapter 1, GICs are not obligated to undertake cooperative transactions with their members as consumers, providers or workers (sec. 1.4(1)), which would be in contrast with their nature as community benefit cooperatives. Implicitly, unlike cooperatives in general (sec. 1.5), GICs are subject to no

22 Cf. P.A. Mori, 'Customer ownership of public utilities: new wine in old bottles', *Journal of Entrepreneurial and Organizational Diversity*, 2013, vol. 2, no. 1, pp. 54 ff.; P.A. Mori, 'Community and cooperation: the evolution of cooperatives towards new models of citizens' democratic participation in public services provision', *Annals of Public and Cooperative Economics*, 2014, vol. 85, no. 3, pp. 327 ff.

limitations on transactions with non-members. Accordingly, they are not obligated to have at least two co-operator members, but simply two members, regardless of whether they are a co-operator or a non-cooperator (sec. 1.3(4)). Implicitly, unlike cooperatives in general (sec. 1.3(5)), they may freely accept non-cooperator members, regardless of any specific provision in their statutes.

The economic activity

Cooperatives are legal entities running an enterprise as specified by the definitions of a cooperative or by the statements of the cooperative objective present in the European cooperative legislation, as well as by the definition of a cooperative in the ICA P. Therefore, legal entities that conduct an activity which is not an enterprise in a strictly legal sense (e.g. grant-making, provision of free services, etc.) cannot be considered cooperatives.

In the definition of a cooperative in PECOL section 1.1(1), the use of 'any' with regard to the economic activity that a cooperative may conduct is deliberate. It should suffice to make clear that cooperatives are in principle business organisations that may be employed to conduct any lawful economic activity, and that legal restrictions in the use of the cooperative legal form to conduct a certain business must be justified in order to be legitimate under the principle of equal treatment.

In fact, some cooperative laws explicitly state that cooperatives are free to conduct any economic activity and operate in any sector of the economy. It is provided for example that: 'Elle exerce son activité dans toutes les branches de l'activité humaine' (art. 1(2) FrCA); 'cualquier actividad económica lícita podrá ser organizada y desarrollada mediante una sociedad constituida al amparo de la presente Ley' (art. 1(2) LC); 'desde que respeitem a lei e os princípios cooperativos, as cooperativas podem exercer livremente qualquer actividade económica' (art. 7(1) PCC)]. But stressing further this aspect in the PECOL has seemed counterproductive because the starting point is that cooperatives are a type of legal entity that acts in parity with the others. Therefore, such a provision may have signaled some sort of weakness in the legal form as developing but yet not fully developed. This explains the choice simply to refer in the PECOL to 'any', without also underlining the cooperative's freedom in regard to the types of economic activity to undertake.

The use of subsidiaries

According to PECOL section 1.1(3), a cooperative exists also when the cooperative enterprise is not run directly by the cooperative but only indirectly through a subsidiary. This possibility is explicitly foreseen by chapter 1, section 2(1) FiCA, according to which the transactions between the cooperative and its members take place directly or the cooperative 'arranges [these transactions] with the help of a subsidiary', and art. 1(3) SCE R., according to which 'an SCE may conduct its activities through a subsidiary'.[23] In other jurisdictions, the possibility to act through a subsidiary is only implicitly granted to cooperatives by legal provisions that allow a cooperative to hold shares in a company: see para. 1(2) GCA; art. 79(1) LC; art. 27-*quinquies* of Italian legislative decree no. 1577/1947; sections 24(2), 100–102, CCBSA). The use of subsidiaries also corresponds to a widespread cooperative practice.

However, in the PECOL, the use of subsidiaries to implement the cooperative objective is subject to restrictions (as in German cooperative law: see para. 1(2) GCA).[24] It is considered possible only if two conditions are met: it is necessary to satisfy the interests of the members, and the members of the cooperative maintain ultimate control over the subsidiary. These two conditions are imposed to prevent the abuse of subsidiaries to the detriment of the interests of the members and more in general of the identity of cooperatives as member-driven organisations. In fact, the subsidiary may be a filter which reduces the possibility for cooperator members to direct and control the enterprise that fulfills their interests. Therefore, if this filter is necessary for the better fulfillment of the cooperators' interests, it may be used – but only on the condition that it is structured in a way that ensures the members' ultimate control over the business through the ultimate control over the subsidiary running it.

Protection of the legal denomination of 'cooperative'

The title of 'cooperative' is protected by PECOL section 1.1(5) following the analogous provisions found in art. 15(2) PCC and art. 2515(2) ICC, among others. Therefore, legal entities that are not cooperatives in their substance may not formally qualify as cooperatives. This would generate confusion in the public and damage the cooperative image.

On the other hand, in the PECOL, cooperatives are required to include the word 'cooperative' in their name, and thus to signal their legal nature (and identity) to the public. This is commonplace in existing European cooperative laws (see, e.g. art. 15(1) PCC and art. 2515(1) ICC).

PECOL section 1.1(5) also contains a reference to the 'universally recognised cooperative values and principles', respect for which is necessary for a legal entity to qualify as a cooperative and use this denomination. The 'universally recognised cooperative values and principles' are also cited in PECOL sections 2.1(2) and 3.1(1). Here, the implicit reference is to the ICA P, which are increasingly playing

---

23 See also, in France, the regulations on merchants' cooperatives and agricultural cooperatives mentioned in D. Hiez, CR France, p. 186ff.

24 Cf. H.-H. Münkner, CR Germany, p. 270.

a role in shaping the legal identity of cooperatives, as demonstrated by their incorporation into the cooperative laws. To give but one example, compliance with the cooperative principles is an element of the definition of a Portuguese cooperative (art. 2(1) PCC). And art. 3 PCC is even more explicit in stipulating that cooperatives must obey the ICA P ('As cooperativas, na sua constituição e funcionamento, obedecem aos seguintes princípios cooperativos, que integram a declaração sobre a identidade cooperativa adotada pela Aliança Cooperativa Internacional'), whose seven principles are entirely reproduced in the same article. Significantly, in the recent reform of French general cooperative law by Law no. 2014-856, reference to some main cooperative principles was added in the definition of a cooperative. Furthermore, according to the English FCA, 'we generally consider something to be a bona fide cooperative society where it is an autonomous association of persons united voluntarily to meet their common economic, social and cultural needs and aspirations through a jointly owned and democratically controlled enterprise' (FCA Guidance 2015, para. 4.10), which is the definition of a cooperative found in the ICA's Statement on the Cooperative Identity. The FCA goes on to affirm that 'this description sufficiently sets out the minimum features of a bona fide cooperative society' (FCA Guidance 2015, para. 4.11), and then that 'reflecting the ICA Statement of Cooperative Identity, we consider it an indicator that the condition for registration is met where the society puts the values below into practice through the principles quoted below', which are the values found in the ICA's Statement on the Cooperative Identity and the ICA P, which are reproduced therein (FCA Guidance 2015, para. 4.12).

SECTION 1.2
LAW APPLICABLE AND COOPERATIVE STATUTES

(1) Cooperatives regulated by special laws for their type of cooperative, including general interest cooperatives, are subject to the general cooperative law only to the extent that it is compatible with their particular nature.

(2) As autonomous organisations, cooperatives are free to govern themselves by their statutes within the limits of cooperative law. For this purpose, 'statutes' includes both the instrument of incorporation and statutes which are the subject of a separate document.

(3) In the case of matters not regulated or partly regulated by cooperative law and cooperative statutes, other laws, including company law, may apply to cooperatives only to the extent that they are compatible with their particular nature.

COMMENTARY

PECOL section 1.2 deals with the sources of cooperative law and their interplay. This is an extremely important point from both a theoretical and a practical point of view.

Usually, national jurisdictions provide a general law on cooperatives: that is, a set of rules applicable to all cooperatives irrespectively of their particular type, sector of activity, etc. What may change (without this determining, in principle, substantial effects) is only the qualification or location of this set of general rules, which in many countries (like those considered for the PECOL: Finland, France, Germany, Portugal, Spain, UK) may be found in a separate act specifically dedicated to cooperatives (normally referred to as the 'law on cooperatives'), while in other countries it may be found within a more general act, including the civil code (as in Italy) or the company code (as, for example, in Belgium).

It is not uncommon for the same jurisdictions where a general law on cooperatives exists to have also special laws on particular types of cooperatives, i.e. subsets of rules applicable only to some cooperatives identified by their particular activity (e.g. cooperative banks, credit unions, agricultural cooperatives, housing cooperatives, etc.), type of mutual relationship with the members (e.g. worker cooperatives), or purpose (e.g. social cooperatives). In general, special laws on particular types of cooperatives exist in almost all jurisdictions, including those considered for the PECOL, while what may vary is the number of these special laws and their scope (France, followed by Portugal, is the most prominent example in this regard, i.e. of a jurisdiction where the number and scope of special laws on cooperatives is so high and broad that these laws end up by reducing the role of the existing general law on cooperatives to its lowest terms).[25]

What should be the relationship between general law and special laws on cooperatives?

PECOL section 1.2(1) resolves this issue by giving priority to special laws over general law (the principle '*lex specialis derogat generali*' is implied in the formulation of PECOL sec. 1.2(1)), but at the same time admitting the supplemental application of general law to special cooperatives on the condition that the former's provisions are compatible with the latter's particular nature (a similar condition for general law to apply to special cooperatives is found in art. 2520(2) ICC). This solution preserves the specificity of special cooperatives, since general law may apply to them only to fill the gaps in their special laws, and on the other hand does not prevent special cooperatives from enjoying the general regulation of cooperatives.

---

25 According to D. Hiez, CR France, p. 165, it is difficult to comprehend French cooperative law as a whole because it is a mix of a general law and several special laws dealing with specific kinds of cooperatives.

The role of cooperative statutes

PECOL section 1.2(2) promotes the autonomy of cooperatives by emphasising the role of cooperative statutes (or by-laws) in the regulation of cooperatives. According to this provision, cooperative statutes have a general power of regulation, being subject only to cooperative law proper; in other words, they can regulate any matter not regulated or only partly regulated by cooperative law. Of course, cooperative statutes may also depart from cooperative law rules that are not mandatory (*ius dispositivum*). Therefore, only mandatory cooperative law limits cooperatives' freedom of self-regulation by their statutes.

Filling the gaps of cooperative law

Like any other body of law, cooperative law (including both general law and special laws) may present a gap in the regulation of its subject matter,[26] which raises the question of how the lacuna must be filled when cooperative statutes do not do so.[27]

This is a very important issue (although, admittedly, the role granted by the PECOL to cooperative statutes partly reduces its significance), since recourse to other bodies of law to fill the gaps in cooperative law may harm the cooperative identity. Conversely, the application to cooperatives of other bodies of law, including company law, may be beneficial to them to the extent that they can thus have access to opportunities granted by law to other types of entities. As Ian Snaith observes, 'While certain differences between company law and cooperative law are necessary for the protection of cooperative identity, others, such as the example of insolvency rescue procedures, simply reflect a failure to update the law applicable to cooperatives which results in obstacles for societies when they operate as businesses in the market place'.[28]

The point must therefore be dealt with carefully so as, on the one hand, to preserve the particular nature of cooperatives, and on the other, to ensure that cooperatives have the same opportunities as other business organisations within a given jurisdiction.

In Spain, in the absence of applicable cooperative legislation, the civil or commercial law most closely related to the nature of the activity in which the cooperative is engaged applies. Nevertheless, the tendency in Spain to take capital-based companies as the company model and extend the rules for these to other companies, irrespective of their nature and objects, needs to be considered.

---

26 Strictly speaking, there is no gap when cooperative law itself makes explicit reference to other sources, such as company law in general or specific rules of company law.

27 Of course, the probability of gaps in cooperative law depends on the degree of completeness of such law. This probability is lower when cooperative law is as comprehensive as, for example, German cooperative law: see H.-H. Münkner, CR Germany, p. 282.

28 Cf. I. Snaith, 'United Kingdom', in Cracogna et al. (eds.), n. 6 above, p. 740.

The PCC (art. 9) provides for the application of the provisions of the Code of commercial companies, and in particular of stock companies, to fill the gaps in cooperative law (including both general law and special laws) to the extent that these provisions respect the cooperative principles.

According to the ICC (arts. 2519 and 2522), company law, more precisely either the law of joint-stock companies or that of limited liability companies, may additionally and residually apply to cooperatives. This is possible only when cooperative law presents a gap and the potentially applicable company law rule is deemed compatible with the particular nature of a cooperative.

Being qualified as 'companies' in the FrCA, French cooperatives are subject to the residual and additional application of company law.[29]

In Germany, Commercial Code provisions may supplement the GCA (although they apply only in very rare cases because the GCA furnishes almost complete regulation).

FiCA is a very detailed and comprehensive law, which, however, contains several explicit references to company law.

The nature of the UK legal system implies that any gaps in the legislation governing cooperatives are filled by common law rules because the company legislation (Companies Act 2006) explicitly does not apply to cooperative societies. This is not a satisfactory solution, as common law rules are not updated due to the subsequent entry into force of company legislation which took their place in regulating companies.

The choice for the PECOL, based on the Italian and Portuguese jurisdictions in particular, has been to admit that other bodies of law, and notably company law, may apply to cooperatives to fill the gaps in cooperative law. To preserve the cooperative identity, however, the PECOL provide that these rules may apply to cooperatives only if they are compatible with their particular nature (PECOL sec. 1.2(3)). Implicit in this last provision is that this particular nature is the one that results from cooperative law (both general and special) and the universally recognised cooperative values and principles.

SECTION 1.3
MEMBERSHIP REQUIREMENTS

(1) The members of a cooperative may be cooperator members or non-cooperator members.

29 As D. Hiez, CR France, p. 169, points out, company law rules may not apply when they contradict cooperative law rules, but it is often difficult to establish whether or not there is contradiction, and judges' poor knowledge of cooperative law often implies a preference for company law.

(2) Cooperator members are natural or legal persons who engage in cooperative transactions as consumers, providers or workers of the cooperative enterprise.

(3) Non-cooperator members are natural or legal persons, such as investors, volunteers, or public bodies, who do not engage in cooperative transactions but are interested in the pursuit of the cooperative objective.

(4) A cooperative shall always comprise no fewer than two cooperator members. A general interest cooperative shall always comprise no fewer than two members, regardless of whether they are cooperator or non-cooperator.

(5) Cooperatives may admit to membership non-cooperator members only if their statutes so provide.

(6) Cooperative statutes may make membership subject to reasonable conditions related to their particular type or objective, without gender, social, ethnic, racial, political or religious discrimination or artificial restriction of membership.

COMMENTARY

In the PECOL a cooperative's participants are referred to as 'members' (sec. 1.3(1)), following in this regard European cooperative laws: see art. 2511 ICC; art. 2(1) PCC; chapter 1, sec. 2(1), FiCA; para. 1(1) GCA; art. 8 LC; art. 1 FrCA; art. 1 SCE R.

The term 'members' is more neutral than 'shareholders' as a company's participants are termed in company law. This is not to state that cooperative members do not, and may not, hold shares of the cooperative capital (as we shall see in PECOL chapter 3), but to highlight their diverse position relative to a company's shareholders. Cooperative members are 'users' of the cooperative enterprise and not just contributors of the capital of the cooperative organisation. In fact, they have the 'double quality' of members of the cooperative organisation and users of the cooperative enterprise (something that is also referred to as the 'identity principle' because members and users are the same people). Furthermore, the term 'members' is the one which more closely reflects the 'personal' character of participation in a cooperative, where rights and obligations are linked to the person of the member and not to the capital contributed/invested by them, differently from for-profit capitalistic companies.

More precisely, the PECOL identify two general categories of cooperative members: cooperator members and non-cooperator members. Cooperator members are those engaging in cooperative transactions with their cooperatives, thereby exchanging goods or services or working with them (sec. 1.3(2)).

In contrast, non-cooperator members (sec. 1.3(3)) do not participate to transact with the cooperative but to support (by contributing capital, voluntary work, etc.) the fulfilment of its objectives.

In general, given that cooperatives pursue a mutual purpose, they are expected to comprise (mainly) cooperator members, while in GICs (which act in the general interest) the presence of cooperator members is not a logical consequence of their particular nature. French law is exemplary in this regard when it stipulates, on the one hand, that: 'les coopératives peuvent admettre comme associés non coopérateurs, dans les conditions et limites fixées par leurs statuts, des personnes physiques, notamment leurs salariés, ou morales qui n'ont pas vocation à recourir à leurs services ou dont elles n'utilisent pas le travail mais qui entendent contribuer notamment par l'apport de capitaux à la réalisation des objectifs de la coopérative' (art. 3*bis*(1) FrCA) and that: 'les associés non coopérateurs ne peuvent détenir ensemble plus de 49% du total des droits de vote, sans que les droits des associés qui ne sont pas des sociétés coopératives puissent excéder la limite de 35%' (art. 3*bis*(e) FrCA), and on the other hand that: 'peut être associé d'une société coopérative d'intérêt collectif toute personne physique ou morale qui contribue par tout moyen à l'activité de la coopérative, notamment toute personne productrice de biens ou de services, tout salarié de la coopérative, toute personne qui bénéficie habituellement, à titre gratuit ou onéreux, des activités de la coopérative, toute personne physique souhaitant participer bénévolement à son activité ou toute personne publique' (art. 19*septies*(1) FrCA).

Accordingly, in the PECOL, for a cooperative to be established, it must have no fewer than two cooperator members (section 1.3(4)); and for it to admit non-cooperator members, a provision in its statutes is necessary (sec. 1.3(5)). But these requirements do not apply to GICs. This does not impede, however, the presence of non-cooperator members, such as investor members, in a cooperative,[30] and on the other hand, participation of cooperator members in a GIC.

In the PECOL the minimum number of members required for the formation and operation of a cooperative is two. The provision ('shall always comprise') makes it clear that a cooperative with only one member (left) cannot operate, and is to be dissolved.

Although the average minimum number of members in European cooperative law is three (see, among others, art. 2522(2) ICC; sec. 2(2)(a) CCBSA; para. 4 GCA; art. 11 PCC), there is no apparent reason to treat cooperatives differently from companies in this regard. What is inconceivable is a cooperative with only one member.[31]

---

30 Non-user investor members, as opposed to user/cooperator members, in cooperatives are provided for in almost all the cooperative laws, as we shall see in PECOL, chapter 3.

31 A cooperative with a sole member is now admissible in Finland: see H. Henrÿ, CR Finland, p. 147.

The number of two, moreover, makes it possible to include secondary (or higher-degree) cooperatives in the same PECOL provision (sec. 1.3(4)); for the operation of secondary cooperatives existent cooperative law usually requires a number of members lower than that for primary cooperatives (see, e.g. sec. 2(2)(b) CCBSA, in relation to sec. 2(2)(a) CCBSA; art. 11 PCC).

As regards GICs, a deliberate choice was made for the PECOL not to follow the French example of compulsory multi-stakeholder membership in collective interest cooperatives (see art. 19*septies*(2), FrCA, according to which: 'La société coopérative d'intérêt collectif comprend au moins trois catégories d'associés, parmi lesquelles figurent obligatoirement les personnes qui bénéficient habituellement, à titre gratuit ou onéreux, des activités de la coopérative et les salariés ou, en l'absence de personnes salariées au sein de la société, les producteurs de biens ou de services de la cooperative').

The PECOL finally state that 'cooperative statutes may make membership subject to reasonable conditions related to their particular type or objective, without gender, social, ethnic, racial, political or religious discrimination or artificial restriction of membership' (sec. 1.3(5)).

Therefore, the PECOL allow cooperative statutes to provide requirements for membership, but at the same time – in order to ensure the open character of a cooperative and to preclude artificial restrictions of membership – they seek to prevent cooperatives from abusing that faculty. This PECOL provision needs to be coordinated and read in conjunction with the one on the admission of new members in PECOL, section 2.2.

SECTION 1.4
COOPERATIVE TRANSACTIONS

(1) Cooperatives pursue their objective mainly through cooperative transactions with their cooperator members for the provision of goods, services or jobs. General interest cooperatives may also do so.

(2) In the conclusion and execution of cooperative transactions cooperatives shall observe the principle of equal treatment of cooperator members.

(3) Cooperative statutes shall include provisions about the participation of cooperator members in cooperative transactions, with particular regard to the minimum extent and/or level of such participation.

(4) Without prejudice to any other legal remedy, failure by the cooperator member or by the cooperative to engage in cooperative transactions is a justified condition respectively for member expulsion and for member withdrawal.

COMMENTARY

PECOL section 1.4(1) identifies the particular acts through which cooperatives seek to achieve their (mainly) mutual purpose, that is, transactions with their cooperator members for the provision of goods, services or jobs. Therefore, section 1.4(1) must be read in conjunction with section 1.1(1). The latter defines the objective of cooperatives; the former the way in which this objective is pursued. Nevertheless, 'mainly' has here a slightly different meaning from 'mainly' in section 1(1).

The use of 'mainly' serves to anchor the cooperative to its institutional objective and typical activity. It serves to place a constraint not only on the cooperative's activity with non-members (in relation to that with cooperator members), but also and more generally on extra-cooperative activities, such as financial activities not directly related to the cooperative enterprise.

The PECOL do not require cooperatives to be fully mutual in the same way that they do not require GICs to be fully outward oriented), which is in line with existing European cooperative law.

It is important that the PECOL give a name ('cooperative transactions') to the typical transactions that take place between the cooperative and its members. Again, this is not a novelty. These transactions are referred to as 'mutual relationships' in the ICC, and 'cooperative acts', or rather, 'cooperative activity' (*actividad cooperativizada*) in the LC. In German scholarship they receive the name of 'purpose transactions on the internal market' (*Zweckgeschäft*) because on the one hand they enact the purpose of the cooperative, and on the other, they are viewed as 'internal', and thus special-market, transactions between the cooperative and its members. Outside Europe, the concept of 'cooperative act' is widespread in Latin America.

PECOL section 1.4(2) is relatively new in European cooperative law, although the underlying idea is commonplace. This provision is found in art. 2516 ICC and is reproduced almost word-for-word in PECOL section 1.4(2) because it is important for the proper functioning of a cooperative (see also art. 16(2)(c) LC, prohibiting member discrimination and founding the 'principle of equality' in case-law). It is connected to the provision and the type of problems solved by following PECOL section 1.4(4), i.e. the obligation for a cooperative to transact with its members, thereby implementing its institutional aim.

A member's right to be treated equally with all the other members may determine the cooperative's obligation to transact with that member when a refusal would be in contrast with the equal treatment rule (but also an obligation not to enter into a contract with a member when this would be in contrast with the duty to treat another member equally). This also has effects on the cooperative's freedom to transact with non-members.

The member's right to be preferred over non-members (a sort of pre-emption right) is easily and broadly acknowledged by Italian legal scholars. Moreover, the Italian Supreme Court has affirmed that 'the mutual aim ... implies the impossibility for the general meeting or the board of directors to dispose of the member's right to participate in the planned benefits of the cooperative activity. Said aim, in a building cooperative, does not permit housing provision to third parties' when this damages member interests, in which case the cooperative's resolution to sell to third parties is null and void as its subject is illicit (Corte di Cassazione, 25/9/1999, no. 10602).

Do members have an obligation to transact with their own cooperative? Or rather, should cooperative law impose that obligation?

In Italy, the law does not state, nor have courts ever affirmed, that the status of cooperative member carries an obligation to transact with the cooperative. There are some scholars, however, who argue that member participation in mutual transactions is a necessary consequence of the cooperative's mutual purpose and the status of a cooperative member. Normally, cooperative statutes, especially in agriculture, explicitly lay down an obligation for the members to provide all their produce (or a given minimum percentage of it) to the cooperative, even providing for penalties in the case of non-compliance.

On the other hand, the PCC (art. 22, no. 2(c)) contains a provision related to this point which imposes a generic obligation upon members but refers to 'what is due', which is not stipulated by law but evidently left for other sources to specify.

In section 1.4(3) the PECOL follow article 15(2)(b) LC, which stipulates the member's obligation to transact with the cooperative to the minimum extent established by the cooperative statutes.

This is probably the best way to deal with this matter because the law could not state a precise, complete obligation in advance, and the contents of this obligation may only be determined by cooperative statutes.

PECOL also follows the LC in connecting (in PECOL sec. 1.4(4)) the obligation to transact with the possibility to expel the member not complying with that obligation. This does not prevent cooperative statutes from dealing with the matter in a more specific manner, since PECOL section 1.4(4) must be understood as a default rule awarding a power and not imposing an obligation to expel. Therefore, cooperative statutes may also provide for a different regulation, e.g. penalties for the non-executing member.

The PECOL also deal with the hypothesis of a cooperative that does not give execution to its institutional objective by engaging in cooperative transactions with its members. In this case the PECOL grant members a legitimate cause for withdrawal.

By contrast, the PECOL do not deal specifically with the issue of the legal nature and regime of the cooperative transactions between the cooperative and its members, whether these transactions are to be considered: (a) pure organisational acts subject to cooperative organisational law only ('monistic' or 'corporate' thesis); or (b) pure contracts subject to ordinary contract law (including, for example, consumer contract law in the case of consumer cooperatives or banking contract law in the case of cooperative banks) ('theory of the double relationship'); or (c) *sui generis* acts, whose regime is to be defined by a combination of cooperative organisational law and contract law. However, the national reports give account of the relevant theories followed in each jurisdiction.

SECTION 1.5
NON-MEMBER COOPERATIVE TRANSACTIONS

(1) 'Non-member cooperative transactions' are transactions between cooperatives and non-members for the provision of goods, services or jobs of the same kind as those provided to cooperator members.

(2) Without prejudice to section 1.4(1), cooperatives may engage in non-member cooperative transactions unless their statutes provide otherwise.

(3) Cooperatives engaging in non-member cooperative transactions shall give those non-members an option to become cooperator members and inform them about it.

(4) When cooperatives carry out non-member cooperative transactions they shall keep a separate account of such transactions. General interest cooperatives may also do so.

(5) Profits from non-member cooperative transactions are allocated to indivisible reserves.

COMMENTARY

Operations with non-members create a problem of regulation in cooperatives, since acting with the members, as explained above, is an essential component of their particular identity. As Hans Münkner observes, 'where cooperative societies carry out purpose transactions with non-members without limits, they lose their special character as self-help organisations of their members and turn into ordinary commercial businesses'.[32]

On the other hand, there are several reasons why cooperatives cannot be required by law to be fully mutual. By transacting (also) with non-members they can remedy a contingent shortage of members' contributions of goods, services or work; they may spread the cooperative idea of business; they may

32 Cf. H.-H. Münkner, CR Germany, p. 270.

try to enlarge membership; or they may want to benefit (also) non-members. Therefore, in general, activity with non-members should not be prohibited *ex ante*, but only limited and/or subject to conditions. These restrictions should, on the one hand, serve as incentives for cooperatives to implement their mutual purpose, and on the other, preserve their distinct identity relative to that of other business organisations.

Following provisions in existing European cooperative law (where, moreover, different regulations may be found depending on the type of cooperative), the PECOL identify different criteria with which to combine the need for cooperatives to act with non-members and the need to protect their identity. Thus, the activity with non-members is permitted within certain limits and upon certain conditions.

Firstly, the activity with non-members must not be the main activity, given that 'cooperatives pursue their objective mainly through cooperative transactions with their cooperator members for the provision of goods, services or jobs' (sec. 1.4(1)); it may be prohibited by cooperative statutes (sec. 1.5(2));[33] it may be conducted only if non-members are given the real possibility to become members of the cooperative (sec. 1.5(3)) and if profits from non-member cooperative transactions are allocated to indivisible reserves (sec. 1.5(5)). In particular, these last two PECOL provisions (the former taken from the English experience of consumer cooperatives; the latter from the LC) prevent the abuse of the cooperative legal form and the 'exploitation' of third parties by cooperator members. The separate account of non-member cooperative transactions, which PECOL section 1.5(4) requires, is necessary for the previous provisions to apply effectively.

Opportunely, PECOL section 1.5(1) clarifies that 'non-member cooperative transactions' are transactions between cooperatives and non-members for the provision of goods, services or jobs of the same kind as those provided to cooperator members. Therefore, the issue of the activity with non-members (in relation to that with the members) only regards the activity by which the cooperative pursues its mutual purpose (i.e. the 'cooperative enterprise' of PECOL sec. 1.1(1)). In housing cooperatives, for example, an 'activity with non-members' is the provision of housing to non-members instead of members. In agricultural cooperatives it is transforming grapes into wine, buying grapes from non-members rather than from members. On the other hand, not 'activities with non-members', subject to conditions and limitations in the PECOL, and in the European legislation on cooperatives, are the work contracts that, for example, the above housing or agricultural cooperatives conclude in order to

[33] Differently, in Italy (art. 2521(2) ICC) and in Germany (para. 8(1), no. 5, GCA), transactions with non-members must be authorised by cooperative statutes; otherwise they are prohibited.

conduct their business, or 'cooperative enterprise', with the members. Indeed, these are only transactions needed to carry out the 'cooperative enterprise' as the institutional activity of a cooperative, and they are not subject to any limitation or condition.[34]

The PECOL only deal with the organisational law of cooperatives in general. But a clarification is necessary. The fact that non-member cooperative transactions are permitted within certain limits and conditions under a substantive regulation of cooperatives does not exclude the possibility that these transactions are subject to the ordinary tax regime instead of the particular one that usually applies to member transactions. On the contrary, this is common in the European jurisdictions. Therefore, also tax law may play a role in discouraging cooperatives from deviating from the pursuit of their mutual purpose.

The preceding regulation of non-member cooperative transactions does not apply to GICs, because their purpose is not (mainly) mutual and therefore does not require transactions with members for its implementation. Consequently, in GICs, the relation between member transactions and non-member transactions does not generate any particular issue of regulation. This explains why GICs are not obligated to keep a separate account of the transactions with non-members, but 'may do so' (PECOL sec. 1.5(4)).

34 In the German context, a distinction is drawn between 'purpose transactions' (*Zweckgeschäft*), i.e. transactions for which the cooperative was formed, and 'counter-transactions' (*Gegengeschäft*), i.e. transactions needed to carry out such purpose transactions. As H.-H. Münkner, CR Germany, p. 270, points out, the problems of transactions with non-members are special when a cooperative enterprise carries out purpose transactions with non-members.

CHAPTER 2
COOPERATIVE GOVERNANCE

With Commentary by Ian Snaith

SECTION 2.1
GENERAL PRINCIPLES OF COOPERATIVE GOVERNANCE

(1) Cooperatives are directed and controlled by or on behalf of their members, who have ultimate democratic control through their governance system.

(2) Cooperative governance reflects their jointly-owned, democratically controlled and autonomous nature. It facilitates operation based on universally recognised cooperative values and principles, including cooperative social responsibility.

(3) The governance organs of a cooperative are structured to pursue economic activities mainly in the interest of their cooperator members. In general interest cooperatives, they are structured to pursue such activities mainly in the general interest of the community.

(4) Cooperative governance structures may vary according to:

(a) the size and type of cooperative enterprise;
(b) the sector in which it operates; and
(c) whether it is a general interest cooperative.

(5) Cooperative governance structures must always ensure cooperative autonomy and member control.

COMMENTARY

The chapter opens in Principles of European Cooperative Law (PECOL) 2.1(1) with a statement about the centrality of the role of members in cooperatives and the importance of ensuring that cooperatives are ultimately controlled by their members, even if functions and powers are divided among a number of organs such as boards and managers. PECOL 2.1(5) focuses specifically on the role of governance structures in upholding the autonomy of the cooperative and member control. Cooperative groups and subsidiaries are dealt with at PECOL 5.2.

PECOL 2.1(1) also defines 'governance' as being concerned with the direction and control of the jointly owned autonomous cooperative enterprise. The core concept of democratic control of cooperatives is emphasised in most of the national laws studied.[1] These principles of governance are important in both cooperatives operating in the interests of their members and those pursuing the general interest. In the case of GICs, democratic governance is perhaps the main feature identifying the organisation as a cooperative.

PECOL 2.1(2) then places cooperative governance in the context of the overall International Co-operative Alliance (ICA)/International Labour Organization (ILO) definition of a cooperative. It links the specifics of governance to the values embodied in the ICA definition. They are both operational (self-responsibility, democracy, equality, equity and solidarity) and ethical. The principle of cooperation among cooperatives is also included. These matters are important in the definition of a cooperative and therefore represent an aspect of the decision-making of the organs of the cooperative. Ultimately, decisions which call the nature of the cooperative into question are to be avoided by the organs whether or not they are constrained by specific legal rules. Therefore PECOL 2.1(2) contains this statement of principle as a requirement to 'facilitate' operation on the basis of the values and principles. The fact that many national laws require a cooperative to comply with the ICA Statement or a similar norm as a condition of registration under the cooperative law reinforces this requirement.[2]

PECOL 2.1(3) emphasises that the centrality of the member control principle also applies to general interest cooperatives (as defined in PECOL 1).[3] If a business entity is to be defined as a cooperative at all, it must be subject to member control, and in the absence of the latter a general interest association or society will not be a cooperative. The distinction concerns the purpose, not the governance structure. For example, while some UK societies registered as community benefit societies will be general interest cooperatives in PECOL terms, others will not. All such societies registered as bona fide cooperatives will be cooperatives. This arises from the nature of registration of societies, which since 1 August 2014 has been as either a bona fide cooperative or as a

1 Cf. D. Hiez, Country Report (CR) France, p. 187, D. Meira, CR Portugal, p. 434; I. Snaith, CR United Kingdom, p. 644.

2 Cf. D. Hiez, CR France, pp. 172–174; A. Fici, CR Italy, pp. 349–350; D. Meira, CR Portugal, p. 414; G. Fajardo, CR Spain, p. 522; I. Snaith, CR United Kingdom, pp. 629–633.

3 Art. 2.1 PCC; art. 1 FrCA; art. 1(1) LC; para. 1(1) GCA; art. 2511 ICC; and FCA Guidance paras. 4.10–4.16.

community benefit society. Community benefit societies may have a stakeholder governance structure with one member one vote, but they will never permit any distribution of surplus to members, and their purpose must always be altruistic rather than being focused on meeting the needs of their own members.[4] In terms of the registration of a society and the use of a name, the Financial Conduct Authority (FCA) Guidance published in 2015 makes it clear that a society must be registered in one category or the other and that neither may use a name referring to the other category.[5]

PECOL 2.1(4) and (5) emphasise the importance of the principle of autonomy, while also acknowledging the need for diverse governance structures. That diversity is necessary to accommodate the variety of cooperatives. For example, in Spain different rules on governance apply to credit cooperatives, insurance cooperatives and agricultural cooperatives.[6] The needs of the different types of cooperative (e.g. consumer, producer, worker) will vary, and so will the needs of those with large or small memberships and those with members across a wide or narrow geographical area. Similarly, the scale and range of the cooperative's economic activities and the number of employees will affect the governance structure that it needs.

PECOL 1.2 indicates the sources of the legally binding rules on cooperatives; and in the case of governance, guidance on best practice (often in the form of Codes of Practice) is significant (see, for example, Co-operatives UK, *Corporate Governance Code of Practice for Consumer Co-operatives*, 2013; Co-operatives UK, *The Worker Co-operative Code*, 2012; and, in Germany, the DGRV Code of 23 November 2010). In the context of companies, that source is also greatly emphasised by the EU Commission (see Recommendation 2005/162/EC and Recommendation 2014/208/EU).

SECTION 2.2
OPEN MEMBERSHIP

(1) Without prejudice to section 1.3, membership of a cooperative must be open to any person able and willing to accept the responsibilities of membership.

(2) Cooperative statutes shall ensure that:

(a) membership applications are dealt with by a designated organ within a reasonable time;

---

4 Sec. 2(2) CCBSA.

5 I. Snaith, CR United Kingdom, p. 636.

6 G. Fajardo, CR Spain, p. 546.

(b) reasons are given for refusal;
(c) the applicant can appeal to the members' meeting if a different organ refused admission; and
(d) the applicant has the right to be heard before a decision is made on the appeal.

(3) No one has a legally enforceable right to join a particular cooperative. The entity responsible for the registration and/or the auditing entity of section 4.3 must ensure that membership is open in accordance with paragraph (1).

(4) Cooperative statutes shall govern the grounds and procedure for termination by either party of cooperative membership. They shall deal, in particular, with:

(a) the notice period required;
(b) any adjustment of capital contribution or other financial arrangements; and
(c) other consequences of such termination.

(5) Termination of membership by the cooperative shall be subject to:

(a) the member having had the right to present their case before the decision was made;
(b) the member's right to be informed of the reason for the decision against them; and
(c) the member's right to appeal to the members' meeting against an adverse decision and to exercise any other legal remedy.

COMMENTARY

PECOL 2.2(1) restates the concept of open membership from the International Cooperative Alliance Principles (ICA P). The rationale and basis of the principle is the avoidance of artificial restrictions on membership to increase the value of the rights of existing members at the expense of potential new members. This is an expression at a high level of abstraction of the purpose of the open membership principle. Those who are already members should not be able to profit from transactions involving people with the same economic relationship with the cooperative by 'closing' membership for that group.

The limitation of the open membership principle to those with the economic relationship on which the cooperative is based is found in the ICA's reference to people 'able to use its services'. This is usually seen as pointing to the type of cooperative. In a consumer cooperative, membership must be open to consumers who buy from it. In a workers' cooperative, all employees must be able to join.

In a producer cooperative, the concept will apply to producers or suppliers. In hybrid (or multi-stakeholder) cooperatives, it will be open to members of more than one of those groups. The ICA limitation of the principle is explicit in arts. 1(3) and (4) of European Cooperative Society (SCE R) and implicit in art. 14(1) SCE R where membership by investor members not expecting to use or produce is permitted only if the Statutes so provide and then only by decision of the members' meeting.

In those legal systems that have special laws for particular types of cooperative, this will be defined more precisely; and in those with only a general law it will usually be found in the statutes of particular types of cooperative (e.g. chap. 2 Finnish Cooperative Act (FiCA); art. 16(1)(d) Portuguese Cooperative Code (PCC); art. 1 Spanish Cooperatives Act (Spanish Law no. 27/1999 (LC)). An example of this is the UK system of model rules provided by cooperative sponsoring organisations which can be used for the registration of new cooperatives for a reduction in the registration fee (see FCA FEES section of FCA Handbook and FCA List of Sponsoring bodies). However, PECOL 2.2(1) expresses a useful abstract rationale for the open door principle and its limits.

Power to decide membership applications

PECOL 2.2(2) indicates that the allocation of power to decide membership applications may be found in the law or the statutes, and it is usually vested in the board with a right of appeal as stated (art. 14(1) SCE R; para. 15(1) German Cooperative Act (GCA); arts. 2527 and 2528 Italian Civil Code (ICC); arts. 21(1) and 38(K) PCC). It uses criteria similar to those found in PECOL 1.3. The importance of due process for those refused or expelled from cooperative membership is reflected in PECOL 2.2(2) and 2.2(5). These require reasoned decisions which are subject to both appeal and the right for the member or prospective member to be heard.

A justiciable right to membership?

PECOL 2.2(3) notes the absence of any subjective or absolute justiciable right to acquire membership of a cooperative. That seems to state the position in most of the systems that we have considered. The open door principle does not give a potential member a legally enforceable individual right to become a member (see, for example, art. 14(1) SCE R, which gives discretion to the organ deciding whether to admit a potential member). However, open membership is a core element of the definition of a cooperative (ICA P1); and it is, for the reason given in the comment on 2.2(1), a central value of cooperatives. In most systems, it is upheld collectively on behalf of potential members by the registering body

(FCA Guidance, paras 4.10–4.16, and comment to PECOL 1.3). PECOL acknowledges and protects that principle.

Termination of membership

PECOL 2.2(4) and (5) indicate that membership can be terminated by either the cooperative or the individual member.

The voluntary nature of membership implies a right for the member to resign, but resignation may require agreement by the directors, a period of notice, or a period of earlier membership, and it may have only partial effect for a period. In addition, payment of money due on shares to a resigning member may not be immediate and may reflect losses by the cooperative. This protects the liquidity of the cooperative and ensures that its capital base reflects its true financial position (art. 16 SCE R; art. 24 PCC; para. 65 GCA; art. 2532(1) ICC; arts. 11, 15, 45(8) and 51 LC). Where, as in some agricultural marketing cooperatives, a member has a separate contract with the cooperative, the resignation of the member will not terminate his or her obligations under that contract if they are expressed to continue after membership ends. Membership will also terminate when the member ceases to exist, for example on the death of an individual or dissolution of a legal entity. It may also be triggered if the member is subject to other insolvency proceedings if cooperative statutes so provide.

Cooperatives usually have the power to expel a member conferred either by law or by the cooperative statutes. PECOL 2.2(5) refers to the procedural safeguards found in the various legal systems (art. 15(3) SCE R; art. 2316 French Law no 47-1775 (FrCA); para. 68 GCA; arts. 2531 and 2533 ICC; arts. 16(2.a) and 26 PCC; art. 18(5) LC and the UK common law rules). The grounds for such termination are left to cooperative statutes because they need to be tailored to the particular circumstances of different cooperatives.

All the national systems provide judicial redress or independent arbitration to deal with expulsion and other disputes. Arbitration or other alternative dispute resolution procedures are commonly used for disputes between a cooperative and its members after internal processes have been exhausted. This conforms to the cooperative ethos, and it acknowledges the value of Alternative Dispute Resolution (ADR) where members have limited funds – as will be the case of some of the people who use cooperatives to meet their needs. Typically, the mechanisms for ADR will be found in cooperative statutes rather than the law. Use is made of arbitration and mediation procedures under general contract or commercial law. However, some provisions of national cooperative law encourage the use of ADR for reasons more relevant to cooperatives than some other enterprises (see e.g. chap. 3 s. 5 and chap. 23 s. 4 FCA; ss. 137–140 of Cooperative and Community Benefit Societies Act (CCBSA)).

SECTION 2.3
MEMBERS' OBLIGATIONS AND RIGHTS

(1) The obligations of cooperator members include:

(a) participation in cooperative transactions to a minimum extent and/ or level, when applicable under section 1.4(3);
(b) the contribution of capital, when applicable in accordance with sections 3.2(1) and 3.2(2);
(c) a minimum level of participation in the governance of the cooperative;
(d) participation in education and training provided for members; and
(e) other obligations imposed by law or cooperative statutes which may, in some cases, include an obligation to bear a proportion of the cooperative's liabilities or losses.

(2) The obligations of investor members include the provision of the capital subscribed but do not include participation in governance. Investor members must respect the limits of their role and the need for cooperator members to control the cooperative.

(3) The statutes of a general interest cooperative shall state the obligations and rights of cooperator and non-cooperator members, including the different roles of different groups in the pursuit of the general interest of the community.

(4) Cooperator members have the following individual rights:

(a) to engage with education and training appropriate to their role in the cooperative;
(b) to participate in the governance of their cooperative, in principle by attending and fully participating in meetings in person, but by proxy if necessary;
(c) to vote in elections for members of the organs or on any issue decided by direct member vote (at a meeting, electronically, or by post);
(d) to stand for election;
(e) to request and receive financial and other relevant information as laid down by law or cooperative statutes;
(f) to receive any compensation on their shares decided under cooperative statutes; and
(g) when applicable, to engage in cooperative transactions and to receive any cooperative refund under cooperative statutes or the law after it is determined by the competent organ.

(5) Together with the number of other members that is laid down by law or cooperative statutes, members have a collective right:

(a) to receive or request any information needed to perform the member's role in their cooperative;

(b) to propose candidates for election as directors or delegates to another organ or meeting;
(c) to require a members' meeting to be called;
(d) to propose resolutions or add matters to the agenda of a members' meeting;
(e) to demand an audit of the cooperative by the auditing entity of section 4.3;
(f) in accordance with procedures laid down by law or cooperative statutes, to amend cooperative statutes and restructure or dissolve the cooperative.

COMMENTARY

The contractual basis of the cooperative as an association is common to all of the systems analysed. So too is the inclusion of members' rights and duties in either the law or the cooperative statutes. For example, art. 5(4) (indent 6) SCE R requires the cooperative statutes to include:

> '- the rights and obligations of members, and the different categories of member, if any, and the rights and obligations of members in each category.'

Obligations

PECOL 2.3(1)–(3) outlines some of the obligations that are imposed on cooperative members. PECOL only deals with those rights and obligations which relate to the very nature of cooperatives by being linked to the ICA definition, values and principles. In order to emphasise the fact that members have obligations as well as rights, the obligations are discussed first.

PECOL 1.4 and 1.5 require a substantial proportion of all transactions by mutual cooperatives to be cooperative transactions with cooperator members.

PECOL 2.3(1)(a) deals with the individual member's obligation to participate economically in the cooperative by using or supplying goods and services. The requirement is usually found in the statutes of particular cooperatives (art. 14(2) SCE R and see commentary on PECOL 3). PECOL 1.4(3) reflects the importance of the requirement, particularly for cooperator members of cooperatives. The obligation will be crucial for the successful operation of certain cooperatives, e.g. agricultural marketing cooperatives which need to ensure that members sell their produce only through the cooperative. As a result, some systems restrict the freedom of the member to resign with immediate effect on the economic relationship (e.g. arts. 2532 and 2533 ICC). An interesting example of the limits on the obligations of cooperative members, the relationship between obligations and rights, and the contractual nature of both, is provided by the French case of

Rennes concerning whether, in changed circumstances when a member's needs were no longer met, the obligation still applied.[7]

Since the economic activity of general interest cooperatives is carried on mainly in the interests of the community, this obligation is not relevant for their members whose rights and obligations will depend on the cooperative statutes – PECOL 2.3(3). PECOL includes this obligation on that basis. Members of general interest cooperatives must never receive any distribution of surplus – PECOL 3.6(7).

PECOL 2.3(1)(b) acknowledges the importance of member contributions to cooperative capital. While the question of whether or not a minimum level of capital is required for the cooperative will be determined by law, any minimum contribution required of individual members will normally be a matter for cooperative statutes (art. 4(7) SCE R, and commentary to PECOL 3) This is sometimes an explicit ground for the expulsion of a member from the cooperative (e.g. art. 2531 ICC) or at least for extending the notice period required for resignation as in para. 65 GCA, and art. 24 PCC.

Similarly, in PECOL 2.3(1)(c) any minimum requirement for participation in cooperative governance is likely to be a requirement of cooperative statutes. It may take the form of minimum attendance at members' meetings. Expulsion and removal from the member register may be based on non-attendance at meetings or the absence of any contact with the cooperative through transactions, voting, attendance at meetings, or voting in elections. National laws provide few concrete examples of this obligation (but see arts. 21 and 22 of PCC). In the case of Spain, the specific obligations for members to attend the meetings of organs of which they were members, and even to accept positions to which they were elected, disappeared from the 1999 LC.[8]

All the laws either lay down quorum requirements for members' meetings or authorise the cooperative statutes to do so: e.g. art. 5(4) (indent 11) SCE R. The quorum requirement effectively imposes the penalty of an inability to make decisions on the members collectively if too many of them fail to attend the members' meeting in person or by proxy.

The PECOL 2.3(1)(d) obligation to participate in education and training links strongly with ICA P5. It is unusual for that obligation to be imposed on members as a condition of membership. Cooperative directors, employees, or managers may have such an obligation by virtue of contract or the cooperative statutes. Because it is important to encourage members to engage with education and training, PECOL chooses to model itself on art. 3 of PCC, which acknowledges the importance of ICA P5. PECOL also follows the PCC's requirement that a mandatory reserve be built up for that purpose (PECOL 3.4(2) and (8) and see art. 97 PCC; arts. 56–58 LC; and, though indirectly, art. 11 of Italian Law

[7] D. Hiez, CR France, p. 196.
[8] G. Fajardo, CR Spain, p. 556.

no.59/1992 for examples of requirements for this in national laws). In Germany, the importance of education and training is emphasised without creating a specific legal obligation, and the requirement for a pre-registration audit plays some role in this.[9] Similarly, the trend in French cooperative laws is towards a greater emphasis on education.[10]

PECOL 2.3(1)(e) indicates the variety of other obligations that may be imposed on members. In particular, it suggests the possibility of provisions requiring members to bear part of the cooperative's losses (art. 16(1) SCE R, and see comment on PECOL 3.6).

Rights

PECOL 2.3(4) notes that the rights of cooperative members are conferred by law or through the statutes of their cooperative and seeks to list the most common individual member rights in both mutual and general interest cooperatives. Many of the listed rights are mirror images of the obligations listed in PECOL 2.3(1).

Participation in education (PECOL 2.3(4)(a)) perhaps fits more easily into the category of rights than into a list of obligations and, even as a right, seems to be funded on a mandatory basis only in certain jurisdictions such as Italy, Portugal and Spain (see commentary on PECOL 2.3(1)(d)). Elsewhere, cooperative societies are permitted to finance or provide education, and in practice many of them do so.

Participation in governance as a right of cooperative members is listed in PECOL 2.3(4)(b)–(d), and it is, in one form or another, present in all jurisdictions. As an individual right, attendance at meetings and voting, either in person or by proxy, on resolutions or in elections is a core right found in virtually all laws; and arts. 52–62 SCE R reflect the general position (chapter 4 FiCA; arts. 1, 4 and 6 FrCA supplemented by the Commercial Code; para. 43, GCA; arts. 2538–2539 ICC; arts. 33–36 PCC; arts. 21–25 LC and, in the UK, s. 14(4) and (5) CCBSA and FCA Guidance paras. 4.10–4.13). Similarly, many of the national laws permit or facilitate the use of sectorial and delegate meetings rather than a general meeting of all members (e.g. art. 63 SCE R; s. 149 CCBSA; arts. FrCA; para. 43a GCA, art. 54 PCC; arts. 5 and 22 LC; and s. 149 CCBSA).

The right to stand in elections, which is usually subject to finding other members willing to propose the individual, is a necessary concomitant of those rights. However, for some roles the right may be qualified to meet the need for candidates in some roles to show a certain level of competence and experience. Generally, the detail of the nomination process is dealt with in cooperative statutes.

---

9 Para. 11 GCA and cf. H.-H. Münkner, CR Germany, p. 313.

10 D. Hiez, CR France p. 202.

The changes made in 2014 to the statutes of the UK Co-operative Group, which have been registered by the FCA as registrar on the basis that the organisation remains a bona fide cooperative, have provided for a majority of the board of directors to be appointed by the board, subject only to endorsement by members without contested elections. Moreover, both those appointed directors and the minority of four 'member nominated directors', whose appointment can be subject to contested elections by members, can be nominated as directors only after approval by a nominations committee of the existing board on the basis of their experience and competence, taking account of the resulting composition of the board in terms of the range of skills and experience it needs, as well as their commitment to cooperatives. This application of the practices and procedures of the UK PLC sector within a cooperative which retains one member one vote resulted from the 2013 commercial and financial failures of the organisation. The changes are controversial among UK cooperative activists, and they illustrate the breadth and flexibility of the concept of member control of cooperatives as applied in the UK.

The individual right to request and receive financial and other relevant information (PECOL 2.3(4)(e)) is a necessary support for the members' participation in governance, since only with access to such information can the direct rights to vote and to participate in meetings be exercised effectively. This is acknowledged in many of the national laws, particularly in respect of financial information. There is an obligation on other organs to publish information to members as well as a right for a certain number of members to demand such information (art. 60 SCE R; hap. 4 sec. 15 and chap. 7 secs. 6–7 FCA; paras. 46 and 59 GCA; arts. 2545 and 2545*bis* ICC; arts. 9, 21.3 and 47 PCC; arts. 16(3) LC). Few laws go beyond the provision of financial information, although the German Law in arts. 31 and 43a provides a right to lists of members and delegates, and the UK law enables members to find similar information by inspecting records held at the society's registered office (s. 30(7) CCBSA).

PECOL 2.3(4)(f) and (g) highlight the economic right of members to receive interest on shares actually declared or decided under the statutes and to engage in cooperative transactions with the cooperative and receive any cooperative refund once the interest and refund have been determined by the appropriate organs. These rights are vital to the functioning of cooperatives other than general interest ones. A right to interest on shares may also apply to some members of general interest cooperatives. These financial or economic rights are dealt with more fully in PECOL 3.3(5) and 3.6 and the comments to those paragraphs.

Cooperatives, including general interest cooperatives, require member engagement in the governance system, but they differ on the economic rights of members, which, apart from the possible right to a modest return on share capital, relate to mutual cooperatives, which serve members and can distribute surplus to them.

PECOL 2.3(5) provides for the additional collective rights of a certain number of members to facilitate the exercise of member control indirectly by ensuring that motions and amendments can be proposed and meetings called by members without requiring the agreement of the board or other elected or appointed officials of the cooperative. Art. 55 SCE R is typical in this respect in defining the number of members required by a combination of a number of members and a proportion of votes.

In most general interest cooperatives and in other multi-stakeholder cooperatives, the governance-related rights of members may involve different roles for different groups of members. For example, employees and users of services may have different voting rights and elect limited proportions of a board to ensure equitable representation of different member interests.

PECOL 2.3(5) attempts to bring together the collective rights of the members in cooperatives, including general interest cooperatives. Collective rights are those that require a number of members for their exercise. For example, calling a special (emergency) members' meeting without board agreement, placing resolutions on the agenda of a members' meeting, deciding through a procedure laid down by law or the cooperative statutes to dissolve or restructure the cooperative or to amend its statutes. These rights support member control of the cooperative and complement the individual rights of members.

The question of the enforcement of the members' rights and duties raises the same issues as in the case of all other private law rights, including those of company shareholders and members of associations. However, the use of alternative dispute resolution systems, such as arbitration and mediation, which either deal with the issue outside the court system or encourage a negotiated solution is common in cooperative laws and statutes and is an aspect of the ethos of cooperation. It also reflects the particular need of those likely to use cooperatives for inexpensive and fast resolution of problems without the need to use the judicial system. Only the model rules for French worker cooperatives,[11] art. 44 LC, and ss. 137–140 CCBSA in the UK go beyond the general availability of ADR for private law disputes by encouraging internal dispute resolution for cooperatives. As a result, PECOL contains no provisions on this issue.

SECTION 2.4
COOPERATIVE GOVERNANCE STRUCTURES: DIRECT MEMBER CONTROL

(1) Cooperative governance structures must ensure that members democratically control the cooperative and can actively participate in

---

[11] D. Hiez, CR France, pp. 207–208.

policy making and major decisions, in principle on a one member one vote basis.

(2) Unless cooperative statutes provide otherwise,

(a) in small cooperatives all members participate directly in making every decision, and
(b) in other cooperatives, governance is divided between a structure or organ giving members ultimate control of the organisation (the 'members' meeting') and one or more boards or committees, responsible for day to day management and accountable to the members.

(3) The powers of the decision-making organs of a cooperative are either:

(a) fixed by law or cooperative statutes, or
(b) can be delegated by the members' meeting on a basis of revocable delegation.

(4) The members' meeting may be organised as one meeting or several separate meetings. In cooperatives with a large or widely dispersed membership or in cooperatives with different categories of members, cooperative statutes may provide for sectorial meetings instead of the general meeting, with members represented by proxies or delegates. Meetings may be actual or virtual.

(5) The members' meeting has power to appoint and remove directors. The members' meeting must have power to make fundamental decisions. Fundamental decisions are decisions about restructuring or dissolving the cooperative, amending its statutes, participating in legal entities or groups, or establishing subsidiaries.

(6) The members' meeting:

(a) receives and considers financial and other information about the economic and cooperative performance of the cooperative, and the activity and the results of companies or other entities in which the cooperative participate, including structures of cooperation with other cooperatives;
(b) appoints and removes financial auditors;
(c) elects and removes members of an elected board or committee; and
(d) exercises any other powers conferred by law or cooperative statutes.

(7) Voting in a members' meeting is in principle on the basis of one member one vote regardless of the capital held.

(8) When necessary for the better functioning of a cooperative, cooperative statutes may confer plural votes not related to capital contribution, and reflecting, for example,

(a) participation in cooperative transactions;
(b) the number of members in particular subdivisions; or
(c) the balanced representation of different member groups.

(9) When cooperative statutes exercise the option in paragraph (8), they must in any case ensure that investor members or a minority of cooperator members do not control the cooperative.

(10) Total plural votes held by any cooperator member can never exceed a certain percentage of all members' votes cast at any members' meeting at which they vote, as defined by the law. However, investor members may have plural votes according to capital limited to a total of a certain percentage of votes cast at the members' meeting at which they vote, as defined by the law.

(11) Adequate notice of the agenda to be considered, the time and the place of meetings ensures that members have the opportunity to attend. Quorum requirements ensure that decisions are not unrepresentative of the membership.

(12) Decisions are made by simple majority of the votes cast but special majorities are required for the fundamental decisions defined in paragraph (5), which are always made on the basis of one member one vote.

(13) Cooperatives must hold annual members' meetings. The designated organ can also convene extraordinary members' meetings between the annual meetings. It must do so if a certain number or proportion of members or an organ so empowered by law or cooperative statutes or the auditing entity of section 4.3 requires it to do so.

(14) In cooperatives with a large or widely dispersed membership a smaller elected body may perform the role of supervising and monitoring the board in a one tier system.

COMMENTARY

PECOL 2.4(1) sets out the democratic control requirements of ICA P2 as the objective of all provisions on the governance of cooperatives.

PECOL 2.4(2) then provides a two-fold classification of direct member control of all decisions: a model sometimes referred to as 'collective', and a model based on the members' meeting which provides ultimate member control and one or more boards, committees or councils responsible for day to day management but accountable to the members. Both choices are subject to the possibility of variation by the statutes of particular cooperatives. Where boards and similar organs are used, a classic dichotomy is provided by the SCE Regulation which furnishes a choice between a unitary board ('administrative organ') and a two-tier board structure consisting of a supervisory board and a management board.

The 'collective' model suits small cooperatives where it is feasible for all decisions to be made by all members. PECOL 2.4(2) gives a default provision which may be changed by the cooperative statutes. It includes the all-member 'collective' model at PECOL 2.4(2)(a) as the purest form of member control but acknowledges that its use will be limited to small cooperatives. Apart from Italy, where some legal scholars believe that a collective structure can be used by cooperatives to which the rules of limited liability companies may additionally apply ('SRL Cooperatives'), most laws require the use of one or more boards or committees in addition to the members' meeting. Some UK worker cooperatives operate in this way by making all members directors comply with the legal requirement that the society or company must have directors (Co-operatives UK, *The Worker Co-operative Code*, 2012). This is a benefit of the liberal approach of UK Business Organisation Law.

That liberal approach is also reflected in PECOL 2.4(2)(b), which leaves room for the unitary board system, the two-tier board and other variations. This reflects the UK system and, in permitting either one- or two-tier systems, the provisions of SCE R.

The unitary board system provides for a single organ to be elected by the members. It has all the powers of day to day decision-making, leaving the annual meeting to receive reports and to make fundamental decisions. Articles 42–48 of SCE R deal with that option and bring together powers of management and representation in one administrative organ. This reflects the systems found in the UK and Finland, and it can be chosen by French cooperatives that use the SA structure and Italian cooperatives (see chapter 5 section 1 FiCA, art. L.225-17 of Fr Code of Commerce, art. 2380*bis* Italian CC).[12] French cooperatives, like French Srl companies, commonly have a structure in which a single manager is appointed by the general meeting, but those using the SA company structure have a board of directors. German cooperatives with fewer than 20 members have been able to choose a unitary board system since 2006 and need only have one board member (para. 24 GCA).[13]

The two-tier system is outlined in articles 37–41 and 45–51 of SCE R, and it is used in Germany for cooperatives with more than twenty members

---

12 Cf. A. Fici, CR Italy, p. 374; D. Hiez, CR France, p. 205; and H. Henrÿ, CR Finland, pp. 152–153; I. Snaith CR United Kingdom, p. 658.

13 Cf. H.-H. Münkner, CR Germany, pp. 288–289.

(see paras. 37–38 GCA).[14] In Spain and Portugal, and for those who choose it in Italy, a version of the system with a supervisory committee mainly concerned with verifying accounts is available as a two-tier system (arts. 38–70 PCC; arts. 21, 32 and 38 LC).[15] In these examples, both the supervisory committee and the board are elected by the general meeting. In the SCE, German and Italian two-tier models, the members elect the supervisory board, and it appoints the separate management organ.

PECOL 2.4(3) highlights another contrast drawn from the legal systems considered. In some systems, such as those of the UK and Germany, the powers and role of a cooperative's decision-making bodies is fixed either by the law or by the cooperative statutes. In others, all power is vested in the members' meeting, which can choose to delegate those powers to other organs, and although this is the usual arrangement and the one contemplated by the cooperative law, the general meeting is ultimately the sovereign body (see, for example art. 33(1) PCC).[16] PECOL acknowledges the two options.

PECOL 2.4(4) acknowledges another range of choices in regard to the functioning of the members' meeting. Cooperatives with a large or widely dispersed membership or with a number of different classes of members, such as employees, users, and suppliers, may need to divide the members' meeting into a number of parts. This can be done on a geographical basis or on the basis of the classes of members, and it may involve either a single 'serial' meeting of members with cumulative voting or a delegate structure. In the case of a delegate structure, the delegates may either be free to make their own decisions on how to vote or they may be bound by the mandate of the members who appoint them. If the delegates are bound, the weighting of their votes at the next level may either reflect the proportionate vote of the members who mandated them or be counted 100% on the side favoured by the majority of appointing members.

Among the national laws considered, German Law illustrates the historical development of the use of delegates by moving from a mandatory full meeting of members to the mandatory use of delegates and back to permitting the use of either system.[17] The use of a single meeting of all members divided into sections to facilitate participation by members in different geographical areas or involved in different business activities is reported to be used in France, particularly for agricultural cooperatives, and it is used by some UK consumer cooperatives.[18] A similar provision can be found in PCC art. 44 as part of a delegate structure.[19]

---

14 Ibid.

15 Cf. A. Fici, CR Italy, pp. 373–375; G. Fajardo, CR Spain, p. 546; and D. Meira, CR Portugal, p. 444.

16 Cf. D. Meira, CR Portugal, p. 437.

17 H.-H. Münkner, CR Germany, p. 284.

18 D. Hiez, CR France, p. 201 below, citing C.rur., art. R.524-16, and I. Snaith (ed.), *Handbook of Co-operative and Community Benefit Society Law*, Jordan Publishing, Bristol, 2014, p. 124.

19 D. Meira, CR Portugal, p. 441.

Article 63 of the SCE R provides a typical example of these possibilities. It permits the statutes of the cooperative to fix a range of such meetings where the cooperative 'undertakes different activities or activities in more than one territorial unit, or has several establishments or more than 500 members'. This provides a good summary of the grounds on which sectorial meetings may be required, and PECOL draws on it, while adding the possibility of different categories of members as another basis for adopting this procedure. PECOL aims to allow flexibility and freedom in a cooperative's own statutes.

The use of proxies to represent members and the use of virtual or electronic means of communication to hold meetings is accepted in most of the legal systems researched for the PECOL (see: para. 43(5) and (7) GCA; arts. 2538(6) and 2539 ICC; chap. 5 secs. 9 and 17 FiCA; art. 10 FrCA; arts. 23 and 24 LC; and s. 14(5) CCBSA).[20]

PECOL 2.4(5) and (6) deal with the items normally addressed by the members' meeting, and they reflect most national laws which empower the members' meeting to appoint and remove directors and make fundamental decisions, as well as the more frequent matters of surplus distribution and receipt or approval of accounts and reports The matter is normally determined by the cooperative law (see, for example, chap. 4 ss. 3 and 14 and chap. 2 sec. 6 FiCA; art. 6 FrCA; para. 24 GCA; arts. 33 and 38 PCC; arts. 28 and 34(1) LC; and s. 14 CCBSA).[21]

In addition, some of the other chapters of the PECOL specifically designate which organs are to make certain decisions: PECOL 3.4(6) requires the members meeting to make decisions about the voluntary reserves, and PECOL 3.6(3) and (6) respectively require the members' meeting to decide on the allocation of surpluses and how to cover losses. PECOL4.4(5) requires the members' meeting to discuss the auditor's report.

PECOL 2.4(7)–(10) emphasises the principle of one member one vote as a key defining feature of cooperatives. The principle is expressed in ICA P2:

> 'In primary cooperatives members have equal voting rights (one member, one vote) and cooperatives at other levels are also organised in a democratic manner.'

Despite the apparently universal requirement of one member one vote for primary cooperatives, many cooperative laws allow plural voting even in primary cooperatives if it produces a more equitable system. That may be justified by

---

20 Cf. A. Fici, CR Italy, p. 370; H. Henrÿ, CR Finland, pp. 150–151; D. Hiez, CR France, p. 200; D. Meira, CR Portugal, p. 441; H.-H. Münkner, CR Germany, p. 285; and I. Snaith, CR United Kingdom, p. 653–654.

21 Cf. G. Fajardo, CR Spain, p. 548; H. Henrÿ, CR Finland, p. 150; D. Hiez CR France, p. 200; D. Meira CR Portugal, p. 441; H.-H. Münkner CR Germany, pp. 285–286; and I. Snaith, CR United Kingdom, pp. 651–652.

the type of member served by the cooperative (for example, cooperatives of entrepreneurs) or, within limits, as an advantage for capital provided. In this respect, PECOL draws on a range of provisions of national laws to extract this principle. Those national provisions tend to show both that exceptions to the general rule of 'one member, one vote' are common, and that they share certain features which PECOL seeks to summarise as principles.[22]

ICC allows a cooperative's statutes to derogate from the rule within limits: plural votes (up to five) may be linked to capital by cooperative statutes in the case of members who are cooperatives or other legal persons. Similarly, the statutes of cooperatives made up of entrepreneurs and enterprises may allow votes proportional to mutual transactions with the cooperative up to 10% of the total vote per member and a total of 30% for all such members; plural votes proportionate to either factor may be awarded for the election of the organ of control: and investor members may have plural votes up to one third of total votes (arts. 2526, 2538 and 2543 ICC). Similarly, paras. 8, 36 and 43 of the GCA focus on cooperatives composed largely of entrepreneur members and limited plural voting for investor members. French Law provides a similar range of pragmatic exceptions to one member, one vote.[23] The Spanish system also displays greater willingness to permit plural voting (based on the volume of cooperative business) where cooperatives have entrepreneurs or businesses as members, or where plural voting is needed to reflect the proportionate weighting of different classes of member (arts. 13, 14, 105 and 107 LC).[24]

Portuguese law strictly limits the extent of plural voting, emphasising that it should not relate to capital contribution and generally linking it to cooperative transactions by cooperators. It also applies a one member one vote system for important or fundamental decisions (arts. 16, 29, 40, 41 and 51 PCC).[25] In the UK, para. 4.15 of the FCA Guidance makes clear the importance of one member one vote as a key element in the interpretation of the phrase 'bona fide cooperative' for the purpose of the CCBSA registration condition, while also acknowledging the diversity of cooperatives and, for example, the particular situation of cooperatives with a number of different stakeholder groups.

PECOL 2.4(7) builds on these features of the legal systems considered and expresses the general principle while emphasising the contrast with joint stock companies, in which voting power is usually linked to capital contribution, thus placing power and control in the hands of investors rather than other stakeholder groups. This is done by expressing the principle as one member one vote 'regardless of capital contribution' (see also art. 59(1) SCE R, which sets out this general proposition).

---

22 See generally: G. Fajardo, CR Spain, pp. 548–550; A. Fici, CR Italy, pp. 370–371; H. Henrÿ, CR Finland, p. 151; D. Hiez, CR France, p. 197; D. Meira, CR Portugal, p. 438.

23 See D. Hiez, CR France, pp. 197–198.

24 See G. Fajardo, CR Spain, pp. 548–550.

25 See D. Meira, CR Portugal, p. 438.

PECOL 2.4(8)–(10) then elaborate on the permitted exceptions to one member one vote based on the national laws studied.

PECOL 2.4(8) lays down the basis of permitted plural votes with examples of acceptable criteria for additional votes. The basis chosen in PECOL is necessity – 'when necessary for the better functioning of the cooperative'. The examples of acceptable bases for plural voting are then set out.

PECOL 2.4(8)(a) deals with participation in cooperative transactions which, as noted above, is a widespread basis for plural voting. That can apply to either primary or secondary cooperatives and links voting power to cooperative inputs (work in a worker cooperative or supplied goods or services in producer cooperatives) or outputs (purchases of goods or services in a consumer cooperative). This system is more common than any other exception to the general one member one vote principle, perhaps because it seems more equitable than one member one vote for cooperatives of entrepreneurs. Art. 59(2) SCE R refers explicitly to this basis for plural voting, chapter 4 section 7 of the FCA permits plural voting without specifying the basis for it; art. 5 of the French Law of 1947 permits it for secondary cooperatives; and some French laws for particular types of cooperative, such as agricultural, artisan and banking cooperatives, allow it for primary cooperatives. Para. 43 of the GCA, like art. 2538(4) of Italian CC and some examples of plural voting permitted by the LC, permits a strictly limited increase in the number of votes on this basis without fully proportionate weighting according to transactions.

PECOL 2.4(8)(b) allows for plural voting based on the number of members in particular subdivisions of a cooperative. This is an indirect reflection of the one member one vote principle. It is most likely to apply to cooperatives with large numbers of members who are widely dispersed geographically. It may also be used by secondary cooperatives to balance the influence of different primary cooperatives in membership of the organisation. In each case, this system will raise questions about how the votes of the members in particular subdivisions are to be assessed. Are the votes for and against a resolution cumulated separately when added together from each subdivision or are all of a subdivision's votes cast in accordance with the view of the majority within that subdivision? PECOL follows arts. 59(2) and 63 SCE R by leaving that choice to the statutes of each cooperative.

PECOL 2.4(8)(c) is most likely to apply to hybrid or multi-stakeholder cooperatives (including, in PECOL terms, general interest cooperatives) where employees, users, suppliers and investors may all have membership. In such cases, voting rights based simply on one member one vote across all types of member would give one or more particular groups unfair dominance in decision-making. For example, the number of user members may greatly exceed the number of employees. Art 59(2) SCE R provides the clearest example, and it permits the practice based on number of members only in wholly or mainly secondary cooperatives ('SCEs the majority of members of which are cooperatives').

PECOL 2.4(9) requires that any plural votes available to investor members be particularly strictly limited. This is intended to reflect the de-emphasis of capital at the heart of the concept of a cooperative. The principle of control by user members rather than investors supports the limitations on the return to capital explored in PECOL 3 and the centrality of denying votes on the basis of capital stake in the cooperative model. The SCE chooses a limit of 25% of total voting rights (SCE R 59(3)). In PECOL 2.4(10) the model of 'percentage of total votes cast' at a meeting is used, but no specific percentage is given because this is a principle rather than a rule. The same approach is taken to minorities of cooperator members.

The above provisions apply equally to general interest cooperatives and mutual cooperatives whether multi-stakeholder based or not.

PECOL 2.4(12) reflects the almost universal practice of requiring a simple majority for decisions other than the fundamental changes listed in PECOL 2.4(5), such as amending the statutes or restructuring or dissolving the cooperative. Article 61(2) and (4) of SCE R are typical of national law provisions on majorities required (66.6% for amendments to the statutes), but they apply a higher (but not lower) national law requirement. They also include a quorum requirement of 50% of those eligible for changes to the statutes at a meeting convened for the purpose, but no special quorum if an inquorate meeting is reconvened.

Similarly, PECOL 2.4(11) requires adequate notice of the business, venue and time of meetings, as well as a quorum to ensure that decisions are not unrepresentative of the membership. This is typical of the approach of national laws. Arts. 5(4), 56 and 57 of SCE R are typical provisions.

PECOL 2.4(13) requires annual members' meetings and ensures that the organ responsible for calling extraordinary meetings can always do that and must do so if a certain number or proportion of members or any organ empowered by law or auditing body requests it. This reflects the general practice found in national laws as expressed in arts. 54 and 55 SCE R.

PECOL 2.4(14) acknowledges the option found in, for example, some of the governance models available under Italian Cooperative Law of interposing a supervisory board, elected by the general meeting, between the directors and the general meeting. The supervisory board has the power to vote as if it were the general meeting of members which it replaces, and it is also given the role of supervising and monitoring the directors. This is particularly appropriate when it is unlikely that all members will be able to participate in frequent members' meetings but the supervisory and monitoring role needs to be carried out on an ongoing basis.

In most systems, mechanisms to protect creditors, or minorities of members or employees are added to the general mechanisms for member control if fundamental restructuring decisions are likely to affect those groups. Classic examples are to be found in the SCE provisions concerning mergers, conversions and the transfer of registered office – see arts. 7, 19 to 34, 35 and 76 of the SCE R.

PECOL 5 deals with governance issues involving secondary and tertiary cooperatives. In particular, PECOL 5.2(4) explains the voting principles to be applied in secondary cooperatives.

SECTION 2.5 COOPERATIVE GOVERNANCE STRUCTURES: MANAGEMENT AND INTERNAL CONTROL

(1) The functions of cooperative boards (if any) include executive management, representation and supervision. The three functions may be performed by one administrative board ('one tier system') or divided between a supervisory board and a management board ('two tier system'). The distribution of powers will be laid down by law and cooperative statutes.

(2) Executive management powers are all those not reserved to another organ. Representation means the authority to represent the cooperative in dealings with third parties and in legal proceedings.

(3) The powers of representation and executive management of the cooperative are allocated to:

(a) the administrative board in the one tier system or
(b) the management board in the two tier system, or
(c) one or more directors or managers.

These powers may be delegated by those on whom they are conferred except to the extent that cooperative statutes provide otherwise.

(4) Supervision is concerned with the economic and social performance of a cooperative. That function involves the internal oversight and monitoring of executive directors or managers. In the two tier system, the supervision and executive functions are carried out by different boards. In the one tier system, subcommittees of the administrative board or of the members' meeting may be used for supervisory purposes. The designated organ will liaise with external auditors as provided in section 4.

(5) Board composition, especially in general interest cooperatives, shall take into account the composition of the cooperative membership, including, for example, by geographical constituency or category of member. Where substitutes have not been elected in advance, the board may have power to co-opt members to fill casual vacancies pending an election.

(6) The majority of members of administrative and supervisory boards shall be cooperator members. The statutes of a general interest cooperative may also provide so.

(7) Law or cooperative statutes lay down:

(a) the maximum and minimum number of members for each board;
(b) the term of office and any limits on the number of terms that may be served;
(c) any requirement for gender balance;
(d) appointment or election procedures; and
(e) the qualifications for board membership which, separately or in combination, must not unduly limit the democratic right of the members to elect, or be elected as, board members. Law or cooperative statutes may also provide grounds for disqualification.

(8) The duties of cooperative board members and managers include an obligation to adhere to the defining values, principles and practices of cooperatives in addition to their obligation to comply with law and cooperative statutes and their duties of honesty, loyalty, good faith, care and skill.

COMMENTARY

As noted in the comments to PECOL 2.4, most legal systems use boards or committees – either the unitary board system or the two-tier board reflected in SCE R. This part of PECOL outlines the functions, powers and composition of organs in each of those systems. However, it also acknowledges the possibility of using the 'collective' model of direct member control of all decisions.

An organ which consists of more than one member operates as a collective body, but it may delegate particular functions to subcommittees or individuals. In the one-tier system, this may include the appointment by the board of specialist audit or supervisory committees. Separate committees to perform particular functions may also be created by law or by cooperative statutes. Boards usually make decisions by simple majority. Procedural matters about board meetings such as convening meetings, quorum, and who chairs meetings are usually laid down in or under cooperative statutes.

PECOL 2.5(1)–(4) define the three key functions of cooperative boards: executive management; representation; and supervision. The separation of these three functions draws on the analysis of the legal systems researched, which, to a greater or lesser extent, explicitly establish these functions or roles.

PECOL 2.5(3) indicates the various ways in which the powers to carry out the representation and executive management functions are distributed under the one-tier and two-tier systems, and those that recognise a role for executive directors or managers as a separate organ of the cooperative rather than the recipients of delegated powers. This follows arts. 37(1), 39(1) and 42(1) of SCE R.[26]

This acknowledges the possibility of having one or more managing directors or managers rather than a full administrative board to carry out the management and representation functions. It allows for the French limited liability company (Srl) system used by some cooperatives. This model is also open to Portuguese cooperatives with no more than 20 members (art. 62(1) PCC).[27] The model with a single member executive organ is distinct from the possibility of delegation by any of the other organs as acknowledged in PECOL 2.5(2). It contemplates a single manager constituting the executive and representative organ under the statutes or the law.

PECOL 2.5(4) concerns the organs that carry out the supervision function in cooperatives. In the two-tier system, this is the function of the supervisory organ. In the one-tier system, it is often the role of a subcommittee of the administrative organ made up of directors who are not personally also executive managers or of a separately elected supervisory board (see art. 39(1) SCE R, Co-operatives UK Code of Practice on Governance in Consumer Co-operatives; chapter 6, secs. 1, 21 and 23 FiCA, para. 38 GCA and arts. 2397–2405 ICC).[28]

PECOL 2.5(5) and (6) concern board composition. The latter should reflect the composition of the membership in general interest and multi-stakeholder cooperatives, while in mutual cooperatives a majority of board members should be members. This is required under para. 9(2) GCA and art. 6 FrCA.[29] These provisions allow some variation in board composition in general interest cooperatives by proportionate constituencies for board composition and for constituencies based on geography or the representation of users, employees, and suppliers. In each case, the PECOL provision is a reflection of the basic principle of member control. The provision for mutual cooperatives represents their purpose of serving their own members on a mutual and self-managed basis.

PECOL 2.5(7) deals with maximum and minimum numbers of board members, the term of office of members of the organ, any limits on the number of terms a person can serve, and any requirement for gender balance. These matters will vary from one context to another. A board should be small enough

---

26 Cf. G. Fajardo, CR Spain, p. 546; A. Fici, CR Italy, pp. 372–376; H. Henrÿ, CR Finland, pp. 152–153; D. Hiez, CR France, pp. 203–205; D. Meira, CR Portugal, pp. 442–443; H.-H. Münkner, CR Germany, pp. 287–288; and I. Snaith, CR United Kingdom, pp. 647–649.

27 Cf. D. Hiez, CR France, p. 203; D. Meira, CR Portugal, p. 443.

28 Cf. A. Fici, CR Italy, p. 373; H. Henrÿ, CR Finland, p. 153; H.-H. Münkner, CR Germany, pp. 287–289; I. Snaith, CR United Kingdom, pp. 657–658.

29 In Germany this may be avoided by admitting 'promoting members' with appropriate expertise who are not part of the cooperative's membership group to allow them to serve on the board – see H.-H. Münkner, CR Germany, p. 289.

for effective operation and large enough to represent a range of members – especially in a multi-stakeholder or general interest cooperative, where member interests may diverge. PECOL does not specify figures. SCE R leaves this to the cooperative's statutes, subject to national law (arts. 37(4) and 42).

Similarly, the term of office provision should balance the need for continuity against the democratic right of members to remove and replace directors. Article 45 of SCE R provides for six-year terms with a maximum of two terms. Many national systems provide for three-year terms, and some allow for the retirement of one third of organ members each year to encourage stability and continuity.[30]

To ensure democratic control by members, appointment or election must either be by the members in a general meeting or directly by members in elections. In both cases, proxy voting and electronic communications should be used to encourage maximum participation. Most systems use the members' meeting option – see, for example, arts. 39(2) and 42(3) SCE R. In the two-tier system, the supervisory board classically appoints the members of the management organ and no-one can be a member of both organs – see art. 36(3) SCE R. Article 37(2) SCE R permits the election of management organ members by the general meeting if national law requires it.

Qualifications for board membership may include membership of the cooperative. This may be extended to a minimum period of membership and may be complemented by a requirement of service on a different organ of the cooperative, such as a regional committee or council, as part of a delegate-based governance structure. A requirement of participation in a particular form of cooperative activity may apply to multi-stakeholder cooperatives. In the case of general interest cooperatives, such a qualification may be replaced by a requirement for connection with a particular geographical region.

Minimum legal capacity requirements, such as age and mental capacity, apply as they do to other legal entities. A minimum level of trade may be required for a mutual cooperative; a minimum capital holding may apply to a mutual or a general interest cooperative. Neither should be set at a level amounting to a serious obstacle to members qualifying. The 2014 reforms to the UK Co-operative Group statutes laid down a requirement for substantial minimum levels of business expertise or experience. The requirement is applied to potential directors by a Nominations Committee of the existing board as a condition of nomination – rules 48 and 51 and Appendix 1 of the rules of the Co-operative Group (2014). A parallel members' council exists in the Co-operative Group,

---

30 Cf. G. Fajardo, CR Spain, p. 553; H. Henrÿ, CR Finland, p. 152; D. Hiez, CR France, p. 205; D. Meira CR Portugal, p. 439; H.-H. Münkner, CR Germany, p. 291; and I. Snaith, CR United Kingdom, p. 657.

and less demanding requirements apply for election to it. Those provisions did not prevent registration of the 2014 amendments by the FCA under ss. 2 and 16 of CCBSA as creating statutes appropriate for a bona fide cooperative.

Any grounds for disqualification as a director will be found in the law or the statutes of the cooperative: for example, personal insolvency, court order of disqualification, or unfitness due to mental incapacity. Others may be added by the statutes of the cooperative.

PECOL 2.5(8) adds the specifically cooperative duties of directors to the duties laid down by law for anyone with such a role in a business entity. Article 51 SCE R aptly summarises the general legal liabilities of organ members thus:

> 'Members of management, supervisory and administrative organs shall be liable, in accordance with the provisions applicable to cooperatives in the Member State in which the SCE's registered office is situated, for loss or damage sustained by the SCE following any breach on their part of the legal, statutory or other obligations inherent in their duties.'

PECOL emphasises the requirement that people adhere specifically to cooperative values principles and practices, as well as complying with the legal and fiduciary obligations that flow from their role in the legal entity. In addition to liability to the cooperative, removal from office is also likely to result from a breach of those duties.

PECOL 2.5(9) specifically acknowledges the particular importance of a minimum level of cooperative training or experience in addition to other relevant professional experience and qualifications. This reflects ICA P7, which requires training and education for elected representatives and managers.

PECOL 2.5(10) states that any remuneration for members of organs or senior managers who participate in governance must be decided or approved by the members' meeting and should take account of the nature of cooperatives and their special features of equity, equality, and de-emphasis of capital. However, the market rate paid to people with particular skills or experience can also be a relevant factor, particularly for managers or executives.

SECTION 2.6
INFORMATION RIGHTS OF MEMBERS AND TRANSPARENCY REQUIREMENTS

(1) Board members and managers shall ensure that the cooperative operates with a high level of transparency and shall give members sufficient clear information to enable them to control the cooperative.

(2) In particular, they shall ensure that full annual accounts and, if appropriate, consolidated accounts are drawn up, audited, and published to members with an annual report and cooperative and financial audit reports as required by law. Such documents shall be available to the public at the cooperative's registered office at a price not exceeding their administrative cost.

(3) Members and applicants for membership have a right to information on their obligations and rights.

COMMENTARY

PECOL 2.6(1) applies the ICA Value of transparency to member control of the cooperative through cooperative governance. It requires that members be given sufficient information to enable them to control the cooperative. Members collectively, or the supervisory or audit organs acting on their behalf, must be given all the information they need to: conduct the business of members' meetings or participate in other democratic processes, such as elections; appoint or remove directors; set the cooperative's business, member promotion, and social responsibility strategies; and decide on changes to the cooperative's statutes or any other fundamental reorganisation of its structure.

Information about subsidiaries of the cooperative is also vital so that members in their meetings and the board are able to ensure that subsidiaries are appropriately controlled in accordance with the requirement of PECOL 1.1(3). Similarly, all members must have access to the audit report under PECOL 4.4(4).

PECOL 2.6(2). Legal requirements in respect of the contents, audit, and publication of information for members and the wider public on the accounting, financial and cooperative performance of a cooperative and the powers of regulators and courts to investigate or inspect cooperatives are dealt with in PECOL 4. For subsidiaries, the law and cooperative statutes governing the preparation, audit and publication of group accounts for cooperatives with subsidiaries play a crucial role in permitting effective member control under PECOL 4.1 and 4.4.

PECOL 2.6(3) Member, director and manager education on members' rights and obligations is vital for the functioning and governance of cooperatives. It should be available either through individual cooperatives or cooperative federations and colleges, and the law should promote and facilitate this by permitting or mandating the use of funds for this purpose.

CHAPTER 3
COOPERATIVE FINANCIAL STRUCTURE

With Commentary by Gemma FAJARDO and Deolinda MEIRA

SECTION 3.1
GENERAL PRINCIPLES OF COOPERATIVE FINANCIAL STRUCTURE

(1) As private legal persons that carry on an economic activity without profits as the ultimate purpose, cooperatives have a specific financial structure aimed at the success of their objectives, with respect to universally recognised cooperative values and principles.

(2) As business organisations, cooperatives can use shares, reserves, loans and other financial instruments as sources of capital, providing they are compatible with their cooperative nature.

COMMENTARY

Cooperatives have a distinct financial structure, as shown below.

The social object of the cooperative, closely linked to its mutualistic vocation, makes it compulsory that the cooperative's financial structure be aimed at promotion of the interests of cooperator members, i.e. at meeting their economic, social and cultural needs. Indeed, unlike commercial companies, cooperatives conduct an economic activity whose aim is not primarily profit but has a mutualistic purpose (see sec. 1.1). However, as outlined in chapter 1, the mutualistic purpose pursued by cooperatives does not mean that they conduct their activity exclusively with their members, since they may also engage in non-member cooperative transactions (see sec. 1.5) which will have consequences on their financial structure.

The financial structure of cooperatives is thus based on a particular logic resulting not only from the specific characteristics of the cooperative objective but also from the necessary obedience to cooperative values and principles.

Cooperatives develop their social object in an organised and professional manner, and, like business organisations, they need to use various management and financial instruments to enhance their efficiency in achieving their goals. To this end, according to the Principles of European Cooperative Law (PECOL), cooperatives can use shares, reserves, loans, and other financial instruments as sources of capital provided that these are compatible with their cooperative nature.

SECTION 3.2
COOPERATIVE SHARE CAPITAL

(1) Cooperatives are established without minimum capital, unless the law or cooperative statutes provide otherwise.

(2) Cooperative statutes may fix a minimum share capital and the minimum amount and nature of the contribution of each member, with respect to the principle of open membership as laid down in sections 1.3(6) and 2.2.

(3) In any case, the share capital is variable, which means that variations in the amount of the capital, due notably to increased or reduced membership, do not require amendments of the cooperative statutes nor disclosures.

(4) Reduction of the share capital below any minimum prescribed may be cause for cooperative dissolution.

COMMENTARY

To start their activity, cooperatives need economic resources, which will be obtained *ab initio* through the contributions of cooperator members to the share capital. These contributions, however, are mere instruments for the development of cooperative transactions, and they do not contribute to determining the rights and duties of cooperator members. *De facto*, in principle, financial rights in a cooperative are determined by (the quantity and quality of) mutual transactions, while governance rights are determined by membership *per se*.

The justification for this instrumental nature of share capital in cooperatives is the fact that cooperatives, in order to conduct their economic activity, need not only their own assets but also, and mainly, the participation of cooperator members in the activity that constitutes their object (cooperative transactions).

As pointed out in PECOL 1, the cooperative operates with its members, who participate in the activity carried out by the cooperative (cooperative transactions). Fulfilment of the cooperative's social object therefore entails that the cooperator members must pay for or provide the goods or services to the cooperative: in Spanish legal scholarship, this set of inputs made by cooperator members to the cooperative is called 'mutualistic capital' ('*masa de gestión cooperativa*'). It is for this reason that, according to art. 52.3 Spanish Cooperative Act (SCA), 'the assets of any kind provided by the members for management by the cooperative and, in general, payments made to obtain cooperative services do not form part of the share capital and are subject to the conditions set by and agreed with the cooperative'. In all the other legal systems analysed, mutualistic capital is not provided for in law.

Moreover, the International Cooperative Alliance (ICA) cooperative principle of economic participation by members does not require share capital in order to incorporate a cooperative. This cooperative principle uses the term 'capital' as a synonym for 'assets', stressing the indivisible assets of the cooperative.

In this context, PECOL's choice, based on the UK legal system, has been to admit the possibility of constituting a cooperative without share capital unless the law or cooperative statutes provide otherwise. It is therefore possible to organise a cooperative without share capital, counting solely on the accumulation of collectively-owned indivisible reserves by cooperator members. In fact, in the UK a cooperative that uses the CLG (Company Limited by Guarantee) structure is not entitled to have any share capital (Companies Act 2006, sections 3.5 and 16(1)–(3)). In the Spanish legal system, there is also the possibility for cooperator members not to make any contribution to the share capital at the moment when the cooperative is established (art. 58.3 of Andalusian Law 2011). In many of the legal systems analysed, it is not possible to set up a cooperative without compulsory contributions by members (see art. 2521, para. 3, no. 4 and 2525, para. 1 Italian Civil Code (ICC); art. 83 Portuguese Cooperatice Code (PCC); chap. 1, sec. 2(1) Finnish Cooperative Act (FiCA); §7.1 German Cooperative Act (GCA); art. 45.2 SCA; art. 27.2 French Law no. 47-1775 (FrCA); art. 3 SCE). At present, the common practice in European cooperative laws is that no one can become a member of a cooperative by buying a share (as in a company). The share contribution is rather an obligation of the person admitted to membership upon application.

In many legal systems, it is now possible to establish a limited liability company with 1 euro, which means that the share capital has lost its relevance (for creditor protection) in general and not just for cooperatives.

Despite the minor importance of cooperative share capital, according to PECOL sec. 3.2(2), cooperative statutes may fix a minimum share capital, and both the nature and minimum amount of the contribution of each member, with respect to the principle of open membership.

Cooperative statutes may fix the nature of the contribution of each member. These contributions to share capital may be in cash or in kind (see, among others, art. 21.1 PCC; art. 45.4 SCA; §7.3 GCA; chap. 2, sec. 6 FiCA).

Contributions in services are usually not allowed as contributions to share capital because the latter is formed solely of assets whose economic value can be assessed (see art. 4.2 SCE).

The minimum share capital operates as a limit on the variability of share capital and on the reduction of the cooperative's assets, thus representing a minimum guarantee for the interests of creditors.

In some legal systems, the requirement of a minimum share capital is mandatory (art. 81.2 PCC; §8.a GCA; art. 3.2 SCE and in most of the Spanish laws). Hence there is an obligation to specify the share capital in the statutes (principle of determination).

In the legal systems of Italy, Finland and the UK, for example, no minimum capital requirement applies to cooperatives. In the Italian legal system, the law requires only that statutes shall indicate the amount of capital subscribed by each member (art. 2521, para. 3, no. 4, ICC) and that the loss of the capital is a cause of cooperative dissolution (art. 2545*duodecies* ICC).

In the French legal system, the requirement of a mandatory minimum share capital depends on the form adopted by the cooperative, taking the legal framework provided in company law as reference. A minimum share capital will only be required if the cooperative takes the legal form of a public limited company (art. 27.2 FrCA).

Under PECOL, the variability of capital is an essential feature of cooperatives. Since cooperatives are governed by open and voluntary membership, capital variability facilitates the entry and exit of members.

The variability of capital is fundamentally influenced by the members joining or leaving the cooperative. However, this equation does not always hold true because members can join or leave by transferring participations in the share capital, which therefore does not change; and the share capital can also be changed without any members joining or leaving. For instance, it can be increased through new contributions made by existing members or by applying surplus or reserves, and it can be reduced through the allocation of losses.

PECOL refers explicitly to the fact that capital variability means that variations in the amount of share capital, due notably to the increase or reduction of membership, do not require amendment to or disclosure of the cooperative statutes.

It has been a common practice in European cooperative law to include variability of share capital in the definition of a cooperative (arts. 2511 and 2524, para. 1, ICC; art. 2 PCC; art. 1 SCA; art. 1.2 SCE).

The main consequence of this variability is the reduced financial quality of the share capital, particularly the economic and social security that the share capital represents for creditors, which can cause difficulties for cooperatives in raising external finance and, on occasion, can lead to undercapitalisation.

This explains why, although the variability of cooperatives' share capital is a recognised feature of their identity, the common practice is to have European cooperative laws comprise measures intended to ensure that the cooperative share capital has a minimum of stability. Examples are: the possibility of deferred redemption for a period of time provided for in the statutes (art. 89.1 PCC; art. 51.5 SCA; art. 2535 ICC; art. 16.3 SCE); the possibility to make deductions from the right to redemption (art. 89.2 PCC; art. 51.2 SCA; art. 2535, para. 2, ICC; art. 18.3 FrCA; art. 16.1 SCE); the application of deductions to the face value of the member's shares whenever losses are attributable to the cooperator member within the financial year in which the right to redemption originated (art. 89.2 PCC); statutory minimum periods of membership; and rules fixing notice periods needed for a withdrawal (art. 24.1 PCC; art. 17.3 SCA; art. 2532 ICC).

Nevertheless, according to PECOL, under no circumstances may these mechanisms suppress the right to withdraw, given the need to respect the cooperative principle of open membership (art. 24.3 PCC and art. 17.1 SCA). This issue is of particular importance and immediacy, given the effects of international accounting regulations on the Spanish legal system, wherein, since the accounting law reform, cooperative law has provided a different criterion for classifying capital contributions, i.e. contributions with the right to redemption in the case of leaving, or contributions for which redemption in the case of leaving can be unconditionally refused by the board.

For PECOL, it is clear that cooperative share capital (like company capital) is and remains equity/risk capital (i.e. funds provided by members in exchange for membership). Notwithstanding the fact that cooperative share capital has many characteristics of debt capital, being equity/risk capital, it is the property of the cooperative and not a sum borrowed from members. In this respect, the issue of international accounting standards has not raised any questions in PECOL.

Cooperative share capital can be increased in various circumstances: by requiring new contributions from the members (art. 46.2 SCA), even if the common practice in European laws is to disallow cooperatives from imposing the subscription of new shares to meet their financial needs when new members join the cooperative (art. 46.7 SCA; art 3.5 SCE); through voluntary contributions from the cooperative members (art. 47 SCA); or by allocating cooperative refunds to the share capital (art. 58.4 SCA; art. 2545*sexies*, para. 3, ICC) or converting available reserves into share capital (art. 2545*quinquies*, para. 3, lit. b, ICC). Allocation of reserves can only be carried out using non-mandatory reserves whose funding does not come from the benefits resulting from operations with non members, as well as from other extra-cooperative sources. In this way, if share capital is increased by the allocation of such reserves, only cooperators who have contributed to such surpluses, and to the exact amount of their contribution, are allowed to participate in the share capital increase.

Cooperative share capital will be reduced by repayment to members who leave the cooperative or by allocation of losses, as pointed out below.

According to the PECOL, reduction of the share capital below any minimum prescribed may be cause for cooperative dissolution (art. 45.8.d) and art. 70.1, both SCA). This will be a means to ensure that the minimum share capital operates as the minimum limit on the variability of share capital, in order to prevent the cooperative's undercapitalisation, and it represents a minimum guarantee for the interests of creditors.

SECTION 3.3
MEMBERS' CONTRIBUTIONS TO CAPITAL

(1) Membership is acquired in accordance with section 2.2. The sole acquisition of shares does not confer the status of member.

(2) Cooperator members contribute equally to cooperative capital unless cooperative statutes provide for another criterion, such as in proportion to participation in cooperative transactions.

(3) The law may allow cooperative statutes to require new members to contribute more capital or a higher contribution than the minimum, to adjust to new conditions in a reasonable manner.

(4) No member may hold a percentage of the share capital higher than the maximum defined by law or cooperative statutes.

(5) The paid-up capital may be paid interest if cooperative statutes so provide and the members' meeting decides to do so. The interest rate may differ according to the nature of the contribution, whether mandatory or optional, and of the category of members providing it, whether cooperator members or other types of members. In any case, the interest rate cannot be higher than a reasonable rate, necessary to obtain and retain enough capital to run the business.

(6) Cooperative shares may be transferred only among members or candidates for membership. The transfer of member shares is always subject to approval by the designated organ as well as to any other conditions laid down in cooperative statutes. Shares subscribed by investor members are not transferable without permission from an organ of the cooperative. Member shares cannot be attached by the personal creditors of the members.

(7) The member who leaves the cooperative may be reimbursed for the nominal value of their shares and their portion of divisible reserves, as provided in the cooperative statutes, which may subject the reimbursement to reasonable conditions. The amount repayable to the member may also take into consideration any outstanding interest or cooperative refunds due to the member and any debts due from the member to the cooperative.

COMMENTARY

Considering that, according to PECOL, it is possible to set up a cooperative without share capital (see 3.2(1)), contributions to capital are not a necessary condition for acquiring membership (see 2.2). To acquire membership, a person must accept the responsibilities of membership (see 2.2.1), in particular he/she must engage in cooperative transactions (see 1.3.2) and be accepted by the designated organ of the cooperative (see 2.2).

However, it is usual for both laws and statutes to establish a contribution to the cooperative's capital as an obligation of members (2.3.1(b)). According to PECOL, contribution to capital is not a condition for membership but may be an obligation to be met by members.

To become a member of a cooperative (either as a cooperator member or as an investor member), the conditions for membership laid down in the statutes must be met (see 2.2).

Taking into account also the ICA cooperative principle of 'member economic participation', which provides for equitable contribution from members to the share capital of cooperatives, PECOL section 3.3(2) states that cooperator members contribute equally to the cooperative capital, while assuming, however, that the cooperative statutes may provide another criterion, such as contribution in proportion to participation in cooperative transactions. Some cooperative laws contain provisions regarding the minimum mandatory contribution to capital (see, among others, art. 81 PCC; art. 2525(1) ICC; para. 4 GCA). In other legal systems, the amount of any minimum contribution to capital that may be required is a matter for the statutes of the cooperative to establish (see, art. 46.1 SCA; §7.1 GCA; No. 4 and 7 of art. 4 SCE).

Some European cooperative laws explicitly state that the minimum mandatory contribution to capital may vary according to the members' participation in cooperative transactions (art. 46.1 SCA; §7.1 and 7.a GCA). The Spanish legal system also provides for the possibility that the minimum mandatory contribution to capital may vary according to the type of member – more specifically according to whether the capital contribution is made by cooperator members or investor members.

In general, the contributions to capital must be paid at the moment of subscription, and the remainder must be paid as provided for in the cooperative statutes or the resolutions of the General Meeting. Contributions in kind must be paid in full. Contributions in cash can be paid in part at the time and the rest at the request of the board, if cooperative statutes so provide (art. 84 PCC; art. 2531 ICC; §7.1 GCA). Finally, it should be noted that, in all cases, the minimum share capital must be fully paid-up at the moment when the cooperative is founded (art. 45.2 SCA).

Not making the contribution to capital or not disbursing it on time may be cause of exclusion, without prejudice to enforcing payment or taking other punitive measures such as suspension of rights (see, among others, art. 26 PCC; art. 46.6 SCA)

The value of the share will be fixed in the statutes. A good practice, worthy of note, set out in the Spanish (art. 49 SCA), Italian (art. 7 of Law no. 59/1992) and German legal systems is the possibility to increase the value of shares by using available voluntary reserves to update their value by offsetting depreciation over time. Share value can likewise be reduced by charging losses.

The law may allow the cooperative statutes to require new members to contribute with more capital or with a contribution higher than the minimum in order to adjust to new conditions in a reasonable manner (sec. 3.3(3)). This possibility can be made effective in different ways: (a) by having new members make a higher contribution to capital to equal their status with that of the contributions made by previous members, or simply by compensating for their depreciation over time; (b) by requiring an admission fee (see, among others art. 90 PCC; art. 52.2 SCA). The admission fee will function: (i) as an outright grant required of every cooperator member and motivated by the expenses that his/her admittance entails which will be borne by the cooperative (cost of installing new work tools, increased maintenance expenses, and any others); (ii) as a way to compensate, in part, for the contribution of existing cooperator members to the common assets of the cooperative.

Use of the expression 'in a reasonable manner' serves to highlight the need to respect the ICA Principle of voluntary and open membership, which will prevent the establishment of excessively burdensome conditions of admission for aspiring cooperator members. Indeed, the establishment of higher admission fees or of a contribution above the minimum may collide with the right of admission.

The Spanish legal system provides for the possibility that, apart from the mandatory contributions required by cooperative statutes or the General Meeting, members can make other non-mandatory (voluntary) contributions. These contributions require the authorisation of the General Meeting or, in some cases, of the Board. The former are the same for every member or proportional to member participation in the cooperative business. These voluntary member contributions confer certain advantages in the return paid, transfer and redemption. Similarly, in the German legal system, the following distinction is drawn: capital subscription as an obligation of membership (compulsory contribution); supplementary contributions at the request of the cooperative (staggered share contributions in proportion to use made of the services of the cooperative enterprise) and laid down in the statutes (§7.a GCA); and voluntary supplementary contributions. In the other cooperative laws analysed, in principle a cooperative cannot require supplementary contributions (or other forms of financial participation) from members unless cooperative statutes authorise the directors to do so, and, even in this case, only up to a certain amount.

Cooperatives can issue financial instruments with fixed, variable, or mixed returns (loans, bonds, equity securities, etc.) (see, among others, art. 21.2 SCA; art. 2526 ICC; art. 87–94, PCC; art. 11, 11*bis* and 19, FrCA; chap. 9, sec. 1 and chap. 10, sec. 1 FiCA), and some legislations still allow the creation of credit sections within the cooperative to meet the financial needs of the cooperative and its members (see, among others, art. 5 SCA).

For PECOL, no member may hold a percentage of the share capital higher than the maximum defined by law or by cooperative statutes. This provision is consistent with the Spanish Law, which establishes that no member can make contributions that exceed a third of the share capital unless that member is a cooperative, a non-profit entity, or a company owned, in its majority, by cooperatives (art. 45.6 SCA).

According to PECOL, it is appropriate to fix the maximum amount of the cooperator member's contributions to share capital, thus avoiding the risk of enabling a cooperator member with an excessive participation in the cooperative share capital to determine, in practice, the cooperative's decisions.

Following the ICA Principle of member economic participation, which prescribes that 'members usually receive limited compensation, if any, on capital subscribed as a condition of membership', PECOL section 3.3(5) states that 'the paid-up capital may be paid interest if cooperative statutes so provide and the members' meeting decides to do so'. This provision is consistent with the common practice in European cooperative law (see art. 2514 and 2545*quinquies*, para. 3, ICC; art. 88 PCC; chap. 1, sec. 2(1), §21a, GCA; No. 1 and 2 of art. 48 SCA; art. 14 FrCA; art. 67 SCE).

In any case, remuneration is not a cooperative member's absolute right. Instead, it is always dependent on a statutory provision, on approval by the General Meeting, and on the existence of positive results in the financial year.

Remuneration of capital is not considered an application of results but rather a cost to the cooperative. The purpose of this compensation is to obtain and retain enough capital to run the business, but, in any case, the interest rate cannot be higher than a reasonable rate, since this operation is not speculative in nature.

According to PECOL, the interest rate may vary according to the nature of the contribution (whether mandatory or optional) and according to the category of the members providing it (whether cooperator members or other types of member – art. 48.1 SCA).

PECOL section 3.3(6) deals with the legal regime of transfer of capital contributions, which may take place *inter vivos* or *mortis causa*.

In the former case, member shares may not freely circulate, which is consistent with the *intuitus personae* that characterises this class of members. Hence member shares may be transferred *inter vivos* only among members or candidates for membership (see, among others, art. 50.a SCA and art. 86 PCC). Transfer of member shares to non-members is not possible. A transfer of member shares is always subject to approval by the designated body, and it is subject to any other conditions laid down in the cooperative statutes.

Consequently, for PECOL, the transfer of member shares is dependent on fulfilment of two conditions: prior authorisation by the cooperative board, which will be a condition of the transfer's effectiveness; and the acquirer's membership of the cooperative or, if not, request for admittance.

For PECOL, shares subscribed by investor members are not transferable without permission from a body of the cooperative.

In the Italian legal system it is explicitly stated that the statutes may even provide for share non-transferability, but in this case members are entitled to withdraw, although not earlier than two years after joining the cooperative (art. 2530.6 ICC).

As to *mortis causa* transfer, the common practice in Europe is to allow transfer to the member's heirs, if they are already members and if they so request, or, if they are not members provided that the conditions for membership, as stipulated in the statutes, are met. Heirs who do not intend or are not able to be members will be entitled to receive the value of the shares of the testator.

Member shares cannot be attached by the personal creditors of the members, but the latter are allowed to seize their reimbursements, interest, and cooperative refunds to collect their debts (see third additional provision, SCA; art. 2537 ICC; §66 GCA). The reason for this prohibition stems from the strictly personal character of the cooperator member's participation in the cooperative and the consequent need to avoid the possibility that, through an enforcement procedure, private individuals who do not meet the conditions for membership, as stipulated in law or in statutes, may become members.

For PECOL (sec. 3.3(7)), it is possible to redeem member contributions to share capital if a member leaves the cooperative. This is a natural consequence of the ICA Principle of voluntary and open membership, and it is the reason for the variability of the share capital (sec. 3.3(3)). Cooperative shares are capital contributions by members to finance the cooperative for the duration of their membership. Hence, taking into account the common European practice, PECOL states that 'the member who leaves the cooperative may be reimbursed for the nominal value of their shares and their portion of divisible reserves, as provided in the cooperative statutes, which may subject the reimbursement to reasonable conditions. The amount repayable to the member may also take into consideration any outstanding interest or cooperative refunds due to the member and any debts due from the member to the cooperative'.

The provision makes it clear that there are limitations on the right to redemption (the statutes may 'subject the reimbursement to reasonable conditions') such as minimum period of membership, a due notice period for members wishing to leave the cooperative, the possibility of deferred redemption for a period of time provided for in the statutes, and the possibility to make deductions from the reimbursement (as we saw in sec. 3.2(3)).

Moreover, capital contributions by cooperator members may not be totally redeemed. In fact, before the member´s capital contribution is redeemed, it must first be liquidated, deducting any losses accountable to the member and any other amounts owed by the member to the cooperative (see, among others, art. 89 PCC; art. 2535 ICC; art. 51.2 SCA).

As mentioned above, the reimbursement may not entail reducing the share capital below the minimum capital laid down in the statutes (see sec. 3.2(4)).

SECTION 3.4
RESERVES

(1) In cooperatives there are mandatory reserves and voluntary reserves.

(2) Mandatory reserves include the legal reserve and other reserves required by law or cooperative statutes, such as the reserve for cooperative education, training and information.

(3) The legal reserve and the reserve for cooperative education, training and information are indivisible, even in the event of cooperative dissolution.

(4) The legal reserve is established by:

(a) a percentage of the net annual cooperative surplus, subject, in principle, to a cap set by law or cooperative statutes;
(b) a percentage of net annual profits, as provided in the cooperative statutes;
(c) and a percentage of other resources, as provided in the cooperative statutes.

(5) The legal reserve can only be used to cover a balance sheet loss that is not covered by other reserves or otherwise, and cannot be used to increase the share capital.

(6) Voluntary reserves are reserves that depend on the collective will of the cooperator members, embodied in a resolution of the members' meeting which determines the mode of their constitution, implementation and liquidation, and in particular their indivisible or divisible nature, also on the basis of individual accounts.

(7) The reserve for cooperative education, training and information is established by:

(a) a percentage of the annual net cooperative surplus;
(b) the part of profits not allocated to the legal reserve;
(c) other resources as provided in the cooperative statutes.

(8) The reserve for cooperative education, training and information is used for the technical and cultural education and training of members, members of the organs, managers and employees of the cooperative, and the provision of information about cooperatives to the general public.

(9) The reserve for cooperative education, training and information can be treated as a separate patrimony if the law so provides.

COMMENTARY

PECOL section 3.4(1) deals with the cooperative's reserves. These are a part of the assets that is not freely available to the management but must be used for specific purposes. According to scholars, given the limited importance of cooperative share capital (see secs. 3.2 and 3.3), the reserves are the financial resource of best quality in a cooperative. They favour implementation of the cooperative's social function and strengthen its financial structure.

PECOL identifies two types of reserves: mandatory reserves and voluntary reserves.

Mandatory reserves include the legal reserve and other reserves required by law or cooperative statutes, such as the reserve for cooperative education, training and information.

In PECOL, the legal reserve and the reserve for cooperative education, training and information are indivisible even in the event of cooperative dissolution (see sec. 3.8).

To be emphasised is that their indivisible nature does not mean that they are non-usable, although the functions performed by indivisible reserves justify limitations in the use of such reserves.

The reasons for the indivisibility of the reserves (mandatory or otherwise) are these: to counterbalance the variable share capital; to increase the creditworthiness of the cooperative and to protect creditors; to avoid speculative winding-up, i.e. present cooperator members' winding up a cooperative in order to share the assets built up by previous cooperator members; and to create common property and solidarity across generations.

The legal reserve is not mandatory or absolutely indivisible in any of the European legal systems considered. In the UK and Finland, there is no legal requirement for indivisible reserves.

Regarding the sources of this reserve, and taking European common practice as reference, PECOL states that this reserve is established: (a) by a percentage of the net annual cooperative surpluses, usually to a certain limit set by the law or the statutes; (b) by a percentage of the net annual profits resulting from transactions with non-members or any activity unrelated to the purpose of the cooperative, as provided in the statutes and without time limits or amounts; (c) and by a percentage of other resources, as defined in the statutes (art. 55 SCA; art. 2545*quater*, para. 1, CC; §7 no. 2 GCA; art. 96.2 PCC; chap. 16, sec. 7 FiCA).

In general, this allocation is not indefinite; rather, it is made until a certain percentage has been reached, as provided by law or cooperative statutes (art. 96.3 PCC; art. 16 FrCA; art. 65.2 SCE; by contrast, no limits are set, for example, by Italian, Finnish or Spanish cooperative law).

The legal reserve can only be used to cover losses which cannot be covered by other reserves and by setting limits (§7 no. 2 GCA; art. 2545*ter*, para. 2, ICC; art. 96.1 PCC). This use of the legal reserve exclusively to cover losses highlights the sole purpose of the legal reserve: to be the first line of defence of the share capital, so that losses arising from the cooperative's business activity do not affect the share capital directly and thus cause its reduction.

As a general rule, the losses compensated by the legal reserve shall refer (mainly) to social losses (losses of the cooperative), excluding, in principle, the losses attributable to the cooperator members (those resulting from their participation in the cooperative's transactions). If the legal reserve is used to cover losses attributable to the cooperator members, the latter may be required to replenish the amount of the legal reserve to the level that existed prior to its use to cover such losses, according to the terms of the resolution adopted by the general meeting (art. 96.5 PCC).

In this regard, the special case of the French cooperative law should be mentioned. In that legal system, some special laws state explicitly that the reserves deriving from transactions with non-members are autonomous. This is the case of farmers' cooperatives (art. L.522-5 al. 3 Rural Code) and artisanal cooperatives (1983 law, art. 25). These reserves cannot be used to cover the losses resulting from the transactions with members. Whereas the Rural Code details the reserves that must be used to compensate these losses, the 1983 law states that if they cannot be compensated by the legal reserve (called the 'indivisible account' in the French law), they must be immediately divided among members or, if this choice is not made, either compensated by the capital or postponed to the next financial year.

Unlike in commercial companies, the cooperative legal reserve cannot be used to increase share capital. As far as cooperatives are concerned, it is PECOL's understanding that increasing the share capital by incorporating reserves cannot be carried out using reserves whose funding includes results of non-member cooperative transactions and results from ownership of company shares or other assets (see sec. 3.7). If the share capital were to be increased by incorporating any such reserves, the cooperator members would end up with either more shares or the same shares with a higher nominal value. Hence, as provided for in section 3.3., the cooperator members who leave the cooperative are entitled to the amount of their contribution to share capital according to the nominal value of the shares. It is therefore evident that increasing share capital by incorporating these mandatory reserves violates the principle of *disinterested distribution* upon winding up.

Voluntary reserves are reserves that depend on the collective will of the cooperator members embodied in a resolution of the members' meeting. Hence they are not a matter of law, but rather of business prudence.

According to PECOL, this resolution of the members' meeting should determine the mode of the constitution, implementation and liquidation of voluntary reserves and in particular their indivisible or divisible nature, also on the basis of individual accounts (art. 98.2 PCC).

In the Portuguese and Spanish legal systems, voluntary reserves can only be established with the annual net surplus that remains after interest on shares, if applicable, has been paid; after the allocations for the various reserves have been made; after losses of previous years have offset, or the legal reserve has been used to compensate for these losses; after the legal reserve has returned to the level prior to its use (art. 100 PCC and art. 58.3 SCA).

Determining the divisible or indivisible nature of the voluntary reserve is of great importance for the following reason: the voluntary reserve must be indivisible if it is established with results from non-member cooperative transactions and results from the ownership of company shares or other assets (see, among others, art. 99 PCC).

The use of the expression 'on the basis of individual accounts' refers to voluntary reserves established from cooperative surpluses which may be distributed among members at membership termination or if the cooperative is transformed or wound up. Even if only cooperator members who have contributed to the formation of such cooperative surplus benefit from this distribution, and only to the precise amount of that contribution, when cooperator members pass a resolution to allocate surplus generated by them to voluntary reserves, individual accounts should be created to identify the contributor and the contribution of each cooperator member to this voluntary reserve fund.

The reserve for cooperative education, training and information is not envisaged in all the legal systems analysed.

In the Spanish and Portuguese legal systems, this reserve is mandatory (art. 56 SCA; art. 97 PCC). The Italian legal system envisages funds, collectively owned by cooperatives, that may serve similar purposes, i.e. the mutual funds of art. 11, Law 59/1992 (mutual funds are those established and administered by cooperative federations for the promotion of cooperation) (art. 2545*quater*, para. 2, CC) or (a specific fund maintained by) the State if the cooperative is not affiliated with any federation.

The existence of this reserve derives directly from the ICA Principle of education, training and information, and from the principle of concern for the community. According to PECOL, the aim of this reserve is to provide for the technical and cultural education and training of members, members of the organs, managers and employees of the cooperative, and the provision of information about cooperatives to the general public.

Indeed, formation of this type of reserve, for this purpose, means that the cooperative is not only an economic organisation but also one with educational and social purposes. This reserve fund will be allocated to cover activities that go beyond the satisfaction of purely individual interests of the cooperative's members and that, although not strictly economic, can produce, directly or indirectly, immediate or deferred economic effects for either the cooperative or the community in which the cooperative operates.

In regard to the purposes of the reserve for cooperative education, training and information, PECOL follows the SCA (art. 56) and stipulates that this reserve can be treated as a separate patrimony if the law so provides. Consequently, this reserve is not attachable except for the payment of debts incurred in fulfilment of its purposes (see sec. 3.5).

SECTION 3.5
MEMBER LIMITED LIABILITY

(1) Cooperatives have legal personality and enjoy patrimonial autonomy.

(2) No member shall be liable for the debts of the cooperative for more than the amount they have subscribed, unless cooperative statutes provide for the liability of the member by guarantee subject to a cap.

COMMENTARY

Cooperatives have a specific legal form or take the form of a partnership or corporation; they are recognised by law; and they have legal personality when they are constituted with the formalities required by law.

Recognition of legal personality will lead, among other consequences, to full patrimonial autonomy: that is to say, the cooperative has its own assets to allocate to fulfil its purposes and respond to its creditors.

The cooperative is liable for meeting its obligations with all its assets. However, some legal systems provide for separate funds to serve specific purposes, in which case the only liabilities in respect of those assets are the obligations generated in meeting those purposes. In Spain and Portugal, the cooperative training and promotion fund can only be used to cover debts arising from fulfilment of its purposes (art. 56 SCA and art. 97.7 PCC). In the UK, it is also possible to allocate part of the funds and assets of the IPS to trusts, in which case they can only be allocated in favour of the beneficiaries of the trust. That would be very unusual, and the existence of such an arrangement would be known to creditors before they contracted with the cooperative.

Moreover, although the laws historically contemplated possible subsidiary responsibility, including unlimited liability of the partners for corporate debts, today the trend is to exclude members from liability for the cooperative's debts.

Nevertheless, some legal systems provide for the possibility that the members' liability for the cooperative's debts may in some cases extend beyond the subscribed capital.

Thus, in France, liability is in principle unlimited for cooperatives established in the form of a civil society; for fishing cooperatives, the liability of the members extends to ten times the subscribed capital (C.rur., art. L, 931-14), or the statutes may define the liability of members (art. 7 FrCA). In Germany, since 2006 the statutes should determine whether members will be responsible for additional contributions in the event of the cooperative's insolvency, and they must specify whether such liability is unlimited or limited to a specific sum (§6 no. 3 GCA). In Portugal, art. 23 PCC establishes that the liability of the cooperator members for the cooperative's debts is limited to the amount of the subscribed capital, although the cooperative's statutes may determine that the liability of cooperators be unlimited or limited in relation to some cooperators and boundless to others. In Italy, since the reform of 2003, cooperatives can only be incorporated as companies with limited liability of members, which implies that only the cooperative with its assets is liable for its obligations, while member liability is limited to the subscribed capital (art. 2518 ICC). In Finland, members may be required by the statutes to make extra payments when necessary to cover a need during normal operations of the cooperative (chap. 13, sec. 1 FiCA). Finally, in the event of liquidation or bankruptcy, the statutes may stipulate an additional limited or unlimited, joint and several liability of the members (chap. 14, secs. 1, 11 and 15 FiCA).

When a member leaves the cooperative, free membership and the integrity of the cooperative's assets must be reconciled. Therefore, if the member is reimbursed, the contributed capital must previously be liquidated (taking the cooperative's equity into account). Likewise, the member can be bound to refund the amount reimbursed if the cooperative becomes insolvent and unable to meet the obligations assumed prior to his or her withdrawal. This responsibility of the member has a double limit: not exceeding the amount that has been repaid, and not exceeding a period starting from the time of repayment, normally set at five years (art. 15.4 SCA or in France: C.Com., art. L.231-6). This responsibility does not apply if the cooperative constitutes a restricted reserve for that period for the amount reimbursed.

SECTION 3.6
ECONOMIC RESULTS FROM COOPERATIVE TRANSACTIONS WITH MEMBERS

(1) The economic results from cooperative transactions with members are 'cooperative surplus' or losses in member cooperative transactions.

(2) Cooperative surplus is the excess of revenues over costs of the cooperative transactions.

(3) By resolution of the members' meeting, the cooperative surplus may be:

(a) distribute to the cooperator members as cooperative refunds in proportion to the quantity and/or quality of their participation in cooperative transactions, either cash or by shares or other financial instruments, or
(b) between indivisible reserves and divisible reserves

(4) Losses in member cooperative transactions are the excess of costs over revenues of cooperative transactions with cooperator members.

(5) By resolution of the members' meeting, losses in member cooperative transactions may be covered:

(a) using the reserves of the cooperative, beginning with the voluntary reserves;
(b) by the cooperator members in proportion to the quantity and/or quality of their participation in cooperative transactions within the limit of the value of the goods and services received.

(6) General interest cooperatives may not distribute cooperative surpluses to their members.

COMMENTARY

As we saw in section 1.1(1), a cooperative is a legal person that carries on any economic activity, mainly in the interests of its members and without having profit as its ultimate purpose; and in section 3.3 we saw that the remuneration of capital is limited and is not considered an application of results but a cost to the cooperative. When cooperatives carry out non-member cooperative transactions, they must keep a separate account of such transactions (sec. 1.5(4)), and the profits from these non-member cooperative transactions must be allocated to indivisible reserves (sec. 1.5(2)).

The economic result of cooperative transactions with members may be positive (surplus) or negative (losses). In any case the General Meeting is the body competent to decide how to distribute this result.

> 'Cooperative Surplus' is the excess of revenue over cost in cooperative transactions:
>
> (a) In service cooperatives, which include consumer and producer cooperatives, prices charged for goods or services delivered to members that are higher than is necessary to cover the cost of the cooperative enterprise, or prices paid for goods or services received by the cooperative from members that are lower for reasons of business prudence or due to market conditions, are provisional prices to be corrected or adjusted when the actual costs are known at the end of the financial year. Refund of the cooperative surplus ('*le trop perçu*') to members at the end of the financial year allows the cooperative to charge for/receive goods or services at near cost.
>
> (b) In worker cooperatives, below-capacity wages paid by the cooperative to worker members for reasons of business prudence or due to market conditions are 'advance payments' on salary (*anticipo*) and subject to final calculation when full information on the income and expenditure of the cooperative enterprise is available. Surplus is paid out as wage supplements.
>
> 'Losses' in member cooperative transactions are the excess of costs over revenues and are shown in the audited balance sheet. They are covered by the reserves, starting with the voluntary reserves. The statutes may stipulate that losses are borne by members:
>
> (a) In service cooperatives, in the form of a reduced (final) price for goods and services delivered to the cooperative or increased charges for goods and services received from the cooperative as calculated at the end of the financial year, when full information on income and expenditure from cooperative transactions is available, in order to provide the goods or services at near cost in retrospect.
>
> (b) In worker cooperatives, in the form of reduced (final) wages paid by the cooperative to worker members.

It should be noted, as we saw in section 1.1(3), that the cooperative enterprise may include an enterprise of a subsidiary if this is necessary to satisfy the interest of the members and if the members of the cooperative maintain ultimate control over the subsidiary. In this case, this rule shall apply to the results of the activity carried out by the subsidiary which is necessary to satisfy the interest of the cooperative members.

The cooperative surplus may be distributed to the cooperator members as cooperative refunds or allocated to reserves (see sec. 3.4). In the distribution of the surplus, the cooperative must obey the following rules. The law regulates surplus distribution primarily by establishing certain compulsory allocations with a view to implementing the social function of cooperatives and strengthening their financial structure.

(a) Reserves may be allocated to either indivisible reserves or divisible reserves. The cooperative must allocate part of its surpluses to a compulsory reserve called the 'legal reserve' (15% art.16.1 FrCA; 30% art. 2545*quater*, para. 1 ICC; 20% art. 58.1 SCA, 5% art. 96.2 PCC or a proportion stipulated in the by-laws, §53.1 and §34.1 GCA). Normally, this allocation is compulsory until the legal reserve is equal to the subscribed capital (art. 16.2 FrCA; art. 96.3 PCC; art. 65.2 SCE or; in Spain, art. 70.2 Valencian Law 2/2015) or reaches a minimum amount (in Finland no less than 2,500 euros (chap. 16, sec. 7 FiCA). Some legal systems have other compulsory reserves. In Spain and Portugal, the cooperative must allocate part of its surpluses to an education and training fund (5% art. 58.1 SCA or 1% art. 97.2 PCC); in Italy, to the mutual fund for cooperative promotion and development (3% of the annual profits, art. 2545*quater*, para. 2 ICC). In France, the development reserve (*fonds de développement*) is compulsory in workers' cooperatives (art. 33.2 L. 78-763).

(b) The cooperative refunds may be distributed to the cooperator members in proportion to the quantity and/or quality of their participation in cooperative transactions, because – as seen earlier – the return complements the provisional price paid or received by the member in the cooperative's transactions (art. 15.1 FrCA; art. 2545-*sexies* ICC or; art. 58.4 SCA). In Finland, the surplus may be distributed only if the statutes so stipulate and within the limits of the statutes according to criteria other than the volume of transaction with the cooperative (chap. 16, sec. 5 FiCA). In France, patronage refund is compulsory for at least 25% of the net surpluses in workers' cooperatives (L. 78-763 art. 33 al. 3), whereas it is forbidden for general interest cooperatives (art. 19*nonies*.4 FrCA). In German law, any distribution of the profit or loss of a financial year to the members must be distributed among them in a particular way: in the first financial year, the distribution is proportional to the payments made on shareholdings; in each successive year it is in proportion to their credit balance, established at the end of the previous financial year as a result of the profit added or loss put down (art. 19.1 GCA).

(c) The distribution of refunds may be made in cash, shares, or other financial instruments. Distribution in shares may be made by increasing the value of the shares or distributing new free shares (art. 2545*sexies*, para. 3, ICC). The latter has been possible in France since 1992, if the statutes so provide, but it is limited to 50% of the available reserves existing at the end of the previous financial year (art. 16 FrCA).

In several countries, cooperative surpluses may not be distributed if and insofar as they are needed to cover existing losses (art. 58. 1 SCA; art. 19.2 GCA, or art. 100.2 PCC) because ensuring the cooperative's solvency should be the priority. For the same reason, a cooperative's surpluses may not be distributed if the cooperative does not cover the required minimum reserve or insofar as the legal reserve level is below that achieved in the previous financial year (art. 19.2 GCA or art. 100.2 PCC).

Losses in member cooperative transactions may be covered by decision of the General Meeting using the cooperative's reserves or by contributions of the cooperator members. In this distribution, the cooperative usually complies with the following rules:

(a) The allocation to reserves must begin with the voluntary reserves (art. 2545*ter* ICC or art. 59 SCA).

(b) The distribution of losses among the members should be in proportion to the quantity and/or quality of their participation in cooperative transactions (art. 59.2.c SCA or art. 96.5 PCC), in the same proportion as for the positive results.

(c) No member should sustain losses that exceed the value of the goods and services delivered or received in the cooperative's transactions. Members should not incur more risk than that derived from transactions with the cooperative in their own interest (in Spain: art. 69 3 Valencian Law 2/2015).

SECTION 3.7
PROFITS AND OTHER LOSSES

(1) Cooperatives may also have other results, including results from non-member cooperative transactions and results from ownership of company shares or other assets. Whatever their origin, these results are allocated to indivisible reserves.

(2) Losses from non-member cooperative transactions and other sources are covered by reserves beginning with voluntary reserves.

COMMENTARY

As we saw in PECOL 1.5 (4), when cooperatives carry out non-member cooperative transactions, they must keep a separate account of such transactions.

The economic results from non-member cooperative transactions (as well as from other extra-cooperative sources) may be called 'profits' or 'losses' to distinguish them from the surpluses or losses from member cooperative transactions.

As a general rule, profits are allocated to indivisible reserves.

Losses are covered by reserves, beginning with the voluntary reserves (see sec. 3.4).

French law does not distinguish profits and surpluses but expressly prohibits both the distribution among members of surpluses (*excédents*) from transactions with customers (art. 15.2 FrCA) and use of the reserves from the cooperative's transactions with non-members to compensate losses from the cooperative's transactions with members. In Italy, only that part of the profits that derives from transactions with members may be refunded (*ristorni*), as Ministerial Communication 53/E of 18 June 2002 has clarified. In Portuguese law, the results from non-member cooperative transactions may not be shared by the cooperator members (art. 100.1, PCC) but must be allocated to indivisible reserves (art. 99 PCC). This provision is also present in the Spanish laws of Extremadura (art. 61.2), Galicia (art. 66.3), Madrid (art. 60.1) and Valencia (art. 68.4).

In many German cooperative societies authorised by their statutes to carry out transactions with non-members (e.g. cooperative banks), there is no separate recording of transactions with members and with non-members. Only where cooperative societies wish to have patronage refund payments recognised by the tax authorities as being tax-deductible operating expenses of the cooperative society, rather than ordinary profit distribution, is the maintenance of separate accounts for transactions with members and non-members one of the conditions. And in agricultural cooperatives the 'purpose transactions' are usually made only with members, so that separate recording of transactions is not important.

Indivisible reserves can be intended to cover losses, as in the case of the legal reserve; but they may also be used for other purposes, such as remunerating capital or financing received, within the limits laid down in the statutes.

SECTION 3.8
LIQUIDATION

(1) In case of liquidation of a cooperative and once paid the cooperative debts, members shall be entitled only to recover the nominal value of their shares and their portion of divisible reserves as provided in the cooperative statutes. The amount repayable to the member should take into consideration, in addition to the nominal value of their shares, any outstanding interest and any other amount due to the member according to cooperative statutes.

(2) Residual net assets shall be distributed in accordance with the principle of disinterested distribution.

(3) In the event of the cooperative losing its legal form through conversion, merger, splitting, or any other restructuring, paragraph (2) applies to assets to the value of the indivisible reserves on the date of this event, unless the new legal entity is subject to the rule in paragraph (2) about the distribution of assets on liquidation.

COMMENTARY

As we saw when a member leaves the cooperative (sec. 3.3(7)), and also in the case of liquidation of the cooperative, members are only entitled to recover the nominal value of their shares and their portion of the divisible reserves as provided in the cooperative statutes. If the divisible reserves have been generated through transactions with members, the allocation should be made in proportion to the transactions with each member. The amount repayable to the member may also take into consideration any outstanding interest or cooperative refunds due to the member and any debts that the member owes to the cooperative (art. 75 SCA). Also in Finland, upon dissolution shares may be paid back at a higher or lower price than subscribed, if the statutes so stipulate.

Residual net assets shall be allocated in accordance with the principle of disinterested distribution, e.g. distributed to the community or other associated cooperatives (3rd principle ICAP). In France they must be assigned to another cooperative or to a social and solidarity economy enterprise (art. 19 FrCA). In the UK, the destination of any surplus assets is governed by the statutes and most cooperatives provide for transfer to other cooperatives, cooperative organisations, or charities and other disinterested destinations. In Spain the remaining assets, if any, must be assigned to the cooperative or federation nominated in the statutes or by the general meeting, or otherwise to the Public Treasury for advancement of the cooperative spirit. If these assets are assigned to another cooperative, they must be kept in the mandatory reserve fund and remain unavailable for fifteen years. If they are received by a federation, the funds must be used to support investment projects promoted by cooperatives. In addition, any member of a cooperative being wound up who intends to join another cooperative may request that his or her proportional part of the remaining liquid assets be deposited in the mandatory reserve fund of the cooperative that he or she is joining, provided that such request has been made before the general meeting approves the final winding-up balance sheet (art. 75.2 SCA). In Portugal, upon liquidation of the assets of the cooperative, art. 114.2 PCC stipulates that the amount of the legal reserve not allocated to covering losses of the financial year and which may not be used for any different application 'can move, with the same purpose, to a new cooperative entity to be formed following the merger or division of the cooperative in liquidation'. But No. 3 of the same article of the PCC states that 'when no new cooperative succeeds the cooperative in liquidation, the application of the mandatory reserve balance will be allocated to another cooperative, preferably from the same city, to be determined by a federation or confederation that represents the main activity of the cooperative.'

The laws sometimes offer other solutions, as in France (art. L.124-14 C.com), where the minister of commerce may allow merchant cooperatives to distribute their assets among their members; for a merchant cooperative whose social object is to run the common administration of a commercial zone, that distribution is even the rule. In the UK, a distribution among the members on the basis of their transactions with the cooperative over a fixed period near the end of its life has been allowed in cooperative society rules and is used by some agricultural cooperative societies. There is a danger that, in the absence of any provision in statutes, the applicable rules (insolvency regime of companies) may lead to distribution according to shareholding. The inclusion of an appropriate provision in cooperative statutes is particularly important. On the other hand, IPSs registered on the basis of operating for the benefit of the community are permitted to 'lock' the assets of the IPS for the purpose for which the IPS has been established. Moreover, upon winding up and during liquidation, the German Cooperative Societies Act allows several options for dealing with the reserves: any surplus in excess of the total credit balance may be distributed among the members on a per capita basis (art. 91.2 GCA); the statutes may prohibit any division of assets, or may stipulate different ratios when dividing assets (art. 91.3 GCA); or members may vote to keep the reserves indivisible and transfer the liquidated assets to 'a natural or legal person for a specific purpose' or 'to the community where the cooperative society was based'. The interest on this fund shall go to charity (art. 92 GCA).

The regulation of the reversion of assets in the case of dissolution also applies to cooperative conversion, merger, splitting, or any other restructuring unless the new entity is also subject to the principle of disinterested distribution.

Some laws establish special rules in these cases. In France, when a cooperative (but not a workers' cooperative) is transformed into a company, the indivisible reserves of the cooperative are allocated to a special reserve of that company which remains indivisible for ten years (art. 25 FrCA). The purpose of this rule is to prevent transformation of the cooperative in the hope of distributing the reserves.

CHAPTER 4
COOPERATIVE AUDIT

With Commentary by Hans-H. MÜNKNER

SECTION 4.1
GENERAL PRINCIPLES OF COOPERATIVE AUDIT

(1) Cooperatives are obligated and entitled to be audited.

(2) The specific aim of cooperative audit is to verify that cooperatives pursue their objectives as defined by the law and their statutes in accordance with section 1.1, and that their structure and activity are consistent with their identity as cooperatives.

(3) Cooperative audit must be conducted by specifically qualified and independent auditors in forms that ensure the autonomy of cooperatives and are consistent with their specific features.

(4) Cooperatives are also obligated and entitled to be financially audited as prescribed by law, according to the nature and scale of their activities, their size, and the need to protect creditors, and other stakeholders in addition to the members and the pursuit of the cooperative objective.

COMMENTARY

Introduction – Overview of Chapter 4

In this chapter, the focus is on audit of cooperative societies as a form of external control supplementing internal audit and member control. Comparing company audit and audit of cooperative societies reveals similarities and differences. As in the case of audit of companies and other commercial enterprises, cooperative audit assesses operational efficiency and economic results, including performance of the management (prudence and care) and compliance with the law. This is done in the form of financial audit. Cooperative audit is different from company audit because, besides assessing the operational efficiency of the cooperative enterprise, the auditors must also assess member-oriented effectiveness by means of management audit in addition to financial audit.

The principles of cooperative audit are derived from national laws and regulations governing audit of cooperative societies in seven EU member states: Finland, France, Germany, Italy, Portugal, Spain and the United Kingdom (UK). In Italy, the Constitution (art. 45) expressly states that the law ensures, through appropriate controls, the character and purposes of cooperatives.[1] This includes ensuring respect of their distinct legal nature as laid down in the organisational law and verifying that cooperatives observe the rules on their function (mutual purpose) and structure (democracy, member participation, member control).[2]

Regarding the sources of the legal framework of cooperative societies, there are different points of departure: the cooperative perceived as a special type of company with variable capital (e. g. in France), as a special type of society (e. g. in the UK) or as an original design (Germany). But all cooperatives have a largely common ideological basis expressed by the Statement of the ICA on the Cooperative Identity including international cooperative values and principles. There are also differences in concept: some view cooperative societies mainly as economic self-help organisations of their members being part of a pluralistic market economy, others perceive cooperatives as social organisations promoting members and non-members and serving the general interest as part of social economy.

There are common development trends. One is the growing size and complexity of cooperative enterprises, which requires adjustment of their legal framework by approximation to the company model regarding governance and financial structure but also concerning the type of audit considered appropriate. Another trend is a growing concern for the community and the environment, with the emphasis on performance as social enterprises, as multi-stakeholder cooperatives serving members of various categories, non-members, and the general interest, adding new, non-financial elements to cooperative audit.

These different backgrounds and concepts of cooperative activities are reflected in the ways in which audit and external control of cooperative societies are regulated in the EU member states. But despite all differences, there are some general principles with effect on regulating cooperative audit that emerge clearly from national legislation and are described in the four parts of this chapter.

Until recently, in four of the seven countries under review (Finland, France, Spain and the UK) the legal regulation of cooperative audit was incomplete and fragmented according to types of cooperative society and branches of activity. In regard to audit of cooperatives, the European Cooperative Society (SCE) Regulation of 2003 does not give guidance. Art. 71 SCE R refers to the national law in force in the EU Member State in which the SCE has its registered office.

---

1 A. Fici, Country Report (CR) Italy, p. 350.

2 A. Fici, CR Italy, p. 397.

The recent trend is to improve the situation by introducing uniform and more complete type-specific legal rules for cooperative audit.

In Finland, the new cooperative law of 2014 is the fourth cooperative law after those of 1901, 1954 and 2001. With 344 articles, the new cooperative law of 2014 is very detailed, with one third of these articles dealing with financial matters. However, the criteria according to which cooperative societies must be audited are laid down in the law on Accounting. According to this law, only large cooperatives must be audited at regular intervals, while other cooperatives may exclude audit and external control through their statutes.

In France, decree no. 84-1027 of 23 November 1984 defined cooperative audit as the critical study of the situation and functioning of the cooperative, taking specific cooperative features into account. Law no. 84-1024 of 2014, introduced in the general law no. 47-1775 of 1947 as arts. 25-1 and following and decree no. 2015-706 of 22 June 2015 deal mainly with cooperative audit, covering the entire range of cooperatives.[3]

In Spain, the constitution of 1978 gives the government power to inspect, penalise, intervene or disqualify cooperatives (arts. 128 to 136 of Real Decreto (RD) 2710/1978 and arts. 150–157 of General Law of Cooperatives (LGC) 1987). In 1989, cooperatives became subject to the General Accounting Plan with orientation on EU Regulations for accounting and auditing. In 2010, rules concerning the accountancy aspects of cooperative societies were adopted (Order EHA/336/2010 of 21 December 2010). The Auditing of Accounts Act contains rules regarding not only financial audit but also special audit of cooperative societies. Information on the contents of annual financial statements can be found in article 19 of the EU Directive 2013/34/EU or article 262 LGC. According to these rules, the analysis of the financial situation of the enterprises shall include, where appropriate, non-financial key performance indicators such as information on environmental matters and employees. In the case of cooperatives, variations in the number of members are included in the management report.[4]

The trend to harmonisation of legal regulations on accounting and reporting of enterprises across their legal forms has recently been stopped with regard to audit. In some EU member states, new rules have been introduced, differentiating cooperative audit from company audit by including non-financial indicators in type-specific co-operative audit. In this way, financial audit is combined with management audit and assessment of social and environmental impact in terms of sustainability beyond corporate social responsibility (expressed in a social report or *bilan sociétal*), fluctuation in membership, proportion of transactions with members and non-members, use of annual surplus, etc.

---

3 D. Hiez, Country Report (CR) France, p. 231.

4 G. Fajardo, CR Spain, pp. 596.

Section 4.1 outlines the rights and obligations of cooperative societies with regard to external control (1); what should be the objectives of external control (2); who should carry out cooperative audit and within what limits (3); and how the right dose of external control of cooperatives can be determined according to their size and nature of activities (4).

General principles of external control of cooperatives

The objective of cooperative audit is to verify that cooperative societies comply with the provisions of organisation law regarding books, accounts and reporting, and that they observe the rules defining their function (member-promotion, mutual aim) and internal structure (democracy).

When designing the right measure of external control and deciding how far it can go, a possible conflict between cooperative autonomy and control by authorities has to be taken into account[5] (sec. 4.1(3)): freedom of choice of the legal form must be granted, but clear rules must be set especially for audit and external control in order to avoid confusion and abuse.

The main concern is to ensure that members exercise ultimate authority also in the field of audit. Because of their special object of member-promotion, cooperatives need a special form of audit to assess their success in member-promotion and their member-oriented effectiveness (see sec. 4.2(2)). Therefore, the general trend to approximate rules of accounting and reporting for cooperatives with company audit should not be followed in case of audit (see sec. 4.2(1) and Conclusion).

Two extremes of regulation can be found in European cooperative legislation:

- In the UK, the only legally required cooperative audit is financial audit; supplemented by discretionary regulatory monitoring and self-regulation, either by a federal cooperative body or other people. Until 2014, there were no specific legal rules on any audit other than the purely financial audit. The new CCBSA of 2014 contains a full set of regulations on the different aspects of cooperative audit, sections 75–99.[6] Every cooperative society must present a revenue account and balance sheet following the principles set out in the Financial Reporting Standards, published by the Accounting Standards Board, and it must appoint one or more qualified auditors in each year of accounts. But despite these new legal provisions, discretionary regulatory monitoring and self-regulation remain important. There are exceptions from these general rules for small societies (secs. 93–96 CCBSA 2014).

[5] D. Hiez *Coopératives, Création, Organisation, Fonctionnement*, Editions Delmas, Paris, 2013, p. 315.

[6] I. Snaith, CR United Kingdom, pp. 692.

- In Germany: Audit of cooperative societies designed as a special type of *'management audit'* with detailed regulation in the law, prescribing management audit in addition to financial audit. Annual (or bi-annual) audit of all registered cooperative societies is mandatory with detailed regulations on the role of cooperative auditing federations in cooperative law (§§53-64c GCA). Auditing federations are special institutions created in the legal form of association to carry out cooperative audit. They have a monopoly to audit all registered cooperative societies with specially trained cooperative auditors employed by the federation but independent in their position as auditors (§55 GCA). For registered cooperative societies, affiliation with an auditing federation is mandatory (§54 GCA).

Between these two extremes, several mechanisms are offered by the national lawmakers to solve the problem of appropriate audit and external control for cooperative societies while respecting their autonomy.

In Italy: Monitoring or *'vigilance'* of cooperatives through the competent ministry (Ministry of Economic Development, MED) as routine inspection is the ordinary form of cooperative revision carried out, normally every two years, by staff of cooperative federations authorised to audit cooperatives affiliated with them. Cooperatives not affiliated with a federation are audited by auditors appointed by the MED. Extraordinary inspection by the MED is carried out whenever the need arises, e.g. in cases of danger, by *'inspectors'* (functionaries of the MED). In the case of serious irregularities in management, recourse to the courts (judicial control) is possible.[7]

In France: *Révision* has two objectives: (i) control of books and accounts and assessment of performance; (ii) analytical examination of the financial situation and of management.[8] In practice, external revision mainly consists of audit of books and accounts together with verification of real performance and compliance with the law, and assessment of whether the society is working in accordance with cooperative principles (e.g. Rural Code, art. 527). Another area of concern is the protection of indivisible assets (reserves) and compliance with the principle of disinterested transmission of assets in the case of dissolution.

For historical reasons, different rules have developed for different types of cooperatives. Although cooperatives need a special type of external control, i.e. *'révision'*,[9] such *révision* used not to be regulated in the law. Some procedures were regulated by a decree of 1984.[10] Full regulation of cooperative audit (*révision*) is of recent date (law no. 84-1024 of 2014, decree no. 2015-706 of 22 June 2015). Today, the general rule is that for some enterprises, including

7 A. Fici, CR Italy, pp. 396–400.
8 Hiez, n. 5 above, pp. 320–321, note 182.13.
9 Hiez, n. 5 above, p. 314.
10 Hiez, n. 5 above, p. 320.

cooperatives, depending on their size and/or legal type, financial audit by a qualified auditor is prescribed. Also before 2014, *révision* was mandatory for registered cooperatives, but without regulation in the general cooperative law of 1947. In 2014, clear rules for cooperative audit by officially recognised auditors were introduced in the general cooperative law to fulfil the already-mentioned two purposes: analytical study of the financial situation and management, and verification of compliance with cooperative principles. The most precise regulations of cooperative audit are contained in the Code Rural (L 527-1), applicable to farmers' and fishing cooperatives.[11]

In Portugal: Responsibility for securing the proper audit of cooperative societies is borne by the members and their elected representatives. After the books were audited in accordance with the 4th EU directive on financial audit, they have to be submitted together with a social report to CASES (António Sérgio Cooperative for Social Economy).[12] CASES, created by decree-law no. 282/2009 of 7 October 2009 as a public interest cooperative, is responsible for overseeing the use of the cooperative form of organisation in compliance with principles and rules concerning the incorporation and functioning of cooperatives. Annually CASES issues a credential supporting the legal incorporation and proper functioning of cooperative societies. Cooperatives should have separate accounts for transactions with members and non-members, but the accounting standards do not cover this issue. The PCC does not provide for an external control of cooperative societies; rather, it leaves control entirely in the hands of the members.[13] CASES cannot be qualified as a regulatory authority with the duty to monitor and supervise the cooperative sector. However, in practice, CASES exercises powers that characterise a regulator. CASES has the power to apply in the courts, through the Public Prosecutor, for the winding-up of cooperatives which do not comply with cooperative principles, e.g. ones that use unlawful means to achieve tax advantages.[14]

In Spain: Cooperatives are subject to twofold external control: by the Administration (arts. 113 and 116 of the Cooperative Societies Act (law 5/2000, infringement of cooperative obligations), and by the specialised cooperative auditors trained at several Spanish universities. There is mandatory audit required by law, by the statutes of the society, by the general meeting, by internal auditors or by a minority of members, as well as voluntary audit called by the board of directors. Adopted in 2010 were special provisions regulating the accounting and auditing of cooperatives (Order EHA/3360/2010). They not only prescribe financial audit but also contain non-financial performance indicators

---

11 D. Hiez CR France, p. 231.
12 D. Meira, CR Portugal, pp. 501–502.
13 D. Meira, CR Portugal, p. 497.
14 D. Meira, CR Portugal, 502.

with which to assess cooperative effectiveness. Such indicators are: volume of transactions with members and non-members, variations in the number of members, activities undertaken in the training of members and staff, and measures promoting cooperative development. Annual reports of cooperatives must contain this cooperative-specific information.[15]

Section 4.1(3) – Qualification of auditors

The qualification required for auditors of cooperative societies depends on the type of audit that they must carry out.

- If cooperative societies are audited in the same way as companies (only financial audit), such audit can be carried out by chartered accountants. The same professional standards apply as required in the case of company audit. No special qualification is required. However, auditors of cooperative societies still need to understand the special governance and financial structure of cooperatives.
- If cooperative societies are audited in a special way including the evaluation of success in member-promotion and supporting sustainable development, specially trained cooperative auditors are needed. They are often trained and employed by cooperative federations in charge of audit and control of affiliated societies.

Cooperative law in Spain may serve as an example of type-specific regulation. External auditors must meet standards of qualification and accountability;[16] they must be independent of the organisation that they audit; and they may not have other direct links with it. All external auditors are enrolled on the Official Register of Auditors of Accounts (ROAC). They must be authorised by the Accounting and Auditing Institute. Authorisation requires an examination on professional competence after theory courses, including the legal system governing cooperatives. However, this is not a subject required for proof of competence, and it is not on the list of subjects to be examined. Evidently, in the case of approved external auditors, there is no guarantee of sufficient knowledge of the cooperative legal and financial system.[17] In practice, in the audit and external control of cooperative societies, the special nature of the cooperative mode of doing business is often neglected.

In the UK, only accepted qualified auditors are certified chartered accountants and members of a recognised supervisory body. Oversight of the quality and

15 G. Fajardo, CR Spain, p. 595.
16 G. Fajardo, CR Spain, pp. 598–599.
17 G. Fajardo, CR Spain, p. 599.

independence of cooperative auditors is exercised by the Financial Reporting Council (CCBSA 2014, sec. 91).

The law must safeguard the independence of cooperative auditors, especially when they are employed by auditing federations, as in Germany. 'Any person who may influence the outcome of the audit, is excluded from the audit if there are reasons to assume that they may cause the suspicion of bias ...' (§55 GCA). Apart from lists of grounds for incompatibility with the exercise of auditing, another way to ensure the independence of cooperative auditors is limitation of the duration of the audit contract and the requirement of rotation.[18]

Generally, there are complaints that auditors lack sufficient knowledge of the way in which cooperatives are structured and operate. The appropriate training of cooperative auditors does not depend only on the scope of legally prescribed audit or control and the tasks of the auditors; it also depends on what is done in cooperative practice. There is consensus that the curricula of general training programmes for auditors and chartered accountants should include introduction to the special problems of auditing cooperative societies.

A special problem in this regard is the combination of audit and advice in the person of the auditor carrying out audit. On the one hand, the auditor may know best what to do to correct identified irregularities or mistakes. On the other hand, the auditor may be biased to criticise and audit a performance of management following the auditor's own advice. A solution could be to supply the '*audit*' and '*advice*' services by different departments of the organisation in charge of external audit.

Section 4.1(3) – Different approaches to audit of cooperative societies

Considering the legal framework provided for audit of cooperative societies in EU-member states, different approaches can be identified:

General reference is made to commercial law or company law, general provisions for all cooperatives in the national cooperative law or special regulations for special types of cooperatives (e.g. France in the case of agricultural cooperatives;[19] audit by certified public accountants or auditing federation, by Commissaires aux Comptes (CCs) employed by a federation or on a list of specialists of the federation). Different professional standards can be observed: certified public accountants, specially trained cooperative auditors, commissaires aux comptes and réviseurs (less qualified than CCs), and lay auditors. After the reform of the cooperative law in 2014, new rules regarding type-specific cooperative audit were introduced and included in the

18 G. Fajardo, CR Spain, pp. 597–599.
19 Hiez, n. 5 above, p. 319.

general cooperative law (art. 25 1 f. general cooperative law of 1947). In Spain, the structure and contents of the annual reports follow the 4th Directive of the EU Council and the Auditing of Accounts Act.[20] In the UK, small cooperatives can use lay auditors to carry out external audit, or they may decide to opt out of audit.

Section 4.1(4) – Special provisions for small cooperatives

Small cooperatives are defined in the cooperative law by the number of members (e.g. in Italy no more than eight, or in Germany no more than twenty), by total of assets, annual turnover or the number of employees. The lawmakers can use several methods to reduce audit costs for such relatively small organisations, e.g. by prescribing a routine audit only every second or fifth year, by reducing the scope of audit to only financial audit, or by simplifying the required annual reports.

In the UK, small cooperatives of certain branches of business, meeting certain financial thresholds and whose statutes do not require full audit, may *'opt out'* of audit, i.e. decide in general meeting to work without external control provided that there are no special reasons to return to routine audit. Small cooperatives with a turnover and assets of less than £5,000 and fewer than 500 members may appoint one or two lay auditors unless the FCA directs them to use qualified auditors for the current year of accounts.[21] There is a trend to exempt some types of smaller cooperatives – with a turnover of less than £5.6 m – from full audit, but some types of small cooperative cannot use such exemption. Small companies enjoy wider exemption than small cooperatives.[22] The CCBSA of 2014 contains special regulations for small cooperatives (secs. 93–96). Small cooperatives may appoint two or more lay auditors to carry out the audit and may submit a simplified audit report. However, this exemption from full audit by chartered accountants does not apply, for example, to housing cooperatives, insurance undertakings and societies with subsidiaries.[23]

In Finland, only large cooperative societies are subject to mandatory audit.

In France, for some types of small cooperatives, audit is optional depending on activity, size of business, number of members and employees; but for collective interest cooperatives (SCICs), full audit is compulsory, whatever their size.[24]

In Portugal, a statutory auditor is always required in the case of agricultural banks and other cooperatives (e.g. consumer cooperatives, housing and

20 G. Fajardo, CR Spain, p. 596.
21 I. Snaith, CR United Kingdom, p. 696.
22 I. Snaith, CR United Kingdom, pp. 695–696.
23 I. Snaith, CR United Kingdom, p. 696.
24 D. Hiez, CR France, p. 234.

construction cooperatives) above a threshold regarding volume of business, number of members and employees).[25]

In Spain, small cooperatives are not obliged to draw up a management report.[26] They may also submit abbreviated balance sheets and are exempted from the obligation to include non-financial information in their reports (art. 285 LSC).[27] However, these exemptions do not apply to all cooperative societies. Cooperatives with organised sections, and in particular with credit sections, and housing cooperatives are subject to full external audit.[28]

In Germany, small cooperatives with a balance sheet total of less than 2 m € must be subjected to audit at least every second financial year, while other cooperatives are audited every year (§53 (1) GCA).

SECTION 4.2
SCOPE AND FORMS OF COOPERATIVE AUDIT

(1) Cooperative audit includes, but is not limited to, the volume of cooperative transactions with members and with non-members; the use and results of subsidiaries; member participation in cooperative governance; member democratic control of the cooperative; the composition of assets; the origin and allocation of the economic results; the amount of the indivisible and divisible reserves; the economic sustainability of the enterprise; the existence of practices of cooperation among cooperatives and of cooperative social responsibility; the level of engagement in cooperative education and training; the manner in which the general interest has been pursued and the stakeholder involvement in general interest cooperatives.

(2) Cooperative audit is conducted through the analysis of books, accounts, balance sheets, reports and other relevant documents, of the cooperative and its subsidiaries, as well as by other means, such as the access of the auditor to the cooperative premises, the interview of cooperative members and members of cooperative organs, and also following a checklist provided by the auditing entity of section 4.3.

(3) Cooperative audit may be ordinary, extraordinary, or special.

---

25 D. Meira, CR Portugal, pp. 497–498.
26 G. Fajardo, CR Spain, p. 596.
27 Ibid.
28 G. Fajardo, CR Spain, 596.

(4) Ordinary cooperative audit is carried out at regular intervals as defined by the law taking into account the size and the type of the cooperative, or by the cooperative statutes if they provide for more stringent intervals.

(5) Extraordinary cooperative audit is carried out whenever requested by a number of members as defined by the law or by cooperative statutes, the union or federation of which the cooperative is a member, the competent public authority, or the cooperative competent organ, by specifying the reasons.

(6) Special cooperative audit is carried out in the event of the cooperative losing its legal form through conversion, merger, splitting, or any other restructuring.

(7) The costs of cooperative audit are born by the cooperative. The costs of extraordinary cooperative audit are borne by those requesting it when no irregularities are found.

COMMENTARY

Section 4.2 defines the contents of type-specific cooperative audit and lists the matters to be included in such cooperative audit: the degree of member-orientation, the use made of economic results, the degree of integration of the cooperative society into cooperative systems, and engagement of the stakeholders in generating positive external effects for the community beyond direct member-promotion in terms of social and ecological effectiveness (1). Section 4.2 also mentions the sources of information to be considered by the auditors. They are usually contained in checklists provided by cooperative auditing federations or other entities in charge of external control of cooperatives (2). Furthermore, the different types of cooperative audit are listed – ordinary, extraordinary and special cooperative audit (3) – and described: the standard case of cooperative audit which, depending on the size and type of cooperative, is carried out at annual or biannual intervals or less frequently, leaving it to individual societies to provide (and pay) for more frequent external audit in their by-laws (4); extraordinary cooperative audit (5); and special cooperative audit (6). Finally, it is explained by whom the costs of audit are borne (7).

Section 4.2(1) – Special features of cooperative external control

External control is necessary to protect the cooperative society as a legal body and as an enterprise, its members, its creditors, and the general public.

Special instruments have been developed by the cooperative movement or by cooperative science to perform type-specific external control and assessment of cooperatives' success in promoting their members.[29] Success in cooperative work is expressed in several forms:

- Success of cooperative societies operating as enterprises on the market is measured by economic results (excess of income over expenditure): *operational efficiency.*
- In transactions with their members (on an internal market, in cooperative transactions) success is measured by *member-oriented effectiveness*. Instruments for measuring member-oriented effectiveness are a promotion plan, proposed by the board of directors and approved by the members in general meeting at the beginning of a financial year, and a promotion report presented by the board at the end of the financial year. It should be mandatory for cooperative societies under cooperative law to present annual promotion plans and promotion reports. However, in practice this is usually not done.

In addition, cooperative success is measured by *success in contributing to social and regional development and in securing sustainable development* (social report, *bilan sociétal*) extending beyond the corporate social responsibility of companies.

If management audit is prescribed, the tasks of the cooperative auditor include the following:

- to monitor the operational efficiency of the cooperative enterprise;
- to understand the cooperative way of doing business and value-oriented management, and to assess member-oriented effectiveness, e.g. service near cost, advantages for members and patronage refund;
- to verify the degree of transparency;
- to monitor the quality of the cooperative enterprise as an employer and in labour relations;
- to monitor the use made of annual surplus and profit; and
- to assess the cooperative society's concern for the community and the environment beyond ordinary Corporate Social Responsibility (CSR).

If special cooperative audit is prescribed, the following additional criteria must be considered as well:

- development of membership within the cooperative group;
- cooperative advantage offered exclusively to members – *'member-value'*; and

[29] The German cooperative literature provides a detailed debate among scholars of proposals for the type-specific external control of cooperatives, e.g. E. Boettcher, 'Die Problematisierung des Förderauftrages in Genossenschaften: Förderplan und Förderbericht', *ZfgG* 1979, vol. 29, pp. 198 ff.; E. Dülfer, 'Welche Relevanz hat der 'Förderauftrag' für die Pflichtprüfung der eingetragenen Genossenschaft?', *ZfgG* 1980, vol. 30, pp. 47 ff.; V. Beuthien and S. Hanrath, 'Den Förderauftrag prüfen – wie soll der Prüfer das machen?', *ZfgG* 1980, vol. 58, p. 85 f.).

- volume of business with non-members in proportion to transactions with members.

To allow control of the economic efficiency and member-oriented effectiveness of cooperative societies, separate accounts must be kept for cooperative transactions with members and with non-members. This makes it possible to distinguish between surplus (earned in cooperative transactions with members) and profit (made in cooperative transactions with non-members and in transactions with business partners), which is important for their different tax-treatments.

Section 4.2(2) – Scope of cooperative audit

There are two basic differences between audit of commercial enterprises and cooperative societies. They regard the purpose of the audit and the type of auditor. In the case of companies, the only legally prescribed form of external control is financial audit. If the shareholders decide to call for a – usually expensive – management audit, they must cover the cost. In the case of cooperative societies, besides carrying out financial audit, the task of the cooperative auditor is to assess the suitability of the business policy to achieving the aim of member-promotion. Usually, cooperative audit is combined with advice on an appropriate future business policy.

Cooperative audit must include a statement of the auditor concerning if, to what extent, and with what result the directors of the cooperative enterprises have pursued the object of member-promotion. In Germany, failure to pursue the object of member-promotion, e.g. by promoting mainly or only the general interest, may lead to *ex-officio* dissolution of the cooperative (§81 GCA). In Portugal, CASES may intervene for similar reasons. Non-compliance with the cooperative principles in cooperative activity is a cause for winding-up the cooperative by judicial means (art. 118(1) PCC).[30] This is also the case in the UK. 'We generally consider something to be a bona fide co-operative where it is an autonomous association of persons united voluntarily to meet their common economic, social and cultural needs and aspirations through a jointly owned and democratically controlled enterprise.'[31] The concepts of community of interest among members and the conduct of business for mutual benefit are central to the registration process of cooperatives in the UK.[32]

In other European countries, like France, Italy and Spain, in the case of social cooperatives, the fact that members' self-help remains the key type-specific feature of all cooperative work is mentioned only indirectly by regulating the composition of the membership group. A certain percentage of members must

30 D. Meira, CR Portugal, p. 502.
31 FCA Guidance 2015, para 4.10, I. Snaith, CR United Kingdom, p. 634.
32 I. Snaith, CR United Kingdom, p. 700.

be user-members and/or worker-members. Cooperatives with only promoting members are not covered by cooperative law. 'A SCIC must have members belonging to at least three of the aforementioned categories and in any case to the categories 1 and 2' (i.e. worker-members and user-members; art. 19*septies* of the French general cooperative law of 1947, introduced in 2001).

As in the case of every enterprise, cooperative audit covers audit of books and accounts (financial or formal audit) in order to check whether books and accounts are correct, complete, duly vouched and in accordance with the law, on the one hand, and assessment of the quality of management in pursuing the special cooperative objectives (management audit or material audit), on the other. Criteria for measuring member orientation are, for instance, the degree of member-satisfaction expressed by the number of new members joining the cooperative society and by withdrawals from membership, and the volume of transactions with members and non-members.

In France, it is left to the by-laws of the individual society to define the scope of external audit.[33] The auditors should undertake an analytical examination of the financial situation and of the management as prescribed for different types of cooperative. Until 2014, there was no uniform regulation but great diversity according to types of cooperative, except in the case of workers' cooperatives, where external audit is prescribed every five years.[34] In the ideal case, the auditor should also verify compliance with cooperative principles and the participation of members, as well as the real performance of the cooperative society, e.g. in the case of agricultural cooperatives, article 527-1 Code Rural.[35]

In 2014, one of the major points of reform of the cooperative law in France was external audit, introduced in the general cooperative law of 1947 by art. 25(1)(1). In the revised general cooperative law, art. 25(1)(1) provides for a special cooperative audit, to verify compliance by cooperatives with cooperative principles and rules and with their mandate of member-promotion.[36] Special inquiry may be invoked for special reasons or in special cases.

In Portugal, the PCC does not provide for an external audit of registered cooperatives and leaves control entirely in the hands of the members. In the new article 43 of law 140/2015 of 7 September 2015, supervision is entrusted to the supervisory board of the society and to a statutory auditor always required in the case of agricultural banks and other cooperative societies above defined thresholds (volume of business, number of members and employees) (art. 70 PCC).

---

33 Hiez, n. 5 above, p. 317, note 181.23.

34 Hiez, n. 5 above, p. 320, notes 182.13 to 182.15.

35 Hiez, n. 5 above, p. 320, note 182.16.

36 D. Hiez, CR France, p. 232.

Section 4.2(2)–(5) – Procedures of external control

Audit procedures are usually prescribed in the law or in regulations.

In §57 of the German Cooperative Societies Act of 2006, the following procedure is prescribed. It can serve as a case study of how external control can be regulated in the cooperative law.

- The board of directors must allow the auditor to inspect books, accounts, documents, cash in hand, securities portfolio and stock of goods.
- The directors must furnish all the information and proof that the auditor requires to conduct the audit in a conscientious manner.
- The auditing federation shall advise the chairperson of the supervisory board in due course of the commencement of the audit. The chairperson of the supervisory board shall inform the other members of the supervisory board in due time of the commencement of the audit and shall call them in the auditing procedure if and when requested by the auditor.
- The auditor shall inform the chairperson of the supervisory board without delay of any important findings on the basis of which s/he deems it necessary for the supervisory board to take immediate measures.
- Immediately after completion of the audit, the auditor must present the expected outcome of the audit orally in a joint meeting of the board of directors and the supervisory board of the cooperative society. S/he can, for that purpose, require the chairperson of the board of directors or the chairperson of the supervisory board to call a meeting. Should the request not be complied with, s/he him/herself may call a meeting of the board of directors or of the supervisory board, indicating the reason for the call. (§57 (1)–(4) GCA).
- The federation must present the outcome of the audit in writing to the chairpersons of the board of directors and the supervisory board, and every member of the supervisory board shall take notice of the audit report (§58 GCA).
- The audit report must be confirmed by the general meeting. The board of directors must submit a certificate of the auditing federation, stating that the audit has taken place, to the Register of Cooperatives (§59 GCA).
- The auditing federation is entitled to call an extraordinary general meeting, chaired by a person appointed by the federation (§60 GCA).

In the UK, reform of the cooperative law in 2014 introduced detailed rules governing the external audit of cooperative societies. However, the audit is still focused on financial aspects. Under these new rules, the auditor must report to the society whether the year's revenue account and the balance sheet are correct, complete, and in accordance with the law. To prepare the report, the auditors are empowered to carry out any necessary investigation.[37]

[37] Sec. 83 CCBAS 2014; I. Snaith, CR United Kingdom, pp. 703–704.

Section 4.2(3)–(6) – Types of cooperative audit

Pre-registration audit

Pre-registration audit is only prescribed in German cooperative law. In the national cooperative laws of some other EU member states, different forms of verification are prescribed to confirm whether the legal requirements for registration as a cooperative society are met.

In Germany, pre-registration audit is a full audit of the new project and its viability (§§11, 11a GCA) together with a verification of whether the requirements for registration are met, e.g. whether the proposed by-laws are in conformity with the cooperative law.

Foreseen in the UK is an investigation by the Financial Conduct Authority (FCA) to confirm compliance with requirements for registration as a cooperative society. This discretionary monitoring (sec. 2 CCBSA 2014) is a check on whether requirements for registration as a 'bona fide cooperative' are met. In 2012, FCA took over this task from the Registrar of Friendly Societies (Financial Services Act 2012). The FCA must be satisfied that the registration requirements are met.[38] With the CCBSA of 2014, the powers of the registering authority have been substantially increased. The FCA must not only be satisfied that the registration requirements are met[39] but also verify continued adherence to cooperative principles. In addition, cooperatives are free to determine the scope of audit in self-regulation under their own rules, or by decision of the directors on whether to monitor performance over and above the minimum requirements. In an attempt to comply with both the letter and the spirit of cooperative principles on three dimensions – cooperative, social and environmental – a list of 10 core performance indicators has been developed. Co-operatives UK published a 'Guide 2013', in which the non-financial and sustainability impact of cooperatives is described, followed by a FCA 'Guidance of 2015'. This means that legally required audit remains basically financial audit supplemented by discretionary regulatory monitoring.

In France, there is no pre-registration audit. But especially where registration requires official assent, e.g. in the case of farmers' cooperatives, fishing cooperatives, workers' cooperatives and general interest cooperatives, after determining whether the new cooperative pursues the legitimate purpose, the supervisory authority must assess compliance of the statutes with cooperative principles. In the case of other cooperatives, there is only a formal check.[40]

In Portugal, there is no audit before registration, but only a public control of the project's legality under the responsibility of the Commercial Registry and

---

38 I. Snaith, CR United Kingdom, p. 701.

39 I. Snaith, CR United Kingdom, pp. 700–701.

40 D. Hiez, CR France, p. 232.

CASES before incorporation and registration of the new cooperative society. There are special rules on the incorporation and functioning of agricultural credit banks, which must be authorised by the Bank of Portugal before incorporation and registration, depending on special registration by that Bank.[41]

There is no pre-registration audit in Spain, but before a new cooperative can be registered, the legitimacy and legality of the new cooperative project are ensured by a notary public, and the Cooperative Registry examines the by-laws/articles of association. Cooperative federations advise founder-members and provide information together with model by-laws vetted by the Cooperative Registry.

Audit and external control of registered cooperative societies

Registered cooperatives are subject to different forms of audit and external control: routine audit or inspection at regular intervals (annual, bi-annual, every five years); special revision, investigation or inquiry (special or extraordinary control) for reasons given in the cooperative law or on demand of entitled petitioners: office-I6holders, a minority of members, the federation to which the society is affiliated, the external auditor, the supervisory authority and creditors. For small cooperatives, light forms of external control are offered up to the right to opt out of audit (UK).[42]

Different types of audit of cooperative societies have developed in the various EU member states.

For example, in the UK there are three categories of external control:[43]

(i) There are only legal rules regarding purely financial audit.
(ii) The FCA must be satisfied that minimum standards of accounts are met, i.e. proper books are kept, a proper system of control is in place, and financial reporting meets standards.
(iii) Discretionary regulatory monitoring and self-regulation on behalf of the society and its members, either by a federal cooperative body or by other people, together with assessment of commercial and cooperative performance beyond accounts.

The powers of the FCA include: requiring the submission of documents and information; ordering investigation by an inspector; convening a special general meeting at members' request. Since 2014, cooperatives, like companies, may appoint inspectors with extensive powers.

---

41 D. Meira, CR Portugal, p. 492.
42 I. Snaith, CR United Kingdom, p. 703.
43 I. Snaith, CR United Kingdom, p. 691.

In Spain the range of cooperative audit extends from mandatory external audit of cooperative accounts required by law or by the articles of association of the society, or by judicial decision, to audit on request of the general meeting, a minority of members or internal auditors and to voluntary audit on request of the board of directors.[44]

Section 4.2(7), 4.3(3)(c) – Audit cost

Where cooperative law prescribes comprehensive (formal and material) audit for cooperative societies, audit costs are higher than if only financial audit were required. Moreover, where the cooperative law prescribes affiliation of registered cooperative societies with an auditing federation, affiliation fees also have to be paid. The auditing entity must ensure that the costs of cooperative audit are reasonable.

In the case of routine audit or special audit called for by a federation or by the supervisory authority, the society audited must pay the fees. If special audit is invoked by an office-holder, a member or creditor, and the audit reveals no irregularities, the petitioner must bear the cost.

There are special tariffs for small and new cooperatives; and there are exemptions of small societies from full audit with the right to present simplified reports and to use *'lay auditors'*, e.g. in the UK (see above sec. 4.1(4)).

SECTION 4.3
AUDITING ENTITY AND AUDITORS

(1) The auditing entity is the entity in charge of the cooperative audit, which conducts it through independent auditors specifically qualified for cooperative audit according to minimum standards established by the law.

(2) Auditing entity may be the state, another public authority, unions or federations of cooperatives or other private entities recognised by the state according to minimum requirements established by the law.

(3) The auditing entity ensures:

(a) continued training of the auditors and provision of a list of them;
(b) compliance with the standards in paragraph (1);
(c) that the costs of audit are reasonable taking into account the activity performed by the auditor, as well as the activity, size and financial capacity of the audited cooperative.

---

44 G. Fajardo, CR Spain, pp. 597–598.

(4) The state ensures compliance with the requirements in paragraph (2) and the obligations in paragraph (3). Any violation may be sanctioned as provided for by the law.

COMMENTARY

In this section, the entities in charge of cooperative audit and auditing standards are defined (1) and (2). In section 4.3(3) the obligations of auditing entities are described: to provide the services of competent auditors at reasonable cost. In section 4.3(4) it is stated that governments must ensure compliance with audit regulations.

Section 4.3(1)-(4)

The power to carry out audit of cooperative societies is given to an auditing entity (e.g. cooperative auditing federation) and to cooperative auditors by the supervisory authority. This authority also lays down the rules with regard to training and experience of auditors. It can also prescribe procedures to be followed when carrying out cooperative audit and collaborating with those in charge of internal control of societies.

The supervisory authority must safeguard the independence and qualification of external auditors and the professional and financial stability of cooperative federations or other entities entrusted with carrying out external audit of affiliated societies. There are special rules to safeguard the independence of auditors (*réviseurs*)[45] and of auditing federations.[46] The supervisory authority has power to cancel the audit licence of an auditor or of a cooperative auditing federation or other entity for reasons laid down in the law (sec. 4.3(3)).

For example, in Spain, since 1989, the structure and content of annual reports have followed the 4th Directive of the EU Council and the Auditing of Accounts Act.[47] Cooperative auditors are usually appointed by the general meeting of the cooperative society for not less than three and not more than nine years, or on request of the cooperative registry, from persons who meet the conditions and are listed in the Official Register of Auditors of Accounts (ROAC).[48]

In the UK, every society must appoint one or more statutory auditors in each year of accounts, to audit its accounts and balance sheet, unless it is subject to an exception (sec. 83 CCBSA 2014). 'Qualified auditor' means a person eligible for appointment as a statutory auditor under the Companies Act 2006.

---

45 Hiez, n. 5 above, p 325, note 182.40.
46 Hiez, n. 5 above, p 325, note 182.45.
47 G. Fajardo, CR Spain, pp. 596–600.
48 G. Fajardo, CR Spain, p. 598; see also sec. 4.1(3), pp. 105–106.

They must be a member of a recognised Supervisory Board (sec. 91, CCBSA 2014) and independent (sec. 92, CCBSA 2014). FCA has power to direct full audit.[49]

Oversight on the performance of auditing entities (super-audit) means auditing of the auditors with regard to quality, independence and effectiveness of audit. Auditing federations are supervised by competent ministries at state level, e.g. in Germany, where the audit licence of a federation can be withdrawn when its financial position is insufficient to finance the operations of the federation (§§64 (1), 64a GCA). In this way, public authorities guarantee compliance with the law, respect of quality standards for external audit, and independence of auditors and auditing federations (sec. 4.3(4)).

Public authorities or institutions in charge of supervision of auditing entities and of registered auditors of accounts must verify whether the federations are authorised to audit, whether their auditors' registrations as cooperative auditors are in line with legal requirements, and whether the auditors participate in ongoing training and whether they respect the rules of the disciplinary system, e.g. in Spain.[50] The German Cooperative Societies Act of 2006 contains full regulation of quality control for auditing federations and their audit staff (§§56, 62, 63a, 63e, 63f, 63g, 64 and 64a GCA). New legal rules on cooperative audit were introduced in France in 2014 and 2015, and in the UK in 2014 (above, p. 2).

SECTION 4.4
CONCLUSION OF COOPERATIVE AUDIT AND EFFECTS

(1) Upon completion of the cooperative audit, the auditor issues an auditing report.

(2) The auditing report, which includes a summary, testifies the auditing activities and findings and may also contain advice on how to deal with deficiencies discovered.

(3) The auditor communicates the auditing report to the cooperative boards. The auditor also communicates the summary of the auditing report to the competent public authority.

(4) The cooperative communicates the summary of the auditing report to all its members and informs them that they may have access to the auditing report provided the member agrees to be legally bound to maintain confidentiality, unless the law provides for its public disclosure.

---

49 I. Snaith, CR United Kingdom, p. 698.

50 G. Fajardo, CR Spain, pp. 597–598.

(5) The auditing report is discussed at the next members' meeting. The cooperative adopts adequate measures to deal with the audit findings.

(6) When irregularities are found, the competent public authority adopts the measures provided for by the law.

COMMENTARY

Section 4.4 summarises the contents of an audit report (1), (2) and describes the procedure to be followed by the auditors after completing the audit: communication and discussion of audit results (3), (4), adoption of adequate measures to deal with audit findings (5) and correction of irregularities (6).

Section 4.4(2) – Links between internal and external control

Audit of cooperatives is a two-way relationship. The persons in charge of audit must be given the right to consult books, accounts, minutes and other documents of the cooperative society and to consult members and office-holders in order to obtain any information needed to carry out their tasks. At the same time, they serve as a source of information and advice for office-holders and members of the cooperative society. The forms and scope of cooperation between internal audit (supervisory board) and external audit or control must be prescribed by the law, e.g. submission of the audit report of external auditors to the supervisory board, follow-up on audit findings, e.g. whether actions have been taken to correct mistakes or irregularities identified during audit and assessment of such follow-up actions.

CONCLUSION

Trends to approximate cooperative audit with company audit and to harmonise national commercial law

Development of the legal framework for audit of cooperative societies in EU member states has followed different paths. But – as stated in the introduction – two general trends can be observed.

As cooperative enterprises working on international markets grow in size and complexity, there is an increasing distance between members and their cooperatives, and growing professionalism among cooperative directors often recruited from outside the cooperative movement. To increase and assess the economic efficiency of such growing cooperative enterprises, legal rules regarding external audit of large cooperatives have been gradually approximated with those of company law, with the main emphasis on financial audit.

Furthermore, there is a general trend to harmonise commercial law in such a way that the differences between the different legal forms of enterprise are levelled. It is claimed that there are no longer good reasons for having special rules for companies and large cooperatives in the fields of accounting, audit, merger, conversion and liquidation.

Rather than following this trend, which weakens the profile of cooperatives, the lawmakers should insist that the tested rules of special cooperative audit are maintained. They make it possible to measure success in member-promotion and sustainable development, and to demonstrate to the members and to the market that the cooperative form of organised self-help still has its place, even in the case of large cooperative enterprises and in a global economy.

In recent years, amendments of the legal rules governing external audit of cooperative societies have shown that type-specific forms of cooperative audit are finding their way into general cooperative law, adding non-financial indicators to purely financial audit, either by amending the general cooperative law (e.g. in France in 2014) or by issuing guidelines for assessing the effectiveness of cooperatives in the fields of member-promotion and promoting social and environmental development (e.g. in the UK by issuing guidelines in 2013 (Co-operatives Europe) and 2015 (FCA Guidance) or by giving institutions special monitoring powers (in Portugal with CASES).

Furthermore, due consideration should be given to the fact that, for new and small cooperatives, audit requirements and audit costs must be kept at a reasonable level. Founder members of self-help projects and group initiatives should not be deterred by complicated procedures and high legal costs but encouraged to opt for the legal form of cooperative society.

CHAPTER 5
COOPERATION AMONG COOPERATIVES

With Commentary by Hagen HENRY[*]

SECTION 5.1
GENERAL PRINCIPLES OF COOPERATION AMONG COOPERATIVES

(1) Cooperatives cooperate among themselves to further their objectives and to support, promote, and develop other cooperatives, cooperation among cooperatives, and the cooperative business model.

(2) The purpose of cooperation is either economic or socio-political or a combination of the two.

(3) Cooperatives cooperate in forms and structures that safeguard their autonomy, are consistent with their specific features, and are guided by the principles of equality, solidarity and subsidiarity.

(4) The law may promote economic and socio-political cooperation among cooperatives as well as with other entities of the social economy.

(5) Cooperatives may not participate in structures of cooperation which prejudice their autonomy and the members' ultimate control of the cooperative.

COMMENTARY

The Study Group on European Cooperative Law (SGECOL) includes cooperation among cooperatives in its suggested Principles of European Cooperative Law (PECOL), which are otherwise limited to the organisational structure of primary cooperatives. It does so because it sees cooperation among cooperatives as part and parcel of the organisational set-up of cooperatives. The purpose of this Introduction to the Commentary on the respective chapter of the PECOL is to shed light on what 'part and parcel' may mean in terms of legal principles.

Cooperation among cooperatives as a specific form of inter-enterprise collaboration is an empirical fact. It predates the emergence of modern cooperatives and their subsequent regulation by law-makers in the second half of the nineteenth century.[1] However, there 'is no simple, widely agreed upon formulation of national or even regional structures.'[2] Indeed, national legal systems display two diverse spectra relating to either economic or socio-political cooperation, or to both at the same time: on the one hand, a spectrum of permitting, facilitating, actively encouraging and supporting cooperation; on the other, a spectrum of regulations on forms of cooperation, varying in their degree of intensity, scope and permanence, and ranging from total integration (e.g. mergers), via groups of cooperatives and other types of enterprises and networks, to contractual arrangements. Obviously, ways of cooperating 'are the product of history and [hence] the names vary.'[3] Not surprisingly, cooperation among cooperatives '... is often the source of considerable controversy within the movement because it invariably raises questions of long-term ambitions, democratic control, institutional competition, and government relationships ...'.[4] For some of these reasons it is also a source of controversy, if not suspicion, outside the cooperative movement. Undoubtedly, '[t]he role of cooperation among cooperatives ... is one of the most important and, in some ways, one of the least well examined dimensions of co-operative experience. ... It is not a challenge that the movement has often met well.'[5]

As far as the elaboration of legal principles of cooperation among cooperatives is concerned, two questions arise: 1. How do cooperative laws deal with this socio-economic and socio-political phenomenon and 2. How should cooperative law deal with the phenomenon?

Like the PECOL themselves, this Introduction to the Commentary on the relevant PECOL therefore goes beyond an empirical compilation and determination of the 'lowest' common denominator of national European laws;

---

1 An extensive account of the history, as well as of the different forms of cooperation among cooperatives and respective support policies, has recently been published by Antonio Fici. Cf. A. Fici, 'La cooperación entre cooperativas en el derecho italiano y comparado' [Cooperation among cooperatives in Italian and comparative law], *Boltetín de la Asociación Internacional de Derecho Cooperativo* [International Association of Cooperative Law Journal], 2014, 103–148. The same *Boletín* contains also other articles on the subject. Cf. also A. Fici, 'Cooperation among Cooperatives in Italian and Comparative Law', *Journal of Entrepreneurial and Organizational Diversity*, 2015, vol. 4, no. 2, 64–97.

2 I. MacPherson, 'Customizing a Patchwork Quilt: Consolidating Co-operative Studies within the University World', in H. Henrÿ, P. Hytinkoski and T. Klén (eds.), *Customizing a Patchwork Quilt: Consolidating Co-operative Studies within the University World. In memoriam Ian MacPherson*, University of Helsinki, Ruralia Institute, Publications 34, Helsinki, 2015, pp. 21–25 (23).

3 Ibid.

4 Ibid., p. 24.

5 Ibid.

it takes an international view, as is required by the very origin of the idea of cooperatives.

As for the first question, and as can be seen from the National Reports, the cooperative law in all the countries concerned deals with cooperation among cooperatives. The regulations on public support range from incentives for cooperation among cooperatives, especially through taxation and special treatment of indivisible reserves, to no mention of such support at all. Whereas the law in some countries contains detailed rules on the objectives, forms and contents of cooperation (for example in Italy, Portugal and Spain), in others it contains no more than a mere implicit reference to (the possibility of) such cooperation (for example in Finland). The law of only one country, Germany, requires membership in audit unions as a condition for incorporation/registration of cooperatives. Apart from this specific case, limited in scope and with a particular historical rationale, the cooperative laws do not establish an obligation to cooperate. As far as the legislators of the Member States of the European Union are concerned, the European Union Council Regulation 1435/2003 on the Statute for a European Cooperative Society (SCE) implies the existence of cooperation among cooperatives, not least because an SCE may be set up by cooperatives and may thus be considered as a secondary cooperative. But the Regulation does not regulate cooperation among cooperatives, i.e. national law applies to cooperation among SCEs; nor does it have any indirect effects on the subject discussed here. Despite the absence of any explicit national or supranational regulation establishing an obligation to cooperate, legislators and others may still have such an obligation if cooperation among cooperatives is an element of the identity of cooperatives and if there is an obligation to ensure that element. This leads to the discussion of the second question. Some authors argue that cooperation among cooperatives is not just an element of the identity of cooperatives; it is consubstantial with them.[6] This may be so in some countries, in fact, and in law. However, on a wider scale the state of cooperation among cooperatives and laws related to it are such that the argument of consubstantiality cannot be sustained. Opinions as to whether cooperation among cooperatives is an element of the identity of cooperatives are divided.[7]

---

6 Cf., for example, A. Martinez Charterina, *Análisis de la integración cooperativa*, Universidad de Deusto, Bilbao 1990, p. 45.

7 Antonio Fici (cf. Fici, *La cooperación*, n. 1 above) defends the opinion that it is so. Against his argument and that of Rosalía Alfonso Sánchez (cf. R. Alfonso Sánchez, 'Los principios cooperativos como principios configuradores de la forma social cooperativa', *CIRIEC-España. Revista Jurídica*, 2015, vol. 27, pp. 49–85), and dealing with cooperative principles in general, cf. Miguel Ángel Santos Domínguez. He is of the opinion that the cooperative principles do not shape the cooperative identity and were therefore not a source of [cooperative] law. Cf. M.A. Santos Domínguez, 'La relación de los principios cooperativos con el derecho', *CIRIEC-España; Revista Jurídica*, 2015, vol. 2, pp. 87–132.

It will be argued here that cooperation among cooperatives is not an element of the identity of cooperatives, but that there is nevertheless an obligation to cooperate.

A normative argument that cooperation among cooperatives is an element of the identity of cooperatives may be found in the 6th Principle of the International Cooperative Alliance (ICA), contained in the 1995 ICA Statement on the Co-operative Identity (ICA Statement).[8] It reads: 'Co-operation among Co-operatives. Co-operatives serve their members most effectively and strengthen the co-operative movement by working together through local, national, regional and international structures.' The title itself of the ICA Statement is indicative that all principles enshrined therein are elements of the identity of cooperatives. Founded in 1895 and today representing around one billion individual members around the world, the ICA is itself the most prominent example of (international) cooperation among cooperatives.

In recurrent statements and reports, the ICA has continuously developed the concept of cooperation among cooperatives as a cooperative principle and explained its rationale.[9] The most recent of these statements is the 1995 ICA Statement.[10] The positive effects of cooperation on the development of cooperatives and the cooperative movement and, conversely, the often poor state of cooperatives where such cooperation does not exist or is deficient lends support to this normative argument. And yet, it may be argued that cooperation among cooperatives is not an essential element of the identity of cooperatives. The rationale for this argument is the exceptional position of the 6th ICA Principle among the ICA Principles. Cooperation among cooperatives finds its limits in the other cooperative principles, primarily the principles of autonomy/independence and democratic control (4th, 2nd and the 3rd ICA Principles respectively) because the ICA Principles are mutually interdependent. Each of them reinforces the others. However, the reverse is not the case: that is, the principles of autonomy/independence and democratic control are not limited by the principle of cooperation among cooperatives. One may therefore argue that cooperation among cooperatives is a means to constitute and protect the other cooperative principles, but that it is itself not a constitutive essential element of the identity of cooperatives. This argument also helps to avoid the conflict with the (human) right of association which would otherwise arise.

---

8 Text of the 1995 ICA Statement on the co-operative identity at: http://ica.coop/en/whats-co-op/co-operative-identity-values-principles. Cf. also the Background paper to the ICA Statement on Co-operative Identity, at: http://www.uwcc.wisc.edu/icic/issues/prin/21-cent/background.html, as well as the ICA Guidance notes to the cooperative principles, at: http://ica.coop/sites/default/files/attachments/Guidance%20Notes%20EN.pdf.

9 For a history of these statements, cf. C. Cano Ortega, 'Una perspectiva actual del sexto principio cooperativo: Cooperación entre cooperativas', *CIRIEC-España. Revista Jurídica*, 2015, vol. 27, pp. 285–331 (288 ff.).

10 Predecessors were the statements of 1937 and 1966.

Arguing that cooperation among cooperatives is not an essential element of the identity of cooperatives is not tantamount to saying that there is no obligation to cooperate or no obligation to regulate on it. Whether or not such an obligation exists depends on the answer to the following questions: What is the legal value of the ICA Statement? Who is bound by it and what is the scope of the obligations that it contains, if any?

The ICA Statement is a text of a non-governmental organisation incorporated under Belgian law as an international non-profit association, in the form of byelaws. As such it binds the ICA members who, according to the wording of the 6th Principle, must cooperate with each other. Within the limits of the law, especially competition law, private law entities may bind themselves and restrict their right of association in the sense of their right not to associate. A systematic interpretation of the 6th ICA Principle, the 1st ICA Principle (Voluntary and open membership) and the 7th ICA Principle (Concern of community) indicates that members of the ICA have also otherwise accepted a limitation of their fundamental rights, and especially their right of association. Whether this obligation to cooperate becomes a legal obligation in cases where the national laws include the ICA Principles or refer to them is doubtful, because the inclusion of principles in a law does not necessarily change them into legal rules.[11]

Prima facie, the ICA Statement binds neither cooperatives, which are not members of the ICA, nor legislators. However, the content of the ICA Statement has been integrated into the 2002 International Labour Organization Recommendation no. 193 concerning the promotion of cooperatives (ILO R. 193).[12] The question is therefore whether the ILO R. 193 is binding upon these actors as far as the cooperative principles are concerned and, if so, what the content of such obligation is.

This Introduction to the Commentary on PECOL chapter 5 is not the place to discuss the legal value of this specific ILO recommendation in detail.[13] Suffice it here to state that, by integrating the text of the ICA Statement into the ILO R. 193, the Member States of the ILO have introduced the text of an international non-governmental organisation, the ICA, into the ambit of public international law. In public international law, the assessment of the legal value of individual

---

11 For a discussion of the relationship between the ICA Principles, legal principles and legal rules, cf. J.L. Moreno, 'Los valores según la Alianza Cooperativa Internacional (ACI)', *CIRIEC-España, Revista Jurídica*, 2014, vol. 25, pp. 371–393.

12 The Promotion of Cooperatives Recommendation (2002), adopted by the International Labour Conference on 20 June 2002. Cf. ILO document 90-PR23-285-En-Doc., at: www.ilo.org/dyn/normlex/en/f?p=NORMLEXPUB: 12100:0::NO::P12100_ILO_CODE:R193. The definition of cooperatives contained in the ICA Statement was integrated in paragraph 2 of the ILO R. 193; the ICA values and principles in its Paragraph 3 and in its Annex.

13 For a detailed discussion cf. H. Henrÿ, 'Public International Cooperative Law: The International Labour Organization Promotion of Cooperatives Recommendation, 2002', in D. Cracogna, A Fici and H. Henrÿ (eds), *International Handbook of Cooperative Law*, Springer, Heidelberg, 2013, pp. 65–88.

norms or entire texts follows criteria other than those applied in national law.[14] Two main arguments support the opinion that the ILO R. 193 is legally binding: its democratic legitimacy and repeated behaviour of states leading to and endorsing[15] the ILO R. 193. The argument of repeated behaviour relates also to states which are not members of the ILO. The relevant parts of the ILO R. 193 are therefore binding on all legislators and, according to Part IV of the ILO R. 193, also on all cooperatives, regardless of whether their country is a member of the ILO or whether they are members of the ICA. The effect for this latter group of cooperatives is that they have the same obligation to cooperate as do the ICA members. As for the content of the obligation of legislators to regulate cooperation among cooperatives, there are two possible interpretations: (a) an obligation to obligate cooperatives to cooperate and/or (b) an obligation of governments to promote cooperation among cooperatives through adequate incentives, without making cooperation an obligation. Interpretation (a) is to be dismissed on the ground that it conflicts with the right to associate. The German law, sanctioned by a decision of the German Constitutional Court,[16] is not convincing. As seen in the case of Italy, for example, the obligation to audit can be made effective through other means, while allowing potential cooperative members to opt for this enterprise form without being forced to adhere to an audit union. Legislators must/should therefore provide for the promotion of cooperation among cooperatives (interpretation (b)) by ensuring that the other cooperative principles, which are equally binding upon them, are at least not weakened, and leave the choice of form and content of this cooperation to the cooperatives. The purpose of this duty to promote cooperation among cooperatives, which is an obligation in the public interest in countries like Spain, is also to compensate for the unequal treatment of cooperatives as compared with capital-centred enterprises to which the regulation of cooperatives leads in some jurisdictions. Examples of such inequalities are legal obstacles to using general growth strategies, like mergers and acquisitions, and to convert into other types of enterprise.

Because the PECOL, especially section 5.1(1), is wider in scope than the 6th ICA Principle, it must be emphasised that the obligation to cooperate or to regulate on cooperation does not extend beyond the scope of the ICA Principle.

The implementation of this obligation to cooperate and to regulate on the promotion of cooperation encounters the dilemma that the more successful cooperatives become in generating their independence and autonomy – at

---

14 For an assessment of the legal value of norms in public international law, cf. M. Virally, 'La valeur juridique des recommandations des organisations internationales', *Annuaire français de droit international*, 1956, vol. II, pp. 66 ff. (reprinted in *Le droit international en devenir*, Presses Universitaires de France, Paris, 1990, pp. 169 ff.).

15 Cf. for examples of such behavior Henrÿ, n. 13 above.

16 Cf. Bundesverfassungsgericht [German Constitutional Court], Decision No. 1759 (19.1. 2001), in *Neue Juristische Wochenschrift*, 2001, 2617.

times because of cooperation – and/or the more they succeed in pursuing their growth strategies individually, mainly through setting up capitalistic subsidiaries, the less they may realise the need to cooperate.[17] Ultimately, however, their success as enterprises based on the cooperative values and principles depends on their cooperation. Cooperation among cooperatives is an effective, possibly the only, means to maintain the principles of autonomy/independence and member control and, through socio-political cooperation, to counteract tendencies towards isomorphisation, more precisely the companisation of all enterprise types,[18] including cooperatives. This companisation is the very opposite of maintaining the cooperative identity, of which cooperation among cooperatives may or may not be an integral element. Cooperation among cooperatives is furthermore an expression of the cooperative value of solidarity. It is the means by which internal solidarity is complemented with external solidarity,[19] as a step towards the even wider solidarity expressed by the 7th ICA Principle of 'Concern for Community'.

With regard to the future, which has already begun, two interrelated major transformations may require imagining radically new types of cooperation among cooperatives: globalisation has prompted the transformation of welfare states into welfare societies and a shift of political power to those actors that possess the technology to collect, appropriate, process and use data (Big Data).[20] These changes may require cooperatives to cooperate and form, together with other actors, especially civil society actors, and with public institutions and new types of private-public entities.[21]

---

17 Which seems to be increasingly the case in France and Germany. It might be worthwhile investigating the extent to which the changing notion of law induces behaviour which is not compatible with solidarity. Cf. M. De Conto, 'A hermenêutica dos direitos fundamentais nas relações cooperativo-comunitárias' [The Hermeneutics of Fundamental Rights in the Cooperative-communitarian Relationship], PhD diss., University of Unisonos, San Leopoldo, Brazil, 2013; H. Henrÿ, 'El derecho de trabajo y la autogestión cooperativa en el contexto internacional global', in G. Fajardo García (dir.) and M.J. Senent Vidal (coord.), *Cooperativas de trabajo asociado y estatuto jurídico de sus socios trabajadores*, Tirant lo Blanch, Valencia, 2016, pp. 33–47.

18 For this tendency, with examples, cf. H. Henrÿ, *Guidelines for Cooperative Legislation*, 3rd revised ed., International Labour Organization, Geneva 2012, Part 1, 2. H. Henrÿ, 'Quo Vadis Cooperative Law?', *CCIJ Report*, 2014, vol. 72, pp. 50–61 (in Japanese; English version with author). A statement also in MacPherson, n. 2 above, p. 23.

19 A. Martinez Charterina, 'Sobre el principio de cooperación entre cooperativas en la actualidad', *Boletín de la Asociación Internacional de Derecho Cooperativo* [International Association of Cooperative Law Journal], 2012, vol. 46, pp. 133–146 (140 f.).

20 H. Henrÿ, 'Tutkimuksen vetäjän Hagen Henrÿn puheenvuoro' [The Research Director´s Turn to Speak], in H. Henrÿ, J. Hänninen, S. Paksu and P. Pylkkänen, *Osuustoiminnasta valoa vanhuspalveluihin* [Light for elderly care from cooperatives], *Kunnallisalan Kehittämissäätiön Tutkimusjulkaisu-sarja* no. 79, Vammalan Kirjapaino, Sastamala, 2014, 113, pp. 9–13; H. Henrÿ, 'Social Justice through Enterprises. The End of the 1972/1973 Conjuncture? A Legal Perspective', *International Journal of Social Quality*, 2015, vol. 5, no. 2, pp. 81–96.

21 H. Henrÿ, 'Superar la crisis del Estado de bienestar: El rol de las empresas democráticas. Una perspectiva jurídica', *CIRIEC-España. Revista Jurídica*, 2013, vol 23, pp. 11–20; H. Henrÿ,

As said, the purpose of this Introduction is to aid understanding of the structure and content of this chapter 5 of the PECOL, which is divided into three sections: 5.1 General principles of cooperation among cooperatives; 5.2 Forms of economic cooperation; and 5.3 Forms of socio-political cooperation.

Section 5.1(1) – Reasons to cooperate

This subsection regulates a four-fold purpose of cooperation. This purpose is in line with, but is wider in scope than, the one contained in the 6th ICA Principle and what is stipulated in paragraph 6(d) of the ILO R. 193.

The first purpose ('further their objectives') lays down the ultimate objective of cooperation among cooperatives – the promotion of the members of the cooperating entities – which, in turn, is the objective of cooperatives according to section 1.1(1). This ultimate objective of cooperation among cooperatives is emphasised several times throughout the PECOL (cf. for example subsection (3) and section 5.2(6)).

Achieving economies of scope and scale and/or political negotiating power (cf. subsection (2)), which is often mentioned as the objective of cooperation among cooperatives, is only an intermediate objective.

The pursuit of this purpose is further strengthened by application of the principle of subsidiarity contained in subsection (3).

The second purpose ('support ... other cooperatives') concerns support for cooperatives which do not participate in the cooperation as such. It is to be understood as support for the pursuit of the objective of these cooperatives, which, again, is the furtherance of the interests of their members.

Another aspect of this purpose is that it takes the cooperative internal solidarity to the outside world, although this is still the cooperative world.

The third purpose ('support ... cooperation among cooperatives') concerns support for the development of the cooperative movement; this is another case of external solidarity.

The fourth purpose ('support ... the cooperative business model') exemplifies more than anything else the specificity of inter-cooperative collaboration. Such a purpose of inter-enterprise cooperation cannot be found for any other enterprise type.

This purpose is not explicitly contained in the 6th ICA Principle. However, it has been discussed for decades in the context of the question of whether or not cooperation among cooperatives has also a political transformative

---

'Positioning yhteisetu cooperatives in the world of cooperatives – a preliminary legal perspective', in M. Rantanen, T. Klén and H. Henrÿ (eds.), *Yhteisetu-osuuskunta – joustava paikallisrakenne muuttuvalle maaseudulle*, University of Helsinki, Ruralia Institute, Helsinki, pp. 42–46, available at: http://www.helsinki.fi/ruralia/julkaisut/ pdf/Raportteja159.pdf.

function.[22] In the aftermath of the so-called financial crisis of 2008 and as part of the Rio + 20 discussions,[23] the question has recently re-emerged. It is reinforced by subsection (4).[24]

Section 5.1(2) – Purpose of cooperation

Often forms of cooperation combine the economic[25] and the socio-political[26] purposes. Typically, however, these purposes are pursued through separate structures.

Section 5.1(3) – Forms and structures of cooperation

This subsection for the first time emphasises the limits of cooperation. The PECOL repeatedly, albeit in various forms (cf. subsection (5) and section 5.2(6), (7) and (8)), emphasise the limits of cooperation set by other cooperative principles, primarily autonomy and independence (4th ICA Principle) of and democratic control (2nd and 3rd ICA Principles) by the members of the cooperating entities. This limitation explains why the notion of cooperation is understood as being antithetical to the notions of concentration and of subordination, as commented below (section 5.2).

Autonomy is not only expressed through the formal by-law autonomy. The principle of autonomy/independence must also be maintained by other means, for example by avoiding unlimited liability in the case of participation of cooperatives in companies.

The reference to the guiding 'principles of equality, solidarity and subsidiarity' reveals a conception of principles in the PECOL which differs from that of the ICA Statement. The ICA Statement distinguishes between values, among which it classifies equality and solidarity, and it establishes a functional link between the cooperative values and the seven (ICA) Principles. We are therefore confronted with three types of principles, namely the ICA Principles, the principles contained in this subsection, and the principles of European cooperative law (PECOL) themselves. This results in a multitude of principles of diverse nature, which renders their relation to legal rules highly complex.[27]

The principle of equality. The principle of equality is a principle which applies also to cooperatives individually, especially in relation to their members.

---

22 Cf. Background paper to the ICA Statement on Co-operative Identity, n. 8 above.

23 Cf. H. Henrÿ, 'Sustainable Development and Cooperative Law: Corporate Social Responsibility or Cooperative Social Responsibility?' *International and Comparative Corporate Law Journal*, 2013, vol. 10, no. 3, pp. 58–75.

24 Cf. the commentary therein.

25 At times called 'inter-cooperation' or 'economic integration'.

26 At times called 'associative' or 'representative'.

27 Moreno, n. 11 above, points to this complexity and the difficulties arising therefrom.

The principle of solidarity. In law, the principle of solidarity materialises in 'obligationes in solidum', i.e. the acceptance of legal obligations knowing that their fulfilment may remain without corresponding advantages.[28] An example is provided by cooperative interbank guarantee schemes.

The principles of subsidiarity. The principle of subsidiarity requires an adequate articulation of the tasks and competences of the structure of cooperation on the one hand, and those of the participating entities on the other. It requires balancing the autonomy of the participating entities with the group discipline necessary to achieve the objectives of cooperation.

Section 5.1(4) – Promotion of economic and socio-political cooperation

As far as cooperation among cooperatives is concerned, this subsection addresses public policy issues in fulfilment of the obligation to promote this cooperation. It recognises the economic and social benefits of cooperation, without, however, suggesting any specific measures.

Typical examples of such promotional measures are special tax regimes for financial contributions to cooperation structures (cf. section 5.2(2)) or support to investments by cooperatives in cooperatives. Governments may also facilitate other types of cooperation, such as the establishment of (tax preferred) cooperative development funds.

This subsection also addresses the promotion of cooperation of cooperatives with social economy entities. A growing number of European countries are passing laws on the social economy.[29] These also serve to facilitate the implementation of policies concerning the cooperation of cooperatives.

Cooperation with social economy entities is another demonstration of the transformative function of cooperation.

Section 5.1(5) – Cooperation which is prejudicial

The PECOL dedicate a separate subsection to the importance of preventing cooperation from becoming a way to compromise the autonomy/independence of, and member control by, the participating entities (cf. the above comment on section 5.1(3). This PECOL includes the obligation for the cooperating entities

[28] As regards the relationship between law and solidarity requiring social justice, it is worthwhile reading A. Supiot, *L'esprit de Philadelphie. La justice sociale face au marché total*, Le Seuil, Paris, 2010; A. Supiot, 'Contribution à une analyse juridique de la crise économique de 2008', *Revue internationale du travail*, 2010, no. 2, pp. 165 ff.

[29] For example France (Loi relative à l'économie sociale et solidaire, 2014); Portugal (Social Economy Law, 2013); Spain (Ley de Economia Social, 2013). See also the 2004 British Act on community interest companies; the 2003 Finnish Law on social enterprises (Law 1351/2003); and the Italian Law on social enterprises 155/2006.

to refrain from any activity that may jeopardise the existence of any of their partners in the cooperation.

SECTION 5.2
FORMS OF ECONOMIC COOPERATION

(1) Forms of economic cooperation among cooperatives include the establishment of:

(a) contractual relationships for the exchange of goods or services;
(b) a secondary (or higher-level) cooperative; or
(c) a cooperative group.

(2) The law may provide for specific treatment of the contractual relationships between cooperatives, including specific tax treatment, in order to promote their establishment.

(3) Two or more cooperatives may establish a secondary (or higher-level) cooperative to conduct an economic activity in the interest of its member cooperatives.

(4) A secondary (or higher-level) cooperative's statutes may provide that each member has a number of votes in the members' meeting in proportion to:

(a) the number of its members;
(b) participation in cooperative transactions with the secondary cooperative; or
(c) according to other criteria but not the amount of capital contributed.

In any event, no member may have more than the maximum amount or percentage of the total number of votes cast in each members' meeting, as defined by the law.

(5) Cooperative transactions between a secondary (or higher-level) cooperative and the members of its member cooperatives are cooperative transactions with members within the meaning of section 1.4.

(6) Two or more cooperatives may establish another type of business organisation to conduct an economic activity in the interest of their member cooperatives, provided that their autonomy and cooperative identity are protected.

(7) Two or more cooperatives may establish a cooperative group to delegate to one of them, to a secondary cooperative, or to another legal type of entity which they control, the power to coordinate or direct their

economic activity, provided that in any case the members' meetings of the member cooperatives retain the power to make fundamental decisions as defined in section 2.4(5). Any member must have the right to withdraw from the group whenever its permanence seems likely to prejudice its objectives or the interests of its members.

(8) Non-cooperative entities may participate in any form of economic cooperation among cooperatives, provided that the cooperatives retain the control of the structure.

COMMENTARY

As a consequence of their being legal persons of private law, and as emphasised in the introductory commentary on section 5.1, the choice of the form in which, and the matters on which, cooperatives want to cooperate must be left to them, regardless of their class, activity, sector[30] or geographical location or the administrative division of the country or, indeed, countries.[31] Cooperatives may agree to form strategic alliances, joint ventures, franchise arrangements, subsidiaries, cooperatives, companies, associations, etc. However, in some jurisdictions this choice is not completely free because it will be determined by the objective (economic and/or socio-political, cf. section 5.1(2)), for the pursuit of which some national laws provide a limited number of legally recognised forms.

Section 5.2 does not consider all forms of cooperation which in some of the jurisdictions are seen as such. The limitation is due, first of all, to the notion of 'cooperation' itself. It is antithetical to the notions of concentration and subordination. Concentration and subordination are typical ways of 'cooperation' among other types of enterprise.[32]

The exclusion of concentration arrangements. Cooperation materialises between at least two independent entities. 'Cooperation' which leads to the dissolution of one entity, for example through merger or acquisition, is not a form of cooperation. Nor is the conversion of cooperatives into another type of legal entity a form of cooperation. Excluded for the same reason are arrangements whereby one cooperative sets up a subsidiary in a form other than a cooperative,

---

30 The ICA itself has for decades underlined the importance of considering the cooperative form of enterprise as a reason for cooperation. Cf. Background paper, n 8 above.

31 This includes international cooperation, both economic and socio-political, which is not mentioned in the PECOL, but which is mentioned in the 6th ICA Principle and in the ILO R. 193 (paragraphs 17(e) and 18(b)).

32 Cf. H. Henrÿ, 'Public International Cooperative Law: The International Labour Organization Promotion of Cooperatives Recommendation, 2002', in Cracogna, Fici and Henrÿ (eds.), n. 13 above, pp. 65–88 (83).

as well as multipurpose cooperatives which pursue several objectives, even if in other cases these objectives are pursued by several cooperatives. Several subsections of section 5.2 clearly express the requirement of at least two cooperatives as cooperation partners.

The exclusion of subordination arrangements. Subordination does not lead to the dissolution of the entities involved. But hierarchical groups which entail loss of independence by the subordinated entities would not comply with section 5.2(7) and are therefore excluded.

However etymologically antonymous the notions of concentration and subordination may be to the notion of cooperation, in practice economic efficiency – where size may matter – needs to be balanced with autonomy/independence; leadership with various forms of democracy (representative, pondered, deliberative, etc.); the pursuit of socio-political impact with political neutrality. It requires overcoming the notional dichotomy by interweaving the structural elements of concentration and cooperation, i.e. hierarchy and networking, without merging the participating entities (heterarchy).

Furthermore, not all 'working together' according to the 6th ICA Principle and paragraph 6 (d) of ILO R. 193 is cooperation. 'Cooperation is not simply about occasional collaboration. Collaboration, though similar [,] works for a single defined objective, whereas co-operation is a more intense commitment and longer term engagement to achieve shared goals.'[33] Cooperation is therefore characterised by three main features: longer-term duration, structure (cf. also the 6th ICA Principle and paragraph 6 (d) of the ILO R. 193), and commitment.

Longer-term duration. This requirement excludes one-time contracts with single objectives from the notion of cooperation.

Structure. The requirement of 'structured' cooperation may exclude, for example, joint ventures.

Commitment. Commitment is understood as legal commitment. Therefore, legally non-binding arrangements, such as codes of conduct, charters, etc. are excluded from the notion of cooperation.

Using these criteria, one may assess whether or not a specific collaboration qualifies as cooperation. For example, forms of cooperation whereby the cooperative is allowed to arrange for its members to be served by another legal entity fulfil the requirements of cooperation only if at least two cooperatives join together to make use of this possibility, and provided that the members of these cooperatives control the other legal entity and have the power to determine the services and how these are produced and provided. Companies controlled by several cooperatives are not a form of cooperation if the participating cooperatives are pure holding cooperatives. Pure holding cooperatives cease to be cooperatives because they lack economic activity and hence there is no

33 Cf. Guidance notes, n. 8 above, 6th Principle, Point 2.

basis for cooperative transactions. Where cooperatives control companies and use them in partial fulfilment of their objectives it may be difficult to ensure control. Cartels and groups, which unite or control legally independent entities, are considered to be forms of cooperation if the members of the participating cooperatives are able to control them, at least indirectly. The same applies to investments by cooperatives in other cooperatives. In joint cooperative groups by contract it may not be clear how the autonomy of the participating entities can be preserved if, through this arrangement, the power to manage is delegated to one or several cooperatives in the group.

Section 5.2(1) – Forms of economic cooperation

The types of items to be exchanged through contracts under subsection 5.2(a) are understood to include knowledge.

Section 5.2(2) – Specific treatment of contractual relationships

As mentioned above, forms of cooperation are meant to last over time. *Prima facie*, one-time contracts do not fulfil this requirement. The formulation 'establishment of contractual relationships' serves to indicate a longer-term duration, a sign of which may be a *de facto* or *de iure* preference (expressed in the byelaws for example) for such contracts over contracts with non-cooperatives. Such contractual relationships can qualify as a 'light institutionalisation' under certain conditions, for example semi-structured joint ventures between cooperatives.

Section 5.2(3) – Secondary or higher-level cooperatives

Cooperation in the form of a cooperative (secondary or higher level), i.e. a cooperative of cooperatives, is the most adequate form of economic cooperation because its structure best accommodates the main conditions of cooperation, i.e. respect for the autonomy/independence of the cooperating entities, and ultimate control by the members of the affiliated entities. This form of cooperation is expressly mentioned as a form to be promoted by governments and by the cooperatives themselves, also internationally, in paragraphs 13, 17(c) and 18(b)(v) of the ILO R. 193, respectively.

Section 5.2(4) – Secondary or higher-level cooperatives´ statutes

This subsection concretises the principle of autonomy/independence and member control. The 2nd ICA Principle alludes to a specific voting rights system in higher-level cooperatives which departs from the one member/ one vote general rule. As regards the attribution of plural voting rights under paragraph (c), 'other criteria' may reflect the heterogeneity of interests of different classes of members, different sectors to which the cooperating cooperatives may belong, etc.

The emphasis on adjustments of the voting rights system must not be construed as precluding further adjustments to the structure of secondary or higher-level cooperatives compared to the structure of primary cooperatives. Adjustments may also be necessary as regards, for example, the minimum number of members (which is usually lower than that required for primary cooperatives) and the composition of the board.

Section 5.2(5) – "Cooperative transactions" in cooperation arrangements

This subsection represents another case of external solidarity.

The risk of violating the principle of subsidiarity (section 5.1(3)) may be heightened in such arrangements.

Section 5.2(6) – Establishment of other business organisations

Such third structures are mainly used to access the financial market or to establish purchase or sales pools.

Section 5.2(7) – Establishment of cooperative groups

In joint cooperative groups in which the power to direct may be delegated to one or several cooperatives in the group, the autonomy of the others may easily be at risk (cf. above Introductory Commentary on section 5.2). The unconditional right to withdraw is therefore a necessary means to prevent this risk from materialising.

Section 5.2(8) – Participation of non-cooperative entities

Again, the text recalls the limitations of cooperation.

SECTION 5.3
FORMS OF SOCIO-POLITICAL COOPERATION

(1) Two or more cooperatives may establish an association or an entity of another legal type to promote their socio-political interests as cooperatives.

(2) These entities pursue their objectives through activities such as representation; assistance and protection; education and training;

advisory services; financial, legal and technical assistance; audit; dispute settlement; support for the creation of new cooperatives or the development of existing cooperatives; and the promotion of the cooperative business model.

COMMENTARY

Section 5.3(1) – Forms of cooperation for socio-political purposes

As cooperatives conduct economic activities, this form may not be chosen for cooperation in the socio-political interest of the participating entities.

Section 5.3(2) – Activities

In part, this subsection reformulates the purpose of cooperation as stipulated in section 5.1. The list of possible activities is not exhaustive. One might add support for research and the devolution of public prerogatives, like registration or the elaboration of feasibility reports, as part of the registration process, as well as the devolution of audit/control powers.

PART II

NATIONAL REPORTS

CHAPTER 6
FINLAND

Hagen HENRŸ*

* I would like to thank Varatuomari Anne Kontkanen, Pellervo Society, for her valuable comments.

Apart from the Act itself, I have used especially Seppo Pöyhönen's book *Osuuskunta ja osuuskuntalaki* [The cooperative and cooperative law], Talentum, Helsinki, 2013.

Finnish cooperative legislation dates back to the beginning of the twentieth century. The first Law on Cooperation [*Osuustoiminatlaki*] was adopted in 1901. The lawmakers of the time thought it of utmost importance to "... pass legislation on economic associations ... as the legal form of stock companies cannot apply to these associations [cooperatives]."[1]

The 1901 Law on Cooperation has been replaced three times, in 1955 with the 1954 Law on Cooperatives ([*Osuuskuntalaki*], 28.5.1954, 247); in 2002 with the 2001 Law on Cooperatives ([*Osuuskuntalaki*], 28.12.2001/1488); and in 2014 with the current Law on Cooperatives ([*Osuuskuntalaki*], 14.6.2013/421, henceforth 'the Act').[2]

The consecutive changes of the cooperative law have related to the substance of the law and to its form.[3]

As regards the substance, the changes introduced with the amendments to the 1954 Law (especially the two major amendments of 1981 and 1989) and with the 2001 law may be summarised as intended to secure the sufficient capitalisation of cooperatives, for reasons of both competitiveness and third party protection[4] and – in order to achieve this – to reduce the legal structural

---

1 A.J Alanen, *Hannes Gebhard*, Yhteiskirjapaino, Helsinki, 1964, p. 217 (translated and adapted by author of this report).

2 Available at: http://www.finlex.fi/fi/laki/alkup/2013/20130421. Contrary to the two previous laws, the Finnish Government has not yet translated this Act into English. The Act is subdivided into 7 parts, 28 chapters and 364 paragraphs (§); the §§ are divided further into subparagraphs, etc. In order to avoid misunderstandings by readers accustomed to English terminology, '§§' are referred to as 'sections'.

3 As regards the 1901 Law, cf. for example J.K. Paasikivi, *Osuustoimintalain pääkohdat* [Main Points of the Law on Cooperation], Helsinki, 1902, available at: http://www.pellervo.fi/kirjasto. Concerning the cooperative law until 1982, cf. C. Olsson, *Osuuskuntaoikeus* [Cooperative Law], Suomen Lakimiesliiton Kustannus, Helsinki, 1982. As regards the 1981 amendments to the 1954 Law, cf. R. Vuori, *Osuuskuntalain muutos 1981* [Amendments to the Cooperative Law 1981], Kirjayhtymä, Helsinki, 1981.

4 The limits the 1954 Law put on financing (member shares only) were seen as the major drawback of this law. Cf. O. Leppänen, 'Osuuskuntalainsäädännön kehityksestä' [The Evolution of Cooperative Law], in *Osuustoiminnan lainsäädäntö, arvot ja kansainvälinen solidaarisuus. Osuustoimintatutkimuksen vuosikirja 2001–2003*, Taloudellisen yhteistyön ja osuustoiminnan tutkimuksen seura Kooperatiivi ry., Helsingin yliopiston Maaseudun tutkimus- ja koulutuskeskus, Mikkeli, 2003, pp. 12 f. (12). The 1981 amendments introduced supplementary share schemes, the possibility to use non-obligatory parts of the reserve fund and parts of the surplus for capitalisation purposes. The 1989 amendments introduced investment shares for members and non-members that are similar to voiceless preferred shares in stock companies and allowed the conversion of a cooperative into a stock company. For more details, cf. J. Laisaari, 'Uusi osuuskuntalaki' [The New Cooperative Law], in *Osuustoiminnan lainsäädäntö*, see above, pp. 8–11.

differences between cooperatives and stock companies to the minimum necessary to maintain the distinctive features of cooperatives. According to the Ministry of Justice, the purpose of the current Act is to further improve the competitiveness of cooperatives by facilitating their foundation, their access to financing and their management, while preserving the minimum cooperative standards.

As regards the form, the amendments to the 1954 Law and the subsequent laws, as well as the amendments thereto, introduced as far as was possible the terminology of the Limited Liability Companies Act ([*Osakeyhtiölaki* 21.7. 2006/62]). This terminology is intended to signify neutral legal figures and to allow use of the abundant literature and jurisprudence on stock companies[5] in the quasi absence of literature and court cases on cooperative law.[6] The reliance on material on stock companies is one of the key reasons for the companisation of cooperatives through legislation.[7] In addition, the following should be noted as far as form is concerned: the 1901 law consisted of 36 sections and was amended twice; the 1954 law consisted of 165 sections and was amended 20 times; the 2001 law consisted of 280 sections, was amended 10 times (of which one major revision in 2007); and the current Act consists of 364 sections. The Act therefore continues the trend of ever greater detail. Even when considering that the number of sections increased because of the insertion into the cooperative law of cross-referenced matters from other laws, especially the stock company law, it remains true that cooperative laws have become ever longer and more detailed over time. Moreover, the frequency of passing a new law and/or amending the

---

5 The change of terminology concerned especially the general assembly, management bodies, loan capital, mergers, scissions, liquidation, penal responsibility and damages. Cf. Laisaari, n. 4 above, p. 10; Leppänen, n. 4 above, p. 13. Another, possibly research-worthy change is the change from 'Law on Cooperation' (1901) to 'Law on Cooperatives' (from 1954 onwards) in order to see whether it was a linguistic change only.

6 The statement relies on Seppo Pöyhönen's findings. Cf. S. Pöyhönen, *Omistajaoikeudet ja omistaja-arvo osuuskunnissa* [The rights of owners and owner value in cooperatives], Talentum, Helsinki, 2011, p. 41. The situation reflects the state of cooperative law research in the country since the 1950s. S. Pöyhönen's books and the ones cited in this report remain exceptions. S. Pöyhönen's doctoral dissertation (cf. above) came after a pause of 50 years. To be especially regretted is the discontinuity of commentaries on the cooperative law. For the past, cf. M. Rapola, and H. Halme, *Osuustoimintalaki selityksineen*, Pellervo-Seura, Helsinki, 1939; Y.L. Hakulinen and M. Rapola, *Osuuskuntalaki selityksineen* [The Cooperative Law with Explanations], Pellervo-Seura, Helsinki, 1954.

7 By 'companisation' I mean the approximation of the features of cooperatives with those of stock companies. The justification given by the Ministry of Justice for the introduction of the one-person cooperative may serve as an example. It argued that the introduction of the one-person company did not cause any problems. Hence there would not be any risk for cooperatives either. Cf. Hallituksen esitys [HE] 185/2012 vp.27, 42. The argument confuses empirical risks for individual cooperative enterprises with the concept of cooperatives. The lack of scientific discussion became also evident during the public debate on the draft bill. Cf. n. 36.

existing one has increased over time, and the number of amendments has risen steadily. Apart from being indicative of a changing legislation technique, the degree of detail in the law may also be indicative of a diminishing consensus on what cooperatives are. At the same time, byelaw[8] autonomy has been extended to include more and more matters. Indeed, most rules of the Act are default rules, including, for example, the section on the objective of cooperatives – so much so that it is impossible to report here on all possible exemptions from the Act through the byelaws. This has widened the margin of interpretation which the elimination of cross-references to other laws was intended to reduce. The wording of the Act therefore does not give a full picture of the 'lived' cooperative law. To my knowledge, and with the exception of the mentioned, rather recent, doctoral thesis,[9] which deals mainly with profit and surplus distribution in larger cooperatives, no legal sociological research has been conducted concerning the extent to which cooperatives are using this byelaw autonomy to depart from what is suggested by the default rules of the Act.[10]

The Act regulates all types of cooperatives in all sectors. The Law on Cooperative Banks and Other Credit Institutions in the Form of Cooperatives [*Laki osuuspankeista ja muista osuuskuntamuotoisista luottolaitoksista*], 28.12.2001/1504) pertains to some organisational features specific to these financial institutions.[11] In addition, there is a special law on housing stock companies ([*Asunto-osakeythiölaki*], 22.12.2009/1599). These laws are not relevant to this report.

Strictly speaking, the Law on European Cooperatives ([*Eurooppaosuuskuntalaki*], 19.10.2006/906) constitutes another source of cooperative law in Finland. This law provides for the necessary changes to acts pertaining to cooperatives in general, and it also implements the EC Council Regulation 1435/2003 on the Statute for a European Cooperative Society (SCE), as far as it concerns SCEs registered in Finland and to which the Act applies by default. Because there are no SCEs registered in Finland, this law is not dealt with here, although there is reason to assume that the EC Regulation led to the creation of a Finnish-type SCE.[12]

8 The term 'byelaw/s' is used to signify the internal rules of cooperatives.
9 Pöyhönen, n. 6 above.
10 Such research would be facilitated to the extent that cooperatives use the model byelaws provided for by their federations or those provided for by the Finnish Government under Chapter 2, Section 3 of the Act.
11 They concern mainly prudential mechanisms.
12 This is at least the implicit conclusion of an EU commissioned assessment of the implementation of the EC Council Regulation 1435/2003 on the Statute for a European Cooperative Society (SCE) according to its Article 79. Cf. 'Study on the implementation of the Regulation 1435/2003 on the Statute for a European Cooperative Society (SCE), 5 October 2010', available at: http:/ec.europa.eu/enterprise/policies/sme/promoting-entrepreneurship/social-economy/ or at: http://www.euricse.eu/node/257. Cf. also J. Mähönen and S. Villa, *Osuuskunta* [The Cooperative], Sanoma Pro, Helsinki, 2014, p. 4.

1. DEFINITION AND OBJECTIVES OF COOPERATIVES

1.1. DEFINITION OF COOPERATIVES

Contrary to the previous law, the Act does not define cooperatives. It simply states in Chapter 1, Section 2 that cooperatives acquire legal personality through registration and in Section 3 that the number of members, the amount of shares and the share capital are variable, and that cooperatives may in addition have stock capital and stocks[13] and that the assets of cooperatives may be distributed only to the extent permitted by the Act.

The previous law defined cooperatives in its Chapter 1, Section 2 as follows: '(1) [A] "Co-operative" is ... an organization whose membership and share capital have not been determined in advance'.[14] The English word 'organization' translated the Finnish word '*yhteisö*'. The word '*yhteisö*', in fact, is otherwise used as a generic term to denote corporations (legal entities, organisations) as a category. This is of relevance because a number of laws apply to this category, for example the Law on the information on enterprises and corporations ([*Yritys- ja yhteisötietolaki*], 16.3.2001/244) and the taxation laws. The consequence is that corporate income tax is, in principle, levied on cooperative profit and surplus in the same way as it is on the profit of stock companies.

The question is whether this change means that cooperatives no longer fall within the category of '*yhteisö*'. But even the category of '*yhteisö*' does not help to categorise cooperatives within the larger group of organisational forms, if that is what is needed and if cooperatives cannot be seen as a *sui generis* category in all respects. The history of cooperative law provides some help in this regard. Although the 1901 Law uses the word 'enterprise' in the definition (instead of 'organization'), there may be no doubt as to the broad consensus at the time on the nature of cooperatives as centred on an association of persons with open membership. As mentioned, the intention of the 1901 legislator was to pass legislation on 'economic associations'. The stated features of cooperatives, namely variable membership and (hence) capital, suggest that this has not changed. According to the general classification of economic organisational forms in Finland, cooperatives are thus 'societies'.[15]

---

13 The term 'share' translates the Finnish word '*osuus*', a typical cooperative financial instrument. The term 'stock' translates the Finnish word '*osake*'. The legislator introduced the latter term to signify a financial instrument, which the previous law had provided for as well, but for which it had used another term [*sijoitusosuus*], arguing that this financial instrument corresponds to voiceless preferred shares in stock companies and should therefore be named as such.

14 English excerpts from the 2001 Law are taken from the 'Unofficial translation © Ministry of Justice, Finland Co-operatives Act (1488/2001; *OSUUSKUNTALAKI*)', available at: http// www.finlex.fi/fi/laki/kaannokset/ 2001/en20011488.pdf.

15 Cf. P.-L. Aro, 'Carrying on a Trade and Forms of Business Enterprise', in J. Uotila (ed.), *The Finnish Legal System*, 2nd ed., Finnish Lawyers Publishing Company, Helsinki, 1985, pp. 101–123 (103).

One could argue that a separate definition clause is not necessary; the definition is something that distils from the entire law. On the other hand, a definition is a guide to many other issues; primarily, of course, a guide through the cooperative law itself. However, the Act remains unclear as to its concept of cooperatives. The possibility to form one-person cooperatives, the possibility to determine a profit-seeking objective, the transferability of membership under certain circumstances, the tradability of shares and stocks, the figure of stock-exchange cooperatives (cf. below), etc., cast doubts on whether the Act conforms to the cooperative values and principles as they have evolved over the past 170 years.[16] There is no reference to the associative character of cooperatives as enshrined in the international definition.[17] The Act regulates 'members'. This does not suffice, however, because it is increasingly argued that stockholders are also to be qualified as members of the stock company. The Act opposes the cooperative as a legal entity to its members. This resolves the difficulty which arises when conceiving the cooperative and its members as a single entity, while, at the same time, separating the cooperative as a legal person from its members. On the other hand, the Act omits reference to the self-help character of cooperatives expressed through the members serving themselves by means of the cooperative enterprise. The Act may be indicative of a change of conception that can also be seen in the Act allowing for one-person cooperatives and in the renaming of the incorporation document as 'incorporation contract'.[18] This indicates a shift from the associative character of cooperatives to a contractual relationship among the members. In comparative law terms, this shift follows a shift of orientation from continental European to Anglo-Saxon conceptions.

The doubts regarding the concept of cooperatives underlying the Act are in part resolved because, in addition to the features stipulated in Sections 2 and 3 of Chapter 1, the Act contains a number of principles which are detailed in the Act. Chapter 1, Section 6, lays down the majority principle [*enemmistöperiaate*].

---

16 Doubts shared by V. Vahtera, 'Millaisille sääntelyratkaisyille Suomen yhteisölainsäädännön kokonaisuudistukset rakentuvat? – esimerkkikinä uusi osuuskuntalaki' [On which legislative principles does the overall reform of the Finnish corporation law rely? – The new cooperative law as an example], *Defensor legis* 2013, n. 4, pp. 626–642 (634).

17 As contained in the 1995 International Cooperative Alliance Statement on the co-operative identity (*International Co-operative Review*, 1995, vol. 88, no. 4, pp. 85 f., available at: http://ica.coop/en/whats-co-op/co-operative-identity-values-principles), ICA Statement, and the relevant Background paper to the ICA Statement, at: http://www.uwcc.wisc.edu/icic/issues/prin/21-cent/background.html. Cf. also the 2001 United Nations Guidelines aimed at creating a supportive environment for the development of cooperatives (UN doc. A/RES/54/123 and doc. A/RES/56/114 (A/56/73-E/2001/68; Res./56)) and the 2002 International Labour Organization (ILO) Recommendation No. 193 concerning the promotion of cooperatives (www.ilo.org/dyn/normlex/en/f?p=NORMLEXPUB:12100:0::NO::P12100_ILO_CODE:R193), ILO R. 193, especially Paragraph 2.

18 The Act changed the previous registration requirement of an 'incorporation instrument' [*perustamiskirja*] to an 'incorporation contract' [*perustamissopimus*] (Chapter 2, Section 2).

It is repeated and detailed in Chapter 5, which deals with general meetings. Another principle is that of of equality ([*yhdenvertaisuus*], Chapter 1, Section 7). This relates to the equal position of the members and the equality of shares and stocks. It is also repeated and detailed in the following chapters, for example in Chapter 5, Section 14 concerning decisions by the general meeting and in Chapter 6, Section 1 concerning the decisions by the board of directors.

Both sections contain principles in the sense that they are subject to specification and modification through the Act or the byelaws. Otherwise, their nature is not clear. Are they legal principles[19] or are they guidelines for interpretation of the law?

Sections 8 and 9 of Chapter 1 are also considered to contain principles.[20] They are however formulated as rules, leaving no margin for interpretation as principles do. Section 8 establishes the obligation of those in leadership positions [*johto*] to act in the interest of the cooperative. According to Chapter 6, Section 1, the leadership consists of the board of directors, as well as the manager and the supervisory committee, if any. It is not clear whether the members of the board of directors and of the supervisory committee have this obligation also individually. In other instances, the Act distinguishes in this respect.[21]

It is understood that the obligation comprises the obligation to act diligently and in the manner required of leaders of enterprises in general.[22] As for the supervisory committee, its inclusion in the leadership may contradict its main task, which is to supervise the board of directors and the manager (cf. below). Furthermore, the obligation relates to the interest of the cooperative, where the main task of the leadership should be to act in the interest of the members (cf. Chapter 1, Section 5). Hence the objective of cooperatives is mediated by the interest of the cooperative itself.

Section 9 establishes the autonomy[23] of the members, in the true sense of the expression: that is, within the limits of the law, the members may determine their affairs freely through the byelaws. The Act contains few mandatory rules. The intention of the legislator was that this autonomy should especially allow access

---

19 As stated by Mähönen and Villa, n. 12 above, p. 8.

20 Cf. N. Lammassaari, and A. Parkkisenniemi, 'Uusi osuuskuntalaki. Osuuskunnan perustaminen ja hallinto' [The new cooperative law. Establishment and governance], Master's degree paper, Oulun Ammattikorkeakoulu, 2014, p. 17; Mähönen and Villa, n. 12 above, p. 8.

21 Cf. for example Sections 17 and 22 of Chapter 6.

22 Cf. Mähönen and Villa, n. 12, above, p. 14.

23 This autonomy, in Finnish '*tahdonvaltaisuus*', is called 'freedom of contract' by some authors. This is not convincing because the Act itself uses the term 'incorporation contract' to designate the basic document underlying the foundation of cooperatives, in Finnish '*perustamissopimus*'. When naming the byelaws with the Finnish term '*säännöt*' the Act does not refer to their being a contract. Another reason for the use of the word 'autonomy' here is, of course, that 'autonomy' and 'freedom of contract' are not identical, although they overlap to some extent.

to financing possibilities. The byelaw autonomy goes as far as setting an objective which is that of stock companies, namely the pursuit of profit maximisation.

1.2. OBJECTIVES OF COOPERATIVES

Chapter 1, Section 5 specifies the objectives of cooperatives as follows: '... The purpose of a co-operative shall be to promote the economic or business interests of its members by way of the pursuit of economic activity where the members make use of the services provided by the cooperative or services that the cooperative arranges with the help of a subsidiary or otherwise. The byelaws may determine another purpose.'[24]

The scope of the interests of the members to be promoted by their cooperative is less broad than that contained in the EC Council Regulation 1435/2003 on the Statute for a European Cooperative Society (SCE) and that in the International Labour Organization Recommendation No. 193 concerning the promotion of cooperatives.[25]

During the discussion of the draft which became the current Act in 2013 there was a public debate on what 'member promotion' means.[26] At the centre of the discussion were patronage refund payments and other distributions. The payment of patronage refunds or other types of distribution to the members are no more than indications of a promotion. Not paying patronage refunds to the members or the absence of other forms of distribution, on the other hand, do not indicate that the interests of the members are not promoted. Determination of whether or not members are promoted is hampered by three facts. First, the Act does not prescribe a specific cooperative audit whereby the question of whether the members have been promoted during the audited period could be answered.

---

24 Translation by the author of this report.

25 Cf. the ILO R. 193, Paragraph 2. This definition is identical with the one contained in the ICA Statement.

26 Cf. (in chronological order) J. Aspara, 'Suurosuuskunnat ovat etääntyneet juristaan' [Big cooperatives have moved away from their roots], *Helsingin Sanomat*, 11.10.2011; Niemelä and Kuisma, 'Vahvoja osuuskuntia tarvitaan' [We need strong cooperatives], *Helsingin Sanomat*, 20.10.2011; L. Laukkanen, 'Osuustoiminnan periaatteet ovat hukassa' [The cooperative principles are lost], *Helsingin Sanomat*, 10.5.2012, C9; L. Laukkanen, 'Osuustoimintayritykset etääntymässä omistajistaan' [Cooperative enterprises move away from their owners], *Länsi Savo*, 11.5.2012, 17; T. Metsä, 'Osuustoiminnan periaatteet pysyvät' [The cooperative principles are not being lost], *Helsingin Sanomat*, 11.5.2012, C7; I. Jussila, 'Tutustukaa osuustoiminnan periaatteisiin' [Acquaint yourselves with the cooperative principles], *Helsingin Sanomat*, 19.5.2012, C9; N. Mattila, 'Yhteishyvä vai imperiumi' [Common good or empire], *Helsingin Sanomat*, 22.6.2012, D4; P Linkola, 'Suomessa ei tunnisteta osuuskuntamallin etuja' [The cooperative advantage is not known in Finland], *Helsingin Sanomat*, 29.7.2012, B; J. Niemeläinen, 'Raha on karannut ihmisten ulottumattomiin' [Money has fled the reach of people], *Taloussanomat*, 2.8.2012, 06:01.

Secondly, the Act leaves it to the byelaws to decide whether the remainder of the surplus after deductions for the reserve fund, among others (Chapter 16, Section 6), is distributed at all, whether it is distributed to members, what form the distribution takes, and how much of the surplus is distributed. It is held that the surplus belongs to the cooperative.[27] The consequences of this view for taxation are obvious. A claim to patronage payments may only be based on a respective decision of the general assembly, which decides upon proposals by the board of directors (Chapter 16, Section 8). The byelaws may therefore stipulate that all or part of the surplus is paid in the form of patronage refunds, in the form of interest on the paid-up shares or stocks, or in the form of a dividend on shares or stocks. Thirdly, the Act does not distinguish between 'surplus' and 'profit'.[28] It uses the term 'surplus' [*ylijäämä*] to signify the positive result. In practice, this has led to the term 'surplus' acquiring the meaning of 'profit'.[29] In addition, there is no rule on, nor is there a recognised practice concerning, how transactions with members should be calculated as opposed to transactions with non-members (in commercial terms or cooperative ones). Separate accounts for members are therefore only necessary as far as patronage refunds are paid; they are the basis for determination of the proportionate shares that the members receive, but not for determination of the amount of the total surplus, because profits are seen as being part of the surplus and may therefore be distributed.

---

27 Cf. Aro, n. 15 above, p. 121; Leppänen, see n. 4 above, p. 14.

28 As do a number of other European cooperative laws, for example the Portuguese cooperative law (cf. J.M. Montolío, 'Legislación cooperativa en la Unión Europea', Madrid: Ministerio de Trabajo y Asuntos Sociales 2000, 6. Finlandia, pp. 245–264 (475)). The distinction followed here is that between 'surplus' (result on transactions with members) and 'profit' (result on transactions with non-members). The term 'non-member' is imprecise as it signifies both those non-members who are provided with the same services of the cooperative as are members and those third parties with whom the cooperative has market transactions. The differentiation between 'surplus' and 'profit' does not only concern the result as such, but also the way this result is produced. Concerning transactions with members: near-cost calculation, on cooperative terms; and concerning transactions with non-members: commercial terms. The price calculation also determines whether members are promoted or not. On the grounds of these strictly interpreted and ideally applied cooperative principles, one could say that there should not be any surplus for distribution to members at all. Another price as compared to the price charged to non-members should be charged to members independently of the priced volume of the individual transaction. In practice, cooperatives in Finland regularly distribute bonuses, cf. Pöyhönen, n. 6 above. Bonuses reward the priced volume of transactions and are not in all respects congruent with the differentiation used here. Their calculation includes profit. Possibly, the differentiation between 'surplus' and 'profit' disappeared with the introduction of the possibility to transact also with non-members. The use of the word 'surplus' [*ylijäämä*] by the legislator cannot, however, be seen as a pure linguistic matter.

29 Cf. for example Leppänen, 'Osuuskunnasta yritysmuotona' [On Cooperatives as Enterprise Form], in *Osuustoiminnan lainsäädäntö*, n. 4 above, pp. 14–17 (14). This explains the income tax treatment of cooperatives and the further harmonisation of the rules on the distribution of surplus with that of profits in stock companies.

The objective clause establishes an obligation of cooperatives to promote the interests of the members with a corresponding subjective right of members to be promoted. The answer to the question of whether the members have an obligation to use the services of the cooperative is less clear. Where the members run a business themselves, competition law needs to be considered. Should a member not conduct any business with the cooperative (over a period of time), this may be reason for the termination of membership. Because the Act itself is silent concerning membership criteria, it gives no answer. The byelaws may provide one.

Transactions with the members are the means to achieve promotion. Legally, membership and transactions are two separate relationships. The Finnish law thus follows the 'double relationship theory'. The transactions take place between the cooperative and its members directly or the cooperative 'arranges [these transactions] with the help of a subsidiary …'. Contrary to the previous law, the Act does not define the term 'subsidiary'. A systematic reading of Section 5 of Chapter 1 and of Section 12 of Chapter 8 results in applying the definition of subsidiaries as contained in Chapter 1, Sections 5 and 6 of the Bookkeeping Act ([*Kirjanpitolaki*], 30.12.1997/1336), i.e. a subsidiary exists when at least 50% of the shares are held by the cooperative. Chapter 8, Section 12 contains also an answer to the question of whether a cooperative may have subsidiaries for purposes other than that of providing services to its members. The purpose clause in Chapter 1, Section 5 does not, however, allow for 'pure holding' cooperatives without any economic activities.

Cooperatives may engage in activities with non-members[30] and in practice most do so, unless the byelaws determine otherwise and imply that non-member business supports the purpose of the cooperative, which is the promotion of its members. The Act does not specify any limitation, nor does it set any parameters for the byelaws in this regard, or specify whether the services of the cooperative may be provided to non-members on the same conditions as they are to members. Because no consequences would ensue, in terms of taxation or profit and surplus calculation for example, this may be a theoretical matter. In practice, many cooperatives differentiate between member and non-member business by granting bonuses to members. However, because membership requirements are often minimal, the difference is more symbolic than real. However, it becomes acute in worker cooperatives, for example, especially when both members and non-members may be workers in the cooperative.

With the exception of the above-mentioned 'Law on Cooperative Banks and Other Credit Institutions in the Form of Cooperatives' there is no organisational law dealing with special objectives such as, for example, social objectives. The 2003 Finnish Act on social enterprises ([*Laki sosiaalisista yrityksistä*],

30 As regards the imprecise use of the term 'non-member', cf. n. 28 above.

1351/2003)[31] does however regulate the substance matter of social cooperatives (work integration of disabled and long-term unemployed persons) in a similar manner to the solutions opted for in other countries, such as Italy and Spain.[32] Because Chapter 1, Section 5 states that the members are free to set their objectives, the cooperative may also serve the general interest.

The freedom to determine an objective other than the one suggested by the default rule (Chapter 1, Section 5) goes as far as fixing the objective of generating profits (cf. Chapter 8, Section 1; Chapter 16, Section 1). This demonstrates the intention of the legislator to increase the scope of default rules to the maximum. Such legislation, however, prepares the ground for consolidation of the laws on different enterprise types[33] because their distinguishing feature is precisely their objective. The organisational and operational rules of the respective laws are no more than mere functions of that objective. The gradual shift by the legislator to less mandatory rules is rather typical of the Anglo-Saxon legal tradition. But, to a certain extent, it is also typical of the French and the Belgian law.

The Act does not limit the choice of the activity. Hence, any licit activity is allowed. Obviously, this freedom to exercise any activity does not exempt cooperatives from the obligation to abide by any law or regulation applicable to the chosen activity.

2. ESTABLISHMENT

Chapter 2 of the Act regulates the forms and modes of the establishment of cooperatives.

A cooperative may be established by at least one person. The minimum number of members is also one. This is not expressly regulated but it follows from the deletion of a respective section on the minimum number of founders and members, respectively, in the previous law, and it is a given for relevant sections of the Act, for example Chapter 5, Section 1 dealing with the meeting of members.

According to Chapter 2, Section 8, the application for registration must be completed within three months from the signing of the incorporation contract. The minimum main content of the incorporation contract according to Chapter 2, Section 2 consists of the following: submission of the byelaws with the contents as prescribed by Chapter 2, Section 3; data on the founding members; their shares; the names of the members of the board of directors; and the names of the auditors and controllers, if any. The details of the registration

31 Available at: http://www.finlex.fi/fi/laki/kaannokset/2003/en20031351.pdf.

32 Cf. the 1991 Italian Law on social cooperatives (381/1991), and the Spanish Ley 5/2011 de Economía Social, especially its Preamble III.

33 Opinion shared by Vahtera, n. 16 above, p. 635.

are regulated by the Law on the Commercial Register ([*Kaupparekisterilaki*], 129/1979).

Registration confers legal personality upon the cooperative (Chapter 1, Section 2 and Chapter 2, Section 9). Those who act on behalf of the cooperative within a specified period before the incorporation contract is signed and before the cooperative is registered, are jointly and severally liable for these acts. The liability arising from such acts transfers to the cooperative upon its registration (Chapter 2, Sections 9 and 10).

Chapter, 2 Section 3 regulates the mandatory contents of the byelaws as follows: indication of the trade name of the cooperative according to the Law on Trade Names ([*Toiminimilaki*], 2.2.1979/128), of the seat of the cooperative in Finland, its field of activity and the financial year, if this is not specified in the incorporation contract (Chapter 2, Section 2). Contrary to the previous law, the Act does not indicate the non-mandatory content of the byelaws. This is in line with the wide byelaw autonomy. On the other hand, the Act thus neglects a possibly important function of the law, which is to assist potential members in setting up their cooperative without the help of a legal expert. This may be the reason why the government is empowered to issue model byelaws by decree (Chapter 2, Section 3).

A special type of cooperative is the stock-exchange cooperative. The Act defines in Chapter 5, Section 2[34] as stock-exchange cooperatives those cooperatives whose shares or stocks may be traded on the stock exchange according to the Law on Trading in Financial Instruments ([*Laki kaupankäynistä rahoitusvälineillä*], 748/2012).

Cooperatives may also merge with cooperatives registered abroad, split, or convert into practically any other type of enterprise, including stock companies, if the usual safeguards concerning especially third party interests are ensured (Chapters 20–22). Because no part of the cooperative capital (cf. the list in Chapter 8, Section 1) constitutes locked-in capital, conversion into a stock company does not pose a problem, still less so if none of the converted capital enjoyed a special tax treatment which would not be available for stock companies. Conversely, practically any other type of enterprise may convert into a cooperative.

3. COOPERATIVE GOVERNANCE

3.1. MEMBERSHIP

Chapter 3 regulates membership. As mentioned, the minimum number of members is one. The Act does not regulate on the personal eligibility criteria

[34] From a systematic point of view, this section belongs rather to Chapter 1.

for membership; however, the byelaws or the board of directors may set these criteria.

Whereas, the byelaws may state that any of the other organs of the cooperative (general meeting or supervisory committee) can be empowered to decide on a written application for membership to be addressed to the board of directors, the admission procedure and the admission criteria can only be set by the board of directors (Chapter 3, Section 1).

The byelaws may establish a right to admission (Chapter 3, Section 1). The Act does not specify the criteria for such a right, which used to be the case under the previous law.

In principle, a member may resign at any time. The byelaws may, however, stipulate a minimum period of membership not exceeding three years (Chapter 3, Section 2). In addition, members have an extraordinary right to withdraw from membership if the general meeting decides to alter their rights to a significant extent or in the case of restructuring (Chapter 5, Sections 21 and 35).

A member may be expelled for contravening membership obligations or on other grounds, as specified in the byelaws. The right to expel lies in principle with that organ which decided on the admission. An appeal against the decision to expel a member can be brought before the general meeting. An appeal against the negative decision of the general meeting can be brought before a court of law or an arbitration panel, if the latter is foreseen by the byelaws as a mode of dispute settlement. The final decision of the court of law or the arbitration panel in favour of the expelled member entitles the latter, besides being reinstated in his rights *ex tunc*, to damages (Chapter 3, Section 3). The Act does not explicitly mention the right to be heard. However, under general principles of Finnish law any contravention against this right would be reason for a court of law to overrule the decision, including that of an arbitrator.

Membership may only be transferred if the byelaws so allow: Chapter 1, Section 4. According to the same Section, members may transfer their shares within the limits stipulated in the byelaws. The transfer is tantamount to a resignation. It ends membership, while the transfer itself becomes effective only if the transferee is admitted as a new member (Chapter 1, Section 4). This rule demonstrates that cooperative shares [*osuudet*] are membership shares and not shares in the sense of shares of stock companies, called 'stocks' for the purpose of this report.[35]

Finally, holders of shares or stocks, other than members, are not members despite their having a number of rights similar to those of members (cf. below). The Act distinguishes between members and shareholders or stockholders.

35 Without over-emphasising language issues, to be noted is that much of the confusion relating to the nature of cooperative shares ensues from using the same word, 'share' to denote different matters, so much so that the debate at international level starts reflecting back on jurisdictions which use/d different words, like the Finnish one. The Act is an example. It replaces the word 'investment share' [*sijoitusosuus*] with 'stock' [*osake*].

3.2. GOVERNANCE STRUCTURE

The mandatory governance structure comprises the general meeting of members, the members and the board of directors (Chapter 6, Section 1). In addition, the byelaws may provide for the establishment of a supervisory committee and for the nomination of a manager (Chapter 6, Section 1). The byelaws may also establish additional organs, Chapter 6, Section 25.

3.2.1. General Meeting

The highest decision-making power is vested with the members (Chapter 5, Section 7). This is underlined by the rule establishing the principle of autonomy (Chapter 1, Section 9.) and by the power of the members, based on a respective rule in the byelaws or a unanimous decision by the general meeting, to exercise the powers of the board of directors or those of the manager in specified cases (Chapter 5, Section 3). The powers of the members are wider in scope and can – at least in theory – be made more easily effective than those of holders of stocks in a stock company

The members decide in an ordinary or extraordinary general meeting. The latter is to be convened according to the byelaws or upon request of the board of directors, the supervisory committee, or a specified proportion of the membership, or the voting rights (Chapter 1, Section 4). The members may also decide without meeting. In this case, decisions are valid only if taken in writing and unanimously (Chapter 5, Section 1). It is not clear how this latter rule relates to the one that allows, within the limits of the byelaws, for participation in the general meeting by post, the internet or other technical means which ensure safeguarding the rights attached to the participation (Chapter 5, Section 17).

The Act uses the term 'general meeting' [*osuuskunnan kokous*] for both the physical general meeting and the unanimous decision-taking in writing without a physical meeting.

If the byelaws so provide, the general meeting may be replaced with a delegate meeting (Chapter 1, Section 6; Chapter 5, Sections 1, and 37–43).

Besides the powers to deliberate and decide, which are attributed by any cooperative law to the general meeting, on issues such as budget, surplus and loss distribution, discharge of the board of directors (Chapter 5, Section 4), election of office holders, matters relating to organisational restructuring and matters the members may request to be dealt with (Chapter 5, Section 6), the main power of the general meeting is that of amending the byelaws (Chapter 5, Sections 29–31 and 34).

Unless the byelaws provide otherwise, up to three members may be represented by a proxy, who may or may not be a member of the cooperative. In so-called 'stock-exchange cooperatives', the byelaws may not restrict this possibility or the number of represented members. Both proxies and members may avail themselves of the help of an assistant (Chapter 5, Section 9).

In addition to the members, non-member shareholders and stockholders may participate in the general meeting if the byelaws so stipulate (Chapter 5, Section 7). A number of cases are exempted (cf. Chapter 5, Section 32). This right may be restricted to participation by post, the internet or another technical means (Chapter 5, Section 17). Non-member shareholders and stockholders have rights to be informed and to ask questions comparable to those of the members (Chapter 5, Sections 22, 23, 25 and 27).

The members of the board of directors, as well as the members of the supervisory committee and the manager, if any, may participate in the general meeting unless the general meeting excludes their participation in specific cases (Chapter 5, Section 11).

In specified cases, auditors and controllers, if any, may attend and speak at the general meeting (Chapter 5, Section 11; Chapter 7, Section 13).

3.2.1.1. Decision Taking

Contrary to the regulation on the board of directors, the Act does not prescribe a quorum for valid deliberations of, and decisions by, the general meeting. A quorum requirement may, however, be included in the byelaws. Theoretically, therefore, the general meeting may validly deliberate and decide with one member present.

In general, decisions by the general meeting are valid if supported by a simple majority. Decisions which alter the rights of shareholders or stockholders require, in addition, the simple majority consent of the respective group (Chapter 5, Sections 30 and 32), where each shareholder and stockholder has one vote unless the byelaws stipulate otherwise. Qualified majorities, up to unanimity, are required for special cases like byelaw amendments, restructuring, decisions which restrict members' acquired rights, or the right to withdraw from membership (Chapter 5, Sections 28–31). The byelaws may set higher majorities.

3.2.1.2. Voting Rights

Each member has one vote. The byelaws may grant more than one vote but any member may have more than 20 times the number of votes of another member only where the byelaws provide that the majority of members must be cooperatives or other legal persons, or where at least one member must be a legal person under public law (Chapter 5, Section 13). The latter criterion may facilitate the establishment of social cooperatives with a strong public interest component where the one member/one vote principle may not suffice for public entities to balance heterogeneous interests of unequal weight. Additional voting rights may be based on the number of shares and/or stocks or on the transactions, i.e. voting rights may also be attached to capital contributions. The purpose of this provision is to attract financial investments. However, it is questionable from the point of view of the cooperative values and principles.

Special rules apply in stock-exchange cooperatives, unless the byelaws stipulate otherwise, Chapter 5, Section 13.

Under specific conditions, the members, like the members of the board of directors, of the supervisory committee and the manager, if any, as well as non-member holders of shares or stocks, have a right to appeal before a court of law against a decision of the general meeting or of the delegate meeting (Chapter 5, Sections 36 and 42; Chapter 24, Section 1). The right of the latter group may be restricted through the byelaws except in cases concerning their shares or stocks (Chapter 24, Section 1 and Chapter 5, Section 32). The right to appeal does not expire if the decision of the general meeting or of the delegate meeting has violated basic rules, as specified in the Act (Chapter 24, Section 2).

3.2.2. Management: Board of Directors and Manager

The management of cooperatives is vested with the board of directors (board), composed of one to five members, unless the byelaws stipulate another number (Chapter 6, Sections 1 and 8). Any matter not within the exclusive power of the general meeting may be – and must be – dealt with by the board.

The board members are elected by the general meeting, unless the byelaws grant this power to the supervisory committee, if any (Chapter 6, section 9). Less than half of the members of the board may be installed through another procedure if the byelaws so stipulate (Chapter 6, Section 9). The Act does not specify what is meant by 'through another procedure'. It is held that outsiders may nominate these board members. The Act does not specify whether the board members have to be members of the cooperative. Chapter 6, Section 10 regulates some eligibility criteria for the board members but it does not answer this question, nor does it lay down any professional qualification criteria for the board members. In principle, at least one member of the board must be a resident in one of the member states of the European Economic Area (Chapter 6, Section 10).

The Act does not determine the term of office of the board members. This may be determined in the byelaws (Chapter 6, Section 11). The organ which nominated the board members may revoke the nomination at any time (Chapter 6, Section 13).

Unless a larger quorum is stipulated in the byelaws, the board may only deliberate and decide if at least half of its members are present (Chapter 6, Section 3). The same rule applies, *mutatis mutandis*, to the majority required for any decision (Chapter 6, Section 3).

The board may exercise the powers of the manager in specific cases or, if the byelaws so allow, in general (Chapter 6, Section 7). The board may devolve a matter which is within its powers or those of the manager for decision to the general meeting or to the supervisory committee (Chapter 6, Section 7).

In addition to the board, cooperatives may have a manager – a member of the board or otherwise – to be appointed by the board unless this power is given through the byelaws to the general meeting or to the supervisory committee (Chapter 6, Sections 20 and 21), if any. In principle, the manager must reside within the European Economic Area.

The manager is responsible for the current operations of the cooperative (Chapter 6, Section 17). S/he has a right to assist and speak at board meetings unless the board decides otherwise for all or specific cases (Chapter 6, Section 18). S/he must inform the board and its members in a manner that enables them to perform their tasks (Chapter 6, Section 17). This rule is of particular importance, given that, in general, modern cooperatives with market links suffer from a triple information gap. There is usually an information gap between the manager and the board, between the board and the supervisory committee and between the supervisory committee and the members.[36]

The board represents the cooperative (Chapter 6, Section 26). The manger may do so but only in matters falling within the scope of the duties assigned to him/her according to Chapter 6, Section 17. The limits on the power to represent are set by the field of activity of the cooperative, which must be determined in the (registered) byelaws (Chapter 2, Section 3). Other restrictions are valid only if they concern the (registered) attribution of a joint right to represent to two or more persons (Chapter 6, Section 28).

The decisions of the representative do not bind the cooperative if the representative acted without fulfilling the general qualification criteria set by the Act, if s/he acted in violation of the registered decision to not act alone, or if s/he exceeded his/her powers and the third party knew or should have known that s/he exceeded his/her powers. The fact that the limitation has been registered is not sufficient proof that the third party knew or should have known the limitation (Chapter 6, Section 29).

3.2.3. Supervisory Committee

The byelaws may provide for the establishment of a supervisory committee composed of at least three members elected by the general meeting. Board members and the manager may not be members of the supervisory committee (Chapter 6, Sections 1, 21 and 23). The supervisory committee has a dual nature.

---

36 Remedied by an obligation of the manager and the board to answer questions of the members during the general meeting (Chapter 5, Section 27).

On the one hand, it is part of the leadership structure (Chapter 6, Section 1), and under certain conditions the byelaws may vest it with management functions. On the other hand, it supervises the work of the board and that of the manger (cf. Chapter 6, Section 21; cf. above discussion). Its powers are limited to setting broad guidelines and it may not interfere in everyday operations (Chapter 6, Section 21).

The board, the members of the board, and the manager must inform the supervisory committee and its members in a manner that enables them to perform their tasks (Chapter 6, Section 22).[37]

4. DISPUTE SETTLEMENT

The byelaws may provide for the resolution of disputes by arbitration (Chapter 26, Section 3). Reportedly, there have been very few arbitration cases. Disputes seem to be settled by mediation.

5. COOPERATIVE FINANCIAL STRUCTURE

Thirteen out of 28 chapters of the Act are devoted, at least partly, to financial matters. By way of comparison, in the 1954 Law four out of eighteen chapters dealt with financing questions. The detailed regulation of financial matters that started with the amendments to the 1954 Law lies in the logic of these amendments and in the motives that inspired the adoption of the current Act. It was to make cooperatives more competitive by allowing for the voluntary issuance of financial instruments besides the membership shares. The legislator wanted the wide byelaw autonomy to bear most on financing questions.

5.1. COMPOSITION OF THE CAPITAL

The equity of the cooperative is composed of tied-up equity [*sidottu oma pääoma*] and free equity ([*vapaa oma pääoma*], Chapter 8, Section 1). The former category consists mainly of the share capital, the reserve fund and the stock capital. All other funds, as well as the surplus of the current and the preceding financial year, form the latter category.

[37] As to the importance of this rule, cf. the above comment on board and manager.

5.1.1. Shares and Stocks

In addition to the obligatory minimum of one share per member (Chapter 9, Section 1), the cooperative may issue shares and stocks for members and non-members (Chapter 1, Sections 2 and 3; Chapter 2, Section 1; Chapter 9, Section 2) unless the byelaws exclude this possibility. However, in principle, only members have residual rights. Under certain conditions, the right to acquire shares and stocks may be restricted to specific persons (Chapter 9, Section 5). The cooperative itself may hold shares and stocks but without any rights being attached to them (Chapter 2, Section 2; Chapter 9, Sections 1 and 2; Chapter 19, Section 1). Shares and stocks may be paid in money or kind [*apportti*], but not in the form of work or services (Chapter 2, Section 6).

The Act does not specify the minimum value of shares and stocks. It does not limit the amount of shares or stocks that a member or non-member may hold, nor does it rule on the proportion of the amount of member versus non-member financing.

The byelaws may stipulate that shares or stocks are of different classes. In this case, the byelaws must specify the difference as far as rights and obligations are concerned (Chapter 4, Section 1). These differences in rights and obligations may pertain, for example, to the subscription price, to the compensation out of the surplus, or to the amount to be refunded upon termination of membership or otherwise.

Neither shares nor stocks grant voting rights in the general meeting (Chapter 4, Section 3), unless the byelaws stipulate otherwise, for all or a specific class of shares or stocks. This means that, in principle, stocks are voiceless (preferred) stocks, as also known in other types of capitalist enterprise types. The Act thus maintains one of the main distinctive features of cooperatives, namely the de-emphasis on capital and the reduced influence of investor interests. However, the effects of the regulation of voting rights should not be over-emphasised. The power of investors, be they non-members or members, can be and is usually exercised in more subtle ways.

The voting rights of members who hold shares or stocks in addition to their obligatory share may be determined according to their holding of shares or stocks in the same way as plural voting rights are determined according to Chapter 5, Section 13 (Chapter 4, Section 3).

Shares which have been acquired voluntarily in addition to the one obligatory share may be returned at any time (Chapter 4, Section 1), and they may be transferred. The effects of the transfer of shares are limited by the rights attached to them at the moment of the transfer, unless the transferee becomes a member or shareholder by decision of the general meeting or unless the byelaws stipulate otherwise. The transfer of stocks may be restricted through the byelaws (Chapter 1, Section 4; Chapter 4, Section 5).

Shares may be converted into stocks; stocks may be converted into shares (Chapter 4, Section 1).

5.1.1.1. Shares

The number of shares and the share capital are variable (Chapter 1, Section 3). This allows for share capital variations; more precisely, for variations in the number of members and/or of the share capital (in the case of members subscribing to and paying for more than the one obligatory share or purchasing voluntary shares) without having to amend the incorporation contract and/or the byelaws. This flexibility is one of the reasons why the cooperative form is increasingly drawing the attention of people who traditionally did not associate with the idea. On the other hand, this variability does not lend itself to protecting third party interests.

Shares are registered with their book value, which may differ by class, unless the byelaws require their registration at nominal value (Chapter 4, Section 4). The byelaws may provide for the issuance of shares at nominal value, the subscription price of which may be higher. In this case, the excess amount may be transferred in part or in total to a free investment fund ([*sijoitettu vapaa pääoma rahasto*], Chapter 2, Section 4). This allows the cooperative partly to refund paid-up shares without reducing the equity that would otherwise be required by the creditors' protection rules (Chapter 8, Section 2). The amount paid on shares in excess of the subscription price is not refunded unless the byelaws or the decision on the issuance of shares stipulates otherwise. The refund may also exceed the subscription price, the criteria being for example the proportion between shares and surplus or other free equity, unless the byelaws stipulate otherwise.

As mentioned, members must acquire one share as a minimum. They may be required by the byelaws to acquire more shares or stocks (Chapter 9, Sections 1 and 2). The byelaws may allow for the increase or reduction of the number of additional shares or stocks to be acquired by the members. Upon issuance of additional shares or stocks, holders of shares or stocks, members or non-members have a right to acquire shares or stocks in proportion to the (type of) shares or stocks that they already hold unless the byelaws stipulate otherwise (Chapter 9, Section 4). These additional shares are refundable upon cessation of membership.

5.1.1.2. Stocks

Unless otherwise stipulated in the byelaws, cooperative stocks differ from the stocks of stock companies insofar as upon dissolution of the cooperative their holders may only claim back, as a maximum, the amount for which they subscribed the stocks. No refund payments on stocks may be made during the lifetime of the cooperative.

It appears that stocks have not been issued by any cooperative so far. There are divergent views as to the reason for this. For some, investors refrain because stocks are not assorted with – proportional – voting rights. Others argue that the Act, although it uses the terminology of the Limited Liability Companies Act, is not comprehensible.[38] Yet another explanation, which is not being considered, is that cooperatives do not opt for the possibility of issuing stocks because they do not want to create a conflict between investor interests and member-user interests. Whilst it is true that the stocks have the features of voiceless (preferred) shares in stock companies, the dynamics of these two enterprise types are different. In cooperatives with shares and stocks heterogeneous interests clash. This is not the case of stock companies, where all shareholders, with or without voice, share a common investment interest.

5.1.2. *Options and Capital Loans*

Based on its byelaws, the cooperative may issue options for members and non-members to receive shares or stocks (Chapter 9, Section 1; Chapter 10, Section 1).

A further financing instrument is capital loans. In the case of liquidation or bankruptcy, refunds on the loan or interest payments may only be made once higher ranking claims have been satisfied (Chapter 12, Section 1).

5.1.3. *Reserve Fund*

Except for the obligatory one share per member, all of the outlined financial instruments are optional, some are variable, and the voting rights attached to them, if any, are not proportional. Their attractiveness is therefore limited. Practice seems to validate this opinion. An exception, as far as creditor protection is concerned, is the legal obligatory reserve fund. Five percent of the surplus, as shown on the balance sheet, must be transferred to the reserve fund until it reaches the minimum amount of 2,500 euros (Chapter 16, Section 7). Thereafter it may grow without limitation if the members so decide. It may be reduced under strict conditions only (Chapter 16, Section 7). Obligatory premium funds and revaluation funds, to which, among others, non-refundable parts of share prices have to be transferred, serve partly to reinforce the function of the reserve fund. The Act does not regulate whether the reserve fund is indivisible, divisible, or divisible under certain circumstances. Notwithstanding possible stipulations in the byelaws, systematic reading of the Act and the rules on taxation gives

---

38 Interestingly, the Ministry of Justice introduced this terminology with the argument that under the previous law, which had already allowed for the same type of investments, making use of this possibility was hampered by a terminology that investors did not understand.

to understand that the reserve fund is divisible. Unrestricted divisibility of the reserve fund is questionable in light of the 3rd Principle of the International Cooperative Alliance.[39]

5.1.4. *Extraordinary Payments and Increased Member Liability*

Members may be required by the byelaws to make extraordinary payments. These payments are not refundable unless otherwise stipulated in the byelaws (Chapter 13, Section 1). Such payments may only be required when necessary to cover a need during normal operations of the cooperative.

Finally, for the event of liquidation or bankruptcy, the byelaws may stipulate an additional limited or unlimited, joint and several liability of the members, per capita, share or otherwise (Chapter 14, Sections 1, 11 and 15), liability to further calls or reserve liability [*lisämaksuvelvollisuus*]. The obligation extends for one year beyond the end of the financial year during which membership ceased (Chapter 14, Section 3). Members may not off-set this obligation against a claim that they may have against the cooperative (Chapter 14, Section 4).

5.2. DISTRIBUTION OF ASSETS

Chapter 16, Section 1 lists the types of assets, and the conditions under which they may be distributed. These are: surplus and free equity; shares; share capital and stock capital, as well as reserve reductions; cooperative's own share and stock acquisitions and transfers; and residual assets after liquidation.

As mentioned, the Act does not distinguish between 'surplus' and 'profit'. Consequently, and if the byelaws so allow, profit on transactions with non-members may be distributed.

Surplus may be distributed among members and non-member shareholders or stockholders according to criteria other than the volume of transactions[40] with the cooperative only if the byelaws so allow and within the limits set therein (Chapter 16, Section 5). Special rules apply in the case of cooperatives with a profit-generating objective (Chapter 16, Sections 1, 5 and 10). The general meeting decides on the distribution and may decide to distribute more than proposed by the board only with the consent of the board (Chapter 16, Section 8).

As mentioned, the claim to patronage payments arises from a respective decision of the general assembly. The Act does not set any criteria for the calculation of the patronage refund. In practice, patronage refunds are calculated in proportion to the price paid on the occasion of the transactions, i.e. quantity

39 Cf. ICA Statement, n. 17 above.
40 This can obviously only apply to members.

and quality are given a price. Cooperatives regularly distribute bonuses. The argument states that these bonuses are proof of the promotion of the members by the cooperative (cf. above).

As mentioned, the Act thus leaves it to the members to decide through the byelaws whether surplus is distributed, what form distribution takes, and how much of the surplus is distributed. The Act leaves it also to the byelaws to decide whether interests and dividends may be paid. The byelaws may therefore stipulate that all or part of the surplus is paid in the form of interest on the paid-up shares or stocks or in the form of a dividend on shares or stocks. This has consequences for taxation.

Upon dissolution, shares may not be paid back at a higher price than subscribed unless the byelaws stipulate otherwise (Chapter 17, Section 1).

Under specified conditions and safeguarding the rights of creditors, the value of the share capital, of the stock capital, and of the reserve fund may be reduced (Chapter 18, Section 1).

6. COOPERATIVE AUDIT

6.1. GENERAL

Audit is understood here in the broad sense of control of compliance by cooperatives with the general law applying to their operations and activities as enterprises, as well as with the cooperative-specific rules and principles. In this sense, registration constitutes an *ex ante* control. Cooperatives must register with the registration authority in order to acquire the status of a legal person (Chapters 1 and 2). The decision to register implies an *ante factum* assessment of the (future) cooperative's constant fulfilment of the legal requirements.

6.2. INTERNAL AND EXTERNAL CONTROL

Further control divides between internal and external control. This paragraph will not repeat some of the already-mentioned internal control mechanisms, such as, for example, the powers of the members and of the supervisory committee (if any) or the possibility to bring an action against a decision of the general meeting under Chapter 24.

At least as important as allowing for the exercise of democratic control rights is the provision to the members of adequate information and knowledge which enable them to exercise their control rights effectively. In complex business enterprises and markets, and especially in the absence of a supervisory committee or a cooperative specific audit, the average member risks not having or understanding this information and knowledge. Education, training and audit are therefore of key importance. The Act does not contain any provision on education and training. Cooperatives are, of course, free to provide education and training and use funds for this purpose. In practice they do so. But the Act establishes a number of rights to be informed, for example basic information on annual accounts must be made accessible to members in due time before the general meeting (Chapter 5, Section 23). In cooperatives with no more than ten members, members have a right to inspect the accounts unless the board refuses this right on grounds that inspection would be detrimental to the cooperative (Chapter 7, Section 14). Members have a right to ask during the general meeting for a special audit (Chapter 7, Section 5).

As regards external control, one should note that a number of acts contravening the law are classified as criminal offences or infractions under Chapter 27 of the Act. In addition, an entire chapter (Chapter 25) regulates the damages to be paid by members, delegates, non-member shareholders or stockholders, as well as the members of the board, the supervisory committee, the manager, auditor or controller, the chairperson of the general meeting and of the delegate meeting in the case of harm caused to each other or to the cooperative, intentionally or negligently. The cases may, in deviation from the general procedural law, also be heard by the court where the cooperative has its seat (Chapter 26, Section 1). The pursuit of these acts and/or related claims can be classified as external (indirect) control.

Furthermore, the decision on the accounts taken by the general meeting must be filed with the Registration Authority (Chapter 8, Section 10), which is an element of external control.

Finally, audit falls within the category of external control. The Act differentiates between auditors and controllers (Chapter 5, Section 4 and Chapter 7), the difference being that the qualification of the former is regulated by the Auditing Act ([*Tilintarkastuslaki*], 13.4.2007, 459), Chapter 7, Section 9), whereas for the latter no specific audit qualifications are required by law.

Audit is only required by law if more than one of the following conditions are given for the current and the immediately preceding financial year: the balance sheet exceeds 100,000 euros, the total sales or comparable revenue exceed 200,000 euros, or the number of employees has exceeded three on average (Chapter 7, Section 2 in connection with Chapter 2, Section 4 of the Auditing Act). Most cooperatives seem to fulfil at least two of these criteria. The byelaws of cooperatives not falling under the Auditing Act may require auditing. In cooperatives which have no auditor, neither by law nor by byelaws, members, by at least one-quarter of the total amount of votes or at least one-third of the votes present or represented at the general meeting, may request that the general meeting elect an auditor (Chapter 7, Section 5). Should the general meeting fail to do so, an auditor must be nominated upon request of a member by the local authority (Chapter 7, Section 5). Furthermore, members who have the backing of at least one-quarter of the total amount of votes or at least one-third of the votes present or represented at the general meeting may request the local authority to conduct an extraordinary audit (Chapter 7, Section 15).

The Auditing Act regulates the scope of the audit. It does not contain any special rules for cooperatives. Cooperative management audit, social and societal audit, as required by some jurisdictions, is therefore not required by law.

Cooperatives must have a controller, elected by the general meeting, if they do not have an auditor and if they do not exclude control through their byelaws (Chapter 7, Section 7). However, a specified minority of the members may insist on having a controller (Chapter 7, Section 7). Failing this obligation, the controller will be nominated by the local authority (Chapter 7, Section 7).

Interestingly, the qualification criteria for the controller (cf. Chapter 7, Sections 9–11) seem to reflect the cooperative values and principles more than is required for the auditor.

7. COOPERATION AMONG COOPERATIVES

The Act does not contain any rules on cooperation among cooperatives. Only one rule indirectly alludes to the existence of secondary or tertiary cooperatives, namely Chapter 5, Section 13, which deals with plural voting rights.

General law regulates cooperation among cooperatives. Depending on the type of cooperation, it is regulated either by organisational law or by contract law. In practice, socio-political cooperation is organised as a two-tier system whereby the second tier is organised as an association. Economic cooperation takes place through central cooperatives.

8. CONCLUSIONS

Painting a more complete picture of the Finnish cooperative law would require exploring the extent to which cooperatives make use of their extensive byelaw autonomy. Furthermore, other legal norms, not to mention taxation, competition law, labour law and accounting standards, which most likely have an impact on the structure and/or operations of cooperatives, may alter the picture.

For more than a century, Finnish legislators have endeavoured to ensure the distinctive features of cooperatives whilst maintaining cooperatives as competitive enterprises. However, as in many if not all jurisdictions, they have not escaped the circle of strengthening the financial competitiveness of cooperatives and jeopardising the identity of cooperatives. What is left of the latter are variable membership and capital. Where surplus is distributed in the form of interests or dividends on shares and stocks and where investors, be they members or not of the cooperative, have a say in the affairs of the cooperative, this identity of cooperatives is at stake. Allowing for the possibility of one-member cooperatives entails that the associative character of cooperatives is lost. In comparative law terms, the reduction to two legal figures, contract (incorporation contract) and ownership, not only means leaving a specific legal tradition behind – which would not be of relevance, –, it may also have consequences in terms of the application of European company legislation to cooperatives in Finland.

Obviously, the consensus on which the original legislator could build when passing the first law in 1901 has faded away. It might have to be found again. Lawyers are increasingly regaining interest in the subject and reflecting on how to re-establish and modernise the distinctive legal features of cooperatives in accordance with rapidly changing globalisation, driven by and driving socio-political and socio-psychological circumstances.

CHAPTER 7
FRANCE

David Hiez

1. DEFINITION AND OBJECT OF COOPERATIVES

1.1. PRELIMINARY REMARKS

1.1.1. General Cooperative Law and Special Cooperative Laws

It is difficult to comprehend cooperative French law as a whole because it is a mix of general law and several special laws dealing with specific kinds of cooperatives. The general law is Act 47-1775 of 10 September 1947 known as the 'cooperation statute'. The purpose of the legislature at that time was to provide a cooperative common law to replace the various previous special laws laid down over a span of fifty years. Indeed, article 30 of the law still states that there will be a codification of cooperative law, and that the 1947 Law will be the first title of the new code. The 1947 Law also contained an original provision regarding normative coordination, since its Article 2 provided that general law would have greater strength than special laws, contrary to the traditional principle *specialia generalibus derogant, non generalia specialibus*. However, that objective was not achieved, and the provision on codification is still in force. The exceptional solution of article 2 has since been repealed by L. 92-643 of the 13th of July 1992, article 2.1.[1]

[1] L. 92-643 of the 13th of July 1992, art. 2.

The consequence is a large number of special laws of such an extent that it is pointless to enumerate them all.[2] Some of the most important examples are the following:

Agricultural cooperatives: Code rural (C.rur.), arts. L.521-1 to L.529-6 and R.521-1 to R.529-2;

Workers' cooperatives: law no. 78-763 of the 13th of July 1978 on workers' cooperative societies; commercial cooperatives: code de commerce (C.com.), art. L.124-1 to L.124-16;

Craft cooperatives: law no. 83-657 of the 23rd of July 1983 on the development of certain social economy activities, art. 1 to art. 34;

Collective interest cooperatives: law no. 47-1275 of the 10th of September 1947, art. 19*quinquies* to 19*quindecies*;

Merchants' cooperatives: C.com. arts. L.124-1 to L.124-16;

Transportation cooperatives: code des transports (C.transp.), arts. L.3441-1 to L.3441-6;

Banking cooperatives: code monétaire et financier (C.mon.fin.), art. L.512-1 to L.512-10, precising that, in the chapter dealing with these cooperatives in this Code, each banking cooperative is submitted to different provisions; for example: C.mon.fin., arts. L.512-2 to L.512-13 for 'banques populaires'.

A cooperative must usually comply with two cooperative laws: the general law and the special law of its family. Theoretically, it is possible to create a cooperative which is not connected with a special law. Such a cooperative is only submitted to the 1947 Law, and is termed a '1947 law cooperative'. These cooperatives are very few in number, mainly because there are some advantages, for example in taxation, to be gained from referring to a special law. Moreover, the general law is not detailed, so that the drafting of its statutes is more difficult.

The complexity derives from the fact that the general law states numerous principles that are explicitly applicable only if the special law does not stipulate another solution. Moreover, even when the general law does not foresee that possibility, the usual interpretation principle requires that *specialia generalibus derogans*. Indeed, special laws often state solutions different from general law: it is not often that there is a fully opposite provision, but the import or the details of the principle differ, so that each family seems to have a fully autonomous special regulation. These specificities can only be understood if each law is related to the history of the corresponding cooperative family.

An example is the possibility to incorporate a part of the reserves in the capital,[3] this possibility is envisaged by the general law,[4] but many special laws

2 There exist about thirty kinds of legally distinct cooperative.
3 For details, see section 3.5.
4 L. no. 47-1775 of the 10th of September 1947, art. 16 al. 3, 4.

derogate the general provision, and often forbid explicitly the incorporation.[5] Moreover, some other special laws exclude a mechanism of the general law and state another: for example, agricultural cooperatives[6] with similar aims but substantially different mechanisms.

In this case, it is difficult to say what the solution is in French law, since they are diverse. This is not an exceptional situation; on the contrary, it is quite common. Of course, it is always significant that the general law states one solution and not another, but when most special laws give another statement, it is superficial to refer to the general statute. In this regard, it would be pointless to itemise all the special provisions. I shall always present the general provision, and describe the most interesting special ones only when they differ, or in order to specify the frequent concrete applications of the general rule.

1.1.2. Cooperative Law and Company Law

French cooperative law, unlike company law, suffers from a lack of interest by doctrine. Whereas Italian, German and Spanish doctrine contains handbooks on cooperative law or substantial developments in more general books, as well as PhD dissertations on the topic, French research is meagre. For example, there exists only one handbook.[7] This is the consequence of the weak autonomy of cooperative law, as well as being one of its causes. Legal doctrine was more developed in the first half of the twentieth century, but the adoption of the law of 1947 closed that cycle. Interest in cooperative law has been renewed with the development of the social and solidarity economy,[8] but still remains modest. This specification is interesting only to show the weakness of the legal cooperative identity, which has strong consequences on its relationship with company law.

Article 1 of the 1947 Law states: 'A cooperative is a company created by several persons willingly associated in order to satisfy their economic or social needs by their common efforts and the creation of the necessary means'. I will detail the meaning of this definition below, but the first specification is that cooperatives are companies. The French word 'société' is very difficult to translate. Indeed, 'société' is in French a generic notion, whereas English distinguishes among different categories, such as company, partnership, but also industrial and provident societies. In business law, the terms 'société' and 'society' are *faux amis*. The precision is important, since it has major consequences, and also because

---

5 L. no. 78-763 of the 19th of July 1978, art. 26*ter*.

6 Code rural et de la pêche maritime (C.rur.), art. L.523-1.

7 D. Hiez, *Coopératives Création Organisation Fonctionnement*, Delmas, Paris, 2013; 2nd ed., forthcoming, Dalloz, Paris, 2016.

8 That development started in 1981, but accelerated in the 2000s, culminating with L. no. 2014-856 of the 31st of July 2014 on social and solidarity economy.

it should not be an evidence of the legal nature of the cooperative. The above statement of article 1 of the 1947 Law was modified in 1992 and 2014, but the first five words, here discussed, remain similar. Therefore, the conclusion is that the qualification of 'company' was adopted in 1947. Before that date, the point was very actively debated. In French law, a *summa divisio* among private legal persons is the distinction between a company and an association. The definitions of companies[9] and associations[10] are opposite to each other: a company aims at the distribution of profits, whereas such distribution is forbidden for an association.

In that context, debate centred on whether cooperatives were companies or associations. The discussion was theoretically important because it was an interesting hard case to specify the distinction between the two groupings. Authors claimed that cooperatives were associations because they did not pursue the aim of profit distribution, even if the doctrine clarified that it was necessary to pay close attention to the articles and practice of each specific cooperative to make the final qualification. Indeed, in the absence of clear solutions from the legislature, the organisation and functioning of each cooperative depended on the wording of its articles.[11] An important and well-known case decided on the notion of 'benefices', included in the definition of both association and company, and categorically delineated the full opposition of association and company.[12] More interestingly, this case concerned a cooperative, more precisely a banking cooperative ('caisse rurale de Manigod'). The judges stated that the cooperative was an association, since it did not distribute profits, even if its byelaws provided for cooperative refunds. But, as highlighted by the doctrine, the qualification was thoroughly dependent on the wording of the cooperative's statutes and could not be extended to all cooperatives. Nevertheless, the conclusion remains that most authors and case law were in favour of the qualification of 'association'.

However, in practice, most cooperatives choose the form of a company. They incorporate the cooperative as a company, using a form provided by company law, derogating it in their byelaws to include cooperative principles. Some special cooperative laws adopted at the beginning of the twentieth century made the same choice, and the only general provisions dedicated to cooperatives, even if cooperatives were not explicitly mentioned in them, were part of company law.[13] The reason for this choice was not political but pragmatic. The 1901 law

---

9 Code Civil (C.civ.), art. 1832.

10 L. of the 1st of July 1901, art. 1.

11 H. Hayme, *Domaines respectifs de l'association et de la société*, thèse Paris, 1907.

12 Cass. réun., 11 mars 1914, S. 1918.1.103 – D. 1914.1.259 – J. Soc. 1915, p. 97 – Rev. Soc. 1915, p. 44.

13 Law of the 24th of July 1867 on commercial companies, title II variable capital companies, arts. 48 ff.; today Code of commerce (C.com.), arts. L.231-1 ff.

on associations concerned the legal recognition of associations but contained no provision regarding their organisation or their economic activities. Therefore, that structure was not very attractive for a firm and, even with its defects, company law offered a more suitable form. An attempt occurred to build a specific regulation for cooperatives, distinct from companies and associations, and a project was launched in the 1930s, but it never succeeded. In the meantime, many special cooperative laws chose simply to refer to company law. Finally, this choice was generalised in 1947, and there is today no longer any discussion in its regard, even if all authors agree that this arrangement is rather strange because cooperatives differ from companies in all main respects.[14]

The classification of cooperatives among companies is not original: what is original, though, is the conclusion drawn from it, which is that cooperatives are in principle subject to company law. In practice, this qualification means that, for all points not covered by cooperative law, company law is applicable. For example, the causes and the procedure of a cooperative's dissolution are regulated by company law. Of course, this application is excluded if the provisions of company law contradict those of cooperative law, but it is often difficult to decide whether or not there is a contradiction. This is decided by judges, and their poor knowledge of cooperative law often explains the preference given to company law.

A major issue is the form of company chosen by a cooperative. Theoretically, the choice is not compulsory, at least not for cooperatives established by reference to the 1947 Law, since this law gives no indication on the matter. But the choice never occurs, for two reasons: first, because the 1947-law cooperatives are very few in number; secondly, because that choice requires full and detailed organisation of the cooperative in the byelaws, which the drafters prefer to avoid. On the contrary, the special laws usually limit the choice of possible forms of company to two options: a limited liability Company ('société à responsabilité limitée', s.a.r.l.) or a public limited company ('*société anonyme*', S.A.). A third possibility is increasingly often proposed: the simplified stock company ('société par action simplifiée', S.A.S). Therefore, the concrete functioning of a cooperative is mainly regulated by company law, in combination with special derogating provisions of cooperative law. A cooperative must usually refer to six sets of provisions: general company law,[15] general commercial company law,[16] variable capital company provisions,[17] the regulation specific to the form of company

[14] R. Saint-Alary, 'Les elements distinctifs de la société coopérative', *Revue trimestrielle de droit commercial*, Paris, 1952, p. 485 f.; J. Mestre, 'Propos introductifs sur l'originalité du droit coopératif', *Revue de la recherche juridique droit prospectif*, 1996, p. 475 f.

[15] C.civ., arts. 1832 ff.

[16] C.com., arts. L.232-1 ff.

[17] C.com., arts. L.231-1 ff.

chosen, the general cooperative law,[18] and the special cooperative legislation applicable to the family to which the cooperatives belongs. It is obvious that the outcome is rather complex.

The only cooperatives with different features in this regard are agricultural cooperatives. Indeed, article L.521-1 of the Rural Code states that 'agricultural cooperative companies and their unions constitute a special category of companies, distinct from civil companies and from commercial companies'. The consequence is that agricultural cooperatives are only subject to general company law, that is to say, Civil Code arts. 1832 to 1844-17. These provisions of the civil code do not deal with many practical questions, notably organisational and financial ones. Consequently, the Rural Code provides solutions to all such matters, so that agricultural cooperative law is far more detailed than any other cooperative statute. Article L.521-1 specifies that agricultural cooperatives have legal personality and full legal capacity, which no other cooperative legislation does. The autonomy of agricultural cooperative legislation must be qualified because, in practice, it is often inspired by the public limited company law as recently reformed.[19] However, this legislation is the only one in French cooperative law which tries to elaborate a full cooperative law; which is the reason why I often refer to it in what follows.

1.2. DEFINITION OF COOPERATIVE

French law gives a definition of cooperatives in general,[20] but it is difficult to clearly distinguish in that provision between the definition itself and the social object. Moreover, the definition has evolved since 1947; first in 1992 to extend its object so that it fit better with all cooperatives, and secondly in 2014 to provide a fully new definition. A major element of this definition relates to the qualification of a company, as explained above.[21] An element lacking in the definition is the variability of capital.

The variability of capital is not included in the definition of a cooperative, differently from other legislations – for example Belgian law[22] and Luxembourg law[23] – whereas, in practice, all cooperatives adopt the variability of capital.

Variable capital companies are regulated by articles L.231-1 to 231-8 of the '*Code de commerce*'. These provisions derive directly from the first legislation

18 L. no. 47-1775 of the 10th of September 1947.
19 D. Hiez, 'Pas de revolution pour les cooperatives agricoles', *Revue des Sociétés*, Paris, 2007, p. 53.
20 L. no. 47-1775 of the 10th September 1947, art. 1.
21 See section 1.1.2.
22 Code belge des sociétés, art. 350.
23 Law of the 10th of August 1915, art. 113.

concerning commercial companies.[24] That law contained eight articles on variable capital companies, the purpose of which was to provide a structure for cooperatives. However, cooperatives were not explicitly mentioned in the law, since cooperatives were reluctant to have their own legislation for fear that it might be a means for the government to control them and restrict their activities. The law of 1947 contained no provisions concerning the variability of capital. Therefore, variable capital is only an option for cooperatives. Theoretically, cooperatives may have a fixed capital, but it would be at odds with fundamental cooperative principles, notably the open door principle, and I know of no example of a cooperative of this kind. The 1947 Law makes only one reference to the variability of capital, which confirms that it is only an option: its article 7 states that cooperatives created as variable capital companies do not have to specify the highest amount of their capital in their articles of incorporation. That provision is only the outcome of a legislative will to reverse a controversial case law ruling[25] which had stated that, if the highest amount of capital was not fixed in the articles, any increase of capital should be submitted to the procedure of capital increase in fixed capital companies.[26]

It appears that the cooperative definition as such is very poor, either referring to company law or making the variability of capital an option. Fortunately, however, if the technical substance of cooperatives is deceptive, there is more detail concerning their social object.

1.2.1. Cooperative Social Object

The cooperative social object is, in French cooperative law, the core of the definition of a cooperative. At first glance, its object is very clear and compliant with the ICA definition and principles.[27]Recently, the French legislature has chosen to highlight the connection between this object and cooperative principles[28] by referring explicitly to some of them in article 1 of the 1947 Law. However, it seems that the consequence of the creation of a new type of cooperative is that the collective interest cooperative ('société cooperative d'intérêt collectif', SCIC) has not been elucidated and has certainly not been integrated into the legal definition.[29]

---

24 Law of the 24th of July 1867.

25 Cass. com. 6 févr. 2007, no 05-19.237, bulletin civil des arrêts de la Cour de cassation (Bull. civ.) IV, no 29; Droit des sociétés, Paris (*Dr. Sociétés*), 2007, 175, comm. Mortier.

26 For an overview: D. Hiez, 'Chronique de droit cooperative', *La semaine juridique Entreprises*, édition Entreprises, (JCP E), 2008, 2373, no. 10.

27 See section 1.2.1.1.

28 See section 1.2.1.2.

29 See section 1.2.1.2.

1.2.1.1. The Definition of Cooperative Social Object

The social object of a cooperative is stated at the end of Article 1 of the 1947 Law. Herein resides the evolution of the article since 1947. In 1947, article 1 stated:

> A cooperative is a company whose main objectives are:
>
> 1. To reduce, for the benefit of its members and by their common effort, the cost price and possibly the selling price of some products and some services, by fulfilling the function of firms or intermediaries whose remuneration would increase this cost price;
> 2. To improve the quality of the products provided to its members or those produced by its members and sold to the consumers.

That definition was an attempt to encompass all the activities of cooperatives, notably through the intent to abolish intermediaries between cooperatives and providers. Nevertheless, the definition has been criticised, since it prolonged the influence of consumer cooperatives whose economic weight, as well as theoretical predominance, were obvious at the time. But the situation had changed, first because of the development of producer cooperatives, and second because of the bankruptcy of French consumer cooperatives in the 1970s. Therefore, the law of 1992[30] added a third object to article 1:

> 3. More generally to contribute to satisfaction of the needs and promotion of the economic and social activities of its members as well as to their training.

Addition is not revision, and the structure of the definition remained the same. For example, it is necessary to distort the provision strongly to make it suitable for workers' cooperatives. Nevertheless, the main features of cooperatives were already present: satisfaction of the members' interests, and the common investment of cooperators in achieving that goal.

In 2014, the definition was redrafted by the law on the social and solidarity economy.[31] It now states: 'A cooperative is a company created by several persons willingly associated in order to satisfy their economic or social needs through their common efforts and the creation of the necessary means'.

There is no substantial change in the meaning of the new provision.[32] The same main elements are present: economic and social means, the common efforts. The modification seems more a simplification and the outcome is positive. However, two items have disappeared: promotion of the activities

---

30 L. 92-643 of the 13th of July 1993, art. 1.

31 L. no. 2014-856 of the 31st of July 2014, art. 24.

32 See below on the collapse with the collective interest cooperative: section 1.2.1.2.

of the members, and their training. The former element can be considered implicit, since the satisfaction of the members' needs consists, for producers' cooperatives, in promotion of their activities. In regard to training, the absence in the definition is compensated by its mention among the cooperative principles to which cooperatives are submitted. It was explicitly introduced for agricultural cooperatives in regard to the board members.[33]

The general object of cooperatives is duplicated in each special law, which defines the special object of the cooperatives regulated by that law. This special object is inspired by the special needs of cooperatives. For example, in law no. 78-763 of 13 July 1978 for workers' cooperatives, article 1, states that: 'Workers' cooperative companies are formed by workers of any category or professional qualification associated to perform together their profession in a firm that they manage directly or through the intermediation of representatives designated by themselves from among themselves'.

A specification is provided by article 1 of the general law: the cooperative performs its activity in any branch of human activity. This is important, since it excludes any limitation according to the activity undertaken. As regards associations or companies, the byelaws state the social object in consideration of the activity, but the law does not provide with such an indication. The general law states that the cooperative may run any activity, but most special laws set, directly or indirectly, the limitations of this activity. However, if a cooperative is not open to a specific activity, the 1947 Law remains available to give generic shape to a cooperative. An example of difficulty and controversy can be found in regard to regulated professions. For example, chartered accountants have encountered difficulties in creating a SCIC. More precisely, there is no cooperative difficulty, but the association of chartered accountants has been reluctant to register a SCIC, arguing unofficially that the cooperation required among cooperatives was in contradiction with the independent of chartered accountants.

But article 1 of the general law of 1947 was also amended in 2014 by the mention of some essential cooperative principles: voluntary and open membership, democratic governance, economic participation of members and their training, and inter-cooperation. This innovation is interesting because it emphasises the relationships between the definition of a cooperative and the cooperative principles, the latter being a means to implement the former. I will not describe all of them here, since they will be analysed in the following sections. Nevertheless, a point must be made regarding cooperative refund, which corresponds to the economic participation of members in the cooperative, since it is specifically a cooperative concept.[34]

There follows discussion of cooperative transactions, which may be analysed as the core of the cooperative social object, since they are the substance of

33 C.rur., art. L.523-1, created by the law no. 2014-1170 of the 13th of October 2014, art. 13 v.
34 See section 1.2.2.

the economic participation of cooperators in the cooperative. This element is mentioned in the article, among cooperative principles, but as such, it is not the cooperative's social object, which is satisfaction of the members' needs. Of course, performing it requires the conduct of transactions between the members and cooperative, but it is logically second. It is true that in French law the qualification of transactions between members and the cooperative is vague. On the one hand, authors insist on the importance of the '*double qualité*' principle, which means that each member is simultaneously an associate of the company and its contractor for the cooperative transaction.[35] This has been recently explicitly stated for agricultural cooperatives: the relationship between the cooperator and the agricultural cooperative of which s/he is a member relies, notably, on the indivisible dual quality of service beneficiary and associate.[36] On the other hand, the two aspects of the relationship remain distinct since each has its own legal qualification. There should be a single contract, the contract of cooperation, but it is difficult to find more than a reciprocal influence of each relationship on the other one. Even if cooperative transactions are the core of the cooperative social object, they cannot be considered as its substance.

1.2.1.2. New Theories of Cooperative Social Object

Legal cooperative thinking is very poor in France, so that there is no real alternative proposal to define the cooperative social object. Interesting discussions took place at the beginning of the twentieth century on the main characteristics of cooperatives and, consequently, on their definition. Debates concerned the possibility of finding a common definition, whereas the relationships between the cooperators and the cooperative were rather different, as was the activity of the former in the cooperative. The interests of consumers were very different from those of enterprises and their common use of the cooperative did not necessarily have the same goals. The democratic principle, the open door, the independence from trade unions, parties or church, the distribution of surpluses, the activity with non-members, all of these questions did not receive the same answers. Depending on the cooperatives to which the authors referred, their analysis could vary. These debates were weakened by adoption of the general law and, today, they are no longer seriously conducted. The only concern of legal thinkers of the past forty years has been to describe the cooperative's specificity and to distinguish it from other groupings. The definition of cooperative has not

35 L. Coutant, *L'évolution du droit coopératif de ses origines à 1950*, éditions Matot-Braine, Paris, 1950, p. 228 ff. B. Saintourens, 'Sociétés coopératives et sociétés de droit commun', *Revue des sociétés*, 1996, p. 1 ff.

36 C.rur., art. L.521-1-1: 'La relation entre l'associé coopérateur et la coopérative agricole à laquelle il adhère … repose, notamment, sur le caractère indissociable de la double qualité d'utilisateur de services et d'associé…'.

been seriously renewed either by updating the distinction with companies,[37] or by comparing it with other groupings such as economic interest groupings,[38] or even by choosing a focus to tackle the cooperative identity.[39]

The innovation has come from practice and the creation by the legislature of a new cooperative: the collective interest cooperative. Partly inspired by the Italian social cooperative, this new form has been established[40] by promoters of the solidarity economy in order to create a bridge between association and cooperative. Its importance is symbolised by its integration into the general law of 1947.[41]

Collective interest cooperatives are first, defined as cooperatives, but their social object differs from the general one, and this has very important consequences, theoretically and practically. Article 19*quinquies* of the 1947 Law states that their objective is 'the production or the supply of collective interest goods and services which contain a dimension of social utility'. The key expression is 'social utility', the definition of which is not yet fully fixed. This concept, as well as that of 'collective interest', is distinct from, and somehow intermediate between, general and individual interest. Consequently, it is considered to fit very well with social solidarity[42] as the third pillar next to the public and capitalist sectors. The concept is often used to assess the activities of social and solidarity economy enterprises, in a perspective opposite to the social impact assessment mechanism.[43] Such a method had been decided for collective interest cooperatives, since their creation was subject to verification of their social utility by the state,[44] but that provision was abrogated in 2012.[45]

In this new kind of cooperative, it is clear that the social object is no longer, or at least not only, the satisfaction of the needs of the members. Here, the cooperative is explicitly targeted on third parties; the beneficiaries of the SCIC are welcome to become members, but membership is not a condition to obtain the services or goods,[46] nor are the services or goods defined in consideration of the members alone. This has major practical consequences, such as the absence

---

37 Mestre, n. 14 above; Saintourens, n. 35 above.

38 H. Azarian, *Coopérative, groupement d'intérêt économique et association*, thèse, Université Paris V, 2000.

39 M. Hérail, *Contribution à l'étude du lien coopératif au sein des sociétés coopératives*, thèse, Université Rennes I, Paris, 1999.

40 L. no. 2001-634 of the 17th of July 2001, art. 36.

41 L. no. 47-1775 of the 10th of September 1947, arts. 19*quinquies* f.

42 D. Hiez and R. Laurent, 'La nouvelle frontière de l'économie sociale et solidaire: l'intérêt général?', RECMA, Paris, 2011, no. 319, p. 36.

43 M. Parodi, 'L'utilité sociale pour éclairer la face cachée de la valeur de l'économie sociale', RECMA, Paris, 2010, no. 315, pp. 40–55.

44 L. no. 47-1775 of the 10th of September 1947, art. 19*terdecies*.

45 L. no. 2012-387 of the 22nd of March 2012, art. 26.

46 L. no. 47-1775 of the 10th of September 1947, art. 19*sexies*.

of cooperative refund.[47] It is the translation of the Italian experience but also an attempt to provide a solution for the big associations, which have important economic activities for which the cooperative form seems more suitable.

The consequence of creating that new kind of cooperative and its integration into the general cooperative law has not been seriously considered. Because of the importance of special cooperative types in French law, authors have merely noted the creation of a new type, without studying its compatibility with the general definition. The two definitions are at least partly contradictory. But it cannot be claimed that the SCIC is an exception, a marginal cooperative, since the legislature made the choice of inserting it into the general law, which is true for no other cooperative except the European cooperative society. The new definition provided by article 1 of the 1947 Law did not take any innovation into account, since it focused only on the needs of the members. Some legislative innovations and cooperative concerns can be mentioned as a starting point for a future and more inclusive definition. First, if the members remain the core of the cooperative, the exclusivism rule has been restricted, and the cooperative may conduct 20% of its transactions with non-members.[48] Secondly, increasing attention is paid to multi-membership, and notably the inclusion of employees among members, for example in agricultural cooperatives.[49] Finally, partly because of the pressure applied by corporate social responsibility interests, cooperatives are increasingly keen to emphasise their attention to the community. Lastly, the SCIC are characterised more by multi-membership than social utility, since the latter is rather extensible and no longer considered as a precise delimitation. The true criterion of the SCIC is comprised more in its regulation itself, notably the obligation to allocate 57.5% of the surplus to an indivisible reserve.[50] In short, there is no longer an opposition between the SCIC and other cooperatives, only a clearer targeting of SCIC on the community. Simply, that unity has not yet been translated into the legal definition.

1.2.2. Cooperative Advantage and Ways to Assign it to Members (Cooperative Refunds)

Cooperative refund is evoked by the general cooperative law,[51] but it is not defined. Generally, it is a distribution of a portion of surplus to cooperators, in proportion to their cooperative transactions with the cooperative. Legally, its distribution is not compulsory for the cooperative. This is discussed by authors,

---

47 L. no. 47-1775 of the 10th of September 1947, art. 19*nonies*, which excludes application of article 15 of the same law.

48 L. no. 47-1775 of the 10th of September 1947, art. 3.

49 C.rur., arts. L.522-3 1 L.522-4; JCP E 2015, 1607, no. 45, obs. D. Hiez.

50 See section 3.5.

51 L.47-1775 of the 10th of September 1947, art. 15.

and it has been debated within the cooperative movement, but the goal may be the development of cooperatives, which may not require the distribution of all the surpluses. The only exception is the workers' cooperative, for which the special law states that at least 25% of the surplus must be distributed to all the employees,[52] that is to say, the cooperators but also non-cooperator employees. The form of that distribution is not defined by law, but it is distinct from the remuneration of share capital. The law proposes three methods of distribution: proportionately to the salary, to the working time, or equally. The attribution to all the employees, members or not, contradicts the qualification of cooperative refund, but that solution is the outcome of a bargain between the workers' cooperative organisation and the government by which the former obtained a tax exemption on the distributed amounts, these amounts being considered as a kind of employee participation in the profits of enterprises. The cooperative refund is certainly rooted in the principle of the economic participation of cooperators in the cooperative, as provided both by the ICA cooperative principles and article 1 of the cooperative general law. That link is obvious in the prohibition of cooperative refund in the SCIC: because the beneficiaries of the goods or services provided by the cooperative are not necessarily, and even not mainly, cooperators, there is no reason to provide for the distribution of surplus in proportion to the cooperative's transactions.

1.2.2.1. Provision and Regulation of Cooperative Refunds

The mechanism of cooperative refund is provided by the general cooperative law. The 1947 Law (art. 15) states that the distribution of the surplus is not possible among the associates, but in proportion to the transactions realised by each member with the cooperative or proportionate to the work that s/he did for it. As such, this provision does not compel cooperative refund, but it forbids any distribution different from that framework. This means that any remuneration of shared capital cannot be considered as distribution of surplus.[53] The proportion established between the distribution and the cooperative transactions implies the prohibition of distribution of surplus related to transactions with clients, i.e. with non-cooperators.[54] This provision is the only example in the general law of a distinct regulation for transactions with cooperators and with non-cooperators, despite the importance of the exclusivism principle.[55] Article 15 contains a last provision which allows the remuneration of the director, that is, the employee in charge of the direction of the cooperative, in proportion to the transactions or the profits, if so provided by the byelaws.

---

52 L. no. 78-763 of the 19th of July 1978, art. 33.

53 See section 3.6.

54 L. no. 47-1775 of the 10th of September 1947, art. 15. al. 2.

55 L. no. 47-1775 of the 10th of September 1947, art. 3; see section 1.3.2.

Special regulations are not usually more precise, except for workers' cooperatives. In these cooperatives, in addition to the mechanism explained above,[56] the law[57] limits the cooperative refund to the workers employed in the cooperative for at least three months during the last annual accounting or who have at least six months of length of service. Moreover, it is possible to favour employees with longer length of service, though within the limit of double the amount.

Finally, some special laws, notably those on agricultural cooperatives, specify that a cooperative refund cannot be attributed to the non-cooperators.[58] The provision can be analysed in relation to the proportion established between the distributed amount and the cooperative transactions: as the non-cooperators perform no cooperative transaction with the cooperative, they cannot receive any cooperative refund. Even if the general law does not provide the same specification, it is uncontested that the rule is general: the general law is silent on this point,[59] since at the time when the provision was drafted, the general law did not recognise non-cooperators, so that the specification was useless. Therefore, only a special provision could allow the distribution of cooperative refund to non-cooperator members, like for example those of workers' cooperatives.[60] More technically, some regulations allow the distribution of cooperative refund by the attribution of new shares, for example in craft cooperatives.[61] If this provision appears neutral, it may be an argument in the debate on the nature of cooperative refund.

1.2.2.2. Concept/Legal Nature of Cooperative Refunds

Because the distribution of cooperative refund is not compulsory,[62] it is determined by factors such as, first, the byelaws of the cooperative, and second the decision taken by the appropriate organ, usually the members' meeting. The various special cooperative laws do not give more details, except that such a distribution is subject to the condition of available surplus; that is to say, the allocation to the reserve comes first.

The pre-eminence of cooperative refunds and returns on shared capital is not clear.[63] In the case of agricultural cooperatives, for example, it is provided that the members' meeting first decides on the distribution of shared capital

56 See above section 1.2.2.
57 L. no. 78-763 of the 19th of July 1978, art. 33 al. 4.
58 C.rur., art. L.522-4.
59 L. no. 47-1775 of the 10th of September 1947, art. 15.
60 See section 3.6.
61 L. no. 83657 of the 20th of July 1983, art. 26.
62 See section 1.2.2.1.
63 D. Hiez, n. 7 above, no. 121.15

return, and then on the distribution of the cooperative refund.[64] This debate is important, both practically and also theoretically. Indeed, the legal nature of the cooperative refund has never been clearly analysed. It can be considered either as a kind of distribution of surplus, or as a payback and an element in the price of goods or services.

The latter qualification relies on strong arguments. It is proportionate to the cooperative transactions and, to use a French expression, it is a '*trop perçu*', that is to say, it corresponds to the amount of money that the cooperator gave to the cooperative to receive a good or a service in addition to the real cost for the cooperative. If it is said that a goal of the cooperative is to provide its members with goods and services at the lowest cost and with the best quality, then any money that the cooperative accounts for at the end of the yearly accounting is an illegitimate surplus. In other words, the cooperators paid too much and the overpaid price must be reimbursed. Obviously, that reimbursement can only be proportionate to the cooperative's transactions, since the excessive amount of money given by the cooperators to the cooperative occurred for the cooperative's transactions.

In the pure French cooperative doctrine, as it was first defined by Charles Gide,[65] this means that a cooperative distributes absolutely no profit.[66] Cooperative refunds are not such a distribution, but even the return on shared capital is only the payment for the service provided by the shareholders with the capital brought. The return may include no dividend, but is only a cost for the cooperative.

This is very important in practice. Indeed, it should imply a wide tax exemption for cooperatives, and should not be considered a revenue for the cooperator, but rather an *a posteriori* reduction of price. This reasoning can be considered as the ground for the exclusion of the cooperative refund from the taxable profit of cooperatives which are not exempt from taxation.[67] However, some case law has found that in order to decide on the application of another provision, the cooperative refund is not a price element but a kind of profit distribution.[68] Therefore, in the end, it is difficult to decide the nature of the cooperative refund in French law. Recently, agricultural cooperatives have faced difficulties because of the complexity of fixing the prices of crops, for which the cooperatives were suspected of being opaque; they have been allowed to include determination of the procedures in their byelaws, but with the additional obligation to provide

64 C.rur., art. L.524-2-1.

65 Ch. Gide, *Les oeuvres de Charles Gide*, vol IV in *Coopération et économie sociale 1886-1904*, edited by P. Devillers, L'Harmattan, Paris, 2001, p. 312 ff.

66 Gide, n. 65 above.

67 Code general des impôts (CGI), art. 214.

68 CAA Nantes, 2 févr. 2012, 11NT00684; D. Hiez, 'Droit cooperative', JCP E, 2013, 1689, no. 9.

individual information for each cooperator.[69] In the end, qualification of the money thus distributed has not been tackled.

1.3. COOPERATIVE SOCIAL OBJECT AND MEMBERSHIP

In 1947, the principle laid down in the law was clear: all members of the cooperative were cooperators, and all the users of the cooperative were members. This was the exact application of the exclusivism principle, with its strictest interpretation.[70] In that context, the situation was clear: there was an indivisible link between cooperative object and membership. The definition of a cooperative still states that the cooperative aims at the satisfaction of the social and economic needs of its members, and this definition contains in itself that indivisible link. The coherence of the general law has, since its adoption, been mitigated by some special laws which state otherwise, but that contradiction is now within the general law itself because of some new provisions. Therefore, it is now necessary to specify the scope of the link between the social object and membership. This concerns both the diversity of members and the exclusivism principle.

1.3.1. The Diversity of Members

In 1947, the general cooperative law recognised only one category of members: the cooperators. In 1992, with the first major reform of the 1947 Law, the legislator created the category of member investor.[71] Hitherto, only very few special cooperative laws had admitted such possibility. It was notably the case of workers' cooperatives: the possibility was already evident in 1915, in the first law on workers' cooperatives,[72] with some restrictions intended to ensuring the control of the cooperative by cooperators. The mechanism remained the same with the major reform of 1978.[73] That mechanism has become part of the general cooperative law, even if its form is not precisely the same.

In 1992, a new article 3*bis* was inserted in the law of 1947. It explicitly stated the existence of these investor members. The provision did not use that wording but defined the new category of members as natural or legal persons who do not aim at the conduct of cooperative transactions with the cooperative, but who wish to contribute to achievement of the cooperative's objectives through the provision of capital. That innovation has been much debated since it created

---

69 C.rur., art. L.631-24.

70 L. no. 47-1775 of the 10th of September 1947, art. 3.

71 L. no. 47-1775 of the 10th of September 1947, art. 3*bis*.

72 L. Coutant, n. 35 above, p. 59 ff.

73 L. no. 78-763 of the 19th of July 1978, art. 5.

a cleavage among the members of the cooperative.[74] Some special cooperative laws exclude the application of the new article 3*bis*, such as the Rural Code for agricultural cooperatives.[75] However, this does not signify the absence of investor members, but rather the application of a special regulation with its own restrictions. I will not deal with these specificities but only refer to the general provision, pointing out that its application is in practice quite rare.[76] The reason for this is probably not the mistrust of cooperatives themselves but the lack of interest among investors, as well as the creation by cooperatives of subsidiaries taking the form of companies.

Article 3*bis* regulates the rights and obligations of the investor members, and determines their relationships with other members. Its main goal is to limit the power of investors in order to protect the control by cooperators. Explicitly, article 3*bis* provides no limitation to the capital that a non-cooperator may subscribe. However, investors may not have more than 33% of the voting rights in the members' meeting, and 49% if the investors are themselves cooperatives. There is no general provision concerning a restriction of investor members on the board; only special indirect provisions deal with this question, for example in workers' cooperatives, in which non-cooperators may not have more than one-third of the seats.[77]

The debate on investor members has hidden the more general question of the diversity of members. Indeed, investor members are not the only category of possible non-cooperators. Many special laws provide for such members, defining them as persons interested in the activity of the cooperative,[78] for example employees in all cooperatives except workers' cooperatives, and retired cooperators.

The only exception concerns a specific cooperative: the collective interest cooperative.[79] In the wording of the regulation adopted in 2001, this cooperative may contain five categories of members: users, employees, volunteers, public bodies, and investors.[80] A collective interest cooperative must comprise at least three of these categories, among which must be users and employees. That provision was redrafted in 2014.[81] The multi-stakeholder perspective of the collective interest cooperative has not been removed, but its precise composition has become more flexible. The members are persons who contribute to the

---

74 B. Piot, 'Une réforme en profondeur de la loi du 10 septembre 1947', RECMA, Paris, 1993, nos. 44–45, p. 36.

75 C.rur., art. L.522-3.

76 D. Hiez, 'Les instruments de fonds propres des coopérative – vingt ans d'innovation législative', RECMA, Paris, 2005, no. 295, p. 20.

77 L. no. 78-763 of the 19th of July 1978, art. 15.

78 C.rur., art. L.522-3.

79 See section 1.2.1.2.

80 L. no. 47-1775 of the 10th of September 1947, art. 19*septies*.

81 L. no. 2014-856 of the 31st of July 2014, art. 33.

activity of the cooperative, and the five categories are now only examples, which means that other categories may be considered. However, the five categories do not remain the same: producers (i.e. undertakers producing outside the cooperative), employees, users, volunteers and public bodies. Therefore, investors have disappeared as such, probably because, in practice, the investors are public bodies. Instead of three minimum categories, a cooperative now contains at least two categories: users, and employees or, if there are no employees in the cooperative, producers.

Although these details are important for the specific identity of the collective interest cooperative, they are less significant for the general cooperative objective. The point in this regard is the focus on the diversity of non-cooperators. Many special laws refer to such members, but these provisions have remained in the shadows. The 2014 law on social and solidarity economy redrafted article 3*bis* of the 1947 Law, and extended the category of non-cooperators. Its definition remains the same: persons who do not aim at the conduct of cooperative transactions with the cooperative but who wish to contribute to achievement of the cooperative's objectives. Nevertheless, two modifications have been introduced. First, employees are explicitly mentioned as possible non-cooperators, even if that was already possible with the previous wording. Second, and more importantly, whereas the contribution to achievement of the cooperative's objective was only foreseen by the subscription of capital, that subscription is now only one example of contribution. This means that article 3*bis* no longer deals with investor members but, more generally, with non-cooperators. All the consequences of that innovation have not yet been drawn.

1.3.2. The Exclusivism Principle

The exclusivism principle means, first, that the cooperative conducts cooperative transactions with its members. This implies two things: on the one hand, cooperators are the core members and their status flows from the addition of their membership and the contract that they conclude with the cooperative to regulate their transactions, and on the other hand, the cooperative should have no cooperative transaction with non-members.

In regard to the status of the cooperator in the cooperative as such, the general cooperative law is entirely silent. This is partly due the fact that the activities are related to the different categories of cooperatives. Otherwise, some explanation can be found in the social object contained in each special law. Nevertheless, this means that there is no general theory on the nature of the legal relationship between the cooperative and each cooperator.

It is uncontroversial that French law complies with this double relationship, or the double quality principle.[82] On the one hand, each member is an associate

---

82 See section 1.2.1.1.

in the cooperative; on the other, s/he is an economic partner. If these two relationships are connected, the technical consequences have not been seriously investigated.[83]

The relationship between the cooperative and its members is firstly defined by the contract, which contains the reciprocal obligations of the two parties. Of course, this applies to the contract itself, but also its regulation by the law, depending on the qualification of the contract. For example, workers' cooperatives conclude employment contracts with their cooperators, cooperative banks make loans, agricultural cooperatives conclude sales, etc. In this respect, labour law or consumer law applies as soon as the legal conditions are fulfilled. The integration of this contract into the cooperative context is not considered to require the application of a different legal regime. In other words, even in a cooperative, the employee or the consumer is a weak party which requires special protection. Sometimes, the cooperative legislation conflicts with other regulations, and difficulties arise in deciding which must prevail; and some solutions stated by case law may be discussed. This concerns, for example, the notion of the annual percentage rate of charge on consumer loans concluded between a cooperative bank and one member. The courts state that the acquisition of shares in the cooperative bank, required to obtain the loan, is included in the calculation of this annual percentage rate.[84] Authors criticise this solution, since it does not take at least two specificities into account: first, the acquisition of shares implies membership and all its rights; secondly, the share may be reimbursed in the case of dismissal. This point is interesting since it shows the limits of the distinct application of the regime of the contract to transactions. It fails to take serious consideration of the cooperative context in which the contract takes place. If the cooperators may appear to be a weak party, it must not be forgotten that they specifically chose to be members of a cooperative to compensate for their weakness by collective action.

In fact, the nature of the contract cannot be reduced to that ordinary qualification, and all the rules of contract law do not apply. For example, in workers' cooperatives, if the obligation to apply for membership has been stated in the byelaws of the cooperative and in the employment contract with a non-cooperator employee, the non-application for membership by a non-cooperative employee implies his/her automatic dismissal,[85] as opposed to labour law.

---

83 D. Hiez, n. 7 above, nos. 31.28 f.

84 Cass. com., 7 févr. 2012, no. 11-10.833: JurisData no. 2012-001699; Contrats, Contrat Concurrence Consommation, Paris (conc. consom.), 2012, comm. 138, obs. G. Raymond; JCP E 2012, 489, note J. Lasserre Capdeville; Cass. 1re civ., 24 avr. 2013, no. 12-14.377: JurisData no. 2013-007986; JCP E 2013, 1408, note J. Lasserre Capdeville; Contrats, conc. consom. 2013, comm. 171, obs. G. Raymond; JCP E, 2013, 1689, no. 18, obs. D. Hiez; JCP E, Paris, 2015, 1607, no. 5.

85 L. no. 78-763 of the 19th of July 1978, art. 9.

The legislation on agricultural cooperatives also provides very interesting examples, and shows the weakening of cooperative identity. A question has arisen regarding the transfer of ownership of the crop brought by the cooperators to the cooperative in order for them to be sold by the cooperative. Until the 1970s and 1980s, it was clear that a cooperative was the representative of its members and that, therefore, the ownership of the crop was never transferred to the cooperative.[86] Until the 2000s, the courts favoured the opposite solution,[87] even if it was never decided that there was a sale contract.[88] The statutes of agricultural cooperatives enforced by a decree of the Ministry of Agriculture state explicitly that ownership is transferred to the cooperative.[89] This solution is important both technically and theoretically: it means that the cooperative is now recognised as an intermediary, which is contrary to its definition in the 1947 Law. It must be specified that, recently, this provision has been considered void because it cannot rely on any legislative provision.[90]

A more general example concerns the exclusion of the cooperative: whereas this is a social decision, i.e. connected with membership of the cooperative, it may rely on the non-execution of the contract between a member and the cooperative.

The question of the obligation to transact with the cooperative is not treated by general law either. It arises differently in different kinds of cooperatives. In workers' cooperatives, for example, to be a cooperator a member must be an employee and, therefore, must supply his/her labour; if s/he is not an employee, s/he can only be investor. In cooperatives of enterprises, such as craft, merchants' or agricultural cooperatives, the obligation to bring or provide oneself with certain goods is the substance of the contract between the cooperative and each member. The obligation therefore exists necessarily, even though the sanction of non-execution may vary.

The equal treatment of members is not stated anywhere, even if it seems to be natural. Nevertheless, it is a question that I have considered and that I would need to check with a rapid empirical enquiry to be absolutely sure. Very few cases refer to that obligation of non-discrimination.[91]

---

86 G. Gourlay, *Cooperatives agricoles*, Litec, Paris, 1983, nos. 73 and 73*bis*.

87 Cass 1re civ., 13 févr. 2001, no. 98-20317 and 98-20319, Bull. civ. I no. 36 p. 22; revue Dalloz affaires Paris (D. aff.), 2002 388, note M. Michalauskas; Rev. sociétés 2001 834, note B. Saintourens; bulletin Joly Sociétés, Paris (Bull. Joly), 2001, §161, note G. Gourlay.

88 Cass. com., 11 juil. 2006, no. 05-13103, Bull. civ. IV no. 181 p. 199; revue de droit rural, Paris (RD rur.), 2006, comm. 332, note J.-J. Barbiéri ; gazette du palais, Paris (Gaz. Pal.), 6 janv. 2007, no. 6, p. 26, note P. Goni; D. Hiez, 'Chronique de droit coopératif', JCP E, 2007, 1907, no. 28 obs. L. Gros.

89 Art. 3 1. of the ratified statutes, enforced by the *arrêté* of the 23rd of April 2008. The transfer of property has become an option for the cooperatives: arrêté of the 31st of March 2016.

90 CE, 11 juin 2014, 3ème et 8ème SSR, no. 365623, inédit; JCP E, 2015 1623, no. 7, obs. D. Hiez.

91 Cass. civ. 1re, 10 avr. 2013, no. 12-11725, inédit; JCP E, 2015, 1623, no. 16, obs. D. Hiez.

The second aspect of exclusivism is the prohibition of cooperative transactions with non-members. The general principle was rigorously stated in article 3 of the 1947 Law, after having been strongly debated at the end of the nineteenth century concerning consumer cooperatives because of tax consequences. Today, the principle is less rigid, and it remains only a distinction between open and closed cooperatives which relates to the clients of the cooperative. Of course, open cooperatives totally respect the open door principle.

Three categories of cooperatives are entirely open: consumer cooperatives,[92] cooperative banks,[93] and workers' cooperatives.[94] Properly speaking, the conditions required for the creation of a workers' cooperative are, in this respect, quite light: two cooperators if it takes the form of a limited liability company or of a simplified stock company, seven if a public limited company. Fortunately, the proportion of cooperators is far higher in practice and in collective interest cooperatives.[95] Note that the solution is similar for the collective interest cooperatives in housing:[96] All other cooperatives are totally or partially closed. The only totally closed cooperatives were, in practice, the merchants' cooperatives,[97] and cooperatives referring only to the 1947 Law. Others are mainly dedicated to their members but a part of their activities may be realised with non-members, usually 20%. A simplification was introduced by the 1947 Law, since its article 3 now stated that proportion as the general rule, and it was extended to the merchants' cooperatives.[98]

The sanction of this restriction is not limited to tax law, even if the non-application of the tax advantage is very efficient:[99] for example, in agricultural cooperatives, if a cooperative has more than 20% activities with non-members, it allows the high council of an agricultural cooperative to disqualify its assent to the cooperative.[100]

Apart from any sanction, the first consequence of cooperative transactions with non-members should be the adoption of specific rules concerning them. The general law is rather poor. Its only statement deals with the prohibition on including in cooperative refunds the surpluses arising from these activities with non-members.[101] Some special laws are more detailed. For example, in craft cooperatives[102] and in agricultural cooperatives,[103] the cooperative must have

92 Law of the 7th of May 1917, art. 2.
93 Only since the 1980s, with the possibility to realise any bank transaction.
94 L. no. 78-763 of the 19th of July 1978, art. 5.
95 L. no.47-1775 of the 10th of July 1947, art. 19*sexies*.
96 Code de la construction et de l'habitation (C.const.hab.), art. L.422-3-2.
97 C.com., art. L.124-2.
98 C.com., art. L.124-2.
99 CGI, art. 207 for example.
100 C.rur., art. L.523-1.
101 L. no. 47-1775 of the 10th of September 1947, art. 15.
102 L. no. 83-657 of the 20th of July 1983, art. 10.
103 C.rur., art. L.525-2.

a special account for the cooperative transactions with non-members. Even if the general law does not provide the same solution, it is required by the special treatment to which these transactions are subject. The new decree has adopted that solution, which now applies to any cooperative.[104] But the above-mentioned special laws go further, and allocate the surpluses from these transactions to a special reserve subject to special rules.[105] These solutions cannot be generalised.

A weakness of French cooperative legislation is the absence of any provision on the definition of cooperative transactions with non-members. Strictly speaking, French law never uses the expression 'cooperative transactions'; it refers only to transactions. Certainly, when the law deals with transactions with non-members, it does not consider any transaction, for example the purchase of a computer by an agricultural cooperative, but there is no proper conceptualisation.

1.4. INDIRECT MUTUALITY (IN COOPERATIVE GROUPS)

The question of the cooperative group is crucial for cooperatives, and is directly connected with its social object. The details will be examined in section 5, but it is useful to explain what is at stake right now. The regulation of cooperative groups has been expected of cooperative organisations for more than a decade, but there has been no agreement on what it is or should be. In practice, the most significant development has adopted the form of subsidiaries, and more precisely capitalist subsidiaries.

This is especially true in the three most powerful categories: agricultural, banking and merchants' cooperatives. In agricultural cooperatives, for example, even if there are no reliable data, it may be half of the activity of the cooperative groups which are achieved in the subsidiaries. Consequently, cooperatives have lobbied for the integration of these activities in their area. In the meantime, they are keen on the flexibility that they find in the capitalist rules and therefore reluctant to develop authentic cooperative groups. The legislature has recently created a cooperative group specifically for workers' cooperatives but it is too early to say if it will be used; and even if it is, the impact will be rather slight, considering the economic importance of these cooperatives.

This evolution began in the 1980s and was, at that time, rather controversial, at least among authors. The strongest arguments against the creation of cooperatives were connected to the cooperative's identity through the question of its social object. Some authors simply denied the validity of such creation and, technically, the defence organised by the cooperative organisations was rather weak.

---

104 Decree no. 2015-594 of the 1st of June 2015, art. 2.

105 L. no. 83-657 of the 20th of July 1983, art. 25; C.rur., art. L.522-5 al. 3.

Nevertheless, the economic impact of the evolution was too important to allow a rational debate. No specific legislation was adopted, and no special provision included in the major reform of 1992, but special provisions were foreseen to secure the mechanism when its legality could not already rely on explicit or implicit authorisations. For example, law 2001-420 of the 15th of May 2001 added three words to the article L.124-1 of the code of commerce for merchants' cooperatives: the activities that a merchants' cooperative may undertake are undertaken by it 'directly or indirectly', that is, through subsidiaries. Agricultural cooperatives legislation has gone further about subsidiaries, and the cooperative is allowed to distribute to its members dividends deriving from the subsidiary.[106] This can be analysed as an increasingly financial perspective of cooperation; it is presented by the agricultural cooperative organisations as an attempt to create a new link between a cooperative's members and its subsidiaries. Anyway, the emergence and the development of subsidiaries has clearly affected the cooperative identity, and the evolution is likely to continue.

2. COOPERATIVE GOVERNANCE

2.1. THE FRAMEWORK OF COOPERATIVE GOVERNANCE

To open this section, the importance of governance must be underlined, and especially the 'one person/one vote' principle. Of course, governance cannot be summarised in that principle, even as the core of its democratic feature. However, it is today a crucial question for cooperatives, for three main reasons. First, it is an easy criterion with which to distinguish cooperatives from companies and something that laypersons can easily understand. Secondly, it is a point of debate with social enterprises, which emphasise more the social purpose of the enterprise and do not pay specific attention to the collective dimension. These two observations explain the emphasis placed by cooperatives on governance to highlight their identity. The third reason for the importance of governance is that it is a relevant example of the possible gap between the rule and its application and its effectiveness. Indeed, many cooperatives, especially the biggest ones, encounter difficulties in applying this democratic principle. Therefore, most of the criticisms addressed to cooperatives focus on governments. In the meantime, aware of the risk of blurring their own identity, cooperative organisations make important efforts to improve their democratic functioning. This section thus has a potentially controversial dimension in the French debate.

To provide a picture of French cooperative governance, I will first describe its framework. Then, I will go into the details of its organisation, starting with

---

106 C.rur., art. L.523-5-1.

its core, the members, continuing with its organs, and finishing with brief discussion of dispute resolution between cooperatives and members.

2.1.1. Cooperative Governance and Cooperative Identity

I have already stressed the link between these two issues; and French law,[107] since the last reform in 2014, highlights it by dealing with these two aspects in the same article 1 of the 1947 Law. Even if there are derogations to the one person/one vote principle, no one claims that there is an attack on the democratic principle itself. The example of the collective interest cooperative is meaningful. Whereas its definition does not fit well with the definition of the cooperative, the same democratic principle applies. Even if the one person/one vote principle may be adjusted, it remains present, and compulsory. It is true that one may wonder whether the democratic principle is part of the cooperative identity, even though not its core. Indeed, the democratic principle is probably the most common rule among all cooperatives. But the democratic principle is far wider than governance, being connected with both financial questions and control and cooperative auditing. Therefore, while democratic governance cannot sum up the cooperative identity, it appears more to be a means to achieve the cooperative objective. However, it still makes an important link with collective interest cooperatives (called 'general interest cooperatives' in the PECOL) and others. Problematically, this questions the link stated between democratic governance and the objective of members' satisfaction, since in collective interest cooperatives, democratic governance is dynamic in the absence of the same objective.

However, French cooperative thought has been elaborated on the basis of that link, perfectly translated into the new article 1 of the 1947 Law.

The definition of the cooperative's object states that the cooperative aims at satisfying the members' needs 'by joint effort of said members'. This feature is very important for governance. Firstly, it refers to the collective dimension of cooperatives, since their internal organisation depends on the collectivity of the members. But, more importantly, needs must be satisfied by the beneficiaries. This means that the cooperative's activities will be carried out by the members, and that cooperatives are managed by the cooperators. This is precisely what is called the 'double quality' principle.[108]

This point is important because it is visible in practical debates, and it requires reference to the nature of cooperatives. One author calls it '*genus cooperatis*'.[109]

107 See above section 1.2.1.1.

108 See above section 1.2.1.1.

109 F. Espagne, 'Restructuration des coopératives, filialisations, fusions, prises de participation', lettre du 8 août 2001; S. De Vendeuil, 'Les entreprises coopératives se modernisent', JCP E 1993, act. 100213.

A good example of such debates concerns the validity of subsidiaries: amid the silence of the law, the latter are considered legal or illegal depending on the opinion of authors concerning the importance of the concept of joint effort of members.[110] Indeed, the common efforts of the members imply their involvement, which is absent in the case of subsidiaries. In other words, the major problem with subsidiaries is the absence of democratic governance and of members' control.

2.1.2. *Cooperative Governance and Company Law*

The connections between cooperative law and company law have been highlighted.[111] However, *prima facie*, there is a clear opposition between cooperatives and companies concerning governance, as illustrated by the one person/one vote principle. Therefore, one might conclude that, about governance, company law has a very marginal application. That would be wrong.

Indeed, the 1947 Law addresses only a few issues relating to governance. It deals with the democratic principle, devotes a few words to the membership and the members' meeting, and no more – and all this in about ten articles, compared to the hundreds in company law. The explanation can be found in the purpose of the legislature in 1947: the aim of this Act was not to establish a full framework for cooperatives, but rather to define the cooperative's specificities as derogations to company law. Many points were considered as neutral and, therefore, possibly extended from companies to cooperatives. It is interesting to note that the last reform of 2014, which has insisted on the specificity of cooperative governance, has automatically reinforced, albeit slightly, the distinction with respect to company law.[112]

Consequently, two sets of issues must be distinguished. Some of them, considered to be connected with the cooperative identity, are ruled by the cooperative law, but most governance issues are seen as the simple regulation of any organisation and consequently neglected by cooperative law. They are therefore only considered by company law. Aside from the 1947 Law, special cooperative laws provide some additional provisions, but most of them are derogations or adjustments to the rules stated in the 1947 Law, and do not give any precision to the topics left to company law.

It must therefore be underlined that important freedom is given to the byelaw drafters. This is not true in company law, notably for public limited companies, for which the legislation is considered to be particularly rigid. By contrast, cooperative law gives important freedom to the byelaws in both

[110] See section 5.5.
[111] See section 1.1.2.
[112] D. Hiez, 'La nouvelle orientation du droit cooperative avec la loi économie sociale et solidaire', *Journal des sociétés*, 2015, no. 128, pp. 28 ff.

the 1947 Law and the provisions dealing with variable capital companies in the Code of Commerce.[113] However, the will of the founders is, first of all, expressed in the choice of the kinds of company that cooperatives will adopt: mainly limited liability companies, public limited companies, and simplified stock.[114] Indeed, general company law contains few provisions on governance because this question depends on the kind of company concerned.

The plurality of applicable laws in cooperative governance causes major difficulties when trying to devise provisions of cooperative law and company law. In principle, cooperative law prevails over company law, since the former is the special law which derogates from the latter. But it is not always easy to determine what the exception is and what the rule is. The remuneration of board members before the 2014 Law is a good example.[115] The 1947 Law contained no provision on this matter, and neither did articles L.231-1 ff. on variable capital companies. Some special cooperative laws contained provisions inspired by the idea of limiting, if not prohibiting, remuneration of the board members. In this case, if there was no provision in the byelaws, two contradictory interpretations were possible: either the special laws containing provisions about remuneration were the expression of an implicit cooperative principle, derogating to the free determination of remuneration in company law, or the special cooperative provisions limiting this remuneration were derogations to a general principle applicable to both companies and cooperatives.

Another question likely to arise is whether there exist rules regarding governance in the byelaws. Theoretically, byelaws can regulate this point to some extent, since cooperative law gives more autonomy to the byelaws than company law does. Nevertheless, choosing a kind of company is an expression of that autonomy. Therefore, it can be analysed as filling the gap in cooperative law by reference to the regulation of the kind of company chosen. Specificities appear for agricultural cooperatives, first of all because they are more distinct from company law, but also because their byelaws are ratified by the Ministry of Agriculture and are therefore compulsory for all agricultural cooperatives. These ratified byelaws have consequently become a significant piece of agricultural cooperative law.

2.2. MEMBERSHIP

Because cooperatives are oriented to their members, their services and also their mechanisms of control, the members are logically the core of the cooperative.

---

113 C.com., arts. L.231-1 ff.

114 I will only refer to these kinds of companies, others being less frequent among cooperatives.

115 The 2014 law introduced a provision on it in article 6 of the 1947 Law: see section 2.4.1.

Therefore, most attention is paid to membership in order to determine who the members are, but also because the manner in which membership is acquired and terminated is highly indicative of the identity of a cooperative. In spite of the importance of membership regulation in cooperative law, the 1947 Law contains only few provisions, referring to the statutes.[116] Therefore, rules must be sought mainly in special cooperative laws, company law, and the provisions on variable companies. This regulation will be described by distinguishing the acquisition and termination of membership.

2.2.1. *The Acquisition of Membership*

The way membership is acquired depends strongly on the variability of capital. I have explained that the general cooperative law does not impose capital variability on cooperatives,[117] even if most special cooperative laws do so, and all the statutes. Therefore I will only deal with variable capital cooperatives.

The cooperative principle stated by ICA is open membership, but its application is very flexible and must be reconciled with control by the cooperative of new applications for membership. The general law of 1947 does not provide any solution, but refers explicitly to the statutes (art. 7).[118] The regulation of variable capital companies is not particularly more precise. It exempts these companies from any publication of the new members,[119] whereas it would require a modification of the statutes in any other company. But, again, there is nothing about the possible conditions laid down to acquire membership. Special cooperative laws go further. Some of them define the possible members,[120] so that applicants who do not comply with the definition cannot be admitted. Even when no such definition is stated, an organ is usually designated to enrol the applicants. This is the case, for example, of workers' cooperatives.[121] The competent organ is the members' meeting, which decides by majority; any application from a worker employed in the cooperative for at least one year must be examined and, if rejected, can be renewed each year. No specification is given concerning the reasons why an application may be rejected, and no appeal is envisaged. The appeal is replaced by the possibility to renew the application. In regard to examination of the application, the common opinion is that the members' meeting has discretionary power, only limited by the prohibition of

---

116 L. no 47-1775 of the 10th of September 1947, art. 7.

117 See above section 1.2.1.

118 Before the 1992 reform, article 3 of the 1947 Law provided for admission by the members' meeting, deciding the conditions required to modify the statutes. That precision has been removed, since all special laws derogated the provision, and, therefore, it was never applied.

119 C.com., art. L.231-3.

120 L. no. 83-657 of the 20th July 1983, art. 6, for example for craft cooperatives.

121 L. no. 78-856 of the 19th of July 1978, art. 7.

discrimination, or abuse of right.[122] Many special laws provide similar solutions, even when some conditions are laid down for membership.[123] When the special cooperative law is silent, no provision can be found in company law, since the regulations on the diverse kinds of possible company deal with the variability of members. Therefore, the only provision is article 7 of the 1947 Law, so that the solution must be found in the statutes. In the case of its silence, and only if the special law gives no other indication, the application is automatically admitted. The discussion has arisen in doctrine because of the debate on whether cooperatives are partnerships or capital companies.[124] The survival of the cooperative, despite the death or bankruptcy of a member, is favourable to the qualification of a capital company, whereas the control of applications highlights the *intuitu personae* and therefore makes the cooperative closer to a partnership. To sum up this point, cooperatives are expected to be open to new applications, but the law attributes them the power to decide whether the applicant fits with the *affection cooperatis*, and this decision is discretionary. Some special laws provide details on the procedure, but the statutes usually have wide latitude in defining it.

Before the 2014 reform, the 1947 Law had established equilibrium between the attacks on exclusivism and the free control of new applications (art. 3). This article stated the exclusivism principle, but recognised the possibility to derogate. However, in this case, it stated also that non-members who had cooperative transactions with the cooperative were to be admitted when applying for membership. While removing the absolute exclusivism principle, the new article 3 also eliminated the mechanism of easy acquisition of membership. Regardless, the old provision did not have significant effects. Special laws did not contradict it, nor do they now; but they do not give any additional provision which should clarify the modes of its application. Furthermore, article 3 itself stated that such admissions must comply with the conditions laid down by the statutes. This did not allow the statutes to contradict article 3 by attributing the cooperative a discretionary power to admit or refuse the applicants, but only to determine the additional elements not provided for by the laws. Only workers' cooperatives law deal with this question.[125] If the applicant has been employed by the cooperative for at least one year (that is to say, s/he is a non-member employee) the application must be examined by the members' meeting.[126] There is therefore an incentive for applications by non-member users but no obligation

---

122 D. Hiez, n. 7 above, nos. 42.16 and 43.22.

123 L. no. 83-653 of the 20th of July 1983, art. 9, for example, for craft cooperatives; C.rur., art. R.522-2, for agricultural cooperatives.

124 L. Coutant, n. 35 above, p. 31 ff.

125 L. no.78-763 of the 19th of July 1978, art. 7.

126 If the condition is not fulfilled, the application may be examined and rejected by the board of directors.

for the cooperative to accept them. Admission to workers' cooperatives must also be voted by the majority, which means that a positive decision must be adopted. But, apart from that special rule, the non-members who perform cooperative transactions with the cooperative are treated like any applicant.

Two special laws organise a transitional membership for new members, named '*période probatoire*' in craft cooperatives.[127] During the period of one year, the cooperator has the same rights and obligations as others, but s/he or the cooperative may terminate membership in the end by derogation to statutory provisions that can impose a longer term for membership. That possibility aims at better knowledge of the obligations of membership before its definitive validation. It is difficult to reach a conclusion as to the usefulness of the provision: it does not seem to be often used in craft cooperatives; and in agricultural cooperatives, where it is perhaps more meaningful because of the usual long-term engagement clause, that possibility was introduced only in 2014. In any case, the purpose of the provision must be assessed by reference to the termination of membership.

2.2.2. *Termination of Membership*

Just as it is possible to become member of a cooperative, it is also possible to terminate membership. There are two circumstances in which membership may be terminated: withdrawal and expulsion.

Withdrawal is a right for members and is one of the main features of cooperatives. It is provided for by the variable capital company law,[128] without any possible statutory derogation. Only financial restrictions can limit it in relation to the regulations on the decrease in capital.[129] Nevertheless, some adjustments are allowed through definition of a minimum period of membership. This is particularly the case of agricultural cooperatives. Neither the law nor the ratified statutes specify the length of the period, and it is often the cause of litigation. The cooperative tends to impose a long-term engagement, while some members withdraw before the term provided.

In order to face the future, a cooperative makes forecasts concerning the amount of transactions that it will conduct, and imposes a fixed-term contract on its members. This contract is the cooperation contract, which both implies the obligation to perform transactions and confers the status of member. Consequently, the member is not allowed to withdraw before termination of the contract.

Several questions arise for which answers can be found mainly by referring to agricultural cooperatives. The first question concerns the maximum contract

---

127 L. no. 83-653 of the 20th of July 1983, art. 9 and agricultural cooperatives C.rur., art. L.521-3.
128 C.com., art. L.231-6.
129 C.com., art. L.231-5.

duration, in order to ensure that the right to withdraw is not indirectly contested. At first, the courts limited the term to fifty years, but it was decided in the 1970s that the contract should not last longer than the duration of professional life (approximately twenty-five to thirty years).[130] Some judges and authors claimed a shorter term, usually ten years,[131] but to date the *Cour de Cassation* has declined that claim.

The second question concerns the circumstances in which a member is allowed to withdraw before termination of the contract. The law only specifies two situations: *force majeure* and justified reason.[132] The law empowers the board to decide if the condition is fulfilled, with a possible appeal before the members' meeting, but a claimant may go before the court to ask for a judicial control.

A similar difficulty occurs when an agricultural cooperative member decides to sell his/her farm before termination of the cooperation contract and the buyer does not apply for membership. On the one hand, ownership of the farm allows the owner to sell; on the other, it can be an easy way for him/her to terminate the contract and evade his/her obligations. Therefore, the law makes the member responsible for the refusal of the buyer to become a member by substitution.[133]

A final provision can be mentioned in regard to workers' cooperatives: the statutes may state, if it is also mentioned in the employment contract, that the non-member employee must apply for membership. In this case, the statutes may decide that the absence of application is considered to be automatic resignation by the employee.[134] This solution is a strong derogation to labour law. In practice, it is not used by workers' cooperatives.

The second instance of termination of the cooperation contract is expulsion by the cooperative. This mechanism, which is exceptional among companies, is also envisaged by the variable capital company regulation.[135] The article subjects the possibility to an explicit statutory provision. The 1947 Law only adds the requirement that the statutes must specify its conditions.[136] The statutes may designate the organ competent to decide on the expulsion when special laws do not specify it. Many special laws do so, but it is difficult to identify a general solution because of the diversity of the special laws on this issue. Nevertheless, the tendency is to substitute the competence of the members' meeting[137]

---

130 D. Hiez, n. 7, nos 91.30 f.

131 M. Hérail, n. 39 above, nos. 39 and 556.

132 C.rur., art. R.522-4.

133 C.rur., art. R.522-5.

134 L. no. 78-673 of the 19th of July 1978, art. 9.

135 C.com., art. L.231-6.

136 L. no. 47-1775 of the 10th of September 1947, art. 7.

137 This principle is stated by article L.231-6 of the Code of Commerce itself. It is still recognised in the old cooperative laws: for example, the law of the 7th of May 1917, art. 1, for consumer cooperatives.

in order to attribute it to the board.[138] The main question remains determination of the circumstances in which a cooperative may expel one of its members. At the beginning of the twentieth century, case law ruled that the members' meeting had discretionary power, meaning that judges could not review the motives justifying the decision of expulsion. That analysis has been cast aside and several special laws specify the requisite conditions. Article R.522-8 of the Rural Code requires, for instance in agricultural cooperatives, 'serious reasons', particularly if the cooperator member has been sentenced to criminal penalties, if s/he has seriously damaged or attempted to damage the cooperative by unjustified acts, or falsified the crop delivered to the cooperative. If the idea of fault provides an acceptable description of the general solutions, it must be interpreted broadly. First, the fault may be committed in performance of the cooperative's transactions, as well as in fulfilling obligations connected to membership. Secondly, the fault may have no direct link with the cooperative; it is sufficient for it to have caused damage to the cooperative.[139]

Finally, procedural conditions have been laid down. They require that the member to be expelled must be summoned to be heard by the organ competent to decide on the expulsion. A recent case nevertheless raises doubts concerning the sanction in the case of absence of summons, since the Cour de Cassation has decided that it cannot make the expulsion void.[140] Of course, damages remain, but if the expulsion is not void, they can only compensate the absence of hearing, which means that they will be far lower.

A link can be established between the evolution of substantial and procedural conditions. Previously, expulsion was considered to be a discretionary power of the group, for which reason it was decided by the members' meeting. But, that analysis has been gradually abandoned: expulsion has become an administrative sanction applied by the board. Consequently, the procedure of the decision has been regulated, and its motivation may be scrutinised.

Finally, the importance of membership is visible in the minimum number of members required to create a cooperative. The number may vary, but the common rule is the prohibition of single-member cooperatives. Farmers' cooperatives require seven members in principle, but four are enough if it is an equipment-sharing or livestock-raising cooperative, and two for a union of agricultural cooperatives.[141] The general cooperative law does not deal with this

---

138 For example, in agricultural cooperatives, or in merchants' cooperatives (C.com., art. L.124-10).

139 For example, falsification concerning a crop delivered to another company has been considered a fault justifying expulsion from the cooperative, because it reveals the dishonesty of the farmer and could create confusion about loyalty of the cooperative: Cass. civ. 1re, 3 mars 2011, no. 10-11.529, NP; Rev. sociétés 2011. 635, note M. Menjucq.

140 Cass. com., 4 déc. 2012, no. 11-27667, inédit; JCP E, 2013, 1031, note B. Dondereau; Dr. Sociétés, Paris, 2013, com. 45, obs. H. Hovasse; JCP E 2013 1703, obs. D. Hiez.

141 C.rur., art. R.522-1.

question, so that an answer can only be found in company law. There, the solution depends on the type of company that the founders have chosen. The distinction is between the limited liability company and the public limited company: the former requires only two members, whereas the latter cannot be created with fewer than seven members,[142] but the threshold of seven was reduced to two in 2015 for public limited companies other than those whose securities are admitted to trading on a regulated market.[143] One difference remains, since the maximum number of members is one hundred in limited liability companies.[144] If the number of members is higher, the company has one year to reduce that number, or to convert to another type of company; otherwise the company is declared void. This limitation makes the limited liability company inappropriate for cooperatives likely to have many members, such as consumer cooperatives. Because they are often quite poor, at least at the beginning, they do not choose the public limited labiality company, which is heavy and expensive, and prefer the form of civil company.[145]

2.3. MEMBERS' RIGHTS AND OBLIGATIONS

2.3.1. Rights and Obligations

Every member has rights and obligations in the cooperative. These rights and obligations concern both the cooperative's transactions and its functioning. The two aspects are connected, and it is not always possible to distinguish them. Moreover, they are interdependent. It could appear that the cooperative's transactions impose more obligations on cooperators, contrary to the functioning of the cooperative. This would mainly create rights. However, what may look like rights are also duties, since participation in the cooperative's governance is also an obligation. Moreover, if the first obligation of cooperators is to participate in cooperative transactions, this also creates rights for them. An example is provided by a recent case.[146] A farmer decided to engage in organic agriculture and then to join an equipment-sharing agricultural cooperative ('Coopérative d'utilisation de matériel agricole'). Thereafter, the European Regulation became more exigent, so that the cooperative's equipment no longer complied with the requirements. Therefore, the cooperator withdrew before the end of its contract, and the cooperative sued him. Considering that the cooperative had an obligation to satisfy its members' needs, and that the new European Regulation

142 C.com., art. L.525-1.
143 Ibid., until the 12th of September 2015.
144 C.com., art. L.223-3.
145 C.civ., arts. 1845 ff.
146 Rennes, ch. 1, 10 juin 2014, no. 13/02341; Jurisdata 2014-022085; JCP E, 2015 1607, no. 13.

was not a '*force majeure*', the court decided that the cooperator was entitled to withdraw because the cooperative had not fulfilled its own obligations. Of course, the obligations of the members are more visible because they are more often not executed, but they also have rights.

2.3.2. *Members' Voting Rights*

The one person/one vote principle is very well known and enforced in French law; it was reinforced in 2014, since it is now, symbolically, mentioned in article 1 of the 1947 Law. It is developed in articles 4 and 9 of the 1947 Law, and some special regulations reiterate the principle.[147] It does not require much explanation. It must nevertheless be emphasised that French cooperative law stipulates equality among cooperators (art. 4) and does not allow any difference in voting rights depending on personal characteristics such as length of membership. The one person/one vote principle is highly symbolic but, in the end, does not sum up the wide scope of democratic control.

More interesting are derogations to the principle, firstly because they demonstrate that cooperative law is not ideological but pragmatic and based on experience, and secondly because they are a barometer of the strength of the principle.

Firstly, the meaning of equal voting right is different in the case of unions of cooperatives.[148] In these, the weight of each cooperator of the union is taken into account in order to ensure equality among primary cooperators. The law offers a choice between two ways to calculate the voting rights of the cooperators: either in proportion to the number of primary members of the various cooperatives, or in proportion to the amount of cooperative transactions carried on by each member of the union (art. 5). The first derogation is not considered, properly speaking, as derogation to the one person/one vote principle, but as a necessary adjustment to a particular situation.[149]

More substantial derogations are present in some special cooperative laws which allow the statutes to attribute more voting rights to some cooperators. This possibility may be found, for instance, in agricultural cooperatives,[150] collective interest cooperatives when they are organised by class of members,[151] or some cooperative banks.[152] These examples remain derogations, but they are sufficiently numerous and varied to mitigate the principle. Nevertheless, apart

---

147 L. no. 78-763 of the 19th of July 1978, art. 14, for workers' cooperatives; L. no.835657 of the 20th of July 1983, art. 14, for craft cooperatives.

148 L. no. 47-1775 of the 10th of September 1947, art. 9.

149 L. Coutant, n. 35 above, pp. 234 ff.

150 C.rur., art. L.524-4.

151 L. no. 47-1775 of the 10th of September 1947, art. 19*octies*.

152 Code monétaire et financier (C.mon.fin)., Art. L.512-5; C.mon.fin., art. L.512-81.

from some cooperative banks, for which the law simply allows a capitalistic voting right, some rules regulate the derogations to the principle. First, the number of additional voting rights may never be proportionate to the subscribed capital; it is instead proportionate to the quantity of cooperative transactions carried on with the cooperative. Secondly, the proportion of voting rights cannot exceed certain limits: for example, 5% for agricultural cooperatives.

Special attention should be paid to the collective interest cooperative, since it furnishes an alternative understanding of the one member/one vote principle that should inspire other cooperative organisations. Article 19*octies* of the 1947 Law reiterates the general principle of article 1. However, it gives it a special meaning when the collective interest cooperative has chosen to function in classes of members; in this case, the principle means that each member has one vote in his/her class. The collective voting right of each class may be defined unequally by the statutes. Three limits are laid down: one class may not have more than 50% of the voting rights; one class may not have less than 10% of the voting rights; and the voting rights may not be proportionate to the subscribed capital. During the negotiations on the 2014 reform, some cooperative organisations lobbied for introduction of a class system as a general provision, for example to welcome and regulate employees as cooperators in cooperatives other than workers' cooperatives. However, they failed.

The strongest derogation to the one member/one vote principle relates to the non-cooperator members (in practice, investors), members usually named 'members of article 3*bis*'. While some specific non-cooperator members were recognised in certain cooperatives before 1992,[153] only workers' cooperatives were generally allowed to have investor members.[154] The general provision on these investor members was integrated into the 1947 Law in 1992.[155] If the new provision is innovative, since it creates a new category of member, its main purpose is to regulate their voting rights. These investors may never have more than 35% of the voting rights. This limit is fixed at 49% if the investors are themselves cooperatives. Within these limits, it is allowed to distribute voting rights among these non-cooperator members in proportion to the subscribed capital. Despite the strong debates in 1992, no serious problem arose in practice, because this category of members is almost non-existent.

The organisation of the members' meeting has not been regulated by the cooperative law as such, even if some provisions deal with it. The general cooperative law of 1947 is almost entirely silent on the matter. Its sole provision concerns distance voting.[156] It allows, if not stated differently in special laws,

153 For example, farmers' trade unions in agricultural cooperatives.

154 See section 1.3.1.

155 L. no. 47-1775 of the 10th of September 1947, art. 3bis.

156 L. no. 47-1775 of the 10th of September 1947, art. 10.

voting by mail. It also states, with the same limit, that members taking part in the meeting by video-conference are taken into consideration for the quorum and calculation of the majority. But it states nothing about the quorum and the majority themselves. Nor does article 7 of the 1947 Law mention these points in its reference to the statutory provisions. Some special cooperative laws give some specifications, for example for merchants' cooperatives[157] and agricultural cooperatives.[158] But most of them do not deal with these questions, or they provide very few rules. In these cases, it is necessary to refer to company law; and, again, the rules will differ according to the kind of company chosen by the cooperative. It is useless to describe the rules in detail.[159] The merchants' cooperatives provide a good example of the general tendency. Firstly, the quorum is fixed at one-third of the members, but at half of the members for modification of the statutes. The required majority is half of members, but two-thirds for modification of the statutes. A different rule is provided for consumer cooperatives, which have the most numerous members, and for which a quorum of one sixth of members is required.[160] However, these rules may differ more or less in other cooperatives, and here is probably one of the best examples of the complexity and opacity of French cooperative law, for which there is no rational justification.

2.3.3. *Mechanisms for Member Control*

Surprisingly, no general provision deals with mechanisms of member control. Of course, some mechanisms may be related to it, but they are not presented as such in the cooperative law. The attention of cooperative law seems to be concentrated on the protection of cooperators against investor members. Besides the limitation of article 3 bis,[161] some provisions aim at limiting the capital subscribed by investors. Thus, cooperative certificates, and non-voting preference shares,[162] may not represent more than half of the equity.[163] Some special laws add further protections related to the minimum participation of cooperators or maximum participation of non-cooperators. For example, in craft cooperatives, if modification of statutes requires a majority of two-thirds of members, it is also stated that this majority must contain at least half of crafts.[164] Similarly, in workers' cooperatives, when there are non-cooperator members, these may not

157 C.com., arts. L.224-8 1 L.124-9.
158 C.rur., art. R.524-15.
159 For an overview, D. Hiez, n. 7 above, nos. 102.17 ff.
160 L. of the 7th of May 1917, art. 4.
161 See section 2.3.1.
162 See section 3.3.2.
163 L. no. 47-1775 of the 10th of September 1947, art. 19*tervicies*.
164 L. no. 83-657 of the 20th of July 1978, art. 16.

constitute more than one-third of members of the board.[165] These rules reveal the fear of domination by non-cooperator members in the cooperative, but, they also reveal the lack of consideration given to the mechanisms necessary to ensure positive control by members on the cooperative. Therefore, it is more useful to indicate them, since many exist in French law, even if they are dispersed.

There is no cooperative general rule concerning the frequency of members' meetings, except for agricultural cooperatives.[166] Company law requires an annual meeting and an extraordinary meeting if an exceptional decision has to be taken. Nor is there a specific rule concerning the call of the members' meeting, usually made by the manager, even though it is also possible for some members to do it themselves: for example, one-fifth of members may convene the members' meeting in agricultural cooperatives.[167] Similarly, nothing special is foreseen concerning the agenda of the meeting, which is usually established by the organ which convenes the meeting.

Some mechanisms are established to favour members' participation in meetings. Postal voting is allowed,[168] even if its framework has not been defined. The only precision introduced by the 2014 reform is a reference to the form regulated for public limited companies. Electronic voting was first regulated in agricultural cooperatives, by copy paste of the regulation for public limited companies. The 2014 reform generalised that possibility with a new provision in article 10 of the 1947 Law, but details are only available for cooperatives which chose the form of public limited company. As in the case of companies, proxies are possible. It is difficult to find a general rule on their limits for they differ considerably according to the kind of cooperative.

The organisation and functioning of administration and/or management is not regulated by the cooperative law as such, even if the 1947 Law provides an unusual qualification. Its article 6 states that the cooperative is governed by representatives ('*mandataires*'). The wording was established in 1947, at a time when the institutionalist theories had not influenced company law; but it has never been changed. It is analysed as the sign of the strong dependence of managers on the members. In practice, however, because the cooperative law is silent on the concrete functioning, cooperatives must refer to the regulation of the kind of company that they have chosen, so that the general provision has no effective consequence. article 6 specifies that managers are appointed and removed by the members' meeting, for a maximum of six years. The only qualification required to take part in the election is membership. The only applicable provision is the maximum length of the representatives' mandates;

165 L. no. 78-763 of the 19th of July 1978, art. 15.

166 C.rur., art. R.524-12.

167 For example, one-fifth of members may call the members' meeting in agricultural cooperatives C.rur., art. R.524-12.

168 L. no. 47-1775 of the 10th of September 1947, art. 10.

and the prevalence of cooperative law, as special, over company law contradicts the solution in principle applicable to limited liability companies.[169]

Another very traditional mechanism is the division of the members' meeting into sections, which vote separately and designate delegates who compose the general meeting of the cooperative. The purpose is to facilitate participation by the members in the meeting, in consideration of the size of the cooperative, its geographic area, and, sometimes, the diversity of business within the cooperative. All meetings take place at the same time with the same agendas. Separate meetings decide each item, and designate delegates who will assemble for the general meeting. Although very attractive in its purpose, especially for big cooperatives, this mechanism is rather complex and its use is decreasing. However, many special cooperative laws provide details on it. Agricultural cooperatives have a particular rule: the section meetings are proposed as an answer to the problem that cooperatives may face in satisfying the quorum requirement:[170] in the section meetings, no quorum is required.

If external control has an important function in the control of members themselves, notably through the information and analysis that it provides to them,[171] a major condition for an efficient effective internal control is the good information of members.

2.3.4. Members' Information

The question of information of members is essential in cooperatives, at least if the democratic principle is to be taken seriously. Nevertheless, there is absolutely no provision on this matter in general cooperative law and very few in special laws. Therefore, the only obligations come from company law. They are very common and do not deserve further attention. The cooperative's members may access the company's documents and may obtain copies of them. However, some changes have occurred, not because of a cooperative claim, but by the extension of recent innovations in company law (inspired by theories of corporate governance) to cooperative law. Agricultural cooperatives first,[172] then the 1947 Law,[173] integrated these considerations. The new general provision imposes on all cooperatives the requirement that the members' meetings take notice of the report on the cooperative's activity; however, it is not stated if the report is written or may be oral. The only more substantial provision is a reference to the obligation of information about the company's social and environmental impact, by the board to the general meeting in public limited companies, extended to

169 C.com., art. L.223-18.
170 C.rur., art. R.524-16.
171 See section 4.4.
172 C.rur., art. L.524-2-1.
173 L. no. 47-1775 of the 10th of September 1947, art. 8.

cooperatives which satisfy the conditions stated in this provision.[174] Overall, the obligation of information stated in the law is poor, and, whereas most reforms result from lobbying by cooperatives themselves, these have been imposed on them as if being a cooperative means, by itself, a concern for the members.

The only interesting obligation of information has been created for agricultural cooperatives, not about the cooperative itself but about the transactions with members. The origin of the innovation is the recent regulation on relationships between producers and traders, in an attempt to improve the situation of farmers facing crisis. The cooperatives have obtained exemption from the obligation of individual contracts, with their compulsory provisions, but they must include the same provisions in their statutes.[175] This provision is supposed to ensure access to the appropriate information for all the cooperators. This general information has been complemented by the obligation for the cooperative to provide each cooperator with individual information about its engagement and its forms.[176] What is interesting here is the conjunction of collective and individual tools to inform about collective and individual businesses. As such, these difficulties are not new.

2.3.5. *Education*

While the information of members is necessary to allow them to exercise effective control on their cooperative, education is crucial as well. However, until very recently, the French cooperative law paid no attention to this point. A change is perhaps on the way. Firstly, the 2014 reform introduced a reference to training in article 1 of the 1947 Law, among the main cooperative principles. Nevertheless, that provision is too general to have any concrete consequence. More technically, for agricultural cooperatives, during the first year of their mandate, training necessary for accomplishment of their mission is proposed to members of the diverse organs.[177] Many questions may arise concerning the application of this new provision, but its purpose is excellent.

2.4. THE DIVISION OF POWERS AMONG THE COOPERATIVES' ORGANS

French cooperative law is unclear on members' obligations and rights, but the choice of the legislature has been clearer concerning the organs of the cooperative.

---

174 C.com., art. L.225-102-1; listed companies and very big cooperatives are concerned.
175 C.rur., art. L.631-24.
176 C.rur., art. L.521-3.
177 C.rur., art. L.524-3-1.

Theoretically, this means broad freedom for a cooperative's founders, since the 1947 Law refers only to the statutes.[178] In practice, however, because nearly all cooperatives are subject to a special cooperative law, and because all special cooperative laws impose the choice among a few kinds of companies, the definition of organs and their relationships are fully provided by the regulation of these companies. Therefore, one finds mainly two organisations (for limited liability companies and for public limited companies).

2.4.1. *Power of a Cooperative's Board and Civil Liability*

Only the distribution of competences between the members' meeting and the board is, more or less, common to all cooperatives, with few authentic cooperative rules. Sovereignty pertains to the members' meeting; leadership to the representatives. Moreover, the prevalence of the members' meeting is stronger in cooperatives than it is in companies, since the collectivity of cooperators is considered to be the cooperative's identity, the cooperative being nothing more than the collectivity of the cooperators. The general competences of the assembly are mainly defined by company law. Article 8 of the 1947 Law attributes to the assembly at least approval of the accounts, reception of the representatives' report, and appointment of the representatives. Other dispersed provisions attribute additional competences to the members' meeting, such as the distribution of surpluses,[179] the designation of the beneficiary of net assets in the case of winding up.[180] Under company law provisions, the members' meeting is also competent to decide when the existence or the nature of cooperative is at stake: dissolution, amendment of the statutes, conversion or merger. Some more specific decisions concern the cooperative's specificities, for instance incorporation of the reserve in the capital, or the issuance of cooperative certificates.[181]

By contrast, administration of the cooperative depends fully on the kind of company chosen. Limited liability companies ('Société à responsabilité limitée') are managed by a director ('*gérant*'), usually only a single natural person, even though this may be several persons. Public limited companies can be organised according to two different systems: either the one-tier or the two-tier system. As for companies, the former system is far more usual in French cooperatives. However, one particular rule introduces part of the two-tier system into medium-sized cooperatives. In workers' cooperatives[182] and craft cooperatives,[183] when

---

178 L. no. 47-1775 of the 10th of September 1947, art. 7.
179 C.rur., art. L.522-4-1 for agricultural cooperatives.
180 L. no. 47-1775 of the 10th of September 1947, art. 19.
181 See sections 3.3.2 and 3.5.
182 L. no. 78-763 of the 19th of July 1947, art. 16.
183 L. no. 83-657 of the 20th of July 1983, arts. 18, 19.

the cooperative has adopted the form of a limited liability company and is composed of more than twenty members, a supervisory board is elected by the members' meeting. Moreover, in the case of craft cooperatives, it is specified that, when there are fewer than twenty members, the same function is fulfilled by the members' meeting itself. The supervisory board is subject to another condition in craft cooperatives: the direction of the cooperative is carried on by a single director if there are fewer twenty members; it is not carried on by more than three directors if there are more than twenty members. This reveals mistrust in a single direction. However collective direction is technically complex, and somewhat dangerous, in limited liability companies, since each director has full competences, and a decision by one director may contradict that of another.

It may be questioned whether the mission of the board in public limited companies differs in cooperatives and capitalist companies. The provisions are the same, but there is no doubt that the 1947 Law imposes another orientation on the distribution of competences between the members' meeting and the board, notably through the generic wording of representatives.

In public limited companies, the board is competent to intervene on any topic, and has to define the company's policy. This does not fit with the spirit of the 1947 Law, since the board members (or the manager) are only representatives of the members. The regulation of agricultural cooperatives, the only one in which governance is detailed, usually inspired by the provisions on public limited companies, states that the board ensures the cooperative's management and correct functioning[184] when the code of commerce states that the board determines the orientations of the company.[185] In other words, it moderates the importance of the board.

In spite of the cooperative's specificities, the institutionalist theories have also influenced cooperative law. Hence, whereas the competences should be defined by the statutes, nobody contests that the code of commerce provisions on engagements *vis-à-vis* third parties are applicable. The clearest rule is for public limited companies:[186]

> In its dealings with third parties, the company is bound even by acts of its board of directors which do not come within the purview of the company's corporate mission, unless it can prove that the third party knew that a specific action was extraneous to that mission or, given the circumstances, could not have been ignorant of that fact, and mere publication of the memorandum and statutes does not constitute such proof.

Traditionally, the counterpart of power is liability. Liability of board members or directors is regulated both by cooperative law and company law. A general

184 C.rur., art. L.524-3-1.
185 C.com., art. L.225-35.
186 C.com., art. L.225-35.

liability principle for managers is provided for in company law, applicable in the absence of a contradictory rule in cooperative law. In limited liability companies,[187] as well as public limited companies[188] and agricultural cooperatives,[189] managers are liable for faults committed at the time of the cooperative's foundation when it implied the nullity of company, for any breaches of the law or of the statutes, and for any errors of management. Cooperative law adds some special liabilities to ensure the application of its own rules. The general law[190] provides for specific liability in the case of infringement of cooperative principles, such as the use of the surplus in contradiction to the rules laid down in the 1947 Law, or infringement of the rules concerning the conversion of the cooperative into a company.

2.4.2. *Board Functioning*

The cooperative's management depends on the kind of company chosen, since cooperative law contains only very general provisions. Therefore, it is again necessary to distinguish between public limited companies and limited liability companies. As explained above, limited liability companies are managed by a director ('*gérant*') and public limited companies by a board of directors. It is permitted to have several directors in limited liability companies, and this allows the involvement of more members in the management. However, it is risky, for in the case of dispute the cooperative may face crisis and, in the worst scenario, may be dissolved by a judge. In public limited companies, the board of directors is composed of at least three members and at most eighteen,[191] the precise number being determined in the statutes. In the case of a tier system, the directorate may be composed of only five directors,[192]

Whatever the form of the company, officers are members of the cooperative.[193] The same provision states that the statutes shall specify the duration of the mandate, which cannot exceed six years. Some special laws provide for a shorter duration, notably for agricultural cooperatives, for which board members are elected for two, three or four years depending on the provision of the statutes.[194]

---

187 C.com., arts. L.223-10 and L. 223-22.

188 C.com., art. L.225-249.

189 C.rur., art. L.524-5-1.

190 L. no. 47-1775 of the 10th of September 1947, art. 26.

191 C.com., art. L.225-17. In agricultural cooperatives, the members are at least three, without any limit; this is fixed by the statutes.

192 C.com., art. L.225-58.

193 L. no. 47-1775 of the 10th of September 1947, art. 6.

194 C.rur., art. R.524-2.

2.4.3. *Mechanism for the Election of the Board of Directors*

The requirement of cooperative membership in order to take part in an organ is a major rule to ensure the members' control, but the cooperative law gives no more details. Only some special cooperative laws are more substantial, notably the 1978 law on workers' cooperatives (art. 1), since it states that cooperatives are managed, directly or indirectly, by their members. But other special laws contain no such provision. The 1983 law on craft cooperatives, refers to the representatives, members or not,[195] but the provision does not deal specifically with the composition of the board. Nevertheless, cooperative laws ensure the control of the cooperatives' members and, more precisely, of cooperators. Indeed, many provisions state that the majority of managers shall be cooperator members, as opposed to non-cooperator members (such as investors). It is even sometimes mandatory that the president be a cooperator.[196]

The only recent requirement comes from company law, more precisely the public limited company regulation, and it concerns age and gender.[197] The legislation on agricultural cooperatives partly duplicates the provisions for public limited companies.[198] These provisions contain an optional rule: two-thirds of the board members shall be aged less than seventy. In any case, the statutes shall contain rules dealing with age. There is no specific provision concerning gender in agricultural cooperatives, but cooperatives which have chosen the form of a public limited company must contain at least 40% of males or females. This rule is new and will not be applicable before 2018. It will only concern public limited companies with at least 500 employees or whose turnover or balance sheet exceeds 50 million euros. In the case of infringement of such rules, the sanction is the voiding of the election, but it cannot mean the voiding of the decisions taken by the wrongly composed board.

2.4.4. *Remuneration of Board Members*

An important question today is the remuneration of the director or board members. Depending on whether the cooperative is viewed as either a firm undertaking business or as a disinterested organisation oriented only to the satisfaction of its members' needs, remuneration will or will not be considered with favour. The point has become more sensitive because the managers' remuneration in big firms is increasingly controversial, and cooperatives are expected to be different. The general cooperative law does not provide a clear

195 L. no. 83-653 of the 20th of July 1983, art. 21.
196 L. no. 83-653 of the 21th of July 1983, art. 18.
197 C.com., art. L.225-19.
198 C.rur., art. L.524-2.

indication; it seemingly does not deal with the remuneration of representatives but of employees in charge of direction. Several special rules are more detailed. Some of them specify that remuneration shall be compensation for the time spent managing the cooperative.[199] The Code of Commerce adds a procedural condition[200] for merchants' cooperatives: the obligation to determine a maximum amount for the global remuneration of board members, and the yearly decision of the members' meeting on the precise remuneration.

The 2014 reform introduced a general provision[201] stating that these positions are unpaid and allow only, when justified, the reimbursement of expenses and the compensation of the time dedicated to administration of the cooperative. Control by the members' meeting is ensured, since it decides each year on the global amount available for these remunerations. Again, the application of the provision shows its imprecision, but the orientation is clear.

2.5. DISPUTE RESOLUTION BETWEEN MEMBERS AND THE COOPERATIVE

In the French tradition, there is a link between the existence of a community and the desire of its members to be judged by their peers; this is still visible within fishing communities (*prud'homie de pêche*). Therefore, arbitration administered by cooperative organisations appears to be the suitable dispute resolution mode. Nevertheless, the general cooperative law contains no provision on the matter. In the meantime, that silence does not preclude arbitration, since it is always possible to conclude an arbitration agreement in the areas in which people are free to dispose of their rights.[202] The Rural Code explicitly allows agricultural cooperatives to conclude such agreements;[203] technically, the precision is useless. In practice, it is among worker's cooperatives that a general organisation of arbitration can be found. Without any special provision in the law, the general confederation of workers' cooperatives (CGSCOP) has inserted an arbitration clause into the statutes that it imposes on its members.[204] The CGSCOP can attract nearly all the workers' cooperatives, so that the arbitration has obtained an important influence therein. In application of that clause, all the members of workers' cooperatives must go before the court of arbitration for any dispute on membership or cooperative transactions.

199 C.rur., art. L.524-3, for agricultural cooperatives.
200 C.com., art. L.124-6.
201 L. no. 47-1775 of the 10th of September 1947, art. 6, para. 2.
202 C.civ., arts. 2059–2061.
203 C.rur., art. L.521-4.
204 Art. 43 of the statutes: *Guide Juridique les SCOP*, Scop Edit, Paris, 2013, p.607.

Interesting questions arise concerning the status of members in these cooperatives. Because arbitration is allowed for disputes about rights that their holders may freely dispose, and because labour law is one topic on which there is no free disposition of rights, there are debates concerned to distinguish questions related to labour law and those directly connected to membership. The problem exists only because French law adds the labour contract to membership, and the competence of the labour judge demonstrates the difficulties that it creates. The best example is the situation of the directors of workers' cooperatives, since these are considered by the law to be employees. Hence the disputes that they may have with the cooperative may go before the arbiter or the judge.

3. FINANCIAL STRUCTURE

3.1. FRAMEWORK OF THE COOPERATIVE FINANCIAL STRUCTURE

3.1.1. The Cooperative Financial Structure and Cooperative Identity

French law complies with the ICA Principles regarding financial structure as it does on other matters. The social object of the cooperative, targeted on satisfaction of its members' needs, is the main explanation of the cooperative's financial structure. It is characterised by pursuit of the development of the cooperators through the cooperative, which means that the financing can only be a tool in that development. Whereas the variability of capital is not compulsory,[205] most detailed rules on financing are related to that variability (notably the important reserves and their partial indivisibility), demonstrating again that this is part of the cooperative identity. The primacy of the person over capital, because of the pursuit of the satisfaction of members' needs, justifies the absence of dividends: the only remuneration of shares consists in interest, and the surpluses may only be distributed through the mechanism of cooperative refund. These principles are safeguarded, when the cooperative is liquidated, by the disinterested distribution principle.

Just as the cooperative identity is opposed to the company's social object, so the financial structures are contradictory. Even the variability of capital, whereas it is allowed for companies other than public limited companies,[206] is in practice used only by cooperatives or by neighbouring companies. The principles and mechanisms evoked above demonstrate the opposition with company

205 See above section 1.2.1.

206 C.com., art. L.231-1.

law. Nevertheless, the evolution of recent decades has been characterised by the importation into cooperative law of techniques deriving from company law. The phenomenon is not typically French; it is perfectly described as the 'companisation' of cooperatives. Based on a claim by cooperative organisations that they lacked financing, a major reform of the 1947 Law was adopted in 1992.[207] None of the cooperative principles was reversed, but most of them were mitigated: admission of investor members, possible incorporation of reserves in the capital, possible conversion of a cooperative into a company, creation of new shares or financial securities. With that reform, the legislature confirmed the 'companisation', but, in practice, the consequences were not significant, since cooperatives did not make significant use of the new facilities.[208] However, 'companisation' did not slow down, but it took another route: the creation of subsidiaries. Anyway, political recognition of the social and solidarity economy, as well as the financial crisis, have redirected attention to cooperative identity, and the new major reform of 2014 did not continue with the orientation of the previous one. Relaxation of the cooperative principles has not been removed, but the experience showed that they did not create particular excesses.

3.1.2. *The Cooperative Financial Structure Regulation*

The cooperative financial structure is laid down in the cooperative law, in the 1947 Law for general principles, and in the special laws for the details on financial structure. Company law is applicable to cooperatives, like the more general law, but in this respect cooperative law clearly contradicts the general law so that there is no room for its application. Nevertheless, some points are not dealt with in cooperative law (or very few): for example, subscription of the capital. The two main points are the minimum capital subscribed, and the liability of members. There are very few provisions on these in cooperative law, and most solutions come from company law. It is not provided by the general company law, but depends on the kind of company chosen by the cooperative.

Finance refers also to taxation and accountability, even if these questions will not be the focus here. In principle, cooperatives are subject to the general law. Some adjustments exist, but they are considered as derogations to the equal treatment principle.

207 L. no. 92-643 of the 13th of July 1992. Major commentaries: M. Jeantin, 'Loi relative à la modernisation des enterprises coopératives', *Revue trimestrielle de droit commercial*, 1993, 119; C. Vienney, 'Identité coopérative et statut juridique', RECMA, Paris, 1993, nos. 44–45, p. 89; G. Gourlay, 'La modernisation des entreprises coopératives par la loi du 13 juillet 1992', *Dr. Sociétés*, 1992, p. 1; B. Piot, n. 74 above.

208 H. Azarian, 'Tentative de bilan d'application de la loi du 13 juillet 1992 à certaines catégories de coopératives', *Dr. Sociétés*, 1998, chron. 11; D. Hiez, n. 76 above.

3.2. THE COOPERATIVE SHARE CAPITAL

3.2.1. The Nature of Cooperative Share Capital

The question of the nature or the function of capital has never been seriously discussed in cooperative law, except to deal with its variability. No cooperative can be created without any capital, even if it can be very low. This point could have been interpreted as the consequence of the feeble importance of capital in cooperatives, compared to the cooperative transactions with members; but it must today be related to the continuous decrease of capital in companies. It is now possible to create a limited liability company with only one euro, and even public limited companies can be created with only 37,000 euros.[209] It is common in cooperatives for the reserves to far exceed the capital itself, and the function and regulation of reserves are probably more characteristic of cooperatives.

The requirement of capital is probably the main difference between cooperatives and mutuals, since mutuals have no capital and cannot have it. Apart from this feature, however, the object and the governance of both organisations are very similar.

The function of cooperative capital has not been studied. Spontaneously, as in companies, it would be considered as the guarantee for the cooperative's creditors. Nevertheless, the doubts that arise concerning that function in companies are far more convincing in cooperatives. Instead of considering cooperatives to be economically weak because of their capital, it would be more exact to wonder whether their capital fulfils an economic function. The function related, in company law, to the governance and the rights of associates has no room in cooperatives; the sole function of share capital is the existence of cooperatives itself and the membership.

Less attention has been paid to the capital itself than to the shares that compose it. Firstly, they are explicitly not a basis for individual rights of members. The only derogation to that principle is that the acquisition is a *sine qua non* condition to acquire membership. Moreover, the original legal nature of the share in a cooperative is highlighted. The capital of cooperatives can only be represented by 'parts sociales',[210] in opposition to 'actions'. Usually, in company law, these 'parts sociales' represent capital in partnerships, whereas 'actions' do so in capital companies. The originality of cooperatives is that, even if they choose the form of a public limited company, which is the most common capital company, do not have 'actions' but 'parts sociales'. The transfer of these 'parts sociales' is very restricted,[211] if not forbidden.[212]

209 C.com., art. L.224-2.
210 L. no. 47-1775 of the 10th of September 1947, art. 11.
211 L. no. 47-1775 of the 10th of September 1947, art. 11.
212 See section 3.3.3.

Moreover, the value of a share is fixed in the statutes, and cannot evolve according to the prosperity of the cooperative. Therefore, the right of redemption of the member refers only to the nominal value.[213]

3.2.2. *The Minimum Cooperative Share Capital*

Even if cooperatives are not legally defined as variable companies,[214] all of them are so in practice, and their legal regime can only be understood on that basis. Before variation, capital must exist. This exigency derives from the structure of the company, and it depends first on company law, subsidiarily on cooperative law. There is no specific rule on limited liability companies, so that they may be created with only one euro. Public limited companies require a capital of 37,000 euros but, for them, cooperative law provides a lower requirement: half of the capital required for capital companies,[215] i.e. 18,500 euros.

Special cooperative laws make some specifications because they define the minimum amount of a share or the minimum number of shares to become a member. These provisions indirectly fix a minimum capital, but it is so low that it is insignificant. In workers' cooperatives, for example created with the form of limited liability companies, the regulation fixes the value of a share at between 15.24 and 76.22 euros,[216] and at least two members are required, so that the minimum capital is 2x15.24 euros, i.e. 30.48 euros.

Apart from these legal requirements, the minimum capital of variable capital companies must be stated in the request for enrolment on the company register.[217] More exactly, the provision requires indication of the amount of capital below which it cannot decrease. This amount cannot be higher than the subscribed capital at the moment of creation, or lower than the legal minimum capital.

No provision considers the payment of special fees to acquire membership, but some special cooperatives do so in order to compensate the efforts made by previous members before the arrival of the new members, from which they take advantage.

3.2.3. *The Consistency of the Cooperative Share Capital*

There is no specific publicity for the capital, but it derives from the general rules on publicity for companies. Firstly, the starting capital is publicised with the

---

213 L. no. 47-1775 of the 10th of September 1947, art. 19; see section 3.4.4.

214 See section 1.2.1.

215 L. no. 47-1775 of the 10th of September 1947, art. 27 al. 2.

216 Decree no. 79-67 of the 18th of January 1979 on the shares issued by workers' cooperatives, art. 1. The amount of the shares is still fixed in francs, so that the legal conversion is so precise.

217 C.com., art. R.123-53.

statutes in the company register.[218] Secondly, the third parties are constantly informed about the variability of the capital, since the cooperative must mention the qualification of 'société cooperative' in any document that it uses[219] and, when it has a variable capital, it must be also mentioned.[220] Then, the evolution of the capital necessarily appears in the accounting, which is publicised to be annexed to the company register, for limited liability companies[221] as well as for capital companies.[222] A recent derogation has been introduced for micro-enterprises, as defined in article L.223-16-1 of the Commerce Code: they do not have to hold the accounting annex,[223] and they may choose to make their accounting not accessible to the public.[224] Indirectly, cooperatives are concerned. Nevertheless, because agricultural cooperatives are not commercial and civil companies, a special provision has been necessary to extend that derogation to micro-agricultural cooperatives.[225]

The cooperative law pays attention to the release of subscribed capital. It takes the possible poverty of members into account, and allows members to release only part of the subscribed capital immediately. That provision is also the consequence of the predominance of man on capital in cooperatives, which requires tofacilitate the acquisition of membership to people unable to release immediately the subscribed capital. Whereas the different forms of companies are regulated differently, the cooperative law provides a general rule.[226] The provision distinguishes contributions in cash and in kind. The former may be released at the subscription for one quarter and completed during the next five years, whereas the latter must be fully released immediately. Company law also envisages this distinction, even if its regulation differs.

Attention is usually paid in companies to the evaluation of goods, when contribution is made in kind. In the silence of cooperative law, company law applies. The mechanism is the external evaluation of the goods by an auditor designated by the associates, imperatively in public limited companies[227] and optionally in limited liability companies[228] if any good's value is less than 30,000 euros[229] and if all of the goods' value is less than half of the share capital; the evaluation of goods is included in the statutes. Unless the associates confirm the evaluation of the external auditor they are responsible for the evaluation.

---

218 C.com., art. R.123-53.
219 L. no. 47-1775 of the 10th of September 1947, art. 22.
220 C.com., art. L.231-2.
221 C.com. art. L.232-22.
222 C.com., art. L.232-23.
223 C.com., art. L.123-16-1.
224 C.com., art. L.232-25.
225 C.rur., art. L.524-6-6.
226 L.no. 47-1775 of the 10th of September 1947, art. 12.
227 C.com., arts. L.225-8 and L.225-14.
228 C.com., art. L.223-9.
229 C.com., art. D.223-6-1.

The general cooperative law makes no provision for contributions in service, so that, in principle, the company law applies. Such contributions are allowed[230] except in public limited companies.[231] However, these contributions are not taken into account for the capital itself, even if they allow the associates to receive dividends.[232] This solution is generally approved because of the difficulty of evaluating them, and the impossibility for creditors to seize them.[233] In the silence of cooperative law, the same rules apply. Nevertheless, there is some resistance against such contributions in cooperatives, since the services provided to the cooperative are the consequence of membership and therefore cannot be part of the capital.[234] The argument is persuasive and may explain the silence of both the law and authors. Some special laws are more precise, notably in the case of workers' cooperatives, since the regulations refer to contributions in cash or in kind as the only ones possible.[235] It should be pointed out, however, that the possible obligation to subscribe new shares, released by a subtraction from salaries, resembles a contribution in service. Moreover, cooperative transactions should not be likened to contributions to the collective benefit of cooperatives, even if these transactions are part of it. There is one situation in which contribution in service is indubitable: a new cooperative – the inhabitants' cooperative[236] – has introduced an original rule for these cooperatives.[237] Their members may contribute in service but these contributions are integrated into the capital. These contributions are specially regulated,[238] and the procedure will be specified by a decree which has not yet been issued.

3.2.4. *The Variability of Cooperative Share Capital*

Since the capital is variable, it may increase or decrease without any amendment of statutes[239] or any publicity.[240] In variation, attention is paid mainly to the decrease in capital, and the reason seems to be the risk of losses for creditors. Several rules apply. First, the capital may not decrease below the minimum capital fixed in the statutes and indicated in the company register.[241] Secondly,

230 C.civ., art. 1832.
231 C.com., art. L.225-3.
232 C.civ., art. 1843-2.
233 Nevertheless, some recent debates have gone further and integrated these contributions in the capital: L. Durit-Pontier, 'Repenser les apports en industrie', *Les petites affiches*, 3 juil. 2002, no. 132; Poracchia, note sous Cass., civ. 1e, 30 mars 2004, Rev. sociétés, 2004, p. 855.
234 M. Hérail, n. 39 above, no. 622.
235 L. no. 78-763 of the 19th of July 1978, art. 27.
236 C.const.hab., L.201-1 ff.; created by the law no.2014-366 of the 22nd of March 2014.
237 C.const.hab., art. L.201-13.
238 Nature of services, date of subscription and of possible transfer.
239 C.com., art. L.231-1.
240 C.com., art. L.231-3.
241 C.com., art. R.123-53.

the capital may not decrease to less than a quarter of the maximum amount reached by the capital since the cooperative's creation.[242] The mechanism is similar for cooperative banks, but the threshold is stricter: three quarters of the maximum capital reached.[243]

A question has arisen concerning the maximum amount of capital: should it be specified in the statutes? In 2007. The Cour de Cassation issued a positive answer.[244] The consequence was as follows: provided that the statutes did not fix a maximum amount of capital, the increase of capital required amendment of the statutes and, if not, was void. The solution was unexpected, useless, and with a doubtful legal grounding. The legislature amended the 1947 Law[245] to reverse the solution.[246]

The purpose of the control of the variation of capital is to take the variability of capital seriously. Variation of membership implies variation of capital. Therefore, the stricter the control on the variation of capital, the less the open-door principle is enforced. In the meantime, the control of capital is a necessity, first for creditors, but also for members. Much debate was provoked in the mid-2000s by the international accounting norms (IAS32), and their analysis of variable capital as debts.[247] To avoid this qualification, it was proposed to restrict the right of withdrawal, so that the cooperative would not be obliged to reduce its capital. In other words, accounting considerations induced substantive amendments. In practice, however, in France, the international accountability regulation had no concrete effect on the legislation. Cooperative banks were the most active in the struggle against the new international regulation, but none of them demanded a legislative amendment; the prohibition on decreasing capital below three quarters of the highest amount of capital is good protection. The only amendment which is claimed to be related to IAS32 concerns the byelaws ratified for agricultural cooperatives to ensure that the cooperative can control the withdrawal of cooperators.[248] The connection is, however, not so clear, or, at least so it has not far had important consequences in practice.

The sanction differs according the rule which has been infringed. Provided that cooperatives are companies, cooperative law is indirectly reluctant to pronounce the dissolution of a cooperative. This may only happen when a provision states so explicitly. This is the case of article 27 line 3 of the 1947 Law if the minimum capital for public limited cooperatives has not been subscribed. The article provides solutions to try to avoid that sanction: if any interested

242 L. no. 47-1775 of the 10th of September 1947, art. 13.

243 Ibid.

244 Cass. com. 6 févr. 2007, no. 05-19237; Bull. civ. IV no. 29; JCP E, 2008, 2373, no. 10.

245 L. no. 47-1775 of the 10th of September, art. 7.

246 L. no. 2008-649 of the 3rd of July 2008, art. 23.

247 J.-C. Detilleux and C. Naett, 'Les coopératives face aux normes comptables internationales: le cas de l'IAS32', RECMA, Paris, 2005.

248 D. Hiez, n. 7 above, no. 91.25.

person may claim it, including the public attorney, the judge may order the dissolution only if the minimum capital is not reached on the day that s/he states, and s/he may grant a six months delay, renewable once, to the cooperative. In other circumstances, solutions are less rigorous and more individual. First, if a member has not released his/her subscribed capital, either the cooperative sues him/her to obtain the payment, or it renounces to the release and, after a formal notice, the membership is terminated.[249] The last circumstance is when a member wants to withdraw, whereas the redemption of his/her shares would decrease the capital below the minimum statutory amount. In this case, a balance must be struck between the various interests: it is not allowed to deprive the member of his/her right of withdrawal, and it is not allowed for the cooperative to decrease its share capital. Therefore, if conditions of withdrawal are fulfilled, the membership is terminated. This means that the member has no further duty towards the cooperative, notably in regard to cooperative transactions. In agricultural cooperatives, it is explicitly the board's task to decide the date of redemption, which cannot be more than five years after the termination of membership.[250] Theoretically, the problem may remain at that date but, in practice, if the share capital had not increased during that time, it is certain that the cooperative will be wound up.

While attention is paid to a decrease of capital because of its danger, an increase is fortunately possible as well. This increase in capital may occur, apart from when the number of members grows, when the cooperative decides to incorporate part of the reserves into the share capital,[251] or when it decides to attribute a cooperative refund through the creation of new shares.[252] It also happens in the case of the subscription of new shares. No provision of the general cooperative law allows a cooperative to impose the subscription of new shares to meet its financial needs. Some special laws may provide for compulsory additional subscriptions. The first case concerns agricultural cooperatives, because of the obligation for any cooperator to hold a number of shares proportionate to its activities with the cooperative.[253] Therefore, if the activity increases, the cooperator will have to acquire new shares. The second case concerns workers' cooperatives, because the acquisition of membership may only be conditioned by the acquisition of one share.[254] As compensation, the statutes may require the acquisition of new shares.[255] However, this requirement must be imposed by the statutes themselves, and does not depend on the decision of any cooperative organ; therefore, it cannot depend on the needs of the cooperative. Nevertheless, in any cooperative,

---

249 L. no. 47-1775 of the 10th of September 1947, art. 12.
250 C.rur., art. R.523-6.
251 See section 3.5.
252 See section 3.6.
253 C.rur., art. L. 521-3.
254 L. no. 78-763 of the 19th of July 1978, art. 6.
255 Ibid.

it is always possible for a member to acquire new shares, with the consent of the competent organ if required, but no member may be obliged to do so.

3.2.5. Structure of Capital and Cooperative Autonomy

Autonomy from state housing cooperatives.

The autonomy of cooperatives is an important ICA Principle which may disqualify an organisation from being a cooperative. In relation to the cooperative object and governance, it is ensured by, and reinforces, the members' control. Hence it resides in the financial structure, with some special provisions. In principle, because members obtain no right depending on the amount of share capital to which they have subscribed, no limit is set on their acquisition. However, even if political equality is respected, important economic differences may allow some members to put pressure on others, and cooperative law paid a special attention to that concern in regard to investor members. However, the only general limit does not concern some categories of members, but rather some categories of financial securities in the capital or in assets. The amount of capital corresponding to non-voting preference shares and to cooperative certificates cannot be more than 50% of the total share capital.[256] In addition, the cooperative certificates cannot be more than 50% of the total capital of the previous financial year.[257]

I have already mentioned the restrictions on the political rights of investors in cooperatives, as well as the maximum participation of some representations of share capital. Some more specifications are provided in special legislation – for example, in regard to workers' or craft cooperatives. The former allow long-time investors to be members. In compensation, the 1978 law provides the guarantee that the cooperators (workers) have the majority on the board (art. 15). A similar solution is stated in the 1983 law for artisanal cooperatives (art. 18). The Rural Code provides a close but more balanced solution. When there are some investors, on the one hand it makes their presence on the board compulsory; on the other, it restricts that presence to one-third.[258]

3.3. THE DIVERSIFICATION OF FINANCIAL SECURITIES

3.3.1. The Different Classes of Shares

The financial structure of cooperatives may seem particularly simple, if one considers the uniformity of cooperative share capital. The financial needs of

---

256 L. no. 47-1775 of the 10th of September 1947, art. 19*tervicies*.

257 L. no. 47-1775 of the 10th of September 1947, art. 19*sepdecies*.

258 C.rur., art. L.524-1.

cooperatives have not been entirely forgotten, but the law focuses on the creation of attractive securities. Until 1992, the cooperative law provided for only one class of shares, which conferred membership.[259] The 1992 law created two new classes of shares inspired by the diversification of shares or stocks in company law. The traditional shares are now named 'A-shares'[260,261] to establish their link with membership and the ensuing obligations of cooperative transactions.

The first new kind of share is a specific benefit share ('parts sociales à avantage particulier').[262] Preference shares may only be subscribed by members, but when subscribed, they are freely transferable among them. They confer on their holders the specific benefits defined in the statutes, in compliance with cooperative principles. The law provides no specification at all of these possible specific benefits. It is uncontroversial that, contrary to the preference shares of company law, the specific benefit may not consist in additional voting rights, since it would not comply with the 'one member one vote' cooperative principle. The benefit is therefore necessarily financial: it can be a higher interest rate, within the general limit provided for by the law,[263] a preferred attribution of interest in the case of low surpluses, a restricted responsibility, a preferred attribution of reserves within the general limit provided for by the law.[264] The aim of this new class is to encourage cooperators to invest by granting them more rights than they would have with basic shares.

The second new class of shares consists of 'non-voting preference shares'.[265] These may be subscribed by any person (a member or non-member), but not cooperators. The holders of such shares will receive interest before any other shareholder. But – and this has been rather controversial in the legislative process – the counterpart is that the holder has no voting rights. This has no effect when the non-voting preference shares have been subscribed by members, since any new subscribed share cannot confer any additional voting rights on them, voting right being independent of the number of shares held. But, in the case of subscription by non-members, this new class of shares means the cooperative comprises the unusual category of full investor member without any political function. The non-voting preference shareholders do not take part in the members' meeting, but they assemble in a special meeting which designates a representative who attends the members' meeting, without any voting rights. However, no limitation on their right may be adopted by the cooperative except with the consent of the non-voting preference shareholders' special meeting.

259 L. no. 47-1775 of the 10th of September 1947, art. 11.
260 In agricultural cooperatives, they are termed 'transaction shares' ('*parts d'activité*').
261 C.rur., art. R.524-14.
262 L. no. 47-1775 of the 10th of September 1947, art. 11 al. 3.
263 See section 3.6.
264 See section 3.5.
265 L. no. 47-1775 of the 10th of September 1947, art. 11*bis*.

Because the political disability of these shareholders is balanced by their economic preference, the former is conditioned by the latter. In other words, if these shareholders do not receive their remuneration for three successive years (because of losses by the cooperative), their voting rights are restored.

No significant amendment has been adopted since 1992 in the financial cooperative system. However, an overall reform of shares was enacted in 2004 for company law,[266] with the purpose of simplifying the numerous classes of shares. To replace the various classes that had been progressively created in company law, the legislature decided to have a single special class of shares – preference shares[267] – whose flexibility allowed them to fit with all the previous mechanisms. No provision dealt with cooperative law, and the issue of whether cooperatives could issue these new shares was discussed.[268] No provision prohibited it, and provided that the issued shares complied with cooperative principles, they could replace the previous specific benefit shares and non-voting preference shares, at least in public limited cooperatives, since preference shares may only be issued by capital companies. Indeed, one cooperative bank decided to issue such preference shares with success in 2012.[269]

3.3.2. Other Financial Securities

Beside the three classes of cooperative shares, the 1992 law created a new financial security: the associate cooperative certificate,[270] which completed the investment cooperative certificate created a few years before.[271] These two classes are very close, the main difference being that the associate cooperative certificates may only be issued by cooperative banks and subscribed by the issuing cooperative's members.[272] These certificates are securities without voting right, and they are freely transferable. The members' meeting of the cooperative decides yearly on their remuneration, which cannot be less than the interest attributed to the shares.[273] However, because they are explicitly defined as attached to a portion of capital, they are subject to the general limitation on the capital's remuneration.[274] Therefore, their attractiveness resides in the conferred

266 Ord. no. 2004-604 of the 20th of June 2004.

267 C.com., arts. L.228-11 ff.

268 D. Hiez, 'L'incidence de l'introduction des actions de préférence sur le droit coopératif', *Dr. Sociétés*, Paris, 2005, étude 8.

269 P. Prud'homme, 'Les actions de préférence d'une société coopérative anonyme', RECMA, Paris, 2013, no. 327.

270 L. no. 47-1775 of the 10th of September 1947, art. 19*tervicies*.

271 L. no. 87-416 of the 17th of June 1987; today L. no. 47-1775 of the 10th of September 1947, art. 19*sexdecies* to 19*duovicies*.

272 L. no. 47-1775 of the 10th of September 1947, art. 19*tervicies*.

273 L. no. 47-1775 of the 10th of September 1947, art. 19*vicies*.

274 See section 3.6.

rights on the reserves.[275] They are issued for the lifetime of the cooperative, but the issuance agreement foresees their possible anticipated redemption.[276]

The last class of financial securities consists of participatory notes ('titres participatifs').[277] These were created by law no. 83-1 of the 3rd of January 1983 in order to facilitate investments in companies held by the state, in cooperatives, and later in mutuals. They are transferable securities. They resemble a mix of shares and bonds. As bonds, they may be redeemed, and their holders assemble in a special meeting, which is a legal person. As shares, their remuneration is partly variable, and their holders receive ample information and consultation.

3.3.3. *The Legal Regime of Shares*

Whatever the kind of company chosen by the cooperative, its shares have a single legal regime, whereas the company may be a partnership or a capital company. However, since there are different classes of shares, their regime may differ. The question of their transfer is therefore regulated differently depending on the class of shares.

A-shares are nominative.[278] Therefore, they may only be transferred with the agreement of the cooperative.[279] The provision refers to the statutes to stipulate if the agreement must be given by the board or by the members' meeting. Some special cooperative laws state it explicitly.[280]

The specific benefit shares are freely transferable among members.[281] It is debatable whether they may be transferred to non-members, since article 11 forbids the subscription by non-members but does not evoke acquisition. The answer is, to me, positive, but it is not certain that there is room for application in practice.

The regime of the non-voting preference shares is not so explicit.[282] The provision only states that these shares may be subscribed or acquired, so that they are certainly transferable. But it is not specified if the transfer is free or requires the cooperative's consent. In the silence of the provision, reference must be made to the spirit of the text or to the nature of the share. Of course, because these shares are targeted on investors, their free transferability is necessary not to deter the latter from subscription. Their nature is not defined, and authors

275 L. no. 47-1775 of the 10th of September 1947, art. 19*duovicies*.
276 L. no. 47-1775 of the 10th of September 1947, arts. 19*novodecies* and 19*sexdecies*.
277 C.com., arts. L.228-36 and L.228-37.
278 C.com., art. L.231-4.
279 L. no. 47-1775 of the 10th of September 1947, art. 11 al. 1.
280 In agricultural cooperatives, the competent organ is the board: C.rur., art. R.523-4.
281 L. no. 47-1775, 10th September 1947, art. 11 al. 2.
282 L. no. 47-1775 of the 10th of September 1947, art. 11*bis*.

have claimed that they are securities.[283] Because the cooperative certificates are explicitly securities,[284] they are also freely transferable.

Neither the general cooperative law nor special ones deal with the transfer of shares *mortis causa*. The grounds for regulating the hypothesis of death of a cooperator are set out in variable capital company regulation:[285] there is no dissolution of the cooperative; it remains without the deceased. This is one of the provisions that mitigates the doctrinal qualification of partnership.[286] The same provision applies in the case of bankruptcy of a cooperator. Agricultural cooperative law duplicates the provision.[287] Therefore, death terminates membership, so that there is no possible transfer, but the heirs may easily apply for membership if they fulfil the required conditions. The solution differs for new shares, since these are not linked to the quality of cooperator, and transferability does not have the same meaning for them. The Rural Code is significant in this regard, since the provision referred to above is situated in a section dealing specifically with cooperators.

3.4. MEMBER CONTRIBUTIONS TO CAPITAL

3.4.1. Obligation to Release Capital

As such, the subscription of capital is an obligation, since it is a condition to become a member. The subscription amounts to at least one share, to which other subscriptions or fees may be attached.[288] In principle, the member must release one quarter of his/her subscribed capital.

Proof of membership is an interesting point, because it highlights the implications of the subscription of shares. If subscription is a condition to become member, its proof also establishes membership. Unlike in companies, the discussion usually arises in cooperatives when a cooperator wants to terminate membership before the end of the agreed period. To escape his/her obligations, the person claims that he/she is not a member. Case law considers the members' register established by the cooperative as valuable proof.[289] But it is not the only possible proof, and execution of the cooperative's obligations and participation in the cooperative's organs are also efficient.

---

283 B. Piot, n. 74 above.
284 L. no. 47-1775 of the 10th of September 1947, art. 19*sexdecies*.
285 C.com., art. L.231-8.
286 See section 1.1.2.
287 C.rur., art. R.522-6.
288 See section 3.2.2.
289 Cass. civ 1re, 18 déc. 2001, no. 99-17.510, Bull. civ. I, no 325.

3.4.2. *Nature of the Contribution*

French cooperative law does not envisage different rights for members depending on the reason why shares have been subscribed, notably if it was a compulsory or voluntary subscription. Rights depend only on the nature of the subscribed shares.[290] These rights are regulated in the case of wind-up,[291] and these provisions are extended to other cases of membership termination.

Apart from the subscription of capital and payment of fees, another case is financial flow between cooperators and the cooperative: the payment for cooperative transactions. To facilitate the relations, the cooperative and the cooperator maintain a running account. This mechanism also exists in company law, but its function is far more important in cooperative law because of cooperative transactions. It suffers reluctance in company law because of the risk of illegitimate financial transactions between the company and its associates. For cooperatives, it is almost a necessity, even if there may be difficulties in distinguishing the flows related to the cooperative's transactions and to membership, such as capital release or cooperative refund.

3.4.3. *Recording*

There are few provisions on recording. There are none in the general cooperative law, and if some can be found in company law, they deal with accounting but not recording. The only recording that is foreseen concerns agricultural cooperatives.[292] The cooperative keeps a record of the cooperators which lists the cooperators and their capital, with specification of the kinds of shares that they hold.

3.4.4. *The Members' Rights on Capital*

In French law, there is no contribution to capital other than shares and cooperative certificates. The rights of their holders depend, therefore, on the classes of rights. Political power is strictly connected to membership, that is to say, to A-shares. Only information may be requested by other holders.[293] In regard to financial rights, shareholders have no right because payment of interest as distribution of the cooperative refund is conditioned to a decision taken by the annual members' meeting. In principle, a member is allowed to withdraw at any time and, in this case, is redeemed of his/her shares. The principle for

290 See section 3.3.1.
291 See section 3.7.
292 C.rur., art. R.522-2.
293 See section 2.3.3.

redemption is the nominal value of the shares fixed in the statutes.[294] The rule has been contested as too rigorous, especially in the case of inflation. In its general attempt to make cooperative investment more attractive, the 1992 reform therefore mitigated the provision by introducing the option for cooperatives to create a special divisible reserve[295] on which outgoing members have rights. This new right has two limits: first, it benefits only a member whose membership has lasted at least five years; second, the added value may not be higher than the rise applicable to a life annuity. Other mechanisms may indirectly increase the rights of members in the case of termination of membership, such as the incorporation of reserves in capital, or the distribution of cooperative refund by the creation of shares.[296] It can be only added that a member is allowed, under the same conditions as for withdrawal, to ask for the redemption of some of his/her shares.[297] This option may even be more open, since it does not imply the termination of membership. Therefore, limits to that termination do not apply. This option is only conditioned by the control on the reduction of capital.[298]

In regard to the holders of special shares or cooperative certificates, these may hold rights, either to preference over ordinary shareholders, or to positive or negative benefits as defined in the issuance agreement.

Agricultural cooperatives law contains an original provision. When such cooperatives have subsidiaries (which they control or not), they may distribute the dividends that they receive, fully or partly, to their members.[299] The distribution may constitute the special benefits of shares defined by the 1947 Law article 11. In this case, these special benefit shares can have been issued as such or derive from a conversion of ordinary shares subscribed by a cooperator in addition to its obligation. The benefit for members is subject to two limits: first, dividends are attributed in priority to compensate losses of the cooperative if there are any; second, the benefit for members may not be higher than 2% more than the general limit for interest to shares.[300]

3.4.5. *Cooperative and Cooperator Liability*

The liability of cooperative members does not differ from the one of shareholders in companies. The members' liability depends on the kind of company; and for the three most common kinds, liability is limited to the subscribed capital. In other kinds of companies, such as civil companies, liability is in principle

294 L. no. 47-1775 of the 10th of September 1947, art. 18.
295 See section 3.5.
296 See section 3.6.
297 C.com., art. L.231-1.
298 See section 3.2.2.
299 C.rur., art. L.523-5-1.
300 See section 3.6.

unlimited. However, either special laws restrict that liability[301] or the statutes may define the liability of members.[302] Reference to the statutory provisions to define the liability of members is absolutely derogatory of any rule, and it may be questioned, with regard to the protection of third parties, since no publicity is provided for them except through the company register.

In practice, in the case of bankruptcy of a cooperative, the members will not be reimbursed for their shares because they will cover the losses. Even if there is no bankruptcy of the cooperative, the members may suffer consequences from the cooperative's losses. They may do so firstly if membership is terminated, but sometimes even before. When membership terminates, the consequence may be that, if there is a loss on the cooperative's annual accounting, the reimbursement of its shares will be reduced proportionately to the losses.[303] However, the statutes may provide that these losses are primarily compensated by an incorporation of divisible reserves. Losses do not affect only members whose membership terminates because they must be compensated provided that members want to avoid wind-up. Whilst general cooperative law does not distinguish among losses, some special laws do, depending on their origin, related or not to cooperative transactions.[304] The former are, in principle, distributed among cooperators in proportion to their cooperative transactions, (art. 24) whereas losses from transactions with non-members are in priority compensated by the reserve supplied with profits from these transactions with non-members (art. 25). This point is closely connected with the status of the diverse reserves, and the absence of general rules makes it difficult to find common provisions for the compensation of losses. Finally, more generally, even after termination of membership, the liability of the member may remain, for five years, for the debts existing at the time of the termination.[305]

3.5. RESERVES

All companies must allocate part of their profits to reserves, but the importance and the nature of these reserves are different for cooperatives. Obviously, this particular regulation is connected to the specificity of capital itself.[306] General cooperative law provides that the cooperative shall allocate 15% of its surpluses to a compulsory reserve, named 'legal reserve'.[307] This allocation is compulsory

[301] For example, for fishing cooperatives, ten times the amount of subscribed capital: C.rur., art. L.931-14.
[302] L. no. 47-1775 of the 10th of September 1947, art. 7.
[303] L. no. 47-1775 of the 10th of September 1947, art. 18 al. 3.
[304] L. no. 83-657 of the 20th of July 1983, arts. 24 and 25.
[305] C.com., art. L.231-6.
[306] See above section 3.2.1.
[307] L. no. 47-1775 of the 10th of September 1947, art. 16.

unless the reserve is equal to or higher than the share capital. This obligation may be completed by the statute, and even when it goes further than the limit and is no longer compulsory, it is not forbidden to maintain the annual allocation. The more hesitation there is about the function of share capital as guarantee for creditors, the more this function is attributed to the legal reserves. The regulations on craft cooperatives even state it explicitly.[308]

Special laws provide specifications. They usually do not derogate concerning the amount of the reserves except in the case of collective interest cooperatives. For these latter, the allocation to the legal reserves is, as a whole, 57.5% of their surpluses.[309] Conversely, other laws set a ceiling, as in the case of craft cooperatives.[310] Moreover, workers' cooperatives benefit from a tax deduction on the sum allocated to the legal reserves.[311] This provision is derogatory and does not refer to a general favour by tax law for cooperative reserves because of their indivisibility. The provision for workers' cooperatives is the outcome of successful lobbying by the workers' cooperative organisation to integrate this allocation to reserves into the tax favour for the contribution by enterprises to the constitution of funds for employees. Because of that tax advantage, workers' cooperatives usually attribute to the legal reserves the maximum amount allowed, that is, one-third of their surpluses.[312]

The general cooperative law does not distinguish between the various legal reserves, even if the wording uses the plural, meaning that the cooperative may create several reserves. Some special cooperative laws are more precise. However, none of them provides for a reserve dedicated to education and training; that possible purpose is not even mentioned. Among the specifications established, the most common concerns the reserve supplied with profits from the transactions with non-members. The agricultural cooperative legislation is particularly significant, since it provides for many reserves, and it thus becomes unclear – revaluing the balance sheet reserve,[313] special indivisible reserve,[314] legal reserve[315] – and article L.523-2-1 refers to at least five reserves or categories of reserves. This does not mean that all these reserves differ, because they are sometimes defined by their content or their regime; but it certainly demonstrates that there is no clear thinking on the detailed functioning of reserves and their role.

308 L. no. 83-657 of the 20th of July 1983, art. 23.
309 L. no. 47-1775 of the 10th of September 1947, art. 19*nonies*.
310 L. no. 83-657 of the 20th of July 1983, art. 23.
311 CGI, art. 237*bis* A.
312 L. no. 78-763 of the 19th of July 1978, art. 33.
313 C.rur., art. L.523-7 al. 1.
314 C.rur., art. L.523-7 al. 2. C.rur., art. L.522-5 al. 3. It is unclear if these two reserves are only one.
315 C.rur., art. L.523-2.

One special reserve must be mentioned, since it is provided for in the general cooperative law.[316] Since 1992, that provision has allowed cooperatives to create a reserve to be distributed among the cooperators who leave the cooperative (withdrawal or expulsion). The right of each member in that reserve, when so stated, is proportionate to his/her contribution to the capital. Nevertheless, it is limited through reference to an official index.[317] Moreover, only members of the cooperative for at least five years have this right. This reserve is not compulsory and its allocation is additional to the allocation to the legal reserve. The creation of this reserve must be provided for in the statutes, which is only allowed if they do not provide for the possible incorporation of reserve in the capital (see below). In practice, this reserve is rare, principally since the incorporation of reserves is more attractive.

The destination of the reserves is not regulated Therefore, in the silence of the law, this destination is free; the only limit concerns its indivisibility. The destination is decided by the board of directors. Some special laws provide restrictions.

First, some special laws stipulate the autonomy of the reserves supplied with the profits from transactions with non-members. This is notably the case of farmers' cooperatives[318] and craft cooperatives.[319] It means that these reserves cannot be used, at least at first, to compensate the losses due to transactions with members. Whereas the Rural Code details the reserves that must be used to compensate them, the 1983 law states that, if these losses cannot be compensated by the legal reserve (designated as indivisible account) they must be immediately divided among members. If they not, they must be either compensated by the capital or postponed to the next financial year. However, it must be noted that no provision of the general law imposes such restrictions, so that these two pieces of legislation appear to be derogatory.

The reserves are indivisible and therefore cannot be distributed to the members, with the exception of the special reserve. This rule had no derogation until 1992, and remains a very strong principle. Besides its traditional place in the general cooperative law,[320] it is now highlighted by the reference in article 1. This provision is more explicit on the meaning of the rule, since it states its purpose: the development of the cooperative and of its members.[321] Moreover, the indivisibility of reserves is considered to be a general feature of social and solidarity economy enterprises, and so is the priority attribution of profits to the

316 L. no. 47-1775 of the 10th of September 1947, art. 18 al. 2.

317 The life annuity, stated by the Ministry for the Economy. It was about 2 or 3%; it is 0.1% for 2016.

318 C.rur., art. L.522-5 al. 3.

319 L. no. 83-657 of the 20th of July 1983, art. 25.

320 L. no. 47-1775 of the 10th of September 1947, art. 16.

321 L. no. 47-1775 of the 10th of September 1947, art. 1.

development of the enterprise.[322] Therefore, it is a condition for a company to be registered as a social and solidarity economy enterprise.[323]

The indivisibility of reserves is stipulated both during the life of the cooperative and at the time of its winding-up. A special solution is provided when the cooperative is converted into a company, a mechanism strictly regulated by the general cooperative law.[324] In this case, the indivisible reserves of the cooperative are allocated to a special reserve of the company, which is itself indivisible for ten years. The purpose of this rule is to deter conversion into a company in order to distribute the reserves among the members. The rule is stricter for workers' cooperatives, for which, in the case of conversion, the cooperative's reserves remain definitely indivisible.[325]

An indirect derogation to the indivisibility was introduced into the general cooperative law in 1992.[326] This article allows the statutes to envisage the possibility of incorporating a part of the reserve into the capital. This new capital has no special nature; nor is it subject to special rules. This increase of the capital implies the issuance of new shares, distributed to the members in proportion to their contribution to the capital, or an increase of the nominal value of each share. Therefore, the increase of capital benefits the members, who will receive the redemption of their shares when leaving the cooperative. Nevertheless, the incorporation is limited by the law. First, this is only possible if provided for in the statutes. Secondly, the decision must be taken by the members' meeting. Thirdly, its amount is limited. The first incorporation may not be more than half of the reserves existing at the end of the financial year before the members' meeting. Subsequent incorporations may not be more than half of the additional amount of the reserves since the last incorporation. Finally, to be noted is that the choice, by the statutes, to allow the incorporation precludes some other mechanisms, such as the creation of a divisible reserve (see above), or the issuance of cooperative certificates.[327]

3.6. SURPLUSES

The general cooperative law does not provide any definition of surpluses. Some special laws are more precise, but their concrete provisions differ from one to another. For craft cooperatives, it is stated that the credit balance of the

---

322 L. no. 2014-856 of the 31st of July 2014, art. 1 I.

323 L. no. 2014-856 of the 31st of July 2014, art. 1 II.

324 L. no. 47-1775 of the 10th of September 1947, art. 25.

325 L. 78-763 of the 19th of July 1978, art. 3*bis*.

326 L. no. 47-1775 of the 10th of September 1947, art. 16 als. 3 and 4.

327 L. no. 47-1775 of the 10th of September 1947, art. 19*tervicies*. That provision is specific to members' cooperative certificates, and it is debated whether it should be extended to the cooperative investment certificates: D. Hiez, 'Certificats coopératifs', *Encycl. Dalloz, rép. Sociétés*, Paris, 2015, nos. 31, 32.

annual accounting, decreased by the delayed losses, are the net surpluses.[328] For workers' cooperatives, they are defined as the net revenue of the financial year minus the overhead expenses and loads of the year, including amortisation and provisions.[329] The differences are not significant, but they illustrate the lack of conceptualisation in cooperative law. The only unanimous opinion concerns the opposition between surpluses and profits, and, indeed, the cooperative law never refers to profits. The distinction has been thoroughly discussed by the French thinker on cooperation, Charles Gide,[330] and it has become the common opinion. Even if profits are not pursued as such, when they exist, it is necessary to state their allocation. As for companies, this is a decision taken by the members' meeting.[331]

The general cooperative law provides some indications;[332] it enumerates the possible allocations, but does not explicitly state their order: reserve fund, interest on shares, cooperative refund, divisible reserve, and subsidy. The first allocation is to the legal reserve, since the law makes it compulsory and states its conditions and extent.[333] It is unclear if the distribution of cooperative refund comes next, or the distribution of interest on shares. General cooperative law refers only to the applicable provisions of the law and, naturally, in their numerical order, so that it does not seem meaningful. If one looks at special cooperative laws, they are not unanimous: for instance, workers' cooperative legislation evokes the cooperative refund before the interest on shares,[334] whereas in the case of farmers' cooperatives a law provides the exact opposite.[335] Indeed, the law usually does not make the order of distribution compulsory; but when it is not silent, it only provides the order of the decisions taken by the members' meeting. Only the allocation to reserves is compulsory. The distribution of interest to shares, as well as the distribution of cooperative refund, is optional, if not otherwise provided in the statutes.

Although the cooperative refund is very important in cooperative thinking (see above 1.2.2), there are relatively few details on its functioning. Therefore, it is mainly up to the statutes to define its conditions. Only the workers' cooperative regulation make its distribution compulsory, for at least 25% of the net surpluses,[336] whereas it is forbidden for general interest cooperatives.[337]

---

328 L. no. 83-657 of the 20th of July 1983, art. 22.
329 L. no. 78-763 of the 19th of July 1978, art. 32.
330 Ch. Gide, n. 65 above.
331 C.rur., art. L.524-2-1.
332 L. no. 47-1775 of the 10th of July 1947, art. 16.
333 See above section 3.5.
334 L. no. 78-763 of the 19th of July 1978, art. 33.
335 C.rur., art. L.524-2-1.
336 L. no. 78-763 of the 19th of July 1978, art. 33 al. 3. See above section 1.3 for the detailed conditions.
337 L. no. 47-1775 of the 10th of September 1947, art. 19*nonies* al. 4.

In French law, the cooperator is not entitled to any cooperative refund. It depends entirely on the decision taken by the members' meeting. Statutory provisions may grant a right to the cooperators, but they must then specify the limits of the mechanism.

Some special laws lay down a special procedure for the attribution of cooperative refunds. For craft cooperatives, for example, if cooperative refunds are allocated, the members' meeting may decide to allocate them not in money but in shares.[338] The attractiveness of the mechanism is that the members receive an advantage and, in the meantime, the cooperative distributes no cash.

The distribution of interest to the shareholders is more detailed. The basic provision is article 14 of the 1947 Law, which sets a limitation on this interest: it shall not be higher than the average rate of return on private company bonds ('taux moyen de rendement des obligations des sociétés privées': TMO).[339] This rate is stated by the Ministry of Economy, and depends on the economic situation. For several years, it was about 4% per year, but it has decreased in recent years and was about 2% in 2015. The principle of the restriction is the main reason to distinguish it from dividends. In fact, the distribution of interest is not a right for members, and statutes may even forbid it. However, this can also be considered a minimum remuneration for the available capital. The general cooperative allows, in the event of insufficient results for a financial year, the deduction of the monies required to complete the interest provided for by the statutes, either from the reserve funds, or from the results of subsequent financial years, without, however, going beyond the fourth subsequent ones.[340] The restriction of remuneration makes investment in cooperative capital not very attractive, which is why the 1992 reform created new shares. The continuous decrease in the average rate of return on private company bonds made the situation unsustainable for cooperatives. An amendment to article 14, allowing the attribution of two points more than the TMO, was voted by the parliament at the end of 2015, but it has been considered illegal by the constitutional court, for procedural reasons. An analogous provision has been adopted.[341]

To be noted is the particularity of workers' cooperatives. Indeed, their legislation explicitly excludes application of the maximum rate stated in the general cooperative law.[342] Instead, these special laws provide for a double proportionate maximum: the money allocated to the legal reserves, and the money distributed as cooperative refunds. Therefore, in practice, principally

[338] L. no. 83-657 of the 20th of July 1983, art. 26.

[339] L. no. 47-1775 of the 10th of September 1947, art. 14. In French cooperative law, this rate is better known as the TMO.

[340] L. no. 47-1775 of the 10th of September 1947, art. 17.

[341] L. no. 2016-1691 of the 9th of December 2016 – art. 113, which has amended art. 14 of L. no. 47-1775 of 10th of September 1947.

[342] L. no. 78-763 of the 19th of July 1978, art. 33 al. 4.

because of the fiscal incentive to maximise the allocation to the reserves, the remuneration of capital is usually, in workers' cooperatives, 33% of surpluses. First, this may be far more than the interests distributed in other cooperatives. Secondly, the proportion established between the interest and surplus makes the mechanism comparable to dividends. This qualification is sometimes debated, even if there is no concrete consequence.[343]

General cooperative law provides for the use of the remainder, if the previous allocations have not exhausted the surpluses.[344] The cooperative has two options: either allocation to a reserve, or attribution in the form of a subsidy, either to other cooperatives or unions of cooperatives, or to works of public or professional interest. This ensures the disinterested principle of cooperative functioning, since no distribution among members is possible, except the restricted legal provisions.

3.7. DISSOLUTION AND LIQUIDATION

There is no specific rule on dissolution in cooperative law except on the allocation of the net assets. Therefore, the applicable regulation is company law. Even farmers' cooperative law, usually more complete, provides for no additional precision. There are no specificities on causes of dissolution, nor about the applicable procedure. The only particularity comes from the variable capital regulation: whatever the form of the cooperative, the bankruptcy of one of its members cannot entail dissolution of the cooperative.[345] The most common cause of winding-up is the bankruptcy of the cooperative itself; the decision of members and nullity of the cooperative are far less frequent causes. In the case of bankruptcy, the procedure is conducted before a judge, and the liquidator must be a person enrolled in the controlled profession of judicial liquidator. In the case of a liquidation decided by the members of the cooperative, there are no special rules. The only restrictions on being a designated liquidator are the prohibition for persons who have been sentenced and can no longer be director of a company.

The only cooperative rules on winding-up deal with the net assets. These net assets are defined, implicitly, as the assets remaining after clearance of the liabilities and redemption of the paid up capital. This definition complies fully with cooperative principles. No distribution is allowed among members, and the assets are attributed either to another cooperative or to a social and solidarity economy enterprise.[346]

343 D. Hiez, n. 7 above, no. 123.15.

344 L. no. 47-1775 of the 10th of September 1947, art. 15.

345 C.com., art. L.231-8.

346 L. no.47-1775 of the 10th of September 1947, art. 19.

Very few specifications are provided by special laws. The main derogation concerns the merchant cooperatives.[347] The Minister of Commerce may allow these to distribute the net assets among their members. For a merchants' cooperative whose social object is to run the common administration of a commercial zone, in the conditions regulated in articles L.125-1 and by the Commercial Code, that distribution among members is even the rule.

4. EXTERNAL CONTROL

4.1. INTRODUCTION

Cooperative audit[348] has developed in French law in different ways according to the type of cooperative type. There used to be almost no common rule on the circumstances in which audit was required, its consequences, or the status of the auditor, not even with regard to the necessity to carry out auditing. These differences can be explained by history, sometimes also because of the particular nature of the cooperative's activities. In the meantime, even if the cooperative audit was considered a support for the cooperative's development, its proximity to other mechanisms of control was highlighted. Moreover, the object of the audit was unclear, since there were very few provisions in the general cooperative law, and the provisions of special cooperative laws were various. In the 1980s, a first attempt was made to create a general legal regime,[349] but the outcome was not very convincing.

One of the major points of the 2014 reform of cooperative law dealt with the cooperative audit.[350] Full regulation was introduced into the general cooperative law.[351] Several points remain unclear, but, now, there is a general regime. It is too early to draw any conclusion on the consequences of the reform, but at least it provides more coherence.

4.2. EXTERNAL AUDIT AND COOPERATIVE AUDIT

4.2.1. General Financial Audit

By principle, French law provides the obligation to carry out an external audit, the substance of which is financial, as imposed by European law. First, every

347 C.com., art. L.124-14.

348 Designated as '*révision*' in French law.

349 D. no. 84-1024 of the 23rd of November 1984 on the cooperative auditing procedure for some categories of cooperatives.

350 L. no. 2014-856 of the 31st of July 2014, art. 25 I 3°.

351 L. no. 47-1775 of the 10th of September 1947, arts. 25-1 ff.; D. no. 2015-706 of the 22nd of June 2015; D. no. 2015-800 of the 1st of July 2015.

enterprise must publish its accounts, with third parties allowed to access them.[352] Only some enterprises, depending on their size and/or their legal type, must carry out a financial audit by a statutory auditor. This general rule applies also to cooperatives. All public limited companies must carry out a financial audit, whereas only limited liability companies do so when they exceed some thresholds.[353] Therefore, there is a difference between the cooperatives which must nominate a statutory auditor and others; and this may impact on the role of the cooperative audit.

4.2.2. *Financial Audit and Cooperative Audit*

Strictly speaking, cooperative audit exists only during the cooperative's life; it is termed 'révision'. Until 2014, most cooperatives were subject to the cooperative audit, except for banking cooperatives and merchants' cooperatives, as well as cooperative established under the single 1947-law, because that 1947-law contained no provision about it. The object of the cooperative audit was very ambiguous, since two different, if not opposite, purposes were provided for.

Most special cooperative laws, which provided for such an audit, defined it as the analytical study of the financial situation and the management ('gestion') of the cooperative. Note that the French word 'gestion', which is translated by 'management', refers to the financial dimension, not to the cooperative's features proper. Nevertheless, the regulation of this audit, provided by *décret* no. 84-1027 of the 23rd of November 1984, was more comprehensive. Its article 1 defined the cooperative audit as the critical and analytical study of the situation and functioning of the cooperative, based on its annual accounts, and considering the cooperative's specific features. The accounts are no longer the object of the control but only its basis. The second paragraph of the same article specifies the frame by stating the purpose of the audit: to verify compliance with cooperative principles, and especially to assess the participation of members in the cooperative's transactions and management. The Rural Code has been even more precise for agricultural cooperatives since 2006. It now defines the audit as control of compliance of their situation and functioning with cooperative rules.[354] The terminology is not fully different but it does not refer at all to the financial aspects. That precision is the consequence of the clear distinction, provided for today, between the financial audit, regulated for agricultural cooperatives with some derogation to other enterprises, notably the authorisation for special cooperative federations to achieve the financial audit itself, and the cooperative audit.

---

352 Some derogations are stated, however, for micro-enterprises: see above section 3.2.3.

353 C.com., art. L.223-35.

354 C.rur., art. L.527-1.

The regulation completely changed in 2014 because introduced into the general cooperative law was a provision which sought to cover the entire range of cooperatives. Whilst it does not provide an explicit definition of the cooperative audit, it serves its purpose: to verify compliance by the organisation and functioning of cooperatives with cooperative principles and rules and with members' interest, as well as with applicable special cooperative regulations, and, if useful, to propose corrections.[355] Therefore, any financial consideration has been removed and the scope is now purely cooperative. The provisions of the decree of 1984 are implicitly abrogated, and, if they are still in force, the provisions of the Rural Code are no longer derogations but only specific modalities.

Some other types of control may occur before the creation of the cooperative, especially when the registration requires official assent. These are not cooperative audit as such, but they have several features in common with it.

4.2.3. Assent for Creation and Cooperative Audit

Audits before registration do not exist as such in company law, so this cannot be applicable to cooperatives either. The only control concerns evaluation of contributions in kind, for which a special auditor may be required. But this is not a general audit. The only general control concerns the very formal compliance with statutes.

Cooperative law does not provide for any audit as such before registration. However, some special cooperatives have to fulfil conditions to be registered as a cooperative. It is stated thus for farmers' cooperatives,[356] fishing cooperatives[357] and workers' cooperatives.[358] Assent was required for the registration of a collective interest cooperative before its registration as a cooperative, but this requirement was abrogated in 2012.[359] Indeed, it was argued that the requirement of an assent, because of its complexity and the risk of not being renewed after five years, was one of the reasons for the small number of these cooperatives created.

In these cases, there is no external audit as such, and its procedure is not regulated. The law specifies only the documents to be provided to the registering body. They are the statutes, the activity of the cooperative, the identities of the members of the board, and some details on the social capital and the value and

355 L. no. 47-1775 of the 10th of September 1947, art. 25-1 al. 1.
356 C.rur., art. L.525-1 and R.525-1 ff.
357 C.rur., art. L.931-11 C.rur. and decree no. 87-368 of the 1st of June 1987 on the assent and control of fishing cooperatives.
358 L. no. 78-763 of the 19th of July 1978, art. 54, and decree no. 93-1231 of the 10th of November 1993 on the recognition of the status of workers' cooperative.
359 See above section 1.2.1.2. The assent was given by the prefect, who determined whether the cooperative pursued social utility.

number of shares. Information concerning the existing subsidiaries must also be provided.

In the case of workers' cooperatives, some additional information is required:[360] the number of shareholders employed in the cooperative[361] and the number of shares that they hold; the number of shares and the identity of the shareholder with the highest number of shares; a list of non-cooperator members, their identities and the number of shares that they hold and their voting rights.

In farmers' cooperatives, the cooperative must provide the list of co-operators and the qualities which entitle them to be such. But here the control is far more important, perhaps because the assent, given by the cooperative movement itself, resembles a cooperativism certificate. Therefore, the cooperative candidate provides two more documents: a report explaining the economic, social and territorial interest of the project, and a certificate provided by a federation competent for the cooperative audit assessing the compliance of the statutes with law, regulation and cooperative principles.[362]

The number and the nature of the documents required can only be understood by considering the purpose of the control. This depends on the special cooperative laws. For farmers' cooperatives, article L.525-1 of the Rural Code states that the registering body must assess compliance with the ratified statutes, as well as with cooperative rules and principles, but also coherence between the project and the economic context. The latter element is very important, since it confers on the registering authority the power to decide on the opportunity of the project.

The other special cooperative laws do not provide such details, and it must be concluded that the control is, therefore, only formal.

Another point must be discussed, because the assent comes after registration on companies' registries: the consequence of the refusal of assent. Indeed, legal personality is conferred by that registration, so that the assent or its refusal has no effect on it.

However, refusal of the assent certainly forbids use of the name of cooperative or, at least, of the special cooperative regulated by the special law. It also deprives the cooperative enterprise of the existing legal benefits, notably from tax law. Nevertheless, the Cour de Cassation has stated, concerning workers' cooperatives, that the status of the director remains regulated by the workers' cooperative legislation.[363] In other words, if, despite the absence of assent, the cooperative carries out its activities, the absence of assent cannot bring any losses to third parties; cooperators are not likely to be considered as third parties.

360 D. no. 93-1231 of the 10th of November 1993, art. 2.

361 Recall that, in workers' cooperatives, there is no rule on exclusivism.

362 C.rur., art. R.525-3.

363 Cass. Soc., 23 September 1992, no. 90-40002, inédit (not published in the Bulletin des arrêts des chambres civiles de la Cour de Cassation).

More specific controls exist because of the follow-up by the registering body. The clearest concerns workers' cooperatives, for which registration on a list established by the Ministry of Labour can be revised each year. For that purpose, the workers' cooperative must provide annual information: first, an update of the information that it provided for the registration, and then the annual accounts and the cooperative audit report every five years.[364] It must also provide information on the distribution of surpluses, and, if any, its subsidiaries. The mechanism is more flexible for agricultural cooperatives. No periodic information must be provided, but the registering body may, at any time, require a control, which can conclude with disqualification of the registration.

4.3. THE CONDITIONS FOR COOPERATIVE AUDIT

The main new provision is the obligation to conduct a cooperative audit for all cooperatives. It used to be considered an obligation specific to some cooperative families, whereas it now appears like a cooperative specificity, with particular consequences for all cooperatives.[365] However, some cooperatives are exempted from the obligation. In practice, the general rule is that the cooperative audit is compulsory only for some cooperatives, by reference to some thresholds, but some special laws provide for a wider obligation. The thresholds for which a cooperative audit is optional, but otherwise provided by the statutes, concern the activity of the cooperative, and consist in the full balance sheet, pre-tax revenue, the number of employees or members.[366] The decree states that the thresholds are two cooperative members and 30,000 euros of pre-tax revenue,[367] but it provides special thresholds for most cooperatives: agricultural cooperatives,[368] merchants' cooperatives,[369] banking cooperatives,[370] consumer cooperatives.[371] For some special cooperatives, the cooperative audit is compulsory, whatever their size: general interest cooperatives,[372] craft cooperatives,[373] housing cooperatives.[374] The regulation is somewhat more complex for workers' cooperatives; they are subject to the general principle, without any concrete threshold, but exempted if, being a limited liability company or a simplified stock company, they are

364 D. no. 93-1231 of the 10th of November 1993, art. 4.
365 See section 4.5.
366 L. no. 47-1775 of the 10th of September 1947, art. 25-1 al. 2.
367 D. no. 2015-800 of the 1st of July 2015, art. 1.
368 C.rur., art. R.525-9-1.
369 C.com., art. R.124-1.
370 C.mon.fin., art. R.512-1.
371 D. no. 2015-800 of the 1st of July 2015, art. 5.
372 L. no. 47-1775 of the 10th of September 1947, art. 19*duodecies*.
373 L. no. 83-657 of the 20th of July 1983, art. 29.
374 C.const.hab., art. L.422-3.

subject to other thresholds and have to designate a statutory auditor.[375] This is confusing, since cooperative audit and audit by a statutory auditor do not pursue the same goal.

The cooperative audit must be conducted, in principle, each five years, provided that the statutes do not require a shorter term.[376]

Apart from this cooperative audit, public bodies perform a general control. The cooperatives must provide, on the request of their dedicated ministry, all justifications that facilitate the control of the compliance of their functioning with the law.[377] These justifications mainly designate their accounts, but also any other useful document. The provision of wrong information is an offence committed by the managers of the cooperative. This rule is specific to cooperatives, and it is related to the special relation between them and the state, a mixture of mistrust and additional control because of their special advantages.

Besides the periodic audit, some occurrences require additional cooperative audits. First, a cooperative audit is compulsory if the cooperative is in deficit for three consecutive years, as well as if in one year the losses are more than half of the maximum amount reached by the capital since the creation of the cooperative.[378] Secondly, the cooperative audit may be required by one-tenth of members, one-third of the administration board or the supervisory board members, the registering body, and the Ministry for Social and Solidarity Economy.[379] Some special laws require additional cooperative audit. For instance, the agricultural cooperative legislation does so in two main situations. Two occurrences require the external audit: first, deciding on the incorporation of reserves into the capital;[380] secondly, preparing for a merger.[381] Indirectly, the workers' cooperative regulation requires such an audit when a cooperative wants to convert into a company.[382]

4.4. THE COOPERATIVE AUDITING PROCEDURE

The cooperative law does not provide many details about the procedure; the decree does to some extent. The general cooperative law states that the president of the court may require designation of the auditor by the manager of the cooperative, under penalty.[383] One may conclude that the auditor is designated

375 C.com., Art. L.221-9 and R.221-5.
376 L. no. 47-1775 of the 10th of September 1947, art. 25-1.
377 L. no. 47-1775 of the 10th of September 1947, art. 23.
378 L. no. 47-1775 of the 10th of September 1947, art. 25-1 al. 3.
379 L. no. 47-1775 of the 10th of September 1947, art. 25-1 als. 4-8.
380 C.rur., art. L.523-1.
381 C.rur., art. L.526-4.
382 D. no. 93-1231 of the 10th of 1993, art. 5.
383 L. no. 47-1775 of the 10th of September 1947, art. 25-2.

by the manager or the board, and not by the members' meeting. This is indirectly confirmed for agricultural cooperatives, since, in the case of merger, the auditor is designated by a common decision taken by all the boards.[384] However, the general rule provided by the decree is designation by the members' meeting;[385] the importance of the choice of the auditor justifies this solution.

The content of the audit is determined by its purpose. It consists in the critical and analytical examination of the cooperative's organisation and functioning with regard to cooperative principles as defined by the 1947 Law, and to applicable special cooperative rules, as well as with regard to analogous enterprises.[386] In order to allow the auditor to achieve his/her mission,the same article obliges the cooperative to communicate all documents necessary for the examination.

The outcome of the audit is the drafting of a report, whose content is determined by the decree.[387] Generally speaking, the report takes the specificities of the cooperative into consideration.[388] More precisely, the report contains: a description of the development and methodology of the audit, a justified opinion on the compliance of the cooperative and, if the report concludes to the non-compliance, proposals for corrections and, if necessary, an order to comply. In the end, the law provides only that the audit report be addressed to the organs of administration and management, and to the central managing body for banking cooperatives.[389] Moreover, it is accessible to all the members and debated in the members' meeting.

4.5. THE CONSEQUENCES OF COOPERATIVE AUDIT

The new provisions pay more attention to the follow-up on the audit. It seems that the legislature feared that the audit was not useful in and of itself, and that it tried to attribute positive consequences to it, through a complex procedure, if the auditor concludes that the cooperative does not comply with cooperative principles and rules and with members' interest, as well as with applicable special cooperative regulations.[390] In this case, s/he may order the cooperative to comply. S/he transfers the proposal received from the cooperative as s/he did for his/her report. If s/he does not receive a significant answer, s/he submits the question to a higher cooperative organisation and, if insufficient, to the court, or to the registering body, the Ministry for Social and Solidarity Economy or

384 C.rur., art. R.526-8.
385 D. no. 2015-706 of the 22nd of June 2015, art. 10.
386 D. no. 2015-706 of the 22nd of June 2015, art. 11.
387 D. no. 2015-706 of the 22nd of June 2015, art. 12.
388 Legal form, size, organisation, activity, special regulation.
389 L. no. 47-1775 of the 10th of September 1947, art. 25-3.
390 L. no. 47-1775 of the 10th of September 1947, arts. 25-3 and 25-4.

the Ministry for the specific cooperative. These three latter bodies are entitled to order the compliance and, if there are no answers within one month, to call an extraordinary members' meeting, which will make the requisite decisions. In the end, if an appropriate functioning is not restored, dissolution may be pronounced. Undoubtedly, the legislature has sought to establish a balance between the autonomy of cooperatives and the necessary public control, but the outcome is far too unclear.

A second outcome has been established for the auto-operative audit, in relation to the inclusion of cooperatives among social and solidarity economy enterprises. For all these enterprises, a guide on good practice shall be adopted by the social and solidarity economy high council, and the members' meetings of all of them will debate on compliance of their enterprise with the guide each year.[391] This has been introduced to try to fill the gap observed between law and practice. And, cleverly, cooperatives have managed to replace that obligation with the mechanism of cooperative audit.[392] The solution is coherent and will exempt cooperatives from being subject to two procedures whose purposes are partly similar.

4.6. THE COOPERATIVE AUDITOR

The general cooperative law does not provide many details, nor do special laws. The recent decree,[393] however, tries to give full regulation of this status, so that I will mainly refer to it in this section.

4.6.1. The Selection of the Auditor

The auditors are natural or legal persons selected by the Ministry for Social and Solidarity Economy for a five-year term, after the cooperation high council's advice, and enrolled on a list accessible through a website (art. 3). They must demonstrate their honesty and their competence (art. 1). This latter consists in three years of experience in cooperative law, economics, finance and management, although persons who have been the representative of a cooperative for two consecutive years are exempted from demonstrating their competence (art. 2 II). The required documents are listed (art. 2) and the procedure is fixed (art. 3). To be noted is that the assent may be attributed to a legal person, provided that it demonstrates its honesty, and the honesty and competence of the natural person that will conduct the audit on its behalf. An indirect control is regulated because, in the case of infringement of cooperative principles and rules or other conditions for assent, the ministry may remove its assent (art. 4).

391 L. no. 2014-856 of the 31st of July 2014, art. 3.
392 L. no. 47-1775 of the 10th of September 1947, art. 25-1 al. 2.
393 D. no. 2015-706 of the 22nd of June 2015.

4.6.2. *The Independence of Auditors*

The independence of auditors is probably the core concern of the legislature, since it is the only point about auditors mentioned in the law; no doubt it has been inspired by the regulation on the statutory auditor. The new legislative provisions do not specify the scope of the independence, but it refers to the decree to ensure that independence. To be noted is that, before the new law, that point was not mentioned. However, some provisions aimed at its achievement, such as the involvement, for the nomination of an auditor, of an independent commission to advise the ministry; removed with many other commissions, it no longer exists. Today, independence is mainly considered by reference to the audited cooperatives. First, it means incompatibilities for the position of auditor:[394] prohibition of the auditor and the natural persons performing the audit on behalf of an auditor legal person, as well as the managers of such a legal person, being manager, member, employee or remunerated service provider for the cooperative during five years after the audit; prohibition on any manager, member, employee or remunerated service provider for a cooperative being designated as auditor or natural person auditing on behalf of a legal person auditor for the cooperative during five years after the end of its relationship. When designated, the auditor must check this incompatibility.

During the audit, the decree provides for other guarantees of independence concerning termination of the audit. The most important is the prohibition of the cooperative terminating the contract when it appears that the auditor is likely to conclude non-compliance and warn the competent organs and bodies.[395] To ensure application of that provision, the decree defines the circumstances in which the auditor may him/herself terminate the contract: definitive termination of his/her professional activity, impelling personal motives such as health or conditions related to his/her independence or objectivity. In such cases, the auditor must submit a special report to the Ministry for Social and Solidarity Economy. Moreover, the audit is then performed by the supply auditor.[396]

The regulation of the independence of auditors is rather broad, and does not provide any guidance on the relationship between auditors and cooperative federations. It seems that auditors may be either fully autonomous from the cooperative organisations or connected with them. The regulation is different for agricultural cooperatives, since the Rural Code explicitly provides for an institutional relationship with cooperative organisations.

---

394 D. no. 2015-706 of the 22nd of June 2015, art. 6.

395 D. no. 2015-706 of the 22nd of June 2015, art. 8.

396 The supply auditor is designated by the members' meeting at the same time and with the same conditions as the auditor him/herself.

The audit is performed by special cooperative federations, and all agricultural cooperatives must be members of one such federation.[397] This means that the financing of auditing federations comes primarily from the cooperatives themselves. However, attention is paid to the independence of the federation. First, to run a cooperative audit, a federation must be certified, through the National Cooperative Auditing Association, by the Minister of Agriculture.[398] This National Association is important because it prepares the rules on auditing and studies all applications to the federation to be auditors. Moreover, it initiates any inquiry that may lead to removal of the assent. The statutes of this association are validated by the Minister of Agriculture.

The structure and organisation of the federation certified to run audits are specially regulated. Firstly, the federation must have a two-tier management system.[399] The management board is only composed of auditors: that is to say, agricultural cooperatives (members) cannot be members. The supervisory board, which nominates the members of the management board, may only be composed of cooperatives that do not use the federation for the legal control of their accounts.[400] Indeed, these federations are competent to perform cooperative audits, but also legal control of accounts,[401] usually performed by the statutory auditor. By derogation to their general regulation, statutory auditors may be employees of an agricultural federation; in this case, they are not allowed to perform any legal control of accounts outside the federation.

The general regulation provides no guidance, although disputes have arisen because of the lack of transparency on the assent of auditors and the free choice of cooperatives. Indeed, a strong financial interest is at stake, notably for the cooperative federations. The agricultural cooperative organisations found equilibrium through recognition of the link between federations and auditors, and regulated it. Certainly, in other cooperatives, publication of the list of auditors on a website of the Ministry for Social and Solidarity Economy will be an improvement.

5. COOPERATION AMONG COOPERATIVES

5.1. INTRODUCTION

In the past, French cooperative law did not enumerate cooperative principles, so that there was no general provision for cooperation among cooperatives.

397 C.rur., art. L.527-1.
398 C.rur., art. R.527-4.
399 C.rur., art. L.527-1.
400 C.rur., art. L.527-1.
401 C.rur., art. L.527-1-1.

This has evolved with the law no.2014-856 of the 31st July 2014 on social and solidarity economy. It has included some principles in the general cooperative law, and one of them is cooperation with other cooperatives.[402] Nevertheless, regulations concerning organisations aimed at this cooperation have existed for a long time.[403] These groupings are primarily aimed at cooperation among cooperatives, but they also enable wider cooperation among social and solidarity economy enterprises.

Two more points are important and will be developed. The first concerns mergers. Like capitalist enterprises, cooperatives take part in the general restructuration process, notably through mergers. The possibility for cooperatives to merge was briefly discussed in the 1980s because there were no general provisions regulating that mechanism. The solution was to refer to company law,[404] since it is the applicable general law. Some special laws have specifically regulated the mechanism for special cooperatives, notably for agricultural cooperatives.[405]

The second point concerns the creation of subsidiaries. This is not related to the cooperation principle. However, it is a means which is used by cooperatives to create networks of enterprises and which raises specific difficulties. The regulation of these subsidiaries is related to most of the questions discussed in the previous sections, but it requires a synthetic approach.

5.2. COOPERATIVE UNION

Union among cooperatives is the technical tool with which to achieve inter-cooperation. It has been provided for in many special cooperative laws since the beginning of the twentieth century, and it was introduced into the general cooperative law in 1947.[406] Nevertheless, this general rule is duplicated by many special provisions dealing with specific cooperative unions. This complexity does not preclude the creation of unions whose members come from different cooperative families.[407] In practice, however, most unions are special unions, that is to say, with members from the same family.

Article 5 of the 1947 Law has been recently modified by the law on social and solidarity economy, but its general purpose and organisation remain similar. Despite the various questions involved, the provision is very brief and there is no case law to complete it. I will refer to provisions included in special cooperative

[402] L. no. 47-1775 of the 10th of September 1947, art. 1.
[403] See section 5.2.
[404] C.com., arts. L.236-1 ff.
[405] C.rur., arts. L.526-3 ff., introduced by ordinance 2006-1225 of the 5th of October 2006.
[406] L. no. 47-1775 of the 10th of September 1947, art. 5.
[407] See section 5.2.2.

laws to clarify the general features. Attention will be paid to a special grouping, dedicated to the political representation of cooperatives: the cooperation high council.

5.2.1. *The Objective of the Union*

The objective of the union is defined very briefly: it aims at the management of their common interests and the development of their activities.[408] Because of the speciality principle applicable to all groupings, which restrains the capacity of legal persons, discussion about the objective of the union deals mainly with the limits of that capacity. The new version of article 5, after the 2014 law on social and solidarity economy, has extended the objective of the union; previously, the management of common interests was the only possible objective. Also to be specified is that the development of members' activities was mentioned in several special laws, so that the addition to article 5 of the law of 1947 is rather a generalisation.

The first remark is that the union is fully targeted on its members, exactly like the primary cooperative itself. This appears in the letter of article 5, as well as through the cooperative nature of the union. Nevertheless, the situation differs, since the members of the union are themselves cooperatives, which means that their purpose is to provide services to their members. Therefore, in the end, the union must be fruitful for the primary cooperators.

To clarify the specific objective of the union, it may be compared to that of the economic interest grouping. The objective of this grouping is to facilitate or develop its members' activities.[409] This is not so different from the union's objective. The most important difference is in the next paragraph, which states that the economic interest grouping's activity must be related to its members' economic activities and be accessory to them. Such restrictions do not apply to cooperative unions, and this allows for a wider objective, also taking into account the reference to management of the common interests of the union's members.

Many special cooperative laws deal with unions, however they are named, and provide some specifications. This is particularly the case of cooperative banks, on which primary banks have lost part of their power attributed to the secondary one, i.e. the regional or national union. In regard to agricultural credit, for instance, the law distinguishes between local and regional agricultural banks, and attributes the conclusion of loans to the local ones.[410] Nevertheless, in practice, the decision to grant a loan is no longer taken at the local level.

408 L. no. 47-1775 of the 10th of September 1947, art. 5.
409 C.com., art. L.251-1.
410 C.mon.fin., arts. L.512-32 and L.512-33.

Moreover, because of general regulations on banks, the powers of the central managing body have become increasingly intrusive.

5.2.2. *The Membership of the Union*

5.2.2.1. Quality of Members

Prima facie, the members of unions are cooperatives, given that article 5 of the 1947 Law states that two cooperatives may create a union. Consequently, it is not possible for natural persons to join the cooperative. Even if the letter of article 5 mentions only the creation of a union, the objective of the latter does not favour any extension, so that no primary cooperator may join the union after its creation.

Nevertheless, the question is more complex in regard to investors. Article 5 of the 1947 Law does not deal with investors, but this also applies to many provisions of the 1947 Law, so that this silence is not very significant. Moreover, because unions are explicitly qualified as cooperatives, the cooperative law is applicable to them, provided that no special provision derogates. Therefore, article 3*bis* of the 1947 Law is applicable, and unions may welcome investors as members, within the limits defined by the general provision. These investors may be cooperatives, but also institutional investors, and even natural persons.

5.2.2.2. Multi-Purpose Unions

No other restriction is provided for in article 5 of the 1947 Law. Therefore, cooperatives may create a union regardless of their social object. In other words, the union may be multi-purpose, since cooperatives may have different objectives. Nevertheless, difficulties arise because of the provisions contained in the cooperative special laws. The Rural Code, for example, specifically regulates agricultural cooperative unions and defines their members as agricultural cooperatives.[411] Because agricultural cooperative unions are subject to a special regulation, such as accounting and more generally financial aspects, it could be argued that the creation of a generic union may evade these rules. Apart from that such a generic union cannot be qualified as an agricultural cooperative union, and provided that there is no fraud, I do not consider the mechanism invalid. However, this choice may have negative consequences: for example, for agricultural cooperative unions, the impossibility to profit from tax exemptions.

Another interesting example is provided by merchants' cooperatives, for which the law distinguishes different unions, notably the union of merchants'

[411] C.rur., art. L.521-1 al. 3.

cooperatives,[412] whose members may only be merchants' cooperatives. However, this confirms the possibility to include different types of cooperatives when the union does not use the title reserved to special unions. The same remarks can be extended to all the specially regulated cooperative unions.

5.2.2.3. Cooperative Exclusivism

Exclusivism requires that cooperatives conduct cooperative transactions only with their members. French cooperative law provides for such a principle, but with some flexibility,[413] and cooperatives are allowed to obtain 20% of their revenues with non-members.

Cooperative unions are subject to the same rule. This means that the union may conduct cooperative transactions with its members, but not with primary cooperators, who are not members of the union.

Some special cooperative laws dealt with this point, especially when exclusivism was absolute;[414] in that case, it was explicitly stated that the cooperators of the union's members could benefit from the services provided by the union.[415] Full exclusivism has been removed, but, in the meantime, extension of the status of possible beneficiaries of cooperative transactions to the primary cooperators of the union's members has been generalised.[416] The solution is interesting, since it transforms the union from a technical, formal grouping of cooperatives into a wide community of cooperators. Moreover, it is more coherent with other provisions applicable to unions that deal with voting rights or cooperative refund.

5.2.2.4. Minimum Membership

Unions are cooperatives and, therefore, subject to the same regulation. The minimum membership is similar in consequence of the application of company law. Therefore, depending on the type of company chosen, the minimum number of members is two or seven.[417] Another special solution is stated by the Rural Code for agricultural cooperatives, since they are not subject to company law. Contrary to agricultural cooperatives, which require at least seven members, agricultural cooperative unions may be created with two cooperatives.[418]

---

412 C.com., art. L.124-5.
413 See above 1.2.2.
414 C.com., art. L.124-2.
415 C.com., art. L.124-5 al. 3.
416 L. no. 47-1775 of the 10th of September of 1947, art. 5.
417 See above 2.2.2.
418 C.rur., art. R.522-1 2.

5.2.3. *Organs*

5.2.3.1. Representative of Members

The question of the representation of members is not really specific to unions, but only unions necessarily face it. By definition, a union is composed of legal persons which designate a representative to take part in the different organs of the union. There is no general provision on this matter. For agricultural cooperatives, the Rural Code states that, when an agricultural cooperative is a member of a union, its board designates the cooperative's representative in the union's organs from among its members.[419] Therefore, it ensures the cooperators' control of the union. If no representative is designated, the president of the cooperative is considered as such. Even if this solution is limited to agricultural cooperative unions, it may be generalised.

5.2.3.2. Members' Meeting

There is no specific statement on the organisation and composition of the members' meeting; it is simply similar to that of any cooperative, but the members are cooperatives. The only specification provided by the law concerns the date of the meeting, for the agricultural cooperative unions.[420] Whereas the meeting must take place within six months from the end of the financial year for cooperatives, unions have three months more. The solution is coherent, since approval of accounts by the unions' meeting may depend on approval by the members of their own accounts. Nevertheless, this is a favour which cannot be extended to other cooperative unions, which remain subject to company law.

The closest attention is paid, regarding the members' meeting in unions, to voting rights. As cooperatives, the unions apply the one person/one vote principle.[421] Nevertheless, a special rule allows the cooperative statutes to adapt the principle to unions.[422] The statutes may derogate the principle, but they are only allowed to adopt two other mechanisms: voting rights may be proportionate, either to the number of the cooperatives' members, or to the cooperative transactions conducted by each cooperative with the union. These two mechanisms raise further questions. As regards the proportion to the cooperative's members, what constitutes a member may be discussed, the doubt being about the assimilation between members and cooperators. The question has

---

419 C.rur., art. R.524-23.

420 C.rur., art. R.524-12.

421 L. no. 47-1775 of the 10th of September 1947, art. 1.

422 L. no. 47-1775 of the 10th of September 1947, art. 9.

been answered in some special laws, notably in the case of workers' cooperative unions, for which the law allows the statutes to proportion voting rights to the number of shareholders employed in each cooperative, i.e. cooperators. The solution must be approved. Nevertheless, another interpretation is required in general law since the law on social and solidarity economy. The new draft of the law of 1947 has retained in article 9 the word 'membre' for the calculation of voting rights in the unions, whilst the expression 'membre coopérateur' has been introduced into the third paragraph of article 1. Consequently, 'membre' seems to be distinct from 'membre coopérateur'. Literal interpretation therefore requires consideration be taken of all shareholders, including investor members.

Given that the statutes attribute voting rights in proportion to business, the question arises as to the meaning of 'business': is it any business run by the cooperative, or is it only cooperative transactions? Apart from practical considerations,[423] the lack of debate is the consequence of the weakness of the notion of cooperative transaction in French law.

Several special laws add a limit on the proportionate attribution of voting rights. In workers' cooperative unions, for example, no member may have more than one-fourth or one-third of the voting rights in the members' meeting, depending on the type of company used by the union.[424] For agricultural cooperative unions, the maximum of voting rights depends on the number of the union's members: if there are more than two members, no member may have more than two-fifths of the voting rights; if there are two members, none may have more than three-fifths.[425]

When the special laws explicitly allow participation in the union by non-cooperators, they often limit their voting rights in the members' meeting. For example, in agricultural cooperative unions, of which any non-cooperative legal person interested in the union's activity may be a member, they may not have more than 20% of voting rights in the members' meeting.[426] Moreover, cooperators must hold more than half of the cooperative's capital.[427]

A similar solution applies to workers' cooperative unions, for which two-thirds of members must be either workers' cooperatives or workers' cooperatives' unions and federations, or credit unions for consumer cooperatives.[428] Moreover, in these unions, workers' cooperatives must hold two-thirds of voting rights in the members' meeting.[429]

423 Usually, the union and its cooperators conduct only cooperative transactions together.
424 L. no. 78-763 of the 19th of July 1978, art. 47.
425 C.rur., art. L.524-4 al. 2.
426 C.rur., art. L.522-2.
427 C.rur., art. L.522-2-1.
428 L. no. 78-763 of the 19th of July 1978, art. 46.
429 L. no. 78-763 of the 19th of July 1978, art. 47.

5.2.3.3. Board

Voting rights in the members' meeting cannot be the only focus of union governance, since it does not fully ensure the control of cooperators. The other point concerns the board. The general cooperative law contains no provision on this matter, but some special laws do, and this should be generalised. As in the case of agricultural cooperatives, non-cooperators in an agricultural cooperatives' union, if any, must be present on the board; but they cannot designate more than one-third of the board members.[430]

5.2.4. Financial Regulation

Again, like cooperatives, unions are subject to financial cooperative regulation. I will only mention a few special rules. First, in agricultural cooperative law, the cooperatives, provided that they have half of the voting rights in a subsidiary,[431] must publish an account which takes these legal persons into consideration. This obligation is not applicable if the legal person is an agricultural cooperative union.[432] Secondly, a special rule is adopted for distribution of the cooperative refund in workers' cooperative unions.[433] Indeed, the mechanism applicable to workers' cooperatives is inapplicable to the union. In workers' cooperatives, the cooperative refund is proportionate to the work performed by the employee in the cooperative.[434] This is meaningless in the union, since the cooperatives, which are the members, may not work for the union. Therefore, by principle, cooperative refund is excluded. The statutes of the union may, nevertheless, replace it with an allocation of a part of surpluses to the members, in proportion to the amount of transactions with the union.

5.2.5. Cooperation High Council

The definition of the objective of the union does not exclude political representation of cooperatives, since this indubitably concerns common interests of cooperatives. Nevertheless, unions are considered like enterprises that pursue economic purposes. It is significant, for example, that the federations of cooperatives (or similar groupings) aimed at this political representation are generally associations.[435]

---

430 C.rur., art. L.524-1 al. 3.
431 C.com., art. L.233-16.
432 C.rur., art. L.524-6-2 al. 3.
433 L. no. 78-763 of the 19th of July 1978, art. 47.
434 Time or salary: L. no. 78-763 of the 19th of July 1978, art. 33 3°.
435 For example, for agricultural cooperatives: C.rur., art. R.527-1.

An official representative institution for cooperatives was established in 1919, but it became dormant. It was resurrected in 1976.[436] Its advice was sometimes compulsory, notably in the procedure for conversion into a company.[437] The law on social and solidarity economy has created a new provision concerning this cooperation high council in the general cooperative law.[438] This innovation must be related to the creation of different institutions in social and solidarity economy, notably the social and solidarity economy high council.[439] The organisation and functioning of the cooperation high council is specified by a decree.[440] The cooperation high council should become more active because its competences have been extended. Its most important new power is, probably, the definition of principles for cooperative audit, and the drafting of its regulation.[441]

5.3. SPECIAL GROUPINGS FOR WORKERS' COOPERATIVES

The question of the cooperative group has been debated for more than twenty years among cooperators. The question arose with the restructuring process, and, in parallel, the creation of capitalist subsidiaries. Some people contested this evolution and called for an authentic cooperative group. Despite the findings of various studies, no precise proposal has emerged. The difficulty stems, at least partly, from the desire of the cooperators to remain within the cooperative area, as well as to benefit from capitalist techniques, such as control. Some innovations have been introduced into cooperative law, but they remain very narrow. For example, in agricultural cooperative law, some aspects of groupings have been regulated, but they concerned mainly accounting.[442]

The social and solidarity economy law created a new grouping inspired by cooperative debates dedicated to workers' cooperatives. It created a new title 4 in the 1978 law: the workers' cooperative grouping.[443] I will describe only its main features.

The purpose behind creation of such a grouping is to enable a cooperative in the grouping to control another cooperative in the same grouping.[444] Indeed, the hope of the legislature is that the capitalist subsidiaries created by some big workers' cooperatives will be converted into worker' cooperatives integrated into such a grouping. But, this possibility is subject to several conditions.

---

436 Decree no. 76-356 of the 20th of April 1976.

437 L. no. 47-1775 of the 10th of September 1947, art. 25.

438 L. no. 47-1775 of the 10th of September 1947, art. 5-1.

439 L. no. 2014-856 of the 31st of July 2014, art. 4.

440 D. no. 2015-562 of the 20th of May 2015.

441 L. no. 47-1775 of the 10th of September 1947, art. 5 al. 4.

442 C.rur., art. L.524-6-2. D. Hiez, n. 7 above, no. 151.32.

443 L. no. 78-763 of the 19th of July 1978, arts. 47*bis* to 47*septies*.

444 L. no. 78-763 of the 19th of July 1978, art. 47*quinquies*.

Of course, a grouping must be created, since a cooperative can control another cooperative only if they are members of the same grouping. The creation of such a grouping requires several conditions. At this stage, an observation is necessary. Despite the word 'grouping', which may be compared to other legally defined groupings, this new legal entity is not a legal person. Title 4 of the 1978 law does not define it, nor considers it as a cooperative. Moreover, the law does not provide for any object, nor create any organ. Hence the grouping is something like an abstraction created by a contract, with consequences on the relationships among its members, but with no substantial existence as such.

Two workers' cooperatives are necessary to create a grouping.[445] These cooperatives must modify their statutes in order to adopt similar provisions on participation in the grouping, membership, distribution of surpluses, forms of control within the grouping.[446] Any future modification of these provisions of the statutes are only possible if accepted by all the members of the grouping.[447] The decision to be part of the grouping is taken by an extraordinary members' meeting. After the creation of the grouping, any new application can only be approved if all the present members agree.[448]

The grouping as such has no specific power, nor any general strategy. It sets only the boundaries of a category of cooperatives, which may have special relationships among themselves. One of them can control the others. But this requires some reciprocity. Indeed, the employees of the controlled cooperatives must hold, as a whole, a proportion of voting rights in the controlling cooperative higher than a percentage defined in cooperatives' statutes.[449] Because this proportion is freely defined in the statutes, nothing forbids a low one. Surprisingly, the minimum voting rights are considered with regard not to the cooperators, but to the employees of the cooperatives.

It is difficult to anticipate the success of this new grouping. Nevertheless, it seems to be a mechanism closely connected to the needs of workers' cooperatives. Consequently, it is not likely to be a basis for definition of a cooperative group.

5.4. COOPERATION BEYOND COOPERATIVES

The political edification of social economy in France in the 1980s has meant the creation of diverse institutions, notably the social economy union. Grounded on cooperation principles, it may be completed by a new grouping which would tackle the question of control.

---

445 L. no. 78-763 of the 19th of July 1978, art. 47*bis*.

446 L. no. 78-763 of the 19th of July 1978, art. 47*bis*.

447 L. no. 78-763 of the 19th of July 1978, art. 47*ter*.

448 L. no. 78-763 of the 19th of July 1978, art. 4 *ter*.

449 L. no. 78-763 of the 19th of July 1978, art. 47*quinquies*.

5.4.1. *Social Economy Union*

The social economy union is a grouping introduced into the law of 1947 in 1985.[450] Its purpose is to facilitate cooperation among diverse enterprises, mainly from the social and solidarity economy. This union is inspired by the cooperative union. It is even stated that these unions are subject to the 1947 Law,[451] whereas they are not cooperatives as such. They have the same objective as cooperative unions; their organisation and functioning are similar. Their particular feature is their membership. Members may be any enterprise, cooperative or not, from the social and solidarity economy, and even companies. No limitation is set on the capital. But voting rights are regulated: 65% of voting rights in the members' meeting must be held by cooperatives, mutuals, associations or foundations, and, if so provided by the statutes, other not-for-profit enterprises.[452] Apart from this frame for the members' meeting, the functioning of the board is also regulated:[453] half of boards and supervisory committees' members must be representatives of the former enterprises.

Despite their attractiveness in books, there are, in fact, few social economy unions. Nevertheless, the legislature has used that legal model to regulate certain activities in housing. First, it has created a social economy union for housing.[454] Its objective is general interest[455] and closely involves the state. Secondly, and more recently, the legislature has created[456] the social economy union for access to ownership.[457] Its purpose is to promote and organise the policy on access to ownership. Again, its connection with general interest implies the strong involvement of the state. I will not detail its organisation and functioning, but only show that this legal person, even if not widely used in practice, may be indirectly useful.

5.4.2. *Social and Solidarity Economy Enterprise Groups*

This section deals only with prospective provisions. It has been proposed, by amendment to the social and solidarity economy law, to create a new group of social and solidarity economy enterprises, but the proposal has not been adopted. However, I mention it because it gives an idea of the expectations concerning creation of a group dedicated to social and solidarity economy enterprises. This group would be regulated in the 1947 Law on cooperation by

---

450 L. no. 47-1775 of the 10th of September 1947, arts. 19*bis* ff.
451 L. no. 47-1775 of the 10th of September 1947, art. 19*bis*.
452 L. no. 47-1775 of the 10th of September 1947, art. 19*bis* al. 3.
453 L. no. 47-1775 of the 10th of September 1947, art. 19*bis* al. 4.
454 C.const.hab., art. L.313-16 ff.
455 Notably the use of a compulsory tax paid by employers for housing.
456 Ord. no. 2006-1048 of the 25th of August 2006.
457 C.const.hab., art. L.215-5 ff.

adding two articles: 19*quarter* and 19*quarter b*. This group would be a special addition to the social economy union, more than being a distinct grouping. Its main objective is to allow coherent coordination of the different members of the union through contractual arrangements. This coherence may derive from exclusive control as defined by the Code of Commerce: common structures able to impose a common commercial or financial policy, the common composition of the organs of the member's union and the union itself. The mechanism of cooperative refund would not be applicable in such unions. The group would have common accounting and reporting obligations.

5.5. SUBSIDIARIES

Generally, subsidiaries are not linked with inter-cooperation. However, there is certainly a relationship between the increasing number of subsidiaries created by cooperatives and the low number of unions or other groupings aimed at inter-cooperation. The recourse to subsidiaries by cooperatives started in the 1980s, and generated a debate in the 1990s. Some prominent authors, specialists in cooperative law, claimed the illegality of such mechanisms in the cooperative world, notably because of the reference, in the legal definition of cooperatives, to the involvement of cooperators in achievement of the cooperative's objective.[458] Some other prominent authors, more specialised in company law, solicited by cooperative institutions for their opinion, defended the validity of the mechanism, notably because of the liberalism principle, which allows everything that is not forbidden.

During the same period, the number of subsidiaries grew very rapidly, mainly in the most economically dynamic sectors, such as merchants' cooperatives and agricultural cooperatives. The Rural Code already regulated that mechanism by requiring authorisation from the public body or its information, depending on the subsidiary's activity.[459] Its regulation also meant the validity of the mechanism. But the question was more debatable when cooperative law was silent, as in the case of merchants' cooperatives. Because of the uncertainty of the point and its economic importance, the legislature modified the definition of the cooperative object:[460] it simply added that the activities may be undertaken by the cooperative 'directly or indirectly', i.e. through subsidiaries.[461] Because

---

458 F. Espagne, 'Restructuration des coopératives, filialisations, fusions, prises de participation', lettre du 8 août 2001; S. De Vendeuil, 'Les entreprises coopératives se modernisent', JCP E, 1993, act. 100213.

459 C.rur., art. L.523-5, now abrogated.

460 C.com., art. L.124-1.

461 S. Grandvuillemin, 'Le statut de coopérative de commerçants détaillants: déclin ou renouveau?', JCP E, 2003, comm. 759 p. 844.

no other modification has been made to the law, there is, for merchants' cooperatives, no regulation of the mechanism, which is, therefore, totally free.

In the absence of any specific provision, the only possible limit on the creation of subsidiaries is the existence of a fraud. Cooperative practitioners generally agree that fraud certainly exists when all the assets, and notably the brand, have been transferred from the cooperative to the subsidiary. The judgement is far too vague, technically insufficient, and requires deeper research. This matter is, to my mind, extremely important, since it questions the practical pertinence of inter-cooperation itself.

CHAPTER 8
GERMANY

Hans-H. Münkner

1. THE COOPERATIVE SOCIAL OBJECTIVE

1.1. INTRODUCTION: COOPERATIVE LAW IN GERMANY

In Germany, cooperatives of all types and business branches are regulated by the Cooperative Societies Act. The German Cooperative Societies Act (GCA) is a pure organisation law only governing the relationship of cooperative societies with their members and with third parties. It does not contain rules regarding competition law and tax law.[1] In the legal definition of societies which may be registered as cooperatives, pursuit of economic activities for the promotion of the economic interests of their members was originally their only legitimate objective. With the amendment of §1(1) GCA in 2006, promotion of members' social and cultural interests is also expressly allowed.

With fewer than 150 sections, GCA is a comprehensive Act regulating all relevant matters without leaving gaps to be filled by other enactments like the civil code or company law. The provisions on the merger of cooperatives (§§93a–s GCA) were transferred to the Conversion Act (Umwandlungsgesetz, UmwG) of 1994: §3(1) no. 3 UmwG, which also contains provisions on the merger of cooperative auditing federations (§§105 ff.), on the division of cooperatives (§§123 ff.), and on the conversion of cooperative societies into other legal forms (§§190 ff. UmwG).[2] The UmwG is a law applicable to business organisations in different legal forms including cooperative societies.

The first draft of the German Cooperative Societies Act was prepared by the lawyer and cooperative pioneer Schulze-Delitzsch in 1860. Inspired by the British Industrial and Provident Societies Act, it became the Prussian Cooperative Societies Act in 1867. In 1889 the national German Cooperative Societies Act came into force, again essentially influenced by Schulze-Delitzsch's writings and elaborated in close collaboration with practising cooperators.[3] Subsequently, amendments were made in 1922/23, 1933/34, 1954, 1973 and 2006 to meet the needs of cooperatives in their practical work. Issues of amendment were: allowing transactions with non-members as an additional objective, meeting the needs of large cooperatives, strengthening the financial bases of cooperatives and allowing cooperatives without members' additional liability, adjusting the governance structure to the requirements of large cooperatives

1 H. Paulick, *Das Recht der eingetragenen Genossenschaft* [The law of registered cooperatives], Karlsruhe, 1956, pp. 26, 27, 31.

2 V. Beuthien, zusammen mit S. Hanrath, 'Den Förderauftrag prüfen – wie soll der Prüfer das machen?' [Auditing management's task of member-promotion, how can this be done by the auditor?] in V. Beuthien (ed.), *Die Eingetragene Genossenschaft, Idee und Wirklichkeit*, Nomos, Baden-Baden, 2013, pp. 51–64, UmwG, Einl. RZ 2, 3. First published in *ZfgG* 2008, 58, pp. 85 f.

3 Paulick, n. 1 above, pp. 25, 26.

(meeting of delegates, increased autonomy of the board of directors) and small cooperatives (simplified organisational structure and audit). Despite several revisions, until 1973 the organisational form of the cooperative society model preserved a relatively clear profile. By amendments made between 1973 and 2006, with attempts to strengthen the organisational and financial bases of large cooperatives, deviations from the original concept were made or allowed within an enlarged autonomy in creating by-laws. This trend and its consequences will be explained in the following five sections.

Many of the amendments made in 2006 were inspired by the EU Regulation for a European Cooperative Society (SCE) of 2003 (European Council regulation no. 1435/2003) for cross-border cooperation. These amendments came into force together with introduction of the SCE Regulation no. 1435/2003 into German law: SCE Ausführungsgesetz (SCEAG) of 2006 (Law on the implementation of the SCE Regulation no. 1435/2003 into German law).[4] The new legal form of the SCE with a registered office in Germany is rarely used. In 2015 there were only 12 SCEs registered in Germany. The more convenient alternative is a cooperative society registered under German cooperative law with international members.[5]

1.2. DEFINITION OF COOPERATIVE SOCIETY

1.2.1. Seen from the Organisation Law Perspective

A cooperative society is a special type of business association and a hybrid between a partnership and a corporation/company (see Figures 1 and 2 below) which combines elements of both together with distinct ones reflecting its special goal and value system.[6]

---

4 M. Geschwandtner and M. Helios, *Genossenschaftsrecht – Das neue Genossenschaftsgesetz und die Einführung der Europäischen Genossenschaft* [The New Cooperative Societies Act and Introduction of the European Cooperative Society], Nomos, Freiburg/Berlin/Munich, 2006, pp. 250–265; Beuthien, n. 2 above, pp. 1393–1414.

5 For a full account of the role of SCE as seen from a German perspective, see O. Korte, 'Die europäische Genossenschaft' [The European Cooperative Society], in M. Helios and T. Strieder (eds.), *Beck'sches Handbuch der Genossenschaft – Recht – Steuern – Rechnungslegung* [Beck's Handbook of Cooperatives – Law – Tax – Accounting], Springer, Munich, 2009, pp. 730–765; H.-H. Münkner, 'Country Report Germany', in *Study on the implementation of the Regulation 1435/2003 on the Statute for the European Cooperative Society (SCE)*, EURICSE/EZAI/CE, Trento, 2010.

6 For more details see H.-H. Münkner, 'Die Rechtstypik der Genossenschaft in den Partnerstaaten der EG' [The cooperative society as a legal type in EU member states], *Genossenschaftswissenschaftliche Beiträge*, 1993, Vorträge/Hefte 32, Institut für Genossenschaftswesen der Universität Münster; H.-H. Münkner, *Cooperative Principles and Cooperative Law*, 2nd revised edition, LIT, Vienna/Zürich/Berlin, 2015.

The purpose of this special organisational type, which distinguishes it from other types of organisation, is defined in §1(1) of the German Cooperative Societies Act (GCA):

Member promotion (*Förderungsauftrag*), i.e. the objective to generate economic and social advantages for members.

- Economic advantages: service near cost, offer of reliable, good quality, cost effective goods and services, access to supply, markets, information, knowledge, technology and loans, refund of surplus in proportion to business done by the member with the cooperative enterprise (patronage refund);
- Social advantages: integration into a group, mutual support and mutual learning, improvement of conditions in the community and contribution to the development of the region.

Elements of partnership: All rights and obligations pertain to the person of the member, not to the amount of capital contribution.

Elements of corporation/company: As an organisation which must be suited to the pursuit of long-term objectives: incorporation, by-laws, governing bodies, variable (open) membership, independent from the individual members, with regulations allowing uncomplicated admission and withdrawal.

Special cooperative elements: Dual nature consisting of two elements: the cooperative group and the cooperative enterprise pursuing the objective of promoting the members of the group by means of a jointly owned, patronised and controlled business organisation.

1.2.2. Seen from the Business Law Perspective

The nature of a cooperative society as an organisation in which owners and users are the same people (principle of identity of owners and users) is seen by Beuthien[7] as the main feature distinguishing cooperatives from other business organisations. The purpose of the enterprise is to promote the members, which entails a promotion-oriented and value-oriented management in contrast to a profit-oriented one. A cooperative enterprise must be efficient and effective in three ways:

- Institutional efficiency of the enterprise: applying modern methods of business administration and management, earning income in excess of expenditure to survive on the market, develop the enterprise and accumulate reserves;

7 V. Beuthien, Wie kapitalistisch darf eine Genossenschaft sein?' [How capitalistic may a cooperative society be?], *Die Aktiengesellschaft*, 2006, no. 3, pp. 53–62.

- Member-oriented effectiveness: being able to promote members by offering them tangible advantages (member value) deriving from membership; and
- Development-oriented effectiveness which contributes to improving the socio-economic and environmental conditions of the community in which the members live and work.

Other differences concern the management style: in contrast to profit-oriented commercial management, cooperative enterprises need value-oriented management with cooperative values, i.e. service near cost, transparency, fair relations with employees and business partners, long-term planning aimed at sustainable development rather than a search for short-term maximum profit.

From the German point of view, cooperative societies are different from non-profit organisations (NPOs). Like every other enterprise, they must earn income in excess of expenditure to be viable business organisations, but they do not aim to create profit for distribution among investors in proportion to contributed/invested capital. As organisations with variable share capital, they must stabilise their equity capital by building up reserves from undistributed surplus which are indivisible. As organisations with the purpose of member-promotion, they distribute part of their surplus among members (in contrast to charities, which are not allowed to do so). The typically cooperative form of distributing surplus to members is 'patronage refund' (*Rückvergütung*) in proportion to business done by the member with the cooperative enterprise as a way to furnish service near cost in retrospect. Cooperatives can also reward their members by paying dividends in proportion to their capital contributions (*Kapitalbeteiligungsdividende*), but as a rule, such dividends are limited, and should not exceed the market rate. According to a new provision in the German cooperative law, also interest can be paid on share capital if the by-laws so provide. However, the term 'interest' is a misnomer, because such 'interest' can only be paid if surplus has been earned by the cooperative enterprise during the financial year (§21a(2) GCA), while interest is a cost factor and must be paid irrespective of any surplus or profit made.

1.2.3. Seen from the Members' Perspective

Expectation of economic and social advantages is the motive for forming or joining a cooperative society. Membership must be worthwhile, i.e. advantages must outweigh contributions. Members have rights of participation and control, as well as the right to elect members of the governing bodies and to be elected.

1.2.4. Definition of a Cooperative Society in German Cooperative Law

The social objective of member-promotion is part of the legal definition and the main criterion determining the form of membership (capital contribution as an

Table 1. System of organisations

	Partnership	Joint stock company
Objective	Building up a jointly owned and managed enterprise for gain	Collect funds for economic investment to finance business for gain
Motivation for membership	Mutual trust among partners, emphasis on good character of partners and their ability to cooperate	Investment of money with a view to making a profit, the person of the investor is not important and may remain anonymous (*société anonyme*)
Financial base	Contributions by partners and their unlimited joint and several liability for the debts of their partnership	Fixed share capital and reserves from undistributed profit
Organisational set-up	Laid down in the partnership agreement	Corporation with by-laws, organs (governing bodies), designed for long-term existence
Members' rights	Based on the person of the partners, rights of participation based the partnership agreement, usually management by the partners themselves	Laid down in the by-laws, usually one share one vote, management by professional directors, rights to participate in the profit in the form of dividends on shares and to benefit from increasing, or lose in the case of decreasing market value of shares
Members' obligations	Contribution of capital or labour according to the partnership agreement, unlimited joint and several liability for the debts of the partnership	Capital contribution in the form of transferable shares, liability limited by shares
Entry and withdrawal of members	Usually not possible during the existence of the partnership, unless provided for in the partnership agreement	Possible and typical for companies and associations designed to achieve long-term objectives
Termination of membership	Usually terminates the partnership, unless the partnership agreement provides otherwise	By selling the shares on the market (stock exchange)

obligation of membership), governance (main goal and overriding task of the directors is member-promotion), and financial structure (capital contribution of members specially designed for this type of organisation, different from the company share), all oriented towards enhancing member-promotion.

In 2006, the objectives of cooperative societies, which by tradition had been defined as promoting the economic interests of the members, were broadened (in line with the SCE-Regulation of 2003) to include promotion of the social and cultural aspirations of the members.

Table 2. The cooperative society as a special legal pattern and a hybrid between partnership and company, society and association

Main objective	Promoting the interests of members by service relations with the jointly owned cooperative enterprise
Motivation for membership	Self-help combined with mutual aid, solidarity and strong social ties among members, emphasis on good character of members
Financial base	Variable share capital and indivisible reserves (asset lock)
Organisational set-up	Corporation with by-laws, organs (governing bodies) and internal democratic structure, and with variable membership designed for long-term existence as in the case of a company or association
Members' rights	Based on the person of the member, rights of participation as in a partnership
Members' obligations	Capital contribution for the duration of membership, use of the cooperative's facilities, liability for the debts of the cooperative society
Entry and withdrawal of members	Possible and typical for cooperatives based on the principle of open and voluntary (i.e. variable) membership
Termination of membership	By withdrawal with a period of notice, or by expulsion. Shares can be redeemed at par value but are not freely transferable

By this amendment, the legal framework of cooperative societies was modified by permitting cooperatives to have promotion of social or cultural interests of their members as their principal objective while, before the revision, having social or cultural goals as additional objectives while mainly promoting the economic interests of their members had always been permitted (e.g. §1(2) GCA).

German cooperative theory distinguishes between surplus earned on the 'internal market', i.e. in business transactions between members and the cooperative enterprise (*Mitgliedergeschäft*), and profit made on the external market with business partners and non-member customers. In cooperative societies as business organisations, service relations with members (internal market) are part of the cooperative identity. Their conditions are laid down in the by-laws or by agreement.

There are legal provisions protecting this model. The cooperative group is protected by the prescription that a cooperative society with less than the legally required minimum number of members (down from fewer than 7 before 2006 to fewer than 3 since 2006 (§4 GCA)) must be wound up *ex officio* and that a cooperative enterprise limited to the sole administration of assets (holding cooperative, *Haltegenossenschaft*) after outsourcing all economic activities to subsidiaries, may be dissolved *ex officio*[8] (§81 GCA).

---

8 V. Beuthien, 'Genossenschaftsgesetz mit Umwandlungs- und Kartellrecht sowie Statut der Europäischen Genossenschaft, Kommentar' [Co-operative Societies Act with transformation

Table 3. Definition of a cooperative society in German cooperative law, §1(1) GCA

Before 2006	After revision of the Cooperative Societies Act in 2006
Definition and types of cooperative societies (1) Societies with a variable number of members, with the purpose of promoting their members' activities in trade and industry by means of a commonly owned enterprise (cooperative socie ties), namely 1. loan and credit associations, 2. commodity associations, 3. associations established for the joint sale of agricultural or industrial products (marketing cooperatives, warehousing associations), 4. associations established for the joint production of goods and the sale thereof on common account (producers' cooperatives), 5. associations established for the joint purchase of victuals or commodities on a large scale and discounting on a small one (consumer cooperatives), 6. associations established to procure objects for agricultural or industrial purposes and use thereof on common account, 7. associations established for the purpose of building houses acquire the legal status of a '*registered cooperative society*' according to this Act.	***The nature of cooperative societies*** (1) Societies with a variable number of members, whose objective is to promote the income or economy of their members or their social or cultural needs by means of a jointly owned and operated enterprise (cooperatives), acquire the rights of a 'registered cooperative society' under this Act.
(2) Membership of societies and other associations, including bodies incorporated under public law, is admissible if and when they are intended to 1. promote the trading and industrial activities of the members of the cooperative society or, 2. serve the non-profit making activities of the cooperative society, without this being the sole or principal objective of the societies.	(2) Membership of societies and other associations (of individuals), including the bodies governed by public law, is permissible if and when they are intended to 1. promote their members' personal economic and business interests, or their social or cultural interests, or 2. serve the public interest goals of the cooperative society, without this being the sole or main purpose of the cooperative society.

Different sizes, needs, situations and problems require different regulations. The revision of the German Cooperative Societies Act in 2006 introduced special provisions for small cooperatives, where contacts between members and the cooperative enterprise are close and personal contacts are important but organisation cost are high. Societies with no more than 20 members may

law and anti-trust law and the EU Regulation for European Cooperatives (SCE), commentary], 15th ed., C.H. Beck, Munich, 2011, §1 GenG, RZ 34, 93–95.

opt in their by-laws to operate with only one person as director (§24(2) GCA) and without a supervisory committee (§9(1) GCA). The intervals of audit are extended from an annual to bi-annual external audit (§53(1) GCA). In large cooperative societies, the by-laws may provide for replacement of the general meeting of members with a meeting of delegates when membership exceeds 1,500. The independence of the board of directors *vis-à-vis* the general meeting had already been increased in 1973. Recruiting external specialists to serve as board members is the rule, although §9(2) GCA prescribes that all office-holders of cooperatives must be members (principle of self-administration). Often, external specialists join as members, and the conditions for admission are adjusted to allow this.[9]

When pursuing a growth strategy, many cooperative enterprises need more funds than the members are able or willing to contribute. From this point of view, the special financial structures designed for user-driven enterprises with the aim of member-promotion are considered by many as 'structural weaknesses' compared with the capital structure of companies. Since 1973, several amendments of the German Cooperative Societies Act have been introduced on recommendation by the cooperative federations to strengthen the equity capital of cooperatives and to make capital contributions to cooperatives more attractive for investors.

The by-laws may provide for:

- admission of investing members (non-using members) (§8 (2) GCA);
- introduction of a fixed minimum capital (§8a GCA);
- plural voting within narrow limits (§43(3) GCA);
- offering to pay 'interest' on capital but only if surplus is made (§21a GCA);
- offering the right of departing members to claim a portion of reserves specially accumulated for this purpose (§73(3) GCA).

1.3. SOCIAL OBJECTIVE – INSTITUTIONAL PURPOSE

In legal terms, member-promotion means an agreement between the members and their cooperative enterprise whereby the enterprise undertakes to render services, to provide or sell goods, etc. or in the case of a workers' cooperative to offer employment on conditions more advantageous than the individual member could obtain. This can be done directly by the cooperative enterprise or through a subsidiary (§1(2) GCA). In return, members agree to comply with the by-laws, to contribute capital, and to use the cooperative's facilities. This arrangement is

---

9 Beuthien, n. 8 above, §9 GenG, RZ 13.

part of the institutional purpose of the cooperative society. It is a self-promotion cycle (*Selbstförderungskreis*).[10]

1.3.1. Interest of Members – Modes of Pursuing Them

A distinction should be drawn between members' interests as owners and those that they have as users of the cooperative enterprise.

From the business perspective, members expect good and reliable services from their own enterprise as a trustworthy and reliable business partner. From the financial perspective, they expect a return of surplus after deductions to cover operating costs and accumulating reserves. Such return typically takes the form of a patronage refund in proportion to business done, and it may be supplemented by a reward of their capital contribution (dividend) at market rate. The allocation of the annual surplus as shown in an audited balance sheet is decided by the members in general meeting/meeting of delegates (§48(1) GCA).

Although the distribution of surplus to members in the form of a patronage refund is the typical cooperative practice, it is not expressly provided for in the German Cooperative Societies Act, and is not widely applied in practice by cooperative banks. Often, this opportunity to demonstrate the unique character of cooperatives is missed, while most cooperatives pay dividends on paid-up share capital – in the same way as companies. One reason may be the relatively complicated rules on having a patronage refund recognised by the tax authorities as a tax-deductible operating cost of the cooperative enterprise (see section 2.1.1).

1.3.1.1. Regulation of Patronage Refund

Patronage refund is not mentioned in the German Cooperative Societies Act. From the tax law perspective, three conditions must be met for recognition of a patronage refund by the tax authorities as a cost that can be deducted from the taxable income of the cooperative enterprise:

- The surplus must have been earned in transactions with members. This means that separate accounts must be kept for business with members and with non-members.
- Surplus due for allocation to members must be distributed to them following the same rules, ensuring that all members receive refunds according to the same ratio. However, where different lines of business can be distinguished, different ratios may be applied.

---

10 M. Helios and T. Strieder (eds.), *Beck'sches Handbuch der Genossenschaft, Recht – Steuern – Rechnungslegung* [Beck's Handbook of Cooperatives, Law – Tax – Accounting], C.H. Beck, Munich, 2009, Einleitung, RZ 17, p. 13.

- The surplus must be paid out to the member.[11] Some cooperative banks have devised a system whereby the members receiving surplus agree to pay it back as a time deposit with low interest rate (pay out – receive back).[12]

1.3.1.2. Concept and Legal Nature of Patronage Refund and Distinction from Dividend

Patronage refund is seen as surplus distribution in proportion to transactions of members with the cooperative enterprise, practically returning to members what has been charged in excess of cost (French: *le top perçu*). If and to what extent such refund is made is decided by the members in general meeting usually following what the board proposes. Once the decision by the members in general meeting has been taken, the members have a claim to receive their part of the surplus. The same applies to dividends on paid-up share capital. However, the dividend is usually credited to the member's share account until the share is fully paid up. Only then is the dividend paid to the member.

From the tax point of view, there is a difference between patronage refund and dividend. A patronage refund of surplus made in transactions with members (on the internal market) means refunding what has been overcharged. A dividend on paid-up share capital is profit distribution, irrespective of where the profit was made, and as such, subject to tax. The law does not set limits on the percentage of dividend on share-capital. But it is agreed under the cooperative principles that, in cooperative societies, the payment of dividends to investors of capital may not become the main concern of cooperative management, and that the dividend should not exceed the market rate.

1.3.1.3. Right to Patronage Refund

The members have no general right to patronage refund, but instead the right or power to participate in voting on the allocation of surplus at the end of a financial year in general meeting or indirectly in the meeting of delegates (§48(1) GCA). Usually, the board proposes how to allocate the surplus and the members in general meeting dispose.

---

11 Beuthien, n. 8 above, §19 GenG, RZ 14, 17.

12 K. Böth, and W. Schütz, 'Praktische Erfahrungen mit der Zinsrückvergütung bei Genossenschaften' (Practical experience with patronage refund in cooperative banks), in H.-H. Münkner and G. Ringle (eds.), *Nutzer-orientierte' versus ‚Investor-orientierte' Unternehmen, Argumente für eine besondere Betriebswirtschaftslehre förderungswirtschaftlicher Unternehmen* ['User-oriented' versus 'investor-oriented' enterprises, arguments supporting a special theory for promotion-oriented enterprises], Vandenhoeck & Ruprecht, Göttingen, 2002, pp. 133–147.

1.3.2. *Different Concepts of Social Objectives*

In Germany, the general view is that pursuit of the objective of member-promotion is a general task of cooperative management which must be defined in detail in each cooperative society's by-laws. This is done jointly by the members in general meeting/meeting of delegates and interpreted as a strategy and guideline for action on a day-to-day basis by the board of directors of the society. Cooperative science has for many years proposed clearer definition of what member-promotion means in an annual promotion plan, drawn up by the board and approved by the members in annual general meetings, and to show the results in the form of a promotion report submitted by the board to the members in general meeting and used as a basis for the next promotion plan in a feed-back-controlled system.[13] However, in practice these instruments are not widely used.

1.4. COOPERATIVE SOCIAL OBJECTIVE; COOPERATIVE MEMBERSHIP AND NON-USER INVESTOR-MEMBERS

The social objective of cooperatives is member-promotion by services offered to and used by members. The principle of identity of owners and users is the main criterion distinguishing between cooperative societies and public companies (*sociétés anonymes*). In cooperative societies, only the cooperative enterprise's potential users of its services qualify for membership. The conditions for membership are usually laid down in the by-laws of each society (e.g. profession, residence, economic activity). While companies can offer their shares to an anonymous market and operate with an unlimited number of customers, the number of persons or legal entities qualifying for membership in a cooperative society and as 'users' is limited.

Whereas companies transact their business on an external market ruled by competition, cooperative societies transact their main business with their members on an 'internal market' where special conditions can be set by the members in their dual capacity as owners and users. Cooperatives are user-owned, user-driven and user-controlled organisations where the owners are also

---

13 E. Boettcher, 'Die Problematik der Operationalisierung des Förderauftrages in Genossenschaften: Förderplan und Förderbericht' [On the problems of implementing the task of member-promotion: Promotion plan und promotion report], *ZfgG* 1979, vol. 29, pp. 47 f.; M. Patera, 'Genossenschaftliche Förderbilanz' [Cooperative promotion balance], in J. Laurinkari (ed.), *Genossenschaftswesen*, Munich, 1991, pp. 201 f.; W. Weber and J. Brazda, 'Promotion Balance Sheet, Promotion Report, Promotion System', in E. Dülfer (ed.), *International Handbook of Cooperative Organisations*, Göttingen, 1994, pp. 736–739. Beuthien and Hanrath, n. 2 above, pp. 51–61.

customers or workers and can agree on special rules and conditions for their cooperation.[14]

According to the classic concept of cooperative organisation, non-users or investors cannot be members, and non-members cannot be users. This does not mean that all members must be active users, but in the law of some countries and in the by-laws of some cooperative societies, inactive members can be expelled. Several amendments have been made to German cooperative law, the last in 2006, allowing cooperative societies to have different categories of members: non-using investor-members, members with different rights, e.g. more than one vote (limited plural voting) and members holding non-voting certificates (*Genussrechte*).[15] Where the Cooperative Societies Act deviates from the clear and simple rules of identity of owners and users and 'one member/one vote', complicated rules are needed to ensure that investor-members do not dominate the user-members, e.g. hold not more than one-quarter of the seats in the supervisory committee (§8(2) GCA), and that plural voting only applies in business matters, while in matters of basic importance like amendment of by-laws, merger, dissolution, the principle of 'one member/one vote' still prevails (§43(3) GCA).

1.5. COOPERATIVE ACTIVITIES WITH MEMBERS

In Germany there is a doctrine outside the law distinguishing an 'internal market' between cooperatives and their members and an 'external market' in the case of transactions of cooperatives with non-members as customers and business partners.[16]

A difference is also envisaged between ordinary market transactions and an organisational relationship between cooperative societies and their members. For the member, there is a dual relationship as owner (property rights) and as user (contract law). Both relationships are influenced by organisation law. In the special case of workers' cooperatives, conflicts may arise between rules of organisation law and of labour law.

---

14 V. Beuthien, S. Hanrath and H.-O. Weber, 'Mitgliederförder-management in Genossenschaftsbanken. Analysen, Erläuterungen, Gestaltungsempfehlungen' [Member-promotion management in cooperative banks. Analyses, explanations, proposals for regulation], *Marburger Schriften zum Genossenschaftswesen*, 2008, vol. 106, pp. 112 f.; P. Hanker, 'Argumente pro und contra aktive Mitgliederförderung aus Sicht der Praxis' [Arguments for and against active member-promotion seen form the perspective of practice], in H.-H. Münkner and G. Ringle (eds.), *Alleinstellungsmerkmale genossenschaftlicher Kooperation – der Unterschied zählt* [Features of uniqueness of working together in the cooperative way], Marburger Schriften zum Genossenschaftswesen 107, Göttingen, 2008, pp. 139–148.

15 Beuthien, n. 8 above, §19 GenG, RZ 23, 28.

16 Beuthien, Hanrath and Weber, n. 14 above, p. 11; W. Grosskopf, H.-H. Münkner and G. Ringle, *Our Cooperative Idea – Mission – Achievements*, LIT, Zurich/Berlin, 2016, p. 59.

When recognising the special relation between cooperative transactions and cooperative membership, how can they be regulated appropriately? Can there be special rules on cooperative transactions that recognise their specificity, e.g. labour relationships in workers' cooperatives?

Another problem is assessment of exclusive advantages for members of cooperatives seen from the perspective of tax law and competition law. Are exclusive advantages for members of cooperatives hidden profit distribution and subject to tax? Must all members be treated equally or can there be special advantages for certain groups of members following objective criteria (e.g. *Mehrhaberprogramm*).[17]

Are members obliged to transact with their cooperative enterprise? This is a matter of the by-laws or of agreement. The cooperative enterprise needs reliable data on users and expected volume of business in order to plan. A workers' cooperative needs the right to contract outside labour to cover peaks of production. The by-laws may provide for sanctions against defaulting or passive members. Members going astray despite commitment to using the cooperative's facilities and causing losses may be liable to pay damages.

In general, this issue is more a matter of education than of legislation. But it is also a question of efficiency of the cooperative enterprise, which must offer competitive services making it beneficial for the member to use a 'cooperative advantage', rather than turning to competitors.

1.6. TRANSACTIONS WITH NON-MEMBERS

The essential feature of cooperative societies that distinguishes them from other business organisations is their objective of furthering and supporting the activities of their members (member-promotion). To understand this feature in the German context it is important to distinguish between two different types of transaction by cooperative societies:

- purpose transactions (*Zweckgeschäft*), i.e. transactions for which the cooperative society was formed, e. g. a cooperative bank accepting savings from and giving loans to members; and
- counter-transactions (*Gegengeschäft*), i.e. transactions needed to carry out such purpose transactions. Counter-transactions are almost always carried out with non-members on the external market. In counter-transactions the cooperative enterprise acts like any other enterprise trying to make good bargains. Income earned from such transactions is ordinary commercial profit.

17 HANKER, above n. 14, pp. 144 f.

Problems of transactions with non-members are special when a cooperative enterprise carries out purpose transactions with non-members, e.g. a consumer cooperative selling consumer goods to members and non-member customers on the same conditions, or a workers' cooperative employing non-members as workers. Such purpose transactions with non-members not only run counter to the institutional purpose of the cooperative society, they also devalue membership and encourage free-riders. Marcus Helios and Thomas Strieder underline that there is an obligation of the boards of cooperative societies to treat members and non-members differently and to offer members a 'cooperative advantage'.[18]

From a German perspective, only purpose transactions with non-members are classified as business with non-members in the strict sense. Such business with non-members is prohibited unless expressly allowed in the by-laws (§8(1) no. 5 GCA).

There are two arguments to justify purpose transactions with non-members:

- to recruit new members by giving non-members the chance to test the advantages of membership and then become members; and
- to use idle capacities in times when transactions with members do not have enough volume to run the facilities of the cooperative enterprise at full capacity in order to avoid losses.

When cooperative societies carry out purpose transactions with non-members without limits, they lose their special character as self-help organisations of their members and turn into ordinary commercial businesses. Under German cooperative law, regulating the issue of purpose transactions with non-members is left to the members in the by-laws. There is a provision in the German Cooperative Societies Act (§81 GCA) which, although it is rarely applied, states that cooperatives failing to meet their institutional objective of promoting the interests of their members can be dissolved *ex officio*.[19]

1.7. INDIRECT MUTUALITY THROUGH SUBSIDIARIES CONTROLLED BY COOPERATIVES

Cooperative societies are permitted under German cooperative law to hold shares in companies (§1(2) GCA). However, there are restrictions. Subsidiaries held by cooperatives are only permitted if their purpose supports the main institutional objective of member-promotion. Economic activities of cooperative enterprises

18 Helios and Strieder 2009, n. 10 above, p. 13, RZ 156, 157, p. 618.
19 Beuthien, see n. 8 above, §1 GenG, RZ 93–95.

cannot be entirely outsourced, so that the cooperative society no longer has a fully operational enterprise, but its economic activity is reduced to holding and administering assets (holding, *Haltegenossenschaft*). There are different views regarding the degree to which such outsourcing of economic activities is permitted without leaving the cooperative model.[20]

In Germany, the most common ways to outsource economic activities are horizontal integration (joint facilities with neighbouring cooperatives) or vertical integration (outsourcing to unions and/or federations, *Verbund*).

1.8. COOPERATIVES WITH PARTICULAR INSTITUTIONAL OBJECTIVES

Cooperative societies must always have the promotion of the interests of their members as their principal institutional objective. Since the 2006 amendment of the German Cooperative Societies Act, which broadened the social objective of cooperatives from promoting the economic interests of their members to their social and cultural interests (§1(1) GCA), this means that cooperatives can also serve the social interests of their members and indirectly or even directly promote common interest, provided that such general interest activity does not become the main objective. Care for the community is one of the international cooperative principles, and it extends beyond normal corporate social responsibility. But under German cooperative law, and for many Germans who classify cooperatives clearly as self-help organisations of their members, general interest cooperatives are a contradiction in terms.

Under German cooperative law and doctrine, general interest organisations in the legal form of registered cooperative society are generally ruled out. The objective of member-promotion is an indispensable element of the legal definition of a cooperative society in §1 GCA and of its organisational structure. Cooperatives are perceived as predominantly user-driven organisations. An organisation in which the majority of members are non-using promoting members, offering their services and facilities to non-members or the general public, cannot be registered as a cooperative society. Where a registered cooperative society changes its objective from member-promotion to serving the general interest, it can be dissolved *ex officio* (§81 GCA).

But there is a change of emphasis on economic and social motives and effects, results and expectations both in cooperative practice and cooperative theory. In attempts to find the right balance between social and economic elements in the cooperative form of organisation, cooperative federations and established cooperatives focus on socially responsible performance of the cooperative

20 Ibid.

enterprise as a business partner or employer and corporate citizen, rather than on its contribution to 'society' and to the common good, referred to as 'member-value' (other than shareholder-value).[21] In new cooperatives offering services to members and non-members, social and economic elements are considered together in efforts to optimise the promotional potential of cooperatives, taking the social functions and effects into account.[22]

1.8.1. *Social Cooperatives*

In Germany, organisations promoting the integration of the economically and socially weak into society and into the labour market exist. However, as a rule, they do so, not in the legal form of a registered cooperative society, but as associations, limited liability companies (GmbH) or foundations with an economic branch. Examples are: Werkstatt e.V. Baden Württemberg; HIS Beschäftigungs- und Qualifizierungs-gGmbH; Stern Radio Beschäftigungs- und Qualifikationsgesellschaft m.b.H. Only a few of such social enterprises exist in the legal form of a registered cooperative society, e.g. Technologie Entwicklung Anwendung eG (TEA eG), Nürnberg[23] and Sozialer Betrieb Sulzbach eG, as an experiment in local economy.[24]

In Germany, there is a special type of cooperative society with a general interest component in the field of housing. Between 1940 (during the Second World War) and 1990 (after German Unification), their activities, and the rules to be followed to receive official recognition as a general interest housing cooperative with tax advantages, were regulated in the Law on General Interest Housing (*Wohnungsgemeinützigkeitsgesetz*, WGG). To promote the construction of low-cost dwellings, housing cooperatives could be exempted from corporation tax, trade tax, and other taxes if the following conditions were met: building only small dwellings, only for rent, charging rent near cost, limitation of share contributions and profit distribution, obligation to use capital for continuous building (foundation-model), use of model by-laws and model contracts.

---

21 N. Göler von Ravensburg, 'Wirtschaftliche und soziale Elemente genossenschaftlicher Kooperation in Deutschland' [Economic and social elements of cooperation in the cooperative way in Germany], in G. Ringle and H.-H. Münkner (eds.) *Genossenschaftliche Kooperation – anders wirtschaften!* [Working together in the cooperative way – doing business differently!], Nomos, Baden-Baden, 2012, pp. 99 ff.

22 Göler von Ravensburg 2012, n. 21 above, p. 113.

23 H.-H. Münkner et al., *Unternehmen mit sozialer Zielsetzung* [Enterprises with social objectives], AG SPAK Bücher, Neu-Ulm, 2000, pp. 93 f.

24 N. Göler von Ravensburg, 'Sozialer Betrieb Sulzbach eG: Ein Experiment der lokalen Ökonomie' [Social enterprise Sulzbach coop.: An experiment of local economy], in H.-H. Münkner and G. Ringle (eds.) *Neue Genossenschaften und Innovative Aktionsfelder – Grundlagen und Fallstudien* [New cooperatives and innovative fields of activity – basic concept and case studies], Nomos, Baden-Baden, 2010, pp. 123 ff.

Communities, churches and enterprises were allowed to acquire shares in such housing cooperatives on behalf of tenants proposed by them. Even since abrogation of the WGG in 1990, housing cooperatives may apply to retain their special tax-status provided that they comply with the rules set by the WGG and their income from other than cooperative housing activities does not exceed 10% of their total income.[25]

In Germany, there are no special legal provisions for social cooperatives like those in Italy, France, Portugal and Spain, which serve members and non-members with the objective of offering employment and social integration to non-members. However, serving the general interest may be pursued as an additional objective (*Nebenzweck*). According to §1(2) no. 2 GCA, besides its main objective of member-promotion, a cooperative society may also 'serve public interest goals of the cooperative society, without this being the sole or main purpose of the cooperative society'. This means that cooperatives do not operate an enterprise oriented to serving the general interest, but an enterprise oriented to serving the interests of its members, and the members themselves decide how this general interest-orientation shall be put into practice.[26] Under German cooperative law, organisations pursuing only the general interest are not allowed to operate in the legal form of a registered cooperative society (§1(1) GCA).

The Germans and their law-makers are not alone in defining cooperatives as member-promotion oriented organisations, as some advocates of 'general interest cooperatives' believe. The International Cooperative Alliance underlines in its Statement on the Cooperative Identity of 1995 that 'self-help' is a cooperative value, and it uses the principle of identity of owners and users in definition of the term 'cooperative society'. Also in the UK, self-help and member-promotion are part of the official definition of a 'bona fide cooperative', and for good reason Community Interest Companies (CIC) and Societies for the Benefit of the Community (BenCom) are seen as distinct categories. CICs and BenComs serve a community other than their own members.[27]

From the British FCA's point of view, an organisation formed by people most of whom do not use its services cannot be a cooperative. In such organisations set up to help others, democratic control would mean that members voted and acted in the interest of a different group of people. Cooperatives must not be entirely self-interested. Members may decide to use resources of their cooperative society for the benefit of the community. However, there is a fundamental difference between, on the one hand, a cooperative society set up by and for the

---

25 Beuthien, n. 8 above, §1 GenG, RZ 75; Helios and Strieder, n. 10 above, §9 GenG, RZ 29 and 30, n. 95, pp. 380, 381, 383.

26 Beuthien, n. 8 above, §1 GenG, RZ 98.

27 I. Snaith, 'United Kingdom', in D. Cracogna et al. (eds.), *International Handbook of Cooperative Law*, Springer, Heidelberg, 2013, pp. 735–757, pp. 740–742.

members who act for self-help but also in the interest of others, and on the other, an organisation set up for general benefit.[28]

The issue of 'general interest cooperative' is dealt with differently in Italian cooperative doctrine and law. In Italy, there are mutual cooperatives and other cooperatives. The mutual purpose is not explicitly defined in the ICC and other cooperative laws. From the Italian perspective, cooperatives are obliged neither to deal prevalently with their members nor to report the volume of their transactions with them. The difference between mutual cooperatives and other cooperatives is perceived as not being relevant under organisational law, but under tax law.[29]

1.8.2. *Cooperatives between Self-Help Organisations and General interest Organisations*

If social cooperatives are located on a continuum between cooperative self-help organisations and general interest organisations, genuine and pure cooperatives with member-promotion as their principal objective can be found at one extreme. Their membership group is exclusively or mainly composed of user-members and/or worker-members, with the possibility of generating external positive effects benefiting non-members or even the general public. At the other extreme are general interest organisations composed only or mainly of promoting or honorary members whose principal objective is to help others.

In cooperatives, self-interest of the individual member and group interests of all members can be combined. Members can pursue their own interests better when cooperating with others who have similar interests. To prevent self-interest and group egoism becoming the only driving forces in cooperatives, the cooperative value system includes social responsibility. Cooperative principles stipulated care for the community long before commercial enterprises accepted the 'corporate social responsibility' often used by them mainly as a marketing tool to boost good will for them.

In Portugal, legislative decree no. of 1998 governing cooperatives of social solidarity mentions self-help of their members as part of the underlying concept (art. 2 (1)). Their membership group is composed of effective members as user-members (art. 4) and honorary members (art. 5) with the obligation to contribute goods and services towards achieving the goals of the cooperative society (art. 5 (1)). These honorary members have rights of access to information to the same extent as effective members. However, they may not elect or be elected to serve as office-bearers but may attend general meetings without voting rights (art. 5 (2)).

---

28 Ian Adderley, Senior Associate, FCA, UK, in a message sent to the author in July 2015.

29 A. Fici, 22 'Italy', in Cracogna et al. (eds.), n. 27 above, pp. 484, 485.

In Italy, the member-orientation of cooperatives can be deduced from the composition of their membership. Law no. 59 of 1992 sets limits on the number of promoting members in the membership group (art. 4): Votes of promoting members may not exceed one third of the total of the votes of all members (art. 4 (2)). Promoting members may be appointed to serve on the board, but the majority of the board members must be co-operators (i.e. user-members or worker-members) (art. 4 (3). What is not expressly mentioned is that the rest of the members of social cooperatives must obviously be user-members and/or worker-members expecting promotion of their interests. It is not clear what the minimum amount of relationship with members must be for such 'other' (i.e. non-prevalently mutual) entities to be recognised as a cooperative society.[30]

In France, in collective interest cooperatives (sociétés coopératives d'intérêt collectif, SCIC), there must be user-members and worker-members apart from promoting members in the membership group; otherwise the organisation does not qualify for registration as SCIC (art. 19*septies*, Law governing cooperative societies of 1947, with amendments up to 2001). This means that promotion of members' interests remains an essential part of the SCIC's objective. art. 3*bis* allows admission of non-using investor-members, with the limitation that investor-members may not have more than 35% of the total votes, or 49% if cooperatives are among the investor-members; but it also allows that third parties (non-members) may make use of the goods and services offered by the SCIC (art. 19*sexies* L. 1947). If the percentage of the capital contributed by promoting members exceeds 35 or 49%, the voting rights of these members are reduced in proportion. According to art. 19*octies* of L. 1947, each member has one vote in the general meeting or in the electoral college to which it belongs. No electoral college may dispose of more than 50% of the total of votes or of less than 10% of the votes.

Where cooperatives pursue the promotion of the social interests of their members as part of their institutional objectives, they can monitor success in achieving this objective by establishing a social council in their by-laws (e.g. Portuguese legislative decree no. 7 of 1998, art. 6). Legally, this council operates as a sub-committee of the supervisory council. The by-laws can also introduce the obligation of the board of directors to present a social report at the end of each financial year and widen the scope of audit to include social audit.

1.8.3. Multi-Stakeholder Cooperatives and Community Cooperatives

The admission of different categories of members, and in particular investor-members but also promoting members, extends the scope of cooperative self-help activities of individuals or enterprises joining forces to help themselves and

30 Fici, n. 29 above, p. 485, n. 15.

their communities and regions. By resorting to organised self-help in groups, multi-stakeholder cooperatives or community cooperatives emerge and are given their particular legal framework e.g. in France and Canada.[31] In such cooperatives all members have as their common interest improvement of the conditions in their community or region.

In the case of multi-stakeholder cooperatives with different categories of members – citizens, employees, investor-members, enterprises working in the community or region, promoters, public authorities – the principle of 'one member/one vote' is modified with regard to election of office-holders. This is to prevent large groups of members that contribute relatively little from dominating by their voting power smaller groups of members making significant contributions. The by-laws of the society may lay down establishment of a committee for the election of board members as a sub-committee of the supervisory council, in which each category of members has an equal number of votes. In this way it is possible to prevent the most numerous sub-group of members from dominating the other sub-groups, which may be the main contributors of capital, know-how and public relations. Such rules have already become part of cooperative law in France and Québec/Canada.[32]

French SCICs may have the following categories of members: (i) workers of the cooperative; (ii) persons normally using the goods and services of the SCIC free of charge or against pay; (iii) every natural person desirous to participate in the activities of the cooperative; (iv) public corporations and their federations; (v) every natural or legal person contributing in one way or another to the activities of the cooperative. However, a SCIC must have members belonging

---

31 H.-H. Münkner, 'Organisierte Selbsthilfe gegen soziale Ausgrenzung, ‚Multi-stakeholder Genossenschaften' (MSG) in der internationalen Praxis' [Organized self-help against social exclusion, 'Multi-stakeholder cooperatives' (MSC) in international practice], in M. Hanisch (ed.), *Genossenschaftsmodelle – zwischen Auftrag und Anpassung: Festschrift zum 65. Geburtstag von Prof. Dr. Rolf Steding* [Cooperative models between mission and adjustment], Berliner Beiträge zum Genossenschaftswesen 56, Institut für Genossenschaftswesen an der Humboldt-Universität zu Berlin, Berlin, 2002, pp. 219–267.

32 France: Loi no. 2001-62, art. 36-I on coopératives d'intérêt collectif, SCIC, amending loi no. 47–1775 du 10 septembre 1947, Titre II*ter*, art. 19*octies*: Every member has one vote in the general meeting or the election committee of which it is part. The by-laws may provide that the members are subdivided into election committees according to their work in the cooperative or their contribution to its existence. Each election committee has an equal number of votes. In this case the by-laws regulate the subdivision of members into election committees, and the number of votes of these representatives in the general meeting in proportion to the members represented or the contributions made. However, no election committee can have more than 50% of the total number of votes or less than 10% of the votes, provided that capital contributions may not be the criterion for attributing votes. Canada: Lois refondues du Québec, Loi sur les coopératives, art. 226.6. 'The user, worker or promoting members form member-groups according to article 83 and each group has the right to elect at least one board member. The cooperatives society can provide in its by-laws that additional members of the board are elected by the general meeting. The number of promoting members among the elected board members may not be more than one third of all board members.'

to at least three of the afore-mentioned categories and must in any case have members belonging to the categories 1 and 2, i.e. user-members and worker-members (art. 19*septies* L. 1947), whose interests must be promoted.

A clear position on this issue is taken by the cooperative law-makers in Quebec, Canada. Canadian cooperatives for solidarity must consist simultaneously of members who are users of the services offered by the cooperative and workers working in the cooperative, and also of promoting members or organisations with an economic or social interest in achieving the goals of the cooperative society (art. 226.1). But if their membership group consists of promoting members only, such cooperatives may be dissolved *ex officio* (art. 226.12).

1.9. INFLUENCE OF THE INSTITUTIONAL OBJECTIVE ON GOVERNANCE STRUCTURE

Under the principle of self-administration, German cooperative law prescribes (§9(2) GCA) that only members can be elected to serve as office-holders (as board members and supervisory council members). However, in the case of board members, this legal provision has lost its effectiveness because it is common practice to recruit specialists from outside the cooperative movement who are admitted as 'promoting members'. They do not originate from the membership-group but are recruited for their professional know-how and experience.[33]

Another amendment of the Cooperative Societies Act of 2006 clarifies a previously unclear issue. Where legal entities are members of cooperative societies, representatives of such legal entities can serve on the governing bodies even if they – personally – are not members.

Under the revised Cooperative Societies Act 2006, investor-members create another cause of concern. There are no provisions preventing investor-members from being elected as board members. In the case of the supervisory council, limits have been introduced to the effect that not more than one quarter of its members may be investor-members, so as to ensure that user-members have the majority and remain in control. According to §8(2) GCA, cooperatives must take appropriate measures to ensure that under no circumstances can investor-members outvote regular members in general meetings.

There are other laws influencing the composition of governing bodies of cooperatives. The workers' co-determination law (*Mitbestimmungsgesetz*) prescribes that, in cooperatives with more than 500 employees, representatives of the employees must be elected by the employees to sit on the governing bodies of cooperative societies, even without being members of the cooperative.[34]

---

33 Beuthien, n. 8 above, §9 GenG, RZ 13.

34 Beuthien, see n. 8 above, §9 GenG, RZ 14, §§1, 6 ff. Mitbestimmungsgesetz (workers' co-determination law).

According to §36(4) GCA, in the case of cooperative banks, there must be at least one member with experience in accounting or auditing among the members of the supervisory council.

1.10. COOPERATIVE SOCIETY AS A HYBRID FORM OF BUSINESS ASSOCIATION BETWEEN PARTNERSHIP AND COMPANY

1.10.1. Common Features of Business Organisations

Common features of cooperative society, partnership and company: All these legal types are business organisations operating in the market. They all need efficient management. They must earn income in excess of expenditure and build up a solid capital base.

Common features of cooperatives and partnerships: Both are based on personal relations among partners/members, social ties and mutual trust. Partners/members are directly responsible for decision making in their group entity. They are personally liable for debts incurred by the jointly owned and operated enterprise.

Common features of cooperatives and companies: Both are characterised by variable membership. They need perpetual succession to exist as organisations independent of the individual members. They have a corporate structure with by-laws, organs (governing bodies) and legal personality by incorporation and are designed to pursue long-term objectives or projects beyond the duration of membership of individual members.

1.10.2. Special Cooperative Features – The Original Design

Cooperative societies are organisations based on their own values and principles and are designed to pursue the specific objective of member-promotion expressed by the principle of identity of owners and users. In contrast to partnerships and companies, which usually carry on business for gain in the open market, cooperatives focus their activities on meeting the needs of their members. Relations between the cooperative enterprise and its members (on the internal market) should be managed according to a policy of service near cost. Cooperatives have an internal democratic structure expressed by the rule 'one member/one vote'. In contrast to companies, where membership can be acquired and terminated by buying or selling shares, in cooperative societies, membership is acquired by admission on members' personal application and only if the applicant meets the qualification requirements specified in the by-laws. The obligation to make financial contributions to the cooperative society results from membership. Membership is terminated from the members' side by giving notice or from the cooperative's side by expulsion with the right of the past member to redeem paid-up share capital.

In their financial structure, cooperatives follow their own rules:

- Shares can only be held by members who are also users of the cooperative's facilities. Shares are not freely transferable and can be redeemed upon termination of membership at par value. The number of shares that can be held by an individual member is usually limited.
- There are four venues for allocating surplus: (i) in form of patronage refund in proportion to business done by the member with the cooperative enterprise; (ii) as a limited dividend on paid-up share capital, if any; (iii) by transfer to indivisible reserves; and (iv) for purposes of general interest.
- After liquidation of the cooperative society, the residual assets cannot be distributed among the members but are transferred to other cooperatives or used for purposes of general interest. In German cooperative law, this matter is left to be decided by the members in the by-laws (§§91, 92(2), (3) GCA).

1.10.3. Cooperatives between For-Profit and Non-Profit Organisations

Discussion of this issue becomes less dogmatic when the term 'profit' is replaced with 'surplus of income over expenditure'. If this is done, there is no doubt that – to be viable – cooperative societies operating an enterprise jointly owned and patronised by their members must make surplus in order to survive in the market and to build up a stable financial base. The term 'non-profit' serves to express that non-profit organisations (NPOs) do not pursue profit-making as their main objective and do not intend to make profit for distribution among rent-seeking investors.

Instead of doing business for gain and to distribute the surplus made among the shareholders in proportion to the shares held by them, cooperatives have developed their own ways to deal with surplus made in transactions with members despite their policy of service near cost *(le trop perçu)*, as discussed above: patronage refund, limited return on paid-up capital, allocation to indivisible reserves, and use for purposes of general interest. Hence, cooperatives can be classified as organisations not serving for profit distribution among the owners of capital or shareholders. Antonio Fici and Chiara Strano[35] describe cooperatives under Italian law as being partly for-profit, partly non-profit organisations.

---

[35] A. Fici and C. Strano, 'Country Report Italy', in *Study on the implementation of the Regulation 1435/2003 on the Statute for the European Cooperative Society (SCE)*, EURICSE/EZAI/CE, Trento, 2010, p. 687.

Under Italian cooperative law, cooperatives may be prevalently mutual or 'non-prevalently mutual'. Prevalently mutual cooperatives are characterised by a partial profit non-distribution constraint.[36] This means that there is a limit on the distribution of dividends on paid-up capital; that the distribution of reserves to user-members is prohibited; and that, in the case of dissolution, the liquidated assets must be devolved to mutual funds.

In Switzerland, cooperatives are classified as NPOs.[37]

1.11. CROSS-BORDER COOPERATION – EUROPEAN COOPERATIVE SOCIETIES IN GERMANY

In Germany, between 2005 and 2015, the total number of newly-formed registered cooperative societies was 2,379, including 12 SCEs, of which 6 were formed in 2014 and 2015. The other SCEs were registered in 2008 (1), 2010 (1), 2011 (2), 2012 (1) and 2013 (1).[38]

The following reasons are given for the limited interest that the SCE has received in Germany so far:

- Lack of need, mainly because there are less complicated alternatives to organise cross-border cooperation.
- Lack of knowledge about the SCE, which is even less known than ordinary cooperatives, especially among founder members of team enterprises, business consultants, tax consultants, associations of entrepreneurs and chambers of crafts, trade and industry.
- The high complexity of the legal provisions, with a hierarchy of norms covering five different levels and options to deviate from the standard German norms.
- Higher minimum requirements regarding the contents of by-laws of SCEs as compared to registered cooperative societies under German cooperative law (eGs).

High complexity results from the incomplete legal framework provided by the SCE Regulation and the method of referring to the national law of the EU member-state in which the SCE has its registered office. Art. 8 SCE-Regulation

---

36 Fici, n. 29 above, pp. 489, 490.

37 P. Schwarz, 'Genossenschaftsmanagement im Dilemma zwischen Profit-, Nonprofit- und Gemeinwohlorientierung' [Cooperative management in the dilemma between profit-, non-profit and general interest orientation], in R. Purtschert (ed.), *Das Genossenschaftswesen in der Schweiz* [Co-operatives in Switzerland], Haupt, Bern/Stuttgart/Vienna, 2005, pp. 195 f.

38 Information obtained from Michael Stappel, Senior Economist, Research and Volkswirtschaft, DZ BANK AG: Gründungen von Genossenschaften in Deutschland 2000 bis 2015, Frankfurt am Main, 2016.

creates this hierarchy of norms with five different levels, which Volker Beuthien[39] summarises as follows:

- First level: Community law – as far as it extends – prevailing over national law (art. 8 paragraph 1, lit. a);
- Second level: Insofar as the SCE Regulation expressly grants autonomy to make by-laws, these European by-laws replace the law of the EU Member States (art. 8 paragraph 1, lit. b);
- Third level: At EU Member State level, as far as left open by the SCE Regulation, there is (a) special legislation introducing the SCE Regulation into national law (SCEAG) art. 8 paragraph 1, lit. c, case i) and (b) the national Cooperative Societies Act (art. 8 paragraph 1, lit. c, case ii);
- Fourth level: Cooperative law under the national legal system (art. 8 paragraph 1, lit. c, case iii);
- Fifth level: By-laws made under national cooperative law.

A publication by Marcus Helios and Thomas Strieder (eds.) (2009) on German cooperative societies from the legal, tax and accounting perspective, contains a full chapter by Otto Korte on 'The European Cooperative Society'.[40]

2. COOPERATIVE GOVERNANCE

2.1. THE LEGAL CONTEXT OF COOPERATIVE GOVERNANCE

2.1.1. Cooperative Governance and Cooperative Identity

From the German perspective, a cooperative society is a special type of business organisation with a legal framework of its own. It has a dual nature, consisting of a cooperative group and a cooperative enterprise. These are linked together by the purpose of member-promotion. As self-help organisations, cooperatives are characterised by the identity of owners and users, those who own the cooperative enterprise established it, or joined it because they seek advantages deriving from membership.

Self-administration is one of the guiding principles of cooperative organisation. Members play a predominant role and the key rights are reserved for them. Officers are elected by the members from among themselves.

Another principle is open and voluntary membership. An organisation pursuing long-term objectives while having variable membership needs a stable

[39] Beuthien, n. 8 above, SCE R Art. 8, RZ 1.
[40] Korte, n. 5 above, pp. 730–765; see also Münkner, above n. 5.

corporate structure with governing bodies (organs) composed of office-holders elected for a limited term of office.

In order to work, plan and develop, the cooperative enterprise needs:

- stability of the cooperative group despite variable membership;
- a stable financial base despite variable share capital;
- a reliable economic framework with a predictable volume of members' use of the joint facilities of the cooperative enterprise;
- leadership and management specially trained to run an efficient business organisation and to use scarce resources efficiently while practising value-oriented cooperative management geared to sustainable promotion of members, taking the social and ecological effects of its activities into account. Cooperatives need a Janus-faced leadership which looks simultaneously in two directions: at the external markets in which they operate like any other business enterprise, and at the internal market, where in transactions with their members, they offer service near cost and/or on favourable conditions;
- special methods to measure success as a business enterprise (operational efficiency) and as a cooperative enterprise (member-oriented effectiveness).

A special code of corporate governance of cooperative societies was developed in 2003 by the German Cooperative and Raiffeisen Federation DGRV.[41] This cooperative corporate governance code was designed mainly for cooperative banks and other cooperatives with full-time directors.

2.1.2. *Cooperative Governance and National Business Organisation Law*

In Germany, cooperative societies are seen and treated by the law-makers as a special type of business association, and they have had their own legal framework since 1889. With about 170 sections, the Cooperative Societies Act is fairly comprehensive. For matters not regulated in the Cooperative Societies Act and not left to the by-laws, the general law of business organisations applies, e.g. the Commercial Code (HGB) and laws on the keeping of books and accounts (Transparency and public information law, TransPuG of 2002).[42] In recent years, partly due to harmonisation of EU-legislation, some matters have been transferred from the Cooperative Societies Act to a special Act on Transformation of Enterprises (UmwG, Transformation Act) applying to all

41 DGRV Geschäftsbericht (annual report) 2003, p. 27, most recent version dated 22 November 2010; see also B. Hilkenbach, 'Corporate Governance Kodex für Genossenschaften, Forschungsinstitut für Genossenschaftswesen an der Universität Erlangen-Nürnberg', *Arbeitspapiere* 30, 2004, Nürnberg, pp. 1, 2 and Annex.

42 Beuthien, n. 8 above, §53 GenG, RZ 9.

legal forms of business organisation, e.g. transformation and merger, division, transfer of assets and change of legal form (old §§93a–d GCA) introduced in 1922 and revised several times until 1993 (§§93a–s GCA), adjusted to practical needs in 1994 by the UmwG of 1994.[43]

In other matters, mainly as a result of growth of primary cooperatives, cooperative law has been approximated to company law, e.g. powers of the board of directors to manage the cooperative enterprise on their own responsibility, only bound by the law and the by-laws, but not by decisions of the members in general meeting or meeting of delegates (§27(1) GCA).

Competition law is relevant mainly in the case of traders' cooperatives. Cooperative banks come under general banking regulations, and housing cooperatives under the laws on building construction and technical matters like safety regulations, labour law[44] and MitbestG (Co-determination law) applied to cooperatives with more than 500 employees.[45]

2.1.3. *Where can Cooperative Governance Rules be Found?*

As business organisations, general rules on corporate governance apply (e.g. corporate social responsibility, CSR). However, the cooperative federations have agreed on a special code of cooperative corporate governance obliging office-holders of cooperative societies to respect cooperative values and principles in their work and in their communication of the cooperative image or brand (*Leitbild*) to their members and to the general public. In 2012, the National Cooperative Academy in Montabaur (ADG) developed a new training programme for value-oriented management offered to senior officers of cooperative societies.[46] Given the focus of cooperative societies on sustainable, ecologically sound, and environment-friendly strategies combined with social responsibility (care for the community) as a matter of principle, awareness of the economic, social and ecological responsibility of cooperative management goes well beyond the general compliance with CSR practised by commercial and capitalist enterprises.

43 Beuthien, n. 8 above, UmwG, pp. 1041 ff.

44 Beuthien, n. 8 above, §24 GenG, RZ 17.

45 Beuthien, n. 8 above, §38 GenG, RZ 5.

46 T. Kring and G. Walther, 'Wider die Glaubwürdigkeitsdefizite in der Führung: Ansätze zur Revitalisierung einer genossenschaftlichen Mitarbeiterführung' [Against credibility deficits in leadership, approaches to revitalizing cooperative staff management], *ZfgG-Sonderheft*, 2012, pp. 49–63.

2.2. THE ROLE OF MEMBERS

2.2.1. Division of Powers Among the Organs of the Cooperative Society

As already mentioned, the distribution of powers among the organs of cooperative societies was changed in 1973, when the elected board of directors was given full autonomy to run the cooperative enterprise: 'The board of directors shall manage the cooperative society on its own responsibility with due consideration to the limitations imposed on it by the by-laws' (§27(1) GCA).

In 1922, steady growth of cooperative societies had made it necessary to replace the general meeting of members with a meeting of delegates (indirect democracy),[47] prescribing that, in cooperatives with more than 10,000 members, the meeting of members was to be replaced by a meeting of delegates, while societies with more than 3,000 members could opt for a meeting of delegates. In 1926, the meeting of delegates became mandatory for societies with more than 3,000 members[48] and in 1973 this figure was reduced further to 1,500 (§43a(1) GCA). This meant that ordinary members lost all their rights of participation in decision-making processes except that of electing delegates and substituting delegates every four years (§43a GCA). Since 1993, in societies with large membership, substitution of the general meeting of members by a meeting of delegates is no longer prescribed by law, but may be introduced in the by-laws.[49] The meeting of delegates must be composed of at least 50 members and their substitutes elected by secret ballot, with conditions for their election being laid down in the by-laws (§43a(4) GCA).

Since revision of the Cooperative Societies Act in 2006, in societies that have introduced the meeting of delegates, the general meeting is no longer replaced completely by the meeting of delegates. The general meeting continues to function in parallel with the meeting of delegates, and the by-laws may stipulate that certain basic rights are reserved for the members in general meeting (§43a(1) GCA) to be decided with a majority of not less than three quarters of votes cast (§43a(2) GCA), e.g. amendment of by-laws changing the objectives, merger, legal form.[50]

Members in general meeting or meeting of delegates have the right to elect and remove their directors and members of the supervisory committee. In the by-laws, the right to elect directors may be delegated by the members to the supervisory committee and/or may be made subject to recommendations by the cooperative federation with which the society is affiliated (§24(2) GCA). If this

---

47 J. Lang and L. Weidmüller, *Genossenschaftsgesetz mit Erläuterungen zum Umwandlungsgesetz, Kommentar*, 37th ed., de Gruyter, Berlin/Boston, 2011, §43a GenG, RZ 1.

48 Paulick, n. 1 above, p. 251.

49 Beuthien 2011, n. 8 above, §43a GenG, RZ 1.

50 Beuthien 2011, n. 8 above, §43a GenG, RZ 2.

is done, the members or their delegates lose their authority to determine the leaders and directors managing the cooperative society on their behalf.[51] They still retain the right to suspend or remove directors if this is not delegated to the supervisory committee (§24(2), (3) GCA).

In 2006, the minimum number of members of a cooperative society was reduced from seven to three (§4 GCA). New rules were introduced with regard to small cooperatives, i.e. cooperatives with no more than 20 members. Such small cooperatives may operate with a simplified structure, i.e. work without a supervisory committee, with only one member serving on the board and the general meeting, or one elected representative replacing the supervisory committee (§§9(1), 24(2) GCA). There are no rules regarding a maximum number of members. Since 1993, the list of members is kept by the board of the society and no longer by the registering authority (local court) (§30 GCA).

2.2.2. *Members' Voting Rights*

Voting rights are exercised at general meetings or at meetings of delegates in person by show of hand or secret ballot (e.g. in the case of election of directors), as the by-laws provide. Since 1973, voting by proxy has been allowed provided that one proxy does not represent more than two members (§43(5) GCA). The possibility to vote in written or electronic form was introduced in 2006 (§43(7) GCA).

Until 1973, the original cooperative principle of 'one member/one vote' was applied without exception. Introduced in 1973 was a moderate form of plural voting that allowed members 'who further the business of the cooperative society in a special manner' to be given up to three votes under the by-laws, provided that certain conditions are met (§43(3) GCA). However, such additional votes are only valid in decisions regarding routine matters, while in the case of decisions on key issues, where a three-quarter majority of votes cast is required, the principle of equal voting power of all members still prevails (§43(3) GCA). The trend to allow plural voting continued in 2006 when in cooperatives in which three-quarters of the members are entrepreneurs, a member could be given up to 10 votes (§43(3) no. 2 GCA). The provisions on plural voting do not apply to cooperative federations or secondary organisations in the legal form of a cooperative society (§43(3) no. 3 GCA).

The cooperative's clear profile as a self-help organisation (principle of identity of owners and users) was blurred in 2006 by allowing the admission

---

51 V. Beuthien, 'Die Genossenschaftsidee im Spiegelbild von Rechtssystem, Unternehmen und Gesellschaft – wie geht es weiter?' [The cooperative idea in the mirror of the legal system, of enterprises and of society – what will be the future development?], *Die Aktiengesellschaft*, 2012, vol. 23, p. 870.

of 'investing members' i.e. non-using members (§8(2) GCA). Admission of 'promoting members' had already been practised under the old law; however, it was quite clear that this meant going against the spirit of the law just as it did in the case of tolerating 'passive members' (e.g. members of dairy cooperatives holding 'dry shares').

The revised Cooperative Societies Act of 2006 contains provisions to prevent the influence of investing members from becoming too strong. Investing members cannot outvote user-members in general meeting or meeting of delegates. In the supervisory committee, the number of investing members cannot exceed one quarter of its total number (§8(2) GCA). In cooperative banks, at least two board members must have professional qualifications as bank managers.[52] One member of the supervisory committee must have expertise in accounting or auditing (§36(4) GCA). There is no provision in the law that prevents investing members from being elected to serve on the board of directors.

New rules regarding voting by corporate members in the general meeting or meeting of delegates, on the board, and in the supervisory committee have been introduced. A corporate member may be represented in cooperative societies by its board members, even if these are not members of the society (§43(4) GCA). 'If a member of the cooperative society is a legal person or a partnership, natural persons authorised to represent them legally may be elected as their delegate' (§43a(2) GCA).

2.2.3. *Mechanisms for Member Control: Meetings; Elections etc*

Decisions and resolutions in general meeting or meeting of delegates are taken by simple majority of votes unless either the law or the by-laws prescribe a larger majority and additional requirements (§43(2) GCA), e.g. for decisions regarding amendment of by-laws, removal of directors, or conversion to a different legal form (§§190, 191(1) no. 3 UmwG, e.g. three-quarters or nine-tenths majority of votes cast (§§193, 194, 260–264 UmwG). Board members may be suspended by the supervisory committee (§40 GCA).

There are no general provisions regarding a quorum; however, such conditions may be stipulated in the by-laws.[53]

2.2.4. *Dispute Resolution between Members and the Cooperative Society*

There are no special rules on resolution of disputes between members and the cooperative society in the Cooperative Societies Act. Each member may take his/her cooperative society to court, and vice versa. However, under general

---

52 Beuthien, n. 8 above, §24 GenG, RZ 8.

53 Beuthien, n. 8 above, §§2 ff., UmwG, RZ 36.

organisation law there is a rule that every member owes loyalty to his/her organisation and should avoid acts damaging the image of the organisation in public.[54] In addition, the by-laws may provide that before going to court, arbitration must be tried.

2.3. MANAGEMENT AND INTERNAL CONTROL

2.3.1. *Powers of a Cooperative's Board or Boards*

Since 1973, there has been a clear division of powers among the board of directors, the supervisory committee, and the meeting of members or delegates. The offices of board member and member of the supervisory committee are incompatible (§37 GCA).

The Board manages the cooperative society on its own responsibility (§27(1) GCA) independently from the decisions of the members. The supervisory committee supervises the board of directors in its management functions (§38(1) GCA) and reports its findings to the members in general meeting or meeting of delegates. It 'convenes such meeting if and when this is in the interest of the society' (§38(2) GCA). 'The supervisory committee may appoint an auditing committee to monitor the accounting process and the effectiveness of the system of controlling, risk management and internal auditing' (§38(1) GCA).

The by-laws may provide that certain important matters of the board's business require the approval of, or must be decided together with, the supervisory committee. However, too close cooperation between these two bodies should be avoided.

The liability of directors *vis-à-vis* a cooperative society for breach of legal obligations is partly regulated by the Cooperative Societies Act (§34 GCA) and partly by the rules of general civil and commercial law.

The board has the duty to give the supervisory committee full information on the management of the cooperative's affairs and the supervisory committee has the right to obtain all information that it needs from the board. A special feature of German cooperative law is the role of cooperative auditing federations. Under the Cooperative Societies Act, to be registered, a new cooperative must be accepted as a member by an officially recognised auditing federation. The auditing federations have the exclusive right to audit affiliated societies, and the scope of auditing includes financial and management audit (e.g. the extent to which the board has promoted the interests of the members). The supervisory committee in charge of internal audit must collaborate with the cooperative auditor of the federation, and it is informed by the auditor of the audit results

---

54 BEUTHIEN, n. 8 above, §18 GenG, RZ 50–56.

(§58(3) GCA). This right to be informed was introduced in 2006. Previously, the auditors only had to send their report to the board of directors.

Basic rules regarding the division of powers among the board of directors, the supervisory committee, and the members' meeting are laid down in the Cooperative Societies Act, with room left for modification of some of those rules in the by-laws. As said, the power to elect and remove the members of the board is often delegated under the by-laws by the members' meeting to the supervisory committee. Under the revised Act of 2006 this does not apply to small cooperatives with no more than 20 members, which may opt to work without a supervisory committee (§9(1) GCA).

In large societies with a meeting of delegates, the position of members in general meeting has been strengthened in the revised Act of 2006 by giving them the right to stipulate in the by-laws that certain decisions are reserved for the general meeting (§43a(1) GCA).

The revised Cooperative Societies Act of 2006 provides that:

- a meeting of members must be convened if this is demanded by at least one tenth of the members (§45(1) GCA);
- a list of candidates for the meeting of delegates can be presented by at least 150 members (§43a(4) GCA); and
- introduction of a meeting of delegates can be revoked, and resumption of a general meeting of members can be requested by at least one tenth of the members (§43a(7) GCA).

Members are entitled to inspect the summary of the audit report (§59(1) GCA).

2.3.2. *Board Functioning, Structure and Composition*

As already mentioned, under German law the board of directors is the executive body in cooperative societies. Since 1973, the board has full autonomy in running the cooperative society and only has to respect the provisions of the Act and of the by-laws. In business matters, the board is not bound by directives from the members in the general meeting or in the meeting of delegates. The board must be composed of at least two directors ('four eyes' principle). The by-laws may provide that certain important matters are to be decided jointly by the board and the supervisory committee or require approval of the supervisory committee.

Until 2006, all cooperative societies had to be organised into a two-tier structure: board of directors and supervisory committee. Since 2006, there have been special provisions for small cooperatives (with not more than twenty members), which can opt for a one-tier structure, so that they have only a board of one director (§24(2) GCA) and without a supervisory committee (§9(1) GCA). According to §57(5) GCA, small cooperatives operating without a supervisory committee have to appoint one member to represent the society *vis-à-vis* the auditing federation (§57(5) GCA).

According to §9(2) GCA, all board members must be members of the cooperative society. With the growing size of cooperative enterprises and the increasing complexity of their operations, it may be impossible to find persons with the requisite qualifications in the membership group. To solve this problem, 'promoting members' are admitted, even if they do not belong to the general membership group, for the sole purpose of making them eligible for service on the board as 'external' directors. Such directors are usually experts in their field but not familiar with cooperative, promotion-oriented and value-based management. Often, cooperative federations recommend suitable candidates.

2.3.3. *Mechanisms for Board Election*

Under German cooperative law the 'four eyes principle' prevails. Each cooperative society must have at least two directors. The board members are only authorised to represent the society jointly if the by-laws do not provide otherwise (§25(1) GCA). In 2006, this rule was softened for small cooperatives, which can now operate with only one director (§24(2) GCA).

In most of the established cooperatives, board members serve full-time and are paid. There is also the option of electing unpaid, honorary directors (§24(3) GCA),[55] e.g. to represent the members' interests on the board of specialists. However, in established cooperatives, this option is seldom used in practice.[56]

The remuneration of board members is usually decided by the supervisory committee or by a sub-committee formed for the purpose. Transparency in this field is limited. Some critics call for transparency to be increased by making the remuneration of board members subject to approval by the general meeting or the meeting of delegates.[57]

Special qualifications are required for directors serving in cooperative banks. General banking regulations require that each cooperative bank must employ at least two board members with full banking qualifications verified by the federal supervisory agency for financial services (BaFin) as bank managers.[58] In cooperative societies with a large number of employees, one board member must be in charge of labour relations (§§1 (1) and 33 (3) MitbestG (co-determination law)).[59]

55 Beuthien, n. 8 above, §24 GenG, RZ 15.

56 H.-H. Münkner, 'Genossenschaftliche Identität und Identifikation der Mitglieder mit ihrer Genossenschaft' [Cooperative identity and identification of members with their cooperative], *Strukturfragen der deutschen Genossenschaften, Veröffentlichungen der DG Bank*, 2012, vol. 17, p. 64.

57 Beuthien, n. 51 above, p. 871.

58 Geschwandtner and Helios, n. 4 above, p. 91.

59 Beuthien, n. 8 above, §24 GenG, RZ 9.

The supervisory committee is elected by the members from among themselves with a minimum number of three. In large cooperatives with more than 500 employees, a workers' representative must be elected by the employees to sit on the supervisory committee even without being a member of the cooperative society (§§1 and 6 MitbestG).[60] A new rule introduced in 2006 limited the number of 'investing members' on the supervisory committee to a quarter of its total number (§8(2) GCA), the purpose being to ensure that user-members have the majority.

Directors of cooperatives must use the 'due diligence and accountability of a conscious management of a cooperative society' (§34(1) GCA). This is interpreted to include the obligation of directors of cooperatives to pursue the objective of member-promotion and to practise value-based management. 'Members of the board failing to comply with their duties are jointly and severally liable to recompense any resulting damage' (§34(2) GCA). The same diligence and accountability is required from the members of the supervisory committee (§41 GCA).

Internal audit is carried out by the supervisory committee. Its annual report to the meeting of members should include an assessment of the board's success in achieving the objective of member promotion. Instruments to make member-promotion transparent have been developed by cooperative research institutes:[61]

- a promotion plan, proposed by the board to the members in general meeting or meeting of delegates, discussed and jointly agreed; and
- a promotion report: presented in the following meeting of members or delegates, showing success in implementing the promotion plan during the financial year including costs and benefits and serving as the basis for the following promotion plans.

However, these instruments are relatively seldom applied in practice.

Development-oriented effectiveness in terms of social activities contributing to the development of the community and the region can be shown in a social balance sheet. This is the specifically cooperative way of showing corporate social responsibility (CSR), as a matter of principle rather than as a marketing tool. Whether this is done in practice is left to the individual society. Some cooperatives mix 'care for the community' with CSR by publishing their engagement in CSR under the heading 'promotion report'.[62]

---

60 Beuthien, n. 8 above, §9 GenG, RZ 14.

61 Beuthien, n. 8 above, §1 GenG, RZ 24 with sources quoted there; Beuthien and Hanrath, n. 2 above, pp. 54–57, 62–64.

62 G. Emmelius and N. Krönlein, 'Mitverantwortung – verantwortliches Unternehmertum genossenschaftlich interpretiert' [Joint reponsibility – Responsible entrepreneurship in the cooperative way], in Ringle and Münkner (eds.), n. 21 above, pp. 68 f.

External audit is carried out by specially trained cooperative auditors employed by cooperative auditing federations. Their audit reports should include assessment of the board's performance with regard to member promotion.[63] However, this is usually not done in detail, if at all. There is a tendency to approximate cooperative audit to the ordinary financial audit of commercial enterprises. This trend is supported by the policy of encouraging cooperative auditors to acquire the qualification of chartered accountant (and thereafter carry out their audit according to what they have learned), as well as by the efforts to harmonise audit regulations at European Union level.

According to §9(2) GCA, only members of the cooperative society are eligible to be board members. The minimum age is eighteen years (full age, §2 Civil Code (BGB),). There are no general rules on maximum age, capital stake, minimum transactions with the society, or length of membership.

German cooperative law does not prescribe that persons elected to serve on the board of a cooperative society need special education and training in cooperative subjects. In the case of cooperative banks, special banking skills are required under banking regulations as a condition for being eligible. But this only refers to banking skills, not to proficiency in cooperative management. Very often, such 'external' directors, i.e. specialists recruited from outside the cooperative system, are fully trained in their field of business but have little knowledge of the special cooperative way of doing business. Such knowledge can be acquired in training courses offered by several cooperative colleges at regional level and by the Academy of German Cooperatives (ADG). However, these special training facilities are not widely used. As a result, many cooperative directors practise what they have learned, i.e. act like their commercial colleagues.[64] Housing cooperatives have established their own academy and offer a special degree course in cooperative estate management.

Procedural matters such as a quorum, how the chair is selected, voting mechanisms, etc. for the board, the supervisory committee and the members' meetings are left to the individual society to regulate in their by-laws or internal regulations. Model rules or regulations are available from cooperative federations.

With regard to the term of office of cooperative board members, good democratic practice would require the rotation of office-holders by limiting re-election to two or three terms of office of two to four years. However, such provisions or practices are more the exception than the rule. According to a survey conducted among cooperative banks in 1990, the average length of service of directors was between 11 and 30 years.[65]

---

63 BEUTHIEN, n. 51 above, pp. 872.

64 KRING and WALTHER, n. 46 above, pp. 49 f.

65 MÜNKNER, n. 56 above, p 96.

2.4. INFORMATION RIGHTS OF MEMBERS AND TRANSPARENCY REQUIREMENTS

2.4.1. *Transparency: Obligation to Inform and Rights to be Informed or to have Access to Information*

In general terms, the directors have the obligation to inform the supervisory committee and the members on business and cooperative matters. The members of the supervisory committee, as well as the members of the cooperative society, have the right to be informed. Cooperative societies usually hold joint meetings of the board and the supervisory committee.

The members have access to information, e.g. they may inspect the list of members (§31 GCA) and the list of delegates (§43a(6), (7) GCA). They have the right to see the summary of the audit report compiled by the external cooperative auditor (§59(1) GCA).

Cooperative societies provide information to members by publishing newsletters available in the main office and branch offices, on notice-boards and on their website or directly by written notice (e. g. §46(1) GCA). Details regarding the information to be provided about both business and cooperative matters are left to the societies. However, annual reports are usually published and made available to members before or during the general meeting or meeting of delegates, where most of the information on the policy and performance of the cooperative society is given by board members and the supervisory committee. Electronic communication is permitted if members opt to use online contracts, e.g. online banking. In other cases, member agreement is required.

2.4.2. *Financial Audit*

There are special rules regarding external audit in the Cooperative Societies Act which differ from those on audit of companies (§§53–64 GCA). Financial auditing is only part of the auditor's duties. Cooperative auditors should also carry out a 'material audit', i.e. a management audit including assessment of success in member-promotion, reasons for mergers, and justification for allocation of surplus to reserves for risk protection and the development of the cooperative enterprise, rather than distributing surplus to members as patronage refunds or dividends on paid-up share capital. The law (§57(4) GCA) prescribes joint sessions of the auditor, the board of directors, and the supervisory committee where the auditor reports on the expected results of the audit. In 2006, provisions ensuring the neutrality and independence of cooperative auditors were strengthened (§55 GCA).

In the revision of the Cooperative Societies Act in 2006, special rules were made for the audit of small cooperatives with a balance sheet total of less than two million euros (§53 GCA). In such cases, external audit is only required every second year and does not have to cover examination of the accounts. It is generally agreed that this new provision reduces audit costs to only a limited extent.[66]

> §53 GCA – Compulsory audit
>
> For the purpose of verifying the economic situation and regularity in the conduct of business of the cooperative society, its facilities, assets, and also management, including the way in which the list of members is kept, shall be subjected to audits in at least every second financial year.
>
> As part of the audits according to par. 1 of cooperative societies with a balance sheet total in excess of one million euros and sales in excess of two million euros the annual accounts must be audited, including the books and status reports. The provisions of the Commercial Code apply accordingly …

With growing size and the greater complexity of business of average cooperatives, there is a tendency to approximate the special cooperative audit (financial and management audit) to the financial audit of companies. For cooperative banks, special rules of banking regulations on audit also apply.

2.4.3. Member Education

There are no legal provisions requiring cooperatives to educate their members, but according to the German cooperative tradition of Raiffeisen, member education is an important aspect of cooperative work. For example, cooperative banks continue to apply Raiffeisen's idea of educating members in the prudent use of money by charging relatively high interest on overdrafts of members' accounts. Generally, there are no systematic programmes for members' education, but those who want to learn more about cooperatives can find plenty of self-study material.[67]

It is regretted by many that cooperative subjects are usually not taught in schools, trade schools and universities. This means that people vaguely know what a cooperative is but little about how one can be formed and how it works. Cooperatives publish newsletters and pamphlets describing the corporate identity '*Leitbild*' of their cooperative society, but it appears that this is not sufficient.

---

66 Geschwandtner and Helios, n. 4 above, p. 153.

67 For example DGRV: How to form a cooperative, Bonn, 1990; BVR. We open the way guidebook for advising and recruiting members, Wiesbaden, 1991; BVR: Membership Strategy: Achieving more together with a practical strategy for members – the six pillar model, 2nd ed., Berlin, 2007; BVR: Membership – a good idea, Berlin, 2007; W. Grosskopf, H.-H. Münkner and G. Ringle, *Our Cooperative Idea – Mission – Achievements*, English translation, Neu-Ulm, 2009, 2nd ed. in German, Wiesbaden, 2012, 2nd ed. in English, LIT Zurich, Vienna, Berlin, 2016.

A special feature of German cooperative law is that it prescribes pre-registration audit by a cooperative auditing federation before a newly-formed cooperative society can be registered (§§11(2) no. 3, 11a(2) GCA). This pre-registration audit usually goes together with coaching the founder-members, informing them and advising them how to plan and run the business of their new cooperative. The pre-registration audit is seen by critics as too expensive and cumbersome for small and new cooperatives, and as a disincentive to choosing the legal form of registered cooperative society for a new business venture.[68] On the other hand, experience shows that the pre-registration audit serves as an effective filter against non-viable or unrealistic projects, failure of which would damage the image of the cooperative movement as a whole.

Efforts are made to inform members of cooperatives by advertising in newspapers and on television, or by propagating slogans like 'Cooperatives are good for everyone' or 'We open the way' in the press and on the internet. Cooperative federations publish quarterly magazines, but these are directed more to cooperative leaders and personnel than to ordinary members.

With regard to their internal structure, modern cooperatives usually do not have a member-relations committee or special member-relations officers (like the consumer cooperatives had in the 1960s and 1970s), but some cooperatives have introduced complaints committees which deal with members' problems and use such opportunities for member information. Large cooperatives hold regional meetings before their meeting of delegates to maintain contact with their members and offer them information about their cooperative. However, such meetings are often used more for information and entertainment than for member education.

Cooperative education of cooperative officers and staff is a precondition for enabling them to educate members. However, such education is often lacking. Regional cooperative colleges are usually more concerned with training in business administration and management than in cooperative education in the strict sense of the term. Therefore, as a rule, special knowledge about the cooperative way of doing business cannot be expected from cooperative personnel. In 2012, the German Cooperative Academy (ADG) in Montabaur launched a new programme for value-oriented cooperative management.[69]

Allocation of surplus in cooperative enterprises is the responsibility of the members in general meeting or meeting of delegates. Members or delegates are free to allocate funds to cooperative education if they wish, but in practice this is more the exception than the rule.

---

68 R. Philipps, 'Possibilities and limits of strengthening the cooperative form of enterprise', in S.H. Mölls and H.-H. Münkner (eds.), *ICA Blueprint for a Cooperative Decade – a Critical Analysis*, Nomos, Baden-Baden, 2015, pp. 65–70.

69 Kring and Walther, n. 46 above, pp. 55 f.

There are good examples of how member education could work in practice. Founder-members planning new projects in the field of renewable energy cooperatives often benefit from contacts with, and advice from, existing energy cooperatives, cooperative banks or cooperative federations.

2.5. ADMISSION AND EXPULSION OF MEMBERS

A 'variable number of members' is mentioned as a characteristic feature of each registered cooperative society in the legal definition provided in §1(1) GCA. Until 2006, there was only one category of members under the law: the user-member (principle of identity of owner and user). As a rule, there is no insistence on active membership, which means that members, who could use the facilities of the cooperative enterprise but for some reason fail to do so, are tolerated. However, in practice, another category of members has been introduced: 'promoting members', i.e. those wanting to support the cooperative society without using its facilities, or those wanting to become eligible as office-holders. Boards of some cooperative societies pursue a policy of discouraging passive membership, but in general the latter is not seen as a serious problem.

In 2006, the revised Cooperative Societies Act introduced a new category of members in contradiction to the principle of identity of owners and users: 'non-using, investing members' (§8(2) GCA).

In this way, internal conflicts over pricing policy, surplus generation and allocation, consolidation or growth of the cooperative enterprise, which are manageable where owners and users are the same people, are brought into the cooperative structure. A number of special provisions have been introduced into the Act to prevent investing members from reaching a dominant position *vis-à-vis* the user-members:

> Appropriate measures shall be put in place to ensure that investing members cannot under any circumstances outvote regular members and that decisions of the general meeting that require, by law or by-laws, a majority of at least three quarters of the votes cast cannot be prevented by investing members (§8(2) GCA).

Rules on admission of new members and appeals against refusal of admission are as follows. Members of a formation committee created to establish a new cooperative society become founder-members by signing the by-laws at the inaugural meeting and the application for registration sent to the registering court. After registration of the society, application for membership follows procedures and conditions laid down in the by-laws. In most cooperatives, applications for admission are made to the board of directors and are decided by the latter. In the case of refusal, the applicant can appeal to the members in general meeting or meeting of delegates (§15(1) GCA). The contents of a declaration of membership are prescribed in §15a GCA. In the case of merger, membership of the merged society is acquired by operation of law.[70]

Open membership implies that members are free to withdraw from the society if they wish (§65 GCA). However, procedures and periods of notice can be laid down in the by-laws. Usually, the period of notice is between three months and two years. If a longer period of notice is stipulated in the by-laws, members belonging to the cooperative for at least one full financial year may withdraw at an earlier date for good reason (§65(3) GCA). In cooperatives of entrepreneurs, the period of notice can be extended to ten years 'for the purpose of securing the financing of fixed assets' (§65(2) GCA). When members have entered into an agreement with the cooperative enterprise to deliver produce or to buy inputs, such agreements must be taken into account when deciding on applications for withdrawal from membership. According to §66 GCA, 'a member's creditor may, for the purpose of having his claim satisfied, exercise the right to terminate membership on behalf of the member' if certain conditions are met.

There are also extraordinary rights of members to withdraw: In the case of amendment of by-laws in respect to important matters listed in §16(2) GCA or in respect of a major change in the purpose of the cooperative enterprise, membership may be terminated by any member protesting against this decision or by any member not present at the general meeting under conditions listed in §67(1) GCA; or if such amendment was decided by a meeting of delegates (§67a(1) no. 2 GCA), membership may be terminated by such member.

In an effort to harmonise the regulations for SCE with national cooperative law, and in an attempt to comply with EU regulations on equity capital, in 2006 the German Cooperative Societies Act introduced provisions allowing cooperatives to opt for a partly fixed share capital (§8a GCA), which is in contradiction to the characteristic cooperative feature of variable capital. If the by-laws provide for such fixed capital, members giving notice may still terminate their membership, but they may have to wait for refund of their paid-up share capital until funds for repayment are available.[71]

Members can be expelled from the cooperative for reasons and by a procedure laid down in the by-laws (§68 GCA). Under general rules of law, such members have the right to be heard and to defend themselves before being expelled.[72]

---

70 Beuthien, n. 8 above, §§2 ff. UmwG, RZ 36.

71 Beuthien, n. 8 above, §8a GenG, RZ 4; Geschwandtner and Helios, n. 4 above, pp. 57, 58.

72 Beuthien, n. 8 above, §68 GenG, RZ 15.

2.6. CONCLUSIONS – MATTERS STILL NEEDING TO BE REVIEWED

In Germany, the main issues in the ongoing discussion on cooperative corporate governance is whether deviations from the characteristic features of the special cooperative legal pattern and approximation to the company model should continue or be avoided, and whether the legal profile of cooperatives as a special type of self-help organisation should be strengthened or blurred further.

With the revision of the Cooperative Societies Act in 2006, the German law-makers aimed at reducing the competitive advantages of the newly-introduced SCE as compared with cooperative societies registered under national cooperative law. They thus yielded to indirect pressure from EU authorities to review and harmonise national cooperative legislation.

According to Beuthien[73], more autonomy should be given mainly to small cooperatives to make by-laws, especially with regard to the powers of the board of directors (§27 GCA). Cooperatives should be allowed to stipulate in their by-laws that one third of those elected to serve on the supervisory committee may be external members with the professional skills required to fulfil their task of effectively controlling the directors.

It is proposed to introduce more elements of the discussion on good governance from company law into cooperative law, e.g. by strengthening the position of the supervisory committee, by giving members more rights and better access to information, introducing on-line voting in general meetings, and ensuring the independence of cooperative auditors even further.[74] Some problems of small cooperatives opting for a simplified structure remain unsolved. Some important matters which have not been dealt with are: transactions with non-members, excessive autonomy of the board of directors, suitable forms of self-administration, and compulsory affiliation of cooperative societies with auditing federations.[75]

Provisions related to voting rights of members are debated. Some critics propose that voting rights in proportion to share contributions should be allowed[76] as in Austria. Some want to return to the clear 'one member/one vote' rule; others want to extend plural voting and introduce special rights for 'stronger' members, e.g. the right to send their own candidates to the supervisory committee. Also discussed is whether no or less stringent limits should be set for voting by proxy. Instead of electing delegates from lists of candidates, which can

---

73 Beuthien, n. 8 above, p. liv; Beuthien, n. 51 above, p. 868.

74 Geschwandtner and Helios, n. 4 above, p. 18.

75 Geschwandtner and Helios, n. 4 above, p. 23.

76 Beuthien, n. 51 above, p. 869.

only be presented by the board, now such lists can be presented also by at least 150 members (§43a(4) GCA). Some prefer election by regions.

It should become an obligation of the board of directors of cooperative societies to prepare a written promotion plan and promotion report, with members having the right to inspect and discuss such plans and reports.

3. COOPERATIVE FINANCE

3.1. INTRODUCTION – COOPERATIVE FINANCE IN THE CONTEXT OF GERMAN COOPERATIVE LAW

Themes to be discussed in this section are:

- the social capital – funds available to the cooperative society;
- members' capital contributions;
- reserves that the cooperative society must or may form;
- how reserves from cooperative economic activities are determined and allocated;
- financing through non-distributed returns or through other contributions from members or non-members; legal/mandatory and voluntary reserves;
- how credit sections are used by cooperatives, or how cooperatives associate with credit cooperatives for financial purposes – vertical integration into the cooperative financial system (*Finanzverbund*).

Two more points have to be analysed:

- the issue of members' liability in relation to financial obligations of the cooperative society, which is no longer a legal must, but a matter of the by-laws;
- what happens to cooperative reserves upon winding-up: is it a matter of by-laws or of members' decision?

3.1.1. Cooperative Financial Structure and Cooperative Identity

In German cooperative law, the legal definition of the term 'Cooperative Society' reads as follows (§1(1) GCA):

> Societies with a variable number of members for the purpose of promoting their members' personal economic and business interests, or their social or cultural interests, by means of a jointly-owned enterprise (cooperative), registered under this Act.

Core elements of this definition are:

- identity of owners and users; and
- the objective of member-promotion by service relations.

From the German perspective, cooperative societies can form their capital in four ways.

Share capital: members contribute capital to their cooperative society as an obligation of a member after having been admitted to membership. Only members may contribute share capital (*Geschäftsanteile*, meaning total amount due, *Geschäftsguthaben*, meaning the amount actually paid or credited to member's share account).

Reserves must or may be created from the undistributed surplus of the cooperative society. Such reserves are mandatory or may be voluntary as regulated in the by-laws (§7 no. 2 GCA). Originally, these reserves were indivisible capital owned by the cooperative society as a legal body and which could not be divided among the members during the existence of the cooperative. Since 1973 a cooperative society may create a special reserve fund of which departing members may claim a portion provided that certain conditions are met (§73(3) GCA).

Cooperatives may exclude distribution of all or part of the annual surplus or pay a dividend on paid-up share capital at the end of each financial year from the surplus earned (§§20, 21 and 21a GCA). The Cooperative Societies Act does not specify how much a 'fair reward' of share capital would be. A cooperative may also allocate surplus to members in proportion to their use made of the cooperative facilities and services (patronage refund in proportion to business done). This typically cooperative form of surplus distribution is not regulated in the German Cooperative Societies Act but it is practised by societies. This is one way to implement the cooperative policy of service near cost in transactions with members. How to dispose of the annual surplus as shown in the audited balance sheet is usually proposed by the board of directors, but it is decided by the members in general meeting.

Members may be required to sign and/or pay additional contributions as prescribed in the by-laws (§7a GCA). Since 2006, such contributions may be in cash or kind (§7a(3) GCA).

Members' additional liability by guarantee in excess of their share contributions for the debts of the cooperative society must be regulated in the by laws or may be excluded (§6 no. 3 GCA, §§119–121 GCA).

Raising capital from external sources is done in accordance with the rules of general law, the Cooperative Societies Act and the by-laws. Much of the funds required by cooperative societies are raised by using the vertically integrated cooperative financial system (*Finanzverbund*) (see sec. 5.3).

Upon the winding-up of a cooperative society, the remaining assets are disposed of in a way prescribed in the Cooperative Societies Act (§§90, 91, 92 GCA) and the by-laws. Disinterested transmission of net assets is only one of several ways to dispose of liquidated assets (§92 GCA).

3.1.2. Financial Structure of the Cooperative and the National Law of Business Organisations

From the German perspective, cooperative societies are a special legal type (*sui generis*) based on a special Cooperative Societies Act of 1889 with amendments up to 2006 covering all types of cooperatives.

In the system of organisations, a cooperative society is – technically – a business association with a legally prescribed objective, namely promoting the interests of its members by means of business transactions. The key distinctive feature *vis-à-vis* other forms of organisations is that, in cooperative societies, owners and users are the same people (principle of identity).

Originally, the position of cooperatives in the system of business organisations and the difference between cooperative societies and investor-driven organisations like companies were very clear – especially with regard to financial structure. Amendments of the Cooperative Societies Act since 1973 have introduced new provisions resembling those of company law, partly by changing the provisions of the law, partly by expanding the power of individual cooperatives to adjust the general legal provisions to their specific needs by amendment of by-laws.

The relations between cooperative societies and their members are regulated by the Cooperative Societies Act, the by-laws, and decisions of the members in general meeting. From the German perspective, there is no doubt that a cooperative society as a legal (incorporated) body operates on its own within the limits set by the law and by the by-laws. From the legal point of view, a cooperative society is not perceived as an agent acting on behalf of its members. German cooperative law contains no special provisions on transactions in and between cooperatives (*'actos cooperativos'*) and no formal agency relationship between cooperatives and their members. All assets brought by members into their cooperative become property of the cooperative society unless they are only lent to the society and come into its possession. The service relations between the cooperative society and its members come under general law (e.g. buying and selling). Only in the case of workers' cooperatives does the problem arise of whether labour law can be replaced by special cooperative service relations.

To sum up:

- Cooperative law applies (not company law).
- In cooperatives, capital is variable.
- Surplus may be distributed as dividends on share capital or patronage refunds in proportion to business done.
- While cooperatives are active, reserves are in principle indivisible, with the exception of §73(3) GCA. How to deal with reserves after liquidation is a matter of the by-laws or of decisions by the members.
- It is possible to allocate surplus or funds to general interest objectives if the members so decide. The annual surplus may also be spent for general interest objectives meeting obligations of Corporate Social Responsibility. How this is done is usually proposed by the board of directors and decided by the members in general meeting.

One way to devote the resources and activities of a cooperative society to general interest objectives is to set up subsidiaries (§1(2) GCA) to pursue goals of public interest, provided that this is not the sole or main purpose.

There have been no changes in the cooperative financial structure due to reform of International Accounting Standards.

3.1.3. *Where can Rules on Cooperative Financial Structure be Found?*

Such rules are found in the Cooperative Societies Act and in the by-laws of the individual society. In Germany, the Cooperative Societies Act is a complete piece of legislation without gaps to be filled by company law. Cooperatives are given autonomy to adjust the general rules of the law to the requirements of the individual society. Depending on the field of operation, other laws on business organisations may apply, e.g. banking law for cooperative banks, competition law for cooperatives of traders. There is a trend towards regulating special matters in special laws applicable to all business organisations irrespective of their legal form, e. g. accounting, audit, merger, conversion and tax.

3.2. COOPERATIVE SHARE CAPITAL

3.2.1. *Essential Nature of Cooperative Share Capital*

Like any other business enterprise, a cooperative society must have a minimum asset base to achieve its objectives. Cooperative share capital is an essential element of this capital base. In Germany, different technical terms are used to denote cooperative members' financial contributions (*Geschäftsanteil*) and the company share (*Aktie*). The minimum amount of a members' financial contribution must be determined in the by-laws (§7 (1)). In German cooperative law, the payment of shares by members is not seen as an investment, but rather as fulfilment of an obligation resulting from admission to membership. Hence, no one can become a member of a cooperative society by buying a share (as in the case of a company), but the share contribution is an obligation of a person admitted to membership upon application.

'The amount up to which individual members may purchase shares (in the cooperative) as well as the payments on the shares which each member is obliged to make; these shall be fixed in terms of amount and time to no less than one tenth of the share' (§7(1) GCA). Since 2006, share contributions can also be made in kind (§7a(3) GCA).

Cooperative shares are linked to membership which – in cooperatives – is open, voluntary and variable. Accordingly, cooperative share capital is by definition variable. It serves as a guarantee for cooperative creditors and cannot be withdrawn at short notice. However, in newly-formed cooperatives, share capital is the only asset available to the cooperative. It takes time to build up reserves from undistributed surplus.

3.2.2. *Assets as a Natural Element of the Cooperative Society*

As a legal body, every cooperative may hold assets, and the Cooperative Societies Act lays down the rules applicable to cooperative assets, e.g. that reserves are indivisible unless the by-laws allow creation of a special reserve fund from which departing members may claim a portion if certain conditions are met (§73(3) GCA). Hence: indivisible reserves are the rule, but with one exception.

3.2.2.1. Regulating Principles of Cooperative Share Capital

The amount of a cooperative share and the method of payment must be laid down in the by-laws (§7(1) GCA). The members can change these rules by amending the by-laws in general meeting. The by-laws and any amendments are published and available for public inspection in the local court keeping the register of cooperatives (§12 GCA).

3.2.2.2. Legal Minimum Share Capital

With the amendment of the Cooperative Societies Act in 2006, a minimum capital may be introduced (§8a GCA) according to the society's needs. The advantage for a cooperative society of introducing minimum capital is that such share capital will be recognised as equity and will not be treated as debt, e.g. by the authority for financial supervision (BaFin) in the case of cooperative banks. The inconvenience for departing members is that they may give due notice and withdraw from the society, but their claim for redemption of their share contribution may be suspended if repayment would bring the share capital below the fixed minimum. The members of cooperative societies have the right to reduce or increase the minimum share capital by amendment of the by-laws.

3.2.2.3. Variability of Share Capital

The amendment of the German Cooperative Societies Act in 2006 allowing introduction of a fixed minimum capital has had the surprising outcome of a cooperative society being defined as an organisation with variable capital but having at least in part fixed capital.

The important cooperative principle of open and voluntary membership usually includes the right of the departing member to claim refund of his/her share contribution at par value. This cooperative principle is not explicitly mentioned in the law but is implied. The Cooperative Societies Act in its amended form of 2006 separates the right of the member to withdraw from his/her right to redeem his/her share contribution if the minimum amount of share capital would be affected. It may happen that some withdrawing members can redeem their share contribution while others cannot. In this case there is no equal treatment of members.

3.2.2.4. Functions of Share Capital

Because cooperatives are associations of persons, their share contribution is an obligation of membership, but the power relations among members are not determined by their share capital contributions. The by-laws may stipulate that voting rights are suspended until the share contribution is paid. Hence, share contribution is an element crucial in establishing members' full rights in the cooperative.

Membership is acquired by application and admission. Until 2006, membership could not be inherited. The heir would represent the deceased member's membership only until the end of the next financial year. Now membership can be inherited without time limit if the heir meets the requirements set for admission of new members (§77 GCA).

For newly-formed cooperative societies, members' contributions are the only capital base. The traditional practice of German cooperatives was to strengthen the creditworthiness of the cooperative society and the solidarity among members by stipulating an additional liability of members by guarantee. This possibility still exists but has become optional (§7 no. 1 GCA).

3.2.3. *Member Contributions to Capital*

3.2.3.1. Obligation to Pay-Up Capital

From the German perspective and under German cooperative law (§§15, 15a GCA), share capital is not a means to become a member, but an obligation of membership after having been admitted. This is an essential difference with respect to company law, where buying a share makes the buyer a shareholder/ member of the company. In cooperative societies, subscribing a share is not a condition for becoming a member. To become a member of a cooperative society, the conditions laid down in the by-laws for membership must be met. After admission upon application (or through inheritance or in the course of a merger), the by-laws can stipulate that the membership rights of the new member can only be exercised after the share contribution has been paid.

This also applies to non-using investing members. They also have to be admitted after application and cannot become members simply by buying shares, for which there is no market and no market price (§8(2) GCA).

3.2.3.2. Types and Nature of Capital Contribution

There is a distinction among capital subscription as an obligation of membership (compulsory contribution), supplementary contributions at the request of the cooperative (staggered share contributions in proportion to use made of the services of the cooperative enterprise) and laid down in the by-laws (§7a GCA), and voluntary supplementary contributions. Whether dividend on share capital is paid from the annual surplus is a matter of the by-laws and of decisions of members in general meeting.

This also refers to capital redemption, with one exception introduced in 2006: when a fixed minimum share capital is laid down in the by-laws, departing members' right of redemption is suspended if refund of the share contribution would bring the share capital below the stipulated minimum amount (§8a(2) GCA).

The nominal value of all shares is equal. The amount of the compulsory contribution by each member may vary depending on objective criteria laid down in the by-laws (payment by instalments, staggered share contributions).

Before 2006, share contributions could only be made in cash. Since amendment of the Cooperative Societies Act in 2006, contributions can also be made in kind (non-cash contributions, §7a(3) GCA). There are no provisions in the cooperative law regarding the valuation of non-cash contributions comparable to art. 4(2) of SCE Regulations of 2003, which admits only contributions of assets suitable for economic assessment.

3.2.4. *Recording*

Cooperative shares are recorded in a register of members and shares kept by the cooperative society. Before 2006, this register was also kept by the local court administering the register of cooperatives. In view of the fact that cooperative shares are not freely transferable, there is no need to issue share certificates, and because payments on shares are not made frequently, there is also no need for share booklets held by members. For each member, the cooperative society keeps a share account in which payments, parts of surplus due to the member, and contributions to losses incurred by the cooperative society are recorded.

3.2.5. *Amount*

Under German cooperative legislation, it is left to the by-laws of the individual cooperative society to fix the amount of share capital which each member must contribute. All members may have to contribute the same minimum amount, but compulsory share contributions can also be staggered in proportion to use made of the facilities and services of the cooperative society (§§7 no. 1 and 7a GCA). Hence, there is a minimum amount of contribution which each member must pay, and there may be a minimum number of shares a member must contribute under a system of staggered share contributions. These matters must be regulated in the by-laws of each society (details to be included in the by-laws, §7 GCA).

3.2.6. *Payment*

The by-laws of the individual cooperative society can stipulate that the full amount of the share must be paid after admission to membership, or a compulsory minimum contribution must be made where shares can be paid by instalments or in kind (§7 no. 1 GCA). In the case of payment by instalments, these must be fixed in terms of amount and time to no less than one tenth of the share. Like all other provisions of the by-laws, also the regulations regarding share contributions can be amended. New members may be required to pay more. Another payment due for new members may be a non-refundable admission fee, e.g. in housing cooperatives. Furthermore, the cooperative society may lay down in its by-laws the amount up to which individual members may purchase shares.

Consequences of default may be loss of membership by expulsion from the cooperative society in a fair and just procedure to be defined in the by-laws.

3.2.7. *Value of Member Contribution*

The value of member contributions can be increased for new members by amendment of the by-laws. It may also be increased by converting optional reserves into share capital. The value of shares can also be reassessed and reduced by amendment of by-laws either by deduction of losses from the individual members' shares or by reducing the value of the shares.

When a member has contributed more than one share, additional shares contributed voluntarily can be withdrawn (*Teilkündigung*) without terminating membership, if the by-laws so allow.

3.2.8. Compensation

The German Cooperative Societies Act leaves the decision on disposal of annual surplus to the members in general meeting (see also section 3.6). It only contains provisions proposing procedures to be followed in the first financial year (§19(1) GCA). The by-laws can exclude any profit distribution among the members (§20 GCA). Payment of interest on share capital is prohibited (§21(1) GCA):

> Interest of a certain amount on the credit balance shall, except provided in §21a GCA, not be paid, even if the contributions made by the member exceed the due amounts' §21(2) GCA: 'Neither can members, having paid more than their due contributions, make claims on other members in the event of loss for the sole reason that the latter have only made these contributions.

A new provision (§21a) contains an exception to this ban on the payment of interest. Closer inspection of this new provision reveals that what is called 'interest' (paid as cost) is in fact a 'dividend' (paid from surplus) payable only if the amount due is covered by retained earnings or by a surplus carried forward (§21a(2) GCA). The typically cooperative form of surplus distribution by way of a patronage refund paid to a member in proportion to business done with the cooperative enterprise is not mentioned in the German Cooperative Societies Act, but it is practised by many societies, occasionally also by cooperative banks.

3.2.9. Redemption

Cooperative shares are capital contributions by members to finance the cooperative society for the duration of their membership. Rules for redemption are laid down in the by-laws. The claim for repayment of the share contribution of a departing member does not depend on the availability of surplus/profit made by the society but must be paid from its assets. There may be a decrease in the value of the share by deduction of losses, if this is decided by the members in general meeting in the form of an amendment of the by-laws. In the case of cooperative societies with a fixed minimum capital, members' claims for repayment of their share contributions are delayed if such payment would reduce the equity capital of the cooperative society below the guaranteed minimum amount.

3.2.10. Transfer

As a rule, cooperative shares are not freely transferable. However, there are several ways to transfer cooperative shares. They can be transferred from one member to another or from a member to a candidate for membership with the approval of the board of directors. Transfer of cooperative shares to non-members is not possible.

The creditors of a member cannot seize the member's cooperative share to satisfy their claim, but they can give notice to the cooperative society to terminate the debtor's membership and claim payment of the equivalent of the share value from the cooperative society (§66 GCA).

Until 2006, cooperatives shares could not be inherited. The deceased member's heir replaced the member only until the end of the next financial year. Then membership was terminated and the repayment of the value of the share was made to the heir. In 2006 the rules on inheritance of shares were amended. Now the heir of a deceased member' share can become a member of the cooperative provided that the conditions for membership as stipulated in the by-laws are met.

3.2.11. Are Political and Economic Rights of Members Linked to their Contributions to Share Capital?

From the German perspective, this is the wrong question. As explained earlier, member's rights are acquired by admission to membership, and the payment of share capital is one of several obligations resulting from membership. However, it can be stipulated in the by-laws that the exercise of membership rights (mainly the right to vote) are suspended until payment of the share contribution has been made.

Indirectly, a link can be established between share contributions and voting power. In cooperative societies prescribing a staggered capital contribution in proportion to the use made of the services or facilities of the cooperative enterprise, and practising plural voting for economically stronger members, staggered capital contributions can be indirectly linked to plural voting.

3.3. RESERVES

Under German cooperative law, every registered cooperative society must build up reserves from undistributed surplus. According to §7 no. 2 GCA, the by-laws of every cooperative society:

> have to provide for the establishment of legal reserves that are to cover any balance sheet loss, as well as the manner in which such reserves are to be established, especially

> the particular portion of the annual surplus which shall be allocated to these reserves, and the minimum amount of the latter up to which allocations have to be made.

Hence, under German cooperative law there are mandatory reserves formed by contributions out of annual surplus as stipulated in the by-laws until a ceiling has been reached. These flexible regulations allow each individual cooperative society to build up reserves as required by practical needs.

To establish voluntary reserves is not considered a matter of legislation, but rather of business prudence. There are provisions fixing methods, a ceiling, and the use of voluntary reserves in the law. Building excessive reserves can be seen as an infringement of the cooperative society's objective of member-promotion and may be criticised in the annual audit report by the auditing federation (§53(1) GCA, see also §34(1) GCA).

Mandatory reserves can only be used 'to cover any balance sheet loss' (§7 no. 2 GCA), i.e. any loss shown in an audited balance sheet. The use of voluntary reserves is decided by the members in general meeting usually after proposals submitted by the board of directors. Such funds can be, and in effect are, often used for education and training, but in Germany it is unusual for cooperative societies to have a special education and training fund.

Until 1973 there was the clear rule that reserves are indivisible during the existence of the cooperative society. This rule still holds for mandatory reserves (§73(2) GCA): The departing member 'is not entitled to any parts of the reserves or other assets of the society, except as provided in par. 3'. Since 1973 cooperatives may stipulate in their by-laws the creation of a special divisible reserve fund of which departing members can claim a portion, provided certain conditions are met (§73(3) GCA):

> In the event of termination of membership, the by-laws may grant members, who have paid-up their share in full, payment of a portion of earnings retained for this purpose from the annual surplus. The by-laws may make this claim contingent on a minimum period during which the member must have belonged to the cooperative society, and may add other requirements and restrict the claim …

There are good reasons for keeping the reserves of cooperative societies indivisible:

- to counterbalance the variable share capital;
- to increase the creditworthiness of the cooperative society and to protect creditors;
- to prevent the present co-operators from winding-up a cooperative to share the fruits of work by previous generations of co-operators – speculative winding-up;

- to create common property and solidarity across generations;
- to build up a trust fund (Raiffeisen: Stiftungsfonds) like a foundation serving cooperative goals.

3.4. MUTUALIST CAPITAL; MASA DE GESTIÓN ECONÓMICA

Within German cooperative law there is no concept of special mutualised cooperative property. Whatever is contributed by a co-operator to his/her cooperative society either becomes property of the cooperative society as a legal body or not. It may also be lent to the cooperative society for use, in which case it remains the property of the co-operator. Business relations between the cooperative enterprise and co-operators are contracts under commercial or private law. Whether the economic relations between the cooperative society and its members are of a special nature or ordinary business relations is not a legal matter but an economic one. On an 'internal market' between the cooperative enterprise and co-operators as users/owners, the cooperative must promote the members, serving members at prices near cost, either by offering special conditions exclusively for members or by returning surplus earned in such transactions partly to members as patronage refund.

Only in the case of workers' cooperatives is it a problem whether labour law (especially those of its provisions protecting workers' rights) can be replaced by special internal cooperative regulations where workers and owners are the same people. Generally, internal cooperative regulations govern the relationship between workers/members and their cooperative society, while relations between the workers cooperative and employed labour (non-members) are governed by labour law protecting them.

The same applies to *'actos cooperativos'* and the conception of cooperative societies as agents acting on behalf of their members and not as special business organisations operating on the market. Under German cooperative law, the cooperative society as a legal body is responsible for its activities with all resources made available by the members – acting directly and not as an agent of its members. The general law regulates:

- who is the owner;
- who acts and has power to act; and
- who is responsible.

Goods provided by the co-operators to their cooperative are either owned by or lent to the cooperative society.

3.5. INCOME FROM COOPERATIVE ECONOMIC ACTIVITY – HOW IT IS DETERMINED AND ALLOCATED

Income from cooperative economic activity is shown in the audited books. In many cooperative societies whose by-laws authorise transactions with non-members (e.g. cooperative banks), there is no separate recording of transactions with members and with non-members.

With regard to the allocation of revenue at the end of the financial year, the general rule is that the board of directors proposes and the members in general meeting decide. Again, there may be special conditions in the case of workers' cooperatives regarding the calculation of salaries and/or profit-sharing outside general rules of labour law agreed upon between trade unions and employers. In all other cases, income from cooperative economic activity is shown in the audited balance sheet, and disposal of such income is either regulated in the by-laws or proposed by the board of directors and ultimately decided by the members in general meeting.

Only when cooperative societies want to have paid-out patronage refunds recognised by the tax authorities as being tax-deductible operating expenses of the cooperative society rather than ordinary profit-distribution, one of the conditions is to keep separate accounts for transactions with members and with non-members. Another condition is that such patronage refund must be distributed in proportion to business done by the co-operators with the cooperative. This must be performed by actually paying such sums to members, and the distribution of patronage refunds must follow the same rules for all members or categories of members.

In German cooperative practice, cooperative banks usually pay dividends on share capital. No distinction is made between transactions with members and with non-member-customers, which are usually recorded together. In agricultural cooperatives, 'purpose-transactions' are usually made only with members, so that separate recording of transactions with members and with non-member-customers is not important.

3.6. FINANCING THROUGH RETAINED COOPERATIVE SURPLUS

Disposal of the surplus as patronage refund after allocation to reserves is a matter decided by the members in general meeting. According to §19(1) GCA:

> The profit or loss of a financial year resulting for the members from adoption of the annual accounts shall be distributed among the members. For the first financial year, such distribution shall be proportional to the payments made on shareholdings; for each successive year, in proportion to their credit balance established at the end of

> the previous financial year as a result of profit added or loss put down. Profit addition shall be made as long as the share has not been paid up.'
>
> 'The by-laws may apply criteria for profit and loss distribution other than those stipulated above, and they may regulate the extent to which profits shall be paid out to the members before the share has been paid up. Profits shall not be paid out until a credit balance diminished by the losses has been replenished (§19(2) GCA).

Co-operators can decide what to do with the refund: have the sum paid out to them, use it to pay for new shares, or donate the sum for a benevolent purpose.

3.7. OTHER MEMBER CONTRIBUTIONS

In some cooperatives (e.g. housing cooperatives), newly-admitted members may have to pay an admission fee or membership fee, a one-time payment to balance the contribution of a new member in relation to what the founder-members and generations of older members have already created. On the other hand, such 'membership fees' go against the principle of solidarity of old and new members by charging a fee allowing new members to enjoy what the old members have already built up. In Germany, claiming payment of periodic membership fees is not a common practice, if applied at all.

3.8. SPECIAL TYPES OF MEMBER CONTRIBUTIONS

There are no financial contributions by non-members to cooperative funds other than loans. However, to meet the increasing demand for funds by growing cooperative societies, a special type of non-voting participation right or certificate (*Genussrechte* or *-scheine*) has been developed, which cooperatives can issue or use. The most common way in which cooperative societies can solve their financial problems is participation in a vertically integrated cooperative financial system (*genossenschaftlicher Finanzverbund*) in which primary cooperatives, regional and national central organisations work together (see section 5.3.1 and Annex).

3.9. CREDIT SECTIONS IN THE FINANCING OF COOPERATIVES

The old Raiffeisen multipurpose cooperatives combining the provision of financial services with agricultural supply and marketing activities to cover all their members' needs in one organisation are largely a matter of the past. Today – with few exceptions – the former rural and urban savings and loan associations have turned into full-fledged banks (Raiffeisenbanken and Volksbanken) operating under banking law and subject to banking supervision in addition to cooperative audit. In 2013, only 129 Raiffeisenbanks with supply and marketing activities still existed out of a total of 1,081 cooperative banks[77] and only 48 of the total of 1,912 housing cooperatives still had their own savings and loan section.[78]

The general rule is that no financial services are permitted without possession of a banking licence. The federal agency for banking supervision (BaFin) closely monitors cooperatives and does not tolerate any infringement of this rule.

3.10. RELATIONS BETWEEN CREDIT COOPERATIVES AND OTHER COOPERATIVES

In Germany, such relations are not a matter of legislation but of cooperative organisation and integration into a vertically integrated cooperative financial system (*genossenschaftlicher Finanzverbund*, see section 3.8 and section 5.3).

3.11. COOPERATIVES AND COOPERATORS' LIABILITY

Under German cooperative law, the importance of cooperators' liability has steadily decreased over the years. Originally, Raiffeisen saw unlimited joint and several liability of all members for the debts of their cooperative society as the only way to make small rural multipurpose cooperatives creditworthy. He valued joint liability of the members as an important element of member solidarity. The legal provisions on co-operators' liability have changed from compulsory and rigid to optional and light. Joint and several liability turned into liability by guarantee and mandatory members' liability into a matter to be regulated in the by-laws. Since 2006, the rules have been as follows: §6 no. 3 GCA:

> Details to be included in the by-laws: details stipulating whether members are liable for additional contributions, should the creditors' claims not be satisfied in the event of insolvency of the cooperative society. If so, whether these are unlimited or limited to a specific sum (amount of liability).

3.12. COOPERATIVE AUTONOMY

In Germany, the state does not control cooperatives, which are left under the guidance of their own auditing federations. The German Cooperative Societies

77 M. Stappel, *Die deutschen Genossenschaften 2014. Entwicklungen – Meinungen – Zahlen* [German cooperatives 2013. Development – Opinions – Figures], Wiesbaden, 2014, p. 42.

78 Stappel, above n. 77, p. 51.

Act gives cooperative auditing federations monopoly in carrying out cooperative audit (§§53 and 55 GCA); makes affiliation of every registered cooperative society with an auditing federation compulsory (§54 GCA); and gives these federations the power to recommend registration of a new cooperative society to the registering authority (local court) and thereby practically to decide whether a new cooperative society can be formed (pre-registration audit; §§11, 11a GCA):

> The application for registration to the local court shall be accompanied by ... the certificate of an auditing federation confirming that the cooperative society is eligible for admission, and an expert opinion of the auditing federation indicating whether in view of the personal and economic conditions, and in particular the financial status of the cooperative society, the interest of the members or creditors of the cooperative society may be jeopardised (§11(2) no. 3 GCA).

According to §81 GCA, the registration of a cooperative society may be cancelled *ex officio* if the objective of member-promotion has not been achieved. Instead of controlling cooperatives, the state conducts a kind of 'super-audit' on the auditing federations (§§56, 63, 63a GCA; section 4.3.2.5). The auditing rights of the federations are granted by the state and may be suspended for various reasons detailed in the law.

There are no provisions in the German Cooperative Societies Act that prevent investing members from being elected to serve on the board of directors and thereby exercising some kind of control over the cooperative society. Such restrictions for investing members only exist with regard to service on the supervisory committee and voting power in the general meeting (§8(2) GCA):

> Appropriate measures shall be put in place to ensure that investing members cannot under any circumstances outvote regular members and that decisions of the general meeting requiring by law or by-laws a majority of at least three quarters of the votes cast cannot be prevented by investing members. ... The number of investing members on the supervisory committee shall not exceed a quarter of its total number.

3.13. WINDING-UP AND LIQUIDATION

The main provisions governing the winding-up of cooperative societies (§§93a-s GCA) were removed from the Cooperative Societies Act in 1994 and included in the transformation law (§3 (1) no. 3. UmwG).

Dissolution of a cooperative society is either decided by the members in general meeting (§78 GCA) or becomes effective when the time limit set in the by-laws for the existence of the cooperative society expires (§79 GCA). Members in general meeting may decide to continue a dissolved society provided that the distribution of cooperative assets among its members remaining after adjustment of debts has not yet commenced (§79a(1) GCA).

A cooperative society is dissolved by court order should the number of members fall below three (§80(1) GCA). Furthermore a cooperative society is dissolved following insolvency (§81a GCA).

Liquidation is effected by the board of directors of the society unless the by-laws or a decision adopted by the general meeting confer this function upon other persons (§83 (1) GCA). Upon request by the supervisory committee or by at least one tenth of the members, liquidators may be appointed by the courts (§83(3) GCA).

After the liquidation proceedings have been closed, the liquidated assets of the cooperative society are distributed. Proven claims must be settled by the liquidator in the following sequence:

- the costs of the liquidation, including remuneration of the liquidator;
- discharge of the liabilities of the society, i.e. settlement of proven claims by the creditors according to the ranking determined by the general provisions of private law;
- repayment of share contributions of the members; and
- payment of dividend, interest or patronage refund for any period during which no dividend, interest or patronage refund was in fact paid.

Upon winding up and during liquidation, the law leaves several options for dealing with reserves:

- any surplus in excess of the total credit balances may be distributed among the members on a per capita basis (§91(2) GCA);
- the by-laws may prohibit any division of assets, or may stipulate different ratios when dividing assets (§91(3) GCA); or
- the members may vote to keep reserves indivisible and to transfer the liquidated assets to 'a natural or legal person for a specific purpose' or 'to the community where the cooperative society was based'. The interest on this fund shall go to charity' (§92 GCA).

3.14. GENERAL INTEREST 'COOPERATIVES'

In Germany, the legally prescribed objective of promoting the economic, social or cultural interests of the members is an essential element of the definition of a cooperative society (§1(1) GCA) and excludes general interest cooperatives from being registered as cooperative societies. This definition is supplemented by §1(2) GCA:

> Membership of societies and other associations (of individuals), including the bodies governed by public law, is permissible if and when intended to

promote their members' personal economic and business interests, or their social and cultural interests, or

to serve the public-interest goals of the cooperative society, without being the sole or main purpose of the cooperative society.

Failure to fulfil the objective of member-promotion may lead to *ex officio* dissolution of a cooperative society (§81 GCA).

As mentioned earlier, there are housing cooperatives serving the general interest (*gemeinnützige Wohnungsgenossenschaften*). They were regulated between 1940 (World War II) and 1990 (Unification of Germany) by a special Law: Gesetz über die Gemeinnützigkeit im Wohnungswesen, WGG (Law on General Interest in the Field of Housing). Under this law, housing cooperatives could be recognised as general interest organisations if they complied with certain conditions, e.g. limitation of surplus distribution, small amount of share contributions, rent near cost, use of model by-laws.[79] This law is no longer in force but still applicable to those housing cooperatives that have already been officially recognised as general interest cooperatives, e.g. where public institutions or enterprises could acquire shares for people of limited means to be accepted by the housing cooperative as tenants. Such cooperatives were (and remain) exempted from certain taxes (e.g. corporation tax, trade tax) provided that they only rent flats to members and exclude acquisition of ownership of such cooperative flats by members, provided further that profit resulting from other business does not exceed 10% of their total annual profit (see above section 1.8.

3.15. SUMMARY

In German cooperative legislation, the structure of the cooperative society as an organisation based on the principle of identity of owners and users was clearly reflected in the Co-operative Societies Act until 1973. Subsequent amendments progressively blurred this clear and specific structure by introducing elements of company law into cooperative law mainly designed to help large and expanding cooperatives to meet their growing need for financial resources. This was also achieved by giving cooperatives more autonomy to adjust their by-laws in order to strengthen their financial base, allowing them to level their typically cooperative profile.

Another new trend is to perceive cooperatives as non-profit organisations (NPOs) not only designed to promote their members' economic interests but also

79 Beuthien, see n 8 above, §1 GenG, RZ 75.

serving the general interest of the community and the cooperative movement as a whole. This deviates to some extent from the ICA Statement of the Cooperative Identity, where member promotion is emphasised as the principal objective of cooperatives. In the seventh cooperative principle (Care for the Community) it is expressly stressed that the authority to decide whether to use the resources of the cooperative to promote general interest or the community are the members, who have to agree to do so, combining self-help with solidarity.

The amendments changing the clear profile of cooperatives as self-help organisations of their members are broadening the objectives of cooperatives in the legal definition (§1(1) GCA) from economic objectives to encompass also the social and cultural interests of the members. They have introduced further new elements into German cooperative law following developments in countries of Southern Europe which have found their way into European cooperative legislation governing SCE, and are aimed at strengthening the financial base of cooperatives by approximating them to companies. For instance, in Italy since 2003 there has been freedom to issue financial instruments of various kinds (equity, debt, or hybrids).[80] Furthermore, an additional exception from the principle of identity of owners and users is now allowed under German cooperative law, namely non-using (investing) members (§8(2) GCA). Transactions with non-members (§8(1) no. 5 GCA) has always been left to the members to decide in the by-laws of their society. Recruitment of specialists from outside the cooperative system to serve as office holders, i.e. not representing members' interests directly but making management and control of growing cooperatives more professional in contravention of §9(2) GCA, has been practised for a long time.

Other amendments of the German cooperative law introduced to strengthen the financial base of cooperative societies:

- make share capital less variable by allowing extension of the period of notice for departing members (§65(2) GCA – up to ten years);
- make it more attractive for 'investing members' to invest their capital in cooperative societies by offering the payment of interest on share capital, which, however, is in fact a dividend (§21a GCA);
- allow part of the reserves to be made divisible (§73(3) GCA);
- allow exclusion of the liability of members in excess of their share contribution (§6(3) GCA);
- allow limited plural voting – which may not be directly but indirectly linked to share contributions (§§8(2) and 43(3) GCA).

In this way, cooperatives are given access to new sources of funds from investing members (§8(2) GCA), by using other financial instruments not regulated in

80 Fici, n. 29 above, p. 491.

cooperative law (*Genussrechte* – non voting participation certificates) and by introducing the purchase of additional shares (§15b GCA).

Other new provisions aim at meeting the need for more funds and try to provide a more stable financial basis for growing cooperative enterprises:

- Making equity capital less variable by introducing a fixed minimum capital below which departing members cannot claim repayment of their share contributions (§8a GCA).
- Making conversion from cooperative society to company or other legal form easier under general law applicable to all types of business organisations (UmwG, *(Transformation Law)* of 1994, with last amendments 2009).
- Stressing audit by professional chartered accountants supplementing or replacing the specific type of cooperative 'material' audit assessing the degree to which the objective of member-promotion has been achieved by the management of the cooperative enterprise by adequately trained and experienced cooperative auditors (§§55(1) and 63b GCA) (see section 4.3.2).

All these new provisions have made it necessary to introduce additional provisions to ensure that the true nature of cooperative societies as self-help organisations (SHOs) of their members is not completely lost and that the essential cooperative features are preserved despite deviations from the original design.

The following provisions have been introduced to prevent non-using (investing) members from becoming too powerful, and to ensure that user-members remain in control:

- limiting the voting power of investing members in the general meeting (§8(2) GCA);
- limiting the number of investing members on the supervisory committee to one quarter of its total members (§8(2) GCA);
- limiting the additional votes under plural voting schemes to three or ten respectively (§43(3) GCA);
- limiting the use of votes under plural voting schemes in general meeting or meeting of delegates in the case of important matters requiring a two-thirds or higher majority of votes (§§44, 45 GCA) and for election of delegates (§43a(1) GCA);
- maintaining the general meeting of members in large cooperatives parallel to a meeting of delegates with power to decide important matters to be defined in the by-laws (§§44, 45 GCA).

The net result of these innovations is that the clear profile of the cooperative society as a legal pattern '*sui generis*' has been blurred by deviating from the following basic rules of the original model:

- one member/one vote;
- variable share capital and indivisible reserves; and
- office-holders elected by the members from among themselves and familiar with the economic interests of the members because of their own practical experience.

Instead of the clear profile of cooperatives as SHOs of their members as contained in the ICA Statement of the Cooperative Identity, cooperatives can be:

- organisations in which structural weaknesses in comparison with companies are partly overcome, while new problems are created; or
- social and general interest cooperatives or NPOs.

There are cooperatives that try to attract investors at the risk of losing their strength as members' SHOs without gaining the strength of investor-driven firms. Most of the new provisions introduced into the German Cooperative Societies Act by amendments in 2006 were inspired by the SCE Regulation of 2003. Although the EU Commission stressed that the latter was not intended to harmonise national cooperative laws, this has in fact happened. In the German case it has been brought about by introducing 'foreign' elements into the Cooperative Societies Act. Some of these new provisions are not mandatory but may be introduced in the by-laws. But in this way the law-makers have sent signals inviting cooperative societies to deviate from the original model. With regard to their financial structure, cooperatives move closer to the company model with mixed results: They may gain access to additional resources, but at the price of losing their unique profile.

From a German perspective, two issues are not included in or governed by cooperative law:

- '*Masa de gestión economica*', mutualist capital, created by member participation in cooperative activity, is not perceived as a special legal issue.
- '*Actos cooperativos*', economic transactions between the members and their cooperative enterprise are legally considered as not being different from economic activity with non-members. The only exception exists in tax law, where cooperatives can claim the surplus made in transactions (purpose-transactions) with members on an 'internal market' and recorded separately from transactions with non-members, distributed equally among members in proportion to business done with the cooperative enterprise as patronage

refund and actually paid out. Such surplus can be deducted as an operating cost from the cooperative's taxable income.

In Germany, the old model of Raiffeisen's multipurpose rural cooperative society combining savings and loan with supply and marketing has become the exception. As already mentioned, in 2013, out of a total of 1,078 cooperative banks, only 129 Raiffeisen banks with commodity sections still existed.[81] All other cooperatives dealing with savings and credit had turned into full banks operating under banking law and banking supervision.

Housing cooperatives used to have a savings and credit section for their members. Also in this case in 2013 out of a total of 1,912 housing cooperatives only 48 remained with their own savings associations.[82]

4. EXTERNAL CONTROL OF COOPERATIVES

4.1. INTRODUCTION: THE SPECIAL GERMAN MODEL OF COOPERATIVE AUDIT

For historical reasons, the external audit of registered cooperative societies and the role of cooperative auditing federations are central issues in German cooperative law.[83] Until today, cooperative auditing federations have had the exclusive right to audit all registered cooperative societies (§55(1) GCA). Pre-registration audit (§11 GCA) and admission for affiliation to a cooperative auditing federation (§54 GCA) are preconditions for registration as a cooperative society by the competent registering court (§11a GCA).

These special provisions on external audit, cooperative auditing federations, and their important role in cooperative development date back to the 1860s. The founding fathers of German cooperatives (Schulze-Delitzsch and Raiffeisen) placed great emphasis on audit combined with advice. They established associations providing advice to people interested in forming cooperatives (the predecessors of today's auditing federations) and wrote text books on how to form and manage cooperatives.[84] This important role of cooperative federations was built into the German cooperative law and is still valid today. According to

81 Stappel, above n. 77, p. 42.

82 Stappel 2014, above n. 77, p. 51.

83 K. Mose, 'Die Einführung der genossenschaftlichen Pflichtprüfung durch das Genossenschaftsgesetz von 1889' [Introduction of mandatory cooperative audit by the Cooperative Societies Act of 1889], *ZfgG* 1989, vol. 39, pp. 114–122, pp. 114 f.

84 For example F.W. Raiffeisen, *Die Darlehnskassen-Vereine als Mittel zur Abhilfe der Not der ländlichen Bevölkerung* [Loan associations as a remedy against the needs of the rural population], 1887, English translation with the title *The credit unions*, translated by K. Engelmann, Raiffeisen Printing and Publishing Company, Neuwied, 1970.

§63b GCA, the legal form of a cooperative auditing federation shall be that of a registered association, and at least one of the board members must be qualified as a chartered accountant (§63b(5) GCA).

However, under present-day conditions, these typically German rules on cooperative audit and the role of cooperative auditing federations (monopoly on carrying out cooperative audit with their own cooperative auditors) have come under pressure. Critics demand that these rules on audit be adjusted to international auditing standards designed for commercial, investor-driven enterprises.

The Cooperative Societies Act prescribes compulsory affiliation of all registered cooperatives with an auditing federation (§54 GCA). A new provision stipulates the procedure for withdrawal from an auditing federation and its consequences: such cooperative societies 'shall be dissolved ex officio' (§54a(2) GCA).

The legal requirement that new cooperatives must be accepted for affiliation with an audit federation before registration has been contested by critics as a violation of the constitutional right of freedom of association. In a judgement, the highest court in Germany has adduced the following arguments to rule that compulsory affiliation with an auditing federation is no such violation. There is freedom to choose between different models of organisation and legal forms. But once this choice has been made, the model must be accepted as it is ruled by law, i.e. in the case of choosing the cooperative society model, this includes compulsory affiliation with a cooperative auditing federation.[85]

4.2. NEED FOR EXTERNAL CONTROL AND DEFINITION OF TERMS

From the German perspective, cooperative societies are classified as business associations and enterprises (*Draheim*: dual nature). Unlike in commercial enterprises, where success and failure can be deduced from the balance sheet, in cooperative societies it is necessary to verify whether the cooperative has succeeded as an enterprise with a specific, legally prescribed objective and as a social group of members.

4.2.1. Definition of Terms

Control, audit and supervision:

- Control: from French 'contre rôle' i.e. keeping a double register and comparing kept copies of roles of accounts; check, verify, regulate;

[85] R. Reinhardt, *Gesellschaftsrecht – Ein Lehrbuch* [Law of organisations – a textbook], Tübingen, 1973, pp. 347, 348, RZ 899, 900; Beuthien, n. 8 above, §54 GenG, RZ 5 and 6.

- Audit: official examination of accounts;
- Supervision: watch with authority, oversee proceedings or progress.

'Control' is the more general term and covers audit and supervision.

Why do cooperative societies as business associations and enterprises need external control? While the management of commercial enterprises must apply scarce resources to make maximum profit (operational efficiency), cooperative management must apply scarce resources to achieve optimal member-promotion. Cooperative management must be promotion-oriented, with member-relations management as a core competency. Unlike investor-driven enterprises, which operate on the market to make profit from commercial business transactions with market partners and customers, in cooperative societies, where the owners of the cooperative society and the users of the goods and services offered by the cooperative enterprise are the same people, cooperative management must distinguish between cooperative transactions on internal markets (in their relations with members) and external markets (in their relations with market partners). There are special technical terms in German cooperative studies to express this difference.

As already explained (sections 1.5 and 1.6), there are cooperative transactions with members, i.e. transactions for which the cooperative society was formed to promote its members (purpose-transactions, *Zweckgeschäft*), and transactions with market partners, i.e. transactions needed to make purpose-transactions possible (counter-transactions, *Gegengeschäft*), e.g. in a consumer cooperative: buying consumer goods from wholesalers or factories (counter-transactions) versus selling the consumer goods to members in the cooperative's stores (purpose-transactions).

In this terminology, counter-transactions are typically transactions with non-members in the broad meaning of the term. Transactions with non-members in the narrow meaning of the term are purpose-transactions with non-members.

4.2.2. *Where can Rules on Cooperative Audit be Found?*

Norms on cooperative audit, auditing federations, auditors, and supervision of auditing federations (super-audit) can be found in Chapter IV of the German Cooperative Societies Act (§§53–64c GCA). These special provisions of cooperative law have been increasingly supplemented by general provisions on audit of enterprises, irrespective of their legal form. In certain cases (e.g. in the case of cooperatives offering financial services) special rules apply. Furthermore, provisions of the Commercial Code supplement the provisions of the Cooperative Societies Act (§53(3) GCA). As a trend, also norms regulating the profession of chartered accountants (e.g. WPO) increasingly apply directly or indirectly to cooperative auditors.

4.3. EXTERNAL AUDIT

4.3.1. General Types of External Audit

The following types of external audit can be distinguished:

- Financial audit – formal audit: verification if books and accounts are correct, complete, duly vouched and in accordance with the law;
- Management audit, audit of substance, material audit: assessment of quality of management in achieving the objectives of the enterprise;
- Cooperative audit: combination of formal and material audit: how have the objectives of member-promotion been pursued? Special features of cooperative management audit are: comprehensive audit allowing assessment of economic efficiency as well as social and ecological effectiveness.

4.3.2. Types of Cooperative Audit

4.3.2.1. Pre-Registration Audit

Pre-registration audit by an auditing federation with a positive result is a legal requirement for registration of a new cooperative society by the competent court. This rule has pros and cons, costs and benefits.

A strong argument in favour of pre-registration audit is evidence that such audit prevents failed cooperative projects which might be detrimental to the reputation of the cooperative society as a business model and to the cooperative movement as a whole. German experience proves that – once the hurdle of pre-registration audit has been overcome – the insolvency rate of new ventures is extremely low (0.5%). Pre-registration audit is seen as an indispensable counter-balance to safeguard creditors dealing with organisations permitted to start business operations without a fixed minimum capital being prescribed by law.[86]

Arguments against pre-registration audit are that it is an additional impediment to be overcome before registration, with cost before starting any activities which causes many founder-members to look for other, more easily accessible and less costly business models and legal frameworks. Cooperative federations have reacted to this complaint by offering help and coaching on the internet during the formative stage of new cooperatives, and by providing special services at reduced cost. Critics of the German model of pre-registration audit point to the fact that the number of new cooperatives is very small compared with start-ups in other legal forms.

[86] Helios and Strieder, n. 10 above, §3 GenG, RZ 86–88, pp. 97–99.

The problem with easy access to the legal form of cooperative society is that when a newly-formed cooperative society fails, this can damage the entire cooperative movement and should therefore be avoided. A balance should be found between protection of the cooperative name against misuse and reasonable conditions for start-ups in the legal form of a cooperative society which do not make it too difficult and expensive and do not discourage founder-members from choosing this legal form.[87]

4.3.2.2. Comprehensive Management Audit

Cooperative management audit is perceived as a long-term audit plus advice including a long-term assessment of promotion success (i.e. success in promoting the interests of the members) on the basis of a 'promotion plan'.[88]

The obligation of the board of directors of a cooperative society to present an annual 'promotion report', i.e. a report on success in implementing the promotion plan, is lacking in German cooperative law.[89]

There are new provisions in the German Cooperative Societies Act requiring the external auditor to present the audit report not only to the board of directors but also to the chairperson of the supervisory committee (§§58(4), 59(3), 60 and 62(3) GCA).[90] A joint meeting of the board of directors and the supervisory committee is prescribed to deliberate on the audit results.[91]

4.3.2.3. Special External Audit

A special external audit can be carried out at the request of:

- a minority of members representing at least one tenth of the membership (§45(1) GCA);
- the supervisory committee (§38(1a) GCA); or
- the auditing federation with which the society is affiliated (§§57(1), 63h GCA).

The German Cooperative Societies Act also provides for *ex officio* cancellation of registration as the ultimate means of correction. Cooperative societies pursuing different objectives (other than promoting the interest of the members), can be dissolved *ex officio* 'upon request of the highest body in the federal state in which the cooperative society is based' (§81(1) GCA).

---

87 Helios and Strieder, n. 10 above, §3 GenG, RZ 84, 85, pp. 97–98.
88 Geschwandtner and Helios, n. 4 above, pp. 150, 151.
89 Geschwandtner and Helios, n. 4 above, p. 64.
90 Geschwandtner and Helios, n. 4 above, pp. 196, 197.
91 Geschwandtner and Helios, n. 4 above, pp. 167, 168.

4.3.2.4. External Audit of Small Cooperatives

There are special rules on a simplified audit of small cooperatives. A 'small cooperative society' is defined in the Cooperative Societies Act as one with fewer than 20 members (§24(2) GCA) and permitted to work with a simplified organisational structure, i.e. without a supervisory committee, which is replaced by the general meeting (§9(1) GCA). For cooperatives with a balance sheet total in excess of two million euros, audits must be carried out every financial year. This means that cooperative societies with a smaller balance sheet total are audited only every second year (§53(1) GCA).

In cooperative societies with a balance sheet total in excess of one million euros and sales in excess of two million euros, the annual accounts must be audited, including the books and the status report. §§316 and 317 of the HGB (Commercial Code) apply. For larger cooperatives, compliance with the provisions of the Commercial Code is mandatory.

4.3.2.5. 'Super-Audit'

Auditing the auditors. Audit of the quality and effectiveness of external auditors is carried out by a public authority (see section 4.9).

4.3.3. Scope of External Audit

The scope and cost of external audit vary according to the objectives to be achieved:

- Financial audit: audit of books and accounts;
- Management audit: Assessment of the management's care and diligence;
- Cooperative audit: Assessment of care and diligence by cooperative management in pursuit of cooperative objectives, i.e. offering best possible member-promotion. Sources for such audit are: minutes of meetings, analysis of decisions, feed-back from stakeholders;
- Comprehensive audit: Aimed at the maximum of transparency, full accounting, including cost of externalities, information on social and ecological costs and benefits.

4.3.4. Independence of Auditors

How independent are cooperative auditors when employed by an auditing federation? New and detailed legal provisions have been introduced into German cooperative law to safeguard the independence of cooperative auditors (§55(2)–(3) GCA).

How independent is an adviser who also carries out audit? Many auditing federations try to separate these two functions by establishing different sections for each of them. However, detailed knowledge of the auditor carrying out management audit enables that auditor also to give well-founded advice.

§62 GCA regulates the accountability of the auditing bodies: They must act in a conscientious and impartial manner and observe strict secrecy.

4.4. DEFINITION OF SUCCESS IN ENTERPRISES

4.4.1. Success in Commercial, Profit-Oriented, Investor-Driven Enterprises

In commercial enterprises, success and failure can be deduced from the balance sheet. Therefore, financial audit is the norm. It does not require the external auditor to look into matters of indoor-management. If the shareholders are not satisfied with the results of management, they can call for a management audit and bear the additional cost. General economic criteria applied are: profit made, return on invested capital earned, short-term financial success (quarterly reports).

4.4.2. Success in User-Driven Cooperative Enterprises

In this case, success criteria are:

- both short-term and long-term promotion of members' interests;
- frequency of members' use of the cooperative's facilities and services;
- volume of business with members and non-members;
- surplus earned despite policy of service near cost on the 'internal market' between cooperative enterprises and their user-members; and
- long-term success, investment in sustainable development, building up solid structures, operating with social and ecological responsibility, and care for the community.

There are problems in carrying out comparative analysis of success in cooperative enterprises due to limited access to data collected during audit, which are treated as confidential. For example, in Germany in the 1990s a research project to study the effectiveness of cooperative audit by analysing audit reports had to be cancelled because access to audit reports was refused. Another project was carried out by Eberhard Dülfer and Jost Kramer in 1991 under the title: *Analysis of weaknesses in German cooperative banks*[92] and showed a large number of recurrent mistakes, mainly in management.

4.5. HOW TO MEASURE SUCCESS IN COMMERCIAL AND COOPERATIVE ENTERPRISES?

In commercial enterprises, success criteria are: operational efficiency and return on investment earned during the period under review. Instruments for measurement are: books, accounts, annual returns and business plans, e.g. balanced scorecard.[93] In cooperative enterprises, three efficiencies can be distinguished: operational, member-oriented, and development-oriented efficiency – a 'tripartite approach'.[94]

A special method for determining and measuring success in cooperative enterprises is to agree with the members on a promotion plan and present a promotion report to the members in general meeting as a basis for the next promotion plan in a feed-back controlled promotion circle.[95]

Objective criteria for assessment of the success of cooperative societies are:

- fluctuations of membership (persons joining and members leaving), statistics on active and passive members;
- the volume of 'purpose-transactions' with non-members.

There are further methods with which to measure success of non-profit organisations. The following are proposed in the ICA Blueprint for a Cooperative Decade: Triple Bottom Line Approach (TBL) and Social Return on Investment (SROI).[96]

---

92 E. Dülfer and J. Kramer, *Schwachstellenanalyse und Frühwarnsysteme bei Genossenschaftsbanken* [Analysis of weaknesses and early warning system in cooperative banks], Nomos, Göttingen, 1991.

93 C.H. Neese, 'Profilierung durch wertebezogenes genossenschaftliches Management – vergleichende Betrachtung der Raiffeisenbanken im Alpenraum' [Gaining profile by value-oriented management – comparative analysis of Raiffeisenbanks in the alpine region], in Ringle and Münkner (eds.), n. 21 above, pp. 229–249, especially pp. 239–243.

94 E. Dülfer, 'Evaluation of Cooperative Organisations', in E. Dülfer and J. Laurinkari (eds.), *International Handbook of Cooperative Organisations*, Springer, Göttingen, 1985, pp. 358–359.

95 Cf. Grosskopf, Münkner and Ringle 2009, n. 16 above, p. 59.

96 International Cooperative Alliance, *Blueprint for a Cooperative Decade, 2012–2020*, 2012, p 18, http://ica.coop/sites/default/files/attachments/ICA%20Blueprint%20-%20Final%20-%20Feb%2013%20EN.pdf.

4.6. DIFFERENCE BETWEEN CORPORATE SOCIAL RESPONSIBILITY (CSR) AND COOPERATIVE CONCERN FOR THE COMMUNITY

In commercial enterprises, CSR is often used as a marketing tool. In cooperative societies, member-promotion is the legally prescribed objective and concern for the community is a matter of principle (7th cooperative principle of the ICA).

Some large cooperatives increasingly operate like their commercial competitors. They place more emphasis on CSR than on member-promotion in the strict meaning of the term and sometimes present 'promotion reports', which are in fact reports on allocations of surplus to CSR projects, e.g. sponsoring associations in the region.

4.7. AUDITING PROCEDURES – HOW TO CARRY OUT AUDIT?

Auditing procedures are regulated in §57 GCA:

> The board of directors has to grant permission to the external auditor to inspect the books and documents, cash in hand, the security portfolio and goods in stock and has to furnish all information requested by the external auditor.

External auditors must be given full access to information. Office-holders of the cooperative society have the obligation to report to auditors and to give them access to any information that they may require.

The external auditor and the auditing federation must inform the chairperson of the supervisory committee of the commencement of the audit, and the chairperson must inform the other members of the supervisory committee (§57(2) GCA). After completion of the audit, the external auditor must inform the chairperson of the supervisory committee without delay of any findings which require measures to be taken (§57(3) GCA). This is done by giving an oral presentation of the expected outcome to a joint meeting of the board of directors and the supervisory committee (§57(4) GCA), and in case of small cooperatives to the general meeting (§57(5) GCA).

In case of undue delay or inadequate information of the general meeting, the external auditor has the right to call a general meeting (§60 GCA). External auditors must work together with the internal control body (supervisory committee) of the cooperative society audited. They must inform, cooperate with, and integrate office-holders of the cooperative society by making them to some extent part of the external audit. The frequency of audit (annual, bi-annual) depends on the size of the cooperative enterprise.

In cooperative enterprises, separate books and accounts should be kept for transactions with members and non-members so that the volume and value of member-promotion can be assessed.

According to Volker Beuthien in a paper entitled 'Auditing management's task of member-promotion, how can this be done by the auditor?' first published in 2008 and contained in a collection of Beuthien's papers published in 2013,[97] the cooperative auditor must verify three aspects of the management's conduct of business with the aim of assessing the structure and performance of the cooperative society not only as an enterprise but also as an association of persons seeking promotion of their economic and other interests by a jointly owned and used cooperative enterprise.

- Is there a promotion plan? Has this plan been discussed and approved by the members?
- Is there a promotion programme and has it been implemented? Did the management offer members the best possible promotion services under prevailing market conditions?
- Has the promotion plan been implemented with success and has the promotion success been communicated to the members in a promotion report?
- Objective criteria for measuring the promotion success are:
- use made by members of the services offered by the cooperative enterprise (frequency of use);
- development of the membership group, new persons joining, members withdrawing, fluctuation within the membership group;
- cooperative advantages, special prices or conditions offered exclusively to members, types, volume, value;
- surplus earned and its allocation in form of patronage refund, dividend on share contributions and reserves;
- the extent to which the allocations to reserves are reasonable, i.e. enough but not too much, creating a kind of 'foundation fund' at the disposal of the board of directors but without member control;
- transactions with non-members (volume, value) compared with transactions with members; and
- efforts to attract customers to become members.

If business done by the cooperative enterprise is mainly geared to making profit in transactions with members and non-members alike with similar conditions for the distribution of dividends on share contributions, this means that the cooperative society fails to comply with its legally prescribed objective of members' promotion by service relations, and that it turns into a 'dividend cooperative'.

97 Beuthien, n. 2 above, pp. 51–61.

4.8. QUALIFICATION OF AUDITORS – WHO CARRIES OUT EXTERNAL AUDIT?

In commercial enterprises, external audit is carried out by chartered accountants or public certified accountants. In cooperative enterprises, external audit is or should be carried out by specialised cooperative auditors.

Cooperative auditors need special training to understand and assess cooperative management and cooperative success or failure. However, there is a trend towards training cooperative auditors like certified public accountants.

General rules on qualification of auditors can be found in special enactments like Wirtschaftsprüferordnung, WPO (law on chartered accountants) and Abschluß-prüferaufsichtsgesetz (law on the supervision of auditors auditing annual reports of enterprises).[98]

A particular problem is ensuring the independence of auditors, especially of cooperative auditors when they are employed by auditing federations. New legal provisions were introduced into cooperative German law in 2006 to safeguard the independence of cooperative auditors (§§55, 56 GCA).

The accountability of auditing bodies is defined in §62 GCA. Federations, auditors and audit firms are obliged to perform their duties in a conscientious and impartial manner and to observe strict secrecy (§62(1) GCA). 'Liability under these provisions cannot be excluded or limited by contract; the same applies to the liability of the federation for persons it employs for performing the audit' (§62(5) GCA).

How to deal with the audit report?

> The auditing report shall be signed by the federation and presented to the board of directors of the cooperative society as well as to the chairperson of the supervisory committee. ... Every supervisory committee member shall take note of the auditing report (§58(2) GCA).

Every member of the cooperative society has the right to inspect the summarised findings of the audit report (§59(1) GCA). At the general meeting, the chairperson of the supervisory committee shall explain the main findings of the auditor or objections raised during the audit (§59(2) GCA).

A full analysis of the effectiveness of cooperative audit and the weaknesses of management in German cooperative banks was provided by Eberhardt Dülfer and Jost Kramer in 1991.[99]

---

98 Geschwandtner and Helios, n. 4 above, pp. 150, 151.

99 Dülfer and Kramer, n. 92 above.

4.9. EXTERNAL SUPERVISION BY PUBLIC AUTHORITIES

'Super-audit' – auditing the auditors: Auditing federations are controlled by public authorities (the competent ministry) which grant and withdraw the audit licence (§§63, 64 GCA), e.g. for lack of a sound financial basis: 'The federation is granted auditing rights by the highest supervisory authority responsible in the federal state in which the federation is based'. ... 'Several federal states may agree on the establishment of a joint authority by ordinance or the extension of responsibilities beyond the territory of one federal state' (§63 GCA). 'Cooperative auditing federations are subject to supervision by the relevant supervisory authority', which takes the measures necessary to ensure that the federation duly fulfils its legal functions and submits auditing reports and other documents (§64(1) and (2) GCA). 'The supervisory authority may strip the federation of its right to audit if the federation can no longer guarantee to fulfil its functions. The board of directors of the federation shall be heard prior to the revocation. The courts named in §63d shall be advised on the revocation' (§64a GCA).

4.10. TRAINING OF COOPERATIVE AUDITORS

§55(1) GCA expressly states that external auditors employed by cooperative auditing federations must be 'adequately trained and experienced in cooperative auditing'. There are problems in familiarising auditors trained as chartered accountants with the special problems of cooperative audit. To be effective, they must understand the theory and know the practice of cooperative work.

There is a trend in law and practice to standardise and unify the qualification of external auditors irrespectively of the legal form of enterprises to be audited. It is intended to prescribe the qualification of chartered accountant for all external auditors.

Another trend is to approximate cooperative audit to company audit, with common rules for large enterprises regardless of their legal form. In such cases, the reasons for the special training of cooperative auditors are no longer valid. This trend is apparent in the Auditing Guidelines (*Prüfungsempfehlungen*) of the German Cooperative and Raiffeisen Federation (DGRV). The second edition (1990) contained a special chapter (C. II. 1) giving suggestions on how to measure the efficiency of a cooperative's management in promoting members, e.g. by comparing conditions offered to members and non-members and by measuring fluctuation of the membership group. In the 3rd edition of *Audit of Cooperative Management* (2005), the DGRV only recommended assessment of the economic conditions of the cooperative society as a basis for offering services to members, and in particular the assets, earnings and risks, i.e. the promotion capacity of the cooperative enterprise, similar to audit of a commercial enterprise.[100]

By means of a new provision, introduced in 1975 and amended in 2004, cooperative law has been brought in line with the law on chartered accountants (WPO) and the law on auditors auditing annual reports of enterprises (*Abschlußprüferaufsichtsgesetz*).[101] Auditing federations are subject to periodic quality control, and the auditing rights of a federation may be suspended if it cannot present a valid certificate of participation in quality control (§63e(1) GCA). In 2006, several new provisions were added to the Cooperative Societies Act. They regulate among other things the implementation of quality control (§§63e, f and g GCA) and special purpose audit for capital-market oriented cooperative enterprises (§63h GCA).

5. COOPERATION AMONG COOPERATIVES

5.1. AUTONOMY OF COOPERATIVES TO COOPERATE, FEDERATE AND NETWORK

The autonomy of cooperatives in cooperating, federating or networking is more a matter of freedom of association than of cooperative legislation. But what reasonable limits can be set by cooperative legislation to preserve the special character of cooperatives, on the one hand and to allow cooperatives to adjust to the presumed and real needs of the global markets on the other?

Many of the provisions of conventional cooperative laws were enacted in order to preserve the unique character of cooperatives as self-help organisations of their members. Today, many professional cooperative managers see such provisions as burdens from the past to be removed if cooperatives are to survive as enterprises, even if this means a low cooperative profile or none at all.

It is often overlooked that preserving a clear profile as a member-oriented and member-controlled organisation may be the competitive advantage which – together with special rules on doing business in cooperative manner – enables cooperatives to succeed as stable and reliable pillars of local development in today's rapidly changing environment dominated by highly mobile and largely anonymous conglomerates.

As independent enterprises, cooperative societies and their federations or networks can use the tool box developed for cooperation among enterprises. But not all forms of economic cooperation designed for investor-led organisations are

100 Beuthien and Hanrath, n. 2 above, p. 52.

101 Geschwandtner and Helios, n. 4 above, pp. 150, 151.

in conformity with the special character of cooperatives. Therefore, cooperatives cannot strengthen their position in the market by levelling or even eliminating their unique profile and their internal driving forces, i.e. member-promotion, member-commitment, and member-support. By approximating themselves to companies and abandoning the cooperative model, such enterprises jeopardise their nature as cooperative societies and demutualise assets accumulated by generations of co-operators. They may survive as enterprises but not as cooperative societies.

In an economic system based on markets and competition, private law elements are the primary factors of regulation. Even where the law on business organisations sets certain standards and rules, private initiative and freedom of association are essential dynamic elements of the German legal system. Private property is protected by the German Constitution,[102] but it is at the same time subject to the obligation that it must be used (also) for the benefit of the public. Cartels are prohibited; mergers are controlled.

Private initiative in undertaking economic activities is encouraged, and it is perceived as the main driving force of economic development. The state furnishes a legal framework within which such private initiatives can be put into practice. On the other hand, private initiative is restrained if this is required to guarantee that legitimate interests and the rights of all actors can be balanced, e.g. by agreement, by property rights, by binding rules of private and – when necessary – public law including penal law. The law of organisations is part of this framework.[103]

There are relatively recent provisions governing cartels and combinations which refer mainly to companies. These provisions are influenced by EU law. The extent to which these provisions also apply to cooperative societies is still debated.

Cooperative societies can use the entire range of forms of cooperation among enterprises: strategic alliances, franchising, networking, including cooperative groups and subsidiaries. Whether cooperative societies can be part of combinations is still debated. The question of whether cooperatives can become dependent on other cooperative or non-cooperative organisations can be answered differently if seen from a legal or cooperative point of view. According to Beuthien the answer is 'yes'.[104]

If cooperatives are to cope with problems of globalised markets and increased competition, they are called upon to build super-structures based on economic reasoning, i.e. strategic networks, when the conventional functional networks

---

102 Grundgesetz, Federal German Constitution, art. 14 (2).

103 D. Schultz and R. Reinhardt, *Gesellschaftsrecht*, 2nd edition, J.C.B. Mohr (Paul Siebeck), Tübingen, 1981, p. 392.

104 Beuthien, n. 8 above §1 GenG, RZ 137–138.

based on voluntary submission to group discipline do not work – as stated in 2005 by Walter Weinkauf, president of the Hessen/Thüringen regional cooperative audit federation in an interview with a leading German newspaper.[105]

Conventional tools with which to organise such cooperative groups based on agreement are:

- a mission statement, which all members of the system support;
- a Charter of Group Discipline within the integrated system (*Charta der Verbunddisziplin*);
- a code of conduct for group members;
- a set of measures and sanctions to ensure compliance.

5.2. TYPES AND FORMS OF COOPERATION AMONG COOPERATIVES

In Germany there are four different types of cooperation among cooperatives:

Cooperative Federation (*Verband*): federative structures operating in the legal form of a registered association (e.V.) (§63b GCA) with the objective of promoting affiliated cooperative societies by means of services like audit, advice, education and training, as well as interest representation/advocacy. Federations exist at regional and national level, and as organisations according to branches of business.

Central cooperative society (*Zentralgenossenschaft*): economic organisations or unions established by cooperatives in different legal forms, usually that of a company owned by cooperatives carrying out joint business activities by branch of business and area of operation (regional and/or national).

Both federations and central societies work together in vertically integrated systems (*Verbund*).

Moreover, German cooperatives work together in cooperative groups, for which they can use all forms of economic cooperation of enterprises provided that they are compatible with cooperative principles.

In what follows, these different forms of cooperation among cooperatives will be discussed under five headings:

- objectives;
- membership;
- governance, including voting rights of members, and representation of the different member groups in the governance structure;
- financial structures;
- control.

---

105 See Annex, pp. 344–345.

5.3. VERTICAL STRUCTURES

5.3.1. Vertically Integrated Cooperative Systems (Verbund)

A vertically integrated cooperative system is defined as a 'planned, voluntary, long-term contractual obligation of economically and legally independent enterprises to cooperate. Such enterprises are usually interrelated in their financial set-up and their leadership'.[106] Such systems are also defined as dynamic cooperative networks.[107]

5.3.1.1. Objectives

The objective of a vertically integrated cooperative system is the long-term promotion of the economic interests of the affiliates and ultimately of the members of affiliated primary cooperatives.[108] The purpose of such integration is to use advantages of large scale and to compensate the low equity and limited market power of member-enterprises while preserving their independence.

5.3.1.2. Membership

Membership is voluntary. Conditions for membership are regulated in the statutes (by-laws) of the system. Only or mainly registered cooperative societies of the same branch of business can join the system.

5.3.1.3. Governance

A German vertically integrated cooperative system works like an inverted combination, with decision-making powers in basic matters running from the bottom to the top. Among the governance problems of such an integrated system are:

- how to balance autonomy of the individual affiliated cooperative society with group discipline;
- how to balance cooperation and concentration;
- how to avoid excessive power of the hub-firm/apex by preserving democratic control; i.e. avoiding uncontrolled hierarchical orders, and preventing the system from turning into a 'cooperative combination';[109]

106 Grosskopf, Münkner and Ringle, n. 67 above, p. 148.
107 Grosskopf, Münkner and Ringle, n. 67 above, p. 150.
108 Grosskopf, Münkner and Ringle, n. 67 above, p. 149.
109 Grosskopf, Münkner and Ringle, n. 67 above, p. 158.

- how to avoid cartel-like behaviour by the system as a whole which violates competition law;
- how to organise democratic control, e.g. voting rights in proportion to transactions within the system, guaranteeing at least one vote to every member, avoiding dominating power of individual members and limiting the power of investors.

5.3.1.4. Financial Structure

Most of the service providers affiliated with the integrated system are organised in the legal form of a company, with the majority of shares held by member cooperative societies. These organisations are owned by primary cooperatives and other member units of the system, which exercise ultimate control. In this way, hostile takeover by external investors is excluded. Income earned from business activities with member cooperatives must be calculated in line with the general objective of member-promotion, i.e. in the ideal case: service near cost.

5.3.1.5. Control

In a vertically integrated cooperative system, control mechanisms include:

- the right to criticise;
- rights of primary cooperatives to be informed;
- democratic elections, discharge and dismissal mechanisms regarding leaders and office-holders;
- limitation of powers of the hub-firm and protection against attempts to weaken democratic processes by hierarchical structures.[110]

Differently from combinations and franchising enterprises, there is usually no business plan of the hub-firm or central organisation aimed at optimal performance by the entire system, and no obligation of the individual partner organisations to follow a common strategy. This is contrary to the principles of subsidiarity and voluntary cooperation. However, even without legally binding obligations to follow the regulations of the system – which critics see as a handicap of system management – effective cooperation can usually be achieved.

Due to proficiency of leadership and the development of group discipline, long-term advantages of an efficient vertically integrated cooperative system are usually not jeopardised if use is made of short-term advantages offered by external competitors. The members of the system must be convinced by advice and performance that the advantages of cooperative autonomy and its

---

110 Grosskopf, Münkner and Ringle, n. 67 above, p. 155.

disadvantages can be balanced for the benefit of all members of the system. In the joint organisation of the vertically integrated cooperative system, members enjoy competitive advantages if the central cooperative organisation is strong. A precondition for successful operation of the vertically integrated cooperative system is that all member units recognise and respect the conditions securing the economic existence of each other.[111]

5.3.1.6. Characteristic Features of Vertically Integrated Cooperative Systems

The characteristic features of a vertically integrated cooperative system are:

- Voluntary membership, i.e. organised solidarity following self-determined rules in own responsibility without obligation to join the system and/or to use its services and
- Subsidiarity, following the three basic rules of an effective integrated system: (i) non-substitution: what small members of the system can handle effectively may not be taken over by larger units of the system; (ii) offering help: what small members of the system cannot handle effectively may be offered by larger units of the system as help; (iii) subsidiarity reduction: when small units of the system are growing, tasks taken over by larger units must be given back to the smaller units when they can handle them effectively by themselves.

5.3.1.7. Infringements of the Rules of Vertically Integrated Cooperative Systems

Typical infringements of the rules of such systems are:

- free-rider behaviour, i.e. using the advantages of the system without making contributions to cover its cost, share the burdens, assume responsibility and comply with the rules;
- deviation, i.e. doing business outside the system, aiming at short-term advantages irrespective of the fact that the integrated system invests considerable efforts in offering services, while such services are weakened by deviation using offers outside the system. Problems arise if the conditions offered within the system cannot compete with offers by competitors;
- infringement of the principle of subsidiarity by the central cooperative organisation entering into competition with primary cooperatives;
- 'harvesting in your neighbours' gardens', i.e. one cooperative doing business in the area of operation of neighbouring cooperatives.

---

111 Grosskopf, Münkner and Ringle, n. 67 above, p. 155.

To deal with such infringements, a charter of discipline within the system is important to show all members their limits and responsibilities.[112]

5.3.1.8. Sanctions for Infringements

Affiliation of a cooperative society with a vertically integrated cooperative system is only justified if member-promotion is also the objective of the system. To make member-organisations comply with the rules of the system, a – written or unwritten – charter of regulations of the system provides for penalties and sanctions in cases of infringement of the mutually agreed rules in order to enforce behaviour in line with the charter.[113]

Acts and omissions constituting violations of the rules and which entail sanctions are usually defined in the by-laws or similar regulations of the member-organisations. Such sanctions can only be imposed by elected bodies and in a procedure considered as just. This includes the right of the accused to be heard.

From the member cooperative's perspective such sanctions are:

- the right to withdraw from the system;
- the right to call for an investigation into the performance of the leading body because of infringement of the regulations of the system.

Sanctions from the perspective of the system are:

- complaints by the auditing federation in the audit report;
- refusal of assistance (solidarity) by the facilities of the integrated system, e.g. of the mutual guarantee fund of cooperative banks, to which member-cooperatives have no legal right in the case of infringement of the regulations of the system;[114]
- expulsion from the system following procedures laid down in the mutually agreed regulations.

In the important sector of German cooperative banks, with 17.7 million of a total of 21.9 million members of cooperative societies,[115] the historic ideological divide between urban Peoples Banks (Schulze-Delitzsch) and rural Raiffeisenbanks has been to a large extent overcome. In 1972, the two national federations DRV and DGV merged into DGRV, and thereafter mergers also occurred at primary cooperative level. This was favoured by two continuing trends: external growth of primary societies by merger across ideological

---

112 Grosskopf, Münkner and Ringle, n. 67 above, p. 156.
113 Grosskopf, Münkner and Ringle, n. 67 above, p. 156.
114 Grosskopf, Münkner and Ringle, n. 67 above, p. 158.
115 Stappel, n. 77 above, pp. 8, 9.

boundaries; and growth requiring professionalisation of management and change from three-tier (local, regional, national) to two-tier systems (local, national) by merger of regional federations among themselves and regional central banks with two national cooperative banks (DZ BANK AG and WZG eG) and in 2016 finally with one national cooperative Bank (DZ BANK AG).

Starting in 1973, the tendency in cooperative law reforms was to strengthen the governance and financial structure of growing cooperatives. This trend continued in the law reform of 2006. However, also special provisions were introduced to meet the needs of small cooperatives: reduction of the minimum number of members from seven to three (§4 GCA), and simplified organisational structures for cooperatives with fewer than 20 members (§9(1) GCA).

5.3.1.9. The Vertically Integrated Financial System of Cooperative Banks

The vertically integrated financial system of cooperative banks (*Finanzverbund*), including the Guarantee Fund of the German Cooperative Banks (Sicherungseinrichtung der deutschen Volksbanken und Raiffeisenbanken), a guarantee scheme based on horizontal solidarity, managed mainly by regional federations and partly by the national apex federation BVR, may serve as an illustration. See also Annex: Walter Weinkauf, 'The Integrated System of German Cooperative Banks Needs New Rules', interview in: *Frankfurter Allgemeine Zeitung*, May 3, 2005, p. 16 (below pp. 71–72).

The Deposit Guarantee Fund of German Cooperative Banks was established in 1929 after the world economic crisis. It has existed in its current form since 1977. Its objective is to protect affiliated cooperative banks against existing or expected economic difficulties. The aim is not only to guarantee deposits but also to protect the bank itself against dissolution.

Although membership of the Deposit Guarantee Fund is voluntary, without membership in the Fund bank licences are not issued. There is no legal right to receive support from the Fund (no insurance against risk). Whether or not support is granted to needy cooperative banks is decided by the board of the respective federation at regional or national level.

The Deposit Guarantee Fund consists of two elements:

- a Guarantee Fund financed by annual contributions of member-cooperatives (0.5 to 2 per mille of the total volume of outlaid loans); and
- a Guarantee System consisting of the combined total of 60% of the sum of member-banks' depreciations for credit risks.

Support from the Fund can take three different forms:

- loan guarantees;

- loans (with interest or interest free);
- grants.

When support is refused, the alternatives for the cooperative bank in need are merger or dissolution.

5.3.1.10. Vertically Integrated System of Housing Cooperatives

German housing cooperatives have their own vertically integrated system with GdW (Bundesverband der Wohnungs- und Immobilienunternehmen – national federation of housing and building enterprises) as the national apex.[116]

5.3.2. Federations

5.3.2.1. Objectives

The objectives of an auditing federation are audit, support, advocacy and dispute settlement/arbitration as stated in the by-laws. According to §63b(4) GCA, these powers are defined in the Cooperative Societies Act as follows:

> [T]he purpose of the federation shall be the auditing of its members and otherwise may also be the common protection of their interests, in particular the maintenance of mutual business relationships. It shall not pursue any other purposes'.

The powers of auditing federations are limited by self-administration and autonomy of its member-societies.[117] Audit plus advice is a combination of financial (formal) audit and management (performance or material) audit typical of cooperative auditing. The criteria for measuring performance are respect for the principles of sound business administration, on the one hand, and the cooperative principles on the other.[118] Cooperative audit serves the interests of the integrated cooperative system as a whole.[119]

An auditing federation cannot influence the performance of affiliated registered cooperative societies by giving orders or making binding proposals. The influence of auditing federations is mainly exercised by advice and the power to carry out performance audit, which can be seen as a kind of self-control.[120]

---

116 Stappel, n. 77 above, p. 7.
117 Lang/Weidmüller, n. 47 above, §53 GenG, RZ 8.
118 Lang/Weidmüller, n. 47 above, §53 GenG, RZ 9.
119 Lang/Weidmüller, n. 47 above, §53 GenG, RZ 10.
120 Lang/Weidmüller, n. 47 above, §53,GenG, RZ 8.

5.3.2.2. Membership

Under German law, every registered cooperative society must be a member of an auditing federation (§54 GCA). Detailed provisions are contained in the German Cooperative Societies Act (§63b(2) GCA):

> Members of the federation can only be registered cooperative societies, or, irrespective of their legal form, enterprises or other associations that are either totally or predominantly owned by registered cooperative societies, or serve the purpose of the cooperative system …

Compulsory adherence of registered cooperative societies to an auditing federation is not considered to be an infringement of the constitutional right of freedom of association. Every group has the right not to adhere to an auditing federation, but if the registered cooperative society is chosen as a legal form for group action, compulsory affiliation with an auditing federation is part of the conditions for registration, and as such it is an integral part of the chosen legal pattern.[121] As a rule, non-cooperatives or individuals cannot become members of an auditing federation.

5.3.2.3. Governance

'The federation shall have the legal form of a registered association' (e.V.) (§63b(1) GCA). According to §25 of the Civil Code (BGB), the governance structures are decided by the members in the constitution (by-laws) of the association. The board must be elected by the general meeting of members (§27 BGB). The general meeting of members is the ultimate authority (§32 BGB). In accordance with the cooperative principle of democratic control, important decisions are taken by the members in general meeting (bottom up). Cooperative federations have an elected president and board, committees and subcommittees, and externally recruited professional managers. There are no external investors.

Over the years, there has been a change in the number of tiers in the structure of auditing federations: from three to two. Like growing primary cooperatives try to reduce their costs, federations have merged across sectors and ideologies. Auditing federations have merged across the borders of federated states and even branches of business. For more details on auditing federations and their role see section 4.

[121] Lang/Weidmüller, n. 47 above, §54 GenG, RZ 4; see also section 4.4, Introduction, pp. 319–320.

5.3.2.4. Financial Structure

The main sources of income for auditing federations are membership fees paid by affiliated cooperative societies and service charges (§61 GCA).

5.3.2.5. Control

In auditing federations, the control mechanisms at the disposal of the members are similar to those used in integrated cooperative systems.[122] In addition, there is a 'super-audit' (audit of the auditors) exercised by the state (state or federal government, §§63, 63a–g, 64a GCA).[123]

5.3.3. Cooperative Groups

In Germany the phenomenon of groups of enterprises including cooperative groups is common. A group is defined as a set of legally independent enterprises under joint leadership and joint control. The group itself is not a legal body. This lack of certainty concerning cooperative groups and groups of enterprises reflects their quality. When cooperatives are grouped together with other legal bodies, the danger arises that those cooperatives may lose their cooperative identity.

The term 'group' appears in the name of the central (national) federation of traders', retailers' and service providers' cooperatives ZGV 'Zentralverband genossenschaftlicher Verbundgruppen', and members of this apex organisation have formed cooperative groups among themselves.

Groups of enterprises used to interest economists more than lawyers. The law of combined enterprises (Recht der verbundenen Unternehmen) has long been vague and is gradually acquiring more precision. Under cooperative law, cooperation among cooperatives has always been considered to be a necessary part of cooperative structure (*Genossenschaftsverbund*). The special term '*Verbund*' is defined as a voluntary network of enterprises linked together by mutually agreed rules.

5.4. HORIZONTAL COOPERATION

Cooperative societies can use the full range of forms of economic cooperation among enterprises developed over the years, and which includes:

- contracts, i.e. cooperation agreements;
- joint ventures;

122 See section 4.3.1.
123 For details see section 4.9.

- daughter societies;
- franchising;
- networking (functional and strategic networking);
- integration (both horizontal and/or vertical integration over several tiers);
- new legal patterns, e.g. producer groups or economic interest groups.

But there are limits. Cooperative societies which have transferred all their economic activities to daughter societies, which only serve as holdings of cooperative assets, and which promote their members by payment of dividends on invested capital (*Haltegenossenschaften*), should not remain on the register. Another limit is crossed if a cooperative enterprise abandons member-promotion as its main purpose.

5.5. CONCLUSION

Working together in cooperative groups is an integral part of cooperative organisation culture, as the principle of cooperation among cooperatives implies.

But it is not possible to level the specific cooperative profile by approximating cooperatives increasingly and without limits to commercial (i.e. investor- and profit-oriented) enterprises in order to compete with commercial conglomerates, combinations, franchising systems and global players of all kinds, and still remain cooperative.

Cooperatives must preserve their unique profile, concentrate on promoting their members,, insist on value-based management and preserve their core-competency, which is member-relations management. Cooperatives must use and further develop their arsenal of weapons with which to fight their investor-driven commercial competitors.

For cooperatives the question is not becoming investor-oriented, shareholder value-oriented organisations opting for companisation (going commercial) and even going public *and* remaining cooperative (i.e. member-value oriented). Rather, the choice is between going commercial and even public *or* remaining cooperative.[124]

This does not exclude a high level of cooperative efficiency in organising business activities and using scarce resources like any other enterprise (economisation). The difference lies in the special objective of cooperative activities, namely to serve their members/users and not (only or mainly) capital owners and anonymous investors.

---

[124] H.-H. Münkner, 'Go public and remain cooperative?', *Boletín Asociación Internacional de Derecho Cooperativo*, nos. 26–27, mayo–diciembre, 1996, Universidad de Deusto, Bilbao, pp. 63–91.

Cooperative groups are part of cooperative organisation culture and must fit into this culture. Guaranteeing this 'fit' is not primarily a matter of legislation but of value orientation. But what is left of cooperative organisation culture?

German cooperative federations, and the German law-makers guided by them, have decided to view cooperatives primarily as enterprises which must compete and survive in the market and which promote their members as far as market conditions permit.

Many cooperative enterprises react to economic change in almost the same ways as their commercial competitors by merger, combination, and the outsourcing of unprofitable activities. They seek new sources of capital to finance growth and the use of modern technologies.

The idea that primary cooperatives are by their nature locally rooted, small and reliable economic units based on personal relationships, and that they can be used as local pillars of stability in times of rapid change and increasing insecurity and as counterpoise against unlimited mobility and unrestricted growth, is seen by most cooperative managers as an illusion. However, when government services and commercial firms withdraw from villages and small towns, new cooperatives are formed for exactly such reasons.

In the search for new approaches to develop cooperative enterprises further and to make them fit to survive in global markets, company-style solutions are seen by many as the only viable options. It is often forgotten that a cooperative enterprise is not an end in itself but rather a means to promote the interests of the co-operators. Instead, it is assumed that the assets of cooperative enterprises are a kind of 'neutralised' capital with 'atomised' ownership by thousands of members and collective reserves. Hence they are assets without effective owner-control.

These assets are often managed by externally recruited managers and professional board members, acting as quasi-trustees on behalf of the members, for whom the interests of the enterprise, the interests of the employees and their own personal interests have priority over the interests of the members which – at best – rank second, if they play a role at all.

In this approach to cooperative management, the internal motivating forces of cooperatives – members' self-interest and self-help by organised group action – cease to work. The cooperative enterprise turns into an 'employees enterprise', following its own rules.

In Germany, voluntary membership of most registered cooperative societies in vertically integrated systems and compulsory affiliation with auditing federations help to preserve the cooperative organisation culture.

ANNEX

Walter Weinkauf, 'Der deutsche Finanzverbund braucht neue Regeln' (The Integrated System of German Cooperative Banks Needs New Rules), interview in: Frankfurter Allgemeine Zeitung, May 3, 2005, p. 16.

According to the opinion of the former president of a regional auditing federation Walter Weinkauf, expressed in an interview in 2005, the integrated system of German cooperative banks needs new rules. It is necessary to reorganise the relationship between the primary cooperative banks and those who provide products and services for them: The entire system – central cooperative banks (DZ BANK AG and WGZ eG), the saving-for-housing organisation and building society Schwäbisch Hall, and the Union Investment Fund – must be put on new bases. 'New rules are needed in order to prevent the integrated cooperative system from suffering further losses of market shares.'

For some time there has been a crisis of confidence among the partners of the integrated system of German cooperative banks. While there has been strong concentration among product and service providers with a *de facto* monopoly, 1,300 primary cooperative banks continue to drift apart in terms of size.

In meetings of delegates of the National Federation of Peoples Banks and Raiffeisen Banks (BVR), often about one quarter of the affiliated banks have refused to follow the leadership of the BVR board. Interest groups have been formed by smaller and larger Peoples Banks and Raiffeisen Banks. Weinkauf warns that 'atomised representation of interests will lead to chaos within the system', and amid rapidly changing markets, he criticises BVR for having opted for the wrong strategy. 'It is the task of a regional audit federation to safeguard the effectiveness of local cooperative banks.' Then the federations will have to supervise compliance with the new rules. However, it is not decided whether the BVR will adopt these new rules.

What Weinkauf wants are more binding rules, efficiency and transparency. It is true that many mergers among primary cooperative banks in recent years have improved cost structures, 'but what we need is more power in marketing'. Weinkauf sees the cooperative banks as cornered between aggressive competitors like financial service providers, on the one side, and car-financing institutions and direct banks on the other. The high interest rates on short-term money with which direct banks lure private customers away from Peoples' Banks raise the question of whether the cooperative integrated financial system would need a direct bank.

The cooperative integrated financial system must react with new rules. 'A local cooperative bank must be able to offer products and services competitive with those offered by direct banks via the internet.' At present, the apex organisation of the Peoples Banks and Raiffeisen banks, the DZ BANK, is unable to make this possible.

Because the DZ BANK is assessed by rating agencies largely on its own, its creditworthiness is determined without considering the local banks and the cooperative deposit guarantee fund serving as a link. 'What we need is rating of the integrated system …' If the DZ BANK could achieve this, it would obtain money on the money market at better conditions. This money could be lent out at low interest rates to Peoples Banks and Raiffeisen banks, which in turn could offer their customers higher interest rates for their deposits.

Plans for a rating of the integrated system will, however, raise even more fears among board members of many primary cooperative banks that they will become members of a combination and lose their autonomy. Primary cooperative banks can sell life-insurance policies or fund certificates of service providers outside the integrated system if the customers want it or if they can earn more. In reaction, the service providers of the integrated cooperative financial system have offered special conditions to large primary cooperatives, annoying the others. 'We cannot turn into an integrated system of brokers' is Weinkauf's advice in this emotional discussion on transparency and increased economisation. 'In the past several years, development trends originating from the markets have increased pressure on primary cooperatives', he admits. An increasingly large share of loans issued by primary cooperative banks no longer shows in their balance sheets, but rather in the books of their partners within the integrated system.

In the interest of the system as a whole, this problem must be considered by offering incentives and exercising control. The People's Banks and Raiffeisen banks should not only receive commissions from products and service providers for new contracts, which tend to favour cooperative banks with a large, largely untapped, potential of customers. Instead, cooperative banks with a high market share should receive annual commissions for having already made good sales. This should have the effect that primary cooperative banks which prefer to sell products and services from outside the system will see this more as a disadvantage. In return, Weinkauf proposes increasing the supervision of the product and service providers of the Peoples Banks and Raiffeisen banks. Irrespective of rating as an integrated system, their products and services must be compared with those of their competitors. Only in this way can it be ascertained that the specialists produce in an efficient manner and offer competitive products to primary cooperative banks.

CHAPTER 9
ITALY

Antonio Fici

1. DEFINITION AND OBJECTIVES OF COOPERATIVES

1.1. INTRODUCTION

In Italian law, the cooperative is a particular type of legal entity – more precisely, a particular type of company with juridical personality – which is subject to a specific set of rules identifying it by a particular aim and structure.

Moreover, in Italian law, several 'legal types' of organisations exist. What characterises and distinguishes a certain legal type is a combination of the entity's purpose and structure, according to the assumption that any organisation is established to achieve a given result in a certain manner.[1]

The entity's purpose is, therefore, one of the most important elements in the classification of the existing organisational types, and Italian law frequently includes the purpose of an organisation in its legal definition. This certainly helps to identify and separate the organisational legal types, and makes a systematic interpretation of organisational law easier. Inquiring into the purpose of a legal entity also helps to interpret its regulation, since entities' regulations should be consistent with their purposes.

The purpose of a legal entity includes both the ultimate objective of the organisation (*scopo-fine*), and the activity by which the organisation aims at pursuing it (*scopo-mezzo*). The activity performed may be the element that permits distinction among legal types of entities that pursue the same final objective. In other instances, and cooperatives may be one of them, the activity performed and the entity's ultimate objective coincide, in the sense that the activity does not play an instrumental role, but its very performance constitutes the final objective of the organisation. While, for example, for-profit companies conduct business (*scopo-mezzo*) in order to distribute profits to shareholders (*scopo-fine*), by conducting business with its members a cooperative may achieve its objectives *per se*, given that – as we shall see – the mutual purpose that characterises Italian cooperatives consists in running an activity that directly satisfies the interests of the members.

1.2. DEFINITION OF COOPERATIVE

The general regulation of Italian cooperatives is set forth in articles 2511–2545*octiesdecies* ICC, as amended by Legislative Decree 17 January 2003, no. 6, reforming company law. Other general legal provisions, however, may be found in separate legal texts (to which we shall refer in this or other sections). Moreover, there are some special laws on particular types of cooperatives (cooperative banks, social cooperatives, worker cooperatives, etc.).

The relationship between general cooperative law and special laws on particular types of cooperatives is governed by article 2520, para. 1, ICC, according to which cooperatives regulated by special laws are also subject to the general cooperative law if it is compatible with their particular nature.

---

1 Cf. G. Marasà, 'Le società', in G. Iudica and P. Zatti (eds.), *Trattato di diritto privato*, 2nd ed., Giuffrè, Milan, 2000, pp. 39 ff.

Furthermore, the regulations of either joint-stock companies (*società per azioni* – SPA) or limited-liability companies (*società a responsabilità limitata* – SRL) may additionally apply to cooperatives, but only to fill the gaps in cooperative law and provided that these regulations are compatible with the particular nature of the cooperative (art. 2519 ICC).

It is also important to recall that the Italian Constitution deals with cooperatives in article 45, para. 1, which reads: 'The Republic recognises the social function of cooperation with mutual character and without private speculation purposes. The law promotes and favours its growth with the most adequate means, and ensures, through appropriate controls, its character and purposes'.[2]

The following analysis will be limited to the cooperative in general, although the regulation of special cooperatives may be important to understand cooperatives in general and to resolve general issues related to this legal form of entity.

The general regulation of cooperatives begins with a provision defining cooperatives as 'societies with variable capital and mutual purpose, registered with the register of cooperative societies under article 2512, para. 2, and article 223*sexiesdecies* of the provisions for the implementation of the present code'.

According to this definition, therefore, essential elements of the cooperative legal type of entity are the mutual purpose (*scopo mutualistico*) and the variable capital. In contrast, although it is now part of the definition as a result of an amendment of 2009, registration is not considered by legal scholars to be an essential characteristic of cooperatives.

The mutual purpose alone already makes it possible to distinguish cooperatives from other companies whose stated purpose is the distribution of profits to participants (according to art. 2247 ICC, 'by a society contract two or more persons contribute goods or services to conduct an economic activity in common, with the aim of sharing its profits').[3]

Yet, even after the 2003 reform of company law, the ICC does not contain an explicit definition of the 'mutual purpose' of cooperatives. Its essence, however, clearly emerges from the overall regulation of cooperatives, and especially from the distinction between 'prevalently mutual cooperatives' (PMCs) and 'other cooperatives' (OCs).

2 All the translations in this article are by the author unless otherwise specified.

3 A point in regard to terminology needs clarification. In Italian law, cooperatives are 'societies' as are other companies, including joint-stock and limited liability companies, and partnerships. Thus, in Italy, 'society' is a general term and legal category which comprises several types of societies and cooperatives. Therefore, if one uses the English term 'company' to translate the Italian term 'society', cooperatives are a type of company and cooperative law pertains to company law.

1.3. THE COOPERATIVE OBJECTIVE – PREVALENTLY MUTUAL COOPERATIVES AND OTHER COOPERATIVES

As stated above, the ICC attributes a mutual purpose to Italian cooperatives, but at the same time it does not define that purpose. The situation was the same before the 2003 reform of company law, although at that time legal scholars and courts were strongly influenced by a passage in the Ministerial Report on the ICC (no. 1025) stating that cooperatives are to be distinguished from other companies because they pursue 'a prevalently mutual purpose consisting in providing goods, services or work opportunities directly to the members of the organisation under conditions more favourable than those that they would find on the market'.

Today, the distinction between PMCs and OCs seems decisive in the interpretation of the mutual purpose. According to article 2512 ICC, PMCs are cooperatives that act prevalently with their members as consumers or users of the goods or services provided by the cooperative (consumer cooperatives), as providers of the goods or services employed by the cooperative in its activity (production cooperatives), or as workers (worker cooperatives).

According to article 2513 ICC, the condition of prevalence must be analytically documented by showing in the cooperative balance sheet that, depending on the type of 'mutual transaction', (a) sales proceeds from the members are more than 50% of total sales proceeds (consumer cooperatives); (b) labour costs for members are more than 50% of total labour costs (worker cooperatives); (c) production costs for goods or services provided by members are more than 50% of total production costs (production cooperatives). By contrast, OCs are obligated neither to act prevalently with their members nor to report on the volume of the activity with them. Unlike OCs, PMCs are also subject to the constraints on the distribution of profits laid down in article 2514 ICC.

The distinction between PMCs and OCs is not particularly important under organisational law (indeed, only the regime of transformation is different), but it is important under tax law, since in general only PMCs are granted a specific tax treatment distinct from and more favourable than that of other business entities (see art. 223*duodecies*, para. 6, of the provisions for the implementation of the ICC).[4]

The definition of PMCs, together with the large group of provisions concerning mutual transactions and relationships between the cooperative and its members, permits identification of the content of the cooperative mutual

4 According to the Ministry of the Economic Development (cf. *Rilevazioni statistiche del Movimento Cooperativo in Italia. Anni 2006–2007–2008*), which is responsible for the Register of cooperative societies, OCs were only 5.07% of total cooperatives in 2008.

purpose in that already delineated in the aforementioned Ministerial Report on the ICC (n. 1025).[5]

Therefore, the institutional purpose of Italian cooperatives is to transact with or employ the members, seeking to maximise their utility as consumers, providers, or workers (and not as owners/investors) of the cooperative enterprise.[6] Consequently, the business enterprise run by a cooperative directly satisfies the members' needs. It is not, as is instead the case in for-profit companies, a pure instrument to maximise, through the subsequent distribution of profits, the return on the capital invested by the company owners (the shareholders).

Nevertheless, a different conclusion should apply to OCs, since they are obligated neither to transact with their members nor to observe limits in the remuneration of the subscribed capital.[7] OCs, in fact, lie somewhere between for-profit companies and genuine cooperatives, that is, PMCs.

---

5 See also art. 1, para. 1, Law no. 142/2001 on worker cooperatives, which – in determining the scope of the law – states: 'The provisions of this law refer to cooperatives in which the mutual relationship regards the provision of labour by the member.'

Current Italian legislation on cooperatives has made any different interpretation of the cooperative purpose very difficult to defend. In the past, before the 2003 reform of company law, there were legal scholars who viewed cooperatives as organisations acting in the interest of an entire category of people with identical needs and not only of members as such (cf. P. Verrucoli, *La società cooperativa*, Giuffrè, Milan, 1958), or as organisations essentially characterised by restrictions on the distribution of profits (F. Messineo, *Manuale di diritto civile e commerciale*, vol. III.I.1, 8th ed., Giuffrè, Milan, 1954, pp. 536 ff.), or by a democratic structure of production (E. Simonetto, *La cooperativa*, Cedam, Padua, 1986, pp. 138 ff.).

Today, the sociological conception of cooperatives, attributable to Verrucoli, would be in clear contrast with art. 2520, para. 2, ICC, which requires a special law for the establishment of non-mutual cooperatives (see sec. 1.9). Therefore, non-mutual cooperatives are 'typical' in the sense that only those specifically provided for by special laws may be established (e.g. social cooperatives under Law no. 381/1991).

With regard to the limits on the distribution of profits, they are the inevitable consequence of the mutual purpose. Given the cooperative's mutual purpose, profit distribution cannot but be limited. The possibility to distribute profits, though limitedly, is in fact to be regarded as a benefit granted by the legislature to organisations pursuing a mutual purpose (consistently with the possibility to act with non-members and thus gain profits in the strict sense), but not as the real essence of the cooperative phenomenon. In theory, law could even prohibit any distribution of profits in cooperatives.

6 Admittedly, however, the objective to maximise the utility of the user-members is not stated anywhere in the Italian legislation. It may be considered implicit because there is no other aim stated by cooperative law, and because users of the enterprise and members/owners of the cooperative society coincide.

7 Even assuming that also OCs must pursue a mutual purpose (as some Italian scholars hold by citing art. 2511 ICC, which defines all cooperatives and not only PMCs), it remains unclear what the minimum amount of dealings with members must be in order to recognise OCs as cooperatives.

1.4. IMPLEMENTATION OF THE MUTUAL PURPOSE AND SOME RELATED ISSUES

Implementation of the mutual purpose requires transactions between the cooperative and its members which in Italian law are termed 'mutual transactions' or 'mutual relationships'. Through these transactions the cooperative fulfils its institutional purpose and the members satisfy their common interests (to obtain certain goods and services, in consumer cooperatives; to sell certain goods and services, in producer cooperatives; to work, in worker cooperatives).

Implementation of the mutual purpose raises several issues. First, one may ask whether it implies an obligation for the parties to transact with each other. Indeed, if the cooperative did not transact with its members and the members with their cooperative, the implementation of the mutual purpose would be impracticable, and the interests of the parties would remain unserved.

Italian law does not explicitly state that cooperative members are entitled to transact with the cooperative, nor that, correspondingly, a cooperative is obligated to transact with (or to employ) its members.

Legal scholars are divided on the matter. Some argue that the mutual purpose implies an obligation for the cooperative to provide goods, services, or jobs to the members, or rather (if one follows the 'double relationship' theory), to enter into a contract with them for their provision. Others reject this interpretation, but admit that cooperative statutes might well provide for such an obligation.

In fact, the conflict between the two opposite views may be resolved if one considers that the cooperative is a legal entity different from and independent of its members. An obligation to transact, therefore, may be conceived of only when it is not in conflict with the interest of the cooperative as an autonomous legal entity. The organs of the cooperative have a discretionary (which does not mean 'free') power to decide whether or not to transact with the members. Hence, a cooperative member's right to transact with the cooperative is to be considered conditional on the actual possibility for the cooperative to undertake mutual transactions. Only when this condition is met does a member's individual right of transacting arise. Undoubtedly, in the case of conflict between a member and the cooperative, establishing when a mutual transaction would undermine or be compatible with the interest of the cooperative as an autonomous legal subject may be problematic. The presence of unobservable and unverifiable information about the use of the discretionary power to transact with the members could make it difficult for a court to adjudicate on this potential dispute.

This issue should be discussed by taking account also of article 2516 ICC. This obligates cooperatives to treat cooperative members equally in the constitution and execution of mutual relationships. A member's right to be treated like all other members may give rise to a cooperative's obligation to transact with the former when refusal to do so would be in conflict with the equal treatment rule (as well as to a cooperative's obligation not to transact with a member when this transaction is in contrast with the duty to treat another member equally).

The member's right to be preferred over non-members as counterparties of the cooperative (a sort of pre-emption right) is more easily and broadly accepted by legal scholars. Moreover, the Italian Supreme Court (*Corte di Cassazione*) has affirmed that 'the mutual purpose … implies the impossibility for the general meeting or the board of directors to dispose of the member right to participate in the planned benefits of the cooperative activity. Said purpose, in a building cooperative, does not permit housing provision to third parties when this damages the members' interests, in which case the cooperative's resolution to sell to third parties is null and void since its object is illicit.'[8]

On the other hand, neither the law nor the courts have ever stated that the status of cooperative member carries an obligation to transact with the cooperative. There are some legal scholars, however, who argue that member participation in mutual transactions is a necessary consequence of the mutual purpose and of the member's participation in a cooperative. Usually, cooperative statutes, especially those of agriculture cooperatives, impose an explicit obligation on members to deliver all their produce (or a minimum percentage of if) to their cooperative, as well as penalties for non-compliance.

As said, the mutual purpose implies mutual transactions *with* the members. It is not clear, however, whether it also implies the duty of the cooperative to act *in the interest* of the members, that is, to maximise their utility as consumers, providers or workers ('mutual benefit' or 'cooperative advantage').

It is frequently claimed in Italy that cooperatives act 'not only with, but also for their members'. This is not explicitly stated by the law. A reference to the members' interests appears only in the already-cited Ministerial Report on the ICC (no. 1025). Nonetheless, the prevailing scholarly opinion is that cooperatives are obligated (due to their institutional purpose and their 'contractual' nature, as well as to the absence of any duty to act in the interest of other subjects) to act in the interest of their members, but this obligation is conditioned by the cooperative's interest, which takes precedence over the members' individual interest in maximising their utility.[9]

---

8 Cass. 25 September 1999, no. 10602, in *Società*, 2000, p. 307; Cass. 4 November 2015, no. 22565, in *Banca dati De Jure*.

9 The Italian Supreme Court held that cooperative members have a specific interest in that the cooperative enterprise is oriented toward the satisfaction of their demand for mutual transactions and under the most favourable conditions possible given the financial constraints in carrying out the enterprise (Cass. 8 August 1999, no. 9513).

1.4.1. *The Mutual Benefit (or Cooperative Advantage) and its Distribution to Members – The Notion and Legal Nature of Cooperative Refunds*

There are two ways in which a cooperative may grant 'mutual benefits' to its members:

(a) immediately, when transactions take place, by applying prices equal to costs in consumer cooperatives, or by awarding remunerations and salaries equal to revenues in production and worker cooperatives; or
(b) subsequently, after approval of the balance sheet, by redirecting to members part of the surplus generated by the cooperative enterprise thanks to their involvement. This second form of assignment of the 'mutual benefit' is called *ristorno mutualistico*, which may be translated as 'cooperative refund' or 'mutual refund'.

Cooperative refunds were not mentioned in the ICC before the reform of 2003. In contrast, they are currently regulated so that the concept thereof arises clearly, as well as its distinction from that of profit distribution, although several aspects still remain uncertain.

First, article 2521, para. 3, no. 8, ICC, while dealing with the minimum compulsory content of a cooperative's statutes, includes the obligation to adopt both rules on profit (*utili*) distribution and rules on the distribution of cooperative refunds (*ristorni*). Therefore, profit distribution and cooperative refund distribution are two different things, requiring two different clauses in the statutes.

Second, article 2545*sexies* ICC stipulates that cooperative refunds must be distributed in proportion to the quantity and quality of the mutual transactions (para. 1), and can also be assigned as free shares of capital or as financial instruments (para. 3). Therefore, cooperative refunds are linked to mutual transactions, and to the volume and characteristics of the latter, and not to the capital held by members. In other words, by distributing cooperative refunds, the cooperative either increases *ex post* the remunerations of its worker-members or provider-members, or reduces *ex post* the prices paid by its consumer-members.[10]

The Italian Supreme Court adopted the same view even before the 2003 reform of company law, stating that: 'cooperative refunds must be distinguished from profits in the strict sense, although both are uncertain because their distribution depends on revenues being greater than costs. While profits constitute a remuneration of the capital provided by each member, cooperative refunds constitute a technical device to allocate the mutual advantage to members

[10] See in this regard art. 12, Presidential Decree no. 601/1973 and art. 3, para. 2, b), Law no. 142/2001.

(lesser expense or greater remuneration) which derives from transactions with the cooperative, thus resulting in a refund to the members of a portion of the price paid for the goods or services acquired from the cooperative (in consumer cooperatives), or in an additional remuneration provided by the cooperative for member performance (in production and worker cooperatives). Given this diversity, cooperative refunds are not subject to the limits set by law on profit distribution'.[11]

Third, as we shall see, profit distribution in proportion to the paid-up capital is a matter separately regulated by the ICC, which confirms that (also) in the Italian legislator's mind cooperative refunds are conceptually different from dividends distributed to members in proportion to the capital. In short, while cooperative refunds remunerate the members' engagement in mutual transactions with the cooperative, dividends remunerate the members' provision of risk capital to the cooperative (as happens in shareholder companies).

While it is clear that cooperative refunds are a particular form of distribution of the entity's surplus, it is not equally clear whether the sums that may be distributed as cooperative refunds are only those generated by member transactions, thereby excluding those deriving from transactions with non-members (in the case of cooperatives that operate also with non-members) and other sources (e.g. financial investments).

The ICC, also after the reform of 2003, fails to clarify this point although there is a rule that obligates the cooperative to report separately in the balance sheet the data referring to the activity with members (art. 2545*sexies*, para. 2), which might be taken as an indication.

In addition, in Ministerial Communication no. 53/E of 18 June 2002, on the specific tax treatment of cooperative refunds, it is stated: 'cooperative refund, that is, the restitution to members of part of the price paid for goods and services or the extra-remuneration for work and in general goods and services provision by members, is possible only if the balance of the activity performed by the cooperative with its members is positive. *What may be refunded is only the documented surplus from transactions with members and not from transactions with non-members*'.[12]

According to a minority scholarly opinion, the sums distributed as patronage refunds should be considered, not as a portion of the cooperative surplus, but as payments of debts to the members which arise after approval of the annual

---

[11] In these terms, Cass. 8 September 1999, no. 9513, in *Giur. comm.*, 2000, II, 317.

[12] Emphasis added. In general, the issue discussed in the main text is relevant in terms of the speculative nature of a cooperative, if one considers that the cooperative surplus from transactions with non-members is the same surplus that for-profit companies distribute to shareholders. Even though in a cooperative it would be distributed according to the volume of mutual transactions and not to the amount of the paid-up capital, this surplus increases the members' welfare not because of their mutual relationships with the cooperative, but because of the 'exploitation' of (third parties on) the market (as companies do).

accounts when the cooperative realises that the price paid by the members or the remuneration awarded to them at the time of mutual transactions were not properly determined in light of the mutual purpose of the cooperative and its duty to act in the best interest of the members, which requires that revenues be equal to costs at the end of each financial year.

This theory would lead to subtracting the sums distributed as patronage refunds from the cooperative surplus (by considering these sums as lower revenues in consumer cooperatives and greater costs in production and worker cooperatives), with significant consequences under tax law, but also in regard to the matter of the compulsory allocations to the legal reserve and to the 'mutual funds'.

This theory is susceptible to a number of criticisms and counter-arguments. Moreover, it is not compatible with the interpretation according to which members do not have a subjective right to patronage refunds, but only a right to be paid the sums that the competent cooperative organ decides to distribute as patronage refunds. The Italian Supreme Court – with the legal scholars' substantial agreement – has affirmed that no legal provision exists which obligates cooperatives to distribute to members the surplus generated by the mutual transactions with them, and that such an obligation cannot be considered implied by the mutual purpose, since cooperatives remain subject to the essential principles of company law according to which they are legal entities with legal personality and their own organisational, efficiency, and enterprise preservation needs. This inevitably means that the discretionary power to deliberate on surplus allocation lies with the general meeting.[13]

In general, no restrictions on the distribution of surpluses as patronage refunds exist (as we shall soon see, limits only regard dividends in the strict sense, i.e. sums that remunerate the capital provided by members),[14] which makes yet more important the issue of the origin of the surplus which may be distributed to members as patronage refund.

1.4.2. *The Remuneration of Capital in Cooperatives*

As stated, Italian cooperative law recognises patronage refunds (although some doubts concerning their precise nature persist) and distinguishes them from dividends, which are separately mentioned and regulated as remuneration of the subscribed capital.

---

13 See Cass. 8 September 1999, no. 9513. The Court adds that this conclusion, however, does not exclude the cooperative's obligation, or rather, the obligation of the majority of cooperative members to act in good faith, so that abusive resolutions not to distribute patronage refunds might be contested by minorities of members.

14 A limit of 30% of the salary applies to worker cooperatives (see art. 3, para. 2, Law no. 142/2001).

Italian law regulates profit allocation first of all by establishing some compulsory destinations, with a view to implementing the social function of cooperatives and strengthening their financial structure, given the limited importance of the capital.

Cooperatives must allocate to a reserve fund (called 'legal reserve') at least 30% of their net annual profits, whatever the amount of this reserve fund (art. 2545*quater*, para. 1, ICC).[15] Cooperatives must also allocate 3% of their net annual profits to the 'mutual funds' of article 11, Law no. 59/1992 (art. 2545*quater*, para. 2, ICC).

With regard to the allocation of the remaining part of profits, PMCs are subject to article 2514 ICC, which strictly limits profit distribution to members. By contrast, OCs are only subject to article 2545*quinquies* ICC (which applies to PMCs as well), according to which the act of incorporation must lay down the maximum percentage of dividends distributable to members (para. 1), and dividends (as well as distributable reserves) may be distributed only if the ratio between net assets and liabilities is higher than one-fourth (para. 2). Different rules may apply to special cooperatives like cooperative banks.[16]

Therefore, PMCs are characterised not only by prevalent mutuality but also by a partial profit non-distribution constraint. Indeed, article 2514 ICC stipulates that PMC statutes must impose (and consequently PMCs must observe):

(a) a prohibition on distributing dividends on the paid-up capital higher than the maximum interest of postal bonds increased by 2.5 points;
(b) a prohibition on remunerating the financial instruments held by cooperative members more than 2 points above the maximum interest applicable to dividends;
(c) a prohibition on distributing reserves to cooperative members;
(d) an obligation to devolve, in the case of dissolution, all assets, subtracting only the paid-up capital and the dividends due but not yet distributed, to the mutual funds of article 11, Law no. 59/1992.

Article 2514 of the ICC requires some comment and clarification.

It is remarkable the care with which the partial profit non-distribution constraint is regulated. It covers not only the periodic distribution of profits (dividends), but also the distribution of accumulated profits (reserves and residual assets). Accordingly, article 2545*ter*, para. 2, ICC states that indivisible reserves may be used to cover losses only after all the other reserves and resources.

---

15 This percentage is 10% for popular banks (art. 32, para. 1, Legislative Decree no. 385/1993) and 70% for credit cooperative banks (art. 37, para. 1, Legislative Decree no. 385/1993).

16 Cf. arts. 32, 37 and 150*bis*, Legislative Decree no. 385/1993.

Prohibitions do not regard investor members, but only cooperative members (or 'cooperators'), i.e. those members who make use of the cooperative enterprise as consumers, providers or workers, thereby contributing to enactment of the cooperative's mutual purpose. When cooperative members are also investor members, which is not prohibited under Italian law, limits apply anew.

It is not clear whether all reserves are indivisible in a PMC, including voluntary reserves that cooperative statutes do not declare indivisible, or only the legal reserve of article 2545*quater*, para. 1, and the voluntary reserves defined as indivisible by cooperative statutes.

Finally, as already emphasised, article 2514 (as well as art. 2545*quinquies*) ICC refers exclusively to profit distribution and capital remuneration, while not applying to patronage refunds.

In Italian law, there are no provisions obligating the cooperative to distribute more patronage refunds than dividends; or obligating the cooperative to give priority to patronage refunds over dividends; or prohibiting the distribution as dividends of the sums generated by transactions with the members. Yet, in theory, these are provisions that reinforce the stated purpose of cooperatives, i.e. their mutuality.

1.5. COOPERATIVE OBJECTIVE AND COOPERATIVE MEMBERSHIP

The mutual purpose of a cooperative requires that its members transact with the cooperative and must therefore meet some requirements, differently from shareholder companies where member features are normally irrelevant.

Italian law obligates cooperative statutes to state membership requirements (art. 2521, para. 3, no. 6, ICC). This is an aspect that may affect the 'open character' of a cooperative, given that a cooperative's decision to refuse the admission of new members may be regarded as problematic only relatively to candidates that satisfy the membership requirements.

Cooperatives are therefore organisations whose members are consumers (in consumer cooperatives), providers (in producer cooperatives), or workers (in worker cooperatives); in other words, they are entities participated in and owned by (natural or legal) persons making direct use of the cooperative enterprise.

Italian law, however, also allows investor members (as 'non-users', members or 'non-cooperators') to join a cooperative and subjects them to specific rules.

Italian law empowers cooperative statutes to identify different categories of members also in regard to the quantity and/or quality of their transactions with the cooperative, as well as to organise its internal structure partially according to this classification of membership, thereby focusing on member categories rather than individual members in shaping its governance.

1.6. MUTUAL TRANSACTIONS WITH THE MEMBERS

As already highlighted, the cooperative's activity with the members fulfils the cooperative objective by transacting with the members, the cooperative accomplishes its institutional purpose.

These mutual transactions raise a number of very complex legal issues. It must be understood whether these transactions are distinct (like any other ordinary 'market' transaction) from the organisational relationship between the member and the cooperative which derives from the subscription/provision of capital.

In other words, the issue is whether mutual transactions (e.g. in a consumer cooperative, the consumer relationship between the cooperative and its members) are to be considered, and therefore regulated, as constituting contractual relationships distinct from the organisational ones between a cooperative and its members (theory of the 'double relationship'). If this were the case, mutual transactions would in principle be governed by contract law rather than organisational law.

Italian scholars and courts adopt the theory of the double relationship, at least with regard to the exchange of goods and services. The Italian Supreme Court, for example, has declared applicable to transport transactions between the cooperative and its members the rules on the extinctive prescription,[17] and the regulations on the sale of goods applicable to purchases within a consumer cooperative (including building cooperatives).[18] Moreover, it has deemed compatible with the particular nature of mutual transactions the possibility for a member to raise the *exceptio inadempleti contractus* claim against the cooperative.[19]

However, both scholars and courts underline that, although the two relationships, contractual and organisational, are separate, they are linked because both are aimed at the pursuit of a common economic objective (as are the 'connected contracts' in the pertinent theory) which may result in reciprocal influence or contamination between contract law rules and cooperative law rules, or in the necessity to adapt the applicable rules of contract law so that they take account of the particular (cooperative) framework in which transactions occur.

On the other hand, the labour relationship between worker-members and a cooperative is governed by a special law (Law no. 142/2001). The existence of a specific law on worker cooperatives partially reduces the extent of the regulatory questions that the issue of the double relationship raises

---

17 See Cass. 7 June 2006, no. 13269, in *Foro it.*, 2007, IV, 1, p. 1237.

18 See Cass. 4 March 2005, no. 4788, in *Giur. it.*, 2005, p. 1855.

19 See Cass. 18 January 2001, no. 694, in *Dir e prat. Soc.*, 2001, p. 62; Cass. 12 December 2014, no. 26222, in *Giust. Civ. Mass.*, 2014.

(e.g. Law no. 142/2001 provides that member withdrawal or legal exclusion terminate the working relationship; that the court competent for the legal disputes between the member and the cooperative is the ordinary tribunal), although this law refers to a further working relationship between the cooperative and its members (art. 1, para. 3, of this law reads: 'a cooperative worker-member establishes … a further working relationship … by which she/he contributes to fulfilment of the social purposes'), thus confirming the theory of the double relationship followed by scholars and courts.

1.7. MUTUAL TRANSACTIONS WITH NON-MEMBERS

As said, implementation of the mutual purpose entails mutual transactions with the members. However, Italian law does not prevent a cooperative from transacting with third parties who are not members (nor is pure mutuality necessary for a cooperative's admission to a specific tax treatment). Both PMCs and OCs may act with non-members – i.e. depending on the type of cooperative, exchange with or employ non-members – provided that their act of incorporation or statutes so permit (art. 2521, para. 2, ICC).[20] Obviously, PMCs must also respect the precise limits that articles 2512 and 2513 ICC set on their activity with non-members. Otherwise, they would lose the qualification as PMCs (art. 2545*octies* ICC).[21]

---

[20] It should be clear that 'activity with non-members' is a precise notion in cooperative theory and legislation. It refers to the same activity as that with the members which characterises the cooperative. For example, in a consumer cooperative, 'activity with non-members' is the sale to non-members of the goods that the cooperative sells (prevalently) to the members. Therefore, a consumer cooperative that buys the goods from a wholesaler (the goods to be later sold to the members) is not conducting an 'activity with non-members' in the sense with which this notion is used in cooperative theory and legislation, although in fact it acts with third parties who are not members. It is this precise 'activity with non-members' which matters when comparison is made in order to qualify a cooperative as a PMC. The activity with non-members may be considered the other side of the coin of the mutual character of the cooperative, in the sense that, if the cooperative aims to act with its members, then the activity with non-members is something in potential conflict with the institutional purpose of this legal type of organisation.

[21] More precisely, art. 2545*octies*, para. 1, ICC states that the status of PMC may be lost in two cases: when the cooperative does not respect the requirement of prevalent activity with the members for two consecutive financial years and/or when the cooperative (cancels or) modifies the provisions of its statutes regarding the profit non-distribution constraints adopted in accordance with art. 2514 ICC. In this case, the cooperative must draw up an extraordinary balance sheet and allocate its assets to indivisible reserve funds (art. 2545*octies*, para. 2 and 3, as amended by art. 10, para. 8, Law 23 July 2009, no. 99): on this subject, see E. Rocchi, 'Sub articles 2512–2514 and 2545-octies', in G. Presti (ed.), *Società cooperative*, Egea-Giuffrè, Milan, 2006, pp. 27 ff.; G. Bonfante, *La nuova società cooperativa*, Zanichelli, Bologna, 2010, p. 75, which report the different line of thought according to which assets should be devolved to the mutual funds of art. 11, Law no. 59/1992. The loss of

A PMC can never exceed these limits on the activity with non-members, not even in the case in which it treats non-members as members. This is confirmed by article 2520, para. 2, ICC, which allows the establishment of non-mutual cooperatives (more precisely, of cooperatives that act with particular categories of subjects, also non-members) only pursuant to a special law providing for them. Of course, a cooperative may choose to qualify as an OC (which does not face explicit barriers in the activity with non-members); in which case, however, it will be subject to a different (and less advantageous) tax treatment.

The particular case of credit cooperative banks is worth mentioning. Credit cooperative banks may be individually authorised by the national banking authority (*Banca d'Italia*) to derogate, for a determined period, from the legal requirement of providing credit prevalently to the members, provided that this is necessary for the bank's financial stability.[22]

1.8. INDIRECT MUTUALITY

As a mutual entity, a cooperative is an organisation that provides goods or services to, or employs, the members, who therefore benefit *directly* from the business conducted by the cooperative. A legal issue that cooperative practice raises is whether a cooperative may fulfil its purpose *indirectly*, that is, through entities (of any legal form, including shareholder companies) that transact with the cooperative's members in order to provide them with goods, services or jobs. In this case, the cooperative acts as a parent entity and not directly with its members; hence, mutuality, if any, is only indirect.

The issue does not find a definite solution in Italian law, which, however, recognises the possibility for a cooperative to hold shares in companies (art. 27*quinquies* Legislative Decree no. 1577/1947). On this basis, some legal scholars argue that a pure cooperative holding is admissible under Italian law.[23] In any event, if not properly regulated by the legislature, this structure would create several problems in terms of members' involvement and protection of the members' mutual interest.

---

the PMC status, and the consequent 'transformation' of the cooperative into an OC, cannot be regarded as an event of conversion (therefore, the pertinent regulation would not be applicable), if one shares the view that conversion only occurs when an organisation of a certain legal type is transformed into another of a different legal type (e.g. from a cooperative into a shareholder company): see on this V. De Stasio, 'La trasformazione delle cooperative', in P. Abbadessa and G.B. Portale (eds.), *Il nuovo diritto delle società: Liber amicorum Gian Franco Campobasso*, vol. IV, Utet, Turin, 2006, pp. 193 f.

22 See art. 35, para. 1, Legislative Decree no. 385/93.

23 According to Bonfante, n. 21 above, pp. 363 ff., the holding cooperative is legitimate insofar as the mutual purpose is indirectly pursued through the subsidiaries.

1.9. SOCIAL COOPERATIVES

In general, Italian cooperatives pursue a mutual purpose as distinct from not only the lucrative purpose of other companies but also the non-lucrative purpose of associations and foundations.

Nonetheless, if the above is certainly true of cooperatives in general, it is not true of special cooperatives. Indeed, article 2520, para. 2, ICC, states that 'the law may provide for the establishment of cooperatives for the provision of goods or services to persons belonging to particular categories also of non-members'. Non-mutual cooperatives, therefore, are admitted only to the extent that a special law provides for them.

One special law that applies the general provision in article 2520, para. 2, ICC, is Law 8 November 1991, no. 381 on social cooperatives. Social cooperatives are non-mutual cooperatives, since they pursue 'the general interest of the community in the human promotion and social integration of citizens through: (a) the management of social-health and educational services; (b) the carrying out of various activities – agricultural, industrial, commercial, or service – for the work integration of disadvantaged people'. Social cooperatives, therefore, do not act in the interest of their members as such, and are closer to social enterprises than to ordinary cooperatives with a mutual aim.[24]

Other non-mutual cooperatives are the *banche popolari*, which are a subtype of cooperatives banks (credit cooperative banks constitute the other subtype). The law applicable, i.e. Legislative Decree no. 385/93, does not obligate the *banche popolari* (differently from credit cooperative banks) to act with their members. For this reason, their nature as cooperatives is debated. In any event, they may be considered non-mutual cooperatives in the framework of article 2520, para. 2, ICC.

Non-mutual cooperatives raise issues in terms of policies in favour of cooperatives. If the mutual aim of cooperatives justifies these policies (as confirmed by the distinction between PMCs and OCs under tax law), then non-mutual cooperatives should be excluded from their scope. Nevertheless, there are non-mutual cooperatives that are relevant to the general interest, for example social cooperatives. Therefore, as happens in Italy with regard to social cooperatives, the law may extend cooperative promotional policies to non-mutual cooperatives when this is justifiable on other grounds, for example in terms of the general interest, social benefits produced by the non-mutual cooperative, etc.

---

24 In Italian law, social enterprises are a precise category of organisations, as identified by Legislative Decree 24 March 2006, no. 155 and now by no. 106/2016 on the Reform of the Third Sector. Cf. A. Fici, 'Recognition and Legal Forms of Social Enterprise in Europe: A Critical Analysis from a Comparative Law Perspective', *European Business Law Review*, 2016, pp. 639 ff.

1.10. COOPERATIVE OBJECTIVE AND GOVERNANCE ISSUES

In Italian cooperative law, the mutual purpose influences cooperative governance. Some rules of cooperative law adapt (or permit to adapt) governance to the entity's mutual purpose.

One example is the possibility for cooperative statutes to derogate from the 'one member – one vote' rule by awarding members more votes in proportion to the quantity and/or quality of their individual mutual transactions with the cooperative.

Another example is the possibility for cooperative statutes to structure the board of directors taking into account different categories of members existing in the cooperative, which are identified according to members' different contributions to the mutual purpose (e.g. members who contribute more and better form one category while the other members form another category).

2. COOPERATIVE GOVERNANCE

2.1. INTRODUCTION – COOPERATIVE GOVERNANCE AND COOPERATIVE IDENTITY

Governance is an essential element of the identity of cooperatives, as several provisions of the 1995 International Cooperative Alliance's (ICA) Statement on the Cooperative Identity (which contains the ICA Principles) demonstrate.

Therein, a cooperative is first of all defined as an 'autonomous association of persons united voluntarily'. 'Autonomy' implies independence from other entities, both public and private; the impossibility for a cooperative to be subject to external control or serve as a pure subsidiary;[25] finally, that the entity's control must lie with the cooperative members, to whom those serving as elected representatives are accountable, as stated in the second ICA Principle.

This is confirmed by the fourth ICA Principle, according to which cooperatives are organisations controlled by their members and 'if they enter into agreements with other organisations, including governments, or raise capital from external sources, they do so on terms that ensure democratic control by their members

25 An entity's external control may be the result of legal or factual arrangements: it may depend on the concentration of ownership rights (majority of votes in the members' general meeting: *ope iuris ownership control*; or even a lower number of votes, which however makes a 'dominant influence' in the general meeting possible: *de facto ownership control*: see art. 2359, para. 1, a) and b), ICC) or on a contract whose purpose is to subject the entity to the domination or dominant influence of other subjects (*contractual control*: see art. 2359, para. 1, c), ICC).

and maintain their cooperative autonomy'.[26] Also the second ICA Principle defines cooperatives as organisations 'controlled by their members', specifying that members 'actively participate in setting their policies and making decisions'.

The definition of cooperatives as 'association of persons' may be interpreted as if membership *per se*, and not the subscribed capital or other factors, must be the guiding principle of cooperative governance. This leads to the democratic member control in the second ICA Principle.

The reference in the definition to the 'voluntary' character of the union among persons means that compulsory membership of a cooperative should not be permitted. This is confirmed by the first ICA Principle when it refers to 'persons ... willing to accept the responsibilities of membership'. It also raises the governance issue of whether cooperative members should in principle be considered free to leave the cooperative, and to what extent the right to a free withdrawal may be constrained by law or cooperative statutes.[27]

According to the first ICA Principle, cooperatives are 'open' organisations; more precisely, organisations open to all persons able to use the services that the cooperative provides, without any discrimination. The governance issue involved here is that of the 'open door' in cooperatives, which will be dealt with later in this report.

The second ICA Principle qualifies cooperatives as 'democratic' organisations, and specifies that in primary cooperatives members have equal voting rights (one member, one vote), without providing for explicit exceptions or mitigations of this principle. Only in secondary or higher-level cooperatives is equality not explicitly required, but more generally a 'democratic manner' of organisation.

A final preliminary remark is that, notwithstanding its central role, governance is only one of the aspects of the overall cooperative identity. Therefore, the relationships between the governance aspects and the other aspects of the cooperative identity deserve careful investigation. For example, if the purpose is key to defining an entity's identity, governance should conform to the entity's organisational purpose, which means, moreover, that when an entity's legal form may be employed to pursue one of several possible objectives,

---

26 This cannot but affect any discussion about 'cooperative groups' as groups of cooperatives led or coordinated by one of them or an entity composed of them. These groups ought to be regulated in such a way as to ensure the autonomy of the comprising cooperatives; which is to say, a balance should be found between autonomy and coordination, e.g. by granting each member cooperative the right to freely withdraw from the group, or requiring that the costs and benefits of the coordination be in any case proportionally divided among the member cooperatives, as happens according to art. 2545*septies* ICC.

27 To be noted is that the contractual nature of a cooperative, and of companies in general, on the one hand is compatible with its voluntary character and moreover presupposes this character; on the other hand, it is not incompatible with possible constraints on (or even exclusion of) member exit because contracts are voluntary acts binding their parties once they are voluntarily entered into.

plural structures of governance should be conceived of for this legal form (e.g. in cooperatives, the governance structure of community-oriented cooperatives, like social cooperatives, cannot be the same as the governance structure of member-oriented cooperatives, i.e. mutual cooperatives like, for example, agricultural cooperatives among farmer producers).

2.2. COOPERATIVE GOVERNANCE AND THE SOURCES OF ITALIAN COOPERATIVE LAW

As already stated, the general regulation of Italian cooperatives may be found in articles 2511–2545*octiesdecies* ICC, which deal specifically with cooperatives as a distinct type of company. Nevertheless, the law of either joint-stock companies (*società per azioni* – SPA) or limited-liability companies (*società a responsabilità limitata* – SRL) may additionally apply to cooperatives to fill the gaps in cooperative law, provided that the rules of SPA law or SRL law, potentially applicable, are compatible with the particular nature of a cooperative (art. 2519 ICC).

More precisely, SPA law applies to cooperatives by default (art. 2519, para. 1, ICC), but a cooperative which is composed of fewer than 20 members or which has net assets not greater than 1,000,000 euros may opt, in its act of incorporation, for the application of SRL law (art. 2519, para. 2, ICC). On the other hand, cooperatives consisting of three but fewer than nine individuals are subject to SRL law (2522, para. 2, ICC).[28]

As a result, another dichotomy appears in Italian cooperative law, which is that between cooperatives subject (additionally and residually) to SPA law (hereinafter 'SPA cooperatives') and cooperatives subject (additionally and residually) to SRL law (hereinafter 'SRL cooperatives'). This dichotomy, unlike that between PMCs and OCs, is highly relevant to the subject of cooperative governance.

Given that Italian cooperative law is rather complete, the applicability of company law to cooperatives does not raise serious concerns in terms of possible 'companisation' of the Italian cooperative. On the contrary, it offers cooperatives a set of opportunities, especially with regard to their governance structure, which is the area where Italian cooperative law presents most of its gaps.

The decision to provide two alternative models – while before the 2003 reform only the regulation of an SPA could apply to cooperatives – was due

28 Therefore, during the life of a cooperative, the applicable regulatory framework may change. This change cannot be regarded as an event of cooperative conversion, even when the change is deliberately caused by the cooperative (which, for example, cancels the clauses of the act of incorporation where SRL law was opted for, thus becoming subject to SPA law). Therefore, the regime of cooperative conversion does not apply in this event.

to the legislature's intention to offer cooperatives, particularly small ones, more flexibility, especially in terms of their governance structure. This is a legislative trend that may be observed in many jurisdictions: that is, treating small(er) and large(r) cooperatives differently as regards their governance structure.

Before entering *in medias res*, there are two more points that must be underlined. First, cooperative statutes also play a role in shaping governance, since Italian law leaves cooperatives (in particular SRL cooperatives) a considerable degree of freedom of self-regulation, even if it is sometimes limited to the choice of one of the options provided by law. Second, the governance of special cooperatives, like social cooperatives of Law 8 November 1991, no. 381, may be affected by the special law regulating them, since special law takes precedence over the ICC, also in light of article 2520, para. 1, ICC, according to which cooperatives regulated by special laws are subject to the general provisions of cooperative law found in the ICC only if these provisions are compatible.

2.3. COOPERATIVE INTERNAL STRUCTURE – ORGANS AND DIVISION OF POWERS (IN GENERAL) – SYSTEMS OF ADMINISTRATION AND CONTROL

Italian cooperatives have a corporate structure, i.e. they are managed by and through organs. Therefore, in general, cooperative members are entitled to take part in the organs and elect their members. Cooperative members hold only few rights as individuals (*uti singuli*), i.e. outside the organs where they may act as members (*uti socii*) and thus exercise their membership rights, beginning with the right to vote in the members' meeting (MM). There are also examples, as we shall see, of the law granting some rights to a group of members that does not constitute an organ.

Before the reform of 2003, Italian cooperatives had limited freedom to shape their internal system of governance: their then regulation only provided for a 'tripartite' model of governance, where powers and responsibilities were shared between the MM, the board of directors (BD) and the supervisory board (SB).

By way of contrast, the current regulation enables cooperative statutes to choose among three different systems of administration and control: the traditional 'tripartite' system and the new 'dualistic' and 'monistic' systems. Except for a few particular provisions, which are specific to cooperatives, the regulation of these systems is the same as that which applies to SPAs.

The default system is the traditional tripartite system because the other systems must be expressly opted for by cooperative statutes. It consists of three organs: the MM (*assemblea dei soci*), the BD (*consiglio di amministrazione*) and the SB (*collegio sindacale*).

Under the tripartite system, the MM is the supreme organ of the cooperative; the BD, appointed by the MM, is the management organ; the SB, appointed by the MM, is the organ of internal control. The SB is not always required. A registered auditor of accounts is not always required because its functions may be carried out by the SB.

The monistic system – similar to, but not coincident with, the one-tier system in the European Cooperative Society (SCE) Regulation of 2003 – does not differ substantially from the tripartite one, except for the fact that the organ of internal control is not directly (and formally) appointed by the MM but by the BD from among its members, and that this organ of control, named 'committee for the supervision of the management' (CSM) (*comitato per il controllo sulla gestione*), is an internal organ (without managing powers) of the BD. When the monistic system is adopted, external financial audit by a registered auditor of accounts is always required.

The dualistic system – similar to, but not coincident with, the two-tier system in the SCE Regulation of 2003 – is rather different from the others and innovative, at least for Italian cooperatives. It consists of three organs: the MM, the surveillance board (SUB) (*consiglio di sorveglianza*), appointed by the MM, and the management board (MB) (*consiglio di gestione*) appointed by the SUB. When the dualistic system is adopted, external financial audit by a registered auditor of accounts is always required.

2.4. THE TRIPARTITE SYSTEM

2.4.1. The Members' Meeting

2.4.1.1. Composition

The MM is a necessary organ of the tripartite system of governance. Cooperative statutes may provide for members' separate meetings (which in some circumstances are mandatory),[29] for example on certain matters or in the presence of particular categories of members. In this case, each separate meeting elects a delegate (who must be a cooperative member) who then votes in the MM (art. 2540 ICC).[30]

---

29 Separate meetings are compulsory in cooperatives with more than 3,000 members and that operate in several provinces, or in cooperatives with more than 500 members and different types of mutual relationships (art. 2540, para. 2, ICC).

30 It is discussed whether delegates may be elected for a determined period of time or necessarily for only one meeting, and whether they may be awarded a discretionary power to vote in the meeting or are bound to the separate meeting's decision upon how to vote: cf. G. Bonfante, 'La società cooperativa', in G. Cottino (ed.), *Trattato di diritto commerciale*, Cedam, Padua, 2014, p. 327; E. Cusa, 'Sub art. 2540', in D.U. Santosuosso (ed.), *Delle società – dell'azienda – della concorrenza*, IV, in *Commentario del codice civile*, directed by E. Gabrielli, Utet, Turin, 2014, pp. 370 ff.

The MM comprises all the members of a cooperative, including investor members.

The MM may be 'ordinary' or 'extraordinary', depending on the matters to be decided. This distinction is important for the MM's organisation and conduct.

2.4.1.2. Powers

In the tripartite system, the MM has the following powers, which all together give the MM a primary role within this system of governance:

(i) to appoint and remove directors (as well as the chair of the BD), and fix their remuneration if it is not established by the cooperative statutes (art. 2542, para. 1, and 2364, para. 1, no. 2 and 3, ICC);
(ii) to appoint and remove the members of the SB and the chair thereof, and fix their remuneration if it is not established by the cooperative statutes (art. 2364, para. 1, no. 2 and 3, ICC);
(iii) to appoint and remove the auditor/s of accounts (art. 2364, para. 1, no. 2, ICC);
(iv) to approve the balance sheet (art. 2364, para. 1, no. 1, ICC);
(v) to decide on how the distributable surplus is to be allocated (art. 2545 *quater*, para. 3, ICC), and whether patronage refunds are to be assigned to members as free capital shares or free financial instruments, instead of in cash (art. 2545*sexies*, para. 3, ICC);
(vi) to decide on the liability of directors and supervisors and on legal actions against them (art. 2364, para. 1, no. 4, and 2393, para. 1, ICC);
(vii) to decide on the appeal by a candidate refused membership (art. 2528, para. 4, ICC);
(viii) to decide on member exclusion if the cooperative's statutes do not confer this power to the BD (art. 2533, para. 2, ICC);
(ix) (in its extraordinary form) to amend statutes (art. 2365, para. 1, ICC);
(x) (in its extraordinary form) to name and substitute liquidators and define their powers (art. 2365, para. 1, ICC);
(xi) (in its extraordinary form) to introduce or suppress in the statutes the clauses on the limited distribution of profits which are necessary for a cooperative to qualify as a PMC (art. 2514, para. 2, ICC);
(xii) (with the majorities required for its extraordinary form) to approve regulations on the mutual relationships between the cooperative and its members (art. 2521, para. 5, ICC);
(xiii) to approve the regulations on the conduct of the MM, if any (art. 2364, para. 1, no. 6, ICC);
(xiv) to authorise directors to perform certain acts if the statutes so provide (art. 2364, para. 1, no. 5, ICC);

(xv) to resolve the liquidation (art. 2545*duodecies* and 2484, para. 1, no. 6, ICC), transformation (art. 2545*decies* ICC), merger and demerger of the cooperative (art. 2545*novies*, para. 2, ICC).

2.4.1.3. Organisation and Conduct

All the members who have been registered in the members' book for at least 90 days have the right to vote in the MM (art. 2538, para. 1, ICC).

Italian law enables members to delegate their power to vote in the MM. However, only other members may be nominated as proxies, and each proxy may not represent more than ten members (art. 2539, para. 1, ICC).[31]

In addition, cooperative statutes may allow voting by post, email or other telecommunication devices, in which case the notice convening the MM must contain the full proposals for decisions (art. 2538, para. 6, ICC).

Pursuant to article 2538, para. 5, ICC, cooperative statutes must establish the quorum and majority requirements, which must be calculated according to the number of votes to which members are entitled (and not to the number of members). The law, however, may provide for mandatory quorums (see, for example, art. 2545*decies* ICC).

In Italian cooperative law, 'each cooperative member has one vote, whatever the value of the share or the number of the stocks held' (art. 2538, para. 2, ICC). Therefore, in a cooperative, voting power in the MM is not related to the amount of capital held, but to membership *per se*.

Nevertheless, cooperative statutes may, in some circumstances and within certain limits, derogate from this rule.

First, cooperative statutes may attribute more votes (but no more than five) to cooperative members who are legal entities, in relation to the amount of the capital held or the number of their members (art. 2538, para. 3, ICC).

Secondly, in cooperatives comprising entrepreneurs or enterprises, the statutes may provide for a member to have a number of votes proportional to its participation in mutual transactions with the cooperative. However, a given privileged member may have no more than 10% of the total votes in each MM; moreover, all privileged members, together, may have no more than one-third of the total votes in each MM (art. 2538, para. 4, ICC).

Thirdly, in the election of the organ of control, cooperative statutes may provide for members to have plural votes in proportion either to the capital held or to the volume of mutual transactions with the cooperative (art. 2543, para. 2, ICC).

---

31 Art. 2539, para. 1, ICC, deals only with SPA cooperatives. It is therefore discussed whether voting by proxy is permitted in SRL cooperatives as well: cf. Bonfante, n. 30 above, pp. 355 f.; E. Cusa, n. 30 above. p. 359.

Finally, cooperative statutes may award plural votes to investor members, although they may not together have more than one-third of the total votes in each MM (art. 2526, para. 2, ICC).

By these provisions Italian cooperative law aims to provide cooperatives with suitable instruments to deal with potential membership heterogeneity. The underlying idea is that plural voting may encourage the participation of investor members and of cooperative members who contribute to the cooperative activity more and better than other members do. This, however, may result in a different principle of cooperative governance – namely, that a single member or category of members cannot control the cooperative – replacing the traditional, and more stringent, democratic 'one member, one vote' principle, to which the ICA Principles refer without exceptions (at least in primary cooperatives).

2.4.1.4. Resolutions

Decisions taken by the MM in conformity with the law and the statutes bind all the members, including absent and dissenting ones (art. 2377, para. 1, ICC).

Decisions taken in contrast to the law or the statutes may be impugned by absent, dissenting or abstaining members representing at least 5% of the total votes in the MM, as well as by the directors and the SB (2377, para. 2 and 3, ICC).

2.4.2. The Board of Directors

The BD is a necessary organ of the tripartite system of governance. It is questioned whether a sole director is permitted in an SPA cooperative.[32]

The BD is composed of the number of members determined by the statutes or the MM within the limits fixed by the statutes (art. 2380*bis*, para. 4, ICC). The majority of directors must be members of the cooperative (or persons designated by member cooperatives) (art. 2542, para. 2, ICC). Unless the MM does so, the chair of the BD is appointed by the BD from among its members (art. 2380*bis*, para. 5, ICC).

BD members are appointed and removed by the MM (art. 2542, para. 1, ICC).

Cooperative statutes may require that directors be selected from among those belonging to different categories of members, in proportion to the interest that each category has in the cooperative's activity. In all cases, those who hold financial instruments may not be entitled to appoint more than one third of the

32 See for a positive answer, A. Bartalena, 'Sub art. 2519', in G. Presti (ed.), *Società cooperative*, Egea-Giuffrè, Milano, 2006, p. 113; and for a negative answer, L.F. Paolucci, 'Sub art. 2542', in Santosuosso (ed.), n. 30 above, p. 385, holding that in this case the sole director must be a cooperative member. As regards SRL cooperatives, see P. Marano, 'L'organo di Amministrazione', in E. Cusa (ed.), *La cooperativa s.r.l. Tra legge e autonomia statutaria*, Cedam, Padua, 2008, pp. 416 f.

directors (art. 2542, para. 4, ICC). This is an interesting option for cooperatives characterised by member heterogeneity (in terms of mutual transactions with the cooperative) or for multistakeholder cooperatives, as social cooperatives potentially are.

In addition, cooperative statutes may provide that one or more directors be nominated by the State or other public bodies. In all cases, the majority of BD members shall be appointed by the MM (art. 2542, para. 5, ICC).

The BD is in charge of management of the cooperative and may perform all the acts necessary to fulfil the cooperative purpose (art. 2380*bis*, para. 1, ICC). BD members represent the cooperative in dealing with third parties (art. 2384 ICC).

The prevalent scholarly opinion is that the BD may not be deprived of its powers in favour of the MM. Hence, while the MM has the general direction of the cooperative, the BD enjoys its power of management in an exclusive way. This, together with the fact that not all of the BD members must be cooperative members, determines a partial modification of the ICA Principle of members' control of a cooperative.

If the statutes or the MM so permit, the BD may delegate its powers to one or more of its members, who thus form an 'executive committee'. Not all the powers may be delegated, including those to draft the balance sheet, those relative to member admission, withdrawal, and exclusion, and those affecting the mutual relationships with the members (art. 2381, para. 4, and 2544, para. 1, ICC).

Resolutions must be taken in the presence of (at least) a majority of directors (but the statutes may provide for a higher quorum) and must be voted by the majority of participants, unless the statutes provide otherwise (art. 2388, para. 1 and 2, ICC). Voting power in the BD may not be delegated (art. 2388, para. 3, ICC), but directors may participate by telecommunication technologies (art. 2388, para. 1, ICC).

Resolutions assumed in contrast to the law or the statutes may be impugned by absent or dissenting directors, the SB, and cooperative members representing at least 5% of the total votes in the MM (2388, para. 4, ICC)

BD members may not perform activities in competition with the cooperative, nor be members or directors or senior executives of competitor companies (art. 2390, para. 1, ICC). BD members must disclose any interest they may have in the operations of the cooperative, in which case the BD must motivate the reasons and convenience of the operation while resolving to perform it (art. 2391 ICC).

Directors must perform their duties with the diligence required by the nature of the activity and their specific qualifications. They are jointly and severally liable to the cooperative for the damages caused by non-performance of their duties (art. 2392 ICC); to creditors for not having complied with the duties regarding the conservation and integrity of the patrimony (art. 2394 ICC); to individual members and third parties for the damages that are direct consequence of their negligent conduct (art. 2395 ICC). Only the delegated directors (and the members of the executive committee) are liable for matters falling within their delegated powers. To be exonerated from said liability, BD dissenting members must promptly annotate their dissensions in the BD's register of meetings and resolutions, and inform the SB's president thereof (art. 2392, para. 3, ICC).

2.4.3. *The Supervisory Board*

The SB is not always a necessary organ of a cooperative adopting the tripartite system of governance. Smaller cooperatives are exempt.[33]

When mandated by law or cooperative statutes, the SB is appointed by the MM and its members may be removed only for a 'just cause' and with the court's approval (art. 2400 ICC).

In SPA cooperatives, the SB is composed of either three or five members, plus two substitutes. They may be cooperative members. In SPA cooperatives, only registered auditors of accounts, registered professionals (such as lawyers and notaries), and law or economics professors may be appointed as supervisors (but in all cases, one supervisor must be a registered auditor of accounts) (art. 2397 ICC). The chair of the SB is nominated by the MM (art. 2398 ICC). There are strict requirements to ensure that SB members do not have interests in conflict with the cooperative (art. 2399 ICC).

The SB must supervise compliance with law, statutes and fair management, and in particular the adequacy of the organisational, administrative and financial structure of the cooperative and its actual functioning (art. 2403, para. 1, ICC). Its components must also attend the meetings of the MM and the BD (art. 2405 ICC).

The SB may also be entrusted by the cooperative statutes with control of financial accounts, in which case it must be entirely formed of registered auditors of accounts (art. 2403, para. 2, ICC).

In order to accomplish its tasks, the SB is given by law ample powers of inspection and control, as well as rights of information.

---

33 More precisely, appointment of an SB is mandatory in cooperatives that: (i) must draw up consolidated accounts (art. 2543, para. 1, and art. 2477, para. 3, a), ICC); (ii) exceed two of the following limits in two consecutive financial years: statement of assets: €4,400,000; proceeds: €8,800.000; 50 employees on average (art. 2543, para. 1; 2477, para. 3, c), and art. 2435*bis*, para. 1, ICC); (iii) issue 'non-participative' financial instruments (art. 2543, para. 1, ICC); or (iv) control a company subject to external financial audit (art. 2543, para. 1, art. 2477, para. 3, b), and art. 2435*bis*, para. 1, ICC). After the repeal of art. 2477, para. 2, ICC, in 2014, it is not clear whether also cooperatives whose capital is greater than €50,000 (the minimum legal capital to establish an SPA) are under this obligation.

Regardless of the obligation to appoint an SB, the cooperative is in any case subject to external financial audit and to cooperative supervision by the State or a federation of cooperatives.

Its resolutions must be taken in the presence of the majority of supervisors and must be voted by the majority of participants (art. 2404, para. 4, ICC).

Supervisors are jointly liable with directors for actions and omissions by the latter if damages would not have occurred had supervisors performed their duties (art. 2407, para. 2, ICC).

2.4.4. *External Financial Audit*

The MM must also appoint at least one external registered auditor for the examination of the accounts, unless, as mentioned, the SB is entirely composed of registered auditors of accounts, in which case it may also be given this further function by cooperative statutes. In SPA cooperatives, the appointment of a registered auditor of accounts is mandatory even in the case of cooperatives not required to appoint an SB.[34]

2.5. THE MONISTIC SYSTEM

The monistic system is an optional system. However, it does not considerably differ from the tripartite one, except for the fact that it does not foresee the SB, but in its stead an internal committee of the BD, named CSM (*comitato per il controllo sulla gestione*), and composed of at least two members who cannot be given executive powers. The CSM is appointed by the BD from among its members, unless the statutes provide otherwise (i.e. that the MM appoints the CSM directly) (art. 2409*octiesdecies*, para. 1, ICC). Its members must possess the same independence requirements as the members of the SB in the tripartite system (art. 2399 ICC). One of the members of the CSM must be an auditor of accounts (art. 2409*octiesdecies*, para. 3, ICC). The CSM has the same functions as the SB in the tripartite system.

Under this system, external financial audit by a registered auditor is always required (art. 2409*noviesdecies* ICC).

The monistic system is the optional system that cooperatives have shown to prefer to the dualistic one, although the tripartite system remains the one most employed by Italian cooperatives. This is probably due to the cost reduction that it brings about, and to scant knowledge of the dualistic system and its potentialities. The monistic system has been criticised by some Italian scholars on the grounds that supervisors are appointed by the selfsame persons that they must supervise. But this criticism seems unconvincing because, in fact, the MM already identifies the supervisors while electing directors. Rather, the monistic system may be an effective system of governance inasmuch as it favours the

34 But there are contrary opinions: see for references Bonfante, n. 30 above, p. 349.

circulation of information between directors and supervisors, since both are parts of the same organ, and, unlike the tripartite system, it always comprises both internal and external audits. It is also claimed that the monistic system allows active members to control the cooperative more than the tripartite one.

2.6. THE DUALISTIC SYSTEM

In this system, the MM has fewer powers than in the two other systems. Among other things, it does not appoint and remove managers and it does not approve annual accounts.

The SUB is the key and qualifying organ of this system of administration. It is appointed by the MM from among its members (art. 2544, para. 2, ICC). It comprises at least three individuals, one of whom must be a registered auditor of accounts (art. 2409*duodecies*, para. 1 and 4, ICC). The chair is nominated by the MM.

Among other things, the SUB appoints (and removes) the MB, supervises its performance (with the same powers, duties and responsibilities as the SB in the tripartite system) and approves annual accounts (although some authors maintain that cooperative statutes may attribute this power to the MM). It may also be granted by cooperative statutes the 'high administrative' power to approve strategic operations and industrial and financial plans drafted by the MB, which however remains responsible for them (art. 2409*terdecies*, ICC).

The MB consists of at least two individuals, who may also be non-members of the cooperative (art. 2409*novies*, para. 2, ICC).[35] It manages the enterprise with the same powers as the BD in the tripartite system. It may delegate its powers to one or more of its members (but not to a committee, according to some authors).

In this system, external audit of accounts by a registered auditor is always mandatory (art. 2409*quinquiesdecies*, ICC).

This system is almost non-existent in practice. Compared to the others, the dualistic system is the one that more divides ownership and control of the cooperative enterprise, since cooperative members in the MM are deprived of significant powers, which are transferred to the SUB. This induces some to argue that, by allowing the concentration and stabilisation of power in the hands of few cooperative members (those in the SUB), it clashes with the cooperative ideal of (all) members' control of the enterprise.[36] Yet, this system may be an interesting alternative in cooperatives where members tend not to participate in the MM (e.g. larger cooperatives). In this case, the members of the SUB may act

---

35 A different view is put forward by BONFANTE, n. 30 above, pp. 343 f., according to which at least the majority of MB members must be cooperative members.

36 This conflict would be exacerbated by the possible provision in the statutes of the election of the SUB in proportion to the capital held or the volume of mutual transactions.

as stable and effective representatives of cooperative members who otherwise, by their limited participation, would let managers exercise excessively uncontrolled power. In other words, in those cases, the dualistic system allows representative or indirect democracy to substitute for a less effective direct democracy.

This system is also interesting because it makes it possible to divide strategic and executive (day-to-day) management – the former entrusted to the SUB and the latter to the MB – in a manner clearer and more transparent than the tripartite system may do. This also makes it possible to combine in a more balanced way the interests of cooperative members (represented in the SUB by some cooperative members) with the interests of the cooperative enterprise as such and of other cooperative stakeholders (represented in the MB by professional managers).

2.7. THE GOVERNANCE OF AN SRL COOPERATIVE

It is very difficult to outline the governance of an SRL cooperative, since the new regime of SRLs, after the 2003 reform of Italian company law, is very liberal, leaving SRL statutes ample freedom to design their internal structure. It must be recalled, however, that the regime of an SRL only applies to cooperatives for matters or aspects not covered by cooperative law and as far as it is compatible.

In general, an SRL cooperative should be able to opt for members' decisions taken outside the MM by written consultation or written consent of the members; a resolution of the MM is necessary only for decisions about particularly important matters, such as amendments of the statutes and substantial modifications of member rights, or when one administrator or one-third of the members so require (art. 2479 ICC). Therefore, the MM is not an essential organ of governance of an SRL cooperative, and it may be doubted that this is compatible with cooperative principles.

Nor is the BD an essential organ. Indeed, in an SRL cooperative, it is possible to entrust administration to two or more cooperative members acting jointly or separately, thus without forming a collective body. In any event, when a BD exists, the statutes may provide that the BD's decisions are taken by written consultation or written consent, i.e. without joint sittings (art. 2475 ICC). Some authors argue that the dualistic and the monistic system are not available for SRL cooperatives, but there is no apparent reason to draw this conclusion.

The SB is necessary in an SRL cooperative under the same conditions as it is necessary in an SPA cooperative. In addition, when required, the SB may be composed of only one member (art. 2477, para. 1, ICC). An external auditor of accounts must be nominated when the conditions for the appointment of an SB are present, and in the case the SB has not be given competence on financial audit.

In an SRL cooperative, a single member has more individual powers than in an SPA cooperative. A sole member has the right to be informed by the directors of the state of social affairs and to consult the social books and documents relative to the administration (art. 2476, para. 2, ICC); a sole member has the right to sue directors for responsibility (art. 2476, para. 3, ICC).

2.8. THE GOVERNANCE OF SOCIAL COOPERATIVES

Social cooperatives are cooperatives instituted and regulated by Law no. 381/1991. In accordance with article 2520, para. 1, ICC, Law no. 381/1991 is a special cooperative law which takes precedence over the general cooperative regulation in the ICC. Nevertheless, Law no. 381/1991 is very concise and does not contain specific provisions on the governance of social cooperatives, which would have been very opportune in light of the fact that social cooperatives present a special purpose compared to ordinary cooperatives: They act in the general interest of the community and not in the interest of their members as such.

The only provisions regarding the governance of social cooperatives which may be found in Italian law are those permitting (but not obligating) social cooperative statutes to provide for the admission of voluntary members (but only up to a half of the total number of members), as well as of private or public entities whose institutional aim is financing and developing social cooperative activities; and that the provision which obligates (and not simply permits) social cooperatives to admit as members their disadvantaged workers if this is compatible with their individual state.

2.9. MEMBER ADMISSION, EXPULSION AND RESIGNATION

Given capital variability, which must be understood as a technical device to facilitate the open character of cooperatives, in a cooperative the admission of new members does not require any amendment of the act of incorporation or the statutes, nor disclosure or filing with the Register of Enterprises (art. 2524, para. 2, ICC).

Admission is regulated by articles 2527 and 2528 ICC as follows:

- the act of incorporation must establish the requirements for the admission of new members and the pertinent procedure, according to non-discriminatory criteria, consistent with the cooperative's purpose and activity;
- admission is subject to approval by the BD, which must justify its refusal within 60 days from the application;
- candidates refused membership may appeal to the MM;
- directors must report on their decisions on admissions in the report on the balance sheet.

Those who run an enterprise in competition with that run by the cooperative may not become members of the cooperative (art. 2527, para. 2, ICC).

The overall regulation of member admission does not entitle third parties to become members of a cooperative, even when they meet the requirements laid down in the act of incorporation. In fact, the interest of third parties in becoming members is protected only indirectly, by imposing upon the cooperative and its organs the aforementioned obligations. Therefore, the 'door' of Italian cooperatives is not 'open', but only 'ajar'.[37]

Third parties' interest in membership is also protected by article. 2527, para. 3, ICC, according to which new (user) members may be admitted in a special category on the grounds of their interest in being trained or involved in the enterprise. This special category of members 'on probation' (as they are referred to by Italian scholars) may not comprise more than one third of total (user) members, and the members belonging to it may enjoy different rights and have different obligations relative to ordinary user members. However, after a maximum of five years, the members belonging to this special category shall enjoy the same rights as the other members.

Capital variability also facilitates member withdrawal, although under Italian law withdrawal is not free (at will). Indeed, under Italian law, members may withdraw only in the cases provided for by law or by cooperative statutes (art. 2532, para. 1, ICC). The law permits member withdrawal only in certain, limited cases (e.g. conversion, transfer of the registered office abroad, and other major changes in the statutes). The cooperative practice, however, is to allow members to leave the cooperative at will, although frequently stipulated in agricultural cooperatives are minimum periods of membership (i.e. until such periods elapse, withdrawal is not permitted) or periods of notice (i.e. withdrawal takes effect after a certain period of time). In all cases, the law establishes, first, that directors may oppose the declaration of withdrawal by the member, who may in this case appeal to the court (art. 2532, para. 2, ICC); second, that member withdrawal takes immediate effect as regards the organisational relationship, while as regards the mutual relationship (of consumption, provision, work) it does so only when the financial year ends if withdrawal has been communicated three months before, or at the end of the next financial year if withdrawal has been communicated later. This last rule is clearly intended to protect the cooperative enterprise against unexpected exits by members and the consequent unforeseen loss of mutual contributions. In cooperatives, in effect, member exit

---

37 More particularly, it is not clear whether the MM may modify the decision of the BD, and thus exact the admission. Similarly, it is not clear what types of legal actions may be taken by third parties if the MM does not reverse the decision and the refusal is unlawful (even less clear is when a refusal may be considered unlawful). In addition, the cooperative's behaviour with regard to the admission of new members may have an impact on the cooperative's revision by the State or cooperative federations.

creates more problems in terms of suddenly lacking mutual exchanges than of capital having to be returned.

Italian cooperative law limits the freedom of members to transfer their shares, for which article 2530 ICC requires the directors' authorisation. Denial may be contested by the member before a court. If the statutes prohibit share transfer, members may freely withdraw from the cooperative if two years after their entrance have elapsed.

Members who do not pay for the subscribed capital may be excluded (art. 2531 ICC). Exclusion may also apply to members who substantially non-perform their obligations toward the cooperative, who have lost the membership requirements, or have gone bankrupt, or have lost the capacity to act legally, and in the other cases provided for by cooperative statutes (art. 2533, para. 1, ICC). Excluded members may appeal to the court. If statutes do not provide otherwise, exclusion terminates not only the organisational relationship but also the mutual relationship between the cooperative and the excluded member.

2.10. OTHER MEMBER RIGHTS OF CONTROL – INFORMATION AND TRANSPARENCY – DISPUTE RESOLUTION – MEMBER EDUCATION

Member control of the cooperative enterprise is exercised in several ways, first of all by the member participating in and voting at the MM and taking part in the other organs of the cooperative. Therefore, discussion of member control in Italian cooperatives would involve the entire governance field as briefly outlined in this report.

There are two more cooperative law provisions which should be mentioned.

The first is article 2545*bis* ICC, according to which one-tenth of the members (or one-twentieth in cooperatives with more than 3,000 members) have the right to examine the register of meetings and resolutions of the BD and of the executive committee if existent.[38] In addition, each member has the right to examine the register of members and the register of meetings and resolutions of the MM.

The second is article 2545*quinquiesdecies* ICC, according to which one-tenth of the members (or one-twentieth in cooperatives with more than 3,000 members) or members holding one-tenth of the capital are entitled to denounce to the court substantial irregularities in the management which are the effect of major violations of directors' duties and may damage the cooperative.

[38] This rule only applies to SPA cooperatives because in SRL cooperatives members hold this right individually.

Information and transparency should be considered general objectives of an adequate cooperative regulation. They should be taken into consideration when regulating all aspects of the cooperative's functioning, from the convening of an MM to the drafting of the accounts. Therefore, it is difficult to report on how Italian law implements the principles of information and transparency because this would involve reiterating the analysis of cooperative governance. Moreover, the most important act in this respect – namely, the balance sheet – is dealt with in another section of this book. Only one further provision is worth mentioning here: article 2545 ICC, which obligates directors and supervisors to report (also) on the criteria applied in management of the enterprise to fulfil the cooperative's mutual purpose.

Italian law comprises no specific provisions on dispute resolution between the cooperative and its members, among the members, between the cooperative and the members of the organs, between the cooperative and third parties, etc. General law applies in this particular regard. In cooperative practice, however, what may be found is the provision in the statutes of an internal organ (or rather, committee) for the 'amicable' resolution of disputes among members or between the members and the cooperative.

In Italian cooperative law, there are no specific provisions obligating a single cooperative to educate and/or train its members, managers, workers, stakeholders and/or the general public, thus following the fifth ICA Principle. However, these activities are certainly performed at a more general level by cooperative federations, thanks to funds provided annually by the associated cooperatives. Indeed, each Italian cooperative must allocate 3% of its annual surplus to the 'mutual funds' managed by the cooperative federation to which the cooperative belongs (in addition, mutual funds are recipients of the residual assets of a dissolved PMC). Mutual funds conduct diverse activities for the promotion and development of the cooperative movement, among which is the professional training of the administrative and technical staff of cooperatives, as well as the funding of research in the field of cooperatives (art. 11, para. 3, Law no. 59/1992).

3. COOPERATIVE FINANCIAL STRUCTURE

3.1. INTRODUCTION

The particular identity of cooperatives, with respect to other types of legal entities, is also the result of specific legal provisions regarding the capital and other financial aspects.

Under Italian law, the matter of cooperative finance is strongly influenced by the general dichotomies between PMCs and OCs, on the one hand, and, although to a lesser extent, between SPA cooperatives and SRL cooperatives, on the other hand.

The presence of special laws on particular types of cooperatives (such as, for example, social cooperatives) must also be taken into account in dealing with cooperative finance.

3.2. COOPERATIVE CAPITAL: NATURE, CHARACTERISTICS AND FUNCTIONS

Italian law requires cooperatives to have a (legal or stated) capital[39] like other types of companies, but the regulation of cooperatives' capital makes it substantially different from the capital of non-cooperative companies, notably joint-stock companies (SPAs). The overall regulation of the cooperative capital modifies its role. In principle, the capital of cooperatives does not determine the extent of a member's ownership rights (first of all, the right to appropriate profits and the right to vote), nor does it serve as an effective guarantee for creditors (due to its variability), but simply as a means of cooperative finance (own resources) alongside others (internal and external resources). This, in fact, reduces (but does not eliminate) the conceptual distinction, in a cooperative, between 'legal capital' and 'assets', which in contrast is clear in companies and company law.

Cooperatives are defined by Italian law as companies with variable capital (arts. 2511 and 2524, para. 1, ICC). Capital variability implies that cooperatives, unlike companies whose capital is 'fixed', may admit new members without amending their incorporation acts or statutes (art. 2524, para. 2, ICC).[40] Nor is such an amendment necessary in the event of member exit (because of withdrawal[41] or expulsion). Capital variability therefore facilitates the admission and exit of members in line with the open character of cooperatives,[42] to the detriment, however, of the interests of a cooperative's creditors, who cannot find sufficient protection in a legal capital thus shaped by law.

---

39 By 'legal' or 'stated' capital is meant an 'amount equal to the aggregate 'par' or stated value of all outstanding shares of a corporation' (*Black's Law Dictionary*, 9th ed., West, Minnesota, 2009, *ad vocem*).

40 This does not mean, however, that third parties are entitled to enter the cooperative.

41 This does not mean that cooperative members are free to withdraw. Under Italian law, members may withdraw only in the cases provided for by law or cooperative statutes (art. 2532, para. 1, ICC).

42 Cooperatives may also decide to issue new shares by amending their statutes, in which case present members have a preemption right on the new shares, unless the members' meeting establishes otherwise (art. 2524, paras. 3 and 4, ICC). In the absence of a members' obligation to buy these new shares, it is not clear why the Italian legislature has contemplated this circumstance. It probably only has a meaning for cooperatives whose capital is fixed or for the fixed part of the cooperative capital (which may include the capital subscribed by investor members, if one believes that it is fixed: see the next footnote). Another possible explanation is that this procedure must be followed when a cooperative intends to solicit new contributions by present members, provided that present members cannot freely subscribe new capital.

In addition, capital variability implies that when a cooperative suffers real losses, its capital shall not be increased and/or reduced like, in contrast, the fixed capital of companies in order to protect creditors who rely on a definite and invariable amount of capital as a guarantee for their credits.

According to some legal scholars, the fact that capital variability is embodied in the very definition of a cooperative makes capital variability mandatory, in the sense that cooperative statutes may not provide for a fixed capital, but at most for a minimum (fixed) capital above which the capital may freely fluctuate.[43]

Indeed, cooperative capital is neither fixed nor stated by Italian law in a (mandatory) minimum amount (contrary, for example, to the European Regulation of European Cooperative Societies, whose minimum legal capital is 30,000 euros).[44] Italian law does not require a cooperative to be set up with, and maintain throughout its entire existence, a minimum amount of capital. It only establishes the minimum nominal value of the capital share that each cooperative member must hold (which is 25 euros: art. 2525, para. 1, ICC), while not requiring the cooperative to maintain during its entire life an amount equivalent to the total of these minimum shares, given that only the loss of the entire capital is cause for cooperative dissolution (art. 2545*duodecies* ICC).

Notwithstanding its variability, a cooperative's capital remains in principle 'equity capital' (as distinct from 'debt capital') because it is composed of contributions in exchange for membership, and because it is property of the cooperative and not of the members to whom it shall be returned only upon exit or liquidation. The fact that, under Italian law, member withdrawal is not free in principle, along with the legal conditions and limits on the reimbursement of the members' contributions, support this classification of cooperative capital. General awareness of that is perhaps the reason why the matter of the international accounting standards (in particular, principle no. 32) has not raised any particular concern in Italy and Italian legal scholarship, contrary to other countries where it has even led to a change in legislation.[45]

Article 7 of Law no. 59/1992 allows cooperatives to allocate a part of their profits to increasing their capital (and thus the members' stocks and individual shares of capital) within the limits of money depreciation. Profits thus allocated

---

43 It is however argued in legal scholarship that the capital subscribed by investor members is fixed, or at least could be shaped as fixed by cooperative statutes, thereby making the cooperative capital divided into two sections: a variable capital subscribed by cooperators (i.e. user-members), and a fixed capital subscribed by investor (non-user) members. If the capital of investor members is fixed, the question arises as to what the regime of this portion of the cooperative capital is. The question should be resolved by taking into consideration the reference to the regulation of SPAs or SRLs.

44 Different rules could obviously apply to certain types of cooperatives in light of the particular economic activity that they conduct, which in Italy is the case of cooperative banks, which in fact are obligated to have a minimum (fixed) capital.

45 On this see L.F. Paolucci, 'Principio contabile internazionale n. 32: la situazione nel diritto italiano', *Revesco*, 2006, no. 3, pp. 92 ff.

do not form part of the cooperative's taxed income (therefore, revaluation of the capital is tax free for the cooperative, while members are taxed only when the capital is returned to them).

A cooperative's capital may also be increased by assigning to members dividends (meant as returns on capital), cooperative refunds (art. 2545*sexies*, para. 3, ICC) or divisible reserves (within the limits of art. 2545*quinquies*, para. 3, b), ICC) as free stocks or shares of capital, rather than in cash or as financial instruments.

Cooperative capital is divided into stocks (*azioni*) or shares (*quote*), whose nominal value cannot be lower than 25 euros or higher than 500 euros (art. 2525, para. 1, ICC).

Stocks or shares are assigned to members in exchange for (and normally also in proportion to) their individual contributions to the (formation of the) legal capital, i.e. to the capital individually subscribed by each member.

Stocks or shares may not be effectively transferred without the authorisation of the directors (art. 2530, para. 1, ICC). Cooperative statutes may even provide for stock (or share) non-transferability, but in this case members are free to withdraw, although not earlier than two years before their entry into the cooperative (2530, para. 6, ICC). In contrast, stocks subscribed by investor members may freely circulate in principle (which is consistent with the lack of *intuitus personae* that characterises this category of members relative to that of cooperators or user-members).

In general, a single member may not hold a capital share greater than 100,000 euros (art. 2525, para. 2, ICC), but there are various exceptions to this rule.[46]

Although the member titles of participation in the cooperative capital are termed 'stocks' or 'shares' like those in a company, they do not have the same role and nature as a company's stocks or shares, since their legal regime is completely different. It is not only a matter of circulation, which in principle is not free as previously stated, but also of ownership rights that participation in the cooperative capital brings about.

Indeed, whereas in a company ownership rights (including both financial and governance rights) normally depend on shareholding *per se* and vary according to the amount of capital held, in a cooperative the capital is neither fully the basis nor the measure of these rights.

---

46 This limit does not apply to the members of a cooperative with more than 500 members if the cooperative has stipulated in its statutes that the maximum limit is 2% of the capital (art. 2525, para. 3, ICC); to members who are not individuals (art. 2525, para. 4, ICC); to members who have made in-kind contributions, including credits (art. 2525, para. 4, ICC); to investor members and other holders of financial instruments with governance rights (art. 2525, para. 4, ICC); to members whose stocks or shares have been augmented by the cooperative through dividends, divisible reserves and cooperative refunds (art. 2525, para. 4, ICC).

More precisely, under Italian law, subscription of a minimum share of capital (25 euros or a greater amount as defined by cooperative statutes) is required for membership, but the amount of capital held does not affect the extent of the ownership rights. In general and in principle (because exceptions may be found), financial rights in a cooperative are determined by (the quantity and quality of) mutual transactions, while governance rights are determined by membership *per se*.

In this section we will only deal with governance rights, while financial rights will be examined throughout the text and in particular in section 3.5.

A fundamental governance right, certainly the most important one, is the right to vote in the MM.

While in Italian company law each stock normally carries one vote, in Italian cooperative law, 'each cooperative member has one vote, whatever the value of the share or the number of the stocks held' (art. 2538, para. 2, ICC). Therefore, in a cooperative, voting power in the members' meeting is not linked to the amount of capital held, but to membership *per se*.

As already highlighted, however, exceptions to this rule may be found in Italian cooperative law, which allows a member to have several votes. What is worth recalling here is that, in some instances, plural votes may be assigned by cooperative statutes on the basis of the capital held, although under given conditions and within certain limits. The pertinent provisions are those in articles 2538, para. 3, 2543, para. 2, and 2526, para. 2, ICC, to which we have already made reference.

According to article 2545*bis* ICC, one-tenth of the members (or one-twentieth in cooperatives with more than 3,000 members) have the right to examine the register of the meetings and resolutions of the BD and of the executive committee, if any (this rule only applies to SPA cooperatives because in SRL cooperatives the members hold this right individually). In addition, each individual member has the right to examine the register of the members and the register of the meetings and resolutions of the MM. Therefore, the capital held is irrelevant also in these latter cases.

In contrast, according to article 2545*quinquiesdecies* ICC, not only one-tenth of the members (or one-twentieth in cooperatives with more than 3,000 members) but also members holding at least one-tenth of the capital are entitled to denounce to the court substantial irregularities in the management which are consequent on major violations of directors' duties and may damage the cooperative.

3.3. MEMBER CONTRIBUTIONS

The concept of company capital, including cooperative capital, is closely connected with that of member contributions. In fact, the cooperative capital is formed by and of the contributions of the members (although, as we shall see, it may subsequently be increased by the cooperative in several ways).

Notwithstanding the difference between cooperatives and capitalist companies, under Italian law member contributions are necessary (albeit potentially not sufficient)[47] for acquiring membership in a cooperative. A share of the cooperative capital is assigned to members in exchange for their contributions, which thus represent the 'price' paid for participation (particularly for engaging in mutual transactions with the cooperative).

By definition, contributions must have the same value as (or higher value than) the nominal (face) value of the stocks or shares assigned as consideration to the members.

Cooperative statutes may provide for a minimum contribution higher than that stated in article 2525, para. 1, ICC (i.e. 25 euros). This contribution may be the same for all members or proportioned to the degree of individual participation in mutual transactions.

Also investor members must contribute to the cooperative's capital if they wish to become members. To be noted is that, in Italian law, the category of investor members and that of the holders of financial instruments do not coincide because the latter includes the former. A cooperative may issue financial instruments of several types; therefore, investors who are not members of the cooperative may be envisaged.

Contributions may be in cash or in kind (including credits). The value assigned to in-kind contributions must be specified in the act of incorporation.

It is discussed whether labour or services may be contributed (in a worker cooperative this would create particular problems, given that the worker cooperative is already composed of worker members).

Although the point is debated in legal scholarship, it seems that in-cash contributions do not need to be paid in advance (i.e. at the time of subscription or acquisition of membership), not even in the measure of 25% which applies to companies. Indeed, article 2531 ICC states that 'the member who does not perform *in all or in part* the payment of the shares or stocks subscribed may, subject to an intimation from directors, be excluded ...'. Legal scholars hold that, in contrast, investor members are subject to the 25% minimum advanced payment rule.

In principle, members may not be requested to provide supplementary contributions (or other forms of financial participation, such as coverage of existing losses or loans), unless cooperative statutes authorise directors to do

47 In light of the membership requirements which a cooperative's statutes may, and usually do, lay down, thereby making the cooperative a type of company characterised by *intuitus personae*, i.e. the relevance of the personal characteristics of members for governance purposes.

so, and even in this case up to a certain amount (which could be calculated by reference to the degree of participation in mutual transactions or the amount of capital already subscribed).

Voluntary contributions should presuppose an offer by the cooperative of new stocks or shares to subscribe, which is something that requires a members' resolution to issue new stocks or shares, taken in accordance with article 2524, para. 3, ICC.

User-members may also subscribe financial instruments issued by the cooperative and thus be (at the same time) investor-members, which is another way for a member to contribute more capital than that necessary to acquire membership. In this case members have a twofold nature, as user-members and investor-members, which may create some problems in terms of governance.

Stocks or shares may not be acquired or reimbursed by the cooperative unless its statutes so authorise, the conditions provided for by article 2545*quinquies*, para. 2, ICC are fulfilled (i.e. the ratio between net assets and debts is higher than a quarter), and acquisition or reimbursement are made within the limits of distributable profits and available reserves as resulting from the last balance sheet (art. 2529 ICC).

Members who leave the cooperative are entitled to have their contributions returned. Losses are to be taken into account when calculating the amount to be returned. Payment must be made within 180 days from the approval of the balance sheet. However, for stocks or shares assigned to members in lieu of the payment of cooperative refunds, dividends and divisible reserves in cash, the payment may be made within five years if the statutes so permit (art. 2535 ICC).

3.4. MUTUAL TRANSACTIONS AND 'MUTUAL' CAPITAL

The concept of 'mutual capital', as developed by the Spanish legal doctrine, is unknown in the Italian legal environment, although it might pose a number of interesting legal issues for Italian legal scholars as well because of its possible consequences under property, tort, or insolvency law.

Certainly, what the cooperative receives from its members during and for the execution of 'mutual transactions' cannot be considered part of its capital, given that members' supply, unlike contributions in the strict sense, has not been received in exchange for membership, but in the carrying out of mutual transactions. Therefore, for example, grapes provided by farmers to a wine cooperative of which they are members do not form part of the wine cooperative's capital. In this case, members are not buying stocks or shares, but are simply performing mutual transactions.

Rather, the issue may be whether the goods provided by the members in the implementation of mutual transactions are to be included in the cooperative's assets.

The answer seems to depend on the legal configuration of the mutual transactions. If they are qualified as separate transactions, the issues that they raise should in principle be resolved by ordinary law and not by cooperative organisational law. Hence, if the transfer of the grapes is legally qualified as a sale of goods, the owner of the grapes is he who must be considered such according to the ordinary regime of sale contracts (e.g. in Italian law, the ownership of grapes is transferred to the buyer when grapes are 'identified': art. 1378 ICC, and thus separated from the kind of pertinence). Therefore, the goods provided by cooperative members in performing mutual transactions remain the members' property or become the cooperative's property depending on the ordinary (contract or property) legal rules applicable to these transactions, regardless of the fact that they take place between a cooperative and its members. Accordingly, the Italian Supreme Court has stated that cash advances paid by the members to a housing cooperative constitute members' credits towards the cooperative, the non-payment of which may be cause of insolvency, with the consequent admission of those credits to the cooperative's bankruptcy status (i.e. its liabilities).[48]

3.5. ALLOCATION OF SURPLUS

Under Italian cooperative law, the allocation of profits is a matter covered by several provisions. First of all, the law prescribes some destinations, with a view to implementing the social function of cooperatives and strengthening their financial structure, given the limited relevance of the capital.

Cooperatives (both PMCs and OCs) must allocate to a reserve fund (named 'legal reserve') at least 30% of their annual net profits, whatever the amount of this reserve fund (art. 2545*quater*, para. 1, ICC).[49]

Cooperatives (both PMCs and OCs) must also allocate 3% of their annual profits to the mutual funds for the promotion and development of cooperation (art. 2545*quater*, para. 2, ICC).

It is not clear whether these compulsory destinations should precede any other allocation including 'cooperative refunds', in other words, whether or not the term 'profits' in article 2545*quater*, para. 1 and 2, ICC, includes the 'cooperative surplus'.

Answering in the affirmative would make the interests of the cooperative (whose stability is reinforced by the legal reserve) and the cooperative movement (whose activity is fostered by the mutual funds) prevail over those of individual cooperative members.

---

48 Cf. Cass. 6 December 2000, no. 15489.

49 Special laws may provide for a different percentage: for example, it is 10% for popular banks (art. 32, para. 1, Legislative Decree no. 385/1993) and 70% for credit cooperative banks (art. 37, para. 1, Legislative Decree no. 385/1993).

With regard to the allocation of the remaining part of annual profits, neither PMCs nor OCs are totally free to decide autonomously, although constraints mostly regard PMCs.

Indeed, PMCs are subject to article 2514 ICC, which strictly limits profit distribution to members. By contrast, OCs are only subject to article 2545*quinquies* ICC (which applies to PMCs as well), according to which the act of incorporation must lay down the maximum percentage of dividends distributable to members (para. 1), and dividends (as well as distributable reserves) may be distributed only if the ratio between net assets and liabilities is higher than one-fourth (para. 2).

Article 2514 ICC stipulates that PMC statutes must impose (and consequently PMCs must observe):

- a prohibition on distributing dividends on the paid-up capital higher than the maximum interest of postal bonds increased by 2.5 points;
- a prohibition on remunerating the financial instruments held by cooperative members more than 2 points above the maximum interest applicable to dividends;
- a prohibition on distributing reserves to cooperative members;
- an obligation to devolve, in the case of dissolution, all assets, subtracting only the capital and the dividends due but not yet distributed, to the mutual funds for the promotion and development of cooperation.

The provisions in article 2514 require some comment and clarification.

Firstly, one can observe how carefully the partial profit non-distribution constraint is regulated. It covers not only the periodic distribution of returns on capital (annual dividends), but also the distribution of retained profits (reserves and residual assets). Accordingly, article 2545*ter*, para. 2, ICC states that indivisible reserves may be used to cover losses only after all the other reserves and resources have been applied to the loss.

Secondly, the restrictions do not regard investor members, but only user members or cooperators (*soci cooperatori*). When user members are also investor members, because they hold financial instruments issued by the cooperative, a limit applies anew.

Thirdly, it is not clear whether all reserves in a PMC are indivisible, including voluntary reserves that cooperative statutes do not stipulate indivisible, or whether indivisible are only the legal reserve of article 2545*quater*, para. 1, ICC, and the reserves established as indivisible by cooperative statutes.

Finally, and more importantly, article 2514 (as well as art. 2545*quinquies*) ICC exclusively refers to profit distribution for capital remuneration ('dividends on the paid-up capital'), whereas a different regulation applies to *ristorni* ('cooperative refunds').

Indeed, Italian law recognises the conceptual distinction between dividends as returns on capital and cooperative refunds as a form of *ex post* remuneration of the mutual transactions. Both are benefits assigned to members, but their legal nature is diverse because each has a different justification – dividends in member capital contribution, and cooperative refunds in member participation in mutual transactions – which affects their legal treatment.

It may suffice to compare article 2514, para. 1, *a*, ICC, with article 2545*sexies* ICC. The former limits, in PMCs, the distribution to cooperators of 'dividends on the paid-up capital'. The latter, specifically dedicated to *ristorni* (the Italian term for 'cooperative refunds'), stipulates that cooperative refunds are to be distributed in proportion to the quantity and quality of the mutual transactions (para. 1).[50]

In general, differently from dividends in PMCs, no restrictions on the distribution of cooperative refunds exist.[51] It remains unclear, however, whether refundable profits are to be considered only those that result after the deduction of compulsory allocations to legal reserve and mutual funds. If this were not the case, fully mutual cooperatives might have neither a legal reserve nor an obligation to contribute to the cooperative movement.

It is also debated whether in cooperatives that operate also with non-members only that part of profits which derives from transactions with members (the 'cooperative surplus') may be refunded or also that part of profits which stems from transactions with non-members.[52]

As regards tax law, a specific regime of tax exemption applies both to sums allocated to indivisible reserves (they are partly exempt) and to sums distributed as cooperative refunds (they are fully exempt, but members pay taxes on the sums thus received).

In conclusion, Italian law draws a clear conceptual distinction between 'dividends' and 'cooperative refunds', but there still remain issues whose resolution would require deriving all the due consequences from that distinction.

---

50 Art. 2545*sexies*, para. 1, ICC helps to interpret correctly art. 2516 ICC, according to which, in the conclusion and execution of mutual transactions, the cooperative must treat members equally. This rule does not obligate the cooperative to treat its members in the same way, but, as clarified by art. 2545*sexies*, para. 1, ICC, to treat its members in proportion to their contributions to the fulfillment of its mutual purpose.

51 A limit of 30% of the salary applies to worker cooperatives (see art. 3, para. 2, Law no. 142/2001).

52 In the first sense, see Ministerial Communication no. 53/E of 18 June 2002, which, in dealing with the specific tax treatment of cooperative refunds, affirms: 'cooperative refund, that is, the restitution to members of part of the price paid for goods and services or the extra-remuneration for work, and in general, goods and services provided by members, is possible only if the balance of the activity performed by the cooperative with its members is positive. What may be refunded is only the documented surplus from transactions with members and not the surplus from transactions with non-members'.

3.6. RESERVES

As stated, every financial year all cooperatives are obligated to allocate at least 30% of their net profits to a 'legal reserve', whatever the amount reached by this reserve (art. 2545*quater*, para. 1, ICC).

Additional reserve funds may be created by the cooperative voluntarily ('voluntary reserves') or following a prescription in their statutes ('statutory reserves').

Italian law does not prescribe a separate reserve fund for the education and training of members, managers, workers, etc., or for the benefit of the community. These objectives are reached in a systemic dimension involving the cooperative movement as a whole: indeed, as stated, each cooperative must provide 3% of their annual profits to 'mutual funds' for the development of promotion of cooperation which are normally managed by federations of cooperatives. Sums thus allocated by cooperatives are exempt from corporate income tax.

Reserves may be either distributable ('divisible' in Italian law) or non-distributable to members ('indivisible').

Indivisible are those reserves that the law or cooperative statutes qualify as non-distributable to members, even in the case of cooperative dissolution (art. 2545*ter*, para. 1, ICC).

The law qualifies as indivisible the reserves of PMCs (art. 2514, para. 1, *c* and *d*, ICC), although it is not clear whether, in so providing, the law intends to refer to the legal reserve only or to any reserve, including voluntary ones, established by PMCs.

Indivisible does not mean non-usable, although the functions performed by indivisible reserves justify limitations in the use of these reserves. Therefore, article 2545*ter*, para. 2, ICC states that 'indivisible reserves may be used to cover losses only after the reserves that the cooperative had destined to increasing the capital and the reserves that may be divided among members in the case of dissolution have been exhausted'.

A specific regime of tax exemption applies to profits allocated (by both PMCs and OCs) to indivisible reserves. These profits are (partially) exempt from the corporate income tax (whose Italian name is *Imposta sul reddito delle società*: IRES).[53] For this provision to apply, reserves must be indivisible to members both during the existence of the cooperative and after its dissolution. As already stated, indivisible reserves may be compulsory (like the legal reserve of art. 2545*quater*, para. 1, ICC) or voluntary. The exemption is subject to restrictions: It does not apply to 40% of the profits; 20% in the case of agricultural

---

53 It should be pointed out that these reserves may be used to cover financial losses – without this producing the loss of the tax measure – but only as long as profits are not distributed before the re-establishment of the reserves (art. 3, para. 1, Law 18 February 1999, no. 28).

and small fishery cooperatives and their consortia; 65% in the case of consumer cooperatives and their consortia.[54] By contrast, all profits allocated by a social cooperative to indivisible reserves are exempt from the corporate income tax.

This exemption also applies to OCs, but limitedly to 30% of the profits allocated to the legal reserve of article 2545*quater*, para. 1, ICC, and on the condition that OC statutes explicitly provide for the indivisibility of said reserve, given that OCs are subject neither to article 2514 ICC nor to the reserve non-distribution constraint provided therein.

3.7. RETAINED COOPERATIVE REFUNDS

A cooperative is not obligated to distribute cooperative refunds to the members. This choice falls within the discretionary power of the MM, on the basis of a proposal by the directors. Consequently, cooperators do not hold a subjective right to cooperative refunds (as a company's shareholders do not hold a subjective right to dividends). On the other hand, a cooperative that never distributes cooperative refunds would act in contrast to its institutional purpose of benefiting members.[55]

Therefore, a cooperative may in principle retain cooperative refunds (or rather, resources that could be distributed as cooperative refunds) and allocate them to the legal reserve or other reserve funds.

The MM of a cooperative is also entitled to decide that cooperative refunds are assigned to members as free stocks or shares of cooperative capital or as financial instruments (art. 2545*sexies* ICC), which is a way to favour the capitalisation of the cooperative without excessively infringing upon the members' subjective interests.

3.8. OTHER MEANS OF COOPERATIVE FINANCE

The legislative reform of 2003 sought to reinforce the financial capacity of cooperatives in several ways. Among other things, it made cooperative capital more attractive for both cooperators and pure investors, and allowed cooperatives to retain cooperative refunds by assigning them to members as

54 The threshold of non-exemption has been recently increased (see art. 2, para. 36*bis*, Decree-Law 13 August 2011, no. 138): this shows a legislative trend towards the approximation of the tax treatment of cooperatives to that of companies. Along the same lines, art. 2, para. 36*ter*, Decree-Law 13 August 2011, no. 138, by changing art. 1, para. 1, Decree-Law 15 April 2002, no. 63, excludes the exemption of 10% of profits allocated to the compulsory legal reserve (i.e. 3% of total annual profits, because 30% of total annual profits must be allocated to the compulsory legal reserve according to art. 2545*quater*, para. 1, ICC).

55 Of course, this is so if there are cooperative refunds to be distributed, because if the cooperative attributes mutual benefits immediately at the time of mutual transactions, members do benefit from the cooperative enterprise and suffer no prejudice at all.

free stocks or capital shares or as financial instruments rather than in cash. The regime of reserves also serves the function of strengthening cooperative finance, as well as that of 'mutual funds', although in a systemic dimension involving the cooperative movement as a whole.

The most important change introduced by the 2003 reform is, however, the general possibility for a cooperative to issue financial instruments of any nature: equity (including stocks to be subscribed by investor members), debt (including bonds), or 'hybrids', and to freely establish their regime as regards the governance and financial rights granted to their holders (art. 2526 ICC). Limits are established with regard to voting power (holders of financial instruments, including investor members, may not have more than one-third of total votes in each MM) and to the attribution of privileges in the distribution of profits and in the reimbursement of the capital (which may not be done using indivisible reserves). Cooperative statutes may even award investor members the right to elect up to a third of members of the BD (art. 2542, para. 4, ICC).

The possibility for SRL cooperatives to issue financial instruments is subject to restrictions: SRL cooperatives 'may offer financial instruments that do not confer governance rights only to qualified investors' (art. 2526, para. 4, ICC). It is discussed whether this provision implies that SRL cooperatives may not issue financial instruments conferring governance rights to their holders (and therefore, may not have investor members), or more narrowly that, in an SRL cooperative, these types of financial instruments may only be offered to qualified investors, whereas no limitations exist with regard to financial instruments conferring governance rights (and therefore to the admission of investor members in an SRL cooperative).

Member loans are another typical instrument of cooperative finance. Italian law allows a cooperative to gather member loans within certain limits (so that the cooperative does not end up acting as a bank: see art. 11, no. 3, of banking law of 1993) and moreover provides for members a (local) tax exemption on the interest received on these loans.

3.9. MEMBER LIMITED LIABILITY FOR COOPERATIVE OBLIGATIONS

After the reform of 2003, cooperatives can only be incorporated as companies with limited liability of members.

The act of incorporation of a cooperative must be registered with the Register of Enterprises maintained by the Chamber of Commerce (art. 2523, para. 1, ICC).[56] Only from the moment of registration is the cooperative considered

[56] Cooperatives must also be registered with the Register of Cooperative Societies maintained by the Ministry of Economic Development.

legally established and acquires the 'legal personality', thus enjoying 'perfect patrimonial autonomy', which implies that only the cooperative with its assets is liable for its obligations, while member liability is limited to contributions, i.e. to the subscribed capital (art. 2518 ICC), and that 'personal creditors of the member may not levy execution on his share or stocks, as long as the cooperative exists' (art. 2537 ICC).

In contrast, before the reform of 2003, both cooperatives with limited liability of members and cooperatives with unlimited liability of members could be established.

3.10. ALLOCATION OF ASSETS AT CONVERSION AND DISSOLUTION

According to article 2545*decies*, para. 1, ICC, only OCs may be converted into another legal type of company.[57] Therefore, cooperatives that are PMCs may be converted only after they have lost this quality, and consequently become OCs, as permitted by article 2545*octies* ICC.[58]

In the event of conversion, the cooperative must devolve its assets to the mutual funds of article 11, Law 59/1992, subtracting only the paid-up capital, the dividends due but not yet distributed, and the additional amount which might be necessary to reach the minimum legal capital of the company into which the cooperative is to be converted (art. 2545*undecies*, para. 1, ICC).[59]

Hence, the conversion of cooperatives into other legal forms is now possible (in fact, before the 2003 reform of company law, it was explicitly prohibited by art. 14, Law 17 February 1971, no. 127) but strongly discouraged by law, which in this manner seeks to limit events of 'demutualisation' or at least to ensure that assets accumulated by the cooperative before transformation remain within the cooperative movement.

---

57 The decision to convert must be approved by a specific majority of members (see art. 2545*decies*, para. 1 and 2, ICC) and entitles dissenting (as well as abstaining and absent) members to withdraw from the cooperative (see arts. 2437 and 2473 ICC, applicable to cooperatives in virtue of art. 2519 ICC).

58 The 'transformation' of a PMC into an OC does not strictly represent conversion. Therefore, assets are not to be devolved to mutual funds but allocated to an indivisible reserve (art. 2545*octies* ICC). This ensures, though in fact only partially and unsatisfactorily (given that indivisible reserves cannot be distributed but can be used, also to cover losses), that cooperators do not exploit for personal reasons the special treatment granted to the cooperative when it was a PMC.

59 For example, up to €50,000 if the cooperative is to be transformed into an SPA. This is, in fact, the minimum capital prescribed by Italian law for establishing an SPA (art. 2327 ICC). Some authors argue that, notwithstanding the letter of art. 2545*undecies*, para. 1, ICC, and on the basis of a systematic interpretation, assets to be devolved to mutual funds are only indivisible reserves: see in this regard Bonfante, n. 21 above, pp. 386 f.

The regulation of assets devolution in the case of conversion also applies to cooperative dissolution, when this cooperative is a PMC (art. 2514, para. 1, *d*, ICC). In contrast, when the cooperative is an OC, only indivisible reserves are to be devolved to mutual funds (arg. *ex* art. 2545*ter*, para. 1, ICC).

3.11. SOCIAL COOPERATIVES

Italian Law no. 381/1991 on social cooperatives states (in art. 3, para. 1) that social cooperatives are subject to article 2514 ICC. Therefore, as regards the distribution of profits, reserves, and residual assets, social cooperatives are treated as if they were PMCs. This seems consistent with their nature as cooperatives acting in the general interest (and not for the members' profit).

Law no. 381/1991 does not contain specific provisions on the distribution of cooperative refunds. However, the fact that the social cooperative acts in the general interest of the community (art. 1) apparently makes the distribution of cooperative refunds to members as such[60] incompatible with its legal nature as a non-mutual cooperative, at least as long as cooperative refunds would grant members benefits that they would not have earned had they transacted (ie., depending on the type of cooperative worked, bought or sold, etc.) outside the cooperative.

In this regard, it is worth noting that Italian Law no. 155/2006 on social enterprise prohibits any enrichment of a social enterprise's members (as well as workers, directors, etc.), including by 'indirect distributions' of profits, as in the case of payments of wages, remunerations, etc., higher than current ones. In principle, a social enterprise must reward its factors of production at market rates, in order to prevent resources from deviating from their principal (common benefit) destination. Imposing a ceiling on the benefits that a member or a director of a general interest cooperative may receive from their participation seems very important in order to protect the general interest purpose of this particular type of cooperative.

4. COOPERATIVE AUDIT

4.1. SOURCES AND GENERAL OBSERVATIONS

Under Italian law, all types of cooperatives are subject to external control. The matter is dealt with in Law 2 August 2002, no. 220, on cooperative vigilance (as regards subjects, contents, forms, procedures, etc.), and partly in the Civil

[60] A different situation would be that in which cooperative refunds are attributed to the beneficiaries of the social cooperative who might also happen to be members.

Code (as regards some possible sanctions: art. 2545-*sexiesdecies* to art. 2545-*octiesdecies*). Special provisions apply to credit cooperative banks (art. 18, para. 1, Law no. 220/2002 and Ministerial Decree 22 December 2005) and may be found for other particular types of cooperatives. Moreover, in some Italian regions (e.g. Trentino-Alto Adige: regional Law 9 July 2008, no. 5) there is an autonomous regulation of cooperative vigilance.

To be sure, the Italian Constitution already refers to the control of cooperatives when it stipulates in article 45 that: 'The Republic recognises the social function of the cooperation with mutual character and without private speculation purposes. The law promotes and favours its growth with the most adequate means, and ensures, through appropriate controls, its character and purposes.'

This provision raises a doubt concerning whether the control of cooperatives (which in any case must be 'appropriate') is a consequence of their character and purposes *per se*, or of State promotion, and therefore whether it is the particular legal nature of cooperatives that *per se* calls for a regime of external public control (to ensure respect of their distinct legal nature), or whether it is the particular promotional treatment awarded by the State to cooperatives that justifies such control. Considering that Italian law subjects both PMCs and OCs to external control, it seems that in Italy the former view is the one adopted, i.e. that the external control is an intrinsic part of the cooperative legal identity, which it aims at ensuring, and not (only) a consequence of State promotion.

Italian legal scholars generally maintain that, under Italian law, cooperatives are the only type of business organisation subject to external control as regards compliance with the organisational law applicable to them. This is correct, although some points should be emphasised.

In fact, on the one hand, cooperatives are the only type of entity (hence, not only of business organisation) subject to external control, because the external control of Italian associations and foundations is not as extensive and pervasive as that of cooperatives; on the other hand, listed companies are subject to a form of control by a special authority (CONSOB) which may involve inquiry into respect for the latter's organisational law.

Furthermore, social enterprises established under Law no. 155/2006 are subject to external control (by the Ministry of Labour and Social Policies). They are so notwithstanding the fact that they are not recipients of a special tax treatment. The control is indeed directed toward ascertaining compliance with the law on social enterprises. This reinforces the idea that the Italian legal system links the public control to the social function of the organisation *per se* (which stems from the pursuit of either a general interest or a mutual aim without speculative purposes).

According to article 2511 ICC, cooperatives must be registered in two separate registers: the Register of Enterprises and the Register of Cooperative Societies (cooperatives obtain a registration number in the latter registry which they must show in their documents and correspondence: art. 7, Ministerial Decree no. 14907/2004). While registration in the former (maintained by the Chambers of Commerce) is necessary for cooperative incorporation, registration in the latter (maintained by the Ministry of Economic Development-Direction General for Cooperative Entities, which, as we shall see, is also responsible for cooperative control) is necessary for the cooperative's eligibility for tax and other benefits (art. 15, para. 1, Legislative Decree no. 220/2002). The Register of Cooperative Societies is divided into three sections: the first for PMCs; the second for OCs; and the third for 'mutual-aid societies' of Law 15 April 1886, no. 3818 (see Ministerial Decree no. 14907/2004). In any event, registration in both registries follows from a single communication by the cooperative to the Chamber of Commerce. Data are then transferred by the latter to the Ministry of Economic Development (MED).

4.2. CONTENTS AND OBJECTIVES

The MED is responsible for the 'vigilance' of cooperatives, which it carries out through 'cooperative revisions' and 'extraordinary inspections' (art. 1, para. 1, Legislative Decree no. 220/2002).

In general, the law states that the purpose of vigilance is to ascertain the 'mutual requirements' (art. 1, para. 2, Legislative Decree no. 220/2002) and that the public bodies responsible perform their tasks 'exclusively in the public interest' (art. 1, para. 4*bis*, Legislative Decree no. 220/2002).

More in particular, according to article 4, para. 1, Legislative Decree no. 220/2002, 'cooperative revision' (which is the ordinary form of control) is intended to:

(i) provide suggestions and advice to cooperative organs so that they can improve the management and the level of internal democracy, with the purpose of promoting members' real participation in social life;
(ii) ascertain the entity's mutual nature, by verifying the effectiveness of membership, members' participation in social life and engagement in mutual transactions with the cooperative, the quality of said participation, the absence of lucrative purposes, and the entity's eligibility for tax, social security and other benefits.

Revision also verifies financial stability and the existence of the prescribed internal regulation on worker members (in worker cooperatives only).

Extraordinary inspections have an even broader scope (art. 9 Legislative Decree no. 220/2002): They verify the general observance of laws, regulations, statutes; the presence of the requirements concerning eligibility for tax, social security and other benefits; regularity of functioning; state of assets, etc.

These rules confirm that the objective of the external control is to verify that the cooperative observes the rules regulating its function (mutual purpose) and structure (democracy, member control, participation, etc.), i.e. its organisational law. Eligibility for tax benefits is only one of the matters subject to control and not even the most important one. Consistently, the control includes advice to cooperatives on how to act properly according to their nature.

In conclusion, control is linked to, and justified by, the distinct legal identity of cooperatives under organisational law. Such control aims at protecting and preserving this legal identity, because it ensures the social function of cooperatives. This also makes it possible to protect the image of a cooperative to the benefit of other cooperatives and the cooperative movement at large.

Of course, given its extent, which involves financial stability, control further protects creditors indirectly, as well as all those who might benefit from reserves accumulated by the cooperative (including the cooperative movement).

4.3. SUBJECTS

All cooperatives are subject to control regardless of whether they are PMCs or OCs, large or small, SPA cooperatives or SRL cooperatives, and also regardless of the activity performed. The only exemptions concern popular banks and insurance cooperatives. Also consortia of cooperatives and cooperative groups are subject to control, and so too are social cooperatives. Cooperative control does not exempt cooperatives from other forms of control by other authorities based on the activity performed and concerning the respect of the regulations thereof (e.g. publishing, insurance, banking, etc.).

The MED is responsible for the 'vigilance' of cooperatives, which it performs through its own employees or employees of other public bodies (art. 7, para. 1 and 2, Legislative Decree no. 220/2002).

However, cooperatives that are members of a National Association of Cooperatives are controlled by the latter through its revisers (art. 2, para. 4, Legislative Decree no. 220/2002). These associations are to be recognised by the MED (art. 3, para. 1, Legislative Decree no. 220/2002). For this to happen, the Association must have at least 2,000 member cooperatives in at least five Italian regions and active in at least three cooperative sectors (e.g. consumer, production, social, etc.) (art. 3, para. 3, Legislative Decree no. 220/2002).

It is worth mentioning that the revisers of the Associations may also control non-associated cooperatives if the MED decides to avail itself of them on the basis of specific agreements with the Associations (art. 7, para. 2, Legislative Decree no. 220/2002).

All revisers must qualify for vigilance through specific training (furnished by the MED or the Associations depending on the case) which should provide them with the competence necessary to perform cooperative revisions.

Extraordinary inspections, on the other hand, are always conducted by the MED through its own functionaries or functionaries from other public bodies (art. 8 Legislative Decree no. 220/2002). These are called 'inspectors' and possess a series of powers of inspection.

4.4. FORMS, PROCEDURES AND OUTCOMES

As said, cooperative vigilance comprises 'cooperative revisions' and 'extraordinary inspections'.[61] The former is the ordinary form of control and normally takes place every two years (every year in the case of social cooperatives). The latter is an extraordinary form and may be carried out at any time by the MED, whenever a need for it arises.

The costs of the ordinary revision are borne by the cooperative (by joining Associations or by contributing to them or the MED), while the costs of extraordinary inspections are borne by the MED.

The entire process of vigilance is documented by minutes, the models of which must be approved by the MED (art. 1, para. 3, Legislative Decree no. 220/2002).

If a cooperative has an urgent need for a certificate of revision, it may explicitly request it from the MED or its Association (art. 2, para. 5, Legislative Decree no. 220/2002). In the meantime, if necessary, it may self-declare that it fulfils the mutual requirements (art. 6 Legislative Decree no. 220/2002). The provision according to which 'Associations have the obligation to subject their member cooperatives to revision' (art. 2, para. 6, Legislative Decree no. 220/2002) shows that revision is for a cooperative both an obligation and an entitlement.

Revision may conclude in one of the following ways:

(i) if no irregularities are found, a certificate of revision is issued (and a copy transmitted to the MED) (art. 5, para. 1–3, Legislative Decree no. 220/2002);
(ii) the reviser issues an injunction to remove irregularities within a certain term (art. 5, para. 4, Legislative Decree no. 220/2002); after that, if the irregularities have been removed, a certificate of revision is issued; otherwise, a sanction is applied;
(iii) if irregularities are found for which a sanction should be applied, the reviser transmits the minutes of the revision to the MED and proposes a sanction.

---

61 There is another form of vigilance for larger cooperatives, namely, the certification of accounts, which however is not worth describing here: see art. 11 Legislative Decree no. 220/2002.

Depending on the situation and the type of irregularity found, those below are the sanctions that may be inflicted:

(a) cancellation from the Register of Cooperative Societies (art. 12, para. 1, *a*, Legislative Decree no. 220/2002): apparently the MED holds that this sanction, although still provided for by law, cannot apply because it has been repealed and/or replaced by others;
(b) suspension of any activity for a semester (art. 12, para. 5*bis*, Legislative Decree no. 220/2002): this applies when a cooperative does not obey the injunction to remove irregularities within the term established, fails to communicate its annual accounting data to the MED, or fails to communicate that it has lost the quality of a PMC. This sanction does not exclude the application of other sanctions;
(c) monetary sanction from 50,000 euros to 500,000 euros (art. 12, para. 5*ter*, Legislative Decree no. 220/2002): when a cooperative subtracts itself from vigilance or in the cases *sub* b) above;
(d) government-appointed commissioner (art. 2545*sexiesdecies* ICC): when a cooperative does not function regularly, especially with regard to the admission of new members (or the violation of the internal regulation on worker members), there ensues revocation of the organs and the appointment of a commissioner (who must be paid by the cooperative) whose task is to remove the irregularities while also running the cooperative's ordinary business;
(e) compulsory liquidation (art. 2545*septiesdecies* ICC): when a cooperative has not operated for two consecutive years, or has not deposited its accounts for two consecutive years (this is a compulsory measure for the MED to adopt in the event that a cooperative has not done so for five consecutive years), or does not or cannot pursue a mutual purpose; this measure can be taken with or without the appointment of liquidation commissioners; it also leads to the cooperative's cancellation from the registers;
(f) substitution of liquidators (art. 2545*septiesdecies* ICC): when the liquidation of a cooperative is conducted in an irregular manner or is excessively delayed.

4.5. PUBLIC CONTROL AND JUDICIAL CONTROL

Cooperatives may also be subject to judicial control upon denunciation of serious irregularities in the management of the cooperative by members who hold at least one-tenth of the capital or by one-tenth of total members (one-twentieth in the case of cooperatives with more than 3,000 members) (art. 2545 *quinquiesdecies*, para. 1, ICC). The recourse to the court must be notified to the

MED. If the MED has already appointed an inspector or a commissioner for the same irregularities, the judicial recourse may not continue. Conversely, if the court has already appointed an inspector or a commissioner for the same irregularities, the procedure before the MED is suspended.

Following article 2409 ICC, the powers of the court and the measures that it may adopt are more or less the same as those that the MED has and may adopt: power of inspection; appointment of a judicial commissioner from which the compulsory liquidation may follow.

On this point, Italian law shows a duplication of external controls which should be avoided in an adequate cooperative legislation.

5. COOPERATION AMONG COOPERATIVES

5.1. COOPERATIVE INTEGRATION IN ITALIAN LAW

Elsewhere we have assessed Italian cooperative law as a sophisticated and cooperative-enhancing cooperative law, as demonstrated by the considerable number of existing cooperatives and the presence of a large and active national cooperative movement.[62]

Indeed, Italian cooperative law promotes not only the establishment of individual cooperatives (thus increasing their total number) but also their integration (thus fuelling a strong and well-organised cooperative movement).[63] Both the 'economic' and the 'socio-political' forms of cooperative integration receive careful attention from the Italian legislature, through measures that both include cooperatives' obligations to the cooperative movement (and, conversely, obligations of the cooperative movement – or rather, of its representative institutions – to cooperatives) and provide legal structures of integration that cooperatives may choose for conducting business together. Although, in principle, economic and socio-political integration are considered by Italian law and have, historically, evolved separately, the latter has progressively involved economic activities to promote the cooperative movement, as we shall see in the following analysis.

---

62 Cf. A. Fici, 'Italy', in D. Cracogna, A. Fici and H. Henrÿ (eds.), *International Handbook of Cooperative Law*, Springer, Heidelberg, 2013, p. 480. According to Euricse, 'La cooperazione in Italia', *1° Rapporto Euricse*, November 2011, the number of active cooperatives as of 31 December 2008 is 71,578, with 1,155,290 employees and €91.8 billion in turnover. The Italian National Institute of Statistics (ISTAT), in its 2011 Industry and Services Census, counted 1,200,585 employees in cooperative enterprises.

63 For a brief history of the subject and further references, cf. S. Zamagni and V. Zamagni, *Cooperative Enterprise*, Edward Elgar, Cheltenham, 2011, pp. 46 ff.

We have referred above to two forms – 'economic' and 'socio-political' – of cooperative integration. The analysis of Italian cooperative law as regards cooperative integration will in fact take these two forms into distinct consideration.

In the cooperative sector, indeed, two main specific objectives of cooperative integration may be identified, to which two distinct forms of integration correspond: The first may be termed 'socio-political'; the second, 'economic'.[64] To quote Charles Gide, 'one [is] to develop the spirit of solidarity among the societies and to guide the co-operative movement; the other to bulk purchases, and, if possible, organise production'.[65] Hence, this distinction is mainly based on the objectives, and not on the nature of the activities necessary to achieve them; activities that therefore may be economic or not, which may also affect, as we shall see, the choice of the legal form for performing the function.

5.2. SECONDARY COOPERATIVES (CONSORTIA OF COOPERATIVES)

A 'consortium of cooperatives' is the traditional form of economic cooperation among Italian cooperatives.[66] Notwithstanding its denomination, which is also found in the legislation, a consortium of cooperatives is in fact a secondary cooperative (i.e. a cooperative of cooperatives) established with the aim of serving its member cooperatives through economic activities that satisfy their particular needs as consumers or providers of the (secondary) cooperative enterprise. Indeed, because it is a (secondary) cooperative, a consortium of cooperatives pursues a mutual purpose as would any other cooperative. Its objective is to conduct an enterprise in the interest of its member cooperatives as consumers or providers of that enterprise. Between a consortium and its member cooperatives, there exist mutual (or cooperative) transactions that are of the same nature as those occurring in primary cooperatives.

The above feature (i.e. the legal nature of consortia as cooperatives) explains why the specific regulation of consortia of cooperatives under Italian law is very limited, so that consortia are subject to the same regulations as primary

64 In the classification made by other authors, a partially different terminology appears, although the substance remains the same. For example, C. Gide, *Consumers' Co-operative Societies* [a translation of the third French edition published in 1917], Co-operative Union Limited, Manchester, 1921, pp. 122 ff., uses 'social' and 'commercial', respectively; G. Fauquet, *The Co-operative Sector* [a translation of the fourth French edition published in 1942], Co-operative Union Limited, Manchester, 1951, p. 28, refers to groups with 'social aims' and groups with 'economic aims'.

65 C. Gide, n. 64 above, p. 122.

66 In the Italian legal literature, see, on this subject (and also for further references), Bonfante, n. 21 above, pp. 349 ff.

cooperatives, with only a few exceptions.[67] This specific regulation either concerns consortia directly or applies to them indirectly, when and inasmuch as the law deals with legal entities or entrepreneurs as possible members of a cooperative (which are the categories of members to which cooperatives that are members of consortia belong).

Consortia of cooperatives may be established given a minimum of three member cooperatives and a minimum subscribed capital of 516 euros.[68] A consortium's statutes may confer on its member cooperatives more than one vote (but no more than five) in the MM in proportion to the amount of the capital held or the number of their members[69] – a structure that deviates (although within certain limits) from the 'one member, one vote' rule. In addition, a consortium's statutes may confer on its member cooperatives more votes in the MM in proportion to the mutual transactions that each cooperative carries out with the consortium. This is, however, limited by the fact that a given privileged member may have no more than 10% of the total votes in each MM; moreover, all privileged members, together, may have no more than one-third of the total votes in each MM.[70] Derogations from the 'one member, one vote' rule in secondary cooperatives are therefore possible and potentially useful in dealing with a heterogeneous membership.[71]

More than for its specific contents (which, as said, are very limited), the regulation of consortia of cooperatives as cooperatives (consisting) of cooperatives is important simply because it exists. Indeed, not only does it provide cooperatives with the ability to form secondary cooperatives (which, in any event, would stem from the circumstance that Italian cooperative law does not limit cooperative membership to physical persons, as may be the case in other jurisdictions) but, more importantly, it also indicates (but does not mandate) the path to economic integration between cooperatives: namely, a structure with the legal form of a cooperative, which, as already stated, should be considered the most natural form of economic integration among cooperatives.

---

67 This is not to state that the specific regulation of secondary cooperatives *should* be limited; rather, the intention is only to give an account of the current state of Italian legislation on this point.

68 See art. 27, paras. 2 and 3, Legislative Decree no. 1577/1947. The minimum number of three members is in line with what European laws provide with regard to cooperatives in general and also with the provisions of Italian law with regard to primary cooperatives (see art. 2522, para. 2, ICC).

69 In fact, this option is given, not only to cooperatives comprised of cooperatives but, more generally, to cooperatives with regard to their members who are legal persons (art. 2538, para. 3, ICC).

70 This rules applies more generally to all cooperatives consisting of entrepreneurs (art. 2538, para. 4, ICC).

71 In addition, they do not conflict with the ICA Principles, where the 'one member, one vote' rule is explicitly referred to only to primary cooperatives, while as regards cooperatives at other levels it is simply stated that they 'are also organized in a democratic manner'.

Under Italian law, however, cooperatives may choose other legal forms for their economic integration, as will be illustrated in the following section.

5.3. COOPERATIVE-OWNED CAPITALIST COMPANIES

Italian law does not prevent cooperatives from establishing limited liability companies (SRLs) or joint-stock companies (SPAs) to which to entrust the economic activities that might serve their interests. Indeed, Italian law allows cooperatives (and consortia of cooperatives) to hold shares or stocks of companies, and even a single cooperative (or consortium of cooperatives) to control them.[72]

This power also allows a single cooperative to establish a 'heterogeneous cooperative group' as a result of controlling and directing one or more non-cooperative companies as subsidiaries (which, in their turn, may control and direct other companies as subsidiaries). Italian cooperatives have made use of this structure to expand their business.[73]

This legal pattern, however, may also be used as an alternative to the secondary cooperative (or consortium of cooperatives) form of cooperative integration, since nothing precludes co-ownership, by a plurality of cooperatives, of the stocks or shares of companies. Two or more cooperatives could thus establish a limited liability or joint-stock company to conduct economic activity in order to satisfy a common interest (e.g. two agricultural cooperatives could establish a company to market their collective produce).

This alternative form of economic integration does not in principle conflict with cooperative identity, since integration would, in any event, be 'horizontal' given that the resulting company would be controlled by the cooperatives (and not the other way round). It leads, however, to a different structure of relationships between the integrated cooperatives, since the resulting entity is subject to company law rather than cooperative law.[74] Therefore, unlike in the

---

72 See art. 27*quinquies*, Legislative Decree no. 1577/1947, which was introduced by art. 18, Law 19 March 1983, no. 72, as well as article 15, Law no. 59/1992.

73 'Heterogeneous' because the group consists of one cooperative (as the parent entity) and one (or more) non-cooperative companies (as subsidiaries). In contrast, a 'homogenous' group is defined such if it consists entirely of cooperatives. The potential for a cooperative to control a company has raised the question of whether a pure holding cooperative (i.e. a cooperative that solely holds stocks or shares of companies) is legitimate under Italian law. The main issue is how to connect a mutual purpose (which, under Italian law, characterises cooperatives) to a cooperative that simply holds companies' capital without directly performing any economic activity with its members. According to Bonfante, n. 21 above, pp. 363 ff., the holding cooperative is legitimate insofar as the mutual purpose is indirectly pursued through the subsidiaries ('indirect mutuality').

74 This also implies that, in principle, the tax treatment (as well as other specific regulations) of cooperatives does not apply to a company controlled by cooperatives but, in contrast, applies

case of secondary cooperatives, integration into a company does not ensure that all cooperatives (or, consequently, all their members) equally control the structure of economic coordination. This creates risks in terms of cooperative identity (of the primary cooperatives) and explains why the secondary cooperative, in addition to being the most traditional form in the history of the cooperative movement, is also usually considered the most natural form of economic cooperation among cooperatives. Nothing excludes, however, that the subsidiary companies are *de facto* (as well as by an appropriate choice of clauses in their statutes) run in a manner that is respectful of the cooperative principles, so as to give each cooperative the real opportunity to participate in their control.[75]

5.4. THE JOINT COOPERATIVE GROUP

A new entity, which was introduced by the 2003 reform of Italian company and cooperative law and which may be relevant to the present discussion, since it seems to allow for a new form of economic cooperation among cooperatives, is the 'joint cooperative group' (*gruppo cooperativo paritetico*), as provided for by article 2545*septies* ICC.

The joint cooperative group is defined by law as a contract whereby two or more cooperatives, which may also belong to different categories, regulate the direction and coordination of their respective enterprises. The legal regulation of the subject is very brief. The law indirectly states that the contract must have a final term; that the group may be directed by one or more cooperatives; that public or private non-cooperative entities may be admitted; and that any cooperative has the right to withdraw without penalty if the conditions of the exchange have become detrimental to its members as a result of joining the group.

The contents, purposes and boundaries of this new entity are still unclear. For example, a legal scholar argues that this contract produces only internal effects among the parties, does not create a legal entity that may have legal relationships with third parties, has no mutual purpose, and does not institute real integration among cooperative enterprises.[76]

What seems more certain is that the joint cooperative group is a flexible structure that may be adapted by the parties to assume many functions and

---

to a secondary cooperative (which may be another practical reason for choosing this more traditional form for cooperative integration).

75 The issue raised in the text has, of course, no relevance for cases in which a consortium of cooperatives controls a company (since, in such cases, there would only be a single parent organisation, that is, the consortium of cooperatives).

76 See in this regard, BONFANTE, n. 21 above, pp. 374 f.

pursue many objectives; on the other hand, this form of integration is based on the 'substantial' equal treatment of all parties involved, with particular regard to the distribution of the group's economic results (rather than its governance, since direction, as said, may be entrusted to one or more cooperatives within the group). Indeed, the law stipulates that the contract establishing the group must state 'the criteria of compensation and the equilibrium in the distribution of the benefits from the common activity'; moreover, it confers on the parties the right to withdraw when participation in the group becomes economically unsatisfactory to them (or, rather, to their members). This also explains why the group has been termed 'joint' (*paritetico*), and even more appropriately should have been termed 'equal' (*paritario*).[77]

If one shares this view, the joint cooperative group may be seen as a true alternative to the secondary cooperative (or consortium of cooperatives) for economic integration among cooperatives. The group under article 2545*septies* ICC is, no doubt, of a more hierarchical character than the consortium, since one cooperative may direct the activity of the others. This might raise serious doubts in regard to cooperative identity (since a cooperative should not be subject to external control); these doubts, however, may be overlooked, considering that in no case may a group share the benefits (and/or the costs) of the common activity unequally among its participant cooperatives and that, in any event, each cooperative may always withdraw from the group at its convenience, thereby making the governance of the group more collaborative than it may initially appear.[78]

5.5. THE NATIONAL ASSOCIATIONS OF THE COOPERATIVE MOVEMENT AND THE MUTUAL FUNDS

Thus far we have dealt with the forms and structures of cooperative integration with regard to economic activity. This section, however, is devoted to the form of integration that we have termed 'socio-political'.

The key subjects of socio-political integration, under Italian law, are the 'national associations of representation, assistance and protection of the cooperative movement', as they are literally referred to by Italian law,[79] and the

---

77 See Bonfante, n. 21 above, p. 369. It is significant that Spanish legal scholarship (see G. Soler, S. Bergia and V. Vasserot, *Regimen jurídico de la sociedad cooperativa del siglo XXI*, Dykinson, Madrid, 2009, p. 553) uses 'equal' (*paritario*) to qualify the cooperative group to which art. 78, para. 1, of Spanish State cooperative law makes reference, since this group is very similar to the Italian cooperative group.

78 Shared governance, in fact, here materialises *ex post* rather than *ex ante*, as in the case of secondary cooperatives.

79 See arts. 11, para. 1, Law no. 59/1992, and 2, para. 4, Legislative Decree no. 220/2002. However, these are usually known as '*centrali*' (in Italian) or 'federations'. The largest ones

'mutual funds for the promotion and development of cooperation' which the former may establish. The cooperative auditing function also plays a fundamental role in shaping an integrated cooperative system in Italy, which, as we shall see, is based on compulsory contributions from individual cooperatives and indirect legal incentives for participation.

National associations may be recognised as cooperative auditing associations by ministerial decree if they have no fewer than 2,000 associated cooperatives based in at least five Italian regions and operating in at least three sections (as defined by the type of mutual relationship) of the national register of cooperatives. In addition, they must give evidence of their qualification with regard to auditing functions.[80]

As already explained, cooperative audit is mandatory for all cooperatives (with only some exceptions), and the legally recognised associations of the cooperative movement play a fundamental role in the cooperative audit. In fact, such associations audit their member cooperatives.[81] In contrast, cooperatives that are not members of any association are audited by the State (*rectius*, by the MED, which also conducts extraordinary inspections when necessary); however, in performing this function, the MED may choose to avail itself of qualified auditors from the recognised associations.[82]

Obviously, this regulation of the cooperative audit generates incentives for cooperatives to become members of an association of the cooperative movement, since being audited by their association is preferable to being controlled by the State or by auditors of associations that they have decided not to join, especially when these cooperatives must, in any case, bear the costs of the audit, as is the case under Italian law.[83] Thus, this regulation certainly helps to reinforce the national cooperative movement, since, although participation in auditing associations is not compulsory, it is strongly encouraged by the cooperative audit regime. Additionally, by performing the auditing function entrusted to them, the auditing associations may contribute to the development of a certain cooperative movement, with certain characteristics and qualities (e.g., in terms of effective member participation, real democracy, etc.).

In accordance with article 3, Legislative Decree no. 220/2002, the same associations eligible for the auditing function may establish mutual funds for

---

are, at present, Confcooperative and Legacoop (which, together with the AGCI, established, in 2011, the 'Alliance of Italian cooperatives', as a structure of coordination among them).

80 See art. 3, Legislative Decree no. 220/2002.

81 See art. 2, para. 4, Legislative Decree no. 220/2002.

82 See art. 7, para. 2, Legislative Decree no. 220/2002. More precisely, the arrangement referred to in the text regards only ordinary audit, namely, cooperative revision, whereas extraordinary inspections are always conducted by the MED through its functionaries or functionaries of other public bodies (art. 8).

83 See art. 8, Legislative Decree 14 December 1947, no. 1577.

the promotion and development of the cooperation.[84] These funds must have the exclusive purpose of promoting and funding new enterprises and initiatives of cooperative development. To this end, they may promote the establishment of cooperatives and consortia of cooperatives, as well as own shares of cooperatives or subsidiary companies established by them. The mutual funds may also fund specific projects for the development of cooperatives and consortia of cooperatives, organise and manage the training of managers of the cooperative sector, or promote studies and research on economic and social topics relevant to the cooperative movement.[85]

What is particularly to be highlighted here is the system of building these funds, which is based on compulsory contributions from the cooperatives belonging to the national association that promoted the institution of the mutual fund. These cooperatives are obligated to allocate 3% of their annual net profits to the mutual funds.[86] In addition, when a cooperative (or, more precisely, a PMC) is dissolved or transformed into another type of company, its residual assets, subtracting only the paid-up capital and the dividends due but not yet distributed, are devolved to the mutual funds.[87]

Cooperatives (and consortia of cooperatives) that are not members of any national association are also subject to these obligations; however, they contribute to a public fund with purposes similar to those of the mutual funds.[88] Again, as observed with regard to the cooperative audit, this is a measure by which Italian law pushes cooperatives to become members of cooperative representative associations.

Along the same lines, state promotion of the cooperative movement also comprises a specific and supportive tax treatment of cooperatives' mandatory contributions to the mutual funds (3%): These contributions are tax-exempt for the funds and tax-deductible for the cooperatives.[89]

Undoubtedly, this regime favours the development of a well-structured cooperative movement as a sort of distinct subject or actor which operates 'beside' (but also, if one considers the role of promotion and control, 'behind'

84 See art. 11, para. 1, Law no. 59/1992. More precisely, these funds are not managed directly by the national association but by an association or a joint-stock company (SPA) established *ad hoc*, in both cases without a profit purpose (art. 11, para. 1). At least 80% of the stock capital of the company so established must be held by the national association (art. 12, para. 1), while if the mutual funds are managed by an association, it is automatically comprised of all the cooperatives and consortia of cooperatives that are members of the national association. On the legal issues raised by this regulation, see recently G. Bosi, *Fondi mutualistici. Un'analisi giuridica ed economica*, Il Mulino, Bologna, 2012, pp. 80 ff.

85 See art. 11, paras. 2 and 3, Law no. 59/1992.

86 See art. 11, para. 4, Law no. 59/1992, and art. 2545*quater*, para. 2, ICC.

87 Art. 2514, para. 1, d), ICC, and art. 11, para. 5, Law no. 59/1992.

88 See art. 11, para. 6, Law no. 59/1992.

89 See art. 11, para. 9, Law no. 59/1992.

and 'above', respectively) the individual cooperatives and their consortia. Compulsory contributions are the distinguishing feature of this cooperative system, and they have the clear objectives of increasing the number of existing cooperatives and of fostering solidarity in the movement (so that existing and larger cooperatives help create new cooperatives or develop smaller ones). It also shows that the development of the cooperative movement may be fostered by the State, not by forcing cooperatives to take part, but, rather, by offering proper incentives to do so. It finally demonstrates that the representative associations of the cooperative movement may also promote it through sophisticated economic activities, such as participation in the capital of cooperative start-ups.

CHAPTER 10
PORTUGAL

Deolinda Meira

1. DEFINITION AND OBJECTIVES OF COOPERATIVES

1.1. INTRODUCTION

The comments that follow focus on the definition and objectives of cooperatives under Portuguese Law.

We will refer to these issues primarily from the standpoint of the Portuguese Cooperative Code (the PCC – 'Código Cooperativo Português')[1] – which also forms the basis for our study – and consider the legal texts governing each of the twelve types of cooperative. According to article 4 of the PCC, there are twelve types of cooperative in Portugal today: consumer, trade, agricultural, credit, housing and building, worker, crafts, fishery, cultural, services, education, and social solidarity.[2]

It is explicitly permitted for one cooperative to operate in areas covered by more than one type: article 4.2 of the PCC distinguishes multi-purpose cooperatives (those covering more than one area of activity) from multi-sector cooperatives (those that carry out activities that are a feature of various types of cooperative within their sector).

It should be noted that cooperatives are granted separate legal status under Portuguese Law by the Constitution of the Portuguese Republic ('Constituição da República Portuguesa' – CRP), which dedicates more than a dozen articles to

---

1 Law no. 119/2015, which was published on 31.08.2015 and came into force on 30.09.2015. The first Portuguese cooperative law was the '*Lei Basilar do Cooperativismo*' (02.07.1867). In 1888, cooperatives came to be governed by the Veiga Beirão Commercial Code. In 1980, the first Cooperative Code (Decree-Law no. 454/80 of 09.10.1980) came into effect, followed by a new Cooperative Code in 1997 (Law no. 51/96), which was, however, amended by Decree-Law no. 343/98 of 06.11.1998; Decree-Law no. 131/99 of 21.04.1999; Decree-Law no. 108/2001 of 06.04.2001; Decree-Law no. 204/2004 of 09.08.2004; and Decree-Law no. 76-A/2006 of 29.03.2006. The current Code (the PCC) came into effect in 2015.

2 Decree-Law no. 335/99 of 20.08.1999 (agricultural cooperatives); Decree-Law no. 523/99 of 10.12.1999 (trade cooperatives); Decree-Law no. 522/99 of 10.12.1999 (consumer cooperatives); Decree-Law no. 24/91 of 11.01.1991, as amended by Decree-Law no. 230/95 of 12.09.1995, Decree-Law no. 320/97 of 25.11.1197, Decree-Law no. 102/99 of 31.03.1999 and Decree-Law no. 142/2009 of 16.06.2009 (credit unions); Decree-Law no. 313/81 of 19.11.1981 (cultural cooperatives); Decree-Law no. 441-A/82 of 06.11.1982 (education cooperatives); Decree-Law no. 502/99 of 19.11.1999 (housing and building cooperatives); Decree-Law no. 312/81 of 18.11.1981 (fisheries cooperatives); Decree-Law no. 309/81 of 16.11.1981 (worker cooperatives); Decree-Law no. 323/81 of 04.12.1981 (service cooperatives); and Decree-Law no. 7/98 of 15.01.1998 (social solidarity cooperatives).

them scattered throughout the constitutional text but nevertheless appropriately developed by means of a set of structuring principles, such as the principle of coexistence of the three sectors: the public sector, the private sector, and the cooperative and social sector (art. 82); the principle of freedom of cooperative initiatives (art. 61); the principle of protection of the social and cooperative sector (art. 80); the principle of the obligation of the State to encourage and support the creation of cooperatives (art. 85); and the principle of compliance with the ICA cooperative principles (art. 61.2 *in fine*).[3]

Company law must also be taken into account, particularly the provisions regarding joint stock companies, considering that article 9 of the PCC on the subsidiary law applicable to situations that are not foreseen in the PCC deals with 'the Commercial Companies Code ('Código das Sociedades Comerciais' – CSC), as long as cooperative principles are respected, particularly those sections that regulate joint-stock companies'. This subsidiary resource of the CSC is dependent on two conditions, however: first, that any solution complies with the cooperative principles, and secondly, within the scope of the CSC, that priority be given to the precepts applicable to joint-stock companies.[4]

1.2. DEFINITION, ESTABLISHMENT, AND LEGAL NATURE OF COOPERATIVES

A cooperative is defined in article 2.1 of the PCC as an 'autonomous association of persons, united voluntarily, of variable composition and capital, which, through cooperation and mutual assistance on the part of its members and in accordance with cooperative principles, aims not at profit but at satisfying the economic, social, or cultural needs and aspirations of said members.'

This definition is based on four distinctive features of this type of legal entity, the first two of which – variability of share capital and variability of the shareholding structure – are formal in nature and the other two – the social object of the cooperative (satisfaction of the economic, social, or cultural needs of members while remaining a non-profit entity) and the management methods of the cooperative (compliance with cooperative principles and cooperation and mutual assistance on the part of members) – are substantive.

---

[3] See D. Meira, 'O quadro jurídico-constitucional do cooperativismo em Portugal', *Cooperativismo e Economia Social*, 2011, 33, pp. 31–46.

[4] For an analysis of this issue, see M.C. Frada and D.C. Gonçalves, 'A acção *ut singuli* (de responsabilidade civil) e a relação do Direito Cooperativo com o Direito das Sociedades Comerciais', *Revista de Direito das Sociedades*, 2009, year I, 4, pp. 888–904; M.M. Rosas, 'A integração de lacunas do Código cooperativo e o recurso ao Direito Societário', in D. Meira (ed.), *Jurisprudência Cooperativa Comentada. Obra coletiva de comentários a acórdãos da jurisprudência portuguesa, brasileira e espanhola*, Imprensa Nacional-Casa da Moeda, Lisbon, 2012, pp. 333–345.

It is worth noting that as cooperatives are defined, compliance with cooperative principles is mandatory for the Portuguese legislator. These principles are embodied in article 3 of the PCC: voluntary and open membership; democratic member control; economic participation by members; autonomy and independence; education, training, and information; cooperation among cooperatives; and concern for the community.[5]

Cooperative principles are thus mandatory in the Portuguese legal system, and are even enshrined in the text of the Constitution. Article 61.2 of the CRP states that: 'Everyone is accorded the right to freely form cooperatives, subject to compliance with cooperative principles.' Article 82.4.a) of the CRP states that the cooperative sub-sector covers 'means of production that cooperatives possess and manage in accordance with cooperative principles.' Hence, a disregard for cooperative principles in business operations is a cause for dissolution (art. 112.1.h) of the PCC).

Cooperatives are legal entities: that is, they have a legal personality distinct from that of each of their members. This definition is taken from article 2.1 of the PCC, which recognises cooperatives as 'autonomous legal persons' – as separate legal entities distinct from the legal personality of their members – and from article 17 of the PCC, which states that a cooperative acquires legal personality at the moment when its incorporation is registered. This means that the legal personality of cooperatives necessarily implies autonomy of assets: a cooperative's assets are distinct and independent from the assets of its respective members.

The incorporation of primary cooperatives must be in writing, and may also involve more stringent formalities ('*forma mais solene*'), if required, 'for the transmission of the assets that represent the cooperators' initial share capital' (art. 10 of the PCC). Secondary degree cooperatives (cooperative unions, federations, and confederations) are governed by 'the provisions applicable to primary cooperatives' (arts. 101 and 107 of the PCC). The incorporation of a cooperative is decided by a meeting of its founding members (art.12 of the PCC). The board of the founders' meeting must take minutes that must mention its social object, assets and rights, and the work or services contributed by the members of the cooperative (art. 13 of the PCC).

The importance of using words or expressions that indicate the entity's cooperative nature is made explicit in article 15.1 of the PCC, which states that: 'the name adopted shall always be followed by the expressions "cooperative", "union of cooperatives", "federation of cooperatives", or "confederation of cooperatives", and also "limited liability" or "unlimited liability", or the respective abbreviations, as appropriate.' The use of the word 'cooperative' (like its abbreviation 'coop.') is not freely available, however; on the contrary, it is 'exclusively reserved for cooperatives and their higher-level organisations, and

5 See R. Namorado, 'A identidade cooperativa na ordem jurídica portuguesa', *Oficina do Centro de Estudos Sociais*, 2001, p. 157.

its adoption by others is a punishable offence, in addition to the corresponding civil liability.' Finally, no. 3 of the same article states that: 'the name shall be registered in the National Registry of Legal Persons.'

Establishment of a cooperative is subject to registration (art. 17 of the PCC and art. 4 of the Commercial Registration Code) and to publication on a public access Internet site (art. 70.1.b) of the Commercial Registration Code).

According to article 11 of the PCC, the number of members of a cooperative is variable and unlimited, but must be no less than three in primary cooperatives and two in higher-level cooperatives. Additional legislation concerning each branch may, however, require a larger minimum number of cooperators.[6]

Having established that cooperatives are legal entities pursuant to article 2 of the PCC, we will now address the issue of to what type of legal entity we are referring, since this type of organisation traditionally falls within several legal categories: collective associations, foundations, and companies ('*sociedades*').

However, despite the fact that they share the status of associations of persons in common, cooperatives are clearly distinguished from associations *strictu sensu*[7] whose legal regime is enshrined in articles 167 ff. of the Portuguese Civil Code. Associations are legal persons that do not have the purpose of carrying out an economic activity in a corporate form, but rather of pursuing a non-profit objective. In the strict sense, the term 'association' is inadequate to describe the cooperative concept, due not only to the business-related nature of cooperatives (art. 7 of the PCC), but also to the fact that the cooperative structure is endowed with features that are not compatible with the typical structures of associations. Two examples of this are share capital, which cooperatives have, but associations do not (art. 81 of the PCC) and member participation in business activities, which is a structural element in the life of cooperatives, as we shall see, but a merely circumstantial one in associations.

Similarly, cooperatives must not be confused with foundations, since the latter are the embodiment of assets, while cooperatives embody an association of people. As a matter of fact, pursuant to article 3.1 of the Framework Law on Foundations ('Lei-Quadro das Fundações'), approved by Law no. 24/2012 of 19 July 2012, a foundation is 'a legal person with a non-profit purpose endowed with sufficient assets and irrevocably assigned to pursuing a social objective.'

The most sensitive issue, however, is determining whether or not cooperatives are companies. Currently, the Portuguese literature seems to favour the notion that cooperatives are clearly distinguished from companies (in the sense of commercial companies, since one of the essential characteristics of companies

---

6 R. Namorado, 'Portugal', in D. Cracogna, A. Fici and H. Henrÿ (eds.), *International Handbook of Cooperative Law*, Springer, Heidelberg, 2013, pp. 635 ff.

7 The term '*association*' can be interpreted strictly or broadly: in the broad sense, 'association' refers to a group of people organised for the purpose of achieving a common goal, including companies (profit economic goal) and associations *strictu sensu* (ideal or economic non-profit goal).

is the distribution of profits (in the sense of capital accruals) among their shareholders.[8] We would like to express a certain disagreement with this doctrinal position. While it is true that article 2.1 of the PCC does not establish the legal nature of the cooperative, and also establishes that the purpose of a cooperative is not to make profit, this does not preclude its classification as a company, albeit a *sui generis* type that is not to be confused with any other kind of company recognised by Portuguese law. We adhere to the doctrine advocating that a profit motive is not an essential element of the definition of the term 'company', but merely a natural one that should be understood in a broad sense that also encompasses cost savings.[9] The essential element is the pursuit of a common economic activity aimed at the economic benefit of members. There is thus some identity between companies and cooperatives, which is the provision of assets or economic benefits for their members. It should be added that the legislator created a commercially-inspired system for cooperatives by applying the rules governing joint stock companies to them (art. 9 of the PCC), subjecting them to registration in the Register of Companies and to insolvency, and allowing them to carry on business with non-members, as we shall explain later.

In short, we believe that cooperatives should be considered companies (if we use the term 'profit' in its broadest sense), even though they have features that are distinct from those of civil and commercial companies, such as the existence of special purposes, including their fundamental mutualist vocation, which we shall discuss in more detail below.[10]

1.3. THE COOPERATIVE OBJECTIVE

Two dimensions are comprised in the cooperative objective: the economic and the social. This is a consequence of the definition of cooperatives in article 2.1 of the PCC, under which the purpose of a cooperative is a non-profit-related intersection of its members' economic, social, and cultural needs by adoption of a style of management that relies on compliance with cooperative principles and on mutual help and cooperation on the part of its members.

---

8 For advocates of this position, see, among others, V.G.L. Xavier, *Sociedades Comerciais. Lições aos alunos de Direito Comercial do 4.º Ano Jurídico*, photocopied text, Coimbra, 1987, pp. 21–23 and J.M.C. Abreu, *Da empresarialidade. As empresas no Direito*, Almedina, Coimbra, 1999, pp. 174 ff.

9 In Portuguese legal writings, we should highlight A.F. Correia, *Lições de Direito Comercial, Vol. II – Sociedades Comerciais. Doutrina Geral*, Universidade de Coimbra, Coimbra, 1968, pp. 19 ff, and J.H.P. FURTADO, *Curso de Direito das Sociedades*, 5th ed., Almedina, Coimbra, 2004, pp. 138 ff.

10 See D. Meira, 'A natureza jurídica da cooperativa. Comentário ao Acórdão do Supremo Tribunal de Justiça de 5 de Fevereiro de 2002', *Revista de Ciências Empresariais e Jurídicas*, 2006, 7, pp. 147–180.

1.3.1. *The Economic Dimension*

The economic dimension is described in article 2.1 of the PCC, which states that it is within the scope of a cooperative to 'meet the needs and economic aspirations' of its members.

Cooperatives are, in fact, enterprises dedicated to the production of goods and services with a rationale that entails the maximisation of results and the containment of costs. The term 'enterprise' is here understood in a broad sense as referring to any form of organisation of human, material, or financial resources that seeks to pursue economic purposes, whether or not they are profitable. We are, therefore, in the presence of a business organisation with stated economic aims that are pursued in an economical manner: that is, one designed to achieve, for the benefit of members, a cost of goods lower than could be obtained by other means. The economic dimension will always be present, even in cooperatives that pursue primarily cultural aims, because these aims meet needs that involve a cost, and thus have a price.

In the PCC, the importance attributed by the legislator to the predominant economic purpose of cooperatives becomes apparent, as illustrated in article 7: 'while complying with the law and cooperative principles, cooperatives may carry on any economic activity freely.'

It is, however, a business entity with the specific aim of pursuing a mutualist purpose, which means that a cooperative's corporate activities are necessarily directed towards its members, who are the main beneficiaries of the economic and social activities that it carries out.[11]

1.3.1.1. The Effects of the Mutualist Scope on the Relationship with Members

The mutualist scope of cooperatives generates a complex legal relationship that emphasises, on the one hand, the obligation assumed by a member to participate in the cooperative's business. and on the other, the return from the cooperative.[12]

Unlike stockholders in a commercial company, in fact, cooperators have an obligation not only to contribute to the share capital of the cooperative, but also to participate in the cooperative's transactions. In this regard, article 22.2.c) of the PCC states that members must 'participate in the general activities of the cooperative and provide the work or services assigned to them.'

---

11 On this issue, see C. Gonçalves, *Comentário ao Código Comercial português*, vol. I, Empresa Editora J. B., Lisbon, 1914, p. 541; and S. Correia, 'Elementos de um regime jurídico da cooperação', *Estudos Sociais e Cooperativos*, March 1966, 17, year V, p. 162.

12 See P. Duarte, 'Reflexos jurídico-obrigacionais da cooperatividade nos negócios jurídicos celebrados pelas cooperativas de habitação e construção', in Meira (ed.), n. 4 above, pp. 483–490.

To achieve the cooperative object, it is therefore necessary that cooperator members supply goods or products to the cooperative (as in an agricultural cooperative); produce goods or provide services within the cooperative (as in worker cooperatives); or pay for goods or services received from the cooperative (as in the case of consumer or housing cooperatives).

As we shall see, this obligation to participate in the cooperative's transactions emerges as the basic mechanism for developing the social object of a cooperative and achieving mutual benefits.

Further business activities and obligations arise out of the relationships established between the cooperative and its members in the course of its mutualist activity, on the legal nature of which the PCC is silent. However, the manner in which they are designated acquires great practical significance, since these activities are characterised as specific businesses with specific functions that do not fit properly into the traditional legal categories. On this view, when members deliver their agricultural products to a cooperative for business purposes, when they provides their work to a cooperative, when a housing cooperative delivers a house to a member, and when a consumer cooperative provides a service to its members, legal transactions of a particular type are always involved, with multiple consequent specificities: the subjects involved in the business (the cooperative and the member); the type of cooperative in question (trade, worker, housing, or other); the mutualist scope underlying the *cooperative social object*, translated into meeting the needs of members.

Given the silence on the part of the legislature, scholars and the courts are divided into two theoretical camps. On the one hand, there are those who share the dualist (or contractualist) theory, according to which this type of business falls outside the cooperative relationship and thus requires an appropriate designation for each case – a sales agreement, an agency agreement, or an employment agreement – and is subject to the relevant regulations. According to this theory, members assume the dual role of stockholder and contracting party. On the other hand, there are those who subscribe to the monistic (or corporate) theory, according to which these obligations and businesses are subsumed into the cooperative relationship as one of its dimensions, and may be seen as corresponding to statutory rights and obligations and being subject to the cooperative rules enshrined in the law and in statutes, internal regulations, and corporate resolutions.[13]

Given also that the PCC did not anticipate the legal category of a cooperative act[14] (which is provided for in Latin American legal systems) that would allow

---

13 See A.A. Martins, 'A relação jurídica entre cooperador trabalhador e cooperativa. Notas sobre a sua qualificação e regime', *Cooperativismo e Economia Social*, 2014, 36, pp. 39–46.

14 On the notion of 'cooperative act' see D. Cracogna, 'O acto cooperativo', *Pensamento Cooperativo – Revista de Estudos Cooperativos*, June 2002, 3, year 3, pp. 175–189.

a resolution of these doctrinal differences, and since this is a legal concept that frames transactions between cooperatives and their members and non-members in furtherance of their purpose, it is our opinion that it is up to the cooperative to choose how it relates with its members within the limits of the law and in compliance with its by-laws.[15] This freedom is understood within the broader scope of the cooperative's ability to choose the means by which it pursues its purpose: that is, the instruments of its mutualist activity.

1.3.1.2. The Effects of the Mutualist Scope in the Relationship with Non-Members

It must be noted, however, that the teleological connection between a cooperative and its members should not be understood in absolute terms: that is, cooperatives should not be considered to be closed organisations that operate solely with their members.

Indeed, the principle of mutuality, which is an underlying and distinctive feature of cooperatives, and one that distinguishes them from other legal entities, does not necessarily mean that a cooperative will conduct its business exclusively with its members: in fact, it may also work with non-members ('*terceiros*').

First, the possibility of entering into a contract with non-members demonstrates the social nature of cooperatives: they will satisfy the interests of their members regarding work, credit, and housing above all, while simultaneously being open for business with outside partners and offering their services to those who share the same needs, even though they are not members. Secondly, this new concept of mutuality makes cooperatives more competitive by enabling them to operate in the market by competing with other businesses in the provision of goods and services to non-members.

In line with this conception, article 2.2 of the PCC states that: 'in the pursuit of their purpose, cooperatives are allowed to conduct business with non-members, subject to any restrictions laid down in the law applicable to each type of cooperative.'

The PCC thereby eliminated the mandatory feature of conducting business with non-members as a complementary activity that was present in the previous legislation, Decree-Law no. 454/80 of 9 October 1980, which stated that cooperatives were allowed to 'carry out business transactions with non-members as a complementary activity.'

Although the law does not define what is meant by 'non-members', it seems to be agreed in the literature that in the wake of the teachings of Rui Namorado, 'from the cooperative point of view, non-members are those who have a business

---

15 In this regard, see R. Guichard, 'Capacidade das cooperativas. Relações entre cooperativas e cooperadores', Meira (ed.), n. 4 above, pp. 521–527.

relationship that is directly related to the performance of the cooperative's primary objective as if they were members, although, in fact, they are not.'[16]

What this means is that the business with non-members to which the legislator refers is of the same nature as that conducted by the cooperative with its members.

It is assumed that transactions with non-members may be subject to limitations in the sector-specific legislation of the various types of cooperative. These limitations are expressly provided for in the following provisions: article 9 of Decree-Law no. 523/99 of 10 December 1999 (trade cooperatives); article 7 of Decree-Law no. 313/81 of 19 November 1981 (cultural cooperatives); article 14 of Decree-Law no. 502/99 of 19 November 1999 (housing and building cooperatives); article 6 of Decree-Law no. 309/81 of 16 November 1980 (worker cooperatives); article 6 of Decree-Law no. 323/81of 4 December 1981 (service cooperatives); and articles 24.2 and 24.3 of Decree-Law no. 24/91 of 11 January 1991 (agricultural credit cooperatives). It is only in this last decree that limitations on credit transactions with non-members are fixed (35% of the cooperative's total net assets, which may be increased to 50% subject to authorisation by the Bank of Portugal).

It therefore follows that, under Portuguese Law, cooperatives are characterised by 'a predominantly, though not exclusively, mutualist purpose and may conduct business with non-members.'[17]

1.3.2. The Social Dimension

The social purpose of a cooperative is not limited to meeting the needs of its members, but must equally attend to the interests of the community within which the cooperative carries out its activity.

The principle of concern for the community is set forth in article 3 of the PCC, which states that: 'cooperatives work for the sustainable development of their communities through policies approved by their members.'

Thus, although they are primarily focused on the needs of their members, cooperatives also work to achieve the sustainable development of their communities pursuant to criteria approved by their members.

This principle is closely connected with another cooperative principle, that of voluntary and open membership; this is the traditional open-door principle as formulated in article 3 of the PCC: 'Cooperatives are voluntary organisations, open to all persons able to use their services and willing

---

16 R. Namorado, *Cooperatividade e Direito Cooperativo. Estudos e Pareceres*, Almedina, Coimbra, 2005, pp. 184–185.

17 D. Meira, 'As operações com terceiros no Direito Cooperativo Português (Comentário ao Acórdão do Supremo Tribunal de Justiça de 18 de Dezembro de 2007)', *Revista de Ciências Empresariais e Jurídicas*, 2010, 17, pp. 93–111.

to accept the responsibility of membership, without gender, social, racial, political, or religious discrimination.' This principle can be considered from two perspectives: firstly, joining must be voluntary, given that it depends exclusively on the will of the member; and secondly, the cooperative must be open to all, as long as candidates for membership meet two requirements: the ability to benefit from the cooperative's transactions, and acceptance of the responsibilities of membership.

The way in which these two principles connect is evident: the traditional open-door policy adopted by a cooperative when accepting new members is justified by a willingness to serve the community in which it has its roots. Taking on members from the area where the cooperative carries out its activities is a constant in this type of organisation, the ultimate goal of which is to meet the needs of the community. This practice reveals the role of cooperatives as generators of stable jobs – not least because, being deeply rooted in their community, cooperatives carry out activities that do not permit relocation – as well as fuel for the entrepreneurial spirit.

Thus, cooperatives have a special responsibility for ensuring that the development of their communities is economically, socially, and culturally sustainable.

Under these principles, cooperatives become involved in the social context, and thus it becomes their members' responsibility to decide on the policies through which this involvement will materialise.

Another principle of enormous relevance in defence of the claim that the purpose of cooperatives falls within the scope of socially-relevant activities is the principle of education, training, and information (art. 3 of the PCC). The law states that: 'cooperatives will provide education and training for their members, elected representatives, managers, and employees so that they can contribute effectively to the development of their cooperatives. They will inform the general public, particularly the young and opinion leaders, of the nature and benefits of cooperation' (art. 3 of the PCC). This principle emphasises the obligation of cooperatives to guarantee the education and training of their members, representatives of their elected bodies, directors, and employees in cooperative-related beliefs and actions. It also includes the duty to inform the general public in order to raise awareness of the nature and benefits of cooperation, which might encourage new, and especially informed, membership.

Finally, it should be noted that this principle is stated in the PCC, where it provides for a compulsory reserve fund 'for the cooperative education and technical and cultural training of members and employees of the cooperative, as well as of the community' (art. 97 of the PCC).

The establishment of reserves for education and training means that a cooperative is not only a business organisation, but also an organisation with social and educational concerns. The aim of this reserve fund is to bear the costs of activities beyond the satisfaction of the purely individual interests of cooperative members. These activities are not strictly of an economic nature, but may result in direct or indirect, immediate or deferred economic effects, both for the cooperative and for the community in which the cooperative operates.

This reserve is one of the most distinctive features of cooperatives compared with other types of enterprise. It generates assets that are allocated to social purposes for the benefit of members, cooperative workers, and the social environment.[18]

Finally, as further evidence of the social dimension of the cooperative object, we should note the principle of the disinterested distribution of assets. This principle is enunciated in article 114 of the PCC, which states that residual assets cannot be distributed among members on winding up. This emphasises the social role of cooperatives and means that in the end assets must be allocated to the promotion of cooperation.

Article 114.1 of the PCC further states that when a cooperative is wound up, any legal reserves that have not been allocated to cover losses in the financial year and cannot be used for any other purpose 'may be transferred with the same purpose to a new cooperative entity to be formed following the merger or division of the cooperative in liquidation.'

Paragraph 3 of the same article of the PCC states, however, that: 'where no new cooperative succeeds the cooperative in liquidation, the balance of the mandatory reserve will be allocated to another cooperative, preferably from the same city, to be determined by the federation or confederation that represents the main activity of the cooperative.'

Paragraph 4 goes even further when it states that: 'as to reserves established under the provisions of article 98 of this Code, in the event of liquidation and where the statutes do not provide otherwise, the provisions of paragraphs 2 and 3 of this article will apply', which means that any free reserves may also be covered by the principle of disinterested distribution.

1.4. COOPERATIVE SURPLUSES

The social object of cooperatives is clearly reflected in the system by which economic results are distributed.

This occurs according to use rather than on the basis of participation in the share capital, as is the rule for commercial companies. This means that returns are made according to participation in the social object: that is, in proportion to the volume of transactions carried out between each member and

18 On this principle, see D. Meira, *O regime económico das cooperativas no Direito Português: o capital social*, Editora Vida Económica, Porto, 2009, pp. 162–167.

the cooperative, and article 3 of the PCC consecrates the general orientation regarding the distribution of surpluses as 'benefiting members in proportion to their business with the cooperative.'

The cooperative surplus ('*excedente cooperativo*') is defined as an amount that members pay to the cooperative in excess of what the cooperative owes to its members in return for member participation in the cooperative's activities. A surplus is thus a result of business that has been carried out between the cooperative and its members and is generated by the members, constituting in this sense 'the result of a tacit waiver on the part of the members of immediate cooperative benefits.'[19]

This definition makes it clear that the concept of cooperative surplus stems from the pursuit of the cooperative's mutualist purpose.

1.5. COOPERATIVE REFUNDS

The cooperative surplus may be returned to members in the manner established by article 100.1 of the PCC, which provides that: 'with the exception of that resulting from transactions with non-members, and after payment of interest on capital contributions and appropriation to any legal or statutory reserve, the annual net surplus may be returned to the members.'

This precept states unequivocally that only cooperative surpluses resulting from transactions between the cooperative and its members can be returned to members. Conversely, economic results from transactions with non-members may not be distributed to members. The basis for this legal regime lies in the fact that, in cooperatives, income from business with non-members is legally regarded as profit and not as a true cooperative surplus, since it does not fall within the scope of the mutualist activity.

Cooperative refunds, which are understood here as the technical means whereby surpluses are assigned to members, are actually a deferred distribution of these same surpluses. This means that, after balancing and calculating net income, members of a cooperative are given back something to which they have been entitled since the beginning of the financial year. Cooperative refunds operate as a retrospective correction by which surpluses – the difference between prices charged and costs, or the difference between net income and advances paid for labour, accurately calculated at the end of each financial year – are returned to those who generated them.[20]

---

19 Namorado, n. 16 above, p. 183.

20 See J.M.C. Abreu, 'Empresas sociais (nótulas de identificação)', *Cooperativismo e Economia Social*, 2015, 37, pp. 373–374.

1.6. THE DISTINCTION BETWEEN PROFITS AND SURPLUSES

In order to understand the specificities of the right to cooperative refunds clearly, it is necessary to distinguish between cooperative surpluses and profits, or between cooperative refunds and dividends.

Indeed, even though cooperative refunds and dividends share the common feature of being sums that are periodically distributed among members/shareholders, they are not equivalent, and have significant differences.[21]

While dividends are a portion of the profits that is distributed among shareholders, cooperative refunds are not distributable profits, but cooperative surpluses: that is, mutual benefits generated by management of the cooperative that are, as we have seen, paid directly to members.

There are, however, other substantial differences deriving from the specificities of the social object of cooperatives that also deserve our attention.

1.6.1. The Criteria for the Distribution of Cooperative Surpluses

One of the primary distinguishing features between cooperative surpluses and profits relates to the criteria for their distribution.

In commercial companies, dividends must be paid in proportion to the shares held by each shareholder.[22] In a cooperative, the surplus generated by each member is a result of the business done with the cooperative and is in proportion to a mutualist exchange whereby each member is due a return (a cooperative refund) in proportion to this exchange. Profits are intended to remunerate a shareholder's investment, and are therefore distributed in proportion to that member's share of the capital, whereas a cooperative surplus is not intended to remunerate capital, but only to compensate members to the same extent as they have contributed to the generation of the cooperative surpluses.

Distribution of cooperative refunds among members is proportional to the business concluded by each of them with or for the cooperative during a given financial year. Since the surplus results from business between the cooperative and its members, and is thus generated by cooperative members, it is understandable that when a return (a cooperative refund) arises, it is made in proportion to the volume of this business, and not to the number of shares each member holds.

---

[21] On the distinction between dividends and cooperative refunds, see D. Meira, 'Revisitando o problema da distinção entre excedente cooperativo e lucro societário', in *II Congresso Direito das Sociedades em Revista*, Almedina, Coimbra, 2012, pp. 353–374.

[22] According to article 22.1 of the CSC, partners participate in a company's profits in proportion to the nominal value of their respective shares in the capital. On this criterion, see P.T. Domingues, 'Capital e património sociais. Lucros e reservas', in J.M.C. Abreu (ed.), *Estudos de Direito das Sociedades*, 12th ed., Almedina, Coimbra, 2015, pp. 194 ff.

The distribution of surpluses in proportion to the business carried out with the cooperative, and not on the basis of participation in share capital, owes its *raison d'être* to the fact that these surpluses represent the cooperative benefits that a member has obtained in precise proportion to the services provided by the cooperative that he or she has used: that is to say, the proportion of the returns allocated to him or her will be in direct relation to the use of these services.

Apart from the general guidelines enshrined in article 3 regarding a distribution of surpluses 'benefiting members in proportion to their business with the cooperative', we find no substantial explicit criteria in the PCC governing the distribution of cooperative surpluses. When referring to the distribution of surpluses, article 100 of the PCC, merely states that they 'may be returned to the members', and in the legislation applicable to the various types of cooperative, we find only general guidelines, and no explicit criterion for the distribution of surpluses. In relation to cultural cooperatives, Decree-Law no. 313/81 of 19 November 1981, states (in art. 8) that distribution will be 'proportional to the work of each member' and that it must comply with 'the criteria defined in the cooperative's statutes or internal regulations.' In the case of worker cooperatives, Decree-Law no. 309/81 of 16 November 1981 stipulates (in article 9) that after calculation of surpluses, 'payments made in advance to members' should be deducted before the distribution of any surplus. Finally, article 9 of the Law governing service cooperatives (Decree-Law no. 323/81 of 4 December 1981) states that in service cooperatives, surpluses will be distributed in proportion to each member's work, according to criteria defined in the statutes and/or internal regulations of the cooperative. In accordance with article 100 of the PCC, after the calculation of surpluses, payments made in advance to members must be deducted before distribution of the surplus.

This means that the legislator has merely outlined general guidelines regarding the allocation of surpluses, and has given cooperatives and their members the task of defining the criteria for allocating surpluses through their statutes,[23] in internal regulations, or at general meetings of the cooperatives.

1.6.2. Cooperative Surpluses are Generated from Business with Members

Unlike cooperatives, commercial companies are not created to do business with partners but to obtain benefits through the establishment of business relations with parties from outside the companies. In commercial companies, therefore, profits are obtained in the market, in transactions with customers, and outside the universe of their members.

---

[23] This possibility of defining rules for the distribution of surplus in statutes is also clear from article 16.2.a) of the PCC, which states that cooperative statutes may also include 'the conditions for the admission, suspension, exclusion, and dismissal of members and their rights and duties.'

Conversely, in cooperatives, as Hans-H. Münkner recalls: 'any surplus accrued from transactions with member-customers at the end of a financial year is not the result of efforts to accumulate profit in the cooperative enterprise at the expense of the member-customers who ... would then try to make profit out of themselves.'[24] The example of worker cooperatives serves as a paradigm for surpluses which are the result of the work of members and are distributed in proportion to the work performed. In the same way, the assertion is fully valid for other types of cooperative: if there is a surplus, it means that the member paid or received an amount above or below market price, thus abdicating any immediate mutual advantage.

To sum up, in commercial companies, economic advantage is generated at the expense of others, while in cooperatives it is generated at the expense of their own members.

1.7. THE ABSENCE OF A SUBJECTIVE RIGHT TO A COOPERATIVE REFUND

As in company law, which places special emphasis on the lack of a subjective right to the actual distribution of profits, in cooperative law it must also be said that inclusion among a cooperative members' rights of the right to a cooperative refund (art. 100.1 of the PCC) does not imply recognition of an (actual) right to have part of the cooperative surplus allocated to a cooperative refund in favour of the cooperator. The use of the words 'may be returned to the cooperators' by the legislator highlights the possibility that the right to cooperative refunds may be waived by a resolution of the General Meeting.

It should be noted first and foremost that in the case of cooperatives, a percentage of the cooperative surplus for a financial year will revert to the legal reserve (art. 96.2.b) of the PCC) and to the reserve for education and training (art. 97.2.b) of the PCC), as well as for the payment of interest on shares (art. 100.1 of the PCC). Only after these allocations and payments have been made is it possible to calculate the cooperative refund (art 100.1 of the PCC).

Moreover, partners in commercial companies may not receive any monies or goods in the form of profit where there are reserves to be created or rebuilt (arts. 32 and 33, CSC). In the same way, it is not possible to distribute surpluses in cooperatives 'before the deduction of any losses from previous financial years or, if the legal reserve to compensate for these losses has been used up, before the reserve has been rebuilt to the level prior to its use' (art. 100.2 of the PCC). In other words, the legislator prevents the distribution of surpluses

---

[24] H.-H. Münkner, *Co-operative Principles and Co-operative Law*, LIT, Vienna/Zurich, 2015, p. 148.

when and insofar as it is necessary to cover losses carried over or to rebuild the legal reserve. In this way, the law consecrates a mandatory regime of coverage of losses under which the surplus for a financial year is allocated primarily for this purpose.

As in commercial companies, with regard to corporate profit (arts. 31, 250.3, and 386.1, CSC), in the case of cooperatives the rules do not establish the automatic distribution of surpluses as a return (cooperative refund), and distribution can therefore not take place without a resolution of the General Meeting. When not provided for in the statutes, resolutions to allocate surpluses must be passed by a majority vote, given that this is the regulation for the approval of most resolutions (art. 40.2 of the PCC and art. 386 CSC, applicable pursuant to art. 9 of the PCC).

Thus, where results for a financial year are positive, the discretionary power of the General Meeting to decide how to allocate surplus becomes clear. On the one hand, the General Meeting may decide freely between distribution among members and the formation of reserves: the General Meeting may be of the opinion that the policy of constituting reserves as a means to finance the cooperative (the major obstacle to distribution) is much more convenient from the point of view of the members and the cooperative. On the other hand, the General Meeting may decide on the temporary retention of a part of cooperative refunds ('deferred return', in the words of Ferreira da Costa[25]), to remedy issues of limited equity. This deferment is in the form of a loan by the member to the cooperative, and the member must therefore provide his or her consent (art. 294.2 CSC, applicable by a remission of art. 9 of the PCC).

This is in line with the principle of the member economic participation (art. 3 of the PCC), which lists three possible destinations for surpluses: (i) 'the development of cooperatives'; (ii) 'support for other activities approved by membership'; and (iii) 'the distribution of surpluses for the benefit of the members in proportion to their transactions with the cooperative.' It follows from this that a return is one of three destinations accepted by the legislator when there is a surplus to be returned, and there is also the possibility of combining either all three destinations or just two of them.

The right to a cooperative refund is, therefore, a derogable right on the part of a member of a cooperative; however, the nature of this right is limited by the general principle of the abuse of rights. Members cannot be refused a cooperative refund without further justification, and refusal cannot be based on extra-social grounds. Were this to happen, the members of the Board of Directors might be subject to actions for liability. The General Meeting, in compliance with general contractual principles – namely the principle of good faith – must

[25] F.F. Costa, *Código Cooperativo. Benefícios fiscais e financeiros*, Estatutos do Inscoop, Livraria Petrony, Lisbon, 1981, p. 94.

justify its decision not to distribute a surplus in the form of cooperative refunds. Thus, the decision to retain cooperative surpluses as assets of the cooperative must be based on 'social interest', particularly on the self-funding needs of the cooperative. It follows that a resolution of this type will be invalid if the majority of cooperative members use their vote to pursue extra-social interests and simultaneously harm the interests of the cooperative.

1.8. THE REMUNERATION OF CAPITAL

Although the legal concept of the cooperative surplus has its roots in the mutualist vocation of cooperatives, the same cannot be said of the remuneration of capital contributions (share capital)[26] referred to in article 88.1 of the PCC, which provides an opportunity for members to obtain a net remuneration of the capital subscribed to as a condition of membership. Remuneration of this kind is not permitted in commercial companies (art. 21.2 CSC). When interest is paid on capital contributions, the total amount must not exceed 30% of the annual net results, as stated in article 88.2 of the PCC. Therefore, a portion not exceeding 30% may be deducted from the annual results or net surpluses to remunerate capital contributions.

The legal regime of remuneration of capital will be subject to a detailed analysis in section 3. At this stage, however, we must consider the issue of whether the legal concept of remuneration of capital contributions constitutes a deviation from the mutualist vocation of the cooperative; it cannot be considered to be a cooperative refund because it is paid in proportion to the capital contributions and not in proportion to participation in the cooperative's transactions.

We believe that this deviation does not exist, since it is the intention of the legislator that the purpose of this legal concept should be to compensate the efforts that capital contributions represent in the minds of the cooperative's members. It is also important not to forget, as Rui Namorado has highlighted, that at the time when a cooperative member underwrites his or her capital contributions, the central motivation is not the profitability of the capital contribution he or she has made, as is the case with members of commercial companies, but participation in the cooperative's social object.[27] A cooperator who limits himself or herself

26 In PCC 'títulos de capital'.

27 Namorado (n. 16 above, p. 162) points out that: 'a member of a company fulfils his or her most important duties for that company, pursuant to article 20 of the CSC, if s/he performs the commitments to which he or she is committed and shares in the losses, where they occur. He or she may even participate in general meetings, but will refrain from any activity that regards him or her as a partner of the company, and must give useful content to his position. He or she will receive dividends in proportion to his or her investment, like any other, thus giving a practical meaning to his or her capacity as a shareholder.'

to underwriting capital contributions ('*títulos de capital*') and refrains from any participation in the cooperative's transactions will not become a full cooperator member, and cannot actually benefit from its advantages. Thus, as we have seen, if surpluses are generated and distributed in the relevant financial year, nothing will be due to him or her, because the distribution of a cooperative surplus, when one takes place, depends on the volume of transactions between each member and the cooperative, and not on the number of shares held by each cooperator.

1.9. INVESTOR MEMBERS

The PCC includes the possibility of statutes that permit investor members (art. 16.1.g) of the PCC). These investor members must not participate in the cooperative's transactions, and are limited to contributing financially to the cooperative.

The admission of investor members is subject to a statutory provision (arts. 16.1.g); 20.1; and 41.1 of the PCC) and must be approved by the General Meeting after having been proposed by the Board of Directors (arts. 20.3 and 20.4 of the PCC).

Article 41.5 of the PCC requires that the statutes identify the 'conditions and criteria' on which the award of a plural vote to investor members depends. However, some restrictions are imposed mandatorily: (i) no investor member may have more than 10% of the votes corresponding to the votes of cooperators; and (ii) investor members may not have total voting rights greater than 30% of the total votes of the cooperators (art. 41.7 of the PCC).[28]

1.10. THE CONSEQUENCES OF A COOPERATIVE'S SOCIAL OBJECT FOR COOPERATIVE GOVERNANCE

One consequence of the fact that cooperatives have a mutualist aim is that their governance will be in the form of participatory governance and oriented towards their members.

What stands out first and foremost is the democratic basis for decision-making, which is considered to be one of most relevant specificities of cooperatives, and which is reflected in their governance. This aspect is based on the principle of democratic member control, as set forth in article 3 of the PCC: 'Cooperatives are democratic organisations controlled by their members, who actively participate in setting their policies and making decisions. The men and

28 On this issue, see D. Meira and M.E. Ramos, 'Os princípios cooperativos no contexto da reforma do Código Cooperativo português', *CIRIEC – Revista Jurídica de Economía Social y Cooperativa*, Monograph No. 77, 2015, pp. 416–422.

women who serve as elected representatives are accountable to the membership. In primary cooperatives, members have equal voting rights (one member/one vote), and cooperatives at other tiers are also organised in a democratic manner.'

Thus, in terms of voting rights, the rule is 'one cooperator/one vote', 'whatever their participation in the relevant social capital' (art. 40.1 of the PCC).

In first-degree cooperatives, a plural vote must always be of an exceptional character, and its admission will always be subject to mandatory rules.

In fact, a plural vote (of cooperators and investor members) can only be accepted in cooperatives that have more than twenty cooperators and that are not worker, handicraft, fishery, consumer or social solidarity cooperatives (art. 41.1 of the PCC).

Moreover, plural voting by cooperators can only be allocated on the basis of the cooperators' activity in the cooperative, and not on the basis of participation in the share capital. Cooperatives of up to 50 cooperators cannot be assigned more than three votes per cooperator (or investor member), and cooperatives with more than 50 cooperators cannot be assigned more than five votes each.

In second-degree cooperatives (cooperative unions, federations, and confederations), the Portuguese cooperative legislator permits plural votes if they are expressly provided for in the statutes, defined in terms of 'objective criteria', and in accordance with the democratic principle (art. 104 of the PCC). Plural voting may be also adopted by cooperatives resulting from associations among cooperatives, or between cooperatives and public-law legal persons (art. 8.3 of the PCC).

The democratic principle reinforces the personal character of cooperatives, which is intimately linked to their mutualist scope: cooperative members are more important than their economic contribution, and decision-making powers do not depend on capital contributions. Each cooperative member therefore has the same decision-making power.

The principle of democratic management by cooperative members also gives rise to the required active participation of cooperative members in the definition of policies and in the cooperative's decision-making process (art. 22.2.c) of the PCC). In cooperatives, direct and active involvement in the business of the cooperative on the part of members – that is, in fulfilling its corporate purpose – is a *sine qua non* requirement, as pointed out above. In many cooperatives, this active involvement will take place mainly in General Meetings, where policy options are discussed, important decisions are made, and significant actions regarding the life of the cooperative are approved (arts. 21.1, a) and b) of the PCC). In other cooperatives, such as production, trade, and housing cooperatives, members will be involved in the daily operations of the cooperative. This direct involvement of cooperators in the cooperative's governance is also a result of the fact that the members of cooperative bodies must be elected from among the cooperative's members (art. 29.1 of the PCC), thus eliminating the possibility that non-members can be a part of those bodies.

1.11. THE PURPOSE OF A COOPERATIVE'S SOCIAL OBJECT IN SECOND-TIER COOPERATIVES AND IN THE EVENT OF AN ASSOCIATION WITH OTHER LEGAL ENTITIES

The PCC provides for different forms of association among cooperatives: merger and division, the formation of secondary cooperatives, and associations of cooperatives and other legal entities.

These forms of association are found in article 3 of the PCC, in which the principle of cooperation among cooperatives is laid out as follows: 'cooperatives serve their members most effectively, and strengthen the cooperative movement, by working together through local, regional, national, and international structures.'

This form of inter-cooperative cooperation, which is based on the aim of increasing both the competitiveness of this type of organisation and its economic potential, leads to the horizontal or vertical integration of activities relating to the cooperative. To this end, articles 109 to 111 of the PCC provide for the merger and division of cooperatives. Finally, article 8.1 of the PCC permits the association of cooperatives with other legal entities, where it states that: 'cooperatives are allowed to associate with other legal persons, as long as the association complies with the cooperative principle of autonomy and independence.' It thus seems that, under certain conditions, article 8.1 allows cooperatives to associate with each and every type of corporate entity. In abstract terms, association with associations, foundations, civil law companies, commercial companies, and other cooperatives is permitted.[29]

It should be noted that the aim of cooperation among cooperatives or the formal association of a cooperative with other legal entities as referred to in article 3 of the PCC is to increase efficiency in the cooperative's service to its members; therefore, the mutualist scope is the ultimate foundation of these processes.

1.12. THE COOPERATIVE OBJECTIVE IN SOCIAL SOLIDARITY AND PUBLIC INTEREST COOPERATIVES

As we have seen, two dimensions are comprised in the cooperative object from a complementary perspective: economic and social.

In the Portuguese legal system, however, we have two types of cooperative in which reconciliation of members' interests (the mutualist scope) and the public

---

[29] On this issue, see J.A. Correia and M.J.R. Dias, 'A associação da cooperativa com outras pessoas coletivas e a transformação encapotada de cooperativa em sociedade comercial: análise dos artigos 8.º e 80.º do Código Cooperativo', in Meira (ed.), n. 4 above, pp. 387–403.

interest is more intense, or assumes certain specificities. We are referring to social solidarity and public interest cooperatives (*'régies cooperativas'*).

Social solidarity cooperatives, which are regulated by Decree-Law no. 78/98 of 15 January 1998, are cooperatives whose activities are concentrated in the area of social services. Their *objective* is a clear mission to offer assistance in situations of social and economic vulnerability, and it is supported by a paradigm of social intervention. They provide assistance to families, children, young people, seniors, disabled and unemployed individuals, and other vulnerable groups, with a view to their professional integration, education, training, and occupational and residential care.

The entire activity of these cooperatives is based on the notion of solidarity, and for this reason they fall within a legal framework that has certain peculiarities. It should be stressed from the outset that the distribution of surpluses among cooperators is impossible, which means that all surpluses revert mandatorily to reserves (art. 7 of Decree-Law no. 78/98 of 15 January 1998) and that the rights, duties and benefits (including tax benefits and access to credit) under the Statute of the Private Institutions of Social Solidarity, as regulated by Decree-Law no. 119/83 of 25 February 1983, as amended and republished by Decree-Law no. 172-A/2014 of 14 November 2014, are extended to social solidarity cooperatives.[30]

The most distinctive feature of public interest cooperatives (*'régies cooperativas'*), which were established pursuant to article 6 of the PCC, is the association of public (the State or other legal persons governed by public law) and cooperative entities (or individual cooperative members) in the pursuit of public interest objectives.[31]

Article 1.3 of Decree-Law 31/84 of 21 January 1984, which establishes the legal framework for public interest cooperatives, states that: 'among others, indicators of public interest purposes are situations in which the carrying out of the cooperative object depends on the use, within the limits of the law, of property in the public domain or in the private unavailable domain of the State, or on the carrying out of business which the Constitution or the law prohibits to private initiative.'

The specifics of the social object of public interest cooperatives (the 'pursuit of the public interest'), which is inseparable from the public nature of some of its members (public participation), justify their exemption from certain cooperative principles. As a matter of fact, according to article 8.1 Decree-Law no. 31/84, participation by public entities in governing bodies is proportional to

---

30 On this issue, see L.L. Martins, 'Breves nótulas sobre o "novo estatuto" das Instituições Particulares de Solidariedade Social no Direito Nacional e no Direito da União Europeia', *Cooperativismo e Economía Social*, 2015, 37, pp. 139–164.

31 On this issue, see R. Namorado, *Horizonte Cooperativo, Política e Projecto*, Almedina, Coimbra, 2001, p. 149.

their weight in the share capital, and the number of votes is also proportional to that capital (which is in conflict with the principle of democratic management by members). Moreover, public entities are given the right to appoint their representatives and to replace them without a resolution by the General Meeting (art. 8.2), and they are also provided with a special resignation system (art. 13).

Deviations from certain specific cooperative principles, with particular emphasis on the principle of democratic control by members, result in public interest cooperatives not being considered to be full cooperatives, but rather 'related organisations' or 'hybrid cooperatives', even though the Portuguese Constitution includes them within the cooperative sector (art. 61.4 CRP).

Finally, it should be noted that despite these specificities, both social solidarity and public interest cooperatives pursue a mutualist scope, which translates into meeting the needs of their members.

2. COOPERATIVE GOVERNANCE

2.1. COOPERATIVE GOVERNANCE AND COOPERATIVE IDENTITY

As highlighted in section 1, it follows from the definition of the term 'cooperative' (art. 2.1 of the PCC) that cooperative governance will be based on compliance with cooperative principles and on cooperation and mutual support among members.

Since the *Cooperative Principles* reflect cooperative specificities and contain the essential features of the cooperative identity, cooperative governance must observe the principles set forth in article 3 of the PCC (the cooperative principles of the ICA).

Furthermore, as mentioned in section 1, cooperative principles are mandatory in the Portuguese legal system, and have even been enshrined in the Portuguese Constitution (arts. 61.2 and 82.4.a) of the CRP).

In this context, it can be said that under Portuguese law, cooperative governance is characterised as participatory governance (due to the *principle of democratic control by members*) oriented towards its members (following the mutualist aim of the cooperative – which stems from the very definition of cooperatives in art. 2 of the PCC), – autonomous and independent (under the *principle of autonomy and independence*), and transparent (due to the members' right to information, enshrined in the PCC, and the control and supervision of the Board of Directors by the General Meeting and Supervisory Board).

Participatory governance stems from the fact that cooperatives are business organisations of a markedly personalistic nature, given the importance granted to cooperators within the organisation. This has led some authors to state that cooperatives should be perceived as 'personalistic entities'. Beyond their distinctive personal character, cooperatives present themselves – under the cooperative *principle of voluntary and open membership* (art. 3 of the PCC) – as organisations that are open to new members (provided that the personal circumstances of the aspiring member are appropriate to the cooperative's social object), which means that cooperatives are set up as 'companies of persons' with a broad social basis. This fact is reflected in cooperative governance, as we shall demonstrate.

This personalistic focus implies active participation in cooperative governance by members: as we shall see, it means that by virtue of the cooperative *principle of education, training, and information* (art. 3 of the PCC), cooperatives promote 'education and training for their members, elected representatives, managers, and employees so that they can contribute effectively to the development of their cooperatives'.

The principle that cooperative governance must be autonomous and independent (art. 3 of the PCC) signifies that relations between cooperatives and the State must not affect the formers' governance. In the Portuguese legal system, as stated in article 85 of the CRP, the State must provide incentives and support for the activities of cooperatives. 'Incentives' means rules that promote cooperative activity, whereas 'support' means administrative measures aimed at the same purpose. Nonetheless, State-supported cooperative activities must not be understood in the sense of State-led cooperative activities. The State's duties cannot, therefore jeopardise the right of cooperatives to pursue their activities freely, and the granting of stimulus and support cannot interfere with their cooperative governance. In addition, external capital sources cannot affect the autonomy of cooperatives or democratic control by their members.

It should be noted that cooperative governance is not restricted to a cooperative's internal relations. Indeed, the very fact that a cooperative pursues goals in both the business and the social areas in such a way that the one complements the other cannot but be reflected in governance of the cooperative. Thus, the paradigm of cooperative governance is in line with the fundamental principles of 'corporate social responsibility' (CSR), and is based on the adoption of best practices regarding organisation, equal opportunities, social inclusion, and sustainable development.

This centrality of social responsibility in cooperative governance (which is closely related to the mandatory observance of cooperative principles and values) may mean that cooperatives adopt codes of conduct which do not exist in the Portuguese legal system.[32]

---

32 See, on this issue, D. Meira, 'Cooperative social responsibility: A Intercultural Analysis', in C. Sarmento (ed.), *In Permanent Transit. Discourses and Maps of the Intercultural Experience*, Cambridge Scholars Publishing, 2012, pp. 127–144.

It is our opinion that in the context of cooperative governance, CSR is not voluntary. In other words, given the cooperative legal framework, namely the fact that a cooperative's bodies must comply with the *principle of concern for the community* (art. 3 of the PCC) – which provides that: 'cooperatives work for the sustainable development of their communities through policies approved by their members' – it should be argued that there is a legal duty on the part of governance bodies, although they are focused on meeting the needs of members, to work to achieve the sustainable development of their communities, according to criteria that they themselves have approved.

In short, the cooperative bodies that are responsible for cooperative governance have a duty to integrate the fundamental values of CSR into their respective activities.

2.2. COOPERATIVE GOVERNANCE AND PORTUGUESE COMPANY LAW

As far as cooperative governance is concerned, apart from the regimes listed in the PCC and the decrees that regulate types of cooperative, company law must also be taken into account, in particular the sections on joint stock companies, since on the subsidiary law applicable to situations that are not foreseen in the PCC, article 9 of the PCC, provides for the possibility of recourse 'to the CSC, as long as cooperative principles are respected, particularly those sections that regulate joint stock companies'. This recourse is, however, dependent on two conditions: first, that any solution reached does not disregard cooperative principles; and second, within the scope of the CSC, that priority should be given to the precepts applicable to joint stock companies.

We can therefore state that with regard to cooperatives governance, article 9 of the PCC points to the application of provisions regulating the governance of joint stock companies contained in the CSC to cooperatives; however, it should be recalled that this subsidiary rule only applies if cooperative principles are not disregarded. We will nevertheless demonstrate that this particular reference to joint stock companies is not in line with various aspects of the cooperative governance regime due to the personalistic characteristics of this type of business organisation.[33]

---

[33] On this issue, see M.E. Ramos, 'Da responsabilidade dos gerentes e gestores das cooperativas', *Cooperativismo e Economía Social*, 2009, 32, pp. 35–54; D. Meira, 'A societarização do órgão de administração das cooperativas e a necessária profissionalização da gestão', *CIRIEC – Revista Jurídica de Economía Social y Cooperativa*, 2014, 25, pp. 162–169.

2.3. THE ROLE OF MEMBERS

2.3.1. The Significance of Cooperator Members

In cooperative governance, the central importance of cooperator members will have significant consequences with regard to the following aspects: equal treatment of members regardless of their financial participation; equal voting rights of all members ('one member/one vote'); the adoption of decisions conditional upon a majority vote; and election of the representatives of a cooperative by its members.

Among these consequences, we should highlight the democratic decision-making process, which is considered one of the most significant peculiarities of cooperatives, and so is reflected in their governance. This aspect is based on the cooperative *principle of democratic member control* as stated in article 3 of the PCC, which establishes that 'cooperatives are democratic organisations controlled by their members, who actively participate in setting their policies and in making decisions. The men and women who serve as elected representatives are accountable to the membership. In primary cooperatives, members have equal voting rights ("one member, one vote") and cooperatives at other levels are also organised in a democratic manner.'

From this principle stems the requirement of active participation on the part of members in the establishment of a cooperative's policies and in the cooperative decision-making process by taking part in General Meetings (arts. 21.1.b) and 22.2.a) of the PCC).

Moreover, for cooperatives, direct and active involvement on the part of members in the activities the cooperative carries out is a *sine qua non* requirement (art. 22.2.c) of the PCC), in compliance with its mutual purpose, as highlighted in section 1.

Democratic control by members is also based on the rule of equal voting rights.[34]

2.3.2. The Division of Power Among Cooperative Bodies

The structure of the governing bodies of Portuguese cooperatives can be characterised as hierarchical and tripartite. Pursuant to article 27.1 of the PCC, the bodies of a cooperative are the General Meeting, the Board of Directors, and the Supervisory Board.

The General Meeting is the highest body of a cooperative, and its decisions are binding on all the other bodies (art. 33.1 of the PCC).

---

34 See D. Meira, 'A relevância do cooperador na governação das cooperativas', *Cooperativismo e Economía Social*, 2013, 35, pp. 9–35.

The Board of Directors is primarily an executive body (arts. 47 and 62 of the PCC), while the Supervisory Board is a control and oversight body (arts. 53, 61, and 64 of the PCC).

As the highest body, the General Meeting may – at any time, and in addition to its exclusive powers, which are set forth in article 38 of the PCC – take over the powers of the other bodies, including those of the Board of Directors. This power vested in the General Meeting distinguishes cooperatives from joint stock companies, in which 'with regard to matters of management of the company, shareholders may act only at the request of the management board' (art. 373.2 of the CSC). Article 27.2 of the PCC states that: 'the cooperative's statutes may still allow for the existence of other bodies, as well as give powers to the General Meeting or the Board of Directors to appoint special committees of limited duration for the performance of certain tasks.'

2.3.3. Member Voting Rights: 'One Member/One Vote' or Variations Thereof

In terms of voting rights, in accordance with the principle of democratic member control, the rule is 'one member/one vote', 'whatever their participation in the cooperative's share capital' (art. 40.1 of the PCC).

The admission of plural voting will always be of an exceptional character and must be subject to a provision in the statutes (arts. 16.1.g), 20.1, and 41.1 of the PCC), which means that it will depend on a consensus in the cooperative act of incorporation or an amendment to the statutes, and this consensus must be expressed in the text of the statutes.

In first-degree cooperatives, there are restrictions regarding the granting of plural voting rights (art. 41 of the PCC).

A plural vote (of cooperators and investor members) will only be admitted in Portuguese cooperatives with more than 20 cooperators, and provided that these cooperatives are not worker, handicraft, fishery, consumer or social solidarity cooperatives (art. 41.1 of the PCC).

A plural vote of cooperators can only be assigned on the basis of the cooperator's activity in the cooperative, and not on the basis of participation in the share capital.

In cooperatives of up to 50 cooperators, more than three votes cannot be assigned per member, and in cooperatives with more than 50 cooperators, more than five votes cannot be assigned per member.

Article 41.5 of the PCC requires the statutes to identify the 'conditions and criteria' on which the award of a plural vote to investor members depends.

Finally, although there is provision for the existence of plural voting rights, certain decisions require that the 'one member (cooperator or investor member)/one vote' rule be maintained. These are the subjects that are included in article 41.4 of the PCC (matters for which approval shall be required by a qualified majority, in accordance with art. 51.1 of the PCC) or any other areas for which the statutes require a qualified majority. On these matters, the rule remains, 'one member/one vote', as they relate to fundamental decisions by the cooperative.

These include matters relating to amendments of the statutes; the approval and amendment of internal regulations; the approval of the merger, division, or voluntary winding up of the cooperative; voluntary membership in cooperative unions, federations, and confederations; and decisions regarding the right to commence civil or criminal proceedings against directors, managers, other agents, or members of the Supervisory Board.

In second-degree cooperatives (cooperative unions, federations, and confederations), the PCC admits plural votes where expressly provided for in the statutes, defined in terms of 'objective criteria' and in accordance with the democratic principle (art. 104 of the PCC). A plural vote may also be adopted by cooperatives resulting from an association of cooperatives, or between cooperatives and legal public law persons (art. 8.3 of the PCC).

2.3.4. Mechanisms for Member Control

Board members are elected from among members for a period of four years, unless a shorter period is provided for in the cooperative's statutes (art. 29 of the PCC).

In the event of vacancy of a corporate office, another member will be appointed: first a substitute, if there is one, and failing that, by a new election.

Since election of members of cooperative bodies is within the exclusive powers of the General Meeting (art. 38.a) of the PCC), it does not seem possible to fill the vacancy by co-option, even if it is subject to ratification by the General Meeting.

Pursuant to article 29.6 of the PCC, the statutes of a cooperative may limit the number of consecutive terms of the board of the General Meeting, the Board of Directors, the Supervisory Board, and any other cooperative body.

The PCC identifies a number of incompatibilities with regard to cooperative governance: no member may simultaneously be a member of the Board of the General Meeting, the Board of Directors, the Supervisory Board, or other elected bodies provided for in the statutes (art. 31.1 of the PCC); and pursuant to article 46.2 of the PCC, members of the Board of Directors and the Supervisory Board cannot carry out any business that competes directly with the cooperative during the period for which they are appointed (unless they obtain authorisation from the General Meeting)[35] or perform any temporary or permanent functions

---

35 The PCC does not clarify the meaning of 'competing activity' or the phrase 'personally exercise'. Regarding the first aspect, article 254.2 of the CSC on the prohibition on competition on the part of managers states that 'any activity covered in the company's object is deemed to be in competition with the company, since it is to be exercised by it, or said exercise has been decided by the shareholders.' This provision applies to joint stock companies by virtue

in the cooperative, whether under an employment contract as a subordinate or independent contractor (art. 398 of the CSC, which applies by reference of art. 9 of the PCC). This latter incompatibility does not apply to cooperatives in which membership involves a compulsory contribution of labour, as in the case of worker, handicraft, and fishery cooperatives.

2.3.5. Dispute Resolution between Members and a Cooperative

It is the sole responsibility of the General Meeting to decide on the exclusion of members and the removal of the governing bodies. It also acts as an appeal body in the event of sanctions imposed by the Board of Directors (art. 38 of the PCC).

Resolutions of the General Meeting may be appealed to the Courts (art. 32.6 of the PCC).

Article 72 expressly provides for liability of directors towards the cooperative. When faced with creditors and third parties, directors will in general terms be held accountable for damage caused directly in the performance of their duties (arts. 73 and 74 of the PCC). There is also provision for the possibility of civil liability on the part of members of the supervisory board and the auditor (arts. 76 and 77 of the PCC). Finally, article 79 of the PCC recognises cooperators as having an active right to take action against the directors for the benefit of the cooperative for liability for the repair of damage suffered, even if the cooperative does not so require.

2.4. THE PORTUGUESE SYSTEM OF GOVERNANCE

2.4.1. The General Meeting of Members: The Deliberative Body of the Cooperative

2.4.1.1. Composition, Convening and Operation

As already mentioned, the General Meeting is considered to be the supreme body of a cooperative. It is composed of all its members, and their resolutions are binding on all bodies of the cooperative and all its members (art. 33.1 of the PCC).

All cooperators and investor members may participate in the General Meeting, subject to one limitation established by the legislature: the cooperator members and investor members must have full enjoyment of their rights (art. 33.2 of the PCC).

---

of an express reference in article 398.5 of the CSC. In the case of 'personally exercise', article 254.3 of the CSC, which regulates the prohibition of competition by managers of companies, states that 'exercise on their own includes participation, whether in person or through a third person to the company involving the assumption of unlimited liability by the manager as well as a participation of at least 20% in the capital or profits of the company in which he or she assumes limited liability.'

The cooperative's statutes may provide for general meetings of delegates (so-called sectorial meetings) (art. 44 of the PCC). These can be organised on the basis of cooperative activities undertaken by the members or based on the geographical areas in which the members live.

Pursuant to article 34 of the PCC, the General Meetings normally meets twice a year, and may meet extraordinarily whenever convened to do so by those in charge (on the initiative of the Chairperson, at the request of the Board of Directors or the Supervisory Board, or upon request of at least 5% (and no less than four) of the cooperative's members).

The General Meeting is convened by the Chairperson of the General Meeting or, in special cases provided by law, by the Committee of Auditors, the General and Supervisory Board, or the Supervisory Board, with at least 15 days' notice (art. 36.1 of the PCC).

The notice must contain at least the following (art. 36.2 of the PCC): an agenda and the date, time, and place of the meeting.

As regards the quorum of General Meeting, article 37.1 of the PCC states that it is defined as 'more than half the members with voting rights or their duly accredited representatives.'

To obtain a quorum, article 40 of the PCC requires a qualified majority for matters listed in paragraph 2, an absolute majority for other matters, and a simple majority for the election of members of bodies.

Given the personal nature of cooperatives, all members have the inalienable right to attend or to be represented at General Meetings, voting by proxy if necessary (art. 43 of the PCC).

2.4.1.2. Powers

Pursuant to article 38 of the PCC, the following matters should be considered to be within the exclusive competence of the General Meeting, in addition to others that may be listed in the statutes: the election and removal of members of the cooperative; review of and voting on the annual report and accounts for the year; the approval and legal certification of accounts; analysis of and voting on budgets and business plans; establishing interest rates to be paid to members; approval of the distribution of surpluses; amendments to the cooperative's statutes; approval of merger, division or voluntary winding up of the cooperative, as well as voluntary membership in cooperative unions, federations, and confederations; decisions on the exclusion of members; the removal of the governing boards from office; establishing the remuneration of cooperative board members; decisions regarding the right to take civil or criminal action against directors, managers and other agents, or members of the Supervisory Board.

It follows from this rule that there is no concentration of management powers in the Boards of Directors of Portuguese cooperatives, and the General Meeting may decide on matters directly related to management of the cooperative activity.

2.4.2. *Management and Supervision Models of Cooperatives*

According to article 28 of the PCC, the management and supervisory board of a cooperative may be structured in one of the following ways: (i) a Board of Directors and a Supervisory Board; (ii) a Board of Directors with an Audit Committee and an auditor; or (iii) an Executive Board of Directors, a General and Supervisory Board, and an auditor.

Each cooperative must choose the management and supervision model it wishes to adopt, and this choice must be moulded on the cooperative's statutes (art. 16.1.d) of the PCC). In cooperatives with 20 or fewer members it is possible to have a sole director (arts. 28.2 and 45 of the PCC) and a single supervisor, insofar as this is provided in the statutes.

2.4.3. *Composition and Responsibilities of the Board of Directors*

Pursuant to the model laid down in article 28.1.a) of the PCC, the management board is a Board of Directors or a sole Director (art. 45.2 of the PCC). The Board of Directors is the executive body of the cooperative, and as such has powers to manage and represent it (art. 47 of the PCC).

In the model laid down in article 28.1.b) of the PCC, the management board is a Board of Directors, which must include the Audit Committee. Members of the Audit Committee are therefore both directors and supervisors. According to article 28.1.b) of the PCC, this model does not permit a sole director (whatever the number of members).

In the model described in article 28.1.c) of the PCC, the management board is an Executive Board of Directors. If the cooperative has no more than 20 members, this management model allows management to be entrusted to a sole director, who must be a cooperator (art. 62.1.b) of the PCC). With regard to the Executive Board of Directors' relations with the General and Supervisory Board, article 63 of the PCC requires that the Executive Board of Directors provide the following to the General and Supervisory Board: (i) at least once a year, information about the management policy that it intends to pursue, as well as the underlying facts and issues that determine their options; (ii) every three months, information on the situation of the cooperative and the evolution of its activity; and (iii) a full annual report on the previous year for the purposes of issuing an opinion to be submitted at the general meeting (art. 63.1 of the PCC).

This model ensures that election of members of the management board will always be the responsibility of the General Meeting, in order to guarantee compliance with the *principle of democratic member control.*

In multi-person elected bodies, the rule that there must be an odd number of members will be enforced. This is the case of a Board of Directors (art. 45.3 of the PCC), a Supervisory Board (arts. 51.1.a) and 51.2 of the PCC), an Audit

Committee (art. 56.2 of the PCC), an Executive Board of Directors (art. 62.1.a) of the PCC), and a General and Supervisory Board (art. 65 of the PCC).

It is our opinion, however, that in cooperatives, the *principle of democratic member control* does not prevent the Board of Directors from being composed of an even number, although it must be conceded that this solution may lead to deadlock situations.

Members of the governance bodies are elected from among the cooperators (art. 29 of the PCC), with the exception of the Statutory Auditor and investor members (art. 29.8 of the PCC).

It is assumed that investor members may join the board but cannot 'represent more than 25% of the number of effective members that make up the body to which they are elected' (art. 29.8 of the PCC). This means that 75% of the total number of members of each of the cooperative bodies must be cooperators. Thus, where a cooperative is managed by a sole director (arts. 28.2; 45.2; and 62.2; of the PCC), this director may not under any circumstances be an investor member. The same applies if the supervisory body is composed of a single member (art. 51.1.a) of the PCC).

Article 32.1 of the PCC on the functioning of the bodies states that: 'in all organs of the cooperative, the chairperson has a casting vote.' This solution, which ultimately, and whatever the subject, gives decision-making powers to the president of the body, may jeopardise the *principle of democratic member control*. If taken literally, it may also lead to a reduction in debate and the weighting of arguments where the objective was to stimulate them through the collegial nature of the Board.[36]

2.4.4. *Delegation of Management Powers*

Article 50 of the PCC allows management powers to be delegated for the 'exercise of certain categories of acts' wherever no provision in the statutes prohibits it. This means that if the cooperative's statutes are silent on the delegation of management powers, the Board of Directors may decide to delegate them.

This delegation of management powers to the 'exercise of certain categories of acts' can only be allocated to members of the management body (art. 50.1 of the PCC). In the absence of a provision in the statutes, the Board of Directors may delegate 'powers of representation of the cooperative for a particular act' to any of its members or representatives (art. 50.2 of the PCC).

Matters relating to the admission and dismissal of members and the imposition of sanctions on them cannot be delegated (art. 50.3 of the PCC).[37]

---

36 D. Meira and M.E. Ramos, *Governação e regime económico das cooperativas. Estado da arte e linhas de reforma*, Vida Económica, Porto, 2014, pp. 33–68.

37 On this issue, see Meira, n. 33 above, pp. 185–188.

2.5. SUPERVISION OF THE COOPERATIVE'S MANAGEMENT

In the Portuguese legal system, cooperatives must have a supervisory body, be it a Statutory Auditor/Supervisory Board, an Audit Committee or a General and Supervisory Board, depending on the model adopted (arts. 28.1, 51, 56, 65 ff. of the PCC).

In cooperatives with more than 20 members, supervision will be the responsibility of a Supervisory Board consisting of a chairman and two members (art. 51.1.b) of the PCC). Because statutory auditing is obligatory for cooperatives (art. 43 of Law 140/2015 of 7 September 2015, which approved the Statute of the Statutory Auditor), supervision will be entrusted to a Supervisory Board and a Statutory Auditor who is not a member of the supervisory board (art. 51.1.c) of the PCC). In the models provided in art. 28.1, b) and c) of the PCC, there will always be a Statutory Auditor, and he or she will not be a member of the supervisory body with the functions described in article 70 of the PCC.

The PCC describes the duties of the members of a Supervisory Board (art. 52), in particular those of care and loyalty. There is, however, no financial literacy or other requirement that members of a Supervisory Board must satisfy; the PCC does not provide mechanisms to ensure stability in office (for example, a prohibition against unfair dismissal); and there are no specific exclusions for membership of a Supervisory Board. It is our opinion, however, that, article 9 of the PCC should be interpreted to mean that the rules governing supervisory boards of joint stock companies should be applied here.

Supervisory board members are recruited from among the cooperators (and optionally investor members) for a period of four years (art. 29 of the PCC). In the absence of any limitations in the statutes, the law does not prevent members of the supervisory board from remaining in office (art. 29.6 of the PCC).

2.6. MEMBERS' RIGHTS TO INFORMATION AND REQUIREMENTS OF TRANSPARENCY

2.6.1. Transparency: The Duty to Inform and the Right to be Informed or Access Information

The value of transparency in governance is central to cooperatives, and is inseparable from active participation in cooperative democratic control. Transparency is ensured first by recognising members' rights to information that provides them with a working knowledge of how business is being conducted and the cooperative's social status and, as a consequence, control of its management.

An active and a passive side can be distinguished within this right to information.

The multiple obligations of the cooperative bodies, including the Board of Directors, to disclose facts and make documents relating to the life of the cooperative available is included in the passive component. Of particular note is the duty to provide information that falls on the Board of Directors by making the management report, the year's accounting documents, the business plan, and the budget for the following year available to members at the headquarters of the cooperative, accompanied by a professional opinion of the Supervisory Board (art. 47.a) of the PCC and article 263.1 of the CSC, which is applicable by reference to art. 9 of the PCC).

The active component of the right to information is enshrined in article 21.1.d) of the PCC, which states that members have the right to request information of the competent bodies of the cooperative and to examine its records and accounts. It follows from this rule that the active information actors are the members and the passive actors the 'competent bodies of the cooperative.'

As for the subject of the right to information, members may obtain information without any limitations on the content of the information requested, with the exception of situations in which the provision of information leads to a violation of the secrecy rules imposed by law (art. 21.3 of the PCC).

The right to information must be exercised during periods and under conditions that are set forth in the cooperative's statutes by the General Meeting or the Board of Directors.

However, given the markedly personalistic nature of cooperatives, whenever the statutes do not provide for it, and in the absence of any resolution by the General Meeting or the Board of Directors, we defend that members may claim their right to information before any cooperative bodies directly, with no limitations as to the conditions of its exercise.

In addition to a general right regarding a cooperative's business and activity, other rights to specific information are included in the right to information, such as in preparation for and during General Meetings.

Accordingly, members have a right to information when preparing for a General Meeting (art. 289 of the CSC (which is applicable by reference to art. 9 of the PCC)), which allows them to obtain the knowledge that they require in order to make a decision and vote. Therefore, taking into account the provisions of article 289.1 of the CSC, prior to the General Meeting, and at least fifteen days prior to the date of the meeting, certain elements that are considered to be essential for voting on a resolution must be available for consultation at the cooperative's headquarters. Among these elements are identification of the members of the governing bodies, the proposals to be presented to the General Meeting by the Board, and the reports and justifications that must accompany these proposals. Before an annual General

Meeting to approve the accounts, a member may consult the accounting information at the cooperative's headquarters, particularly the management report and the accounts.[38]

Members also have a right to information during the General Meeting, and may demand to be given information on the matters being deliberated (art. 290.1 of the CSC, by reference to art. 9 of the PCC). The lack of availability of this information to a member makes an appeal against the resolution possible, as is the case with commercial companies (art. 290.3 of the CSC, by reference to art. 9 of the PCC). Application of this rule in the CSC by reference to article 9 of the PCC is, however, subject to one condition: the right to information is not dependent on ownership of a certain percentage of the share capital (as is required for the exercise of a minimum right and the collective right to information on a joint stock company), because this would imply a violation of the *principle of democratic member control* by the cooperative's members; this right to information is an individual right of each member, thereby granting every single member the right to request information from the cooperative bodies.[39]

A decision by the Board of Directors to refuse to provide information requested by members or the provision of false, incomplete, or non-clarifying information can be appealed against before the General Meeting (art. 21.2 of the PCC).

This may, however, create a problem when an attempt is made to convene an Extraordinary General Meeting to consider a refusal by the Board of Directors to provide information to a member: in article 45.3 of the PCC, the cooperative legislator has established a rule that unless the cooperative's statutes or the laws applicable to the various types of cooperative state otherwise, these extraordinary General Meetings may only be convened by its Chairperson on his or her own initiative at the request of the Board of Directors or the Supervisory Board, or by a petition by at least 5% of the members, but in any event no fewer than three. Still, the right to information is seen as a right of individual members, which makes it imperative to introduce a legislative amendment to guarantee that in the event of a violation of the right to information, any member may require that a General Meeting be convened so that he or she is able to enforce his or her rights.

It is also not expressly provided in the PCC whether this recourse to the General Meeting is necessary or optional, and therefore if, when faced with a breach of the right to information, a member may immediately request an

38 See M.P. Almeida, 'O segredo bancário e o direito à informação nas cooperativas de crédito (Acórdão do Tribunal da Relação de Évora, de 22 de março de 2012)', *Cooperativismo e Economía Social*, 2013, 35, pp. 293–306.

39 On this issue, see H. Salazar, 'O direito à informação dos cooperadores no âmbito das cooperativas', in Meira (ed.), n. 4 above, pp. 347–357.

investigation with a view to obtaining the requested information (this application for an investigation is set forth in article 292 of the CSC, which is applicable to cooperatives by reference to article 9 of the PCC).

2.6.2. *Financial Audits*

The PCC does not provide for external audits of cooperatives.

The explanation for this closed control system results is the fact that the Portuguese legislator has placed the control mechanisms of cooperative governance exclusively in the hands of members through their participation in the activities of the cooperative and in General Meetings (through the exercise of voting rights) by giving them a broad right to information and establishing the rule that the members of bodies (including the Supervisory Board) should be members of the cooperative.

It should be noted that although the existence of a Statutory Auditor is anticipated, he or she cannot join the supervisory board. In fact, in the case of cooperatives that are obliged to have statutory auditing – see article 43 of Law 140/2015 of 7 September 2015, which approved the Statute of Statutory Auditors – supervision will be entrusted to a supervisory board and a Statutory Auditor, who is not a member of the supervisory board (art. 51.1.c) of the PCC). In the models provided in article 28.1, b) and c) of the PCC, there must always be a Statutory Auditor, but he or she cannot join the supervisory board.

The functions of the Statutory Auditor are described in article 70 of the PCC. They are to verify the bookkeeping and accounting records and the documents that support them; to verify the extent of cash flows and inventories of all kinds of goods or assets belonging to the cooperative; to check the accuracy of the accounting documents; and to check whether the accounting policies and evaluation criteria adopted by the cooperative lead to a correct evaluation of its assets and results.

2.6.3. *Member Education*

Article 3 of the PCC enshrines the principle of education, training and information, and states that: 'cooperatives provide education and training for their members, elected representatives, managers, and employees so they can contribute effectively to the development of their cooperatives. They inform the general public – particularly young people and opinion leaders – on the nature and benefits of cooperation.'

As highlighted in section 1, this principle emphasises the vital importance of education and training in cooperatives.

In terms of cooperative governance, education and training should: (i) provide the members of the cooperative with knowledge about the cooperative's principles and values: namely to induce them to actively participate in their cooperative, to deliberate properly at meetings, and to elect their bodies consciously and monitor their performance; (ii) to teach the leaders and managers of the cooperative to exercise the power they have been given properly and to preserve the trust placed in them by the other members, to obtain knowledge of the cooperative and show a level of competence in keeping with the responsibilities of their office; (iii) to provide workers with the technical expertise needed for proper performance; (iv) and finally, to foster a sense of solidarity and cooperative responsibility in the community in which the cooperative operates.

As also mentioned in section 1, this principle manifests itself in the PCC through the dedication of a compulsory reserve 'for the cooperative education and technical and cultural training of members and employees of the cooperative, as well as of the community' (Art 97 of the PCC).

Management of this reserve fund is a specificity of cooperative governance to which the PCC devotes particular attention.

Thus, pursuant to article 97.3 of the PCC, 'models to implement this reserve will be determined by the General Meeting', and, although it is not expressly mentioned by the legislator, it is our belief that it is also within the powers of the General Meeting to control how this reserve is spent. From this it follows that the General Meeting is the competent body for establishing the basic guidelines for application of this reserve fund. Ordinary management of the fund is the responsibility of the Board of Directors, as the manager of the cooperative, since article 97.4 imposes the duty on the Board of Directors 'to include a training plan for the implementation of this reserve fund in the annual business plan.'

Article 97.5 makes it possible for the General Meeting to allow the Board of Directors to hand over all or a part of the 'reserve to a higher-tier cooperative, subject to the latter's pursuing the purpose of the reserve and having a business plan in which the former cooperative is involved.'

Finally, by the same terms, article 97.6 enshrines the possibility that a part or all of this reserve may be dedicated to 'education and training projects that jointly or separately involve the cooperative concerned and to (a) one or more legal persons governed by public law; (b) one or more non-profit private law legal persons; and (c) one or more cooperatives.'

2.7. ADMISSION, RESIGNATION AND EXPULSION OF MEMBERS

Another cooperative principle with important legal consequences in cooperative governance is the *principle of voluntary and open membership* – the traditional *open-door principle* (art. 3 of the PCC). This allows for a variable number of members (art. 2.1 of the PCC speaks of 'variable composition') and for a variable share capital (art. 81.1 of the PCC).

The principle of voluntary and open membership incorporates two aspects: people join voluntarily and are free to leave whenever they wish.

Given the mutualist aim of cooperatives, anyone who is interested and meets the admission requirements must be able to become a member of a cooperative and benefit from the services it offers.

In order to do so, a prospective member must apply to the Board of Directors of the cooperative for admission (arts. 19.1 and 47.d) of the PCC). In this regard, Rui Namorado argues that 'any restriction on the free entry of new members must derive from the very nature of the cooperative and not from an arbitrary judgment of rejection, which is potentially discriminatory because it is based on individual preferences'.[40] What must be checked, in particular, therefore, is the ability of a candidate to remember to use both the services of the cooperative and to carry out the work his or her inclusion in the cooperative involves, as well as to accept the cooperative's culture and values.

The Portuguese cooperative legislator has established that the statutes of each cooperative must contain admission requirements for members (art. 16.2.a) of the PCC). If a candidate satisfies these conditions, the proposed admission is still subject to approval by the Board of Directors (art. 47.d) of the PCC), and a resolution is mandatory for the acquisition of membership.

It cannot, therefore, be considered that there is an actual subjective right to be admitted as a member.[41] Various authors have treated this as an ordinary legal expectation: that is, an active position that although legally significant, lacks the assurance mechanisms of subjective rights.[42]

In Portuguese Law, the General Meeting acts as an appeal body with regard to the admission or rejection of new members (art. 38.k) of the PCC).

The *principle of voluntary and open membership* also relates to the right of members to leave: this right is what Sérvulo Correia has called the 'freedom of resignation'.[43] Indeed, pursuant to article 24.1 of the PCC, members are granted an actual right to leave or resign.

---

40 R. Namorado, *Os Princípios Cooperativos*, Fora do Texto, Coimbra, 1995, p. 61.

41 However, actual rights of admission to prospective members derive from certain additional provisions of the PCC: see article 6 of Decree-Law no. 303/81 of 12.11.1981 (crafts cooperatives), article 8 of Decree-Law no. 309/81 of 16.11.1981 (worker cooperatives), and article 8 of Decree-Law no. 323/81 of 04.12.1981 (service cooperatives). After clarifying that the admission of members may only be refused 'on the basis of a visible incapability on the part of the prospective member to carry out his or her activity or of an absence of demand for this activity for the time being in the pursuit of the cooperative's aim', it states that 'in any case, admission cannot be refused on any of the grounds set forth in the preceding point to people who, pursuant to an employment contract', perform work for the cooperative for more than two years. In line with this, article 8 of Decree-Law no. 509/99 of 19.11.1999 (housing and building cooperatives), after providing in paragraph 1 that 'housing and building cooperatives can only condition the admission of new members on the existence of programmes into which candidates can be integrated', states that 'no housing and building cooperative may use the option provided in paragraph 1 ... for more than three consecutive years.' On this issue, see J.M.C. Abreu, 'Deliberação de dissolução de cooperativa. Anotação ao Acórdão do STJ de 28/6/2011', in Meira (ed.), n. 4 above, pp. 567–568.

42 In this regard, see for all Namorado, n. 16 above, p. 21.

43 Correia, n. 11 above, p. 127.

Free membership also implies that no member may be arbitrarily compelled to leave the cooperative. The PCC deals with expulsion ('*exclusão*') in article 26.

Members must be expelled by a resolution of the General Meeting. Article 38 of the PCC states: 'It is the exclusive competence of the General Meeting: ... k) To deliberate on the expulsion of members ... while also functioning as an appeal body ... in relation to sanctions imposed by the Board of Directors.' It follows that the Board of Directors has no jurisdiction over the expulsion of members.[44]

Expulsion must be based on a 'serious and culpable' breach of the cooperative law, the cooperative's statutes, or its internal regulations (art. 26.1 of the PCC), and must be preceded by the relevant written procedure, which must contain an indication of the offences, their classification, the evidence produced, the defence of the accused party, and a proposal for application of the expulsion measure.[45] The reasons for expulsion and the rules governing the procedure must be clearly expressed in the cooperative's statutes so that each member knows from the outset under what circumstances he or she may run the risk of being expelled, thereby ensuring the member's procedural rights of defence. It is clear, therefore, why article 16.2.a) of the PCC states that cooperative statutes may also include 'the requirements of admission, suspension, expulsion and resignation of members and their rights and duties.'

3. COOPERATIVE FINANCIAL STRUCTURE

3.1. COOPERATIVE FINANCIAL STRUCTURE AND COOPERATIVE IDENTITY

When analysing the financial structure of cooperatives in the PCC, we are confronted with its singularity and complexity, which is derived from the *Cooperative Identity* as defined by the International Cooperative Alliance (ICA), which is based on a set of principles (the *Cooperative Principles*), in a set of values (the *Cooperative Values*) that embody these principles, and in a *Notion of a Cooperative*.

As highlighted in section 1, the definition of a cooperative (as set forth in art. 2.1 of the PCC, closely in line with the ICA's definition) is based on four distinctive features of this type of legal person that are fundamental for understanding the singularities of the cooperative financial structure.

---

44 On this issue, see A.S. Martins, 'A Direção exclui e a Assembleia Geral aprova (Sobre deliberações inexistentes e nulas)', in Meira (ed.), n. 4 above, pp. 439–443.

45 See A.A. Martins, 'A relação jurídica entre cooperador trabalhador e cooperativa. Notas sobre a sua qualificação e regime', *Cooperativismo e Economía Social*, 2014, 36, pp. 46–51.

The two first characteristics – variability of share capital and variability of the shareholding structure ('an autonomous association of freely associated persons of variable composition and capital') – are formal. The others – the social object of the cooperative ('aimed not at profit but at satisfying the economic, social, or cultural needs and aspirations of said members') and the management style of the cooperative enterprise ('through cooperation and mutual assistance of its members, and in compliance with cooperative principles') – are of a substantive nature.

As highlighted in sections 1 and 2, cooperative principles are mandatory in the Portuguese legal system and have even been enshrined in the Portuguese Constitution (arts. 61.2 and 82.4.a) of the CPR); hence, a disregard of the cooperative principles in business operations is a cause for dissolution (art. 112.1.h) of the PCC).

It should also be mentioned that the mutualist scope, which is an underlying and distinctive feature of cooperatives, and one that distinguishes them from other legal entities, does not necessarily mean that cooperatives conduct their business exclusively with their members: they may also carry out activities with non-members. In accordance with this concept, article 2.2 of the PCC states that: 'in pursuit of their objects, cooperatives are allowed to conduct business with non-members, subject to any restrictions laid down in the law applicable to each type of cooperative'.

This opportunity to develop business with non-members has important consequences at a cooperative financial structure level, as we will demonstrate.

The financial structure of cooperatives is therefore based on a logic of its own that results from its *Cooperative Identity*: namely from the required compliance with cooperative principles. An ongoing effort on the part of the legislature to adapt Cooperative Principles to new market needs is, however, evident throughout the PCC and its accompanying legislation, as we shall see throughout this report.

This adaptation is essentially justified by the need felt by cooperatives to use their financial resources efficiently and to seek new funding sources, and it has led to a move towards the legal regime of capital-based companies.

As cooperatives are based on the leading role played by their members, they mainly live by doing business with them, and are not affected by the logic of the maximum profitability of the capital invested in them (thus distinguishing them from capital-based companies), but it is also true that today cooperatives are faced with the great challenge of resorting to all necessary means to be efficient on the market, thus becoming more similar to capital-based companies, while also preserving their identity. It should therefore be kept in mind first that the legal framework cannot act as an inhibitor on a cooperative's development, and second that any innovations to be introduced (which point towards a move in the direction of the legal framework of capital-based companies) should not mischaracterise cooperatives.

3.2. THE LEGAL CONTEXT OF THE FINANCIAL STRUCTURE OF COOPERATIVES

Chapter V (arts. 80 to 100) of the PCC contains a comprehensive set of rules on the financial structure of cooperatives.

The special regimes established in the twelve legal decrees that regulate each of the twelve types of cooperative must also be taken into consideration.

Company law must also be taken into account. Article 9 of the PCC points to the application to cooperatives of provisions contained in the CSC regulating the financial structure of joint stock companies. It should be remembered, however, that this subsidiary rule only applies if cooperative principles are not disregarded.

We will also take into account Law no. 30/2013 of 8 May 2013, the so-called '*Lei de Bases da Economia Social*' (LBES), a framework law on the social economy, which was unanimously approved by the Portuguese Parliament on 15 March 2013.[46]

With regard to the accounting regime, it should be noted that there is no specific or differential accounting treatment of cooperatives in the Portuguese legal system compared to commercial companies: in fact, the Accounting Normalisation System ('*Sistema de Normalização Contabilística*' – SNC)[47] applies to cooperatives (art. 3.1 of the SNC), which has led to a critical reaction in the legal literature, since the SNC was conceived as specifically for conventional capital-based companies,[48] and therefore not taking into account the specific features of cooperatives, namely the variable nature of their share capital deriving from the right to a reimbursement of capital contributions in the event of withdrawal by a cooperator.

Moreover, there are specific accounting rules in Portugal for 'non-profit entities' in Decree-Law no. 36-A/2011 of 9 March 2011. Article 5.2 of this Decree, however, expressly excludes cooperatives from application of this regime. This is incomprehensible, as it is agreed both in the literature and in case law that cooperatives are non-profit entities, at least as regards their main objectives, and that they do not distribute economic or financial profits to their respective members, as we can see throughout this study.

Based on the provisions of article 2 of the Law on the Defence of Competition (Law no. 18/2012 of 8 May 2012), all economic activity carried out by the public, private, or cooperative sectors, whether permanently or occasionally, is subject

---

46 On this point see D. Meira, 'A Lei de Bases da Economia Social Portuguesa: do projeto ao texto final', *CIRIEC – Revista Jurídica*, 2013, 24, pp. 21–52.

47 Approved by Decree-Law no. 158/2009 of 13.07.2009.

48 Pursuant to article 3.1 of Decree-Law no. 158/2009 of 13.07.2009, the SNC must apply to the following entities: companies incorporated under the CSC, individual firms regulated by the Commercial Code, individual limited liability establishments, public companies, cooperatives, complementary groups of companies and European Economic Interest Groupings.

to the law on competition. Article 12 of the LBES should be recalled here, however, where it states that social economy entities are subject to the 'European and national rules that apply to general interest social services within the scope of their activities, without prejudice to the constitutional principle of protection of the social and cooperative sector'. The wording of this regulation has raised many questions, but it appears to mean: (i) integration into the social economy sector (as in the case of cooperatives), which does not mean that an entity is not subject to national and European rules on competition; and (ii) that the spirit of the law is to allow these social economy entities, as well as general interest social services, not to be subject to national or European rules on competition wherever it would prevent them from pursuing their objective, which is the pursuit of the general interest.

3.3. COOPERATIVE SHARE CAPITAL

3.3.1. *The Essential or Non-Essential Nature of Cooperative Share Capital*

In the Portuguese legal system, it is not possible to create a cooperative without share capital. Hence, the initial share capital must be determined in the cooperative's statutes (art. 16.1.f) of the PCC). Moreover, a cooperator is only considered to be a member after he or she has contributed to the share capital (art. 83 of the PCC).

In order to start developing their activity, cooperatives require economic resources, which are initially obtained by the contributions of cooperators to their share capital (arts. 83 to 85 of the PCC). Contributions to capital are, however, a mere instrument for the development of cooperatives' activity, and do not contribute towards determining the rights and duties of their cooperators, as we shall see. Moreover, owing to its variability, share capital plays a very tenuous guarantee role as far as creditors are concerned, as we will also illustrate later.

Justification for the instrumental nature of share capital in cooperatives lies in the fact that in order to develop their economic activity, cooperatives need not only their own assets but also the participation of cooperators in their transactions. We will refer again to the significance pointed out in section 1 of both the *Cooperative Principles* in the activities of cooperatives and their mutualist scope as regards their object.

3.3.2. *Assets as a Natural Element of Cooperatives*

While the essential nature of share capital might be questioned, the same is not true of cooperatives' assets: effectively, cooperatives are granted legal personality and autonomy with regard to their assets (art. 17 of the PCC), and this was taken into account by the legislator when regulating their establishment, operation, winding up, and liquidation, and the distribution of assets.

In cooperatives, the notion of assets has the same features as it does for companies, with one specific element (which we will mention briefly here and develop further later on, when we discuss the issue of reserves) that arises out of the clear distinction between cooperatives' divisible and indivisible assets. Divisible assets are that portion of the assets that corresponds to the share capital each cooperator brings to the cooperative, and under certain conditions the portion of voluntary reserves defined by the cooperative that may belong to the cooperator. Indivisible assets are those assets that correspond to the legal reserve and the reserve for education and training, and they maintain their absolute indivisibility both during the life of the cooperative and when it is wound up (arts. 99 and 114 of the PCC).

It should be noted, finally, that the PCC does not make any further provision for pecuniary or non-pecuniary contributions – made by cooperators while participating in cooperative transactions (mutualist capital) – as part of the assets, an issue that we will discuss further below.

3.3.3. *Regulating Principles of Cooperative Share Capital*

In order for share capital to be able to fulfil its purpose adequately, it is governed by the principles provided for in its specific legal regime: namely, the principle of determination, the principle of unity, the principle of publicity, and the principle of effective correspondence.

It should also be noted that the variability of the cooperatives' share capital derives from the *principle of voluntary and open membership*, as opposed to the *principle of stability* that characterises the share capital of companies.

The variability of share capital will not be analysed at this point, but the remaining principles will now be considered in some detail.

3.3.3.1. The Principle of Determination

As highlighted above, the initial share capital must be established in the cooperative's statutes (art. 16.1.f) of the PCC).

Accordingly, if we take the provisions of article 16.1.e) of the PCC into account, it appears that share capital is an essential reference in a cooperative's statutes with regard to the following: the amount of initial share capital; the amount of admission fees, if any are payable; the value of share contributions; and the minimum share capital to be subscribed by each cooperator.

3.3.3.2. The Principle of Unity

Like companies, cooperatives must have a single registered share capital that includes members' contributions expressed as their overall value. This is a result of the legislator's use of the definite article 'the' when reference is made to 'the amount of initial share capital …' in article 16.1.f).

In cooperatives, unity of share capital is inherent to the unity of the legal subject, and so the subscribed share capital – the total sum of the contributions by its members – will always be unique, despite its variability.

3.3.3.3. The Principle of Publicity

The principle of publicity results from the need to render public and publicise the share capital of cooperatives. The establishment of a cooperative will thus be subject to commercial registration (art. 17 of the PCC and art. 4 of the Commercial Registry Code).

Accordingly, since references to the amount of initial share capital, the amount of admission fees (if any are payable), the value of capital contributions (shares), and the minimum capital to be subscribed by each cooperator and how it is paid are mandatory in a cooperative's deed of incorporation, these elements are subject to publication. Any person may therefore request oral or written information on these elements regarding the share capital of the cooperative from the competent Commercial Registry Office, and may also request a certificate containing such elements (arts. 75 to 78 of the Commercial Registry Code).

Non-members may, however, only discover the value of the nominal share capital, which corresponds to the minimum initial share capital, and not that of the accounting or actual share capital (resulting from subscribed contributions at any given moment), due to its variability.

It could be argued that interested parties may have access to the amount of accounting or actual share capital by consulting the cooperative's accounting documentation, which is required to be deposited at the Commercial Registry Office; however, under the Portuguese legal system, cooperatives are not required to deposit their annual reports and accounting documents at the Commercial Registry Office, as article 4 of the Commercial Registry Code sets out the details regarding cooperatives that are subject to registration, and these do not include those relating to accounts, as is expressly provided for in the case of companies (art. 3.n) of the Commercial Registry Code).

It is our opinion that this absence of a specific provision as to the filing of cooperatives' annual accounts does not permit the Commercial Registry to play a real role in financial publicity, an omission that we believe is unacceptable, because it undermines the guarantee function that share capital could have for creditors.

3.3.3.4. The Principle of Effective Correspondence

The PCC takes a number of steps to ensure that there is a correlation between the amount of share capital and a cooperative's assets: the obligation to value contributions in kind (art. 84.4 of the PCC); the imposition of a minimum amount for contributions to share capital (arts. 82 and 83 of the PCC); the requirement of a minimum share capital (art. 81.2 of the PCC); limitations on compensation for shares to the existence of positive results in a financial year beyond limits as to its amount (arts. 88.2 and 100. 1 of the PCC); and the possibility of allocating losses in the case of reimbursement of capital contributions (art. 89.2 of the PCC).

The principle in question also manifests itself through the establishment of mandatory reserves of an indivisible nature. In fact, although they are equity accounts, it is mainly these reserves that will function as mechanisms for the protection of creditors in a cooperative, thus reducing the weaknesses in the guarantee function of the cooperative's share capital and weaknesses resulting from its variability. As we will see, reserves are one of the most important components of a cooperative's financial structure.

3.3.4. The Legal Minimum Cooperative Share Capital

The minimum share capital principle is explicitly established in the Portuguese legal system. Accordingly, under article 81.2 of the PCC, the statutes must establish the cooperative's minimum share capital, which may not be less than 1,500 euros, although the complementary legislation regulating each branch may impose a different minimum.

The minimum share capital of a cooperative must be included in its statutes and operate as the minimum limit for the variability of share capital in order to avoid under-capitalisation, thus representing a minimum guarantee of creditors' interests. Pursuant to article 16.1.f) of the PCC, this is a mandatory provision in the statutes.

While the accounting or actual share capital of cooperatives is variable, the minimum share capital is stable, because it is public knowledge, as it is registered at the Commercial Registry. Cooperatives therefore guarantee to non-members that the share capital will always be at least equal or superior to that recorded at the Commercial Registry, regardless of the current level.

In this context, redemption of contributions cannot affect the minimum share capital. Accordingly, article 89.3 of the PCC states that the statutes may provide that, when in any financial year, the amount of shares to be repaid exceeds a certain percentage of the amount of share capital established in the statutes, redemption will be subject to a resolution by the Board of Directors. Reasons must be provided for a suspension of reimbursement, if any, and it is subject to ratification by the General Meeting (art. 89.4 of the PCC).

However, for the minimum share capital to have an adequate guarantee function, it is necessary to attribute a different legal regime to it based on the following assumptions.

First, a reduction of the share capital to an amount below the minimum share capital will lead to the cooperative's being wound up and subsequently dissolved. The PCC does not expressly provide for this type of winding up.

Second, the Portuguese legal system does not establish the possibility for creditors of a cooperative to file a legal objection to a reduction of share capital to an amount lower than the minimum share capital based on the losses arising out of it when claiming their rights, provided that they have requested that cooperative pay their credits or an appropriate guarantee and their request has not been granted.[49]

3.3.5. *Variability of Share Capital*

3.3.5.1. Mechanisms to Reduce the Effects of the Variability of Share Capital

The variability of share capital is included in the definition of a cooperative (art. 2.1 of the PCC) as a consequence of the principle of voluntary and open membership (art. 3 of the PCC).

Cooperators are granted the right to withdraw, as laid down in article 24.1 of the PCC;[50] this right is reflected in the consequent redemption of the member's contributions to the capital. Article 89.1 of the PCC states that: 'a cooperator who withdraws is entitled to a refund … in the amount of the member's contribution to share capital, based on the face value of the shares.'

Cooperatives are thus characterised by a structural variability with regard to both their cooperators and their share capital (art. 81.1 of the PCC). The main consequence of this variability is a reduction in the financial quality of share capital – namely in the economic and social security that share capital represents for creditors – thus potentially causing difficulties with raising external funding and on occasion leading to under-capitalisation.

In this context, the PCC establishes a series of mechanisms to lessen the effects of a cooperator's resignation with regard to the redemption of the membership contribution, namely:

(a) the possibility to defer redemption for a period of time provided for in the statutes, or additionally, for no more than one year (art. 89.1);
(b) the possibility to make deductions from the right to redemption (art. 89.2) by applying deductions to the face value of the member's shares wherever

[49] On this issue, see D. Meira, 'Contributos legislativos para a criação de empresas cooperativas: a livre fixação do capital social', *CIRIEC – Revista Jurídica*, 2015, 26, pp. 27–52.

[50] Article 24.1 of the PCC states that: 'cooperators may ask to terminate their membership under the conditions established in the statutes or, where not expressly stated otherwise, by giving thirty (30) days' notice, provided that any debts and liabilities of the member are satisfied.'

losses are attributable to the member during the financial year in which the right to redemption originated;

(c) minimum periods of membership and rules in the statutes fixing the notice periods needed for withdrawal (art. 24.1). Cooperators may therefore ask to terminate their membership under the conditions established in the statutes or, when not expressly stated otherwise, at the end of a financial year, by giving 30 days' notice, provided that any debts and liabilities of the member are satisfied. A failure to comply with minimum periods of membership or notice periods may lead to compensation for loss and damage;
(d) the regime of the external liability of cooperators (arts. 23 and 80), which we will discuss later;
(e) the minimum share capital (art. 81.2);
(f) the legal regime governing mandatory reserves (arts. 96 ff.);
(g) the possibility that the statutes may provide for the above-mentioned suspension of redemption (art. 89, nos. 3 and 4 of the PCC).

Nevertheless, under no circumstances may these mechanisms suppress the right to withdraw (art. 24.3 of the PCC). If one takes account of the fact mentioned above that share capital is variable, this means that it may be increased by new members' contributions and reduced due to the redemption of member contributions to capital without the need for an amendment of the cooperative's statutes.[51]

Finally, it must be noted that the PCC does not provide for any minimum asset guarantees to creditors.

3.3.5.2. Specific Aspects of Reductions in Cooperatives' Share Capital

Reductions in cooperatives' share capital are subject to the same legal regime as joint stock companies, with certain specific aspects. A cooperative's share capital may be reduced by a reimbursement of shares in the case of the resignation, exclusion, or death of a member (provided that the heirs do not wish to, or cannot, become cooperators).

Under the terms of articles 24 and 26 of the PCC, a reduction in share capital will take place whenever a member terminates his or her membership, whether by withdrawal or exclusion, and under these circumstances the member is entitled to redemption in the amount of his or her contribution to the share capital at the face value of the shares. In case of the death of a member, the heirs

---

[51] On this issue, see, D. Meira, 'As insuficiências do regime legal do capital social e das reservas na cooperativa', in *I Congresso Direito das Sociedades em Revista*, Almedina, May 2011, pp. 129–155.

or legatees are entitled to repayment of the member's contribution to the share capital (art. 86.5 of the PCC).

Even though the PCC includes no express provision, it is our view that reductions in share capital may also occur wherever the General Meeting rules that losses attributable to cooperators should be deducted from contributions to share capital. Share capital may therefore be reduced by a resolution by the General Meeting to cover losses in a financial year. The Legal Regime of Mutual Agricultural Credit Institutions expressly mentions this possibility in article 17.6, where it states that: 'the share capital of cooperative banks may also be reduced by way of a resolution of the General Meeting where a reduction in capital will cover losses, in which case articles 94 to 96 of CSC shall apply *mutatis mutandis*.'

The PCC does not expressly provide that a reduction of share capital below any prescribed minimum may be a cause for dissolution of a cooperative, an omission which we believe is open to criticism, considering the significance of share capital variability, as we have illustrated above.

By reference to article 9 of the PCC, however, and taking the commercial company framework into consideration, a resolution to reduce share capital to an amount below the legal minimum amount is allowed provided that such a reduction is followed by an increase in share capital to an amount equal to or higher than the minimum share capital within 60 days following the resolution to reduce the share capital (art. 95.2 CSC).

3.3.5.3. Specific Aspects of Increases in Cooperatives' Share Capital

(a) Increases in Cooperatives' Share Capital by the Allocation of Reserves

As far as cooperatives are concerned, it is our understanding that allocations of reserves can only be made by using non-mandatory reserves that are not funded with profits from transactions with non-members.

In support of our opinion, we refer to article 99 of the PCC, which states that mandatory reserves and reserves resulting from profits from transactions with non-members are not divisible. If share capital were to be increased by the allocation of any such reserves, cooperators would end up either with more shares or with the same number of shares, but with a higher face value (art. 92 of the CSC). As we know, however, a cooperator who wishes to leave a cooperative (by withdrawal or exclusion) is entitled to 'the amount of the member's contribution to the share capital at the face value of the shares' (art. 89 of the PCC). It is therefore evident that increasing share capital by an allocation of mandatory reserves breaches article 99 of the PCC and article 114 of the PCC (which provides for the disinterested return of reserves on winding up). Furthermore – and even if the above-mentioned rules are disregarded – it must be pointed out that the purposes of legal reserves are provided in the legislation, and these purposes do not include additions to share capital, as we shall discuss further below.

As far as statutory reserves are concerned, on the other hand (art. 98.1 of the PCC), we believe that they may be used to increase capital as long as the resolution to increase share capital by the allocation of reserves is simultaneously a resolution to amend the statutes.

In the same manner, reserves set up by a resolution of the General Meeting under the terms of article 98.2 of the PCC may be used to increase share capital by the allocation of reserves.

Still, it must be stressed that these reserves are not mandatory, but are the result of surpluses derived from transactions with cooperators. Accordingly, if share capital is increased by the allocation of these reserves, only those cooperators who have contributed to the surpluses are allowed to participate in the share capital increase, and then only as to the exact amount of their contribution.

For a share capital increase of this kind to be carried out, minutes of the resolution of the General Meeting attended by all the beneficiaries describing the exact terms of the increase in capital are sufficient.

Finally, the specific situation of agricultural credit cooperatives must be considered. Here, the law provides for increases in share capital by an allocation of reserves available for the purpose as long as the shares issued for the share capital resulting from the allocation of reserves are handed to the credit cooperative or the credit cooperative and associates in proportion to the capital they held prior to the increase (art. 16, nos. 1 and 5 of Decree-Law no. 24/91 of 11 January 1991).

(b) Increases in Cooperatives' Share Capital by Contributions in Cash or Kind

Increases in cooperatives' share capital may be concluded through contributions in cash or in kind.

This form of share capital increase is characterised by an increase in the cooperative's assets. This is why we can speak of an actual increase in share capital, due to the increase in cooperative assets that complements the new contributions in kind. Such an increase in share capital may be the result of new members joining the cooperative or a consequence of the *principle of voluntary and open membership* or a resolution by the cooperative's bodies.

In the first case, an increase in a cooperative's share capital does not mean amending the statutes. Minutes of the resolution of the General Meeting describing the exact terms of the increase in share capital are sufficient. It must not be forgotten, however, that the specific purpose behind new members joining the cooperative is the promotion of the cooperative's basis rather than increasing capital.

It is now time to describe increase in cooperatives' share capital that results from a resolution by the General Meeting in detail. This type of increase in share capital is achieved by a vote of members by a resolution by the General Meeting with a qualified majority of two-thirds of the votes cast (arts. 38.g) and 40.2 of the PCC), except where the Board of Directors is granted this power in the statutes (art. 85 of the CSC, by reference to art. 9 of the PCC).

However, no cooperator can be forced to contribute to any increase in share capital unless he or she is willing to do so: this principle is clearly stated in article 86.2 of the CSC, which applies to cooperatives through article 9 of the PCC. This means that contributions to increases in capital are not mandatory for cooperators. This position has been supported by the courts, which have ruled that the PCC imposes mandatory contributions to share capital exclusively at the time the cooperative is formed[52] and that General Meeting resolutions to increase a cooperative's share capital are invalid with regard to cooperators who have not agreed to contribute.[53] Not agreeing to do so means that the cooperator voted against, abstained, or was not present at the time the resolution was passed. It is also our understanding that a cooperator who does not agree is entitled to resign on the terms and within the periods set forth in article 24 of the PCC.[54]

When this form of increase in share capital is open to non-members, they do not automatically become members by making a contribution. Verification of compliance with the requirements to acquire membership is necessary in such cases. The same is not true, however, when this form of increase in capital is open to non-members whose liability is limited to their contributions to capital and thus who do not participate in the activities of the cooperative: that is, investor members (art. 20 of the PCC).

3.3.6. *The Functions of Share Capital*

We will now analyse the functions of share capital in cooperatives in comparison with the functions of share capital in companies, so as to assess the differences in the roles of share capital in these two legal entities.

3.3.6.1. The Political and Economic Rights Granted by Member Contributions to Share Capital

Share capital is a means of becoming a member of both companies and cooperatives.

52 Ruling of the Supreme Court of 16.12.1993 (Colectânea de Jurisprudência, Ano I, Tomo III, p. 189).

53 Ruling of the Court of Appeal of Évora of 10.10.1995 (Colectânea de Jurisprudência, Ano XX, Tomo IV, p. 275).

54 On this issue, see P.T. Domingues, 'O aumento ou agravamento de obrigações impostas aos cooperadores', in Meira (ed.), n. 4 above, pp. 327–331.

Subscription of a minimum of three shares is a mandatory requirement in order to acquire membership (art. 83 of the PCC), although this may not be enough, as we will demonstrate below.

Nevertheless, in cooperatives, the participation of cooperators in share capital merely influences their right to compensation for capital contributions (art. 88 of the PCC) and their liability for the cooperative's debts (art. 23 of the PCC). In all other cases, there is no relationship between economic rights and the amount of contributions to share capital; financial rights are determined by the quantity and quality of the cooperator's participation in the cooperative's transactions.

As highlighted in section 2, the organisational structure of cooperatives is established by taking into consideration the majority of members, and not the majority of the share capital: members of cooperative bodies are elected from among their cooperators (art. 29 of the PCC).

Furthermore, in the General Meeting, which is the highest-ranking body of cooperatives and is attended by all cooperators in full enjoyment of their rights (art. 33 of the PCC), share capital is not a quorum or majority requirement. Resolutions of the General Meeting are passed with the number of cooperators as a determining criterion, regardless of the capital that they represent (art. 40 of the PCC).

Even when a plural vote is given to cooperators in the statutes in accordance with article 41, this will always be attributed on the basis of the cooperator's participation in the cooperative's transactions (art. 41.2 of the PCC).

Also, as said in section 2, in second-tier cooperatives (cooperative unions, federations, and confederations), a plural vote is defined by an 'objective criterion' and in accordance with the above-mentioned democratic principle (art. 83 of the PCC). Accordingly, plural voting in second-tier cooperatives is proportional to the number of members of each participating entity or to the volume of the cooperative's activity carried out with the cooperative, thus also signifying that share capital is still not a relevant factor.

In cooperatives, participation in surpluses is assessed in relation to members' participation in the cooperative's transactions. Surpluses are distributed to cooperators in the form of a cooperative refund and in proportion to the transactions that each member carries out with the cooperative in a given financial year, and not proportionately to the member's contributions to the share capital (art. 100.1 of the PCC).

Another fundamental right of cooperators is the right to participate in the cooperative's transactions, as provided for in the statutes. This participation is, however, carried out in consideration of the cooperator's economic capacity or needs rather than the cooperator's participation in the cooperative's share capital.

3.3.6.2. The Role of Capital in Productivity

Share capital represents the means by which cooperators pool their resources to carry out the economic activity of their choice. In this sense, the aim of share capital is to contribute towards setting up a production structure, thereby playing a role in productivity.

In the same way, share capital also influences productivity in cooperatives. Transactions by a cooperative are not possible without a minimum of economic resources. At the time when a cooperative is formed, this funding is made up of members' contributions to the share capital, which will later be strengthened by contributions from new members, new contributions, and especially the results of the cooperative's economic activities. This is why initial assets are required by law through the mandatory minimum share capital, and why the reserves that become the funds to be used in the consolidation and development of the cooperative are imposed.

Similarly, this role in productivity justifies the fact that a minimum share capital for cooperatives is imposed by law. Making a minimum share capital a legal requirement reveals a concern regarding productivity on the part of the legislator, who in this manner guarantees the feasibility and survival of the cooperative for the benefit of its cooperators and creditors.

3.3.6.3. The Role of Capital as a Guarantee

The role of a cooperative's share capital as a guarantee is irrelevant when considered from the point of view of static information to non-members, because due to the *principle of voluntary and open membership*, this information is only accurate as regards the statutory minimum capital, and as we have noted above, minimum share capital is not properly protected under Portuguese law. Conversely, when considered from a dynamic point of view, it is our understanding that share capital (understood here as the amount held at a certain moment rather than the statutory minimum) has a role of guarantee. This is the case first of all because cooperators' capital contributions are not totally redeemed.

The share of capital of a cooperator who wishes to leave a cooperative is paid after settlement of the losses that appear 'in the balance sheet of the financial year in which the right of redemption originated' (art. 89.2 of the PCC). Furthermore, in cooperatives, it is not possible to distribute refunds in a financial year that closes with losses. Article 100.2 of the PCC does not allow a distribution of surpluses among cooperators until losses from previous financial years have been compensated. In the same way, a surplus cannot be distributed if the legal reserve has been used to compensate for losses and is not yet 'at the level prior to its use', which, as we shall see later, has to do with the guarantee role played by legal reserves. Furthermore, in cooperatives in which cooperators' liability is unlimited, non-members are guaranteed not only by the assets of the cooperative, but also by the assets of those cooperators (arts. 23 and 80 of the PCC).

Nevertheless, this role of share capital as a guarantee from a dynamic point of view is still fairly fragile. For creditors, what is really important is the business carried out with members and non-members, as well as the cooperative's mandatory reserves.

3.4. MEMBERS' CONTRIBUTIONS TO CAPITAL

Contributions to capital are an obligation to be met by members (art. 83 of the PCC). They are a necessary condition for becoming a member, although they may not be enough, since cooperators must also take part in the cooperative's activities (art. 22.2.c) of the PCC). In the case of investor members (art. 20 of the PCC), a member acquires membership by contributing to the share capital, but does not participate in cooperative activities, which means that, for these investor members, a subscription of share capital is enough to become a member.

3.4.1. *Obligation to Pay Up Capital*

The PCC provides solely for those mandatory contributions to share capital that are a pre-requisite for the acquisition of membership. The PCC does not, therefore, distinguish between mandatory and voluntary contributions. Nevertheless, by reference to article 287 of the CSC (pursuant to art. 9 of the PCC), it is possible, we believe, that the statutes of cooperatives may impose the obligation on some or all cooperators to make further contributions (accessory contributions) apart from the mandatory ones, as long as the essential elements of this duty are established, and as long as the statutes specify whether these contributions are free of charge or for consideration.

Under Portuguese law, certain cooperatives have mandatory contributions of capital and labour (art. 85 of the PCC). This is the case of craft cooperatives (art. 5 of Decree-Law no. 303/81 of 12 November 1981), worker cooperatives (art. 7 of Decree-Law no. 309/81 of 16 November 1981) and service cooperatives (art. 7 of Decree-Law no. 323/81 of 4 December 1981). These rules state that contributions in labour are in the form of provision of the cooperator's professional services to the cooperative in accordance with the rules established by the General Meeting or the Board of Directors. Only members who 'after having joined the cooperative become incapable of working because of accident, illness, or age' are exempt from this mandatory contribution of labour. In these cooperatives, acquiring and maintaining membership are mandatorily dependent on the member's contribution to the cooperative in capital and labour. The contribution in labour is part of the legal act by which the acquisition of membership is carried out, and is thus a necessary element of the acquisition of membership, although it is not part of the share capital.

3.4.2. *Types and Nature of Capital Contribution*

Cooperators' contributions to share capital may be in cash or in kind (art. 84.1 of the PCC).

Under the terms of article 84.4 of the PCC, contributions in kind are assessed by the General Meeting of Incorporators or the General Meeting following a proposal by the Board of Directors. If the value of these entries is higher than 7,000 euros per member or 35,000 euros in total contributions, it must be assessed by a Statutory Auditor (or by the Auditing Firm) pursuant to the terms of article 28 of the CSC.

Contributions in services are not permitted as contributions to share capital (art. 85 of the PCC). The reason for excluding them is that 'labour' is not a quantifiable amount that can easily be expressed as a money value, and therefore does not perform the guarantee role that capital does. Nevertheless – and even though contributions in services cannot be understood as a contribution to share capital – this does not mean they have no value as a contribution to the cooperative. We would therefore say that they are contributions in labour, with special characteristics, but not share capital.

3.4.3. *Registration*

The law states that securities representing share capital are known as '*títulos de capital*' (cooperative shares) (art. 82 of the PCC). They are registered securities (art. 82.2 of the PCC).

Under the terms of article 82.3 of the PCC, 'securities representing cooperative share capital may be represented in book-entry form, and so the provisions of Title II of the Portuguese Securities Code apply to these securities, *mutatis mutandis*.'

Just like shares in joint stock companies, shares in cooperatives are simultaneously securities that are part of the cooperators' assets and debt securities. Unlike shares, however, shares in cooperatives cannot be traded on the securities market: that is, on the Stock Exchange. This is due to the impossibility of separating a cooperator's participation from his or her person.

3.4.4. *Amount*

The cooperative principle of 'member economic participation' provides for an equitable contribution to the share capital of cooperatives from their members. Here, the legislation on cooperatives has established that as a rule, the minimum contributions to capital to which each cooperator subscribes are defined in either the complementary legislation applicable to the various types of cooperative in the cooperative sector[55] or the statutes. In any case, they may never be below the equivalent of three shares (art. 83 of the PCC).

Share capital is divided into securities the value of which cannot be below 5 euros each (art. 80.1 of the PCC), and each cooperator must have a minimum contribution of three shares.

Portuguese cooperative law does not set any maximum limit on the number of shares that may be held by each cooperator, an omission that might be understood as a means of making the funding of cooperatives easier. Because this omission means that no maximum limit is set on cooperator participation, however, it carries with it the risk of allowing a cooperator with an excessive participating interest in the cooperative's share capital to affect the decisions of the cooperative, not legally but actually.

3.4.5. Payment

With regard to honouring the duty to make contributions to capital, the law lays down that 10% of capital in cash must be paid up upon subscription (art. 84.2 of the PCC). Deferrals of contributions to capital in cash are admitted as long as payment is completed within a maximum of five years (art. 84.3 of the PCC). This possibility to defer contributions is limited to contributions in cash, and does not apply to investor members (art. 84.5 of the PCC).

Contributions in kind must be made at the time of the incorporation, and may not be deferred beyond that date.

Although the PCC is not explicit on this issue, it is our understanding that a deferral of this kind is only possible if the face value of the contributions in cash and kind initially made by the cooperators is at least equivalent to the legal minimum capital.

The percentage of contributions in cash that may be deferred is calculated in relation to each contribution and not to the total of contributions that can be deferred. This means that until the date of incorporation, each cooperator must contribute at least 10% of his or her contribution in cash.

Cooperators' mandatory contributions to capital are only considered to be overdue after they have been asked by the cooperative to comply with their

---

55 The minimum individual capital in agricultural cooperatives is 100 euros, and in multi-purpose cooperatives, members must subscribe as many minimum contributions to capital as the number of sections to which they belong (art. 6, nos. 2 and 3 of Decree-Law no. 335/99 of 20.08.1999, as amended by Decree-Law no. 23/2001 of 30.01.2001). In the case of cooperative banks, the minimum individual capital is 500 euros (art. 15 of the Legal Regime of Cooperative Banks). The minimum individual capital for trade cooperatives is 100 euros (art. 8 of Decree-Law no. 523/99 of 10.12.1999). The minimum individual capital in housing cooperatives is 100 euros (art. 6 of Decree-Law no. 502/99 of 19.12.1999).

obligation within a period of between 30 and 60 days. The Board of Directors may send a warning to cooperators whose contributions are overdue by recorded mail and grant them a further period of over 90 days in which to pay their debt, with interest for late payment. All these rules result from the subsidiary application of the provisions of nos. 2 to 4 of article 285 of the CSC.

An overdue contribution may lead to a cooperator being excluded (art. 26.2 of the PCC). A penalty of loss of shares in favour of the cooperative does not apply to cooperators (art. 26.9 of the PCC): this rule states that the provisions of the last section of no. 1 of article 24 of the PCC (ongoing responsibility to fulfil the obligations of cooperative members) apply to the excluded cooperator, as well as the provisions in article 89 of the PCC (that is, the right to settlement of a contribution to share capital).[56]

Overdue payments will affect the distribution of surpluses to cooperators (art. 27, nos. 4 and 5 of the CSC, which applies to cooperatives as a subsidiary matter, pursuant to art. 9 of the PCC). Surpluses may therefore not be distributed to cooperators whose payments of subscribed capital are overdue. They are credited as offsetting their debts – the only case in which the law allows compensation for debts of capital.

Furthermore, the law grants cooperative creditors the power to subrogate and demand from cooperators payment in favour of the cooperative of all contributions in debt, including those that are not overdue but where payment is necessary to maintain credits (art. 30 of the CSC, applicable as a subsidiary matter pursuant to article 9 of the PCC).

Finally, it must be noted that the total amount of contributions in cash made prior to incorporation of a cooperative must be deposited in a bank account opened in the name of the future cooperative (art. 277, nos. 3 and 4 of the CSC, applicable pursuant to art. 9 of the PCC).

3.4.6. The Value of Members' Contributions

Increases or reductions in the value of the shares of a cooperative may occur when the share capital is increased or reduced. This is not expressly provided for in the PCC, but is regulated by the CSC by reference to article 9 of the PCC.

This means that when capital is increased by the allocation of statutory reserves or non-mandatory reserves, the cooperators will pass a resolution in the General Meeting either to issue more shares or to keep the same number of shares but with a higher face value (art. 92.1 of the CSC), or else the cooperators will pass a resolution on the terms required for amendments to the statutes to

56 Conversely, in joint stock companies, a shareholder who fails to honour his or her debts after having been asked by the company to do so loses the shares for which payment is overdue and the payments made for those shares to the company (art. 285.4 of the CSC).

incorporate the reserves and issue new shares corresponding to the increase in share capital, which will be allocated to the cooperative free of consideration.

Where an increase in capital is carried out through new contributions in cash or kind, with regard to the criterion adopted for the distribution of these increases among cooperators, the CSC states at article 266.2.a) that each cooperator receives the amount proportionate to the participation he or she holds at the time, or 'one below that amount, if he or she specifically requests it.'

It is only when increases in capital are open to non-members that the issuance of new shares becomes compulsory, while if share capital is to be subscribed solely by the cooperators, the increase may simply result in a corresponding increase in the value of the existing shares. From this we conclude that in the case of an increase in capital of this type, cooperators will end up either with more shares or with the same number of shares, but with a higher face value.

3.4.7. Compensation

As we saw in section 1, one of the peculiarities of the share capital of cooperatives is the possibility of compensation for cooperative shares referred to in article 88 of the PCC, which translates into the possibility that members may obtain net compensation based on the capital underwritten as a condition of membership. This type of compensation is not permitted in commercial companies (art. 21.2 of the CSC).[57] When interest is paid, the total amount should not exceed 30% of the annual net results, as stated in article 88.2 of the PCC. Therefore, a portion not exceeding 30% can be deducted from the annual results or net surpluses to compensate for shares.

However, as mentioned previously, this compensation is dependent on the fulfilment of two conditions: a provision in the statutes and the existence of positive economic results.

First, the statutes of the cooperative may provide for payments of interest, or they may provide otherwise (art. 88.1 of the PCC); this gives compensation for shares the optional character with which it appears to be regulated. Where there is a provision in the statutes, it falls within the exclusive competence of the General Meeting to establish the interest rate payable by the cooperative to its members (art. 38.e) of the PCC), but this rate may never be speculative, since the *principle of member economic participation* limits compensation (art. 3 of the PCC).

[57] Article 21.2 of the CSC, in support of the principle of the intangibility of capital shares, establishes that 'contractual clauses that assign interest or other rights to a social partner in return for his or her capital or industry are forbidden.' The only possible retribution is profits, where any exist and if they are distributed.

Second, compensation of shares will be dependent on the existence of positive results. Article 100.1 of the PCC states that: 'with the exception of those from transactions with non-members, annual net cooperative surpluses remaining after the payment of interest on shares and allocations to the various reserves may be returned to the cooperator members.' However, a distribution of a surplus among cooperator members (and consequently the payment of interest on shares) may only be made after 'losses from previous years have been covered or after the legal reserve has been used to compensate for these losses to rebuild legal reserves to the level prior to their use' (art. 100.2 of the PCC).

Finally, we should stress that the purpose of this compensation is to reward cooperators for the efforts that the shares represent, thereby simultaneously constituting an incentive for cooperators to invest more significant capital.[58]

3.4.8. Redemption

As already mentioned, a cooperator who resigns is entitled to reimbursement of his or her shares in the cooperative according to their nominal value within the period specified in the statutes or, complementarily, within one year.

This nominal value, plus interest, is what the cooperator is entitled to for the last financial year for his or her share of the surplus and non-mandatory divisible reserves, after deduction, where applicable, of the losses attributable to him or her as revealed in the balance sheet relating to which the right to reimbursement arose (art. 89 of the PCC).

From the wording of the rule, is apparent that cooperators are entitled to the reimbursement of their capital contributions calculated according to their face value and not their actual value, thus avoiding the possibility of giving cooperators the right to liquidate the theoretical actual value of their participation in the assets of the cooperative.

This question is an important one, since in the case of commercial companies, any compensation to be paid to a withdrawing partner is calculated in accordance with article 105.2 of the CSC, which leads in turn to article 1021 of Portuguese Civil Code (liquidation of shares), which states that the value of the shares will be established based on the state of the company at the time when withdrawal occurred or the effects produced by the fact that determined the liquidation.

We should bear in mind, however, that in cooperatives, as in commercial companies, assets can be revalued, or revenues can be allocated to voluntary reserves, which may increase the actual value of the cooperative's assets above the nominal value of its share capital. As a consequence, the actual value of the share capital will be higher than its nominal value.

---

58 See D. Meira, 'O regime de distribuição de resultados nas cooperativas de crédito em Portugal. Uma análise crítica', *Boletín de la Asociación Internacional de Derecho cooperativo*, 2015, 49, pp. 106–109.

In the case of a winding up of a cooperative, cooperators are only entitled to recover their share capital and any corresponding interest (art. 114 of the PCC).

It should be noted, finally, that the PCC provides mechanisms to ensure early large-scale reimbursements that may considerably reduce the assets of the cooperative.[59] In this regard, as already mentioned above, article 89.3 of the PCC establishes that the statutes may provide that when the amount of capital contributions to be reimbursed in a financial year exceeds a certain percentage of the share capital established in said statutes, redemption will be subject to a resolution of the Board of Directors. Pursuant to article 89.4 of the PCC, reasons must be provided for suspensions of reimbursement and they are subject to ratification by the General Meeting.

3.4.9. *Transfer*

Ownership of shares (‘*títulos de capital*’) is not separable from the status as a cooperator. This explains why in cooperatives, restrictions on the free transfer of shares to persons outside the cooperative are the rule and not the exception.

Article 86 of the PCC provides that shares are only transferable with the permission of the Board of Directors or, if the cooperative's statutes so require, of the General Meeting, provided that the acquirer or successor is already a cooperator or has requested admission by satisfying the required conditions.

In this way, the legislator has made the transfer of shares, whether *inter vivos* or *mortis causa*, dependent on the fulfilment of two conditions: prior authorisation from the cooperative board, which is a condition of the effectiveness of the transfer; and that the acquirer must be a member of the cooperative or, if he or she is not, must request admission.

In the latter case, an application for admission may only be made if the prospective cooperator meets the conditions required for this case, which will vary according to the type of cooperative in question.

Authorisation for a transfer will be given as a rule by the Board of Directors, although it will be a power of the General Meeting if the statutes so state. Purchasers who are not yet cooperators will need to request admission explicitly.[60]

If the transfer of the shares is requested by a cooperator, the cooperative's bodies (the Board of Directors or the General Meeting, as provided in the statutes) must act to grant or refuse authorisation within 60 days, after which time the transfer is deemed to be valid and effective (art. 86.2 of the PCC).

---

[59] See M.F. Ribeiro, ‘Os interesses do cooperador demissionário e a tutela do património dos credores da cooperativa’, in Meira (ed.), n. 4 above, pp. 375–386.

[60] See A.S. Martins, ‘Ser (cooperador) ou não ser: eis a questão! Comentário ao Acórdão do Tribunal da Relação de Coimbra de 10 de setembro de 2013’, *Cooperativismo e Economía Social*, 2014, 36, pp. 133–147.

A refusal of consent must be substantiated,[61] first to avoid setting an absolute rule that binds the shareholder to his or her shares and, second to understand the procedure followed by the cooperative's bodies in the exercise of control of the compliance of the transfer with the interests of the cooperative.

A transfer of shares *mortis causa* poses a number of complex problems in the case of cooperatives. With cooperatives that are structured according to contributions of labour, it is necessary for the heir or group of heirs to acquire the objective requirements for being members of the cooperative. There is a true subjective right on the part of the heirs to be shareholders and to be automatically granted the position occupied by the deceased in the cooperative. If the capacity of a cooperator cannot be attained by the heirs, one proceeds with the liquidation of the entry, under the terms of article 89 of the PCC, of who takes the place of the deceased cooperator (art. 86.5 of the PCC).

As regards the *modus operandi* of a transfer, article 86 of the PCC distinguishes between transfers *inter vivos* and *mortis causa* and, within the transfer, between titled shares and non-titled shares (shares in dematerialised format).

An *inter vivos* transfer of titled shares will operate by endorsement of the title to be conveyed signed by the transferor and the acquirer, which binds the cooperative and is recorded in the Registry Book. As for the transfer of non-titled shares, the transfer system of book entry securities provided for in the Portuguese Securities Code ('*Código dos Valores Mobiliários*') is followed, *mutatis mutandis*, operating through registration on the acquirer's account as recorded in the Registry.

In turn, *mortis causa* transfers proceed with the submission of documentary evidence of the capacity of the heir or legatee and are recorded in the *Registry Book* in the name of the holder. With regard to the transfer of titled shares and non-titled shares the legal regime provided for *inter vivos* transfers applies, with some adjustments.

In the Portuguese legal system, cooperatives can only acquire their own shares free of charge (art. 87 of the PCC).

The PCC does not address the issue of the destination of shares acquired by a cooperative for free, but it is our opinion that in the absence of provisions in the statutes defining the final destination of these shares, there are several possibilities open to the cooperative: withdrawal, with the subsequent reduction of share capital by the nominal value of the shares acquired; disposal to cooperators or others; or retention in the hands of the cooperative.

---

[61] According to article 329.2 of the CSC (which applies to cooperatives under article 9 of the PCC), 'where the contract does not specify the grounds for refusal of consent, it is lawful to refuse it on the grounds of any material interest of the company, and the reason for refusal must be stated in the resolution.'

If the cooperative chooses to repay or sell its shares, a prior resolution of the General Meeting will be required.[62] For as long as the shares belong to the cooperative, all rights inherent in them are deemed to be suspended (art. 324.1.a) of the CSC, applicable pursuant to art. 9 of the PCC).

It should be noted, finally, that the existence of shares must be properly communicated and publicised, and that the Board of Directors of the cooperative must register the following in the relevant annual report: (i) the number of shares purchased during the financial year and the reasons for the acquisitions (provided that they must be acquisitions without consideration); (ii) the number of shares sold during the financial year and the reasons for the sales made; and (iii) the number of shares of the cooperative held by it at the end of the financial year (art. 324.2 of the CSC applies, *mutatis mutandis*, pursuant to art. 9 of the PCC).[63]

3.5. RESERVES

The PCC envisages the existence of five types of reserve: a legal reserve, a reserve for education and training, a reserve provided for in the subsidiary legislation applicable to each type of cooperative, the reserves required by the cooperative's statutes, and the reserves established by resolutions of the General Meeting.

The first two types of reserve are mandatory, the third will be mandatory or not according to guidelines from which it derives, and the last two are voluntary, because they depend on the collective will of the cooperators as embodied in the statutes or a resolution of the General Meeting.

3.5.1. Mandatory Reserves

3.5.1.1. Legal Reserve Fund

Article 95 of the PCC constitutes the legal basis for the legal reserves of cooperatives. Paragraph 1 of this provision of the law clearly provides that this reserve is intended exclusively to cover any yearly financial losses. Thus, the fate of the legal reserve will be more restricted in a cooperative than it is in a commercial company: according to article 296 of the CSC, legal reserves in

---

62 As stated in article 320.1 CSC (applicable by virtue of art. 9 of the PCC), the sale of a cooperative's own shares requires a resolution of the General Meeting, which must include: (i) the minimum number and, if any, the maximum number of shares to be sold; (ii) the period, not exceeding 18 months, from the date of the resolution, during which the sale can be made; (iii) the terms of the sale; and (iv) the minimum price or other consideration for the disposal in return for payment.

63 See D. Meira, 'O regime de transmissão dos títulos de capital na cooperativa', *Cooperativismo e Economía Social*, 2011, 33, pp. 283–290.

commercial companies may be used not only to cover losses, as in cooperatives, but also to increase share capital, which cannot happen in the case of cooperatives, as we have shown previously.

This use of legal reserves exclusively to cover losses in the financial year highlights the main – and in the case of cooperatives, the only – purpose of legal reserves, which is to function as a first line of defence of share capital, thus preventing losses arising from the business activity of the cooperative directly affecting the share capital and leading to its reduction. With the existence of the legal reserve, losses will first be covered by the assets of the reserve.

However, in order for the legal reserve to perform this function adequately, a hierarchy must be established among the reserves, with the legal reserve as the last stage: that is, for the purpose of covering losses it will only be used after the other reserves have been exhausted (art. 96.4 of the PCC).

Paragraphs 1 and 4 of article 96 of the PCC refer to losses in the current and previous financial years, but do not specify the origin of these losses. It is our understanding, however, that these losses relate to social losses (losses by the cooperative) to which its assets may be allocated. Losses attributable to the cooperator must be excluded, since they result from participation in the cooperative's transactions.

In the event that the legal reserve is used to cover losses attributable to a cooperator member, that member may be required to restore the amount of the legal reserve to the level existing prior to its use to cover these losses according to the terms of the resolution adopted by the General Meeting (art. 96.5 of the PCC).

With regard to the sources of this reserve (admission fee and annual net surplus), the legislator has established a percentage that 'may not be less than 5%' (art. 96.2 of the PCC). The law has therefore been followed if this percentage is applied. However, this percentage is referred to as being 'not less than', which implies that the statutes of the cooperative or the General Meeting may prescribe a higher percentage than this. Indeed, it is our opinion that a more rapid build-up of a legal reserve will have the beneficial effect of strengthening the assets of the cooperative due to the higher proportion of surplus allocated to it.

Establishment of the reserve will cease to be mandatory from the time it reaches 'an amount equal to the share capital achieved by the cooperative in the financial year' (art. 96.3 of the PCC).[64]

3.5.1.2. The Reserve for Education and Training

The reserve for education and training is governed by article 97 of the PCC, and is also mandatory.

64 See D. Meira, 'A reserva legal nas cooperativas', *Revista de Ciências Empresariais e Jurídicas*, 2011, 19, pp. 7–25.

Paragraph 1 of this provision states that: 'it is mandatory to establish a reserve for educational, cultural and technical training of the cooperators of the cooperative and the community.' As highlighted in section 1, the existence of this reserve derives directly from the principle of education, training, and information and the principle of concern for the community. The formation of this type of reserve for this purpose indicates that cooperatives are not only economic organisations, but also have educational and social purposes. This reserve fund is allocated to cover activities that go beyond satisfaction of the purely individual interests of its members, activities that although not strictly economic, can directly or indirectly produce immediate or deferred economic effects either for the cooperative or for the community in which the cooperative operates. For example, an appropriate use of this reserve might be to train leaders of the cooperative or to increase community awareness of the benefits of the cooperative model, with a consequent increase in the number of cooperators.

According to article 97.2 of the PCC, the following is allocated to this reserve: the part of the admission fee that is not tied to the legal reserve; at least 1% of the annual net surplus derived from transactions with cooperators (this percentage may be higher if the statutes or the General Meeting see fit);[65] grants and subsidies that are specifically designed for the purposes of the reserve; and profits from transactions with non-members that are not allocated to other reserves.

This reserve is not attachable except for the payment of debts incurred in the fulfilment of its purposes (art. 97.7 of the PCC).

3.5.1.3. Voluntary Reserves

We will now address the reserves that depend on the collective will of the cooperators as embodied in a resolution of the General Meeting, at which the mode of formation, implementation, and liquidation of voluntary reserves is determined. The legislator refers to them in article 98.2 of the PCC.

Of note are the voluntary reserves provided for in the subsidiary legislation, such as social reserves of housing and building cooperatives[66] and reserves

---

65 We must stress the system of allocation of the reserve referred to in Decree-Law no. 24/91, 11.01.1991 (Banks of Mutual Agricultural Credit), which provides in art. 44.2.c) that the annual net surplus will be affected '5% maximum, to reserves for cooperative training and education and for mutualism, according to what is decided by the General Meeting, pursuant to a proposal by the Board of Directors.'

66 Pursuant to article 13 of Decree-Law no. 502/99 of 19.11.1999, this reserve will be allocated to cover the life risks and permanent disability of cooperators and the provision of other benefits of a social nature, since the cooperative has a technical, financial and economic capability to this the effect. In cooperatives in which a reserve such as this has been created, the creation of an individual account will be required.

for retirement supplements that may be stipulated in the statutes of fishery cooperatives.[67]

Voluntary reserves can only be established with any annual net surplus remaining after interest on shares, if applicable, has been paid, after allocations for the various reserves have been made, after losses of previous years have been off-set, and, when the legal reserves have been used to compensate for these losses, after the legal reserve has been reset at the level prior to its use (art. 100.2 of the PCC).

Voluntary reserves established for economic results arising from transactions with non-members are not susceptible to division between the cooperators (art. 99 of the PCC), and being made up of surplus from operations with cooperators, they may only be distributed to cooperators who have performed, with the cooperative, operations from which surpluses have resulted and in the precise measure of the proportion of the contribution of these operations.

Because it is certain that only cooperators who have contributed to the formation of this surplus can benefit from a distribution and then up to the exact level of their contribution, it is our opinion that where cooperators decide to allocate an amount of surplus generated by them to voluntary reserves, it should be identified who generated them and the amount of the contribution of each cooperator to the voluntary reserve fund.

The potential distribution of voluntary reserves raises a significant problem relating to the system described in article 114.4 of the PCC, whereby in the event of a liquidation of the cooperative, these reserves will only be divisible if the statutes so provide. Nevertheless, article 86.5 of the PCC refers to the right of successors to the share of non-mandatory reserves, and article 89.2 of the PCC establishes that a resigning cooperator is entitled to a share of non-mandatory divisible reserves. It will therefore be of interest to know whether the successors of a deceased member or resigning members will have the right to share in the fund if the statutes are silent as to the possibility of distribution of voluntary reserves in the event of liquidation of the cooperative. Our interpretation is that in this case, successors or resigning members will not have a right to a proportion of these reserves because of the risk of creating a situation of inequality for members who remain in the cooperative until the cooperative has been dissolved and will not, under these circumstances, have any right in a distribution of these reserves.[68]

---

67 Article 9 of Decree-Law no. 312/81 of 18.11.1981 states that: 'fishing cooperatives may have a reserve for retirement supplements for their cooperators, and its manner of formation, application, and liquidation will be determined in the statutes.'

68 D. Meira, 'A repartição de reservas não obrigatórias decorrente da demissão de cooperador', in Meira (ed.), n. 4 above, pp. 499–504.

3.6. MUTUALIST CAPITAL

The definition of cooperatives in article 2.1 of the PCC leads to their absolute instrumentality, in the sense that they have no purpose in and of themselves, and no autonomy. Cooperatives are means to meet the individual needs (of each and every one) of the cooperators who assist each other within and through them. Cooperatives are intended to operate with their members, who participate in the activities developed within them. We should recall that article 22.2.c) of the PCC states that cooperators 'participate in the general activities of the cooperative and provide the work or services that they must carry out.'

This relationship between cooperators and cooperatives is legally complex, and stresses, on the one hand, the obligation assumed by the cooperator to participate in the activity of the cooperative and, on the other, the consideration of the cooperative designed to meet the needs of the cooperator. Realisation of the social object of the cooperative will therefore entail the cooperators' paying or providing goods or services to the cooperative.[69] In the legal literature, this set of inputs brought into the cooperative by cooperators is called '*mutualist capital*'.

The Portuguese legislation on cooperatives is, however, silent on the question of mutualist capital.

3.7. THE CALCULATION AND ALLOCATION OF REVENUES FROM A COOPERATIVE'S ECONOMIC ACTIVITY

The problem of calculating and distributing revenues is dealt with extremely poorly in both the PCC and the regulations on the various types of cooperative.

In section 1 we pointed out that:

(a) surpluses may be returned to co-operators; because this right to refunds may be waived by a resolution of the General Meeting, there is no subjective right to a refund;
(b) given the members' economic participation in a cooperative's transactions, the distribution of surpluses among cooperators will be made in proportion to the activity or transactions conducted with the cooperative to which they belong (the value of purchases or services consumed in the case of consumer cooperative or users of services, or the value of transactions performed or products delivered in the case of agricultural or trade cooperatives) or in proportion to the work provided by each member (as in the case of cooperative work, in which distributions of surpluses generated

69 See D. Meira, 'A participação de um cooperador na atividade de uma cooperativa agrícola. Anotação ao Acórdão do Tribunal da Relação de Coimbra de 17 de abril de 2012', *Cooperativismo e Economía Social*, 2013, 35, pp. 315–326.

by members is deducted from the surveys previously received 'on their behalf');[70]

(c) the economic results arising from transactions with non-members may not be shared by the cooperators (art. 100.1 of the PCC), and nor may any other extra cooperative results: they must be allocated to indivisible reserves (art. 99 of the PCC), as they are legally regarded as profits;[71]

(d) a percentage of the cooperative's surplus for a financial year in transactions with cooperators will be allocated to the legal reserve (art. 96.2.b) of the PCC) and the reserve for education and training (art. 97.2.b) of the PCC), as well as to the payment of interest by shares (art. 88 of the PCC);

(e) only after these allocations and payments have been made is it possible to calculate any refunds (art. 100.1 of the PCC);

(f) the legislator prevents the distribution of surpluses where and to the extent that they are necessary to cover accumulated losses or to reconstitute the legal reserve (art. 100.2 of the PCC).[72]

3.8. FUNDING THROUGH RETAINED COOPERATIVE REFUNDS

Where there are positive revenues for a financial year, the extent of discretionality available to the General Meeting will be unequivocal as regards their allocation.

On the one hand, the General Meeting may choose freely between distribution to cooperators or the formation of reserves. The General Meeting may consider a policy of building reserves with a view to self-financing (the major option opposing distribution), which might prove much more convenient from the point of view of cooperators and the cooperative alike.

On the other hand, the General Meeting may decide to retain part of the individual refunds temporarily to tackle a lack of sufficient capital. This deferral of refunds will be classified as a loan from the cooperator to the cooperative and should therefore be consented to by the cooperator (art. 294.2 CSC, by reference to art. 9 of the PCC).[73]

All this is in harmony with the principle of member economic participation (art. 3 of the PCC), which points to three possible destinations for the surplus: (i) 'development of their cooperatives'; (ii) 'support for other activities approved by the membership'; and (iii) 'distribution of the surplus for the benefit of the members in proportion to their transactions with the cooperative.'

---

70 Decree-Law no. 313/81 on cultural cooperatives and Decree-Law no. 309/81 on worker cooperatives.

71 See N. Aguiar, 'A tributação do rendimento das cooperativas em Portugal', *Cooperativismo e Economia Social*, 2014, 36, pp. 55–80.

72 See Meira, n. 21 above, pp. 353–374.

73 See Costa, n. 25 above, p. 94.

3.9. MEMBERS' CONTRIBUTIONS FOR PURPOSES OTHER THAN SHARES AND MUTUALIST CAPITAL

The Portuguese legal system provides for the possibility that cooperators may be asked to make other contributions that will not add to the share capital. These members' contributions constitute the 'admission fee' provided for in article 90 of the PCC, pursuant to which 'the statutes of a cooperative may require payment of an admission fee, which may be payable at once or in instalments.' This is an outright contribution, since the cooperator does not receive any rights in return, and unlike contributions to the share capital, the cooperator receives no compensation for the admission fee. In addition, in the financial organisation of the cooperative, the admission fee becomes an asset of the cooperative and not part of its share capital, so that the cooperator is not entitled to recover it in the case of withdrawal. Thus, article 90.2 of the PCC states that the amount of the admission fee 'will be allocated to mandatory reserves, as indicated in the statutes, within the limits of the law.' A minimum of 5% of the value of the admission fee will be allocated to the legal reserve until it 'reaches an amount equal to the share capital achieved by the cooperative in the financial year' (art. 96.3 of the PCC). The remaining value of the admission fees must be allocated to the reserve for education and training (art. 97.2.a) of the PCC).

The requirement of a fee on the admission of a cooperator functions as follows: (i) as an outright grant required of every cooperator member and motivated by the expenses borne by the cooperative that his or her admission entails (the cost of installing new working tools, increased maintenance expenses, and others); and (ii) as a way partially to compensate the contribution made by the existing cooperator members to the common assets of the cooperative.

Of course, one should always bear in mind the *principle of voluntary and open membership*, which prevents the establishment of conditions for admission that are excessively burdensome for aspiring cooperators. Indeed, the establishment of high admission fees constitutes an obstacle to the right of admission. We consider it a negative development that the Portuguese cooperative legislator has eliminated the maximum value of the admission fee: a ceiling for the fee based on share capital, which was then defined by a percentage of the share capital reported on the last approved balance sheet, ceased to exist in the 1980 Code (art. 27).[74]

3.10. OTHER SOURCES OF FUNDING

The Portuguese legal system provides the possibility that the General Meeting may decide on other forms of funding that do not include share capital and that may take the form of issuing investment securities or bonds (art. 90.1 of the PCC).

---

[74] See Meira and Ramos, n. 36 above, pp. 120–122.

Investment securities are financial instruments inspired by the profile of 'participating shares'.[75] As stated in article 91.1 of the PCC, the General Meeting is responsible for passing a resolution to issue investment securities, as well as for determining 'with what goals and under what conditions the Board of Directors may use said product.'

The legislator identifies certain investment securities in article 91.2 of the PCC, namely: those giving entitlement to annual compensation, consisting of a fixed portion and a variable portion; those that confer the right to a reimbursement premium on their holders, which are either fixed or dependent on revenues; those with an interest and reimbursement plan, which vary depending on revenues; those that are convertible into shares ('*títulos de capital*'), provided that the holder can be admitted as a cooperator; and those that have a share premium.

Investment securities may be subscribed to by persons outside the cooperative, even though they grant the cooperators an option of pre-emptive subscription rights for convertible investment securities (art. 91.4 of the PCC). Cooperatives may not, however, acquire investment securities themselves unless they do so free of charge, as in the case of the acquisition of shares (art. 91.5 of the PCC).

Finally, investment securities issued by cooperatives can be treated as bonds as to the part that is not regulated by the PCC (art. 91.6 of the PCC).

Article 92 of the PCC states that the General Meeting is responsible for issuing investment securities, determining the interest rate, imposing a nominative character and transferability of securities, and establishing the terms that are binding on the shares.

The legislator has, however, imposed limits on the issuance of investment securities. Thus, article 92.4 establishes that such issuance may not exceed the amount of the existing paid-up capital in accordance with the last approved financial statements plus any amount of increased capital paid after the closing date of these financial statements. Moreover, paragraph 5 of the same article prohibits any resolution involving the issuance of investment securities, 'while the previous issuance has not been fully subscribed.'

In the event that a public subscription of investment securities is approved, article 93 of the PCC requires that it be 'preceded by an external audit of the cooperative, subject to the regime established by law for this type of issue.'

As to the rights granted to underwriters of investment securities, article 92.3 of the PCC provides that even if they are not members (cooperators or investor members), they may nevertheless participate in General Meetings – without voting rights – provided that the General Meeting so agrees.

---

75 Equity securities created pursuant to Decree-Law no. 321/85 of 05.08.1985 are tendentiously perpetual shares that conferring the right to compensation with two components: one fixed and one variable.

The compensation from these investment securities is mixed, and consists of a fixed part and a variable part, thereby distinguishing them from bonds with compensation consisting only of a fixed part.

With regard to the depreciation of investment securities, the legislator has established in the interests of the financial stability of the cooperative that they will only be reimbursed 'in the event of liquidation of the cooperative, and only after payment of all other creditors of the cooperative or, if it so decides, after the expiry of at least five years since its completion, on the conditions defined for the issue' (art. 91.3 of the PCC).

As determined by article 95 of the PCC, cooperatives are also entitled to issue bonds according to the standards established by the CSC, since this does not prejudice the *Cooperative Principles* or the provisions of the PCC.

3.11. CREDIT SECTIONS IN THE FUNDING OF COOPERATIVES

In the Portuguese legal system, despite the fact that provision is made for multi-purpose cooperatives (those covering an area of activity of this type of cooperative or one that is directly related or connected) and multi-sector cooperatives (those that engage in various types of cooperative within the cooperative sector) in the adoption of an internal organisation by sections – created and governed in operational terms in the statutes of the cooperative (arts. 13 and 19 of Decree-Law no. 335/99 of 20 August 1999 (agricultural types of cooperatives); art. 4 of Decree-Law no. 523/99 of 10 December 1999 (multi-sectoral trade cooperatives); art. 3 of Decree-Law no. 522/99 of 10 December 1999 (multi-sectoral consumer cooperatives); art. 4 of Decree-Law no. 502/99 of 19 December 1999 (multi-sectoral housing and building); and art. 3 of Decree-Law no. 7/98 of 15 January 1998 (social solidarity cooperatives)) – no express provision is made for credit sections for the funding of cooperatives.

3.12. RELATIONS BETWEEN COOPERATIVES AND CREDIT COOPERATIVES

Under the Portuguese legal system, credit cooperatives are limited to the agricultural sector, despite a demand on the part of scholars for the establishment of credit cooperatives beyond that scope.

Only agricultural credit unions can currently operate, therefore. Their purpose is primarily to perform 'agricultural credit functions in favour of their associates' and also 'the exercise of other actions inherent in banking' (art. 1 of Decree-Law no. 24/91 of 11 January 1991). Article 28.2 of the same Decree-Law, however, allows 'credit transactions with non-members' to be carried out, but sets a limit for these transactions, which is 35% of the net assets of the agricultural bank. In accordance with article 28.3, this limit may be raised to 50% with the authorisation of the Bank of Portugal; however, this can only happen 'in duly justified exceptional cases, taking into account, in particular, the level of deposit taking and the capacity for and limitations on the growth and efficiency of agricultural banks' and 'on a proposal from the 'Caixa Central' in the case of associated agricultural credit unions.'[76]

Agricultural credit unions can freely associate with regional unions and national associations (art. 49 of Decree-Law 24/91 of 11 January 1991).

3.13. THE LIABILITY OF COOPERATIVES AND COOPERATORS

As already mentioned, cooperatives have a legal personality distinct from that of each of their members (art. 2.1 and art. 17 of the PCC).

This legal personality necessarily entails patrimonial autonomy: that is, the cooperative has its own assets distinct from and independent of the assets of its members.

Patrimonial autonomy will first mean that the assets of the cooperative are its sole support of liability for debts arising out of its business, and second that account is not taken of other goods for these debts, but only of these assets. On this subject, and regarding the liability of cooperators for the debts of the cooperative, article 23 of the PCC establishes that liability 'is limited to the amount of the subscribed capital, notwithstanding the fact that the statutes of the cooperative may state that the liability of cooperators is unlimited, or limited for some and unlimited for others.' It thus follows that the liability of cooperators will be limited to the amount of capital subscribed, so that only the assets of the cooperative will answer for its debts. Once the subscribed capital has been fully paid up, no other liability may be required of the cooperators by lenders to the cooperative.

The law accepts, however, that the statutes of each cooperative may decide that the liability of cooperators, or some of them, is unlimited, and unlimited liability of cooperators will constitute an additional guarantee for non-members who contract with the cooperative, thereby increasing the means of safeguarding the creditors of the cooperative. This unlimited liability for the debts of the cooperative will only exist if provided in the statutes. If the cooperators' liability for the debts of the cooperative is provided for in the statutes, this liability will be subsidiary to that of the cooperative and joint and several among the liable cooperators.

The possibility of charging a cooperator for losses resulting from his or her participation in the cooperative activity, as referred to in article 89.2 of the PCC, is a separate issue. As we have seen, cooperators are subject not only to an

[76] See A.P. Quelhas, 'O Terceiro Sector na encruzilhada do Sistema Financeiro. O caso das Caixas de Crédito Agrícola Mútuo e das Caixas Económicas em Portugal', *Boletim de Ciências Económicas*, vol. XLVIII, Universidade de Coimbra, Coimbra, 2005, pp. 199–259.

obligation to pay for the share capital of the cooperative, but also to an obligation to participate in the cooperative's transactions (art. 22.2.c) of the PCC).[77]

Losses that have their origin in members' cooperative transactions are not social losses from a legal or accounting point of view, however, but losses of the cooperator. Hence these losses, which originate from the exercise of an activity carried out on behalf of cooperators, must be charged to the cooperators themselves (art. 89.2 of the PCC). Conversely, losses produced by activities with non-members and all other losses will be social losses, and will be borne exclusively by the social assets (art. 35 and art. 80 of the PCC).

It should be noted that the regulations in the PCC relating to the system of allocating these losses to the cooperator are very vague: they do not establish limits on these allocations, which may therefore be unlimited, and they do not establish at what point losses should be charged, namely if they should be accounted for in the period in which they are generated or if they may be postponed to subsequent years.

In relation to the position of the creditors of a cooperator regarding the assets of a cooperative, the rule is that in no case may private creditors of cooperators claim payment from the assets of the cooperative, even to the extent of the cooperator's shareholding. In fact, in cooperatives, private creditors of a cooperator cannot be assigned his or her shares in the cooperative (and so shares cooperators hold cannot be pledged in satisfaction of claims against them) (art. 86.7 of the PCC). The reason for the prohibition against pledging shares originally derives from the strictly personal nature of the cooperator's participation in the cooperative and the consequent need to prevent persons lacking the requirements of the law or the statutes from becoming members of the cooperative as a result or by virtue of an executive action. Furthermore, it prevents the cooperative from being placed in a situation of economic hardship through an intervention by private creditors of cooperators, which might happen if those creditors had the right to demand payment of the capital contributions of the debtor cooperator and the prompt payment of the relevant amount. However, the interests of a private creditor of the cooperator will be met to the extent that a creditor can assert its right to refunds, to compensation from shares, to the liquidation value of capital contributions in the case of reimbursement (due to the withdrawal of the cooperator or the winding up or liquidation of the cooperative), or to the assets that comprise amounts due to the cooperator (unless the statutes of cooperative provide otherwise).

Moreover, under no circumstances may a private creditor of a cooperator require that the cooperative be wound up.[78]

---

77 See D. Meira, 'Da possibilidade de imputação de perdas ao cooperador numa *régie* cooperativa', *Cooperativismo e Economía Social*, 2015, 37, pp. 78–85.

78 See Meira, n. 18 above, pp. 128–133.

3.14. AUTONOMY OF COOPERATIVES

The cooperative principle of autonomy and independence states that: 'Cooperatives are autonomous, self-help organisations controlled by their members. If they enter into agreements with other organisations, including governments, or raise capital from external sources, they do so on terms that ensure democratic control by their members and maintain their cooperative autonomy' (art. 3 of the PCC).

This principle has a dual goal: first, to ensure that relations between cooperatives and the State do not lead to their being exploited, and second, to ensure that the capital inflow from external sources jeopardises neither their autonomy nor democratic control by their members.

In the Portuguese legal system, there are specific rules regulating the relationship between cooperatives and the State.

Articles 80 and 85 of the CRP rule that the State determines the legal framework for regulating the activity of cooperatives. In particular, the law establishes the tax and financial benefits as well as the creation of privileged conditions in terms of access to credit and technical assistance.

Article 5.f of the LBES also enshrines the principle of autonomous and independent management in relation to the public authorities and other entities outside the social economy as one of the guiding principles of the social economy. Later, article 9 of the LBES establishes that in its relations with these entities, the State must 'encourage and support the creation and activity' of cooperatives (art. 9.a) of the LBES); 'ensure the principle of cooperation, considering, especially in the planning and development of public welfare systems, the material, human and economic capacity utilisation of social economy entities, and their levels of technical competence and insertion in the economic and social fabric of the country' (art. 9.b) of the LBES); and 'ensure the necessary stability of the relations established with social economy entities' (art. 9.d) of the LBES).

In turn, articles 87–89 of the PCC attribute to the '*António Sérgio Cooperative for Social Economy*' ('*Cooperativa António Sérgio para a Economia Social*' – CASES) a set of public law powers over cooperatives, including the power to monitor the use of the cooperative form, the power to accredit cooperatives (issuing credentials proving their lawful establishment and operation), and the power to require the administrative winding up of a cooperative independently or its judicial winding up by the Public Prosecutor's office.

As a consequence of all these principles and standards, the State must encourage cooperativism, but not impose it.

On the other hand, this same requirement of autonomy aims to ensure that capital inflows from external sources do not call into question the independence or the democratic control by the members of cooperatives. Accordingly, no investor member may hold more than 10% of the total votes of the cooperators, and investor members cannot have a total of voting rights in excess of 30% of the total votes of cooperators (art. 41.7 of the PCC).

3.15. WINDING UP AND LIQUIDATION

Winding up is a modification of the legal status of a cooperative characterised by its entry into liquidation. The cooperative will retain its legal personality until registration of the conclusion of the liquidation process (art. 160. 2 of the CSC, applicable by reference to art. 9 of the PCC) and from the time of winding up onwards, the words 'in liquidation' must be added to its name (art. 146, nos. 2 and 3, of the CSC, by reference to art. 9 of the PCC).

Winding up is a consequence of verification that there is a cause for winding up, but not all causes operate in the same way. Article 112 of the PCC lists voluntary winding up resulting from a resolution of the cooperators, administrative winding up and compulsory judicial winding up.

Causes of voluntary winding up are the necessary and sufficient conditions for a cooperative to be wound up. The following will lead to a voluntary winding up of a cooperative: exhaustion of the social object; expiry of a time period, if the cooperative has been established temporarily; verification of any cause for extinguishment in the statutes; merger by integration, incorporation, or division; or a resolution of the General Meeting.

A winding up by merger, integration, incorporation, or division can also be requested through judicial means by unions, federations, or confederations of cooperatives, in accordance with article 109.5 of the PCC.

Pursuant to article 112.3 of the PCC, the causes for an administrative winding up depend on the occurrence of the following facts: the absolute impossibility of continuing the object or a lack of coincidence between the object actually being pursued and the object expressed in the statutes; or a reduced number of members below the legal minimum for a period exceeding twelve months, provided that the reduction is not temporary or occasional.

After the occurrence of any of these events, the administrative procedure to wind up of the cooperative can be initiated at the request of any cooperator or successor-in-interest or any creditor of the cooperative or any creditor of cooperators with unlimited liability. Where the cooperative's activity does not match the object stated in the statutes, CASES may request the competent Registry Office to commence the administrative winding up procedure (art. 118.2 of the PCC).

According to article 112.4 of the PCC, winding up is declared in an administrative winding up procedure initiated *ex officio* by the competent Registry Office in the following instances: a failure to deliver an income tax form for two consecutive years, as communicated by the tax office to the competent registration office; communication by the tax administration to the

Registry Office of the absence of any effective activity observed in terms of tax legislation; and communication by the tax administration to the Registry Office of an unofficial declaration of cessation of activity in accordance with the tax legislation.

Winding up may also become effective by a resolution of the General Meeting (arts. 38.i) and 112.1.f) of the PCC). This resolution must be passed by a qualified majority of at least two-thirds of the votes cast, but winding up will not occur if the minimum number of members required to incorporate the cooperative is willing to declare that they will ensure its continuity (art. 40.2 of the PCC).

The existence of a final court decision declaring the insolvency of a cooperative constitutes grounds for compelling a winding up by judicial process. This ascertains that the operations of the cooperative do not comply with the *Cooperative Principles* and that it systematically uses illegal means to pursue its objectives or makes use of the cooperative form to achieve undue legal benefits (art. 112.1, g) and h) of the PCC).

Pursuant to nos. 1 and 2 of article 113 of the PCC, the winding up of cooperatives, whatever the reason, involves the appointment of a Winding Up Board that is responsible for the liquidation of the assets. The General Meeting that decides the winding up elects a Winding Up Board, on which it confer the necessary powers within the established time limit and carries out the liquidation.

When the liquidation has been completed, the Winding Up Board submits the accounts to the General Meeting, to the Registry Office, or to the Court, as appropriate, and prepares a project for dividing the balance from the liquidation in the form of a chart (art. 113.7 of the PCC).

Depending on the particular case, the last General Meeting, the Registry Office, or the court designates who will have custody of the cooperative's books, papers and documents, which must be kept for a period of five years (art. 113.8 of the PCC).

Let us now focus on the question of the destination of the assets in liquidation. It should be noted first that the assets cannot be divided until all the debts of the cooperative have been paid or seized (art. 154 of the CSC, by reference to art. 9 of the PCC).

The remaining assets will be divided in accordance with the provisions of article 114.1 of the PCC: once the expenses of the liquidation process have been paid, any surplus is applied immediately in the following order: (i) payment of wages and benefits due to employees of the cooperative; (ii) payment of any remaining debts of the cooperative, including the redemption of investment securities, bonds, and other potential benefits due to cooperative members; and (iii) redemption of capital contributions.

Upon liquidation of the cooperative's assets, article 114.2 of the PCC stipulates that any amount of the legal reserve that is unaffected by the need to cover losses for the financial year and cannot be used for a different application 'can move, with the same purpose, to a new cooperative entity to be formed following the merger or division of the cooperative in liquidation'. Article 114.3 of the PCC has established, however, that 'where the cooperative in liquidation is not succeeded by a new cooperative entity, the application of the balance of the mandatory reserves will be allocated to another cooperative, preferably from the same city, to be selected by a federation or confederation that represents the main activity of the cooperative.' Article 114.4 goes even further, providing that 'the provisions of numbers 2 and 3 of this article will apply to the reserves established, pursuant to article 98 of this Code, to liquidation if the statutes say nothing', which means that this regime may also cover voluntary reserves if the statutes are silent.

This impossibility of distributing residual assets in the event of a liquidation derives from the social function that cooperatives are required to fulfil, and means that following the liquidation, they should be used for the promotion of the cooperative movement (the so-called principle of disinterested distribution).

As regards the question of determining the rights of a cooperator in the event of the liquidation of a cooperative, the PCC states that in the event a cooperative is wound up, cooperators will be entitled only to recover their contributions to the share capital (art. 114.1.c) of the PCC). Therefore, in a cooperative, we do not refer to '*final profits*' or '*liquidation*'[79] as in commercial companies, because, as we have seen, part of the cooperative's assets cannot be appropriated by its cooperators.

Notwithstanding the fact that the PCC and the complementary legislation are silent regarding the criteria for distribution both among cooperators and with reference to the remaining assets, we believe that under the cooperative *principle of member economic participation*, these criteria would be calculated with regard to the extent of participation in the cooperative transactions.

Finally, as we have mentioned previously, article 114.1 of the PCC states that there is an order of preference in sharing the remaining assets, with the employees of the cooperative in a preferred position as to payment of their wages and other benefits, followed by payment of the remaining debts of the cooperative, including the redemption of investment securities, bonds, and any other benefits due to the members of the cooperative, and finally redemption of the members' capital contributions.

---

79 Final or liquidation profits are those that derive from determination of an excess of assets over liabilities at the end of the liquidation process (art. 156 ff., CSC). Considering that the commercial company may eventually expire, the right to participate in the profits resulting from art. 21.1.a) of the CSC is encompassed in the right of shareholders to participate in the final or liquidation profits.

3.16. SPECIFIC ASPECTS OF THE FINANCIAL STRUCTURE OF SOCIAL SOLIDARITY COOPERATIVES

As we saw in section 1, social solidarity cooperatives, which are regulated by Decree-Law no. 78/98 of 15 January 1998, are cooperatives whose activities are concentrated in the area of social services. Their social object consists of a clear mission to assist in situations of social and economic vulnerability, supported by a paradigm of social intervention. They provide assistance to families, children, young people, seniors, disabled people, the unemployed, and other vulnerable groups with regard to their professional integration, education, training, and occupational and residential care.

Because the entire activity of these cooperatives falls within a framework of solidarity, the legal regime that establishes its financial structure has certain specific features. The impossibility of distributing surpluses to members (which means that all surpluses must be allocated to reserves (art. 7 of Decree-Law no. 78/98)), and the extension of the rights, duties, and benefits (including taxation and access to credit) to these cooperatives of social solidarity as foreseen in the Statute of the Private Institutions of Social Solidarity,[80] regulated by Decree-Law no. 119/83 of 25 February 1983, as amended and republished by Decree-Law no. 172-A/2014 of 14 November 2014, should be especially highlighted.

4. CONTROL OF COOPERATIVES

4.1. INTRODUCTION – THE NEED FOR INTERNAL AND EXTERNAL CONTROLS

In the Portuguese legal system, cooperatives are subject to two levels of control: internal and external. Internal control is exercised by members and bodies of cooperatives, while external control is exercised by the courts, administrative authorities (regulators and supervisory), and auditors.

As in other previous sections, with regard to cooperative control we will make reference to the PCC, the twelve pieces of legislation governing each of the twelve types of cooperative, the constitutional framework of the Portuguese cooperative sector, the LBES, and the legal framework of commercial companies as regards cooperative control, as provided in the CSC by reference from article 9 of the PCC.

There are several reasons that justify the need for control of cooperatives, both internal and external.

---

80 This extension is planned and permitted by Law no. 101/97 of 13.09.1997.

4.1.1. *The Principle of Positive Discrimination in Favour of Cooperatives*

One of the grounds for the internal and external control of cooperatives is the *principle of positive discrimination* in favour of the cooperative sector, which is enshrined in both the CRP and the LBES.

Article 85.1 of the CRP expresses the State's commitment to and support for the creation and activity of cooperatives when it states that: 'the State will stimulate and support the creation and activities of cooperatives' and where, in article 85.2, it ensures that 'the law defines the fiscal and financial benefits to be enjoyed by cooperatives, as well as preferential terms and conditions for obtaining credit and technical assistance'. The above-mentioned stimulus results mainly from legislative measures that increase interest in the activities of cooperatives, while support will be the result of administrative measures aimed at facilitating the specific features of that activity.

For its part, the LBES establishes that the public authorities shall 'promote the creation of mechanisms to strengthen the economic and financial self-sustainability of entities of the Social Economy, in compliance with the terms of article 85 of the Constitution of the Portuguese Republic' (art. 10.2.b) of the LBES).

This constitutional rule establishes the *principle of protection of the social and cooperative sector*, which, in turn, is to be the foundation for the adoption of distinct solutions in the areas of taxation, access to credit, technical assistance, and others for cooperatives.

From this constitutionally-established positive discrimination we may draw the conclusion that if relations between the State and cooperatives in Portugal were exactly the same as those between the State and private companies, the CRP would not be complied with. This is why the State may decide freely on tax issues or on granting other benefits to cooperatives, but is not constitutionally authorised to grant them any support. The same applies support at the technical and credit levels.

The LBES adds that promotion of the social economy (cooperatives have always been the strongest branch of the social economy) by the public authorities will also include:

- 'supporting the creation of new social economy entities and the diversity of social economy initiatives by triggering innovative responses to the challenges faced by local, regional, national, or any other communities, and by removing obstacles to the formation and development of economic activities of social economy entities' (art. 10.2.c) of the LBES);
- 'promoting research and innovation in the social economy and training social economy entities, as well as access on the part of these entities to technological innovations and organisational management practices and processes' (art. 10.2.d) of the LBES);

- and 'deepening the dialogue between public authorities and representatives of the social economy at a national and European level, thus promoting mutual knowledge and the dissemination of good practices' (art. 10.2.e) of the LBES).

Promotion of the social economy also means providing these entities with 'favourable treatment in terms of taxation that the law defines as taking into consideration the entities' nature and foundation' (art. 11 of the LBES).

This more favourable differentiated treatment of cooperatives accentuates the need for more effective and appropriate external controls. The LBES realises this where, in article 8, it highlights the importance of transparency and the subsequent supervisory mechanisms of the activities of social economy entities.

Accordingly, ensuring transparency is the State's responsibility, in such a way that when 'articulated with the organisations that represent social economy entities, it develops mechanisms of supervision to guarantee a transparent relationship between the entities and their members in an effort to optimise resources, namely through the utilization of supervisory structures that are already in use' (art. 9.c) of the LBES).

4.1.2. *The Need to Protect the Indivisible Assets of the Cooperative*

As discussed in section 3, one of the specific features of the assets of cooperatives is the clear distinction established between their divisible and indivisible assets. Divisible assets consist of the portion of the assets that corresponds to the share capital that each cooperator brings to the cooperative and, under certain conditions, by the portion of voluntary reserves defined by the cooperative that eventually belongs to the cooperator. Indivisible assets are those corresponding to the legal reserve and the reserve for education and training, and they maintain their absolute indivisibility both during the life of a cooperative and at the time it is wound up (arts. 99 and 114 of the PCC).

We should recall that this impossibility of distributing the residual assets in the event of liquidation derives from the social function that the cooperative is called upon to fulfil, and means that after liquidation, their destination must be the promotion of the cooperative movement (the so-called principle of disinterested distribution).

Control of respect for this principle is of great importance in the context of the cooperative movement.

It will first be up to cooperative federations and confederations to carry out these controls, although the PCC does not explicitly mention it, except that article 108 of the PCC states that cooperative federations and confederations 'have the purposes of representation, coordination and provision of services, and may carry out any activity permitted by law that is consistent with cooperative principles.' These controls must be included within the segment of the norm that refers to the conduct of 'any activity ... consistent with cooperative principles.'

As we shall see below, in Portugal this type of control is mainly carried out by CASES.

4.1.3. *The Need to Protect the Cooperative Identity: Controls of Compliance with Cooperative Principles*

In the Portuguese legal system, the cooperative principles are mandatory (art. 2.1 of the PCC), and are even enshrined in the Constitution. Article 61.2 of the CRP states that: 'everyone is accorded the right to freely form cooperatives, subject to compliance with cooperative principles.' In turn, article 82.4 of the CRP states that the cooperative sub-sector covers 'the means of production that cooperatives possess and manage in accordance with cooperative principles.' Hence, disregard for the *Cooperative Principles* in the activities of a cooperative is a cause for compulsory judicial winding up (art. 112.1.h) of the PCC).

In particular, it will be up to CASES to request, through the Public Prosecutors and the appropriate Court, the winding up of cooperatives whose operations do not comply with the *Cooperative Principles* (art. 118.1.a) of the PCC). In this case, we are dealing with a form of external control of the cooperative structure.

4.1.4. *The Need to Protect the Mutualist Scope*

Article 2.2 of the PCC states that: 'in pursuit of their objects, cooperatives are allowed to conduct business with non-members, subject to any restrictions set forth in the law applicable to each type of cooperative.'

Transactions with non-members may be subject to limitations in the sectorial legislation covering the various types of cooperative. Limitations are expressly provided for in the following: article 9 of Decree-Law no. 523/99 of 10 December 1999 (trade cooperatives); article 7 of Decree-Law no. 313/81 of 19 November 1981 (cultural cooperatives); article 14 of Decree-Law no. 502/99 of 19 November 1999 (housing and building cooperatives); article 6 of Decree-Law no. 309/81 of 16 November 1980 (worker cooperatives); article 6 of Decree-Law no. 323/81 of 4 December 1981 (service cooperatives); and article 24, nos. 2 and 3, of Decree-Law no. 24/91 of 11 January 1991 (agricultural credit cooperatives). Only in this last decree are limits on credit transactions with non-members set out (35% of the cooperative's total net assets, which may be increased to 50% subject to authorisation by the Bank of Portugal).

To preserve the mutualist scope – preventing the conversion of a cooperative into a *de facto* for-profit company – Portuguese cooperative law obliges the allocation of financial results arising from transactions with non-members that may not be distributed among cooperators (art. 100.1 of the PCC) to indivisible reserves. The basis for this legal regime is that in cooperatives, the economic results of transactions with non-members must be legally regarded as profit and not as a true cooperative surplus, since these transactions are not carried out as a part of a mutualistic activity.

To this end, cooperatives must have separate accounts that allow surpluses from activities with members to be distinguished from profits obtained from transactions with non-members or other extra-cooperative activities. These separate accounts also permit a cooperative to account for its divisible and indivisible assets without the risk of confusion.

Where there are no separate accounts, cooperatives must at least implement a system that will facilitate the determination of a presumptive coefficient of mutuality based on which all surpluses and the amount of profits will be calculated, calculating the amount that can be distributed among cooperators as a surplus and the amount of extra-cooperative results that must be allocated to indivisible reserves.

The PCC and the accounting standard applicable to cooperatives (the SNC) are silent on this issue, so that as Portuguese law currently stands, it is possible not to adopt different accounting treatments for transactions with cooperators and non-members, with consequent difficulties in terms of controls over the cooperative's activities.

The issue of controlling compliance with the limitations on transactions with non-members and the indivisibility of profits is extremely important in order to prevent any risk of demutualisation that might, if it were to occur, give rise to a civil liability claim against the members of the Board of Directors and the Supervisory Board, and ultimately be a reason for the cooperative to be wound up (art. 118.2 of the PCC).

4.1.5. The Need to Protect the Interests of Creditors

As we saw in section 3, the rule for cooperatives is that only the assets of a cooperative are available to its creditors, and the liability of its cooperators is therefore limited to the amount of their subscribed capital (arts. 23 and 80 of the PCC).

In this context, it is of extreme significance to creditors of a cooperative to obtain accurate information regarding the probity of the accounts, the existence and/or solvency of the cooperative enterprise, the existence of any fraud, and the cooperative's compliance with its legal obligations.

As we will see later, obtaining this information presents an obstacle for creditors due to the lack of an obligation to file annual reports and accounting documents with the Commercial Registry (art. 4 of the Commercial Registry Code).

The protection of creditors is also ensured through the mechanism of directors' liability (provided for in art. 73 of the PCC), which will be discussed later. We anticipate, however, that under this rule, the members of the Board of Directors and the Supervisory Board will answer to creditors of the cooperative when the assets of the cooperative become insufficient to satisfy their claims due to a failure to comply with legal or statutory provisions for their protection, particularly in cases involving distribution of legal or other mandatory reserves among cooperators, or the distribution of a fictitious surplus.

4.2. EXTERNAL CONTROLS ON REGISTRATION OF THE INCORPORATION OF A COOPERATIVE – CONTROLS OF LEGALITY

In the Portuguese legal system, there is no prior control of the formation or registration of a cooperative. This means that any public control of legality, which is the responsibility of the Commercial Registry and CASES, only takes place upon registration of the incorporation of the cooperative with the *Commercial Registry* and CASES.

Effectively, the incorporation of a cooperative follows a process that is structured primarily into three phases:

(a) act of incorporation and statutes (arts. 10 to 16 of the PCC);
(b) registration (art. 17 of the PCC and art. 4 of the Commercial Registration Code);
(c) publication (art. 70.1.b) of the Commercial Registration Code).

The incorporation of primary cooperatives must be conducted in writing, and may also involve more formality if required 'for the transmission of the assets that represent the cooperators' initial share capital' (art. 10 of the PCC). Secondary cooperatives (cooperative unions, federations, and confederations) are governed by 'the provisions applicable to primary cooperatives … as regards everything that is not specifically regulated in this chapter' (arts. 101 and 107 of the PCC).

The incorporation of a cooperative is subject to registration (art. 17 of the PCC and art. 4 of the Commercial Registration Code) and to publication on a public access internet site (art. 70.1.b) of the Commercial Registration Code).

The incorporation and operation of agricultural credit banks must be authorised in advance by the Bank of Portugal, and they depend on special registration at the Bank of Portugal as to a set of acts (arts. 4 to 10 of Decree-Law 24/91 of 11 January 1991).

In addition to the registration referred to in article 17 of the PCC conferring legal personality, cooperatives are subject to other registrations, and must send CASES a copy of all documents referring to their incorporation (art. 116.1 of the PCC). CASES issues an annual credential attesting to the legal incorporation and proper functioning of the cooperative (art. 117.1 of the PCC).

4.3. MANAGEMENT AUDITS OF COOPERATIVES

4.3.1. Controls of the Efficiency of Management of a Cooperative

There are three indexes for assessing the effectiveness of the management of cooperatives, which are therefore subject to internal and external controls of the level of satisfaction of the cooperators' economic, social, and cultural needs; the ability of the cooperative to ensure the conditions for the sustainability and efficient use of its financial resources; and the quality of the cooperative's relations with the community.

The first index of effectiveness relates to the achievement of the cooperative's social object. The purpose of cooperatives is to 'meet the needs and economic aspirations' of their members (art. 2.1 of the PCC). First and foremost, it will be up to the cooperators, individually or collectively, to control the pursuit of the social object through their participation in the cooperative's transactions (art. 22.2.c) of the PCC) and as members of the cooperative (arts. 21, 29, 33 and 38 of the PCC). In turn, it will be up to the Board of Directors, as the cooperative's management body, to carry out all acts required for the activities included in the cooperative's object (arts. 47 and 62 of the PCC). Finally, it is up to the Supervisory Board, the Audit Committee, or the General and Supervisory Board to monitor the adequacy of the business organisation for attaining its social object (arts. 53, 61, and 66 of the PCC). Externally, this scrutiny is the responsibility of CASES (arts. 116 and 118 of the PCC).

The second index relates to the economic efficiency of the management of the cooperative, especially as embodied in the management report and financial year accounts and other related documents, which are produced annually by the Board of Directors and examined and voted on annually by the General Meeting, and which are the subject of an opinion by the Supervisory Board (art. 38, a) and c), art. 47.a), and art. 53 of the PCC). We will discuss this in greater depth and develop the discussion further below.

The third index relates to the social dimension of the cooperative's object. As we have discussed in sections 1 and 2, the social object of a cooperative is not limited to meeting the needs of its members, but must also be attentive to the interests of the community in which the cooperative carries out its activity.

Thus, although primarily focused on the needs of their members, cooperatives work to achieve the sustainable development of their communities, applying criteria that have been approved by their members.

As highlighted in section 2, given the legal framework of cooperatives – namely the fact that the activities of their bodies must comply with the *principle of concern for the community* (art. 3 of the PCC, which asserts that 'cooperatives work for the sustainable development of their communities through policies approved by their members') – it should be argued that there is a legal duty on the part of the governance bodies, although they are focused on meeting the needs of the members, to work to achieve the sustainable development of their communities, according to criteria they themselves approve.

Accordingly, the bodies responsible for cooperative governance have a duty to integrate the fundamental values of the CSR into their respective activities, and this duty is subject to both internal (the responsibility of the General Meeting and the Supervisory Board) and external (the responsibility of CASES) controls. As a consequence, the Board of Directors of a cooperative must draw up a social report, which must be approved by the General Meeting and sent to CASES for the purpose of issuing the credentials proving the legal incorporation and proper operation of the cooperative (art. 116.c) of the PCC).

4.3.2. *The Role of Cooperators in Controlling Cooperative Management*

The PCC attributes a very important role to cooperators in the control of their cooperative: (i) through their participation at general meetings (by the exercise of their voting rights); (ii) by giving them a broad right to information; and (iii) by establishing the requirement that the members of the cooperative's bodies be cooperators. Consequently, members of cooperative bodies are elected by the General Meeting from among the cooperators (art. 29 of the PCC), and it is also the responsibility of the General Meeting to dismiss these members (art. 38.a) of the PCC).

It is the sole responsibility of the General Meeting (which is composed of all the cooperators) to consider and vote on the management report and accounts for the financial year as well as the opinion of the Supervisory Board, to assess the legal certification of accounts, if any, to approve and vote on the budget and activity plan for the following year, to establish the interest rates payable to members of the cooperative, and to approve the form of distribution of surpluses (art. 38 of the PCC).

As outlined in section 2, the General Meeting is the supreme body of cooperatives, and its decisions are binding on the remaining bodies (art. 33.1 of the PCC). From this primacy of the General Meeting it follows that it may arrogating to itself the powers of other organs, particularly those of the Board of Directors, at any time and in addition to its exclusive powers set forth in article 38. This power of the General Meeting distinguishes cooperatives from joint stock companies, in which 'on matters of corporate management, shareholders may only act at the request of the Board' (art. 373.2 of the CSC).

Scrutiny of the performance of the Board of Directors and Supervisory Board by the members of a cooperative occurs particularly at the time when the management report and accounts for the financial year are assessed (art. 38.b) of the PCC). Indeed, it may happen that the management report and accounts for the financial year denounce or indicate the conduct by the cooperative of unlawful, wrongful and harmful acts, which may support a liability action against the members of the Board of Directors and Supervisory Board (arts. 73 to 79 of the PCC).

In addition to the annual control the General Meeting exerts over the Board of Directors, cooperators may also exercise their right to information individually or collectively. As outlined in section 2, we can distinguish an active component and a passive component of this right to information.

The multiple obligations of the cooperative's bodies, including the Board of Directors, to disclose facts and make documents relating to the activities of the cooperative available are included in the passive component. Of note here is the significant duty of information that falls on the Board of Directors to make the management report, the financial year accounting documents, the business plan and the budget for the following financial year available to members at the cooperative's head office, accompanied by an expert opinion from the Supervisory Board (art. 47.a) of the PCC and art. 263.1 of the CSC, applicable by reference to article 9 of the PCC).

The active component of the right to information is enshrined in article 21.1.d) of the PCC, which states that members have the right to request information from the competent bodies of the cooperative and examine its records and accounts.[81]

4.3.3. The Main Object of Controls: The Cooperative's Accounts (Financial Audit)

4.3.3.1. The Preparation of Documents Presenting the Accounts

Portuguese law requires all business owners to maintain commercial accounting records and to prepare balance sheets and accounts (arts. 29 and 62 of the Commercial Code and arts. 65 and 66 of the CSC), and these duties extend to cooperatives, with certain specific aspects, as we will see.

The reporting obligation, which is the responsibility of the Board of Directors (art. 47.a) of the PCC), correlates with a right of cooperators to inspect this accounting, not to be confused with cooperators' right to receive information or to consult documents.

Thus, in addition to the duty to prepare accounting documents and records, the members of Boards of Directors are obliged to submit these documents to the competent bodies of the cooperative, namely the General Meeting and the Supervisory Board, Audit Committee or a General and Supervisory Board.

---

[81] On this issue, see Meira, n. 34 above, pp. 9–35.

Accounting documents and records include the management report and accounts for the financial year (balance sheet, profit-and-loss account, notes, and other documents).

In addition to the financial effects of past events, the annual report includes very significant non-financial information so that the zeal with which the Board of Directors performs its duties in relation to the resources entrusted to it can be evaluated. It is an extremely important document in liability lawsuits (both civil and criminal) against the members of management bodies.

The descriptive and analytical content of cooperatives' management reports and accounts will not be identical to those of commercial companies, given the specific nature of cooperatives' transactions and the calculation of their financial results. These reports must therefore specifically state the criteria applied in the management of the cooperative in order to attain its mutual scope and the volume of transactions carried out with cooperators (transactions with members) and non-members (transactions with non-members). This last aspect proves extremely important in order to prevent phenomena of demutualisation of cooperatives, ensuring compliance with the cooperative principles, as outlined above.

4.3.3.2. Specifics of the Filing of Accounts in the Portuguese Legal System

As highlighted in section 3, in the Portuguese legal system, cooperatives are not required to file their management reports and accounts for the financial year with the Commercial Registry. Article 4 of the Commercial Registration Code sets out the facts relating to cooperatives and registration, and they do not include those relating to accounts, as is expressly provided in the case of commercial companies (art. 3.n) of the Commercial Registration Code).

This lack of foresight regarding management reports and accounts means that the Commercial Registry does not perform the function of financial advertising as fully for cooperatives, an omission that we believe to be open to criticism because it limits the control creditors can exercise over cooperatives.

Cooperatives are also required to submit both their management reports and accounts to CASES after obtaining approval from the respective General Meeting, as well as a Social Report, which is a prerequisite for obtaining credentials attesting to their legal incorporation and proper operation (arts. 116 and 117 of the PCC). In this context, CASES has allowed creditors of a cooperative claiming a legitimate interest to query the accounting documents of cooperatives deposited there. The PCC does not, however, make it clear whether filing can be treated as a registration of cooperatives designed to make their legal status public; and therefore the question might be asked as to whether these documents are protected by confidentiality (in the sense that they were sent by the cooperative for the particular purpose of obtaining the credentials).

4.3.4. *The Audit/Statutory Audit*[82]

The PCC does not provide for an external audit of cooperatives. As we interpret it, this closed control system is a result of the fact that the Portuguese legislator has placed the control mechanisms for cooperative governance exclusively in the hands of members through their participation in the activities of the cooperative and in General Meetings (by the exercise of their voting rights) by giving them a broad right to information and establishing the rule that the members of bodies (including the Supervisory Board) must be members of the cooperative.

As highlighted in section 2, in the case of cooperatives that are obliged to submit to statutory auditing – see article 43 of Law 140/2015 of 7 September 2015, which approved the Statute of Statutory Auditors – supervision will be entrusted to a Supervisory Board and to a Statutory Auditor who is not a member of the Supervisory Board (art. 51.1.c) of the PCC). In the models provided for in article 28.1, b) and c) of the PCC, a Statutory Auditor will always exist, but he or she will not join the Supervisory Board.

The functions of the Statutory Auditor are described in article 70 of the PCC. They are as follows: to verify the bookkeeping, the accounting records and the documents that support them; to verify the cash flow and inventory levels of all kind of goods and assets belonging to the cooperative; to check the accuracy of the accounting documents; and to check whether the accounting policies and evaluation criteria adopted by the cooperative lead to a correct valuation of assets and results.

The intervention of a statutory auditor is always required in the case of agricultural banks and the Central Bank, which, pursuant to article 37 of the Legal Framework of Mutual Agricultural Credit and Cooperative Credit Scheme (RJCAM), must engage an auditing firm run by a chartered accountant. Similarly, although it refers to the legal certification of accounts, we should mention article 42-A, which was added to the RJCAM by Decree-Law no. 142/2009 of 16 June 2009.

This is also a requirement for cooperatives above a certain size.

Agricultural cooperatives (art. 11 and the chart attached to Decree-Law no. 335/99 of 20 August 1999, as amended by Decree-Law no. 23/2001 of 30 January 2001), trade cooperatives (art. 10.1 of Decree-Law no. 523/99 of 10 December 1999) and consumer cooperatives (art. 7.1 of Decree-Law

[82] In this study, we use these two concepts interchangeably, and yet they are different: while the term 'Statutory Audit' refers to situations in which audited accounts for statutory auditor are the result of a legal requirement, the term 'Audit' refers to an accounting control resulting from a statutory or contractual provision.

no. 522/99 of 10 December 1999) are compelled to obtain legal certification of their accounts if they exceed two of the following limits for two consecutive years:

(i) total balance sheet: 1,500,000 euros;
(ii) total net sales and other income: 3,000,000 euros;
(iii) average number of employees during the year: 50.

Housing and building cooperatives (art. 11.1 of Decree-Law no. 502/99 of 19 November 1999) will also be bound to obtain legal certification of their accounts if they exceed two of the following three limits for two consecutive years:

(i) total number of cooperators: 500;
(ii) total equity capital: 1,000,000 euros;
(iii) total financial statements: 5,000,000 euros.

Finally, the statutory auditor is civilly liable to the cooperative and its cooperators and creditors for damage caused to them by his or her wrongful conduct (art. 77 of the PCC).[83]

4.3.5. *The Inadequacy of the Accounting Tools Used by Cooperatives to Compile their Accounts*

In preparing their accounts, cooperatives are subject to the SNC.[84] The application of the SNC to cooperatives' accounts of introduces certain difficulties because it is an accounting model geared to commercial companies, and does not address the specific aspects of transactions by cooperatives.

As highlighted in section 3, the Cooperative Principles of voluntary and open membership and member economic participation hinder understanding of the share capital, whether the goal is maintaining the share capital or the distribution of profits.

On the other hand, according to the SNC, the information that is provided must be sufficient to evaluate the performance of an entity, in particular its profitability, which is inadequate with regard to the actual information needed by cooperatives and their users, since the primary purpose of cooperatives is to meet the economic and social needs of their members (mutuality) and not to make a profit.

---

[83] See A.M.G. Rodrigues, 'A alteração das exigências de certificação legal de contas para as entidades que aplicam a NCRF-ESNL', *Cooperativismo e Economía Social*, 2014, 36, pp. 294–297.

[84] Approved by Decree-Law no. 158/2009, 13.07.2009.

Furthermore, in the SNC, the privileged user of the information disclosed in the financial statements is clearly the investor. The information prepared is based on assumptions that are very much conditioned by the logic of profitability and results distributed to investors, which is inadequate for the logic of cooperatives, which is based on a mutualist purpose, and where distributions of cooperative surpluses are made in proportion to the transactions carried out by each member.

Finally, income statements are dedicated to the economic and financial performance of the corporate entity at the expense of the economic and social performance which is a feature of cooperatives, which does not facilitate the capture of many of the objectives of cooperatives, which are alien to the logic of profit.[85]

4.3.6. *The Control Exercised by the Supervisory Board*

One of the main mechanisms of internal control is the organisational supervision structure.

As we highlighted in section 2, the Supervisory Board, Audit Committee, or General and Supervisory Board (depending on the model adopted – arts. 28.1, 51, 56, 65 ff. of the PCC) will assess compliance with the law and the statutes, the formal audit (verification of the correctness of entries and accounting procedures), and the material audit (assessing the quality of management in relation to business objectives) of the cooperative (art. 53 of the PCC).

As a body of control and supervision, the Supervisory Board must be *independent*, the understanding being that its members cannot be associated with any specific interest group within the cooperative, and that their impartial analysis or decision may under no circumstances be subject to being influenced (art. 414.5 of the CSC, by reference to art. 9 of the PCC).

How is the independence of the Supervisory Board members ensured in cooperatives?

From the outset, the legislator established a regime of incompatibilities in article 31.1 of the PCC, according to which 'No cooperator may be simultaneously a member of the General Meeting, the Board of Directors, the Supervisory Board, and any other elected body provided for in the statutes.'

However, this is not sufficient to ensure the independence of the body, which should also be a result of the possession of appropriate professional qualifications and experience to perform the duties. As a matter of fact, unlike in company law, Supervisory Board members are recruited from among the cooperators (and optionally the investor members) (art. 29.1 of the PCC), thus

---

85 See A.M.G. Rodrigues, 'Os novos desafios da contabilidade para organizações da economia social que aplicam o SNC', *Cooperativismo e Economía Social*, 2010, 32, pp. 115–140.

not taking into account the possibility of non-members being able to join, which may represent an obstacle to the professionalisation of the body. Furthermore, there is no financial literacy or other requirement that some or all the members of the Supervisory Board must satisfy.[86]

In the Portuguese legal system, and as mentioned in section 2, resolutions of the General Meeting are binding on all bodies of the cooperative and on all its members (art. 33.1 of the PCC). This means that if resolutions of the General Meeting are binding on the Supervisory Board, as appears from the law to be the case, then the independence of this body will be undermined.

The prohibition against removal from the Supervisory Board without just cause is another way of ensuring its independence (art. 60.1 of the PCC).

4.3.7. The Liability of Members of the Board of Directors and Supervisory Board as an Instrument of Control

The democratic liability of members of the management and supervisory bodies is an important instrument of control in cooperatives.

Article 71 of the PCC on the liability of directors towards the cooperative provides that Directors will respond to the cooperative for the damage caused by acts or omissions in breach of their legal or statutory duties or of internal regulations or resolutions of the General Meeting, unless they can prove that they acted without fault.

These are cases of contractual civil liability, and it is therefore to be expected that there will be a presumption of fault as regards the cooperative. Furthermore, there are certain cases of illicit behaviour that may serve as a basis for directors' liability of the, such as: (i) the performance on behalf of the cooperative of acts that lie outside the object or interests of the cooperative, or allowing acts such as these to be carried out; (ii) the payment of amounts not due from the cooperative; (iii) non-recovery of sums payable where the limitations period for their payment expires; (iv) the distribution of fictitious surpluses in breach of the PCC, the additional legislation applicable to the various branches of the cooperative sector, or the statutes; and (v) the abusive use of their mandate, whether or not it involves the use of goods and credits of the cooperative, for their own benefit or for that of other persons.

Approval of the management report and accounts by the General Meeting does not imply renunciation by the cooperative of its compensation rights against the directors, unless the facts constituting the liability were expressly brought to the attention of the members of the cooperative prior to approval (art. 71.4 of the PCC).

---

86 On this issue, see D. Meira and M.E. Ramos, 'Um roteiro para a reforma da governação e do regime económico das cooperativas portuguesas', *Cooperativismo e Economía Social*, 2014, 36, pp. 88–89.

Article 73 of the PCC deals with the liability of directors with regard to a cooperative's creditors, and states that directors are liable to these creditors where, due to a failure to comply with the legal or statutory provisions for their protection, the assets become insufficient to satisfy their respective claims. In particular, directors are liable to the cooperative's creditors where the assets of the cooperative become insufficient due to their own fault because of: (i) distribution of the legal reserve to the cooperators; (ii) distribution of other mandatory reserves; and (iii) distribution of a fictitious surplus.

Unlawful and negligent performance on the part of directors will not suffice, however: it is a requirement that the assets of the cooperative became insufficient to satisfy the cooperative's creditor's claims due to the breach of these provisions. The insufficiency of assets for this purpose is not equivalent to insolvency.

In general terms, directors are liable to cooperators and third parties for damage they cause them directly in the performance of their duties (art. 74 of the PCC).

Liability among the various directors is joint, which reinforces the position of those to whom compensation is due (art. 75 of the PCC).

There are also instances of civil liability of members of the Supervisory Board and the Statutory Auditor (arts. 76 and 77 of the PCC), who are subject to the same rules as those applicable to members of the Board of Directors, and who are jointly liable with the directors for their acts or omissions in the performance of their duties if the damage would not been produced if their supervisory obligations had been satisfied.[87]

4.3.8. *The Control Exercised by CASES*

Under the Portuguese law system, there are no regulatory authorities for the cooperative sector or the social economy sector in general. The regulatory authorities are public law legal persons, and have the characteristics of independent administrative entities, with powers to regulate economic activity in defence of the general interest, to protect the rights and interests of consumers and to promote and defend competition in the private, public, cooperative and social sectors (Law no. 67/2013 of 28 August 2013). These entities have the power (which is more or less extensive, depending on the sector) to regulate, supervise, enforce, and sanction.

Although it cannot be classified as a regulatory authority, CASES exercises some of the typical powers that characterise a regulator in practice because its duties are to monitor the cooperative sector and to supervise the sector and its mode of operation.

---

87 See M.E. Ramos, 'Da responsabilidade dos diretores e gerentes de cooperativas – uma introdução', *Cooperativismo e Economia Social*, 2010, 32, pp. 35–53.

CASES was created by Decree-Law no. 282/2009 of 7 October 2009. It is a public interest cooperative, and is responsible for overseeing the use of the cooperative format in compliance with the principles and rules concerning its incorporation and operation.

Thus, pursuant to article 117.1 of the PCC, it is the responsibility of CASES to issue certification of the legal incorporation and proper operation of cooperatives annually. For this purpose, cooperatives must send CASES a copy of all elements relating to their duly-registered acts of incorporation and amendments to their statutes, as well as their annual management reports and accounts following approval by the General Meeting, together with a social report where the law requires them to produce one (art. 116 of the PCC).

Technical and financial support to cooperatives from public entities is subject to the credentials issued by CASES (art. 117.2 of the PCC).

In accordance with article 118.1 of the PCC, CASES must request the Public Prosecutor, through the courts, to wind up cooperatives that do not comply with the *Cooperative Principles*, that systematically use unlawful means for the pursuit of their purpose, or that resort to the cooperative format in order to obtain improper tax or other benefits offered by the public authorities. CASES must also apply to the Commercial Registry for an administrative winding up procedure for cooperatives whose activity does not coincide with the purpose stated in their statutes.

Finally, it is the duty of CASES to collect evidence relating to cooperatives or cooperative sector organisations so that it can maintain updated data on them with regard to incorporation, legalisation, amendments, and activities.

5. COOPERATION AMONG COOPERATIVES

5.1. INTRODUCTION

Economic globalisation, the rise of major international economic groups, and extreme market saturation have forced Portuguese cooperatives to increase in size in order to be more competitive, and many small- and medium-sized cooperatives often have to engage in integration processes and vertical and horizontal cooperation to survive in the competitive market that surrounds them.

In this regard, article 61.3 of the CRP provides that 'Cooperatives … can be grouped into unions, federations, and confederations or other forms of organisation provided by law.'

In the same vein, article 7.1 of the LBES states that: 'social economy entities may organise themselves freely and group themselves into associations, unions, federations, or confederations that represent and defend their interests.'

In turn, the PCC allows various forms of articulation among cooperatives: multi-sector cooperatives (art. 4.2 of the PCC); mergers of cooperatives (arts. 109

to 110 of the PCC); the incorporation of cooperatives 'of a higher degree or the second degree' (arts. 101 to 108 of the PCC); and the association of cooperatives with other legal persons (art. 8 of the PCC).

All these forms are founded on article 3 of the PCC, which states the principle of cooperation among cooperatives, and provides that 'cooperatives serve their members most effectively and strengthen the cooperative movement by working together through local, national, regional, and international structures.' This principle establishes a duty of mutual cooperation among cooperatives (inter-cooperation) that has the aim of continuing the interests of cooperators and the community in which the cooperative operates.

The concept of inter-cooperation that will be adopted in this report is nevertheless broader than the cooperative principle underlying the above definition, since we believe that this concept can cover both relations among cooperatives and relations between cooperatives and other legal persons.

In all these cases of inter-cooperation, and as stated in article 3 of the PCC, the aim is to increase the effectiveness of how a cooperative serves its members, with its mutualist scope being the ultimate foundation for these processes.

In the Portuguese legal system, two classification criteria for inter-cooperation can be identified.

The first distinguishes between formal and informal inter-cooperation. According to Rui Namorado, informal inter-cooperation results in a set of contractual relationships that reflect an economic or another, more or less regular, form of collaboration and does not lead to a loss of individuality on the part of each cooperative.[88] Formal inter-cooperation translates into the integration of cooperatives into higher-tier structures or into associations by cooperatives with other legal persons, resulting the creation of another legal person of a cooperative or other nature.

Inter-cooperation may take one of two forms: horizontal inter-cooperation (between cooperatives from the same or different branches, or between cooperatives and other legal persons); and vertical inter-cooperation (cooperative groups and second-tier cooperatives).

5.2. HORIZONTAL INTER-COOPERATION

5.2.1. Multi-Sector or Multi-Purpose Cooperatives

The idea that cooperatives may extend across all sectors or branches that are relevant to meeting the needs of their members is a manifestation of inter-cooperation.[89]

88 See in this regard, Namorado, n. 40 above, p. 95.

89 See in this regard, J.S. Leite, *Princípios Cooperativos*, IN-CM, Lisbon, 2012, p. 70.

Multi-sector cooperatives, which were only introduced in a full form in the 1996 Portuguese Code, are cooperatives that develop specific activities across various branches of the cooperative sector (art. 2.4 of the PCC). It should be recalled that in accordance with article 4.1 of the PCC, the current branches in Portugal are consumer, trade, agricultural, credit, housing and building, worker, crafts, fishery, cultural, services, education and social solidarity.

As we will see, recognition of this multi-sectorality also extends to cooperative unions (art. 82 of the PCC).

As mentioned in section 3, multi-sector or multi-purpose cooperatives may adopt an internal organisation that is divided into sections created and governed in terms of their operations, by the cooperative's statutes (arts. 13 and 19 of Decree-Law no. 335/99 of 20 August 1999 (agricultural cooperatives); art. 4 of Decree-Law no. 523/99 of 10 December 1999 (multi-sector trade cooperatives); art. 3 of Decree-Law no. 522/99 of 10 December 1999 (multi-sector consumer cooperatives); art. 4 of Decree-Law no. 502/99 of 19 December 1999 (multi-sector housing and building); and art. 3 of Decree-Law no. 7/98 of 15 January 1998 (social solidarity cooperatives)).

Finally, it should be mentioned that multi-sector cooperatives that have chosen one particular branch as a reference point with a view to integration into cooperatives of a higher tier (art. 4.2 of the PCC) have legal requirements that are intended to safeguard issues relating to the representativeness of federations and confederations of cooperatives (art. 106.3 of the PCC).[90]

5.2.2. The Association of Cooperatives with Other Legal Persons

The association of cooperatives with other legal persons may be in the form of a horizontal inter-cooperation that has the aim of enhancing the business of the legal persons involved, and so this type of association can be characterised as an inter-cooperation with an economic purpose.

We are excluding cooperative groups and subsidiaries controlled by cooperatives from this horizontal inter-cooperation, but both will be subject to further discussion below.

An analysis of the association of cooperatives with other legal persons requires that we first deal with one of the specificities of the Portuguese legal system, which is the prohibition against converting cooperatives into commercial companies, given the constraints this ban imposes on the types of association that cooperatives may access.

---

90 On multi-sectoral cooperatives, see R. Namorado, *Introdução ao direito cooperativo. Para uma expressão jurídica da cooperatividade*, Almedina, Coimbra, 2000, pp. 191–195.

5.2.2.1. Preliminary Issue: The Issue of the Prohibition Against the Conversion of Cooperatives into Commercial Companies

Article 111 of the PCC states that: 'the conversion of a cooperative into any form of commercial company is null and void, as are all acts that seek to thwart or circumvent said legal prohibition.'

This prohibited form of conversion is heterogeneous, since the converted legal entity was not originally a commercial company.[91] Furthermore, the prohibited conversion includes both a formal cooperative conversion or a conversion by extinguishment, in which the original legal person is dissolved and replaced by another that succeeds it.

The legislator also forbids *covert conversions*, which are understood here as being any acts that allow cooperatives to access the regime of commercial companies.[92]

Two main arguments have been raised by legal theory against the admissibility of conversions:

(i) the dogmatic argument: the causal heterogeneity of the two legal persons;
(ii) the public order argument: difficulties with maintaining the control by the public authorities that is imposed on the activities of cooperatives (this control could no longer be carried out if a conversion were to be accepted) and the possibility that the cooperative format might initially be used to obtain the benefits granted by the legislator to cooperatives, including tax benefits, followed by a conversion into a company.[93]

The first argument is based on the idea that the mutualist scope is essential to cooperatives and consequently that a cooperative cannot adopt a for-profit purpose through its conversion into a commercial company without triggering its dissolution. This idea, which has been defended in Portugal by Raúl Ventura, is based on a conceptual and interpretative rule according to which conversions of legal entities with different purposes are not permitted. The author invokes the essential difference in purpose between cooperatives

---

91 On these distinctions, see F.M. Correia, *Transformação de Sociedades Comerciais – Delimitação do Âmbito de Aplicação no Direito Privado Português*, Almedina, Coimbra, 2009, pp. 245 ff.; and M. Lanz, 'Transformação de Sociedades. A Problemática das Transformações Heterogéneas', *Revista de Direito das Sociedades*, 2010, year II, nos. 1–2, p. 244.

92 R.A. Subtil, M. Esteves, M. Ilhéu and L.M. Martins (*Legislação Cooperativa Anotada*, 2nd ed., Vida Económica, Porto, 2005, p. 100) consider that in the light of article 111 of the *PCC*, a cooperative cannot turn into any type of non-cooperative legal person, otherwise it might eventually turn into a commercial company at a later stage.

93 On this argument, see Correia, n. 91 above, pp. 251 ff.

and companies: the mutualist scope of cooperatives and the profit aims of commercial companies.[94]

This understanding is founded on the fact that the prevailing legal theory in Portugal argues that cooperatives are clearly distinct from commercial companies since one of the essential characteristics of commercial companies is the distribution of profits (in the sense of capital accruals) among their shareholders.[95]

As we see it, the most sensitive issue that arises in the case of a conversion of a cooperative into a commercial company is the protection of the indivisibility of the cooperative's mandatory reserves.[96]

As has been highlighted in previous sections, one of the specific aspects of cooperatives lies in the distinction that has been established between cooperatives' divisible and indivisible assets. Divisible assets are that portion of the assets that correspond to the share capital that each cooperator has brought to the cooperative and, under certain conditions, to the share of voluntary reserves defined by the cooperative that belongs to the cooperator. Indivisible assets include those corresponding to the legal reserve and the reserve for education and training, and they maintain their absolute indivisibility both during the life of the cooperative and when it is wound up (arts. 99 and 114 of the PCC).

Assuming the conversion of a cooperative into a commercial company, this indivisibility regime must be applied, and so if the conversion of the cooperative into a commercial company has been deliberated, the regime described in article 114.3 of the PCC must be applied, which establishes that 'application of the amount of the mandatory reserve reverts to another cooperative, preferably from the same city, to be determined by the federation or confederation that represents the main activity of the cooperative', but not to a commercial company.

As we have mentioned previously, this impossibility of distributing residual assets in the event a cooperative is converted into a commercial company derives from the social function cooperatives are called upon to fulfil, and means that their destination must be the promotion of the cooperative movement (the so-called principle of disinterested distribution).

Our analysis of the regime of horizontal inter-cooperation in this report cannot disregard the fact that, in the Portuguese law on cooperatives, the conversion of cooperatives into commercial companies is prohibited.

---

94 R. Ventura, *Fusão, Cisão, Transformação de Sociedades. Comentário ao Código das Sociedades Comerciais*, Almedina, Coimbra, 1990, pp. 430 ff. In the same sense, see Namorado, n. 90 above, pp. 237–240.

95 As advocates of this position, see, among others, Xavier, n. 8 above, pp. 21–23 and Abreu, n. 8 above, pp. 174 ff.

96 For an opposition to transformations based upon this argument, see Abreu, n. 8 above, pp. 184–185.

5.2.2.2. Means of Associating Cooperatives with Other Legal Persons

Article 8.1 of the PCC provides for 'the association of cooperatives and other legal persons, provided that this association respects the cooperative principle of autonomy and independence.'

From this rule, it follows that:

(i) cooperatives can associate with two categories of legal persons: legal persons of a cooperative or non-cooperative nature (associations, foundations, civil companies, commercial companies, and others); and
(ii) this association may or may not result in the creation of another legal person.[97]

Legal persons created by associations of cooperatives are cooperative that must not be confused with second-tier cooperatives.[98] The legislator may be referring to first-degree cooperatives; this is reinforced by article 8.3 of the PCC, which expressly allows the extension of the voting regime of higher-tier cooperatives to legal persons resulting from an association between cooperatives.

Under article 8 of the PCC, cooperatives may also join a consortium or an association in the form of a partnership (Decree-Law no. 231/81 of 28 July 1981) or participate in a complementary group of companies (Decree-Law no. 43/73 of 25 August 1973).[99]

5.2.2.3. Maintaining the Autonomy of the Cooperative as a Necessary Condition

Under article 8.1 of the PCC, maintaining the autonomy and independence of a cooperative is a necessary condition for its association with other legal persons.

The aim of this autonomy and independence will be to ensure that the cooperative's association with other legal persons calls into question neither the independence of the cooperative nor its democratic member control. We are therefore referring to autonomy in the existence and winding up of the cooperative (which could be jeopardised if unlimited liability is being assumed) and to autonomy in the management of its business and assets.

It is clear that only an individual assessment will determine whether or not autonomy is affected in the case of the cooperative's association with other legal persons.

---

97 On the terms of a cooperative's association with other legal persons, see Correia and Dias, n. 29 above, pp. 389–394.

98 In this sense, see Namorado, n. 90 above, p. 201.

99 Regarding the admissibility of the participation by a cooperative in a complementary group of companies, see the Opinion issued by the 'Conselho Técnico da Direcção-Geral dos Registos e do Notariado' dated 24.04.2001, in *Boletim dos Registos e Notariado*, May 2001 ('*Parecer da Direcção-Geral dos Registos e do Notariado de 24 de abril de 2001*').

It seems safe to say that the assumption of unlimited liability by a cooperative in its capacity as a partner of a commercial company may undermine the cooperative's autonomy.[100]

However, we disagree with Rui Namorado's position when he argues that observance of the principle of autonomy would not be compatible with the integration of a cooperative into a commercial company in which it did not hold a majority position.

As highlighted by Anacoreta Correia and Maria João Rodrigues, the rule advocated by Rui Namorado was bound to be mitigated, because if several member cooperatives are involved, not all of them can hold a majority of the shares.[101]

The maintenance or loss of autonomy therefore needs to be investigated on an individual basis. We may, however, point out some examples: consider the case of a cooperative that allocates a significant portion of its assets to entering a commercial company that has a subordination agreement with another partner, or the case of a cooperative that replaces a branch that performs essential activities for its operation with a commercial company, which no longer has the majority of votes following a capital increase, or the case of the execution of a shareholders' agreement by the cooperative that affects its voting rights in a constituted company that is valid under article 17 of the CSC.[102]

5.2.3. *Integration through a Merger Among Cooperatives (Horizontal Inter-Cooperation)*

Portuguese law has always allowed cooperatives to merge.

In a merger process, we witness the full economic and legal integration of the participating entities. Merger is therefore presented as a mechanism for cooperative integration.

Pursuant to article 109 of the PCC, mergers of cooperatives may be come about through integration or incorporation. A merger by integration takes place when two or more cooperatives, with a simultaneous extinction of their legal personality, form a new cooperative that assumes all the rights and obligations of the merged cooperatives (art. 109.2 of the PCC).

A merger of cooperatives can only be validly carried out by a resolution of at least two-thirds of the votes of the cooperators present or represented at an extraordinary General Meeting convened for the purpose (arts. 38.h) and 109.4 of the PCC).

---

100 See, in this sense, the Opinion issued by the 'Conselho Técnico da Direcção-Geral dos Registos e do Notariado', dated 24.04.2001, see n. 99 above.

101 See Correia and Dias, n. 29 above, p. 395.

102 Examples mentioned by Correia and Dias, n. 29 above, pp. 395–396.

Article 109.5 of the PCC provides a mechanism for forced mergers by incorporation. Subject to a prior favourable opinion from CASES, higher-tier cooperatives may legally demand the merger of one or more third-tier cooperatives, and will assume all the rights and obligations of the cooperatives that are integrated into them or with which they have a significant connection when any of the following circumstances occurs:

(i) if the absence or inactivity of the governing bodies is identified for a period longer than 12 months, or where it is impossible to elect them;
(ii) if activities unrelated to the social object of the cooperative are carried out on a repeated basis.

One significant and complex issue in the Portuguese legal system is whether a cooperative can merge with a commercial company (heterogeneous mergers), since the PCC only refers to homogeneous mergers (mergers between cooperatives). Legal theory considers that a merger such as this is not legally viable in the Portuguese legal system,[103] since article 111 of the PCC prohibits the conversion of a cooperative into a commercial company, and deems all acts that seek to counteract this prohibition to be null and void (and a heterogeneous merger of this kind would be one of these acts).

It is our understanding that, in light of article 111 of the PCC, a merger will not be possible if the merged legal entity is a commercial company, but will be legally viable if the merged legal entity is a cooperative: because the CSC says nothing about mergers of commercial companies with cooperatives, if a resolution of approval by a qualified majority of at least two-thirds exists, a heterogeneous merger of this kind should be permitted.

5.3. VERTICAL INTER-COOPERATION

Vertical inter-cooperation takes place through subsidiaries controlled by cooperatives, cooperative groups and second-tier cooperatives.

5.3.1. *The Possibility of Cooperatives Forming Companies*

The association of cooperatives with other cooperatives deserves particular attention with regard to the establishment of a commercial company or the constitution of a single shareholder limited liability company ('*sociedades unipessoais por quotas*') by a cooperative.

103 See, in this sense, Ventura, n. 94 above, pp. 34 ff.

Cooperatives, associations, or companies may be born out of the association of a cooperative with non-profit legal entities. Associations or companies may also be created from the association of a cooperative with for-profit legal entities, provided that this association does not undermine the autonomy of the cooperative (art. 8.1 of the PCC). We find no restriction in the corporate legal regime on participation by a cooperative in a commercial company, since neither article 980 of the Portuguese Civil Code nor the CSC (except for cases in which the CSC requires that the partner have a certain corporate form, as in the system of affiliated companies, particularly with regard to companies in a group relationship) poses any obstacle to access by a cooperative to a partner in a commercial company.

In this context, cooperatives may create companies, including commercial companies.[104]

Cooperatives may not, however, constitute any kind of commercial company. Indeed, given the rules in article 8 of the PCC (namely the prohibition against loss of autonomy) cooperatives cannot assume unlimited liability in commercial companies. We are therefore of the opinion that not all types of company (or the types of liability permitted by them) will be accessible to cooperatives. Cooperatives cannot be a partner in a general partnership or be a general partner in a limited partnership. In the case of a limited liability company, cooperatives cannot assume liability for company debts in their statutes, on the terms mentioned in article 198 of the CSC.

Another issue that has been discussed by scholars and in the courts relates to the possibility of a cooperative itself creating a commercial company, more specifically a single-shareholder limited liability company (*sociedades unipessoais por quotas* (Arts 270-A ff. of the CSC)), since this is the only case of a single shareholder status that is (at least originally) permissible for a cooperative limited partner.

Against this possibility, it is argued that the cooperative would take on all aspects of the structure of a true commercial company, with a consequent breach of article 111 of the PCC, which, as we have seen, prohibits the conversion of a cooperative into a commercial company. It is felt that the creation of a single shareholder limited liability company by a cooperative involves a complete transmutation of the cooperative itself – which when compared with the above-mentioned legal prohibition against conversion (art. 111 of the PCC) avoids this

[104] The question is not clear in the case law, where the emphasis is on arguments that defend the position that participation by a cooperative in a commercial company constitutes a violation of the rule in article 2.2 prohibiting cooperatives from pursuing a profit, a theory that was defended by the Public Prosecutor in a judgment by the Court of Lisbon dated 29.09.2005. On this judgment, see Correia and Dias, n. 29 above pp. 387 ff.

legal prohibition by seeking the creation of a single shareholder limited liability company.[105]

In its favour, it is argued that:

(i) the incorporated company enjoys autonomy of assets and the sole shareholder (the cooperative) has limited liability;
(ii) the company and the cooperative are two separate legal entities, with separate accounts;
(iii) the company and the cooperative have different tax regimes and therefore the tax benefits afforded to the cooperative are not applicable to the company;
(iv) the sole shareholder (in this case the cooperative) controls the single shareholder limited liability company.[106]

It will always be necessary to ensure, however, that the commercial company's profits are not appropriated by individual cooperators and must be allocated to the cooperative indivisible reserves. The oversight of any business that may exist between the sole shareholder and the company is due from CASES pursuant to article 115 of the PCC.

5.3.2. The Difficult Question of the Legal Framework of a Participation Relationship between a Cooperative (Partner) and an Established Company

Scholars have framed the relationship between a cooperative partner and a company set up as an operation with non-members ('*terceiros*') by taking into account the provisions of article 2.2 of the PCC, which states that: 'in pursuit of their objects, cooperatives are allowed to conduct business with non-members, subject to any restrictions set forth in the law applicable to each cooperative branch.'

As previously highlighted in section 1, even though the law does not define what is meant by a third party ('*terceiro*') it seems to be settled doctrine that in the wake of the teachings of Rui Namorado: 'from the cooperative point of view, non-members are those who have a business relationship that is directly related to the pursuit of the cooperative's primary object as if they were members, although, in fact, they are not'.[107] This means that the business conducted with

---

105 See the Opinion issued by the 'Conselho Técnico da Direção Geral dos Registos e do Notariado' dated 25.02.2000, in *Boletim dos Registos e Notariado*, May 2000.

106 On these arguments, see the Opinion issued by the Conselho Técnico da Direção Geral dos Registos e do Notariado, n. 99 above.

107 Namorado, n. 16 above, pp. 184–185.

non-members the legislator is referring to is of the same kind of business as that being conducted by the cooperative with its members.

In light of this concept of non-members ('*terceiros*'), the classification of shareholdings in companies as a transaction with non-members does not seem to be adequate.

Such shareholdings should unquestionably be described as an extraordinary activity, since they are outside the cooperative's social object in cases where they correspond to a mere investment by the cooperative.

In many cases, these equity interests in commercial companies are related to the development of activities that are preparatory or complementary to the economic activities developed between the cooperative and its members. The cooperative's aim is to obtain a segmentation of the activities that make up its social object by transferring one or more of these activities to a subsidiary controlled by the cooperative.

Several questions arise in this regard, and merit reflection.

First, the establishment of subsidiary companies by Portuguese cooperatives is a strange concept, since cooperatives benefit from a more favourable tax treatment than commercial companies in Portugal.[108]

If the purpose is the segmentation of activities, why not form a multi-purpose cooperative?

Furthermore, the concept of *indirect mutuality* is not defined in the Portuguese legal system, and we have doubts as to whether it is admissible. From a legal perspective, the cooperative is a shareholder or member of the subsidiary company and therefore has a shareholding: that is, a 'unitary set of current and potential rights and obligations of a shareholder (as such).'[109] One of those rights relates to profits generated from the subsidiary company's activity. Profit is an equity increase created directly within the legal sphere of the company (objective profit) that is intended to be subsequently distributed among its partners (subjective profit),[110] because a distribution of profits cannot be made without a company resolution (arts. 31, 250.3, and 386.1 of the CSC).

In this context, admitting the possibility that the cooperative can continue its mutualist scope indirectly through a subsidiary company and classifying some of the results of this activity as a cooperative surplus will to some extent mean disregarding the legal entity of the commercial company (subsidiary) in which

---

108 See, in this sense, J.A. Rodrigues, 'La integración cooperativa en el marco jurídico português', in R. Chaves, G. Fajardo and R. Namorado (eds.), *Integración Empresarial Cooperativa*, CIRIEC, 2003, pp. 51–55.

109 J.M.C. Abreu, *Curso de Direito Comercial, Vol. II – Das Sociedades*, 2nd ed., Almedina, Coimbra, 2007, p. 207.

110 On this distinction, see P.T. Domingues, *Variações sobre o capital social*, Almedina, Coimbra, 2009, p. 264.

the shareholding has been taken. The cooperative and the subsidiary are two separate legal entities with autonomous assets.

In this sequence, if there is a company resolution approving distribution of the profits from the activity carried out by the subsidiary company among members, the distribution becomes a part of the assets of the cooperative in the form of extraordinary results because they were not generated from transactions with members or non-members, even though they refer to activities that constitute the social object of the cooperative. Therefore, they must be subject to the same profit regime as that relating to transactions with non-members and cannot be appropriated by individual cooperators, and are allocated to the indivisible reserves.

5.3.3. *Cooperative Inter-Cooperation through the Creation of Cooperative Groups*

The PCC is silent on the issue of cooperative groups. Thus, if one takes into account the provisions of article 9 of the PCC, which contains a reference to the CSC, which is immediately applicable to anything that is not specifically provided for in the PCC, and since the solution does not infringe cooperative principles, we must reflect on arrangements for cooperative groups that are consistent with those principles to which Portuguese cooperatives may have access.

Company groups can take four forms in the Portuguese legal system: (a) relationships of simple interest (mere participation); (b) relationships of reciprocal ownership interest; (c) relationships by a dominant position; and (d) group relationships.

If we consider on the one hand that the reference to the CSC must comply with the *Cooperative Principles*, and on the other that cooperatives can associate with other legal persons of a cooperative or non-cooperative nature provided that it does not lead to a loss of autonomy (art. 8.1 of the PCC), cooperative association arrangements that translate into any form of subordination of the cooperative to the interests of others are prohibited. In fact, the cooperative principles of autonomy and independence and the principle of democratic member control prevent cooperatives from being controlled entities in a company group dominated by another legal entity.

5.3.4. *Second-Tier Cooperatives*

Vertical inter-cooperation also takes place through cooperatives of higher levels – unions, federations, and confederations of cooperatives, as foreseen in Chapter VI of PCC ('Unions, Federations, and Confederations'), articles 101 to 108.

This is the most natural form of vertical inter-cooperation since it presents no risk of a lack of compliance with cooperative principles, namely the principle of democratic member control and the principle of autonomy and independence.

Historically, the first reference to these forms of inter-cooperation may be found in the Cooperative Code of 1980 (Chapter IX – 'Unions, Federations, and Confederations', articles 78–83).

In the 1980 Code, this type of inter-cooperation was structured on the basis of a pyramidal criterion, according to the rule that 'cooperatives of a lower grade must group together in the next higher grade', and a geographical criterion, based on the rule that unions have a regional dimension, while federations and confederations have a national dimension.

It therefore establishes that:

(a) at a regional level, cooperatives of the first tier in the same branch of the cooperative sector are grouped into cooperative unions;
(b) at a national level, unions, either alone or in conjunction with first tier cooperatives from the same cooperative branch, are grouped into federations of cooperatives;
(c) at a national level, federations are grouped into confederations that represent various branches of the cooperative sector.

The Cooperative Code of 1996 introduced some changes to this model, which are explained in part by the introduction of multi-purpose cooperatives, which, as we have seen, develop their own activities from among various branches of the cooperative sector. This change was maintained in the current Cooperative Code (of 2015).

The scope of cooperative unions is therefore no longer necessarily regional: they are allowed to create other unions among themselves. The possibility of forming cooperative unions that group first-degree cooperatives or associations of various branches of the cooperative sector is also contemplated (art. 102 of the PCC).

The scope of federations of cooperative is also no longer necessarily national. A federation can admit cooperatives and cooperative unions of branches of the cooperative sector other than those that define the scope of the federation. Mergers of federations representing different branches of the cooperative sector are also permitted (art. 106.4 of the PCC).

As for confederations, affiliations of first-degree cooperatives are admitted on an exceptional basis (art. 107 of the PCC).

There are two cooperative confederations in Portugal: agricultural federations and the mutual agricultural credit banks in the CONFAGRI (National Confederation of Agricultural Cooperatives); the CONFECOOP (Portuguese Confederation of Cooperatives) has all the other branches as a potential scope. There are 21 federations of cooperatives and 67 cooperative unions covering various cooperative branches.

5.3.5. *The Incorporation and Economic Regime of Unions, Federations, and Confederations*

Under article 101.1 of the PCC, unions, federations, and confederations of cooperatives acquire legal personality upon registration of their incorporation, therefore confirming *the principle of the constitutive nature of registration* contained in article 17 of the PCC.

By this regulation, the legislator emphasises that the structures that comprise unions, federations, and confederations retain their legal personality.

The legislator requires a minimum of two first-tier cooperatives in order for a union of cooperatives to be constituted (art. 102.1 of the PCC). No reference is made to the minimum number of members either for federations or for confederations.

In terms of the economic regime, the provisions applicable to first-tier cooperatives apply to higher-tier cooperatives (art. 101.1 of the PCC).

5.3.6. *The Features of Unions, Federations, and Confederations*

In Portugal, there is no strict division between the economic and representative features of these three distinct types of higher-level cooperatives, although the representative function is primarily assumed by federations and confederations. In this regard, article 101.2 of the PCC provides that '... all cooperative structures of a higher tier lawfully represent the entities that comprise them.'

Pursuant to article 103 of the PCC, the purposes of unions are economic, social, cultural, and technical assistance to their members.

In the case of federations and confederations, articles 106 and 107 of the PCC state that their aims are representation and coordination and the provision of services to their members.

The legislator has set forth these functions in article 108 of the PCC. Federations and confederations may exercise any activity under the law and in compliance with the cooperative principles, namely:

(a) to represent, defend, and promote the interests of member organisations and the cooperative sector;
(b) to provide services of an economic and social character to their member organisations;
(c) to promote and encourage inter-cooperation between their members and the various branches of the cooperative sector;
(d) to encourage and promote cooperative training and education, with the power to manage reserves for the education and training of members, given that article 97.5 of the PCC makes it possible for the General Meeting

of a cooperative to allow the Board of Directors to deliver all or part of the 'amount of this reserve to a higher-tier cooperative on the condition that it furthers the purpose of the reserve in question and has a plan of activities in which that cooperative is engaged;'

(e) to spread cooperative values and principles, and to promote the cooperative model;

(f) to negotiate and conclude labour agreements;

(g) to mediate the resolution of conflicts among their members and between their members and their cooperators.

It should be noted, finally, that both federations and confederations must satisfy a number of requirements in order to be recognised as representatives of the cooperative sector that corresponds to each: (i) federations must prove that they have more than 50% of primary cooperatives from the cooperative branch corresponding to the social object of the federation definitely recorded as members (art. 106.3 of the PCC); and (ii) confederations must prove that they include at least 50% of the federations of the cooperative branch or branches corresponding to the social object of the confederation definitely recorded as members (art. 107.1 of the PCC).

CHAPTER 11
SPAIN

Gemma FAJARDO

1. DEFINITION AND OBJECTIVES OF COOPERATIVES

1.1. INTRODUCTION

When examining Spanish cooperative law, irrespective of the topic under study, the first salient factor is the coexistence of different laws governing cooperatives. Spain is divided into a number of Autonomous Communities, each of which has assumed exclusive competence in cooperative matters within its own boundaries. As a result, 16 of these 17 autonomous regions have passed a Cooperatives Law.[1]

---

[1] The regional legislation in force at the time of writing comprises the Cooperative Laws of Andalusia (Law 14/2011 of 23 December), Aragon, (Law 2/2014 of 29 August), Asturias (Law 4/2010 of 29 June), the Balearic Islands (Law 1/2003 of 20 March), Castile La Mancha (Law

This multiplicity of laws coexists with a national Cooperatives Law, Law 27/1999 of 16 July 1999 (hereinafter LC), which applies to cooperatives that do not concentrate the greater part of their activity with their members in any particular Autonomous Community (LC art. 2). Moreover, the national law is applied in addition to that of the Autonomous Community in the event of any lack in the latter law (Spanish Constitution of 6 December 1978, art. 149.3).

Moreover some types of cooperative are subject to special laws, as in the case of credit cooperatives,[2] insurance cooperatives[3] or transport cooperatives.[4]

The LC is also the reference of other laws regulating the taxation and accounting of cooperatives, such as the Fiscal System for Cooperatives Law no. 20 of 19 December 1990 (hereinafter LRFC), and the Order EHA/3360/2010, of 21 December 2010 adopting the Rules concerning the accountancy aspects of cooperative societies. However, the Communities of Navarra and the Basque Country have their own tax laws on cooperatives.

In view of this situation, the examination of Spanish cooperative legislation in this book is based on national Law 27/1999, this being what we may call the common legal system, but also takes the peculiarities of the current regional laws into account.

1.2. THE LEGAL CONCEPT OF COOPERATIVE

The Spanish national Cooperatives Law of 1999 states that a cooperative is a society set up by people who associate to conduct business activities directed at meeting their economic and social needs and aspirations, on the basis of freedom to join and to leave voluntarily, and with a democratic structure and operating democratically in accordance with the principles drawn up by the International Co-operative Alliance, as provided for in this Law (LC art. 1).

The concept of a cooperative is very similar in all the other Spanish laws. In all of them: a cooperative is described as a 'society' (*sociedad*, which also means company) made up of persons who 'associate' (form a partnership), although some of these laws avoid the word 'society' and replace it with 'association',

11/2010 of 4 November), Castile and León (Law 4/2002 of 11 April), Catalonia (Law 12/2015 of 9 July), Extremadura (Law 2/1998 of 26 March), Galicia (Law 5/1998 of 18 December), Madrid (Law 4/1999 of 30 March), Murcia (Law 8/2006 of 16 November), Navarre (Law 14/2006 of 11 December), the Basque Country (Law 4/1993 of 24 June), La Rioja (Law 4/2001 of 2 July), Cantabria (Law 6/2013 of 28 October) and Valencia (Law 2/2015 of 15 May). Despite also having exclusive competence on this matter, the Canary Islands do not have their own cooperative law.

2 Law 13/1989 of 26 May 1989 and Royal Decree 34/1993 of 22 January 1993.

3 Law 20/2015 of 14 July on Regulation and Supervision of Private Insurance.

4 Law 16/1987 of 30 July 1987, Royal Decree 1211/1990 of 28 September 1990 and Order of 23 July 1997.

'group of people' or simply 'enterprise' (Andalusia, Balearic Islands, Madrid, La Rioja and Valencia).

The definition expressly refers to the objective of the cooperative: to satisfy its members' economic and social needs and aspirations by conducting business activities. Definitions of the concept in the legislation also frequently mention that these activities are carried out jointly by the members or with the members' participating as workers, consumers or providers of goods or services (Andalusia, Aragon, Galicia, Madrid, Basque Country or Valencia).

While the above is the main objective of the cooperative, it is not the only one. The definitions provided in these laws often include improving the surroundings or the community as a complementary objective of a cooperative. This complementary purpose, not expressly mentioned in the definition of cooperatives found in the current Spanish national law, has traditionally formed part of the concept in Cooperative Laws (*Ley de Cooperativas* 52/1974 of 19 December and *Ley General de Cooperativas* 3/1987 of 2 April, hereinafter LGC).

The definition normally also mentions some of the characteristics which are most clearly identified with cooperatives, such as voluntary and open membership, democratic management, or distributing surpluses in proportion to the members' participation. In all cases, it refers to applying the cooperative principles of the International Co-operative Alliance (ICA).

The International Co-operative Alliance's Statement on the Co-operative Identity can usually be found in the definition of cooperatives. On occasion, the definition is copied from the Identity Statement (Balearic Islands, Madrid). Other laws refer to the cooperative values (Balearic Islands, Madrid, La Rioja or Valencia) or principles (national law, Andalusia, Aragon, Balearic Islands, Cantabria, Catalonia, the Basque Country, Castile La Mancha, Castile and León, Galicia, Madrid, Murcia, Navarre, La Rioja or Valencia) or even copy them word for word (Murcia or Valencia).

1.3. THE OBJECTIVE OF THE COOPERATIVE

As we have seen, the definition of cooperatives includes their purpose, doing so in terms very similar to those of the ICA Statement on the Co-operative Identity: to meet their members' economic and social needs by engaging in economic activities, conducted as a business, in which the members participate directly as consumers or as providers of goods or services.

In fact, the legislation entrusts cooperatives with pursuit of various goals:

- meeting their members' economic needs and aspirations;
- meeting other social aspirations of their members;
- concern for the community.

The main aim of the cooperative is to meet its members' economic needs and aspirations by engaging in business activities with the direct involvement of the members.

The business activity carried out in the cooperative with the members taking part is termed the 'cooperative activity' or 'cooperativised activity'. The laws do not usually define it and its content can be very diverse.[5] The legislation usually refers to it when describing the various types of cooperative.[6]

However, cooperatives must also meet other needs and aspirations of their members; those of a social nature, such as improving conditions in the community. For this purpose the law requires cooperatives to allocate part of their surpluses and profits to a fund for training, education and promotion. Law 27/1999 calls this fund the Education and Promotion Fund and states that it must be used to train and educate members and employees in the cooperative principles and values, or in specific subjects concerned with their activity: to disseminate cooperativism; to promote relations among cooperatives; to drive cultural, professional and welfare advancement in the neighbourhood or in the community in general; to improve the community's quality of life and development; and to take action to protect the environment (LC art. 56).

In Spanish law, a cooperative's objectives differ from those of other entities such as companies (*sociedades*) in the strict sense of the word.

A company (*sociedad*) is defined as a contractual arrangement whereby two or more persons undertake to pool money, goods or labour 'with the intention of sharing the gains among themselves' (Civil Code of 1889, CC. article 1665) or 'obtaining a profit' (Code of Commerce of 1885, C.Com. article 116).

Consequently, companies are defined as for-profit entities because they are set up to conduct an activity with which to obtain profits in order to share these profits among their members. In contrast, cooperatives are set up to conduct an activity in order to meet the needs and aspirations of their members in the best conditions, rather than to obtain profits for themselves.

Although the legislation sometimes terms cooperatives 'societies', properly speaking their mutual and non-profit nature prevents them from being

5 An exception is Valencia, where article 2 of the regional law states that: 'For the purposes herein, cooperativised activity means the activity consisting of all the contributions and services in which the cooperative engages with its members on a non-profit basis in pursuit of the purpose of the cooperative.' For ample information on cooperativised activity cf. G. Fajardo, *La gestión económica de la cooperativa: responsabilidad de los socios*, Ed. Tecnos, Madrid, 1997, pp. 75–241, or C. Vargas, 'La actividad cooperativizada y las relaciones de la cooperativa con sus socios y con terceros', *Revista Aranzadi de Sociedades*, 2006, Monograph No. 27, pp. 94–104.

6 For instance, the object of worker cooperatives is to 'provide members with jobs, by means of their direct, personal efforts, ... through the shared organisation of the production of goods or services for third parties' (LC art. 80.1), while that of service cooperatives is 'to provide supplies and services or produce goods and carry out transactions directed at economic and technical improvement of the members' professional activities (LC art. 98).

considered either civil societies (*sociedades civiles*) or commercial companies (*sociedades mercantiles*). Nonetheless, it could be argued that if a cooperative also conducts activities with non-members, it ought to be considered a company,[7] particularly if it allows all or part of the profits to be shared among its members.[8]

Nevertheless, to date the law has not classified cooperatives as either civil societies or commercial companies, and they are excluded from registration in the Company Register (*Registro Mercantil*).[9] Furthermore, the reason that the autonomous regions can regulate cooperatives is precisely because they are not considered to be either civil societies or commercial companies, since the State reserves exclusive jurisdiction in both civil and commercial matters (Spanish Constitution, art. 149.1, 6th and 8th). This argument was used by the Supreme Court (*Tribunal Supremo*) to deny the commercial nature of cooperatives in the Judgement of 1 February 1992 (STS), see *Repertorio Aranzadi* legal compendium (RA) No. 867).

1.3.1. Satisfying the Members' Needs and Aspirations

The members' needs and aspirations that the cooperative must meet, as well as how this should be done, must be set out in its statutes.[10]

There are times when the members' aim is to obtain a particular service not offered by the state or the market. On other occasions, the state or the market

---

7 Article 124 CCom states that production, credit or consumption cooperatives will only be considered commercial companies and subject to the provisions of the Code when they engage in non-mutual acts of commerce.

8 Cf. M. Vergez, *El Derecho de las cooperativas y su reforma*, Civitas, Madrid, 1973; M. Paniagua, *Mutualidad y lucro en la sociedad cooperativa*, McGraw-Hill, Madrid, 1997, and *La sociedad cooperativa. Las sociedades mutuas de seguros y las mutualidades de previsión social*, Marcial Pons, Madrid, 2005, p. 94; F.J. Martinez Segovia, 'Sobre el concepto jurídico de cooperativa' in *La sociedad cooperativa: Un análisis de sus características societarias y empresariales*. Coord. Moyano, Universidad de Jaén, 2001 pp. 41–76; or M.J. Morillas and M.I. Feliú, *Curso de Cooperativas*, 2nd ed., Tecnos, Madrid, 2002, pp. 78–82.

9 The Code of Commerce (art. 16) states that entry in the Company Register is required for sole traders, commercial companies (*sociedades mercantiles*) and other entities expressly required by law to register, such as credit and insurance cooperatives (Company Register Regulation, RRM, art. 81) and cooperatives that engage in wholesale or retail trade (Ordering of Retail Trade Law, LOCM, additional provision No. 4).

10 The Statutes must state the objectives of the cooperative (LC art. 11). This entails referring to the activities in which the cooperative will engage in pursuit of its purposes – as other cooperative laws more explicitly recognise (LGC 1987 or Andalusia's Cooperatives Law). In other words, the cooperative's purpose and the activities to be undertaken in order to achieve it must be specified. For instance, the statutes of a worker cooperative should contain: 'The object of the cooperative shall be to provide its members with work in the best possible conditions. To this end, the cooperative shall engage in the activity of … and in any other which is complementary to or dependent on the said activity'.

can provide the service but the members wish to obtain it on better conditions (better quality or price).

Whatever the case, in a cooperative it is the members as a group that participate directly and jointly (co-operate) in the activity undertaken (the cooperative activity), either as consumers or as providers of goods or services. But they do so through the legal person of the cooperative.

Accordingly, the cooperative is said to manage the interests of its members or act on their behalf. This is a way of acting very different from that of a commercial company acting as intermediary in the market, which is why legal doctrine considers it a 'cooperative act' (*acto cooperativo*) in contrast to an 'act of commerce' (*acto de comercio*).[11]

In a consumer cooperative, the members buy jointly through the cooperative, and the cooperative manages purchases for its members;[12] in a worker cooperative the members work together, rather than being engaged by the cooperative to work,[13] and the cooperative sells the products of its members or makes purchases for them.[14] In general, the legislation refers to the cooperative management of the goods delivered by the members (LC art. 52.3).

Cooperative management or service management[15] is more characteristic of relations of collaboration than of intermediation. It is considered by legal

---

11 The Code of Commerce does not define acts of commerce, merely stating that: 'Acts comprised in this code and any other acts of an analogous nature shall be held to be acts of commerce' (art. 2). We have also seen how the Code of Commerce excludes cooperatives from commercial company status owing to their non-engagement in this type of act. According to the legal doctrine on acts of commerce, the characteristics of these acts in the Code of Commerce are the presumed profit motive and speculative purpose in acting as a trade intermediary. Cf. F. Vicent Chuliá, *Introducción al Derecho Mercantil*, vol. I, 23rd ed., Tirant lo Blanch, Valencia, 2012, p. 889, and doctrine cited therein. On the nature of the cooperative act, see: A. Salinas Puente, *Derecho Cooperativo*, Ed. Cooperativismo, México 1954, p. 156; W. Bulgarelli, *Elaboracao do Direito Cooperativo*, Ed. Atlas S.A., Sao Paolo, 1967, p. 107; D. Cracogna, 'El Acto Cooperativo', in *Estudios de Derecho Cooperativo*, Ed. Intercoop, Buenos Aires, 1986, p. 20, and 'Inexistencia del vínculo laboral en la Cooperativa de Trabajo: Fallo esclarecedor de la Corte Suprema', *La Ley* T. 2010-A, p. 290; or E. Cuesta, *Derecho Cooperativo*, Abaco, Buenos Aires, 1987, p. 106.

12 This is why the law states that: 'Deliveries of goods and provisions of services by cooperative societies to their members, whether produced by the cooperative or acquired from others to fulfil its objects, shall not be considered sales' (LC, additional provision no. 5.3) and why in housing cooperatives the building belongs to the members as a group, through the cooperative, until individual ownership of the dwelling is 'adjudicated' (LC art. 89.3).

13 The law states that the cooperative provides its members with jobs, but the cooperative/worker relationship is one of membership not labour: there is no work contract between them (LC art. 80.1).

14 Farmers cooperatives store, process, distribute or market the products from the cooperative's farms and those of its members (LC art. 93.2b).

15 A term attributed to Fauquet and employed by most legal doctrine in Spain (see I. Trujillo, *Cooperativas de Consumo y Cooperativas de Producción*, Aranzadi, Madrid, 2000, p. 43).

doctrine to be a mandate without representation or indirect representation.[16] This is why the member must pay the price of the goods acquired for him/her by the cooperative and is entitled to collect the sum obtained from the sale of his/her goods or services by the cooperative. However, this is not an individual right but rather a right that pertains to the membership as a whole, which is why it is the members who decide, at a General Meeting, how to meet payments and how to distribute the income obtained through their joint or cooperative activity.

1.3.2. The Cooperative Advantage

The cooperative advantage obtained by the member is not always a quantitative advantage, as we have already mentioned, because it often consists exclusively of the ability to receive the service provided by the cooperative, and in other cases it is the quality of the service that leads the member to form the cooperative or to join it.

Irrespective of the advantages that a person may receive as member of a cooperative, what is certain is that obtaining them requires that person to take part in the cooperative's activity. This involves providing goods or services to the cooperative or obtaining benefits or services from it. These services, goods and benefits are normally remunerated.

The way in which they are remunerated varies according to the type of cooperative. Because cooperative management is management to serve members, it might be thought that until the financial year closes and the income and expenses are known, it would not be possible to determine the value of the goods or services provided by the member or the benefit or service provided by the cooperative. For this reason, some cooperatives wait until the end of the year to determine the value of the members' consumption or services, so that when it is included in the accounts under income or expenses, as appropriate, the result of the year is zero (this is known as 0 surplus).

This method has the advantage of bringing the member the maximum advantage from participation in the cooperative's activity but the disadvantage of not generating a result that can be assigned to reserves or a taxable amount on which company tax can be charged.

---

16 Cf. F. Manrique Romero and J. M. Rodriguez Poyo-Guerrero, 'La cooperativa: garantías formales para su eficacia en el tráfico', *Revista de Derecho Notarial*, 1980, nos. 109–110, pp. 61–65; F. Vicent, 'Ley General de Cooperativas', *Revista de Derecho Privado*, 1994, vol. XX, no. 3. pp. 305–312; J. Mateo Blanco, *El Retorno Cooperativo*, Ed. Escuela Universitaria de Estudios Sociales, Universidad de Zaragoza, 2003, pp. 171–221; N. Paz Canalejo, *Ley General de Cooperativas*, vol. 2, EDERSA, 1990, pp. 148–149; G. Fajardo, *La gestión económica de la cooperativa: responsabilidad de los socios*, Ed. Tecnos, Madrid, 1997, pp. 75–103 and pp. 241–245; M.L. Llobregat, *Mutualidad y empresas cooperativas*, Ed. Bosch, Barcelona, 1990, pp. 222–224; or J.F. Martinez Segovia, 'La relación cooperativizada entre la sociedad cooperativa y sus socios: naturaleza y régimen jurídico', *Revista de Sociedades*, 2005, no. 25, pp. 203–234.

Because of this, both the substantive and fiscal legislation on cooperatives (for different reasons) require these benefits to be assigned a provisional value (an advance) before closing the financial year, calculating them more or less objectively to give a positive year-end result.

Cooperative legislation has used various preliminary evaluation systems to calculate the members' participation:

(a) market price;[17]
(b) price no higher than market price;[18]
(c) effective settlement price.[19]

The tax rules mainly value transactions between cooperatives and their members at market value,[20] and exceptionally, deliveries by members to farmers' cooperatives at the effective settlement price, which in practice makes it possible not to generate a surplus (LRFC art. 15).

Depending on the valuation of the members' contribution, the cooperative may have a larger or smaller surplus, or may even have incurred losses. When the legislation requires the service to be valued at market prices or no higher, it corrects the tendency towards a zero surplus or the generation of losses.

When the difference between the income and expenses generated in the cooperative's activity (the activity conducted with the participation of the members) is positive it is called a surplus (*excedente*).

---

17 The LGC 1987 states that the following shall be considered current expenses: the sum of the goods delivered by the members for cooperative management, valued at the mean market price at the time of delivery, even if the members have not been paid advances for these or the advances were lower in value; and the sum of the advances to the working members and worker members, valued according to the salaries normally paid in companies engaged in similar activities in the area where the work is performed, even if the advances actually paid are lower (art. 83.1 a). The cooperative laws of Aragon and Navarre now employ similar expressions in general to assess the value of goods delivered by the members.

18 The law of the Basque Country considers the following expenses: the sum of the goods delivered for cooperative management, valued at no higher than market prices, and the sum of the advances to the working members to a total sum no higher than normal salaries in the area for the respective sector of activity (art. 66.2 a). Similar expressions are used in the legislation of Valencia, Extremadura and Asturias.

19 This is the case of the national law of 1999, which allows as expenses: 'The sum of the goods delivered by the members for cooperative management, valued no higher than the effective settlement prices, and the sum of the advances to the working members' (art. 57.2 a). Most of the regional legislation has copied this rule, which does not influence the value that can be placed on them: see the laws of Madrid, Catalonia, Castile and León, the Balearic Islands, Murcia, Castile La Mancha and Andalusia.

20 According to this law, the cooperatives' transactions with their members in pursuit of their objects shall be entered at market value. Market value means the normal price of the goods, services and benefits as agreed between independent parties for such transactions; and the sum of the advances to the working members shall be calculated according to the normal salaries in the same sector of activity that they should have received if their situation were that of employees (art. 15.2).

It should be noted at this point that cooperatives may also engage in other types of activity on their own account, independently from their activity with their members. We will look at this in more detail below. These activities can be the same as in the cooperative's objects but carried out with non-members, or they can be other types of activity. The legislation usually terms these activities 'extra-cooperative' or 'extraordinary'. It has also traditionally called the positive results of these activities 'profits' (*beneficios*) rather than surpluses.

Traditionally, until the Basque law was passed, cooperative legislation required the results of the cooperative's activities with its members to be differentiated from those obtained from other activities. It also required the profits obtained by cooperatives from these extra-cooperative or extraordinary activities to be assigned to non-distributable reserves for developing and strengthening the cooperative, whereas the year's surpluses from activities with the members, after assigning certain sums to legal and voluntary reserves, could be distributed among the members who had generated them by participating in these activities. The law termed the current surplus that the members agree to distribute a 'patronage refund' (*retorno*).

The Basque Country's cooperatives act changed this rule and required the surpluses of cooperatives to be determined in accordance with the rules and criteria established for capital-based companies (art. 66).[21] The Basque law does not differentiate between transactions with members and with others, or between profits and surpluses. According to this law, at least 30% of the positive results of the year, which it also calls 'surpluses', must be assigned to non-distributable reserves, and the rest may be assigned to distributable reserves or distributed between the members as 'patronage refunds' (art. 67). If the results are negative, the losses can be assigned to reserves, to share capital or to the members (art. 69).

Since the Basque law was enacted, most new Spanish cooperative laws have allowed results not to be separated if so provided in the statutes,[22] but in general they continue to be kept separate.

This is partly because, in order to receive favourable fiscal treatment, Spanish tax legislation requires the results to be separate and the profits from extra-cooperative and extraordinary activities to be applied to non-distributable reserves (LRFC art. 13.10). Basque fiscal law, does not make the favourable tax treatment of cooperatives conditional upon this requirement.

Since then, other cooperative laws have begun to use these concepts indiscriminately despite continuing to require separation of the results. For instance, they sometimes call even the transactions with non-members

21 Both Law 1/1982 of 11 February 1982 and that currently in force, which dates from 1993.

22 LC 1999 and those of Andalusia, Asturias, Castile La Mancha, Castile and Leon, Galicia, Madrid, Murcia or Valencia.

'cooperativised',[23] or all the positive results of the year 'surpluses',[24] or allow both surpluses and profits to be distributed as 'patronage refunds'.[25]

However, laws are still to be found that only allow the surpluses of cooperative activities (meaning the positive results derived from the cooperative's activity with the members), to be distributed as 'patronage refunds'.[26]

This tendency to unify results has also affected negative ones. Since the Basque law, for instance, most of the cooperative legislation provides for the possibility of assigning any losses to the members.[27] While it could be argued that members should assume part of the losses generated through the cooperative's activity, losses which are sometimes the consequence of having overvalued their services, there is no justification for allocating losses generated by extra-cooperative and extraordinary activities to the members, since the member is not responsible for the cooperative's debts and losses.

1.3.2.1. Provision for and Regulation of Patronage Refunds

In spite of the confusion over the meaning of the term 'patronage refund' as used nowadays, the fact is that all the Spanish cooperative laws provide for and regulate the refund, and do so in fairly similar terms.

First, they provide that the refund shall be credited to the members in proportion to the cooperativised activities that each member has carried out with the cooperative and not in proportion to the capital invested.

Secondly, they set out how the patronage refund might be paid to the member,[28] although they usually leave the final decision on this to the statutes or the General Meeting.

Whether or not to distribute patronage refunds is a decision that pertains to the General Meeting. The law usually recognises the members' right to a patronage refund 'if any' (LC art. 16.2 d), in other words conditionally, as will be seen below.

---

23 The laws of Andalusia, Aragon, Asturias, Castile and Leon, Catalonia and Murcia, for instance.

24 For instance, the laws of Aragon, the Balearic Islands and Extremadura. The Catalan law, in article 66, calls extraordinary profits (from restatement of the balance sheet or capital gains on transferring tangible or intangible fixed assets) a 'surplus', and that of Galicia differentiates the surplus from the extra-cooperative profit but uses the term 'extra-cooperative surplus'.

25 The national law states that: 'The surpluses and extra-cooperative and extraordinary profits available after payment of tax liabilities shall be applied, as provided in the statutes or as resolved by the General Meeting for each financial year, to cooperative refunds to the members, ...' (art. 58.3). Most of the other laws employ similar expressions.

26 The laws of Madrid and Valencia.

27 The laws of Extremadura, Madrid and Valencia can be cited as exceptions.

28 The ways to pay the patronage refund that are mentioned usually include cash, increasing the members' capital contribution or allocating it to a remunerated and reimbursable patronage refunds fund.

1.3.2.2. Patronage Refunds Compared to Dividends in Commercial Companies. Remuneration of Capital in Cooperatives

Having seen how the concepts of 'surplus' and 'patronage refund' have evolved and the diversity of situations that the laws of Spain present, it is easier to understand the difficulty of defining what is meant nowadays by 'patronage refund'.

The patronage refund may be said to be that part of the positive result of the financial year (surplus, or surplus and profits) that the General Meeting agrees to distribute among the members.

The traditional concept of the patronage refund found in the Cooperatives Law of 1987, which is still retained in the laws of Valencia or Madrid, is clearly differentiated from that of dividends in a commercial company.

This is partly because, being part of the surplus rather than of profits, the patronage refund is a complement to the advance that has been received or paid. Consequently, the patronage refund should only be distributed among the members who participated in the cooperative activity in the financial year in question and only in proportion to the participation of each. If the result is negative, its distribution among the members should follow the same criterion.

In this traditional view of patronage refunds, if the cooperative engages in other activities on its own account rather than in the interests of its members (transactions with non-members or of other types), its behaviour resembles that of any conventional company. The profits obtained through such activities are the result of the cooperative's management and of the employment of its own resources, so that there is no reason to make their distribution among the members conditional on the transactions effected with each member in that financial year. For the same reason, if the members are not responsible for the cooperative's debts and have already paid up the capital subscribed, then losses should only be covered by the assets of the cooperative.

The concept(s) or definitions of patronage refunds currently found in Spanish legislation include not only a complement of the advance due to or from the member but also part of the profits obtained through the cooperative's own account operations. This situation brings the patronage refund closer in concept to the dividends of a commercial company, since it shares their origin (profits) in part. However, the distribution of the patronage refund retains its classic features, as it must be distributed in proportion to the cooperativised activity of each member – although this criterion could coincide with the profit distribution criterion of a limited liability company.[29]

---

[29] A *sociedad anónima* must distribute its dividends in proportion to the capital paid up by the members, but in a *sociedad limitada* the distribution is proportional to the member's participation in the capital 'unless otherwise provided in the Statutes', Capital-Based Company Law (*Ley de Sociedades de Capital*, LSC) No. 1, of 2 July 2010, art. 275.

Moreover, there is another important difference between patronage refunds and dividends. Dividends are the way in which members are compensated for their investment in the capital of commercial companies, whereas cooperatives have their own way of compensating their members for their capital investment: paying interest on it. In a cooperative, the members receive interest on their provision of capital and patronage refunds on their participation in the cooperative activity.

Remuneration of the capital contributed by the members takes the form of interest and is shown in the accounts as a current expense. According to the legislation, the member is entitled to receive interest on his or her contributions to the capital 'if applicable' (art. 16.2 e). The reason is that this remuneration is subject to certain conditions and limitations set out in the law:

1. The statutes must state whether the compulsory contributions to capital give entitlement to accrued interest on the part that has effectively been paid up (LC art. 48.1).
2. Remuneration of voluntary contributions is subject to the conditions and limitations set out in the agreement through which they originated (LC art. 48.1).
3. Remuneration of capital contributions is conditional on the existence of positive current results prior to distribution and the maximum sum of this remuneration is limited to the said positive result (LC art. 48.2).
4. Remuneration of capital contributions cannot exceed 6 points above the legal interest rate.[30]
5. The General Meeting decides the interest rate that may be applied to the share capital (LC art. 21. 2 d).

In view of these rules, it might be asked whether the General Meeting or Board of Directors is entitled to decide whether or not interest is paid on the capital. This question is important, because the recently introduced accounting rules that apply to cooperatives state that if the cooperative society is obliged to remunerate the share capital, this share capital shall not be considered shareholders' equity but liability (Order EHA 3360/2010, Second Rule (Norma Segunda) 1.1.2.1).

Exceptionally, some laws provide for other ways to recompense the capital invested. The law of Valencia allows remuneration of the capital contribution of certain members who do not take part in the cooperative activity (investor or associate members) not to be based on the receipt of interest but on participation in the surpluses not exceeding 45% of these.[31] Other regions simply refer the

[30] The legal interest rate for 2016 is 3% (Law 48/2015). The maximum interest that could be paid on the capital contributed by the member would be 9% per annum.

[31] The law of Valencia, article 28.2 notes that if the Statutes so permit, up to 45% of the year's surplus may be allocated to distribution among the associate members in proportion to the

remuneration of investor members' capital contributions to the provisions of the statutes or to the terms agreed by the parties (law of Madrid, art. 28.2).

1.3.2.3. Patronage Refunds: A Conditional Right

As explained above, Spanish law considers patronage refunds to be a conditional right of the members. The national law states that the member has a right to the patronage refund 'if applicable' (*en su caso*). This right can be conditional on:

- provisions in the statutes, as the law allows them to waive the distribution of patronage refunds.[32]
- the existence of positive results for the year, whether surpluses or (sometimes, as we have seen) profits.
- the General Meeting's resolving their distribution.[33]
- certain reserves having been covered.[34]

Payment of patronage refunds raises some problems.

The first is that patronage refunds can only be distributed if the results for the financial year are positive. Companies with share capital can distribute dividends out of current profits or freely-distributable reserves (LSC art. 273.2). In principle, cooperative legislation does not allow for this possibility, and some laws even state expressly that patronage refunds must be made out of the available surplus.[35] However, in other cases this possibility should be considered, since the law allows freely-distributable reserves to be created, and these could even be distributable among the members.

---

paid-up capital. In this case, the year's losses must also be borne by the members in the same proportion, up to the limit of their capital contribution. The laws of Catalonia (art. 27.c 8th), Castile La Mancha (art. 25.3) and Asturias (art. 25.2) have subsequently made similar provisions.

32 On occasion, through their statutes, cooperatives do waive patronage refund payments. It is sometimes provided for in law and at other times required, as in cooperatives classed as 'non-profit entities' (LC first additional provision). These are cooperatives that manage collective benefit or publicly owned services or engage in economic activities for the purpose of integrating people who suffer social exclusion into the labour market. They also renounce the distribution of surpluses, payment of interest above the legal rate and payment of their officers, and limit their workers' remuneration.

33 The General Meeting possesses exclusive competence to examine the cooperative's management and to approve the annual accounts, management report, and allocation of the available surpluses or of losses (LC art. 21.2 a).

34 For example, the law of Valencia requires the cooperative to set up and maintain an obligatory reserve for the purpose of strengthening, developing and guaranteeing the cooperative; this reserve must be a sum at least equal to the share capital provided for in the statutes, and until this sum has been reached, the surplus and profits may not be assigned to any other purpose, interest may not be paid on the capital, and the capital contributions may not be updated (art. 70.1).

35 As in the laws of Andalusia, Castile La Mancha, Extremadura, Galicia or La Rioja.

The second question is whether it is acceptable for the General Meeting to repeatedly agree not to distribute patronage refunds. Cooperative law has not foreseen this possibility, but the criterion employed by Spanish jurisprudence in relation to the right to receive dividends,[36] could be considered applicable, although with one distinction: the cooperative advantage is not achieved through patronage refunds alone, and an advantageous valuation of the member's participation in the cooperative activity could justify not distributing patronage refunds, or even expressly waiving them in the statutes.

Lastly, there is the question of whether it is possible to recognise the member's right to patronage refunds on part of the surplus in the statutes, in such a way that if surpluses exist the General Meeting would have to recognise this right.[37] While this eventuality has been possible until recently, we believe that the recent reform of the accounting rules reduces the chances of this practice surviving. Indeed, as we saw in relation to the remuneration of capital, if the General Meeting is obliged to distribute patronage refunds, then the cooperative's share capital is classified as a liability (Order EHA/3360/2010, Second Rule 1.1.2.1).

1.4. COOPERATIVE OBJECTS AND MEMBERSHIP

If the cooperative is an association of persons who unite to conduct business activities in common with the purpose of meeting their economic and social needs and aspirations, it is comprehensible that, as we saw, the law should require the statutes to identify the objectives of the cooperative and what activity it will conduct with its members in order to fulfil these objectives (LC art. 11.1 c). It also requires the members to be in a position to take part in and benefit from this activity. Consequently, membership is conditional on the ability to take part in the activity.[38] Moreover, the law establishes both the obligation of members to take part in the cooperative activity (LC art. 15.2 b) and their right to do so

36 The Capital-Based Companies Law states that members have the right to share in the distribution of the company's gains and in the assets resulting from its liquidation (LSC art. 93 a). The jurisprudence has interpreted that this rule does not give rise to a subjective right to the dividend unless the General Meeting resolves to distribute it (Supreme Court judgements (STS) of 30 November 1971, RA No. 5019, and 30 January 2002, RA No. 2311.

37 The jurisprudence has also accepted that the statutes may establish the obligation to distribute a minimum percentage provided that a net profit exists and is distributable to all the members or to a particular class of shares in the capital-based companies (STS of 5 July 1986, RA No. 4412).

38 Article 12 of the national law states that 'depending on the cooperativised activity', both natural and legal persons can be members and that the statutes shall establish the requirements for acquiring membership in accordance with the provisions of that law. As we have also seen, the cooperative laws set out the requirements for membership according to the different types of cooperative.

(LC art. 16.2 c), and declares that it is obligatory for a member who can no longer take part in this activity to leave the cooperative.[39]

The statutes must establish the classes of membership, the requirements for acceptance and voluntary or compulsory withdrawal, and the system to be applied (LC art. 11.1 j). They must also regulate the internal disciplinary rules, classifying the breaches and penalties, the procedure for imposing penalties, and loss of membership (LC art. 11.1 m). Members can be penalised or even expelled from the cooperative for not fulfilling their obligation to take part in the cooperative's activity.[40]

Hence membership of a cooperative is closely linked to involvement, whether as a consumer, a worker or a supplier of goods and services. However, the degree of attachment is not the same in every case, as it depends on the greater or lesser participation required of members by the provisions of the statutes or the resolutions of the cooperative.[41]

In view of the diversity of the members, those who take part in the cooperative activity are termed 'cooperating members' or 'user members'. Their involvement can be for an indefinite or a fixed term: since the Cooperative Law of 1999, if the statutes so provide and the General Meeting so resolves, temporary members may be admitted.[42]

---

39 Members who cannot take part in the cooperative activity must leave the cooperative; if they do not resign the Board of Directors shall resolve to expel them, acting on its own initiative or at the request of any member (LC art. 17.5). However, under certain conditions these members may continue to be attached to the cooperative as investor members (*socios colaboradores*) (LC art. 14.4), also known in other laws as members with leave of absence (*socios excedentes*) or inactive members.

40 According to LC article 18.4, the penalty of suspending membership rights shall only be regulated in the statutes for cases in which the member falls behind on his or her financial obligations or does not take part in the cooperativised activities, as set out in the articles. The courts have ruled on many occasions in favour of penalties imposed on members for breach of their obligation to participate as set out in the cooperative's articles and resolutions: see Supreme Court judgments of 14 January 1976 (RA No. 4468), 6 October 1994 (RJ 1994/7462); 2 February 1995 (RJ 1995/1221); 2 June 2006 (RJ 2006/3066). On this and other minor case law see G. Fajardo, *La gestión económica de la cooperativa: responsabilidad de los socios*, Ed. Tecnos, Madrid, 1997, pp. 81–82; C. Vargas, 'La actividad cooperativizada y las relaciones de la cooperativa con sus socios y con terceros', *Revista Aranzadi de Sociedades*, 2006, Monograph No. 27, p. 98; L. Gallego, 'Medios económicos y disciplinarios para combatir el incumplimiento de los socios de participar en las actividades de las cooperativas agrarias', *Revista de Estudios Cooperativos*, 2011, no. 104, pp. 63–101.

41 Some cooperative laws even recognise what is known as the principle of exclusivity, whereby members must deliver the entirety of their output to the cooperative (law of Extremadura, Madrid, Valencia and Andalusia).

42 LC article 13.6 allows 'fixed-term attachment to the cooperative' provided that the total number of such members is no more than one-fifth of the indefinite-term members in the membership class in question. The compulsory share capital contribution demanded of this type of member may not be greater than 10% of that required of indefinite-term members and shall be reimbursed when the member leaves the cooperative at the end of the fixed term. Other legislations use a clearer term: 'temporary member' (law of Asturias, art. 24; Castile La Mancha, art. 23; or Castile and Leon, art. 28).

It is also possible for a single cooperative to fulfil the purposes of different classes of cooperative and therefore have different types of cooperating members: worker members and consumer members, for instance. The national law calls this type of cooperative 'integral cooperatives' and says that they have plural cooperative objectives.[43] Their decision-making bodies must include representatives of the different activities included in their objects (art. 105).

As well as cooperating or user members, cooperatives can also have employee members (*socios de trabajo*). This is only possible in cooperatives where work is not the typical form of involvement and only if their existence is provided for in the statutes. It is not possible in worker cooperatives and communal farming cooperatives (LC art. 13.4). The Law states that the 'cooperativised activity' of these members shall consist of their personal performance of work in the cooperative. Consequently, they are members who coexist with other consumer or supplier members. The Cooperatives Law only establishes one rule to ensure the equitable participation of these members in the economic and social rights and obligations and guarantee them a minimum remuneration for their work. In every other respect, these members are governed by the same rules as the 'worker members' of worker cooperatives.

Lastly, the legislation also recognises the existence of members who are not involved, or nor fully (as in the law of Andalusia or Madrid), in the typical cooperative activity of the cooperative objects but contribute to achieving them by providing capital or in other ways. The different laws employ different terms for these members, but the one most often used for investor members is contributor member (*socio colaborador*) (LC art. 14). These members share in the capital of the cooperative and in return receive limited economic and political rights.[44]

1.5. COOPERATIVE ACTIVITY WITH MEMBERS: REGULATION

As we have seen, the cooperative can engage in any lawful economic activity in pursuit of its objectives (LC art. 1.2). The economic activity of the cooperative

---

43 The same term is used in Asturias (art. 185), the Balearic Islands (art. 140), Castile La Mancha (art. 153), Madrid (art. 122), Murcia (art. 129) Navarre (art. 80) Cantabria (art. 128) and Catalonia (art. 136). Other names used in other regions are 'mixed cooperative': Andalusia (art. 106) and Aragon (art. 71) and 'multipurpose cooperative' (*cooperativa polivalente*) in Valencia (art. 86).

44 The laws usually differentiate between different classes of non-cooperating members: inactive (*inactivos*) (Andalusia, the Basque Country, Castile and Leon, Madrid); on extended leave of absence (*excedentes*) (Aragon, Catalonia, Galicia, La Rioja); associate (*asociados*) (Balearic Islands, Extremadura, Madrid, Murcia, Navarre and Valencia); and contributor (*colaboradores*) [investor members] (Andalusia, Aragon, Asturias, Castile La Mancha, Castile and Leon, Catalonia, Galicia, Madrid, Navarre and La Rioja).

and the members' involvement in it are mainly regulated by the provisions of the cooperatives law and the cooperative's own statutes. The latter have to state the object of the cooperative, the rights and obligations of its members and its disciplinary rules (LC art. 11).

The law obliges the members to take part in the cooperative activities carried out by the cooperative to fulfil its objectives, to at least the minimum extent set out in its statutes (LC art. 15.2 b); the penalties for no doing so can even include the member's expulsion from the cooperative (LC art. 18. 4 and 5). However, when there is due cause the Board of Directors can exonerate the member from this obligation to the extent appropriate to the circumstances.

For the same reason, loss of the conditions required for membership, in other words, for taking part in the cooperative activity, is cause for compulsory withdrawal from the cooperative, which can be resolved at the instance of any member or of the Board of Directors (LC art. 17.5).

Involvement in the cooperative activity is not only an obligation, it is also a right. The law provides that members have a right to take part in all the cooperative's activities without discrimination (LC art. 16.2 c).[45]

As we have seen, the cooperative legislation also regulates how the results of the financial year should be calculated and allocated and how the member's involvement in the cooperative should be valued (LC arts. 57–59). It also describes the different types of cooperative, defines their objects and sets out the basic regulations, referring their further development to the statutes, the internal rules and the resolutions of the decision-making bodies.

However, as regards regulation of the transactions between the cooperative and its members, the national law (art. 52.3) states that the goods of any kind delivered by the members for cooperative management and, in general, payments to obtain cooperative services, shall be subject to the conditions decided and agreed with the cooperative society.[46] This rule would seem to allow the possibility of the cooperative's making individual agreements with its members about the conditions in which they will take part in the cooperative activity.

On the basis of this rule, there is a thesis that cooperatives can manage the interests of their members (service management) or contract directly with them

---

45 The courts, on several occasions, have recognised the right of the member to take part in the economic activity of the cooperative while still a member, even when there is cause to proceed with his or her expulsion. Among others see STS of 16 October 1989 (RA No. 6921) and 21 March 1990 (RA No. 1717). According to this Court, the member can only be deprived of the right to take part in the economic activity of the cooperative as a result of the breaches and disciplinary procedure set out in the Statutes.
See G. Fajardo, *La gestión económica de la cooperativa: responsabilidad de los socios*, Ed. Tecnos, Madrid, 1998, pp. 78–79.

46 The Supreme Court pronounced its judgement on this rule on (STS) 27 January 1986, stating that these conditions 'can be set both individually with each cooperative member and through general conditions that the members accept when they join the cooperative, with reciprocal rights and obligations stemming from the bond so created'.

to meet their needs. In this minority view, there is a two-pronged contractual relationship between the cooperative and its members: the partnership relationship, on the one hand, and, in the sphere of the cooperative's activity, on the other, a relationship that depending on the different cases could be considered purchase and sale, mandate, lease, etc. The thesis of a two-pronged contractual relationship is not held in relation to worker cooperatives, as both the legislation and the case law state quite clearly that the relationship is exclusively one of partnership,[47] but it is held in relation to other types of cooperative.[48] Legally it is based on the above-mentioned LC article 52.3, and also on the new accounting rules.[49]

However, if the possibility of negotiating the transaction conditions individually with the members is accepted, it should be remembered that these conditions cannot give rise to discrimination between the members (LC art. 16.2 c) and that the jurisprudence has ruled that what is known as the 'principle of equality' between the members must prevail.[50]

The regional cooperative laws have improved on this rule and the most recent among them state that: 'Cooperativised relations with the members entered into by the cooperative shall be subject to the conditions set out in the Statutes, the Internal Regulations or, where applicable, in the resolutions of the General Meeting. Otherwise, these relations shall be subject to stipulations agreed individually between the cooperative and each member, but the society must always observe the principle of equal treatment when establishing the conditions that will apply.' (art. 29.3 of the law of Asturias or art. 34.3 of the law of Castile La Mancha).

---

47 LC article 80.5 and SSTS of 3 July 2009 or 13 October 2009, among others.

48 Cf. I. Trujillo ('Las relaciones mutualistas entre socio y cooperativa desde el Derecho de Sociedades y el Derecho de Contratos: una jurisprudencia en construcción', *Cuadernos de Derecho y Comercio*, septiembre, 1998, no. 26, pp. 117–120) argues for a contractual relationship of exchange between consumer cooperatives and their members, but played out in the context of the company, recognising the influence that the law, the Statutes and the Resolutions of the governing bodies exert in shaping this relationship, as well as the principle of equal treatment. In reply, C. Vargas ('La actividad cooperativizada y las relaciones de la cooperativa con sus socios y con terceros', *Revista Aranzadi de Sociedades*, 2006, Monograph No. 27, pp. 163–172) criticises the contractual character of the mutual relation, whether as a separate contract or as an allied (or linked) contract, on the basis that the partnership contract and the mutual relations have the same cause.

49 Order EHA/3360/2010 approving the rules on accounting aspects of cooperative societies describes the services between members and the cooperative as 'acquisitions' and marginally regulates 'Transactions on the members account', but only if 'no acquisitions or sales of goods have taken place' between the cooperative and its members (Eighth, No. 4). M. Paniagua, *La sociedad cooperativa. Las sociedades mutuas de seguros y las mutualidades de previsión social*, Marcial Pons, Madrid, 2005, p. 88 analyses these grounds, but in relation to the previous accounting rules.

50 Among others, see SSTS of 26 January 1983, 27 January 1986, 11 April 1987 or 26 February 2009.

1.6. ACTIVITY WITH NON-MEMBERS

Spanish cooperative laws have always allowed for the possibility of carrying out the cooperative activity with non-members, although only in certain cases and with certain limits and conditions: it must be provided for in the statutes, the sum is limited, results must be kept separate, and the profits must be assigned to non-distributable reserves.[51]

These limitations are also due to the traditionally very broad recognition of the open-door principle or free entry into the cooperative.

Article 4 of the national law now expressly governs transactions with non-members. It allows them if provided for in the Statutes, subject to the conditions and limits set by the law as discussed below. However, it adds that in exceptional circumstances that endanger the financial viability of the cooperative the latter can apply to the competent ministry for permission to expand its activities with non-members beyond the legal limits, to the sums and for the time given in the authorisation, depending on the attendant circumstances.

The law imposes different limitations on transactions with non-members according to the type of cooperative. Four criteria may be mentioned here. Consumer cooperatives have no limits on their transactions with non-members (art. 88). Business and professional services cooperatives can engage in transactions with non-members up to a maximum of 50% of the total transactions undertaken with members (arts. 93.4, 94.2, 98 and 99). Housing cooperatives cannot offer dwellings to non-members but can provide commercial premises and other goods and services (art. 89).[52] Lastly, in worker cooperatives the number of hours per year worked by employees with a work contract may not exceed 30% of the total hours per year worked by the worker members. The law makes some exceptions to this percentage, such as employees who explicitly refuse to be worker members.[53] In worker cooperatives, if the limits set by the

[51] Spain's first Cooperatives Law of 1931 also provided for the possibility of the 'overpayments' collected by a consumer cooperative to be refunded to non-member consumers (art. 19) and non-member workers of worker cooperatives to be paid their share of such overpayments (art. 25).

[52] Because of the financial and building sector crisis that has hit Spain, exceptions have recently been made to this rule so that housing owned by housing cooperatives on which construction began before this law came into force may be sold or rented to non-members provided that this is approved by the General Meeting and that these transactions do not exceed 50% of those made with the members. This new rule has been adopted both by the Spanish State (Second transitional provision, of Social Economy Law 5/2011 of 29 March) and by several of the autonomous regions.

[53] Article 80.7 also excludes workers brought into the cooperative through subrogation or taken on in activities subject to that subrogation; substitutes for worker members or employees on extended leave of absence, temporary incapacity sick leave, or maternity, adoption or fostering leave; workers in subordinate or dependent workplaces; workers taken on to be

law are exceeded, employees with indefinite-period work contracts and over two years' length of service must be accepted as worker members, if they so request, within six months of being entitled to exercise this right, provided they meet the other requirements in the statutes (LC art. 80.8).

Breach of these rules can be penalised by the Work and Social Security Inspectorate (LC arts. 113–116), but the main consequences are fiscal.

Fiscal System for Cooperatives Law 29/1990 (LRFC) classifies cooperatives into protected and especially protected. The difference is based on a number of criteria: whether the cooperative works in particular sectors, the members' financial strength and its 'greater closeness to the mutual principle', as the Preamble to this law says.

All cooperatives established in accordance with cooperative law are fiscally protected, meaning that they are exempt from or are allowed relief or special rates on various taxes.[54] However, they lose these advantages if their transactions with non-members exceed the cases allowed in law or if they breach the rules on separate accounts for these transactions and assigning the results obtained from them to the Obligatory Reserve Fund (LRFC art. 13.10).

Especially protected status is given to workers, farmers, communal farming, maritime and consumers and users cooperatives that meet certain requirements, including one that limits the volume of transactions with third parties. For example, for a worker cooperative to be especially protected the number of employees with indefinite-period contracts may not exceed 10%, but if there are fewer than 10 members one worker may be employed (LRFC art. 8.3). In a consumer cooperative the sales to non-members may not be greater than 10% of the cooperative's total sales, or 50% if so provided in the statutes. However, if a consumer cooperative has at least 30 worker members and at least 50 consumer members for each worker member, there are no limitations on the transactions with non-members. These cooperatives enjoy considerable fiscal advantages compared to other cooperatives and to commercial companies.[55]

made available to user companies when the cooperative is acting as a temporary employment agency; workers with work practice or training contracts; or work contracted for under any provision to promote the employment of people with physical or mental disabilities.

54 They are exempt from the Capital Transfers and Documented Legal Acts Tax (*Impuesto sobre Transmisiones Patrimoniales y Actos Jurídicos Documentados*) on a number of operations such as acts of constitution, capital increase, merger and breakup; constitution and cancellation of loans; or acquisitions of assets and rights that become part of the Education and Promotion Fund. Company Tax is paid at 20% on cooperative results (transactions with members) and the general rate of 35% on extra-cooperative results. They also enjoy 95% relief on the assessment of a number of local taxes as well as other benefits (LRFC art. 33).

55 As well as the advantages that protected cooperatives enjoy, specially protected cooperatives have Capital Transfers and Documented Legal Acts Tax exemption on acquisitions of goods and services to be used to fulfil the cooperative's purposes and 50% relief on the total Company Tax due (LRFC art. 34.2).

1.7. COOPERATIVE ACTIVITIES CONDUCTED THROUGH A SUBSIDIARY

Cooperatives necessarily have to conduct their activity with their members, although non-members can also take part in it. However, cooperatives often provide their services to their members indirectly, through a subsidiary or other cooperatives.[56]

The Cooperatives Law allows them to set up companies, groups, consortia or unions amongst themselves or with other natural or legal persons, public or private, and to sign agreements in order to fulfil their objectives better and to defend their interests (LC art. 79.1).

Together with other cooperatives, they may set up a second-tier cooperative or a cooperative group.

Second-tier cooperatives must be set up by at least two cooperatives. Their objectives can be to promote, coordinate and pursue their members' shared economic goals and to strengthen or even integrate their economic activities (LC art. 77). This article expressly provides that a second-tier cooperative can become a first-tier one.

Cooperative groups are made up of a number of cooperative societies headed by a company (the *sociedad cabecera de grupo*) that may or may not be a cooperative, which exercises powers or issues instructions that the cooperatives in the group are obliged to obey, so that unity of decision-making ensues (LC art. 78).

The law also expressly mentions that cooperatives can sign agreements to cooperate with each other with a view to fulfilling their objectives. By virtue of these agreements the cooperative and its members can engage in supply transactions, delivering products or services to the other cooperative that is party to the agreement, and these shall be considered the same as cooperativised transactions with its own members, although the entirety of the results must be assigned to the cooperative's obligatory reserve (LC art. 79.3).

When determining the results of the financial year, the income received from investments or financial holdings in cooperative societies, or in non-cooperative companies when these conduct activities that are preparatory, complementary or subordinate to those of the cooperative itself, are considered cooperative results to all effects and purposes (LC art. 57.3 a). This means that they contribute to

[56] Extensive information on cooperative integration, second-tier cooperatives and cooperative groups can be found in J.M. Embid, *Concentración de empresas y Derecho de cooperativas*, Ed. Universidad de Murcia, 1991 and 'Los grupos cooperativos', *CIRIEC – Revista Jurídica de Economía Social y Cooperativa*, 1995, no. 7, pp. 221–231; and R. Alfonso, *La integración cooperativa y sus técnicas de realización: las cooperativas de segundo grado*, Monograph No. 167, Tirant lo Blanch, Valencia, 2000.

creating surpluses; so they receive more favourable tax treatment and can be distributed among the members.

To determine the taxable amount for Company Tax, the fiscal law distinguishes between cooperative and extra-cooperative results, as mentioned above. It considers the income and refunds that a cooperative receives through its holdings in other cooperatives to be 'cooperative income' (LRFC art. 17.5) and those from investments or financial holdings in non-cooperative companies to be 'extra-cooperative income' (LRFC art. 21.2).

1.8. OTHER COOPERATIVE OBJECTIVES

As we saw at the beginning of this chapter, Spanish cooperative law recognises that all cooperatives have various objectives: satisfaction of their members' economic and social needs and, complementarily, concern for the community and environment.

In relation to the first and principle objective, we have seen that in pursuing its objects the cooperative can also benefit non-members:

- directly, because the law allows cooperatives, within certain limits, to conduct the same transactions with non-members as with members; and
- indirectly because thanks to its being easy to join a cooperative, anyone who is interested in benefiting from the services it provides can access them by applying for membership (the open-door principle).

As for complementary objectives, we also saw that some laws expressly recognise them in the very definition of a cooperative. However, all the cooperative laws without exception require them to devote part of their surpluses to training,[57] cooperative promotion and public benefit purposes such as disseminating cooperativism, cultural, professional and welfare advancement in the neighbourhood or in the community in general, and improving the quality of life and development of the community and taking action to protect the environment (LC art. 56.1).

It may therefore be said that although cooperatives must mainly attend to mutual goals, to a lesser extent they also fulfil public benefit purposes.

Spanish cooperative legislation also regulates a model known as a social initiative cooperative, which is not unlike an Italian social cooperative. In the Spanish national law these are defined as non-profit cooperatives which

---

[57] Normally, between 5 and 10% of the surpluses. Exceptionally, the laws of Andalusia and Valencia also provide that part of the extra-cooperative profits (25% and 50% respectively) can also be used for these purposes.

irrespective of the class to which they belong have as their objects either the provision of welfare services through health, education, cultural or other activities of a social nature, or the conduct of any economic activity with the purpose of integrating those who suffer any kind of social exclusion into the labour market and, in general, meeting social needs that are not being attended to by the market (LC art. 106.1).

These cooperatives undertake activities that could be described as being of public benefit,[58] but the nature of their activity does not change their cooperative nature. Social initiative cooperatives can belong to any of the classes of cooperative, and the legislation that applies to them will be that which applies to their class (LC art. 106.3). Consequently, the activity in question will be conducted mainly to attend to the needs of its members, whether these be consumers, users, providers or workers.

The only peculiarity of social initiative cooperatives compared to any other cooperative engaged in the same activity is that they must have been classified as a 'non-profit entity'. This classification depends on meeting certain requirements such as not distributing surpluses or profits to their members, not paying more than the legal rate of interest (currently 4%) on the capital, unpaid cooperative office-holders and limitations on the salaries of the workers (members or otherwise), which may not exceed 150% of the levels set out in the applicable sector agreement (*convenio colectivo*).

In some cases it is also necessary to engage in public benefit activities in order to be classed as a non-profit organisation.[59] In spite of these requirements, the fiscal legislation for non-profit organisations (Law 49/2002 of 13 December 2002, art. 2) does not apply to non-profit cooperatives, as it is only applicable to foundations and associations (whether of public or private benefit) that are classed as being of public utility.

1.9. MEMBERS' RIGHTS AND PARTICIPATION IN COOPERATIVE ACTIVITIES

The extent to which the members take part in the cooperative's activity mainly influences the allocation of the positive and negative results of the

---

58 Ruling on the taxation of non-profit organisations, Law 49/2002 describes the following, among others, as being public benefit purposes: '[purposes] of social assistance and social inclusion, civic, educational, cultural, scientific, sporting, health, labour, development aid, advancement of volunteering, advancement of social action, defence of the environment, advancement and care of those at risk of exclusion for physical, economic or cultural reasons ... encouragement of the social economy ...' (art. 3.1).

59 This requirement is only found in the national law (first additional provision) and in those of Aragon, Murcia, Galicia and Madrid. In the others it is not a condition for being classed as a non-profit organisation.

financial year,[60] and the distribution of the distributable reserve funds when a cooperative is wound up.[61]

However, Spanish law-makers are increasingly frequently recognising that voting at the General Meeting may also be proportional to the volume of cooperativised activity carried out by the members.

This possibility, which has always been recognised for second-tier cooperatives, has gradually been extended to first-tier ones as well, mainly for business services cooperatives such as farmers or transport cooperatives. Voting in proportion to the cooperativised activity is usually limited as regards both the maximum number of votes that a single member may cast and the percentage of the members as a whole that this may represent.[62]

In contrast, it should also be mentioned that members that do not take part in the cooperativised activity (investor members, inactive members, etc.) have a smaller part in the decision-making bodies (both percentage of votes and cooperative officers).[63]

1.10. CONCLUSION

The main objective of a cooperative in Spain is to satisfy its members' economic and social aspirations in common by means of an enterprise in which they participate as providers, consumers or workers. The cooperative also has the complementary object of improving its surroundings (concern for community).

The cooperative provides services to its members and does so in their interest, although it operates in its own name on the market. The economic relations

60 The national cooperatives law states that refunds are due to the members in proportion to the cooperativised activities performed (art. 58.4) and that the losses assigned to the members shall be distributed in proportion to the transactions, services or activities that each member carries out with the cooperative (art. 59.2 c).

61 According to LC (art. 75.2 c) these funds are distributed in accordance with the rules set out in the Statutes or by resolutions of the General Meeting, or otherwise in proportion to the activities with the cooperative performed by each member in the past five years or, if the cooperative is more recent, since its founding.

62 The national cooperatives law provides that in first-tier cooperatives the Statutes may establish the right to multiple voting rights weighted in proportion to the volume of cooperativised activity for members that are cooperatives, companies controlled by cooperatives or public bodies, in which case the number of votes per member may not exceed one-third of the total votes of the cooperative (art. 26.2). In farmers, services, transport and maritime cooperatives, the statutes may provide for the possibility of weighted multiple voting rights, in proportion to the volume of the member's cooperativised activity, which may not be more than five votes and no one member may be assigned more than one-third of the total votes (art. 26.4).

63 For example, according to the national law, the total votes of contributor members (investor members) may not be more than 30% of the votes in the cooperative's corporate decision-making bodies.

between cooperative and member are governed by the provisions of the law, the statutes and the resolutions of the governing bodies, but they could also be decided contractually provided that equality among the members is respected.

The cooperative must manage to satisfy its members' needs in the best financial conditions. When the member pays for or receives an advance on the service provided, the close of the financial year may show a surplus. The members, at the General Meeting, decide whether this surplus is to be refunded to the members or assigned to reserves. However, Spanish law always requires part of the surplus to be allocated to a reserve for member and worker training, the advancement of cooperativism and community development, and another part to the compulsory reserve, which must serve to strengthen the cooperative as a business. Normally, both reserves are wholly or partly non-distributable. The cooperative can also provide services to non-members and undertake other activities on its own account. These activities must not be priorities for the cooperative.

Like any business, cooperatives need capital, and the members are the first who must contribute it. Nevertheless, their capital contributions are paid interest, although the amount is limited and is conditional on the existence of profits and on the General Meeting's approval. Unlike commercial companies, however, the cooperative is controlled democratically (one member/one vote), or if not, through voting rights in proportion to the members' participation in the cooperativised activities, but never in proportion to their share capital contribution.

Cooperatives possess features that differentiate them clearly from commercial companies and justify a legal framework of their own, both nationally and at the European level, that is appropriate to their economic function.

2. COOPERATIVE GOVERNANCE

2.1. THE LEGAL CONTEXT OF COOPERATIVE GOVERNANCE

2.1.1. Cooperative Governance and Cooperative Identity

As we saw when discussing the cooperative identity, democratic control by the members is one of the defining features of cooperatives.

The Spanish cooperatives law 27/1999 of 16 July 1999 (LC), when defining cooperatives, declares that they have 'democratic structure and functioning, in accordance with the principles stated by the International Co-operative Alliance, as provided for in this law' (art. 1.1).

It also lays down that the members have the right and the duty to take part in the organs of the cooperative and in its activities (LC arts. 15 and 16).

2.1.2. *Cooperative Governance and National Business Organisation Law*

Spanish law applies different business organisation rules according to whether or not the members have unlimited liability for the company's debts.

Where their liability is unlimited, the law only requires the cooperative's statutes to define who is responsible for managing and representing the company and allows the members to organise themselves as they wish in all other respects. In principle, unless expressly agreed otherwise, all members may take part in the management of the company; they must all come to an agreement to take decisions; and they are all entitled to examine the state of the administration and of the accounts (arts. 125–144 C.Com).

In all other cases, taking commercial companies – mainly public limited companies (PLC) and limited liability companies – as the model, ever since the public limited company law (*Ley de sociedades anónimas*) of 1951 and the limited liability companies law of 1953 the law has laid down detailed rules on the organs of the company and their composition, powers and decision-making procedures. These companies have two organs: the General Meeting (*Junta General*), the decision-making organ composed of all the members (shareholders) assembled together, and the administrative organ, which manages and represents the company.[64]

In 2010, the consolidated text of the capital-based companies law (LSC) laid down joint rules for the corporate organs of PLC and limited companies.

According to this law, capital-based companies must have two organs of government, the General Meeting (art. 159) and the administrative organ (art. 209 LSC). The latter may be a sole director, or various directors acting jointly and severally or jointly, or a Board of Directors. The model of administrative organ must be established in the company statutes.

As well as the general rules, Spanish company law also covers some special cases such as single-member companies (*sociedad unipersonal*),[65] new limited companies (*Sociedad limitada nueva empresa*)[66] or European companies (SE)

---

64 A PLC used also to be subject to inspection of the accounts by the *censores de cuentas*, an internal audit body composed of shareholders that lacked independence and professionalism. This changed when Spain joined the European Economic Community and passed Auditing of Accounts Law 19/1988 of 12 July 1988 and Law 19/1989 of 25 July 1989, which made PLCs and limited companies subject to a system of verification of accounts by professional independent external auditors and abolished the *censores de cuentas*.

65 Company formed by a sole proprietor who exercises the powers of the General Meeting and whose decisions, recorded as minutes, are carried out by that member or by the company's directors (art. 12 LSC).

66 A subtype of limited liability company created by Law 7/2003 of 1 April 2003 in order to simplify the requirements for company formation as much as possible. It may have an administrative organ composed of one or more persons but may not have a Board of Directors (art. 447 LSC).

registered in Spain.[67] The latter may choose a one-tier or two-tier system, stating which has been adopted in its company statutes.

The Spanish legislation on cooperatives provided from the start that all cooperatives should have a General Meeting (*asamblea general*) of members, a Board of Directors (*consejo rector*) and internal auditors (*interventores de cuentas*) and its management (*dirección*). In primary cooperatives with more than a certain number of members or level of capital, credit cooperatives and secondary or higher-degree cooperatives, a manager became obligatory.

The LGC 1987 retained the General Meeting and General Meeting of delegates, the Board of Directors and the manager, as well as the internal auditors as a necessary organ, although the latter became compatible with external auditing.

The present cooperatives law introduced important changes compared to the previous legislation. The rules governing the manager have disappeared; a sole director in cooperatives with fewer than 10 members is possible (art. 32) and internal auditing is no longer obligatory if the cooperative is subject to external auditing (art. 39).

2.1.3. *Where are Cooperative Governance Rules Found?*

The rules on corporate governance are found in the legislation on cooperatives. As well as the national law of cooperatives (law 27/1999) and the 15 regional cooperatives laws, specific rules can be found for particular types of cooperatives such as credit cooperatives,[68] insurance cooperatives,[69] agricultural cooperatives,[70] or European cooperative societies (SCE).[71]

Hence, cooperative legislation in Spain has its own system of organisation and regulation which is differentiated from the provisions for capital-based companies. However, over the years a certain narrowing of the differences in their regulation has taken place. In credit cooperatives, for instance, voting rights in proportion to capital are now allowed.

The legislation on capital-based societies is not applicable by extension to cooperatives apart from a few express referrals to it in relation to contesting resolutions (LC art. 31.5), the liability of directors (*consejeros*) and internal auditors (*interventores*) (LC art. 43) or non-cash contributions to the capital of the cooperative (LC art. 45.4). Nevertheless, they may be applicable by analogy in the combination of circumstances envisaged in the Civil Code (art. 4).

---

67 This type of company was regulated in Spain by Law 19/2005 of 14 November 2005 on the Societas Europaea registered in Spain, which transposed Council Regulation (EC) No. 2157/2001 of 8 October 2001 into Spanish law.

68 Law 13/1989 of 26 May 1989, on credit cooperatives, and Royal Decree 84/93 of 22 January 1993.

69 The Regulation and Supervision of Private Insurance, Law 20/2015 of 14 July 2015.

70 Law 13/2013 of 2 August 2013 promotes integration among agricultural cooperatives.

71 Law 3/2011 of 4 March 2011, governing European Cooperative Societies registered in Spain.

A European Cooperative Society (SCE) that is registered in Spain is governed by law 3/2011 of 4 March 2011 (LSCE) and can choose between a one-tier (Board of Directors) or two-tier (management and supervisory board) system of administration, in similar terms to a European Company (SE).

2.2. THE ROLE OF THE MEMBERS

2.2.1. The Division of Powers Among the Organs of the Cooperative. Powers and Role of the General Meeting

As we have seen, law 27/1999 states that the organs of the cooperative are the General Meeting, the Board of Directors and the internal auditors.

The General Meeting is the assembly of the members held to deliberate and adopt resolutions on the matters which the law or the cooperative's statutes have placed within its competence, and the decisions it adopts are binding on all the members of the cooperative (LC art. 21.1).

The Board of Directors is the collegial organ of governance. Its responsibilities include but are not confined to, senior management, supervising the managers and representing the cooperative society, subject to the law, the cooperative's statutes and the general policy guidelines set by the General Meeting (LC art. 32.1).

The internal audit body is the organ that supervises the cooperative. Its functions, as well as those entrusted to it by the law, are those allotted to it by the cooperative's statutes, in accordance with its nature, that are not expressly entrusted to other corporate organs (LC art. 38.1).

Spanish cooperatives laws do not all require an internal audit organ (it may be optional),[72] and the Catalan law allows cooperatives with two or three members to have a single organ which acts as both General Meeting and Board of Directors (art. 55.4). It should also be pointed out that many Spanish cooperatives laws continue to lay down rules for the management (*dirección* or *gerencia*) of the cooperative,[73] which is an obligatory organ in credit cooperatives, and on other non-obligatory organs such as the legal advisor (*letrado asesor*) or the worker-members' representative committee known as the social committee (*comité social*).

As noted above, the General Meeting is the assembly of the members held to deliberate on and adopt resolutions on matters which the law or the articles place within its jurisdiction.

---

72 For instance, it is an optional organ in the cooperatives laws of Andalusia, Castile La Mancha, Galicia and the Valencia Region.

73 This is the case in the cooperatives laws of Andalusia (art. 47), Aragon (art. 41), the Balearic Islands (art. 55), Castile La Mancha (art. 65), Castile and Leon (art. 55), Catalonia (art. 62), Extremadura (art. 39), Murcia (art. 54), Navarre (art. 39), La Rioja (art. 56) and Valencia (art. 48).

The law employs two criteria to define the powers of the General Meeting: First, it lists a series of powers that are reserved exclusively to the General Meeting (LC art. 21.2). Secondly, it provides that the General Meeting shall set the general policy of the cooperative and may discuss any other matter of interest to it, provided that it is included in the agenda of the meeting, but may only adopt obligatory resolutions on matters that the law does not reserve exclusively to another organ of the cooperative (LC art. 21.1). This second criterion makes it necessary to consider what powers are exclusive to the Board of Directors, which we will examine in section 2.3.1.

Nevertheless, the law adds that unless otherwise provided in the cooperative's statutes, the General Meeting may give instructions to the Board of Directors or make the Board's adoption of decisions or resolutions on certain matters subject to its authorisation.

The powers that the law reserves exclusively to the General Meeting include: (i) examining the management of the cooperative and approving the annual accounts, management report and allocation of the profits or losses of the financial year; (ii) appointing and removing directors, internal auditors, external auditors, liquidators and members of the appeals committee, if applicable, and the amount of remuneration of directors and liquidators; (iii) amending the cooperative's statutes and approving and amending the internal regulations; (iv) approving new obligatory contributions to the share capital, allowing voluntary contributions, updating the value of the contributions, setting the sums to be contributed by new members, establishing joining or periodic fees and the interest rate to be paid on the contributions to capital; (v) issuing debentures and participation certificates; (vi) approving the merger, split, conversion or winding-up of the cooperative; (vii) adopting any decision that entails substantial changes to the economic, social, organisational or functional structure of the cooperative; h) setting up or joining secondary cooperatives, cooperative groups, representative bodies or economic collaboration formulas; (viii) taking legal action against the directors, auditors and liquidators on behalf of the cooperative; and (ix) other decisions arising from legal provisions or the statutes of the cooperative. None of the above powers may be delegated, other than those that may be delegated to a cooperative group (LC art. 21.3).

2.2.2. Member Voting Rights: One Member/One Vote or Variations from it

Whereas the maxim in shareholder-based companies is that voting rights are in proportion to the capital contributed by each shareholder, voting in cooperatives has always been democratic.

In primary cooperatives each member had one vote and in secondary or higher-degree cooperatives, if provided in their statutes, the members' votes may be proportional to their part in the cooperative activity and/or to the number of members in the member cooperative.

Law 27/1999 introduced important changes in this area. First, it altered the differentiation between primary cooperatives, made up of natural persons, and secondary cooperatives, composed of cooperatives. Nowadays, both types of cooperatives may have both natural and legal persons as members.[74] Multiple voting rights are associated more frequently with legal person members. Secondly, a complex system was adopted to decide the votes vested in the members, based on a number of criteria (LC art. 26):

In primary cooperatives, if so provided in the statutes:

In farming, services, transport and maritime cooperatives, in other words, ones that are made up of entrepreneurs or professionals, weighted multiple voting rights are allowed in proportion to the volume of cooperativised activity engaged in by the member (natural or legal person), but may not exceed five votes. No member may cast more than one third of the total votes.

In any type of cooperative, members that are cooperatives, companies controlled by cooperatives or public bodies may be allowed weighted multiple votes in proportion to the volume of their cooperativised activity. In this case there is no limit on the votes vested in any one member but their combined votes may not exceed one-third of the total number of votes in the cooperative.

In cooperatives with different classes of member (ones with employee members,[75] investor members,[76] or integral,[77] or mixed cooperatives)[78], plural or fractional votes may be assigned so far as is necessary to maintain the proportion of the General Meeting that the cooperative's statutes lay down for each class of member. The law also regulates a specific type composed of

---

74 Primary cooperatives must have at least three members (LC art. 8.1), who can be natural or legal persons, public or private, including joint owners (*comunidades de bienes*) (LC art. 12.1). Secondary cooperatives, on the other hand, must comprise at least two cooperatives (LC art. 8.2), but other public or private legal persons, sole traders and employee members may also join them (LC art. 77.1).

75 Cooperatives other than workers' cooperatives may have employee members. LC art. 13.4 states that if the cooperative's statutes allow this class of members, they must establish criteria that will ensure these members a fair, weighted participation in the rights and obligations, both financial and corporate (information, voting, eligibility for office). The same rules apply to these members as to the worker members of worker cooperatives.

76 All types of cooperatives may have investor members who do not participate directly in the cooperative activity but contribute to achieving it and may be allowed voting rights. LC art. 14 states that the combined votes of this membership class may not exceed 30% of the votes in the organs of the cooperative.

77 Integral cooperatives are those that fulfil the typical purposes of different classes of cooperatives within a single cooperative, as established in their statutes. The different activities of the cooperative must always be represented in its decision-making bodies (LC art. 105).

78 Mixed cooperatives, as mentioned in LC art. 107, are those that have members whose voting rights in the General Meeting may be decided exclusively or preferentially by the capital that they contribute. These members may cast up to 40% of the votes and their shares may be freely negotiable. The sum of the votes of these members and any investor members may not exceed 49% of the total votes in the cooperative.

different classes of members: the communal farming cooperative (*cooperativa de explotación comunitaria de la tierra*).[79]

In the above cases, the total multiple votes must be fewer than half the number of members.

In secondary cooperatives, if provided in the cooperative's statutes, the members' votes may be proportional to their participation in the cooperative activity and/or to the number of members in the member cooperative. No member may have more than one- third of the total votes unless the cooperative has only three members, in which case the limit rises to 40%, or only two members, when agreements must be adopted unanimously. The votes vested in members that are organisations other than cooperatives are also limited to under 40% of the total votes. The aim is to ensure that the control of a secondary cooperative remains in the hands of the cooperatives.

The multiple voting rights allowed in the above cases cease to be effective and the one member/one vote principle applies in the circumstances provided for in the cooperative's statutes and when the members entitled to multiple votes waive this right for a General Meeting or any other vote.

To determine the number of votes per member when multiple voting is allowed, the main criterion employed is volume of business done with the cooperative. In farmers' cooperatives that engage in a number of economic activities, the statutes frequently assign votes in proportion to the number of sections or activities in which the member takes part (marketing, processing, credit, etc.).

Voting rights in proportion to capital are also found in Spanish cooperatives legislation, as in the cases of investor members, capitalist members of mixed cooperatives or members of credit cooperatives.

2.2.3. Mechanisms for Member Control: Meetings, Elections, etc.

As we have seen, democratic control of the cooperative entails the members' assuming an active role in policy-making and decision-taking, with equal voting rights, and that those who manage the cooperative render accounts to the other members.

The General Meeting is the deliberating and controlling organ of the cooperative. All members are entitled to speak and vote at the General Meeting.[80]

---

79 LC art. 26.5 provides that in these cooperatives each worker member shall have one vote and members who cede the use of assets to the cooperative may have multiple or fractional votes, depending on the valuation of the assets ceded, but the voting rights of any one member may never reach five times the fractional vote vested in another member in the same class.

80 Law 27/1999 provides that investor members are entitled to speak and vote, but not all cooperatives laws recognise these rights, leaving provision in this respect to the cooperative's statutes, as in the Valencia region's cooperatives law (art. 28).

The General Meeting can address all the matters that the members wish but, as we have seen, may only adopt resolutions on matters that are not reserved to the Board of Directors and are included in the agenda.

2.2.3.1. Classes of General Meeting

Spanish cooperatives legislation differentiates among different classes of General Meeting. LC (art. 22) distinguishes regular or Annual General Meetings (*asambleas generales ordinarias*), extraordinary or special General Meetings (*asambleas generales extraordinarias*) and delegate General Meetings (*asambleas generales de delegados*).

The main purpose of the Annual General Meeting is to examine the management of the company and approve the annual accounts (if appropriate), although other matters within its powers may be included in the agenda. All other meetings are extraordinary.

Delegate meetings are held if the cooperative's statutes provide for this possibility when circumstances make it difficult for all the members to attend the General Meeting. In these cases, the members must be allotted to preparatory meetings (*juntas preparatorias*) where they debate the matters included in the agenda, may make non-binding proposals and must appoint from among those present the delegates who will attend the delegate General Meeting and decide the maximum number of votes that each delegate may cast in the General Meeting, the nature of the delegates' mandate and its term, which may not be greater than three years.[81]

Sector meetings or assemblies of the members of a section are another type of meeting. They take place in cooperatives which pursue their objectives through economic activities under independent management, with separate assets and differentiated operating statements. These cooperatives have common accounts and a General Meeting, but the decisions within specific sections are adopted by assemblies of the members of that section. The General Meeting can suspend sector meeting resolutions it considers contrary to the law, the cooperative's statutes or the general interests of the cooperative (LC art. 5).

2.2.3.2. Convening the General Meeting

The Board of Directors must convene the Annual General Meeting within 6 months of the end of the financial year. If it does not, the internal auditors or

81 The rules for delegate General Meetings are set out at length in Cooperatives Law (LC art. 30).

any member may ask a court to convene it (LC art. 23). Extraordinary General Meetings may be convened by the Board of Directors or by a court at the request of members representing 20% of the total votes.[82]

Notice of the meeting must be posted at least fifteen days and at most two months beforehand on the notice board of the cooperative headquarters and of each of its workplaces, although the cooperative's statutes may allow other forms of written communication that will ensure it is received.[83] If the cooperative has over 500 members the notice must also be published in a newspaper with a large circulation in the area.

The matters to be included in the agenda are decided by the Board of Directors, the internal auditors and members representing at least 10% of the total or 200 members (LC art. 24).

It is not necessary to convene the General Meeting if all the members of the cooperative are present in person or by proxy and unanimously agree to form a universal General Meeting and approve the agenda (LC art. 23.5).

2.2.3.3. Holding the General Meeting and Adopting Resolutions

The quorum for holding the General Meeting when first convened is over half the votes of the cooperative present in person or by proxy.[84] At the second time convened[85] it is at least 10% of the votes or 100 members or, if the cooperative's statutes so allow, whatever number of members is present in person or by proxy (LC art. 25). The cooperative's statutes may also require a minimum number of user members to be present in person or by proxy. If the cooperative's statutes provide for this possibility, the General Meeting may be held telematically.

As a general rule, the General Meeting must adopt resolutions by a simple majority of over half the valid votes, but at least two thirds of the votes present or represented by proxy are required to adopt resolutions to amend the cooperative's statutes, join or leave a cooperative group, or convert, merge, split, wind up or reactivate a cooperative (LC article 28). In elections for directors, voting must be by secret ballot.

---

82 In a capital-based company, in all cases, members representing at least 5% of the capital may ask for a General Meeting to be convened (LSC art. 168).

83 Capital-based companies can convene the General Meeting through their website or by placing an announcement in the Official Journal of the Company Register (*Boletín Oficial del Registro Mercantil* – BORME), and in a newspaper with a large circulation in the province (LSC art. 173).

84 Members may be represented by another member, who may not stand proxy for more than two members (LC art. 27).

85 In Spain, meetings are convened for two times on the same day with a short interval between the two times.

2.3. MANAGEMENT AND INTERNAL CONTROL

2.3.1. *Power of a Cooperative's Board or Boards*

The Board of Directors is the governing body of the cooperative and is responsible for its management, for supervising the managers and for representing the cooperative.

It is a necessary organ of the cooperative and has evolved quite considerably in recent years.[86]

First, the extent of the gradual reduction in the number of members required to set up a cooperative has favoured administrative organs composed of a sole director or of various directors acting jointly and severally or jointly.[87] This is only allowed in small cooperatives (fewer than 10 members).

Secondly, there has been a clearer demarcation of the powers of the different organs. Law 27/1999 states that all powers not reserved to other organs of the cooperative by law or by the cooperative's statutes are the responsibility of the Board of Directors, including, where applicable, amendment of the cooperative's statutes to change the registered office within the same municipality.[88]

The Board's powers to represent the cooperative extend to all acts related to the activities that comprise the objects of the cooperative, and any limitations imposed by the cooperative's statutes are without effect in respect of third parties (art. 32.1). The representative of the cooperative is the chairman of the Board of Directors or, if absent or unavailable, the vice-chairman.

Lastly, European cooperative societies registered in Spain may opt in their statutes to organise their administration according to either a one-tier system (the administrative organ is the *consejo rector* or Board of Directors) or a two-tier system of management (*dirección*) and supervisory board (*consejo de control*) as provided in articles 11–19 LSCE.

2.3.2. *Board Functioning, Composition and Liability*

The functioning of the Board of Directors must be set out in the cooperative's statutes or decided by the General Meeting. It is normally laid down in the

---

86 The exception, as we saw in section 2.2.1, is the Catalan law, which provides that cooperatives with three members shall have a single organ combining the functions of the General Meeting and the Board of Directors.

87 It has now become usual to require only three members to set up a cooperative, and the laws are being changed to allow worker cooperatives to be formed by only two members.

88 In section 2.2.1 we saw the powers that the law reserves to the General Meeting, which, moreover, may not be delegated (LC art. 21.3).

internal regulations. However, the law states that the Board of Directors must be convened and that it must adopt its resolutions by over half the votes cast. Each director has one vote and the chairman has the tie-breaking vote (LC art. 36.4).

The cooperative's statutes must specify the composition of the Board of Directors. The number of directors may not be fewer than three and there must be a chairman, a vice-chairman and a secretary. In cooperatives, it is common for positions on the Board to be reserved for members of sections or for investor or employee members. The cooperatives law also provides that when a cooperative has more than 50 employees with an indefinite-period contract and has an employee representatives committee (*comité de empresa*), the Board of Directors will have a member who is an employee chosen by that committee (LC art. 33). This representation of the employees is not required in capital-based companies.

Since the passing of Law 3/2007 of 22 March, on the effective equality of men and women, some cooperatives laws include a reminder of the need to guarantee a balanced presence of men and women in the administrative organs.[89] In other cases, this is recommended by codes of governance.[90]

The directors are chosen by the General Meeting, as we will see in section 2.3.3. The cooperative's statutes can provide that up to one-third of the directors may be qualified experts who are not members (LC art. 34.2).

The incompatibilities, incapacities and prohibitions for directors are laid down in the law (LC art. 41). For instance, the positions of director, internal auditor and member of the appeals committee are mutually incompatible and no person may be a director of more than three primary cooperatives.

If the cooperative must incur any liability to any director or any relative of a Director, this must be authorised by the General Meeting and the interested party may not take part in the voting. Acts and contracts performed without due authorisation can be annulled (LC art. 42).

The cooperative's statutes may provide for remuneration of the directors, in which case they must establish the system and criteria by which the General Meeting decides the remuneration. In all cases directors will be reimbursed for the expenses incurred in the course of their duties (LC art. 40).

The liability of the members of the Board of Directors of a cooperative is the same as that of the Board of Directors of a capital-based company.[91] They must

89 For instance, see the Galician cooperatives law (art. 43.4).

90 Article 75 of Law 3/2007 states: Companies that are required to present full profit and loss accounts shall endeavour to include a number of women on the Board of Directors that will make it possible to attain a balanced presence of men and women within a period of eight years from the date on which this law comes into force.

91 As provided LC (art. 43), with express reference to the legislation that applies to public limited companies (LSC arts. 236 to 241).

answer to the cooperative, its members and its creditors for any damages they may cause through acts or omissions contrary to the law or the cooperative's statutes or by neglecting the duties inherent to their office (LSC art. 136) All members of the Board of Directors that adopted the resolution or carried out the damaging act are jointly and severally liable unless they can prove that they took no part in its adoption or execution, expressly opposed it, were unaware of its existence or had exercised due diligence to avoid the damage occasioned (LSC art. 237).

2.3.3. Mechanisms for Board Election and Removal

Directors are elected by the General Meeting by the greatest number of votes in a secret ballot (LC art. 34.1).[92]

The election procedure must be laid down in the cooperative's statutes or internal regulations. However, law 27/1999 lays down certain measures that must be complied with, such as the following: The chairman, vice-chairman and secretary will elected by the Board of Directors from among its members or by the General Meeting, depending on the provisions of the cooperative's statutes. If a legal person is elected director, it must appoint a natural person to carry out the functions of the position. Appointment as a director takes effect from the moment of accepting office.

The cooperative's statutes must also lay down the duration of office, which must be between 3 and 6 years. Re-election is allowed (LC art. 35.1). Removal of the Board of Directors is total and simultaneous unless the cooperative's statutes provide for partial renewal.

The General Meeting may resolve to remove the directors even if this is not on the agenda. In this case, the resolution must be adopted by majority of the votes in the cooperative unless the cooperative's statutes set a lower majority for justified cases. In other cases, the Board may be removed by a simple majority (LC art. 35.3).[93] Directors may also resign at any time, but their resignation does not become effective until it has been accepted by the Board of Directors or the General Meeting.

---

92 Except for the director representing the employees, who is elected by the employee representatives committee as we saw in section 2.3.3.

93 The law lays down different rules for capital-based companies. LSC (art. 223) states that directors may be removed from office at any time by the General Meeting even when their removal is not on the agenda. This resolution requires a simple majority. However, in limited liability companies the company statutes may demand a larger majority, which may not be greater than two thirds of the votes vested in the shares into which the company's capital is divided.

2.4. INFORMATION AND PARTICIPATION RIGHTS OF MEMBERS AND TRANSPARENCY REQUIREMENTS

2.4.1. Right and Obligation of Members to Take Part and Member Education

Spanish cooperatives laws have hitherto considered that participating in the organs of the cooperative is the right and the duty of every member.[94] However, the requirement that members attend the General Meetings and those of the other organs of which they are members has disappeared from Law 27/1999, currently in force.

Studies have shown that members take little part, except in worker cooperatives, and recommend adopting measures to strengthen their involvement.[95] Such measures undoubtedly include education, training and information for both members and the managers. The fifth principle of the ICA Statement on the Co-operative Identity is relevant here. This principle emphasises the vital importance played by education and training within cooperatives.

For this purpose, Spanish cooperatives law requires cooperatives to assign part of their surpluses and profits to training and educating their members. For instance, law 27/1999 states that at least 5% of the cooperative's surpluses must be assigned to the education and promotion fund (*fondo de educación y promoción*) (LC art. 58). This fund must be used for the activities set out in the cooperative's statutes or decided by the General Meeting that have the purpose of training and educating the members and employees in the cooperative values and principles.[96] In order to achieve these ends, the cooperative may work with other companies and organisations and may provide part or all of their funding. However, at the end of the financial year the management report must detail the sums employed for this purpose, the activities carried out and the organisations

94 For instance, the previous cooperatives law (LGC 1987) required members to attend the meetings of the General Meeting and of the other collegial organs of which they were members, to accept the positions to which they were elected, unless there was just cause to excuse them, and to take part in the training activities (art. 34). At the same time, they were entitled to elect and be eligible for positions on the organs of the cooperative, to make proposals and speak and vote on the adoption of resolutions by the General Meeting and other organs of which they were members and to receive the necessary information to exercise their rights and fulfil their obligations (art. 35).

95 For example, see A. Mozas, 'La participación de los socios en las cooperativas agrarias: una aproximación empírica' [Member participation in farmers' cooperatives: an empirical approximation], *CIRIEC-España. Revista de economía pública, social y cooperativa*, 2002, no. 40, pp. 165–193; or I. Vidal, 'La participación de los socios y el gobierno de las cooperativas de consumo en España' [Member participation and the governance of consumers' cooperatives in Spain], *Boletín CIES*, September 2010, no. 83.

96 This fund may also be used to spread the cooperative movement, promote relations between cooperatives, promote culture, work and social and health care in the neighbourhood or the community at large, improve the quality of life and development of the community and take action to protect the environment.

entrusted with this (LC art. 56). Large cooperatives usually set up foundations to which they assign the funds set aside for these purposes. Smaller cooperatives sometimes transfer these funds to their respective cooperative federation so that these purposes can be addressed jointly.

2.4.2. *Transparency: Obligations to Inform and Rights to be Informed or to Access to Information*

Spanish cooperatives legislation gives members the right to receive the information they need to exercise their rights and fulfil their obligations, regulating the exercise of this right in detail. LC (art. 16.3) for instance, distinguishes between a right to information at the request of a member and at the request of a group of members.

The former has the right to receive a copy of the cooperative's statutes and internal regulations and amendments to these, the right to free access to the cooperative's books,[97] the right to information in relation to the matters to be addressed at the General Meeting,[98] the right to request and receive a certified copy of the resolutions of the Board of Directors that affect him or her particularly and the right to request and receive information on the progress of the cooperative.

A group of members that represent 10% of the total of the cooperative, or 100 members if the cooperative has more than 1,000, may request and receive all the information they consider necessary from the Board of Directors.

In certain cases the Board of Directors may refuse to give this information unless a majority vote of the General Meeting supports the request.

Spanish cooperatives legislation has not yet included mostly[99] the right to information through the cooperative's website or communication between the cooperative and its members by electronic means, as has been recently allowed by the capital-based companies law.[100] Nevertheless, it is normal practice for

97 The member has the right to access the register of members and the General Meeting minute book and, on request, may obtain a certified copy of the resolutions adopted by the General Meeting.

98 Members have the right to examine the documents that will be presented to the General Meeting before it is held, particularly the annual accounts, management report, proposed distribution of results and reports of the internal and external auditors, which documents they may view at the headquarters and in the workplaces specified in the cooperative's statutes. They also have the right to request further details of such information as they may consider necessary in relation to the items on the agenda, either in writing prior to the General Meeting or verbally during the meeting.

99 However, the most recent cooperative laws already regulate the corporate website of cooperatives (Cooperative Law of Valencia, art. 6; and Cooperative Law of Catalonia, art. 7).

100 Law 1/2012 of 22 June 2012 has added a new section to the capital-based companies law regarding websites and electronic communications within companies (arts. 11*bis*, 11*ter* and 11*quáter*).

cooperatives to have a website and to use electronic communications in their relations with their members. However, studies show that the information provided on their websites targets the market more than the members.[101]

2.4.3. The Supervisory Board and the External Financial Audit

As we saw in section 2.1.2 above, Spanish cooperatives legislation also provides for an internal audit organ (*intervención* or *interventores*) to supervise the cooperative. Its functions are established by the cooperative's statutes and it may not trespass on the powers of the other organs (LC art. 38).

Law 27/1999 requires the internal auditors to examine the annual accounts and management report before they are presented to the General Meeting, unless the cooperative is subject to external auditing (LC art. 39).

The Law on auditing of accounts 22/2015 of 20 July 2015 (LAC) requires all organisations – whatever their legal form – that meet the conditions set out in its first additional provision to undergo this review process.

This law applies equally to cooperatives and to capital-based companies. The cooperatives law recalls this obligation (LC art. 62) and states that if the cooperative is not obliged to have its accounts independently audited, members representing 5% of the total may request the cooperatives register to appoint an external auditor to examine the annual accounts of a particular financial year at the expense of the cooperative.

2.5. ADMISSION, RESIGNATION AND EXPULSION OF MEMBERS

Spanish cooperatives legislation recognises voluntary and open membership as a distinguishing feature of cooperatives (LC art. 1).

Law 27/1999 requires the cooperative's statutes to establish the classes of membership, the requirements for acceptance and resignation or obligatory loss of membership, and the system to be applied. They must also establish the right to reimbursement of the members' contributions and rule on loss of membership (LC art. 11).

The law recognises the members' right to resign (LC art. 16.2) and sets out rules for the admission of new members (art. 13), the resignation of members

---

101 See J. Julia, F. Polo and G García, 'La información divulgada a través de internet por las cooperativas' [The information published on the Internet by cooperatives], *CIRIEC-España. Revista de economía pública, social y cooperativa*, 2004, no. 49, pp. 167–192; or E. Bernal and A. Mozas, 'Evaluación del uso comercial de la World Wide Web por parte de las cooperativas de segundo grado españolas' [Evaluation of the commercial use of the World Wide Web by Spanish secondary cooperatives], *Revista española de estudios agrosociales y pesqueros*, 2008, no. 219, pp. 181–202.

(art. 17), the liabilities of members who leave (art. 15.4), the expulsion of members (art. 18.5), the new members' contribution to capital (art. 46.7) and reimbursement of contributions to members leaving the cooperative (arts. 51 and 45.8).

The following may be members of the cooperative: natural or legal persons that are able to take part in the cooperativised activity with the aim of satisfying their economic needs or aspirations (cooperating or user members); employee members (*socios de trabajo*) of a consumer or supplier cooperative, who work for the cooperative, become members of it and contribute their work to the cooperativised activity (LC art. 13.4); and investor members (*socios colaboradores*), who are natural or legal persons that are unable to carry out or participate in the cooperativised activity but can contribute to attaining it in some way, such as by contributing capital (LC art. 14).

Application for membership of the cooperative must be made in writing to the Board of Directors, which must make its decision, giving reasons, within three months. If the Board does not reply within this period, the application is considered to have been approved. If it is refused, appeal may be made to the appeals committee or to the General Meeting, where the applicant will be heard (LC art. 13). The cooperative's statutes must set the minimum contribution to capital required for acquiring membership, the form and due dates of payment, and the criteria for setting the obligatory contribution to capital to be made by new members (LC art. 11). Nevertheless, the law contains some rules on these matters, such as what assets may be contributed to the capital and how they are to be valued, and limiting the contribution of any one member to one-third of the share capital (LC art. 45). Regarding new members, Law 27/1999 states that they must make the obligatory contribution to capital that the General Meeting has decided upon. The amount of this contribution may not be greater than the value of all the obligatory contributions that the longest-standing member of the cooperative has made, updated by the retail price index (art. 46.7). New members may also be required to pay a non-refundable joining fee (*cuota de ingreso*), which may not be greater than 25% of the obligatory contribution to capital demanded to acquire membership (art. 52).

A member may resign from the cooperative at any time by giving written notice to the Board of Directors. The notice given may not be greater than one year and the penalty for failure to give due notice may be a payment of compensation for damages. The Board of Directors has the power to decide whether the resignation is or is not justified and its effects. If the Board does not issue a statement within the required period of three months the resignation is considered justified.[102] The cooperative's statutes may require the members

[102] The cooperative's statutes must set out the cases in which resignation is or is not justified, but the law states that if a member opposes a resolution of the General Meeting which entails accepting costly obligations that are not contemplated in the cooperative's statutes,

to undertake not to resign voluntarily without due cause before the end of the financial year or within a period which may not be greater than five years (LC art. 17).

It is obligatory for a member who no longer meets the conditions for membership provided for in the law or in the cooperative's statutes to lose his or her membership (*baja obliga*toria). However, in these cases the member may continue to be associated with the cooperative through investor membership (LC art. 14). A member may only be expelled for a very serious offence (LC art. 18.5).[103]

The law also rules on repaying capital to members who leave the cooperative. Since the reform effected by Law 16/2007 of 4 July 2007 on reform and adaptation of commercial legislation in accounting, it is possible for part or all of the capital of the cooperative not to be refundable to departing member.[104] If the capital is refunded the sum must previously be settled (*liquidado*), deducting the losses assignable to the member. If the resignation is unjustified as a result of not having remained in the cooperative for the required period, a deduction not exceeding 30% may be made from the sum resulting from settlement of the obligatory contributions. Repayment to members can be postponed for up to 5 years from the date of their leaving (or up to one year if the cause is death). During that period, the member is entitled to payment of interest on the sum at the legal rate. The cooperative's statutes may provide that if new members join the cooperative in the meantime, the new capital contributions may be made by acquiring those that are pending repayment (LC art. 51).

2.6. DISPUTE RESOLUTION BETWEEN MEMBERS AND THE CO-OPERATIVE

Spanish cooperatives laws usually refer to the possibility of the cooperative's statutes' providing for an appeals committee (*comité de recursos*) to be created to process and decide on appeals against the penalties imposed on members by the Board of Directors and in other cases envisaged in the law or the cooperative's statutes.

that member's resignation within 40 days of having knowledge of the resolution shall be considered justified (LC art. 17.4).

103 The cooperative's statutes must lay down the internal disciplinary rules and describe the offences and penalties and the procedures for penalising and expelling a member (LC art. 11).

104 Spanish cooperative laws provide for two classes of contributions, those with a right to repayment on leaving the cooperative and those for which the Board of Directors may unconditionally refuse repayment. The law also envisages the possibility that even if all the contributions are refundable, the cooperative's statutes may set an annual limit on the amount that can be repaid, and any reimbursement in excess of the limit must be authorised by the Board of Directors (LC art. 45.1).

Article 44 of law 27/1999 regulates this organ and its composition and functioning. Its decisions are final and immediately effective but can be contested as though they had been adopted by the General Meeting.

The decisions of the appeal committee, like those of the General Meeting and the Board of Directors, may be contested in the commercial law courts.

Moreover, cooperatives legislation usually contains a reminder that disagreements or arguments that may arise in cooperatives – between the Board of Directors or managers, the appeals committee and the members, even during the settlement or liquidation period – may be submitted to arbitration, and if the dispute mainly affects the cooperative principles, then resort may be had to amiable composition (LC 10th Additional Provision).

Arbitration is regulated in the Arbitration Law 60/2003 of 23 December 2003. In particular, article 11*bis* of this law covers *arbitraje estatutario*, whereby the statutes of capital-based companies may include an arbitration clause for conflicts within the company.

The statutes of cooperatives frequently include an arbitration clause and some regional governments, such as Valencia or the Basque Country, offer an arbitration service for cooperatives.

3. COOPERATIVE FINANCE

3.1. THE LEGAL CONTEXT OF COOPERATIVE FINANCIAL STRUCTURE

3.1.1. Cooperative Financial Structure and Cooperative Identity

Cooperative laws in Spain usually define the cooperative in terms which are very similar to those of the ICA Declaration on the Cooperative identity, reflecting some of the specificities of its financial structure.

Thus, for example, national law 27/1999 defines the cooperative as a company established by people who associate to perform entrepreneurial activities intended to satisfy their economic and social needs and aspirations, adding that every lawful economic activity can be organised and conducted through a company established pursuant to this law (art.1).

From this definition we may note that the cooperative performs a function of service in its members' interest, for which it can conduct any kind of lawful economic activity.

The initial articles of this law also pay special attention to operations with non-members, to the sections and to types of cooperatives.

As seen in section 1, the law allows cooperatives to carry out the same activities and services with non-members as with members, but only if so provided in the statutes and under the conditions and with the limitations established by law (art. 4).

The sections allow the cooperative to organise different socio-economic activities with autonomous management, separate assets and differentiated operating accounts, always subject to the cooperative's general accounts (art. 5).

In some cases the economic activity conducted by the cooperative establishes its cooperative type (housing, education, credit, transport, etc.).

According to its type, its legal framework may vary.

In all other cases, special provisions for the different types of cooperative are found in the general cooperative law itself.

3.1.2. Where are Cooperative Financial Structure Rules Found?

Cooperative law in Spain widely regulates the financial structure of these entities.

In addition to regulating operations with non-members and different sections of the cooperative, it regulates the cooperative members' economic rights and obligations, the economic regime of the cooperative (share capital, social funds and financial year) and its accounting system, dissolution and liquidation.

It also regulates the forms of economic collaboration, cooperation and integration between cooperatives and other companies and between different types of cooperative, taking into account the economic activity that they carry out: housing, agricultural, communal use of land, sea, transport, insurance, health, education, credit, care services or comprehensive cooperatives. Multi-purpose cooperatives are characterised by conducting two or more activities, achieving specific aims of different cooperative types.

The cooperative statutes (*estatutos*, articles of association) must establish the minimum share capital, the mandatory minimum contribution to share capital for each cooperative member, the manner and time of payment; the accrual or non-accrual of interest on the mandatory contributions to capital, the rights and obligations of the members and, particularly, the right to redemption of the contributions and rules for their transfer.

The cooperative statutes must comply with the law, and it should be noted that the law contains numerous rules on economic aspects, as explained below. Their great detail is justified by the fact that the Spanish legal system does not contain an adequate frame of reference in company law that could be applied by extension.

Cooperatives' accounts were always regulated by the cooperatives law, whereas trading company accounts were regulated by the Commercial Code.

Nevertheless, when Spain joined the European Economic Community in 1986, the rules for companies were modified considerably in order to incorporate the Directives concerning accounts and accountancy.

The directives which exclusively affected capital-based companies (public limited companies, limited liability companies and limited partnerships) were incorporated into commercial law by Law 19/1989 of 15 July 1989, which modified the Commercial Code and the special laws which regulated public and private limited companies.[105]

The title of the chapter in the Commercial Code that regulates this matter was changed from 'Traders' Accounting' (*Contabilidad de los Comerciantes*) to 'Entrepreneurs' Accounting' (*Contabilidad de los Empresarios*) but continued to regulate only commercial companies, making no reference to cooperatives or any other legal form of enterprise. The General Accounting Plans follow these rules, which were targeted on capital-based companies.

The accounting reform of those years did not bring any improvement for cooperatives, which were initially left aside. However, the cooperatives laws passed from 1980 onwards stopped regulating cooperative accounts and referred to the provisions of the Commercial Code.[106] As a result, the cooperative is subjected to a legal framework that does not take its characteristics into account. This obliges cooperatives to keep two sets of accounts, one formal (in accordance with commercial accounting legislation) and the other real, in order to continue acting as a cooperative (remunerate capital as a cost, apply advance payments and separate the results of operations with cooperative members from those with non-members.

This situation changed with Order No. 3614 of 2003 (now Order No. 3360 of 2010) which approved the rules on accounting aspects of cooperative societies, adapting the General Accounting Plan (GAP) to the specificities of cooperatives.

Finally, we must also bear in mind that cooperatives in Spain are governed by the Tax Regime for Cooperatives Law (Law 20/1990 of 19 December 1990), which indirectly affects their financial structure. In addition to regulating some tax benefits, this law establishes technical rules for adjustment to company tax in matters such as the valuation of operations carried out by the cooperative with its members, determining the cooperative results (with the members) and extra-cooperative results (with non-members), the status of income and deductible and non-deductible expenditure, requirements for the Cooperative Education and Promotion Fund, or updating the contributions to capital. Compliance with these rules is important for entitlement to the corresponding tax treatment, thus conditioning how cooperatives conduct their economic activity.

---

105 Directive 78/660/EEC on the annual accounts of certain types of companies; Directive 83/349/EEC on consolidated accounts; Directive 86/635/EEC on the annual accounts and consolidated accounts of banks and other financial institutions.

106 Thus, article 67 of the Cooperatives Bill (*Proyecto de ley de cooperativas*) of 24 June 1980 provided that cooperatives should keep organised accounts appropriate to their activity in accordance with the Commercial Code. This reference has been repeated in all the subsequent national and regional cooperatives laws.

3.2. THE COOPERATIVE SHARE CAPITAL

3.2.1. The Essential or Non-Essential Nature of Cooperative Share Capital

A cooperative is created to respond to certain needs and interests of its members. To do so, it may not need to have assets of its own at an early stage. It should be remembered that a cooperative develops its economic activity mainly through the members' contributions of goods, services and money to that activity. The cooperative may start generating assets by keeping part of the results obtained from the said activity. Thus, it could be said that share capital is not essential to the cooperative.

However, share capital plays an important role in determining cooperative member status because a capital contribution is necessary to become a member.

According to Spanish law the cooperative adopts a variable capital structure but, as we shall see, this has been changing in recent years.

The variability of the share capital makes it easy for members to join and leave the cooperative but in turn decreases the stability of its assets. This has been compensated for with certain measures that we will examine later, such as a minimum capital requirement, the liability of departing members, and indivisible reserves.

Given the weakness created by the variable share capital, cooperatives have concentrated their own resources in reserves. In Spain these reserves must be generated constantly throughout the existence of the cooperative and cannot be distributed to the members even if the cooperative is dissolved.

But despite the minor importance of its share capital, the cooperative is required to create it, to establish in the cooperative statutes the minimum capital that must be maintained, and to set the minimum capital contribution required for membership. Furthermore, since the 1990s many cooperative laws have been requiring a minimum capital in order to form a cooperative. This capital is normally set at 3,000 euros, which is the same amount as required to create a limited liability company in Spain.

The cooperative's capital is far from resembling the capital of public limited companies, however. The members of the cooperative are not investors who bring their assets to an entrepreneurial activity in order to obtain profits from it. The purpose of cooperative members is to participate in the activity in order to fulfil certain needs and interests, and the capital contribution is more like a charge or contribution that entitles them to participate in that activity. Therefore, and also given the limited rights conferred by share capital, the members of a cooperative do not have any great interest in making new contributions to share capital.

However, despite its low significance in the normal development of the cooperative, this amount, together with the reserves, form the cooperative's assets and, ultimately, the resources with which the cooperative has to comply with its obligations and responsibilities towards non-members. Spanish lawmakers have not taken any specific measures to ensure the preservation of this amount as a guarantee for non-members, or if they have, the measures have been insufficient. Now, however, the minimum share capital established in the statutes does offer guarantees to creditors of the cooperative, and it is normally subject to preservation measures similar to those for public limited companies, as we shall see in section 3.2.6.

3.2.2. Assets as a Natural Element of the Cooperative

The cooperative must not only create a share capital with the contributions of its members but as it generates surpluses, and possibly also profits, it must also create and increase mandatory reserves.

The cooperative must create assets independent from those belonging to its members; these assets will be devoted to developing its activity and backing its commitments.

However, the cooperative will also have assets provided by its members at its disposal that there is no reason to include in the cooperative's own assets, such as money to build houses for its members or buy goods for them, or the goods produced by the members to be sold or processed by the cooperative. These goods are managed by the cooperative for the account of its members, and are not usually included among the assets of the cooperative, although the law does provides that these goods may previously become assets of the cooperative. Thus, article 52.3 LC states that assets of any kind provided by the members for management by the cooperative and, in general, payments made to obtain cooperative services do not form part of the share capital and are subject to the conditions set and agreed with the cooperative society. Other laws, like those of the Valencia, Asturias or Castile La Mancha regions, indicate clearly that those goods and funds are not considered share contributions and do not form part of the cooperative's assets unless otherwise provided in its statutes.

The indivisible reserves are another particular characteristic of the cooperative's assets. Spanish cooperatives law provides for a mandatory reserve and a cooperative education and promotion fund.

Traditionally, the mandatory reserve has been built up year by year with part of the cooperative surplus of that financial year and its functions have been to contribute to consolidating the cooperative and to provide guarantees to non-members.

The education and promotion fund has adopted several names, but its function is to contribute to the education of the members, workers and managers of the cooperative, and to promote cooperativism. Traditionally, in each financial year it has received part of the cooperative surplus and the profits from operations with non-members and extraordinary operations.

Any other voluntary reserve set up by the cooperative was also indivisible.

Nowadays, this system has undergone important changes. The mandatory reserve (or mandatory reserve fund) no longer has always to be increased indefinitely because some laws require this until a certain percentage has been reached; and it is no longer necessary to allocate all the profits to this reserve, as 50% is now sufficient. Also, some laws allow partial distribution to members who leave or if the cooperative is dissolved. The education and training fund is indivisible and not attachable except for the payment of debts incurred in the fulfilment of its purposes.

Lastly, the voluntary reserves may be distributable if so provided in the statutes or decided by the General Meeting.

3.2.3. Regulating Principles of Cooperative Share Capital

In general, the cooperative's share capital is variable; therefore, its amount is not reflected in the cooperative's statutes but in its accounts. The minimum share capital, which is a stable and specific amount, will appear in the statutes; this is a matter we shall discuss in the next section.

The real or accounting capital of the cooperative will appear in its balance sheet and must be presented at the Annual General Meeting.

If the cooperative announces its share capital to the public, the law requires it to be done with reference to a specific date, stating the paid-up sum (art. 45.7 LC).

As for the effectiveness of the capital, the law takes several steps to ensure a correspondence between the amount of capital and the assets of the cooperative. Thus, when the cooperative is founded, proof must be provided of its payment (art. 10 LC) and of the parties (founding members) having subscribed the minimum contribution to become members and paid up at least the proportion required by the statutes.[107] The share capital must be the sum of the contributions made or committed to by the members of the cooperative.

If non-cash assets have been contributed, their registration data, if any, must be recorded, as must the identities of the persons contributing them. Also, the law is concerned to ensure that these assets be valued and their existence guaranteed by demanding experts' reports and making the members of the Board liable for their valuation, as we shall see in section 3.3.3.

---

[107] At the moment when the cooperative is founded at least 25% of the share capital must be already paid up and the minimum share capital provided for in the cooperative statutes must always be fully paid up (art. 45.2 LC). The remaining capital must be paid within the period defined by the cooperative statutes or by the general assembly (art. 46.3 LC). Spanish national law requires full payment of voluntary contributions to the share capital, but other laws limit that requirement to 25%.

3.2.4. *The Legal Minimum for Cooperative Share Capital*

Spanish cooperative law has always provided for variable share capital above a minimum that must be set in the cooperative statutes. In principle, the founding members are free to set the minimum capital, except in the case of credit, insurance and transport cooperatives; but since the Basque Country law of 1993, cooperatives laws from several other regions have generally demanded a specific minimum share capital in order to found a cooperative. In general, this amount is set at 3,000 euros, which is the amount required to found a limited liability company.

The minimum share capital must be fully paid up when the cooperative is founded (art. 45.2 LC) and represents a limit to the variability of share capital and to reduction of the cooperative's assets.

One reason is that reducing the capital to an amount below the minimum is, in certain cases, cause for dissolution, as we shall see below. Another is that if the accounting assets of the cooperative drop below the minimum capital due to losses, the statutes must be changed in order to reduce the minimum capital requirement (art. 45.8 LC).

Finally, if the minimum capital reduction is caused by a reduction of share capital due to repayment of contributions to a cooperative member who is leaving, the reduction resolution cannot come into force without certain guarantees being made in favour of the creditors. These guarantees are similar to those for public limited companies (art. 333 LSC). Thus the reduction cannot take place within a period of three months from the date when the creditors are notified. During this period, the ordinary creditors may oppose execution of the reduction resolution if the cooperative does not provide guarantees of payment.

3.2.5. *The Variability of Share Capital*

The variability of share capital is a legal instrument which makes it easy for members to join or leave the cooperative. Therefore, since cooperatives are governed by the open door principle, the variability of capital has always been an essential feature of cooperatives in Spanish law, to such an extent that it has been included in the definition of a cooperative (art. 1 LGC 1987) or included among its most important principles or characteristics (art. 2 LGC 1974).

The variability of capital is fundamentally influenced by the members joining or leaving the cooperative. However, this equation is not always true, because members can join or leave by transfers of participations in the capital, which therefore does not change, and the capital can also be changed without any members joining or leaving. For instance, it can be increased by new contributions made by existing members or by applying profits or reserves, and it can be reduced by the allocation of losses.

Nowadays the law still recognises the variability of the cooperatives' capital as a feature of their identity, but with important limitations. First, in order to promote the stability of capital, the regulation of the transfer of shares between members and non-members was improved, as we shall see in section 3.3.10. Later, with the reform of the accounting law by law 16/2007 (as we have seen in section 2.5), other measures were adopted such as, if a member decides to leave the cooperative, making redemption of that member's contributions to capital conditional on the agreement of the board (art. 45.1 LC), or even forcing the members to purchase the contributions to capital made by the member who is leaving (art. 85.3 LC).[108]

Despite these measures and their importance, the share capital of cooperatives is still variable and therefore will increase or decrease without the need for permission or public registration of these modifications.

The cooperatives law provides for the capital to be increased in several circumstances:

(a) By requiring new contributions from the members. The law allows the General Meeting to resolve, by a simple majority, on new mandatory contributions by the members (art. 46.2 LC). The resolutions of the General Meeting are binding on all members without exception (art. 20 LC). However, any member who is dissatisfied with the resolution adopted may leave, and this leaving will be classified as justified.

(b) When new members join the cooperative. Indeed, as stated in article 46 7 LC, members who join the cooperative must make the required contribution to share capital established by the General Meeting in order to acquire membership.[109]

(c) Voluntary contributions by the cooperative members. Apart from the mandatory contributions required by the cooperative statutes or the General Meeting, the members can make other non-mandatory (voluntary) contributions. These contributions require the authorisation of the General Meeting, or in some cases the Board.

(d) Unlike other cooperatives laws,[110] the national law does not state this explicitly, but it does allow the patronage refunds credited to the cooperative members to be paid by incorporating them into the share capital (art. 58.4 LC). This must be done through a resolution adopted by the Annual General Meeting and implies increasing the capital contribution of the cooperative members who generated the right to the patronage refund by that same amount.

---

108 This legal measure was provided for cases where the members of a workers' cooperative have been obliged to leave due to economic, technical, organisational or production causes.

109 The cooperative statutes must establish the criteria for setting the mandatory contribution by new cooperative members.

110 Like the cooperatives law of Valencia (art. 68), Aragón (art. 58.4) or Asturias (art. 98).

(e) Finally, the capital may be increased by distributing divisible reserves among the cooperative members. This is expressly provided for in some cooperatives laws, which also state that the distribution must be made in proportion to the cooperative member's participation in the cooperative activity within the last five years.[111] Spanish national law provides for the existence of divisible voluntary reserves but does not rule on how to make that distribution or on its proportion. This lack of regulation does not prevent the distribution of reserves to be made by increasing the cooperative members' contribution to capital.

Regardless of the reason for the contribution of capital, including the acquisition of capital share certificates, no member of a first-tier cooperative can have contributions that exceed a third of the share capital, unless that member is a cooperative, a non-profit entity or a company owned in its majority by cooperatives (art. 45.6 LC).

In turn, capital will be reduced by repayment to members or by allocation of losses.

(a) *Repayment to members who leave.* One of the main features of cooperatives is that people join them on an open door basis (art. 1 LC). This means that cooperative members have the right to leave voluntarily (art. 16.2 f LC) at any moment by giving notice in writing to the Board (art. 17.1). However, cooperative members can also be obliged to leave if they fail to meet the requirements for membership. This loss of membership must be agreed by the Board, acting *ex-officio* or at the request of any cooperative member, after hearing the member concerned (art. 17. 5 LC). Finally, members can be penalised by expulsion from the cooperative in the event of committing a very serious offence, according to the procedure provided for in the law (art. 18 LC).

In all these cases the cooperative member may recover all or part of the contributions he or she has made to the capital of the cooperative. Unlike the LGC 1987 which mentioned the members' right to be refunded their contributions to capital (art. 35.1 g), the current national cooperatives law mentions the right to 'liquidation' of the contributions to share capital (art. 16.2 e LC). Other cooperatives laws refer, more correctly, to the members' right to receive liquidation of their contribution if they leave or if the cooperative is wound up.

In fact, this is a right to redemption of the capital contributed but only once the settlement has been drawn up, since the calculation must take into account the balance sheet of the financial year in which the member leaves (art. 51.1 LC). Thus, the contributions made by the cooperative member may have been reduced by an allocation of losses or application of deductions. The latter can be applied

111 Cooperatives law of Valencia (art. 71.3).

for non-compliance with the minimum period of membership (in the case of the national law) or unjustified termination of membership (in the case of other cooperatives laws).[112] In any case, the law requires the cooperative statutes to regulate the 'right to redemption of the members' contributions' (art. 11. 1, l LC) in accordance with the rules it lays down.

This right to the redemption of the liquidated capital may be subject to conditions if the cooperative statutes make redemption subject to the authorisation of the Board, as provided in article 45.1 LC, or if the cooperative statutes provide for freely transferable participation shares, as in some regions of Spain.[113]

(b) *Allocation of losses.* The capital can be reduced by allocation of losses. In theory, the share capital should only be reduced by losses after all the voluntary and mandatory reserves have been exhausted. However, Spanish cooperative law has traditionally regulated the allocation of losses of the financial year to the cooperative members and has provided that this should be effective through deductions from their contributions to share capital on some occasions and on others through reducing the paid-up capital. The latter case is an internal compensation because the cooperative member is still a debtor, but it is now classed as a contribution to capital pending payment.[114]

Insofar as the cooperative member owns the goods managed by the cooperative, he or she must assume the economic consequences of that management. Therefore, if a value initially assigned to these goods is different from the definitive value, it must be possible to attribute the positive (surplus earnings) or negative (losses) difference to that member.

Exclusively in this sense, losses may be allocated to the cooperative member at the end of the financial year in proportion to his or her participation in the activity.

It is a different matter when the cooperative, acting in its own name, generates losses and these, after clearing the reserves, are allocated to capital, thus reducing the member's participation. In this case the member must not assume any liability apart from the loss of his or her capital if – as is usually the case – the cooperative member is not liable for the corporate debts.

---

112 In these cases, unjustified leaving must be distinguished from expulsion. In the former, the law does not allow cooperative statutes to allow deductions of more than 20% of the amount of the mandatory contributions to be repaid, while in the latter the deduction cannot be higher than 30%.

113 Like the law of Andalusia (art. 61.1) or Asturias (art. 92).

114 For instance, the cooperatives law of Valencia refers to 'payment through the proportional reduction of the amount paid in mandatory contributions to the share capital' (art. 69.2). More recently, the cooperatives law of Asturias provides that 'if payment through reduction of the contributions to the share capital is agreed, that deduction shall first be made from the cooperative member's voluntary contributions, if any, and then from his or her paid-up mandatory contributions' (art. 99.4).

However, most of the cooperatives laws refer to the allocation of losses to the cooperative members without making any distinction according to the origin of those losses and without limiting their amount.[115]

3.2.6. *The Functions of Share Capital*

In the cooperative, share capital only fulfils some of the functions that are assigned to share capital in public limited liability companies and limited liability companies.

As regards its organisational function, we have already seen that the contribution of capital determines membership. For cooperating members, this contribution is a necessary but insufficient condition. The applicant must also be able to participate in the cooperative's activity.

Apart from the acts of joining or leaving the cooperative, share capital does not determine any other organisational feature of the cooperative relating to the cooperating members, except in credit cooperatives, where the law allows voting rights to be proportional to the capital contributed by the member.

On the other hand, in the case of investor or contributor members, meaning those that do not participate in the cooperative activity, the contribution of capital can be the criterion that determines their rights, both economic and political, as we shall see in section 3.3.11.

As for the guarantee function, we have already noted that the share capital of the cooperative does not fulfil that function due to its variability, but the amount of minimum capital provided for in the statutes does fulfil it.

Finally, regarding the productive function of capital, we have also mentioned its lower significance due to the importance in cooperatives of the so-called mutualist capital (*masa de gestión cooperativa*), which is the set of assets managed by the cooperative and fully available for it to fulfil its purpose. However, it should also be noted that in practice there is a tendency to reinvest the available surpluses due to the fact that the cooperative members have different sources of income from the cooperative: interest from their contribution to capital, advances for their work or for contributing other assets, discounts on their purchases, etc. The reinvestment can be made by applying the surpluses to reserves or capital.

Normally, the reinvestment of capital has found greater acceptance in many cooperatives because it can be individualised, because it is redeemable, and because of the traditional indivisibility of the reserves. This scenario has changed in recent years. It is possible to create individualised distributable reserves and

---

115 Exceptionally the Andalusian law limits the cooperative member's liability in the event of allocation of losses, to the capital contributed (art. 69) and that of Valencia limits it to the capital contributed, acknowledged advances and the sum of the credited divisible reserves (art. 69.2).

the share capital is no longer necessarily redeemable when a member leaves the cooperative.

3.3. MEMBER CONTRIBUTIONS TO CAPITAL

3.3.1. *Obligation to Pay Up Capital*

Each member of a cooperative must make a minimum mandatory contribution to the share capital in order to become a member. In the case of cooperating members, the cooperative statutes must indicate the capital contribution that the member must make to acquire and maintain membership. In the case of investor members, it is the General Meeting that determines the contribution to be made.

The minimum mandatory contribution to capital that must be made by each cooperative member can be different according to the type of member and also according to the member's participation in the cooperative activity. Failure to comply with this obligation will cause mandatory termination of membership due to non-fulfilment of the requirements for membership (art. 17.5 LC).

In addition to this initial contribution, the General Meeting can resolve at any moment to require new capital contributions, but only from cooperating members. In this case, any member who has not voted in favour of the resolution can leave the cooperative by giving written notification to the Board within a period not exceeding 40 days (art. 17.4 LC).

3.3.2. *Types of Contribution*

Traditionally, the Spanish cooperatives law has drawn a distinction between mandatory and voluntary contributions to capital.

Mandatory contributions are the ones that the cooperative member is required to make in order to participate in the economic activity and in the organs of the cooperative. All the members must contribute in equal conditions or in proportion to their participation in the activity. Normally, these contributions are not remunerated or the remuneration is minimal.

Voluntary contributions are freely made by the member provided that the cooperative has authorised them. These contributions are often better remunerated and are more easily transferable.

The regulation of their payment and remuneration differs in the different laws. According to the national law they must be fully paid-up from the moment of subscription and their remuneration cannot be higher than that of the last-agreed voluntary contributions or, by default, than that of the mandatory contributions. Other laws accept a minimum payment of 25% and give the cooperative more freedom to decide their remuneration.

The introduction of the investor member into the legislation opens up several options for defining these members' participation in the share capital. Some laws limit these members' maximum participation in the capital,[116] while others only limit their political rights (voting, eligibility for office). As for the type of contribution that they make, it is not defined in the national law, which only mentions that they must pay the contribution determined by the General Meeting and that new contributions to capital cannot be demanded of these members.

After the accounting reform by Law 16/2007, the cooperatives law provides another criterion for classifying capital contributions: voluntary or mandatory contributions can be contributions with the right to redemption in case of leaving, or contributions for which redemption in case of leaving can be unconditionally refused by the Board.

The contributions where redemption can be unconditionally refused by the Board (known as 'B contributions') possess some advantages once the cooperative member has left and redemption of his or her contributions has been refused. They have precedence to receive the remuneration provided for in the statutes whenever the General Meeting resolves to pay interest on the capital or distribute patronage refunds. Also, if new members join the cooperative their contributions to capital must be made through the acquisition of B contributions when redemption has been requested because their holder has left the cooperative.

3.3.3. *Nature of the Contribution*

The general rule in Spanish cooperatives law is that contributions to capital by the cooperative members must be made in legal tender. However, they can be made in goods and rights if so provided in the statues or resolved by the General Meeting.

These goods must be eligible for economic valuation. Future contributions of services are not allowable as contributions to capital.

In the case of non-cash contributions to capital, it will be the Board that sets the valuation after consulting one or several independent experts appointed by the Board.

The board members are liable for five years for the authenticity or existence of such contributions and for their assigned value.

The cooperative statutes can submit the valuation made by the Board to ratification by the General Meeting.

As for regulation of their delivery and of the provisioning and transfer of risks, the same rules are applied to non-cash contributions as to contributions to public limited companies, by explicit reference in the cooperatives legislation.

---

116 According to the national law, the contributions made by contributor members can never exceed 45% of the total contributions to the share capital.

3.3.4. *Accreditation*

There are numerous possibilities for accrediting the contributions made by the member to the cooperative capital. The national cooperative law only requires that the form of accreditation, as well as its variations, must be provided for in the cooperative statutes. It explicitly forbids considering them as securities.

The regional laws usually refer to their accreditation through registered securities, participation passbooks, certification of the register of members, or entries in the accounts. More recently, since the accounting reform by Law 16/2007, with the intention of facilitating the transfer of contributions, some laws provide for the possibility of these being documented as securities, registered or otherwise.[117]

3.3.5. *Amount*

As we have seen, every member, or at least every contributor member, must make a mandatory contribution to share capital. In addition, voluntary contributions to capital by cooperating or investor members are allowed.

The minimum mandatory contribution to become a cooperative member will initially be determined by the cooperative statutes. Thereafter, according to the national law, the contributions by new members will be determined by the General Meeting (art. 46.7 LC) and cannot exceed the value of the initial and subsequent mandatory contributions made by the most senior member of the cooperative, updated according to the general consumer price index. Other laws use other criteria to determine the maximum contribution to be made by new members, allowing this amount to be set according to the assets or reasonable value of the company.[118]

This minimum mandatory contribution can be different according to the type of member or his or her participation in the cooperative activity.

Voluntary contributions allowed by the cooperative can be added to the mandatory ones. The total sum of both contributions by each member cannot exceed a third of the share capital, except when the members are cooperative companies, non-profit entities or companies with majority ownership by cooperatives. Other laws raise this general limit to 45%, and also make an exception for cooperative members that are public entities.[119]

Investor members are not subject to this limitation regarding the maximum contribution of each member. Their only limitation is on the total amount of

117 See the laws of Asturias (art. 81) or Castile La Mancha (art. 74.5).
118 This is the case in the laws of Andalusia (art. 58.2) and Aragon (art. 49.5).
119 As in the law of Andalusia (art. 54.3).

capital that may be contributed by all the investor members. In the national law, the limit is 45% of the total contributions to capital (art. 14). In other laws there is no limit to their contribution to capital, only to their political rights.[120]

When determining the amount of the contributions to capital by the members of the cooperative, one must also consider that it can be increased in two ways: by applying the cooperative surpluses to capital and by updating the value of the contributions, as we shall see below.

3.3.6. *Payment*

In general, in Spanish cooperative law at least 25% of the contributions to capital must be paid for at the moment of their subscription and the remainder must be paid as provided in the cooperative statutes or by the General Meeting. However, there are important exceptions to this general rule. Non-cash contributions must be paid in full, as must voluntary contributions to capital according to some laws, like the national one. Finally, it should be noted that in any case the minimum share capital must be fully paid-up from the moment that the cooperative is founded.

A cooperative member who does not make the payments within the set period shall be overdue automatically as a result of the due date and in consequence – according to the law – must pay the cooperative the legal interest on the amount owed and compensate the cooperative for damages caused by the delayed payment. In addition, until the situation is solved, the member's rights can be suspended and he or she can be expelled, without prejudice to claiming the amount pending payment through the courts (art. 46.6 LC).

3.3.7. *The Updating of Capital Contribution*

Cooperative law regulates the updating of contributions differently in different laws. Traditionally, cooperative legislation used to provide for the members' contributions to be updated to compensate for their depreciation over time and allow increases in line with the growth of the Consumer Price Index (CPI). This update could be made through an account that could be replenished with the gains generated by balance sheet adjustments (art. 77 LGC 1987).

Since the Cooperatives Law of 1999, it is considered that the gain generated by balance sheet adjustment can be used to update the value of the contributions to capital, but this update no longer refers to the CPI, only to the gains obtained (art. 49 LC).

120 As in the law of Valencia (art. 28).

3.3.8. *Compensation*

Remuneration of the paid-up contributions to capital is treated differently according to whether the contributions are mandatory or voluntary.

In the first case, the cooperative statutes will establish whether the contributions give a right to receive interest. In the second case, it will be the agreement to accept them that will set the remuneration or the procedure to define it (art. 48.1 LC). In any case, remuneration is not a cooperative member's absolute right but one that is subject to approval by the General Meeting.

Remuneration of the contributions is subject to other conditions: it can only happen if there are positive results available in the financial year, and the compensation cannot exceed an amount related to the legal interest rate published half-yearly in the State Official Gazette (BOE). According to different laws, it can range from 3 to 8 points above that interest rate.

Remuneration of capital is not considered an application of results but a cost to the cooperative. However, as we have seen, its existence and amount depend on the existence of positive results. In contrast, in some regions the remuneration of capital does not require the existence of positive results as long as there are reserves available for this purpose.[121]

3.3.9. *Redemption*

Redemption of the capital if a member leaves the cooperative is a natural consequence of the variability of the share capital and the open door principle (as we saw in section 2.5). However, insofar as redemption leads to a reduction in the cooperative's total assets that could jeopardise its solvency and its capacity to meet its creditors' claims, the law has included some safeguards.

First, before the member´s capital contribution is redeemed it must first be liquidated, deducting any losses accountable to the member and any other amounts owed by the member to the cooperative from the paid-up sum.[122] Other possible deductions include penalties if the member leaves without justification, or before the end of the agreed period of membership, or has been expelled.[123]

---

[121] As in the law of Valencia (art. 58).

[122] As stated in article 51.2 of the LC: 'From the credited capital contributions there shall be deducted all losses attributed and attributable to the member, as recorded in the balance sheet of the year of membership termination, whether those losses were incurred in that financial year or have been carried over from previous years and are still to be offset.'

[123] According to the national law (art. 51.3), in the case of unjustified termination before the end of the agreed membership period a deduction may be applied to the amount resulting from the liquidation of mandatory contributions. The exact percentage will be specified by the articles of association but may not exceed 30%.

These amounts can only be deducted from mandatory contributions, not from voluntary ones.

Secondly, the law also extends liability for some of the cooperative's debts to a member who has received reimbursement of his or her capital contributions on termination of membership. This liability is personal and subsidiary to that of the cooperative, as well as being limited in its amount (up to the total reimbursed) and duration (five years after termination of membership). Furthermore, this liability is also limited to debts incurred before the membership was terminated (art. 15.4 LC).

The moment when capital redemption becomes effective depends on whether or not the Board of Directors may deny capital reimbursement unconditionally (type B contributions). If not, total capital reimbursement must be completed within five years from the membership termination. If the member has died, this period is reduced to one year after the member's death has been notified to the cooperative. Should the Board of Directors be allowed to deny capital reimbursement, it will take place at the Board's discretion, after which the same periods as described above will apply.

In any case, once the Board of Directors has agreed on reimbursement and on the total amount to be reimbursed, the former member is entitled to interest at the legal rate, paid annually together with at least a fifth of the total to be redeemed (art. 51.4 LC).

When two or more members are to be reimbursed, capital redemption shall take place in order of termination date, except for type B capital contributions, which shall be redeemed in order of the reimbursement request dates or, if no request has been made, in order of termination date (art. 51.6 LC).

3.3.10. Transfer

Transfer of capital contributions (or participations) may take place *inter vivos* or *mortis causa*.

In the first case, voluntary transfer is possible among cooperative members and to those becoming members within three months of the transfer (art. 50 a LC). Some laws allow living members to freely transfer capital to their relatives and heirs.[124] Although these capital contributions cannot be purchased by the cooperative, the legislation of some Spanish regions, especially after the accounting reform by Law 16/2007, does allow such transactions in order to simplify capital redemption after membership termination.[125]

---

124 See the law of Aragon (art. 53.3).

125 As in the law of Andalusia (art. 61.2) and Aragon (art. 53.6).

The law does not provide for compulsory transfer of capital contributions as a result of the enforcement of securities (attachment and seizing of assets). According to all the legislation dealing with cooperatives, the members' personal creditors hold no right over the cooperative's assets or share capital, as these are unseizable (LC third additional provision).[126]

Mortis causa transfer may take place in favour of the member's heirs if these are already members and so request it, or, if they are not members, after joining the cooperative within six months from the member's death. If no transfer of the late member's capital contributions takes place, the corresponding amount will be given to his/her heirs (art. 50 b LC).

In no case does the legislator impose limits or conditions on the value of share capital transfers, the sole exception being the law of Andalusia, which requires a contribution to the mandatory reserve fund of 10% of the profit made by the member through the free transfer of capital when compared to the amount that would be due in the event of capital liquidation (art. 70).

3.3.11. Economic and Political Rights Acquired through Capital Contribution

As already pointed out, share capital contribution is a mandatory requirement for membership, but as a general rule it does not confer any rights other than collecting interest on the paid-up amount if so provided in the cooperative statutes (articles of association) or the General Meeting (depending on whether the contributions are mandatory or voluntary).

However, share capital contribution may be the criterion for determining the economic and political rights of investor members[127] and cooperative members in credit cooperatives.[128]

Another type of cooperative that should be mentioned at this point is the mixed cooperative. It is regulated by several cooperative laws following the 1993 Basque law and is characterised by the presence of members whose voting rights in the General Meeting (up to a maximum of 49% of all votes) are exclusively or preferentially determined by their contribution to the share capital (art. 107 LC). This capital will be represented by securities or book entries called *partes sociales con voto*, which may be transferred freely and will be governed by the legislation regulating the stock market. Each member's rights and duties are defined by the cooperative statutes and, by extension, by the legislation dealing with public limited companies. The share of the profit or loss for the year of these voting capital shares is proportional to their voting rights.

---

126 On the other hand, members' creditors are allowed to seize their reimbursements, interest and patronage refunds to collect their debts.

127 Art. 14 LC, and law of Valencia (arts. 28.2 f), Catalonia (arts. 66.4 and 27.c.8) and Andalusia (art. 25.4).

128 Articles 8 and 9.2 of Credit Cooperative Law.

3.4. RESERVES

Spanish cooperative legislation has traditionally distinguished three types of reserves – the mandatory reserve, the education and promotion reserve (formerly education and welfare fund – *Fondo de Educación y Obras Sociales*) and voluntary reserves. None of these may be distributed among the members, even if a member leaves or the cooperative is wound up. Nowadays the three types of reserve can still be found, but in some cases they are distributable.

It is worth mentioning that the law sometimes refers to these reserves as funds or reserve funds. In short, they are a part of the assets that is not freely available to the management but must be used for specific purposes.

3.4.1. Mandatory Reserve Fund

The mandatory reserve fund (MRF) must be used for the consolidation, development and guarantee of the cooperative and may not be distributed among the members, even if they leave or if the cooperative is wound up. Some legislation, however, has recently allowed for its partial distribution, in cases of membership termination,[129] or total distribution, if the cooperative is wound up or transformed.[130]

The MRF is made up of a percentage of the surpluses for the year and all the profits (or part of them in some legislation), the amounts deducted from the mandatory capital contributions at the time of membership termination, the one-time joining fees paid by new members (*cuotas de ingreso*), and the profit obtained through inter-cooperative transactions (art. 55 LC).

3.4.2. Education and Promotion Reserve Fund

The education and promotion reserve fund (EPF), entered under liabilities in the balance sheet, is an allocation of funds that is built up from a portion of the surplus for the year and from the fines that the cooperative may impose on its members. In compliance with the state level law, at least 5% of the surplus for the year is to be allocated to the education reserve (art. 58.1).

The specific use of this fund must be defined, either by the cooperative statutes or by the General Meeting, among the purposes established by law, such as the training and education of members and workers in the cooperative principles and values or in specific matters concerning corporate activities and working life; the dissemination of the cooperative spirit and the advancement

---

129 Such is the case in the law of Andalusia (art. 70) if so provided in the cooperative statutes and whenever these do not envisage free transfer of the contributions.

130 In the law of Andalusia (art. 70).

of inter-cooperative ties; the cultural, professional and social advancement of the local community and society in general, improving the quality of life and development of the community and environmental protection. There has been a notable evolution in the purposes of this fund, from education and the advancement of the cooperative spirit to the adoption of recommendations on corporate social responsibility.[131]

In order to achieve those aims, cooperatives may collaborate with other companies and organisations, applying all or part of the resources in this fund (art. 56 LC).

In all cases, the Annual Report must provide a detailed account of the sums allocated to this fund and of the activities carried out, including the organisations involved.

Like the mandatory reserve fund, the education and promotion reserve is non-distributable, even if the cooperative is wound up, and not attachable. It is a separate group of assets intended for the fulfilment of its stated purposes and is only responsible for the debts arising from these.

The funds of the education and promotion reserve are intended to be used during the year that generated them. If they are not used in full, the law requires them to be clearly identified and the credit to be invested in savings accounts or government bonds in the year following the allocation of funds, the interest on which shall be used for the same purposes. These accounts cannot be used as collateral for credit or loan operations (art. 56.6 LC).

3.4.3. *Other Types of Voluntary Reserves*

The law also allows for the creation of other types of voluntary reserves for specific purposes.[132] Indeed the national law refers to the possibility of setting up voluntary reserve funds, which may or may not be distributable among members at membership termination or if the cooperative is transformed or wound up. These funds will be provisioned from the available surplus and profits, at the discretion of the General Meeting.

3.5. MUTUALIST CAPITAL (MASA DE GESTIÓN COOPERATIVA)

A cooperative achieves its corporate objectives through the participation of its members in economic activity. Members may contribute with property or funds, or provide a service. This group of assets forms the mutualist capital, known as

---

131 For example, the law of Andalusia (art. 71) considers this fund an instrument to serve the corporate social responsibility of cooperatives.

132 Like the Reimbursement Fund in the law of Murcia (art. 77) and the Depreciation Fund in that of Navarre (art. 46).

the *masa de gestión cooperativa* in Spanish legal doctrine. Though managed by the cooperative, these assets belong to the members, except when their purchase by the cooperative has specifically been agreed.

The nature of the economic relationship between the cooperative and its members, as well as its legal regime, are beyond the scope of this paper and have already been analysed in section 1. Instead, what follows is a description of the management mechanisms used by cooperatives to increase their capital and reserves, for which assessment of the members' participation in the cooperative activity is a key aspect.

The value obtained through the assets and services provided by the members and the price paid for the assets and services that the member demands of the cooperative will usually depend on their market value. The law, however, requires a value to be defined from the start, in order to obtain positive results to build up reserve funds and establish a tax base for the company tax. Depending on the legal system, there are several methods to determine that value, ranging from objectively fixed to effectively applied values, or even maximum limit values (as we saw in section 1.3.2). The latter is the case in the Basque law, probably the most elaborate system, according to which all assets provided by the members for cooperative management shall be valued no higher than their market value and the advances paid to worker members may not surpass the usual remuneration paid in the surrounding area in that sector of economic activity (art. 66.2 a).

Since cooperatives must record the amounts received from and paid to their members as income and expenditure respectively, at the close of the financial year the results may be positive (surplus), negative (loss) or neutral (zero surplus). In any case, it is up to the General Meeting to decide how to manage those assets, as explained in the following section.

3.6. REVENUE FROM COOPERATIVE ECONOMIC ACTIVITY. HOW IT IS DETERMINED AND ALLOCATED

In order to determine the results for the year, cooperative law has usually required a distinction to be made between the economic activity conducted by the cooperative with its members (cooperative results), that carried out between the cooperative and non-members (extra-cooperative results), and extraordinary results unrelated to the purpose of the cooperative (as we saw in section 1.3.2).

The reason for this distinction has been based on the need to establish the value of the member's share in the cooperative activity. This is important because it allows the results to be distributed according to each member's contribution to them. Moreover, this distinction makes it possible to identify the profit obtained through extra-cooperative activities, and therefore find out whether these are core activities or subsidiary to the fundamentally cooperative purposes. That distinction may also lead to a differentiated use of the results, such distributing surpluses but allocating the profits to building up shared assets. It may also lead to different tax treatment depending on their origin.

The current cooperative legislation in Spain provides an extensive array of cases in relation to this matter. In general, the results are to be determined in accordance with the general accounting plan, but distinguishing between cooperative and extra-cooperative results at the least. An exception is the 1993 Basque cooperatives law, which states that cooperative results should be determined in the same way as for capital-based companies, making no distinction between cooperative and extra-cooperative business.

Since then, all Spanish cooperative laws have gradually incorporated the possibility of considering all results together if so provided in the cooperative statutes. However, not distinguishing the results has tax implications for cooperatives, as their global results are unable to benefit from the reduced company tax rate applicable to the surplus resulting from cooperative transactions with members, which is the reason why this option is never put into practice. The Basque cooperative law is different because the Basque Country has its own tax law which grants all cooperative results a lower tax rate than for capital-based companies. Unlike the Basque legislation, in the rest of Spain cooperatives distinguish between cooperative and other (extra-cooperative and occasionally extraordinary) results, but the contents of this classification may differ from one regional law to the next.

The cooperative results are those derived from the cooperative's ordinary business, whereas the extra-cooperative results are obtained from its ordinary business conducted with non-members, from sources unrelated to the cooperative's specific purposes, from investments or holdings in other companies and from capital gains arising from the sale of fixed assets.[133]

Spanish cooperative legislation also offers a wide array of possible applications of the results. Until some years ago, only the surpluses could be distributed among members after replenishing the MRF and EPF. As already mentioned, however, the legislation has already made considerable changes to these rules.

In the national law, 20% of the surplus after deducting any losses from previous years and before company tax must be assigned to the MRF and 5% to

---

[133] Regional cooperative laws have gradually expanded the concept of ordinary results by including results from other companies partially owned by cooperatives if their businesses are preparatory, complementary or subsidiary to that of the cooperative. In workers' cooperatives, many regional laws also include the results derived from activities with non-members, though within certain boundaries.

In order to determine the results, the law also mentions some expenses to be taken into account, such as the value assigned to the assets and services the members contribute to the mutualist capital and the remuneration of capital contributions, special participating shares, bonds and other sources of funding. These expenses are deducted from the cooperative income or from all income (when extra-cooperative results are not separately identified).

the EPF (cooperative education and promotion fund), whereas 50% of profits after deducting any losses from previous years and before company tax must be assigned to the MRF. The remaining available surpluses and profits shall be assigned, as set out in the cooperative statutes or decided each year by the General Meeting, to patronage refunds to the members, distributable and non-distributable (*indivisible*) voluntary reserve funds and increasing the mandatory funds. Patronage refunds must be credited in accordance with each member's contribution to the cooperativised activities.[134] The cooperative statutes or the General Meeting may define an annual bonus to be paid to its wage-earning employees, the amount of which shall be set according to the results of the financial year (art. 58 LC).

If the cooperative's results do not distinguish between members and non-members, the allocation of the results is modified. In the Basque Country (art. 67), 20% of positive results must be assigned to the MRF and 10% to the EPF; in Asturias (art. 98), 35% of all positive results must go to the MRF and 5% to the EPF; in Valencia (art. 65.3), 5% must be allocated to the EPF and the rest to the MRF.

Cooperative statutes must define the criteria for offsetting losses, which may be entered in a special account to be set against future positive results in the following seven years. This must also be done in a certain order regulated by law.

The national law does not distinguish between cooperative and extra-cooperative losses in establishing this order and indicates that all losses may be set against the voluntary reserve funds. The mandatory reserve fund may cover losses in proportion to the surpluses and profits allocated in the previous five years. Any remaining losses not covered by these funds may be assigned to the members according to their contribution to the cooperative's economic activity. Losses assigned to members may be met through direct payment or deductions from their capital contributions, or from any financial investment they have made in the cooperative that allows for this deduction. The General Meeting may also decide to finance losses through the patronage refunds that may be due to the member in the following seven years (art. 59 LC).[135]

---

134 In the regional cooperative laws the percentages may be different. For instance, in Valencia (art. 68) 20% of the surplus must be assigned to the MRF until this fund reaches a total equal to the share capital, and 5% to the EPF, while all extra-cooperative profits and 50% of extraordinary profits must be assigned to the MRF. In Catalonia (art. 64), the MRF and EPF must receive 30% and 10% of the surplus respectively. In Andalucía (art. 68), 20% of the surplus is allocated to the MRF until it totals 50% of share capital, and 5% to the Training and Sustainability Fund, while 25% of the profits must be assigned to the latter and 25% to the MRF, though this last allocation may be used, if so decided by the General Meeting, for productive investment, inter-business cooperation and integration, or internationalisation.

135 The law of Andalusia (art. 69) also pools all losses, regardless of their origin, and allows for the use of voluntary reserves as well as of 50% of the mandatory reserve. The rest must be covered by members up to the total amounts of their capital contributions. Conversely, the law of Valencia (art. 69) separates the losses by their origin and only allows members to be

3.7. FINANCING THROUGH RETAINED COOPERATIVE REFUNDS

A traditional source of finance for cooperatives has been retaining the patronage refunds credited to the members, for a limited period, with or without remuneration. The national law is silent on this matter, though it states that the cooperative statutes, or failing these, the General Meeting, shall decide how the patronage refund credited to each member shall be paid (art. 58.4). Other laws refer to the Patronage Refunds Fund and limit its remuneration and duration. In all cases it is distributable in accordance with the rules decided by the General Meeting.

3.8. MEMBERS' CONTRIBUTIONS TO PURPOSES OTHER THAN SHARE OR MUTUALIST CAPITAL

This section deals with contributions, other than to share capital or mutualist capital, that the members must make in order to finance the cooperative.

Cooperative legislation has usually included the possibility of demanding one-time joining fees or regular membership fees. The current cooperatives law mentions these contributions in article 52.

Both one-time and regular membership fees are non-refundable and do not form part of the cooperative's capital. The amounts payable may vary according to the different membership type, whether the member is a natural or legal persons, or in proportion to participation in the cooperative activity.

One-time joining fees are usually required from new members, together with the corresponding capital contribution. The maximum amount that can lawfully be demanded varies, though the national law states that this fee may not be higher than 25% of the mandatory capital contribution invested by the joining member. One-time fees are intended to make up for the economic effort made by the existing members in building up assets and to compensate for the benefit that the new member will obtain from them. The legislation has usually limited this fee to a certain percentage of the capital contribution, as in the national law, though some regional laws have used different criteria, relating it to the fees demanded of existing or former members, updated according to the Consumer Price Index,[136] or to the volume of non-distributable reserves. In the latter case,

charged for cooperative losses, not extra-cooperative or extraordinary losses. It also limits the amounts demanded from members to the advances allotted in the year, their paid-up capital contributions and their share of distributable reserves.

136 See the Catalan law (art. 61).

the maximum fee is calculated by dividing these reserves by the number of members or by the capital contributions.[137]

Regular fees may be demanded at any time, if so decided by the General Meeting. They may be used for different purposes, from covering losses to financing investments. Members who voted against them are exempted from paying them if they terminate their membership within forty days following notification of the decision (art. 17.4 LC), otherwise they are obliged to pay these fees (art. 15. 2 a LC).

3.9. OTHER SOURCES OF FINANCE

In addition to the members' capital contributions, the mutualist capital, undistributed patronage refunds and one-time and regular membership fees, cooperative legislation provides for other specific or generic sources of financing, such as bonds, participation certificates and special participating shares. The General Meeting has the sole power to issue these (art. 21.2 e LC).

The national legislation merely states that cooperatives may issue bonds, though other regional laws add that these are non-convertible. Bonds issued by public limited companies and other organisations, as well as their legal framework, are regulated by Law 211/1964 of 24 December. Despite being a source of funds that has traditionally been applicable to cooperatives, in practice it is not used. Recently this law has been repealed by Law 5/2015 of 27 April, which refers the regulation of the issue of bonds by cooperatives to Capital Companies Act (art. 54.1 LC).

Cooperatives are allowed to issue participation certificates, which may be regarded as transferable securities and carry the right to the remuneration fixed at the time when they were issued, which must be in accordance with the development of cooperative activity, and possibly also a fixed interest rate. The issuance agreement must define a repayment term and other applicable norms, and, in compliance with the national law, may entitle bearers to attend the General Meeting as speaking but non-voting participants (art. 54.2 LC).

Special participating shares are subordinated debt instruments. If so provided by the cooperative statutes (articles of association), the General Meeting may resolve to issue these securities in order to obtain new sources of finance from members and non-members, with a maturity of at least five years. If the cooperative is wound up before maturity they will be classed as part of the share capital. In spite of this, they may be refundable, at the cooperative's discretion, through the mechanisms laid down for limited liability companies in cases of

[137] These are the criteria followed by the laws of Aragon (art. 55) and Asturias (art. 93), among others.

capital reduction due to repayment of capital contributions to the members. The 1993 Basque cooperatives law was the first to introduce this possibility of obtaining new equity, as variable capital is recorded in the accounts as liabilities. This instrument has been mainly used by *Mondragón Corporación Cooperativa.*

Cooperative legislation also admits of any other voluntary funding formula for members or non-members, by any other legal arrangement, including joint accounts, which are governed by provisions laid down by the Commercial Code.

3.10. LIABILITY OF THE COOPERATIVE AND ITS MEMBERS

Cooperatives are based on the principle of universal liability, according to which they are liable with all their present and future assets. A major exception to this rule, however, as already mentioned, is the cooperative training and promotion fund (EPF), which is unseizable; it can only be used to cover debts arising through the fulfilment of its purposes.

It must be remembered that cooperatives manage assets that do not belong to them but to their members (economic management mass or mutualist capital). Cooperatives manage their members' assets in order to pursue their social ends; therefore those assets must be used for specific purposes and should not answer for any debts unrelated to those ends. Both the legislation and jurisprudence provide clear examples of this asset discrimination. The national law, for instance, when dealing with housing cooperatives, considers the different sections (also called 'phases' or 'promotion stages') as separate assets, in such a way that the assets of one phase or stage cannot be used to cover any debts incurred by the others (art. 90 LC). This separation of assets depends not only on the existence of specific legal regulations, but also on the clearly identifiable entry of assets in public registers.

Regarding the regulation of member liability, if it is true that cooperative articles of association have had freedom to choose between limited or unlimited liability of the members, it is no less true that limited liability is currently the most widespread type of member liability, so much so that other types, namely unlimited and mixed liability, have progressively disappeared from the legislation.

Consequently, members only answer for cooperative debts with the share capital that they have subscribed, their one-time and regular membership fees, and their contributions to the mutualist capital. It is no exception to this rule that members should be held personally accountable for the consequences of their participation in cooperative activity, or that for five years after membership termination they should be accountable on a subsidiary basis for cooperative debts incurred during their membership, to the extent of the part of the assets that they were repaid at membership termination.

As already pointed out, however, it is unfortunate that some Spanish cooperative laws, like the national law, hold members accountable for any type of loss without limitation.

3.11. DISSOLUTION AND WINDING UP

Cooperatives shall automatically be dissolved at the end of the duration established in the original articles of association, unless this term has previously been extended. In every other case, the dissolution must be voted by an ordinary or extraordinary majority of the General Meeting, depending on whether or not there is a cause established by law or by the articles of association.

In accordance with the law, dissolution may be due to total and unjustified inactivity of the management bodies or of the cooperative for two years; decrease in the number of members or in the share capital to under the minimum required by law, without replenishment in the course of one year; fulfilment of the social object or the utter impossibility of carrying it out.

Under any of these circumstances, the Board of Directors must convene a General Meeting within one month following the detection of the cause, in order to approve the dissolution resolution. This resolution may be adopted by ordinary majority, except when the articles of association require a majority by a higher percentage. If the Directors do not convene the General Meeting on their own initiative, any member may request them to do so. If they fail to comply, or if the General Meeting does not adopt the dissolution resolution, any interested party may request the cooperative's dissolution by a judge.

A cooperative may also be dissolved as a result of a resolution adopted by the General Meeting that entails a complete split, a merger with or absorption by another organisation, or that resolves its dissolution despite the absence of any causes provided for in the law or in the cooperative statute. In the latter cases, the dissolution resolution must be adopted by a two-third majority of all the members present or represented at the General Meeting.

Once dissolved, the cooperative goes through a winding-up period (except in cases of splitting, merger or absorption). Until reimbursement of the members' capital contributions has begun, however, the cooperative may resume operations if the cause of the dissolution is no longer present and a re-launch agreement is adopted by two thirds of the members present or represented at the General Meeting (art. 70 LC).

The duties of the liquidators are similar to those in capital-based companies – they must keep and take custody of the books, carry out pending operations, collect receivables and pay creditors, etc.

After all the cooperative's debts have been paid, the remaining assets shall be distributed in compliance with the law, without prejudice to any agreements on subordinated financial assets. The legislation usually establishes a distribution order.

First, the EPF must be assigned to the cooperative federation to which the cooperative belongs, or otherwise to any other as voted by the General Meeting or to the Public Treasury for the advancement of the cooperative spirit.

Secondly, the members' capital contributions must be reimbursed, after the addition or deduction of any profits or losses from previous years. The distribution shall start with the contributor members and voluntary contributions, followed by mandatory contributions.

Also refundable are the amounts in the voluntary reserves that are distributable according to the articles of association or through a resolution of the General Meeting, following the criteria laid down in the same or otherwise in proportion to each member's activities with the cooperative in the previous five years.

Finally, the remaining assets, if any, must be assigned to the cooperative or federation nominated in the articles of association or by the General Meeting, or otherwise to the Public Treasure for the advancement of the cooperative spirit.

If these assets are assigned to another cooperative, they must be kept in the mandatory reserve fund and remain unavailable for fifteen years. If they are received by a federation, the funds must be used to support investment projects promoted by cooperatives. In addition, any member of a cooperative being wound up who intends to join another cooperative may request that his or her proportionate part of the remaining liquid assets should be deposited in the mandatory reserve fund of the cooperative that he or she is joining, provided that such a request has been made before the General Meeting approves the final winding-up balance sheet (art. 75.2 LC).

3.12. CHARACTERISTICS OF THE FINANCIAL STRUCTURE OF NON-PROFIT COOPERATIVES

In accordance with Spanish cooperative legislation, some cooperatives may be classified as non-profit cooperatives and therefore be regulated by a specific legal framework, including particular finance mechanisms.

The cooperatives that may request non-profit status comprise those that provide services of general interest or in public ownership, as well as those that pursue economic activities leading to the integration of socially disadvantaged or excluded people into the workforce and include certain clauses in their cooperative statutes (articles of association).

Classification as a non-profit cooperative is of very little consequence for cooperatives, because, as the law specifies (LC 9th additional provision), they remain subject to the same tax regime as other cooperatives and not to that for non-profit institutions. They may, however, bid for public tenders in which that classification is either a requirement or an assessment factor.

According to the state cooperative law (LC first additional provision), in order to be classified as a non-profit cooperative, the cooperative statutes must establish the following:

- No positive financial results of any kind may be distributed among members.
- Neither mandatory nor voluntary capital contributions may bear interest higher than the legal interest rate, though their value may be updated.
- No position on the Board of Directors is remunerated, without prejudice to any refunds for expenses incurred by the directors in the course of their duties.
- The salaries and wages paid to worker members, employee members and employees must not exceed 150% of the remuneration set by the sector's collective labour agreement for the same duties and occupational status.

4. EXTERNAL CONTROL OF COOPERATIVES

4.1. THE CONTROL OF COOPERATIVES – WHAT SHOULD BE CONTROLLED AND WHY?

The objective of the cooperative is principally to satisfy the needs and aspirations of its members under the best possible conditions. However, it also has to address other objectives such as training and educating its members and workforce, disseminating the cooperative spirit and promoting culture, welfare and professional advancement in its neighbourhood, as well as improving the quality of life, community development and environmental protection.[138]

To achieve these objectives, the members delegate the top management, representation of the cooperative, and supervision of the managers to particular persons, who are normally members (art. 32 LC). These persons form the Board of Directors.

In return, the Board of Directors must account to the members for its actions at least once a year. By law, it falls exclusively to the General Meeting to review the management of the society and approve the annual accounts, the management report and the allocation of available surpluses or of losses (art. 21.2 LC). These matters form the minimum content of the Annual General Meeting (art. 22.1 LC).

The Board of Directors is not subject to this annual control alone, however, because the law recognises that members have a wide-ranging right to information which they can exercise at any moment, either individually or in a group (arts. 16.3 and 16.4 LC).

---

138 To pursue these goals, part of the financial year's results must be allocated to the education and promotion fund (art. 56 LC).

However, it is not only the members that have an interest in controlling the cooperative's management. Like any company, cooperatives need to keep monitoring their documents and accounts in order to retain a clear vision and precise knowledge of their financial situation and results and be able to adopt more appropriate decisions in the future. The accounts are not only indispensable for the company, however, as they are also needed by other market participants (stakeholders).

Spanish law requires all enterprises to keep their books in order and to draw up the company's annual accounts at the close of the financial year. This obligation also applies to co-operatives.[139]

Nevertheless, the control mechanisms are not confined to giving the members an account of the management and the accounting results, as this information has to be verified by independent experts (audits) and made known both to the members and to other interested parties (publication).

In Spain, unlike other countries such as Germany, there cannot be said to be a pre-registration audit when the cooperative is formed. Instead, setting up the cooperative necessarily involves a notary public to ensure the legitimacy of the partners and the legality of the act. Subsequently, the Cooperatives Registry must examine the articles of association before registering the cooperative and may deny registration if they do not comply with cooperative law (art. 7 of Royal Decree 136/2002 adopting the Cooperatives Register Regulations – RRC). On occasion, the founding members consult the cooperative federations, which can provide information and model articles of association that have normally been guaranteed to be legal by the Cooperatives Registry.

4.2. TYPES OF CONTROL: INTERNAL AND EXTERNAL

As in any company, there can be different types of control of cooperatives depending on who exercises the control (members or persons from outside the cooperative) and on whether the results are only reported to the members and workforce or are made available to the public.

Internal control refers to that exercised by the members. Cooperatives have always been subject to internal control by the members, whether through the Annual General Meeting, as mentioned above, or through specific supervision bodies made up of members: *Comisión de Inspección de Cuentas* (Decree-Law

---

139 The obligation on co-operatives to keep accounts was introduced by the Cooperation Regulations of 1971 (art. 8 of Decree 2396/1971 of 13 August 1971). Previously, accounts were only required of cooperative unions, unions formed by legal persons and cooperatives operating on a national scale and were optional for other cooperatives (art. 8 of Decree of 11 November 1943).

of 4 July 1931); *Consejo de Vigilancia* (Cooperation Act of 2 January 1942) or *Interventores de Cuentas* (Royal Decree – 2710 of 16 November 1978).

On 25 July 1978, the Council of the European Communities adopted the Fourth Directive on the annual accounts of certain types of companies. This directive coordinated the provisions concerning the structure and content of annual accounts and management reports, the valuation methods used and publication of the documents, mainly for public limited companies and private limited companies.[140]

Since the transposition of the Fourth Directive into Spanish law (Law 19/1989 of 25 July 1989 and its application to all companies irrespective of legal form, internal auditing has played a very limited role compared to the general requirement to submit the annual accounts to external auditing by independent experts (*auditoría*).

Different solutions are found in co-operative legislation:

(a) In some cases the internal control body remains obligatory, under the name of *interventores* (controllers) or, in the Basque Country, *comisión de vigilancia* (supervisory committee). This is the situation in the national law (art. 38) and in most of the regional laws, although it may sometimes be dispensed with when the cooperative has few members. For instance, it is not required in Catalonia if the cooperative has three members, or in the Basque Country if there are fewer than 100 members.
(b) In other cases a control body is only contemplated if so provided in the articles of association. This is the situation in Andalusia, Aragon, Castile La Mancha, Galicia and Valencia.

In all cases, the members of these bodies are chosen by the General Meeting from among the members, although a minority of non-member experts is also allowed. Their functions are those set out in the law and others assigned to them by the articles of association. All the Spanish legislations agree in declaring that their function is to supervise the annual accounts and management report and that they shall issue a report and place it at the disposal of the members prior to the General Meeting that is to approve the annual accounts. The different cooperative laws envisage different consequences in the absence of this report. In the national law, the meeting cannot be convened until the report is issued or the date by which it must be issued has passed (art. 39.2 LC). The previous LGC 1987 and several of the regional laws (Castile-Leon, Extremadura) state that the resolution approving the annual accounts can be challenged if the controllers had not presented their report.

140 Directive 2013/34/EU of 26 June 2013 has repealed the Fourth Directive and extended its scope to cover partnerships and limited liability partnerships.

However, the controllers' report is not required when the cooperative's accounts are audited externally.

Some laws also assign other functions to this body, such as examining how the cooperative is performing, and the decisions taken by the Board of Directors and the manager; warning the Board and manager when they are not complying with the policies adopted by the General Meeting or with good business management criteria (law of Valencia, art. 54); and reviewing the books, convening the General Meeting, supervising elections or even suspending the directors if they give grounds for disqualification (law of Country Basque, art. 53).

External control of cooperatives has also existed since the first Cooperatives Act of 1931 set up an official body in charge of inspecting cooperatives and overseeing them when necessary (art. 38.1), and obliged cooperatives to send it their annual accounts for statistical purposes and to facilitate the inspection effected by a competent official (art. 39.1).

Following the Constitution of 1978 public control persisted in the law in measures such as the government's power to inspect, penalise, intervene or disqualify a cooperative.[141] The legislation currently in force continues to regulate not only measures to foster cooperatives but also inspection (art. 113 LC), penalties[142] and disqualification of cooperatives (art. 116 LC).

Apart from the above methods of controlling cooperatives, external control by auditors was introduced when the EEC's Fourth and Eighth Directives were transposed into Spanish laws 19/1989 and 19/1988 respectively.

Law 19/1989 transposed the directives concerning companies, including the Fourth Directive, and amended the Commercial Code and other commercial laws. The amended Commercial Code's rules concerning the obligation to keep accounts, extended this requirement to 'entrepreneurs' (*empresarios*).[143] As this entails that all enterprises, whatever their legal form, are governed by the Commercial Code accounting rules, it repealed the existing accounting rules contained in the cooperative legislation.

In turn, the Auditing of Accounts Act (Law 19/1988) transposed the Eighth Directive concerning the approval of persons responsible for carrying out the statutory audits of accounting documents. Since that date, Spanish cooperative laws have stated that cooperatives are obliged to have their accounts and management reports audited in the manner provided for in the Auditing of Accounts Act (current Law 22/2015 of 20 July- LAC).

---

141 See articles 128–136 of RD 2710/1978, or articles 150–157 of LGC 1987.

142 Article 115 LC provided for penalties, but this rule was subsequently repealed. Currently, offences in co-operative matters are set out in article 38 to 40 of Legislative Royal Decree 5/2000 of 4 August 2000, the Revised Text of the Offences and Penalties in the Social Order Act (essentially a labour law_.

143 *Empresario* is a concept broader than 'entrepreneur' (its literal translation), as it covers public and private enterprises, including civil-law partnerships; mercantile companies (like traders); and other enterprises such as those founded on a mutual basis (like co-operatives).

4.3. COOPERATIVES SUBJECT TO EXTERNAL AUDITING

Spanish cooperative laws oblige cooperatives to have their accounts and management reports audited in the manner provided for in the Auditing of Accounts Act and pursuant regulations, or any other applicable statutory provisions, and also as established in the articles of association or resolved by the General Meeting or the financial controllers (*interventores*). Additionally, if the cooperative is not subject to external auditing, a minimum number of members[144] may request the Registry of Co-operative Societies to appoint an external auditor (*auditor de cuentas*) to examine the accounts of a particular financial year provided that no more than three months have elapsed since the close of that financial year. The cost of this audit must be borne by the cooperative in all cases (according to art. 62.2 LC), or only if the audit uncovers irregularities in the documents examined (in the Balearic Islands or Castile and Leon), or – in Andalusia or Madrid, but also according to the Commercial Code (art. 40.2 CCo) – only if such irregularities are fundamental (*esenciales*).

The cooperatives that are subject to external auditing according to the current Auditing of Accounts Act are:

(a) Those that issue securities which are listed for trading on regulated markets, such as debentures, participation certificates or special participating shares (arts. 53 and 54 LC).
(b) Credit and insurance cooperatives.
(c) Those that receive subsidies or grants from government bodies or European funds with an accumulated value in excess of 600,000 euros in the financial year.
(d) Those that engage in contracts with government bodies with an accumulated value in excess of 600,000 euros if this represents over 50% of their net annual turnover.
(e) Those that exceed the limits established in the Capital-Based Companies Act for drawing up an abbreviated balance sheet (*balance abreviado*) from their accounts. Under article 257 LSC, companies that meet at least two of the following conditions at the close of each of two consecutive financial years may draw up an abbreviated balance sheet:
    (i) Total assets no greater than 4,000,000 euros;
    (ii) Net annual turnover no greater than 8,000,000 euros;
    (iii) Mean number of employees during the financial year no greater than 50.

144 This number varies in the different laws. Reference is usually made to the same percentage of members as required to convene the General Meeting, while others specify a percentage that can range from 5% of the members (in the national law, art. 62.2) to one-third of the members (in that of La Rioja, art. 80).

For their part, cooperative laws usually require external auditing of the accounts of cooperatives that have organised sections, particularly if one is a credit section, and of housing cooperatives.

4.4. LEGISLATION APPLICABLE TO EXTERNAL AUDITS OF COOPERATIVE ACCOUNTS

The legislation that applies to external auditing of the annual accounts of cooperatives is mainly found in the following texts:

(a) In the Commercial Code of 1885 (C.Com), Title III 'On the accounts of entrepreneurs' requires all enterprises to draw up their annual accounts (art. 34 C.Com) and lays down the basic structure of the accountancy model to be used (documents, definition of assets, accounting principles, valuation criteria, etc.). It also states that all entrepreneurs shall be obliged to submit their company's annual accounts to external auditing when so resolved by the competent court (art. 40 C.Com).

(b) As regards the preparation, external auditing, filing with the Registry and publication of their annual accounts, cooperatives are subject to the cooperative laws. Both the national Cooperatives Act and the regional laws regulate such aspects of the annual accounts as the Board of Directors' obligation to prepare them, the possibility of doing this in abbreviated form under the same conditions as for public limited companies, the requirement that the management report must reflect any variations in the number or members,[145] and filing of the accounts and other documents with the Cooperatives Registry. As regards external auditing, the cooperative laws refer to the provisions of the Auditing of Accounts Act.

(c) The Spanish General Accounting Plan implements the Commercial Code rules regarding accounting principles, accounts tables, definitions, annual accounts and valuation rules. The main provisions currently in force in this matter are the General Accounting Plan (*Plan General de Contabilidad* – PGC) adopted by RD 1514/2007 of 16 November 2007 and the General Accounting Plan for Small and Medium Companies (PGC-PYMES) adopted by RD 1515/2007 of the same date. When the cooperatives became subject to the General Accounting Plan (Law 19/1989), the government was authorised to adapt this plan to them.

---

145 The Madrid region's Cooperatives Act adds that in this report the directors must explain with total clarity how the cooperative is performing, realistic expectations, the uses to which the cooperative education and promotion fund has been put, variations in the number of members, associate members and investor members, and information on important events that have taken place since the closing date (art. 66.3).

This adaptation initially took place through Order ECO/3614/2003, since repealed by Order EHA/3360/2010 of 21 December 2010 adopting the Rules concerning the accountancy aspects of cooperative societies. The purpose of these rules is to delimit the net assets of the cooperative, develop the concept of cooperative share capital, define the contributions made by members, classify the obligatory reserve fund according to whether or not it is compulsory and regulate subordinated debts repayable on liquidation of the cooperative, the education, training and promotion fund, preparation of the profit and loss account, recording of transactions with members and non-members, and distribution of the results.

Rule thirteen states that the annual accounts of cooperatives shall be drawn up in accordance with the PGC or PGC-PYMES, as applicable, and the additional information specific to cooperatives referred to in the previous rules must be included in the annual report.

4.5. EXTERNAL CONTROL: AUDITS

The Auditing of Accounts Act defines auditing as the activity that consists of reviewing and verifying the annual accounts and other financial statements or accounting documents with the purpose of issuing a report on the reliability of the same with effects in respect of third parties (art. 1.2 LAC).

4.5.1. Types of Co-operative Audit

Having looked at the auditing regulations and focusing now on external audits in cooperatives, the following types of audit may be distinguished:

(a) Mandatory audit – statutory requirement. The Auditing of Accounts Act (1st additional provision) states the circumstances in which all companies are required to have their accounts audited. Other laws, such as the various Cooperative Acts, also require external auditing of cooperative accounts in certain situations.

(b) Mandatory audit – required by the articles of association or by a resolution of the General Meeting or the internal auditors. The cooperative is also obliged to submit its accounts to external audit when so provided by the articles of association, decided by the General Meeting or requested by the internal auditors.

(c) Mandatory audit – requested by a minority. If there is no external auditing obligation, cooperative members representing a certain percentage of the total may request the Registry of Cooperative Societies to appoint an external auditor to review the accounts of a particular financial year, provided that no more than three months have elapsed since the close of that financial year.

(d) Mandatory audit – judicial decision. As noted above, the Commercial Code provides that all enterprises are obliged to submit the company's annual accounts to external audit if so decided by the competent court's accepting the well-founded petition of a person who has proved a legitimate interest. In this case the court will require sufficient surety (guarantees) to defray the court costs and audit expenses, which shall be met by the petitioner if the audit finds no fundamental defect or irregularity (art. 40 C.Com).

(e) Voluntary audit The cooperative, through its Board of Directors, may voluntarily request to be audited at any time, as the law states that external auditing may carried out on a mandatory or voluntary basis (art. 1.1 LAC).

4.5.2. Scope of the Audit

The cooperative legislation confines itself to stating that auditing of the annual accounts and management reports of cooperatives is obligatory (art. 62 LC), but barely mentions the subject any further.

The annual accounts are listed in the Commercial Code (art. 34) and described in the following sections of that code and in the General Accounting Plans. The annual accounts comprise the balance sheet, profit and loss account, statement of changes in equity, cash flow statement and annual report. Moreover, rule 13 of Order EHA/3360/2010 approving the rules concerning accounting aspects of cooperative societies requires the annual report on the accounts of the cooperative to contain the specific information listed in that Order so that it will give a true and comprehensible picture of the cooperative's assets, financial situation and results.

As regards the management report, the cooperative legislation barely mentions its content, and so does the Commercial Code. To discover its content it is necessary to refer to article 19 of Directive 2013/34/EU on annual financial statements, or article 262 LSC.

The management report must contain a fair review of the development and performance of the company's business and of its position, together with a description of the principal risks and uncertainties that it faces. The analysis shall include financial and, where appropriate, non-financial key performance indicators, such as information on environmental matters and employees. Cooperative laws usually only add that the management report must include variations in the number of members (art. 61.3 LC).

However, smaller companies are exempted from the obligation to include non-financial information (art. 258 LSC).

According to, article 20 of Directive 2013/34, the management report must include a corporate governance declaration that refers to the governance code and practices applied by the company, the operation of the corporate bodies, members' rights, composition of the Board of Directors, etc. However, this information is only required of companies that are quoted on a regulated stock market, and cooperatives do not fall within its scope.

4.5.3. Procedure

Auditing of the accounts must necessarily be performed by an external auditor (*auditor de cuentas* – 'auditor of accounts') or an audit company, that must issue the corresponding report (art. 1.3 LAC).

The auditing process starts when the auditor is appointed. This appointment is generally the responsibility of the General Meeting and must be made before the end of the financial year to be audited. The auditors are appointed for a specific period of time, lasting no less than three financial years and no more than nine, although they may be reappointed annually by the General Meeting. In exceptional cases provided for in law, the Cooperatives Registry or the courts may be requested to appoint an auditor to review the accounts of a particular financial year (art. 62.3 LC).

The appointment must be made from among the natural or legal persons that meet the conditions mentioned in section 6 and are listed in the Official Register of Auditors of Accounts (*Registro Oficial de Auditores de Cuentas* – ROAC) of the Accounting and Account Auditing Institute (*Instituto de Contabilidad y Auditoría de Cuentas* – ICAC) (art. 7.1 LAC).

After the close of the financial year, the cooperative's Board of Directors must draw up the annual accounts, management report, and proposal for allocation of the results – surpluses or losses – within a maximum period of three months from the closing date (art. 61.2 LC).

The accounts and management report must be reviewed by the financial controllers (internal auditors) or, if applicable, submitted to external auditing. The auditors' report must be drawn up within one month of receipt of the accounts and management report (art. 39 LC).

The organisations audited are obliged to provide all the information necessary for the auditors to carry out their work, and also any that may be demanded by the person who is to draw up the auditors' report (art. 6 LAC).

The law also lays down the required content of the auditors' report (art. 5 LAC).

Once the auditors have concluded their report, the Board of Directors must convene the General Meeting to examine the management of the company and approve the annual accounts if appropriate.

Within a month of approval of the accounts, the Board of Directors must present certification of the resolution of the General Meeting approving the accounts and the allocation of results, attaching a copy of each of the accounts and of the management report – and also of the auditors' report if external auditing is obligatory or has been carried out at the request of a minority of members – for filing with the Registry of Cooperative Societies (*Registro de Sociedades Cooperativas*) (art. 61.4 LC).

As a result of the business in which they engage, some cooperatives (mainly credit and insurance) are also required to file these documents with the Registry of Companies (*Registro Mercantil*). In these cases, the Registry of Cooperative Societies notifies the Registry of Companies that these cooperatives have filed their accounts (art. 28.3 RD 136/2002 adopting the Cooperatives Register Regulations – RRC).[146]

Lastly, it should be pointed out that the Register of Cooperative Societies is public (art. 3 RRC) and that publication may be made by means of a certificate or an extract (*nota simple*) or by displaying the register entry (arts. 34 and 35 RRC).

4.6. EXTERNAL AUDITORS – QUALIFICATIONS, INDEPENDENCE AND ACCOUNTABILITY

4.6.1. Qualifications

External audits may only be carried out by an auditor of accounts or audit company that is registered with the Official Register of Auditors of Accounts (ROAC).

The requirements for ROAC registration are: legal age, Spanish or other European Union member state nationality, no criminal record of any intentional offence, and having obtained the relevant authorisation from the Accounting and Account Auditing Institute (*Instituto de Contabilidad y Auditoría de Cuentas* – ICAC) (art. 9.1 LAC). ICAC authorisation requires:

- A university degree.
- Having taken theory courses and acquired practical training in the financial and accountancy area for a period of three years, two of which were spent in training placements with auditors or audit companies in Spain or any other European Union country.
- Having passed a professional competence examination organised and recognised by the state. The law lists the subjects to be examined. They include company law, laws governing other organisations and governance; civil, commercial, fiscal and insolvency law; and labour and social security law. Those who hold an officially-recognised university degree regulated by the Spanish Universities Act (*Ley Orgánica de Universidades*) are excused from examination in the subjects they passed in order to obtain their degrees.

---

[146] However, the Co-operatives Act of the Murcia region provides that the accounts shall be filed with the Registry of Companies and the documents proving filing with the Registry of Companies shall be filed with the Registry of Co-operatives (art. 83.5).

ICAC's Resolution of 12 July 2012 set out the conditions that must be met by the theory courses for training auditors. The part devoted to the laws governing companies and other organisations must include the study of civil societies and commercial companies, types of commercial company, public limited companies (formation, variations in capital, conversion, merger, dissolution and liquidation), control and publication of the annual accounts of public limited companies; private limited companies – fundamental legal aspects, foundations – fundamental legal aspects, and, finally, notions of the legal system governing cooperatives, foundations and other non-profit organisations.

However, the legal system governing cooperatives is not a required subject in the examination of professional competence. In Order ECC/682/2013 of 15 April 2013 convening the professional competence examination required for ROAC registration, the list of legal subjects to be examined in the part concerning the law of companies and other organisations omitted the legal system governing cooperatives, foundations and other non-profit organisations.

Evidently, then, the system by which professionals are approved as external auditors of cooperatives does not guarantee sufficient knowledge of the cooperatives' legal and financial system because 'notions of the legal system governing cooperatives' is a required subject of study, but knowledge of it is not a requirement for passing the professional competence examinations.

4.6.2. *Independence and Liability*

In performing their duties, external auditors and audit companies must be independent of the organisations that they audit and of any others that are directly or indirectly linked to the latter. The law therefore provides a series of safeguards that range from the auditor's obligation to refrain from auditing where his or her independence may be compromised,[147] to establishing grounds for incompatibility with the exercise of auditing, limiting the duration of the audit contract and requiring rotation,[148] prohibiting termination of the audit contract without due cause, and prohibitions after completing the auditing work.

Auditors and audit companies are liable to the full extent of their assets for damages arising from breach of their obligations. When an auditor carries out an audit on behalf of an audit company, they shall be jointly and severally

---

147 The Auditing of Accounts Act gives a long list of grounds for incompatibility. The cases in which the auditor or audit company is presumed to lack the necessary independence include relations of employment, supervision or agency with the organisation to be audited or associated companies, direct or indirect financial interests in them, family ties and provision of legal services, among others. These incompatibilities extend to all persons or organisations directly related to the auditor or audit company or that are part of a network to which they belong.

148 Despite the disputed possibility of extending the auditors' appointment, after seven years of contracts the auditor must be changed for at least two years if the audited organisation is of public interest or its turnover is in excess of 50 million euros.

liable. Liability proceedings must be brought within four years of the date of the auditors' report.

Without prejudice to their above liability, auditors and audit companies are obliged to provide surety in proportion to their turnover, in the amount set by the Ministry of the Economy and the Treasury.

4.7. EXTERNAL SUPERVISION BY PUBLIC AUTHORITIES

Auditors and audit companies are subject to public supervision, which is exercised by the Accounting and Account Auditing Institute (ICAC), an independent body attached to the Ministry of the Economy and the Treasury.[149] This supervision includes authorisation and ROAC registration, adopting ethical, quality control and technical standards, ongoing training of auditors, quality control, the investigation system and the disciplinary system.

The ICAC supervises the accounts auditing activity *ex-officio*, inspecting the auditors and investigating their actions. For this purpose, it conducts technical and quality control operations. ICAC has the power to impose sanctions. The Auditing of Accounts Act sets out the offences and their respective penalties.

4.8. CONTROL OF THE PURSUIT OF COOPERATIVE OBJECTS

The obligation to keep accounts, draw up annual accounts, and audit them provide financial information of interest to members and others, but it does not report sufficiently on whether the cooperative is fulfilling its objectives or making progress towards them.

As discussed in section 1, according to Spanish law cooperatives have a basic objective, which is to meet the needs of their members, and a complementary objective (derived from the cooperative principles but also required by law) that concerns training, promoting the cooperative spirit and sustainable development of their communities.

- the specifically cooperative or social information that cooperatives are legally obliged to provide nowadays comprises:
- the information regarding the particular aspects of co-operatives required by the accounting standards (Order EHA/3360/2010), contained in the annual report (annual accounts);
- the information on variations in the number of members provided in the management report.[150]

---

149 http://www.icac.meh.es/.

150 The Madrid region's Co-operatives Act 4/1999 also requires the management report to give a clear explanation of the cooperative's performance, realistic expectations, and the uses to which the cooperative education and promotion fund has been put (art. 66).

The Cooperatives Act 1/2003 of the Balearic Islands envisages the possibility that the cooperative may prepare a social balance sheet if so provided in the articles of association. According to the preamble to the Act, this balance sheet must make it possible to assess the fulfilment of the objectives set, the relations between the cooperative and its members, its social participation, collaboration with other cooperatives and contribution to its social environment, as well as reporting on the cooperative's strengths and weaknesses. The social balance sheet shall be submitted together with the annual accounts for the General Meeting's knowledge and approval (art. 88).

In Spain, many cooperatives voluntarily draw up social balance sheets, either alone or as part of a network.[151] These balance sheets may focus on the cooperative values and principles, like the Cooperative Social Balance Sheet certified by ICA-Americas,[152] or on the Corporate Social Responsibility structure (financial, environmental, social and responsible management aspects) adapted to the social economy, as advocated by CEPES, the association that represents cooperatives at the national level. To this end, CEPES places a measurement tool at the cooperatives' disposal.[153]

Quite apart from the voluntary basis on which these analyses may be drawn up, the fact is that the law ought to require cooperatives to give an account not only of their financial results but also of their fulfilment of the objectives for which they were founded. A recent PhD thesis at the University of the Balearic Islands concluded that it should be a legal requirement for the annual accounts of cooperatives to be accompanied by information on the extent to which the social objectives proposed have been met, that this information should be included in the annual report, and that the annual accounts should be filed with the Company Registry.[154]

If it is decided to integrate the cooperative and social information with the financial information, consideration needs to be given to the most appropriate instrument for this purpose, since not all cooperatives are required to prepare a management report. Another consideration is whether this information, too, should be assessed by external auditors or if internal verification would be acceptable, at least when the cooperative is not required to be audited. Lastly,

---

151 This is the case of the regional network REAS (*Red de Economía Alternativa Social y Solidaria* or Network of the Social and Solidarity Alternative Economy). REAS not only provides a method for drawing up social balance sheets, it also carries out social audits. See http://www.economiasolidaria.org/red_redes and http://www.auditoriasocial.net/.

152 http://www.aciamericas.coop/Balance-Social-Cooperativo-2394.

153 See the CEPES corporate social responsibility manifesto (*El manifiesto CEPES ante la responsabilidad social empresarial*) at http://www.cepes.es/pagina_cepes=7#> and the RSE. COOP measuring tool at http://www.cepes.es/index.php?pagina=pagina_blanca&id=8.

154 J.I. Genovart, 'Aspectos económico-contables de las sociedades cooperativas' [Financial and accounting aspects of co-operative societies], PhD thesis, available at: http://www.tdx.cat/bitstream/handle/10803/111331/tjgb1de1.pdf?sequence=1.

as regards the persons who should exercise this control, internal control of cooperatives can only be effective if the internal auditors or members of the control committee are independent of the directors. Consequently, it is important to employ external experts. As regards external auditors, if they are called upon to audit cooperatives they should be required to have a better knowledge of the structure and workings of this form of company.

5. COOPERATION AMONG COOPERATIVES

5.1. INTRODUCTION

In order to defend their interests and improve the service that they provide to their members, cooperatives usually cooperate with other organisations, both public and private, whether or not they are cooperatives. Such cooperation can be occasional, by entering into an agreement, or it can be more intense, through longer-term agreements, setting up new joint ventures, or integration into existing organisations.

As the purpose of such structures can be economic or merely representative, Spanish law makes a distinction between representative integration cooperative structures and economic integration cooperative structures. In both cases, however, the law considers that promoting, stimulating and developing these structures is a task in the public interest. The previous Cooperatives Act of 1987 added 'guaranteeing the freedom and autonomy of the cooperative' (LGC art. 150). One of the dilemmas of integrating cooperatives is how to make their right to association (which could lead to a strong commitment to integration) compatible with their autonomy (which forms part of their identity) and with benefiting their members (their main purpose).

In what follows, we shall examine the different forms of cooperation and integration among cooperatives – or with majority participation by cooperatives – envisaged by Spanish cooperative law and assess their compatibility with the cooperative identity and, particularly, with the principles that Spanish cooperative law should obey.

5.2. FORMULAS FOR COOPERATION AMONG COOPERATIVES. RECOGNITION AND PROMOTION

Inter-cooperation can have two aims: to represent the interests of member cooperatives and promote the cooperative movement, or to promote their economic interests and those of their members. The former case is known as 'associative' or representative' integration, and the latter as 'inter-cooperation' or 'economic' integration.

Both are recognised by Spanish law as models to be promoted.

Cooperative laws in Spain usually include a title on cooperative associationism that envisages different forms of cooperation, such as unions, federations or confederations, and a specific chapter on economic cooperation. The main economic cooperation formulas normally regulated in the cooperative legislation are intercooperation agreements, second-tier cooperatives, and cooperative groups.

The law does not confine itself to acknowledging these forms of cooperation between cooperatives but actually encourages them. For instance, article 108 LC (on promoting cooperativism) considers 'the promotion, stimulation and development of cooperative societies and their economic and representative integration structures' to be a task in the general interest. This same law contains a number of measures to promote them, such as: (i) the education and promotion fund (*Fondo de Educación y Promoción* – FEP) that cooperatives are obliged to set up with a proportion of their positive results must be devoted, among other purposes, to promoting inter-cooperative relations (LC art. 56.1 b); and (ii) if the cooperative is wound up, the non-distributable equity must be placed at the disposal of another cooperative or an association of cooperatives (LC art. 75.2).

It should be noted, however, that the distinction between these two models of cooperation (associative and economic) is not always clear.[155] Experience shows that associations which were created to represent the interests of their members have later engaged in economic cooperation or have even become second-tier cooperatives,[156] or cooperative groups.[157] The opposite also holds true because organisations which were set up to pursue economic integration frequently end up representing their member cooperatives on representative bodies.[158]

---

155 On this point, see A. Martinez Charterina, *Análisis de la integración cooperativa*, Universidad de Deusto, Bilbao, 1990 p. 47.

156 For example COARVAL (http://coarval.com/), initially the supplies section of the union of agricultural cooperatives of Valencia province.

157 For example INTERCOOP (http://www.intercoop.es/), initially the union of agricultural cooperatives of Castellón province.

158 As in the case of the Spanish retail cooperatives' union UNIDE (http://web.unide.es/) and the industrial group Mondragón Corporación Cooperativa (http://www.mondragon-corporation.com/), which both act as their respective sectors' representatives in the Spanish Confederation of Social Economy Enterprises, CEPES (http://www.cepes.es/socios_miembros).

5.3. ASSOCIATIVE OR REPRESENTATIVE INTEGRATION: UNIONS, FEDERATIONS AND CONFEDERATIONS

Cooperatives can freely and voluntarily join together in unions, federations and confederations to defend and promote their interests. Spain's national Cooperatives Act (LC) regulates cooperative associationism in articles 117–120.

5.3.1. *Free and Voluntary Membership*

Because cooperatives have formed associations ever since they were first founded, cooperative associationism is said to be 'consubstantial' with the cooperative phenomenon.[159]

During the Franco dictatorship, cooperatives in Spain were automatically enlisted in their respective associations.[160] Today, a resolution of the General Meeting is needed for a cooperative to join or leave a representative association, but a simple majority of the members is sufficient unless the cooperative statutes set a higher percentage.

5.3.2. *Structure of the Cooperative Movement*

The Spanish expression *movimiento cooperativo* ('cooperative movement') refers to the associative phenomenon which is specific to cooperatives.

Traditionally, Spanish legislation distinguishes among unions, federations and confederations, but it does not prevent cooperatives from joining other types of association in accordance with the right of association.

Unions are made up of at least three cooperatives of the same class. Federations are formed directly or indirectly (through unions) by at least ten cooperatives, of different classes, and confederations must be composed of at least three federations.

These organisations are set up along geographical and sectoral lines. Their memorandum of association must list the founding organisations and must be filed with the Registry of Cooperatives, and any subsequent change in their membership must be notified to the Registry. For their name to include a reference to a specific geographical area, they need to show that their membership directly or indirectly covers at least 20% of the cooperatives registered in that area.

---

159 See A. Martinez Charterina, n. 155 above, p. 45.

160 See F. Vicent Chuliá, 'Ley General de Cooperativas', *Revista de Derecho Privado*, 1994, vol. XX, no. 3, p. 954.

Cooperatives may also form or join associations with other social economy organisations, as specifically provided for and encouraged by the Social Economy Act (LES art. 7).

5.3.3. *Legal Regime of Associative Entities*

Unless the Registry gives a reasoned decision to deny the application, these organisations acquire legal personality one month from having applied to file their memorandum of association with the Registry of Cooperatives.

The functions of associations that represent cooperatives include representing and defending the general interests of the cooperatives and their members; encouraging cooperative promotion and education; using conciliation to settle disputes between member cooperatives and between these cooperatives and their members; organising advisory services, audits and legal and technical assistance; and acting as representatives and interlocutors with public bodies and organisations.

Cooperative associations are not companies but they are allowed to conduct economic activities that bring in revenue. According to the Associations Act, any such profits must be applied exclusively to the association's aims and may not be distributed among its members, or related persons or bodies, nor ceded free of charge to any natural or legal person seeking a profit (LOA art. 13.2).

Some of the more active associations conduct economic activities (normally advisory) that make a profit, However, the main source of income for these organisations is government grants and subsidies, as discussed below.

They also receive membership fees from their affiliated cooperatives and can receive all or part of the latter's education and promotion fund (FEP). The law states that in order to fulfil their education and promotion purpose, cooperatives may cooperate with other companies and organisations and may contribute all or part of this fund to them (LC article 56.2). On the basis of this provision, many cooperatives allocate these funds to foundations set up for social, cultural or scientific purposes, as in the case of credit cooperatives.[161] Recently, since most of the government aid to the cooperative movement has dried up, there has been a move to remember and boost the cooperative associations' internal funding mechanisms. For instance, the law to encourage agricultural cooperative integration (Law 13/2013 of 2 August- LFICA) has amended the previous criterion by adding that such contributions may be made to the union or federation to which the cooperative is affiliated, to fulfil functions that match those of the education and promotion fund.

161 http://www.fundacioncajamarvalencia.es/es/comun/, http://www.fundacioncrj.es/, www.fundacioncajaruraldesegovia.es/, www.fundacioncrg.com/, https://www.fundacioncajaruralcastillalamancha.es/.

5.3.4. *Promoting the Cooperative Movement*

As mentioned above, the law considers promoting the cooperatives' representative integration structures to be a task in the general interest (LC art. 108) and sets out specific mechanisms for their member cooperatives to fund these organisations, such as contributing their FEP funds, as just discussed, or adjudicating the residual assets to them when a cooperative is wound up.

When a cooperative ceases to exist, and in other situations (special merger or conversion) where the law requires the cooperative's non-distributable equity to be allocated in the manner provided for in the event of liquidation, the procedure is as follows: (i) the funds in the FEP are placed at the disposal of the federation to which the cooperative is affiliated; if it is not affiliated to any, the General Meeting may designate the federation to which they shall be allocated. Failing designation by the General Meeting, the funds are allocated to the national confederation of cooperatives of the class to which the cooperative being wound up belongs, and if no such confederation exists, to the public treasury with the purpose of allocating them to setting up a fund for promoting cooperativism (art. 75.2 a); (ii) after paying the debts, reimbursing the members' contributions to capital and paying the members their share of the distributable reserves, the residual liquid assets are placed at the disposal of the cooperative or federative body expressly named in the cooperative's statutes or designated by a resolution of the General Meeting. Should one not be named or designated, they shall be allocated to the national confederation of the relevant class and if no such confederation exists, to the public treasury (art. 75.2 d).

However, there are specific measures that the government can use to promote cooperative associations: both fiscal measures and direct aid to defray their operating costs and those of their actions to promote the cooperative movement.

Cooperative associations can benefit from favourable tax treatment in two ways: (i) as associations they are entitled to the benefits offered by the Non-Profit Organisations Tax Regime Act (Law 49/2002),[162] or failing these, by the Company Tax Act (RD Leg. 4/2004, article 120–122); (ii) as cooperative associations, article 36 of the Cooperative Tax Regime Act (LRFC) grants certain tax advantages.

Every year, in pursuance of Order TIN/3440/2009 on promoting the social economy, the Spanish state and its autonomous regions call for applications for

---

162 This special regime applies to associations declared of public utility. One of the aims that these associations may have is to promote the social economy (art. 3).

subsidies to defray the cooperative associations' operating costs and those of the social economy promotion activities that they undertake.[163]

5.4. ECONOMIC INTER-COOPERATION: FROM COOPERATION TO BUSINESS INTEGRATION

5.4.1. *Possibilities for Inter-Cooperation*

Economic cooperation between cooperatives covers a wide range of possibilities. Cooperatives can pursue their object (of meeting the needs of their members) directly or, indirectly, through agreements with cooperatives or other bodies or by joining more complex and stable organisations.

Law 27/1999 (LC) regulates second-tier cooperatives (art. 77) and cooperative groups (art. 78) and declares that cooperatives of all types and classes, in order better to fulfil their objects and to defend their interests, may enter into contracts and agreements and form companies, groups, consortia, and unions among each other or with other natural or legal persons, whether public or private (art. 79).[164]

This possibility has proved particularly useful for cooperatives, alone or with other bodies, to set up special purpose vehicles, mainly capital-based companies and economic interest groupings (EIGs), which allow them to hive off or broaden their activities, expand abroad or initiate integration processes.[165]

---

163 These activities can cover studying, educating in and disseminating cooperativism (G. Fajardo, 'El fomento de la 'economía social' en la legislación española', *Revista de Estudios Cooperativo, REVESCO*, no. 107, pp. 58–97).

164 This provision omits to mention that, to these ends, cooperatives may also join existing organisations of these kinds and overlooks the fact that a cooperative may also become a member of a first-tier cooperative. With some exceptions, first-tier cooperatives may be composed of natural or legal persons, whether public or private (LC art. 12). In these cases the cooperative statutes may make exceptions to the principle of one member/one vote and allow the cooperative weighted multiple voting rights in proportion to the volume of cooperativised activity (LC art. 26.2). The first-tier cooperative may be a business services cooperative (R. Alfonso, 'Posibilidades y regulación de los procesos de integración en España (Cooperativas de Segundo Grado, Grupos Cooperativos, Fusiones)', in R. Chaves, G. Fajardo and R. Namorado (dir.), *Integración Empresarial Cooperativa*, CIRIEC, 2003, p. 27), but not necessarily so.

165 There are notable cases of cooperatives that have set up commercial companies to enter foreign markets, as in the case of ANECOOP, which has subsidiaries in Spain, France, the United Kingdom, the Netherlands, the Czech Republic, Poland, Russia and China (http://www.anecoop.com/es/red-internacional), or that of MCC, which has 147 subsidiaries in Europe, Asia, America and Africa (http://www.mondragon-corporation.com/sobre-nosotros/magnitudes-economicas/). See R. Server and E. Meliá, 'Caracterización empresarial de los grupos y otras formas de integración cooperativa al amparo del nuevo marco legislativo', *REVESCO*, 1999, no. 69, p. 211; A. Celaya, 'Estructura y problemática jurídica de la Corporación MCC', *Anuario de Estudios Cooperativos*, Universidad de Deusto, 1992, p. 124; or J.M. Luzarraga and I. Irizar, 'La estrategia de multilocalización internacional de la

Lastly, it should not be forgotten that cooperatives can also be involved in larger business integration and disaggregation processes. For instance, the law regulates mergers, splits and conversions of second-tier cooperatives into first-tier ones, as discussed further on.

Spanish legal writers view the concept of business integration as covering cooperation agreements, concentration operations and joint ventures.[166] Researchers studying cooperatives also sometimes identify inter-cooperation and integration,[167] or they see integration as a manifestation of the principle of inter-cooperation.[168] In the present author's opinion, integration is not always an example of cooperation or inter-cooperation.[169] It is an instance of concentration among cooperative enterprises through the creation of a new jointly-owned company (cooperative or otherwise) with a unified management, in which the partners in the new company may or may not retain their own personality. If they maintain their separate personalities we are speaking of cooperative groups, and if they do not, of mergers.

5.4.2. *Powers of the General Meeting*

The decision to take part in the above-mentioned processes must be taken by the General Meeting,[170] by a simple majority of the votes cast, except in the cases

Corporación Mondragón', *EKONOMIAZ. Revista Vasca de Economía*, 2012, no. 79, p. 114. Another case is that of Cooperativa Sanitaria Lavinia, founded by doctors and sole shareholder ASISA (http://coopsalud.blogspot.com.es/2007/01/desarrollo-del-cooperativismo-sanitario.html), a PLC which is the third-ranking insurance company operating in Spain in terms of market share (http://www.segurosalud.org/seguros-ranking-de-companias-.html).

166 R. Alonso Soto, 'Las formas de integración, concentración y cooperación empresarial y el derecho de la competencia', in J.C. Sáenz García de Albizu, F. Oleo Banet and A. Martínez Flores (coord.), *Estudios de Derecho Mercantil. En memoria del Profesor Aníbal Sánchez Andrés*, Civitas, Madrid, 2010, p. 117.

167 P. Borjabad, *Manual de Derecho Cooperativo. General y Catalán*, Ed. Bosch, Barcelona, 1993, pp. 290–292.

168 Alfonso, n. 164 above, p. 19.

169 G. Fajardo, 'Inter-cooperación e integración cooperativa en la legislación española', in J. Juliá, E. Meliá and R. Server (dir.), *Cooperativismo Agrario y Desarrollo Rural*, Ed. Universidad Politécnica de Valencia, 2005, p. 602.

170 The law states that the General Meeting has the sole power to decide on: (i) founding second-tier cooperatives and cooperative groups, or joining existing ones; (ii) participating in other forms of economic cooperation as envisaged in article 78; (iii) merger, split and conversion; and (iv) any resolution that entails a substantial modification of the economic, social, organisational or functional structure of the cooperative (LC art. 21.2). Curiously, the decision as to whether a modification to the cooperative's structure is substantial is left to its statutes, giving rise to uncertainty when a form of integration that has not been foreseen in the statutes is mooted: will the cooperative be able to implement it, or will it be able to do so without needing a resolution of the General Meeting?

of merger, split, conversion or joining or leaving a cooperative group, which require the favourable vote of at least a qualified majority (LC art. 28.2). It is questionable that such important decisions as setting up or joining a second-tier cooperative should not require greater agreement among the members, but this can always be required by the cooperative statutes. Moreover, it is not clear whether a member who disagrees with the decision can leave the cooperative 'with due cause'. Classing the resignation as being justified only has financial consequences in terms of reimbursing the member's capital contribution. The laws mention certain causes that they consider justified,[171] but others can be provided for in the cooperative statutes.[172]

5.4.3. *Financial and Fiscal Consequences*

Cooperation or integration with other organisations, cooperative or otherwise, can give rise to profits or patronage refunds. The national Cooperatives Act imposes certain conditions on the uses to which they may be put. In principle, these profits are classed as extra-cooperative, and 100% or 50% of them must therefore, by law, be allocated to indivisible reserves. However, if they have been obtained through investments or shares in cooperatives, or in companies that are not cooperatives but engage in activities that are preparatory, complementary or subordinated to those of the cooperative, they are considered cooperative results (surpluses). This means that: (i) most of them can be distributed to the members; and (ii) from the tax point of view, the results obtained from cooperatives and (complementary) companies are taxed more favourably, as surpluses rather than profits.[173] Nevertheless, the Cooperative Tax Regime Act, which predates the Cooperatives Act, employs a different criterion for calculating company tax: it considers interest and patronage refunds arising through the cooperative's membership of other cooperatives as constituting cooperative revenue (art. 17), and income derived from investments or financial participation in non-cooperative companies as constituting extra-cooperative

---

171 Opposition to a General Meeting resolution that entails assuming highly onerous liabilities or charges not initially envisaged in the cooperative statutes (art. 17.4); certain resolutions to modify the cooperative statutes, such as changing the class of cooperative (art. 11.3); and resolutions that entail certain structural modifications such as merger, split or conversion (arts. 65, 68 and 69).

172 J. Pulgar, 'La pérdida de la condición de socio en el marco cooperativo: su baja y expulsión', in J.C. Sáenz García de Albizu, F. Oleo Banet and A. Martínez Flores (coord.), *Estudios de Derecho Mercantil. En memoria del Profesor Aníbal Sánchez Andrés*, Civitas, Madrid, 2010, pp. 1056–1058.

173 According to the preamble to the law, the purpose of this rule is to encourage the cooperative's participation in the different stages of the production process.

revenue (art. 21). In short, the tax rules only allow the tax treatment for cooperative activity to benefit the results obtained through cooperation among cooperatives.[174]

Lastly, the law requires the benefits of the legislation on company grouping and concentration to be applied to concentrations of cooperatives,[175] whether by merger, setting up second-tier cooperatives, or temporary joint ventures (LC art. 79.2).

5.5. SECOND-TIER COOPERATIVES

5.5.1. Functions of Second-Tier Cooperatives

A second-tier cooperative is the natural outcome of cooperative integration,[176] as already mentioned, and it is the arrangement that offers cooperatives the broadest possibilities owing to its flexibility. According to the Cooperatives Act of 1987 (LGC), the purpose of second-tier cooperatives was to fulfil the shared economic aims of their member cooperatives (art. 48.1). The Act of 1999 broadened their sphere of action considerably, and their object can now be to promote, coordinate and pursue the shared economic aims of their member cooperatives and to strengthen and integrate these members' economic activities (LC art. 77.1) In short, a second-tier cooperative can act as a cooperative (carrying out activities with the aim of satisfying the needs of its members or promoting their interests), as a group of companies (coordinating its member's activities or assuming their management), or even as a business integration mechanism in the full sense of the expression if any or all of the activities previously carried out by its members are conducted in its name instead.[177] It is also possible for a single second-tier cooperative to assume all the above roles, depending on the activities involved.

174 This discrepancy arose because the possibility of integration was extended to non-cooperatives in 1999. As a result, Spanish legal writers have called for the tax legislation of 1990 to be reformed to adapt it to the new situation. Cf. Server and Melía, n. 165 above, p. 214; N. Paz Canalejo, *La sociedad cooperativa ante el reto de los mercados actuales. Un análisis no sólo jurídico*, Informes y Estudios, Ministerio de Trabajo y Asuntos Sociales, 2002, p. 241; and C. Vargas, 'Integración y diferenciación cooperativa: de las secciones a los grupos de sociedades', *Boletín de la Asociación Internacional de Derecho Cooperativo*, 2010, no. 44, p. 166.

175 This legislation is mainly found in Law 18/1982 (the Company Groups and Temporary Joint Ventures Act) and Law 27/2014 of 27 November on Company Tax, arts. 44–47.

176 Alfonso, n. 164 above, p. 25.

177 At which point, some second-tier cooperatives convert to first-tier cooperatives.

5.5.2. *Members and Legal System*

Previous cooperative legislation only allowed second-tier cooperatives to have cooperatives as members.[178] In 1993 an attempt was made to remedy this drawback by creating integration cooperatives (*cooperativa de integración*) which were also allowed to have members of other types – from the social economy, or publicly-owned, or companies with social economy or public sector shareholders – provided that cooperatives made up the majority of members and votes.[179]

Later, the Cooperatives Act of 1999 only required two cooperatives to set up a second-tier cooperative, allowed other legal persons (public or private) and natural persons (sole proprietors and employee members) to be active members (*socios cooperadores* or cooperating members) and, naturally, also allowed non-user investor members (*socios colaboradores* or contributing members). As a result of this extension of membership, the 1999 Act (repeal provision 2) abolished integration cooperatives.

Until the reform effected by the Law on Agricultural Cooperative Integration (LFICA) in 2013 there were no classes of second-tier cooperatives.[180] Today, however, any of the classes provided for in law may be adopted provided that all the cooperatives in the second-tier cooperative belong to the same class (LC art. 6.2).

Article 77 LC is devoted to second-tier cooperatives. A striking feature of the rules on second-tier cooperatives is the legislators' concern to prevent their coming under the control of non-cooperative members or of any single member. Consequently, they include a series of limitations:

- non-cooperative entities may not exceed 45% of the total membership (LC article 71) nor 40% of the total votes (LC art. 26.6).
- no member may hold over 30% of the share capital, 'except in joint ventures with an equal ownership structure' (LC art. 77.1.3) which are set up by two or more cooperatives holding equal shares. If the cooperative statutes allow weighted voting, no member may hold more than one-third of the voting rights, or more than 40% if the members number three, and unanimity is required in the case of two members only (LC art. 26.6).

---

178 Since the 1987 Cooperatives Act (art. 148), second-tier cooperatives made up of agricultural cooperatives have also been allowed to join agricultural partnerships (*Sociedad Agraria de Transformación*, SAT).

179 Integration cooperatives are regulated by RD 84/1993.

180 As an exception, the cooperative legislation has allowed second-tier cooperatives to be classed as health cooperatives (*cooperativa sanitaria*) if their members include at least one cooperative of this type (LC art. 102.3).

5.5.3. Promotion of Second-Tier Cooperatives

Since economic integration among cooperatives is also a task in the general interest (LC art. 108), the legislation sets out a number of measures to foster second-tier cooperatives.

As already mentioned, income from investments or financial participation in cooperatives is considered cooperative results (LC art. 57.3.a), which favours second-tier cooperatives and their cooperative members.

When a second-tier cooperative is wound up, the residual non-distributable assets must be transferred to the fund of the same nature of each of its member cooperatives,[181] divided between them in proportion to the cooperativised activity with each in the past five years or, if fewer, since the constitution of the second-tier cooperative (LC art. 77.4).

From the tax point of view, there are no more benefits attached to setting up a second-tier cooperative than those to which it is entitled because of the type of cooperatives that it unites. It is fiscally protected, like all cooperatives, and is especially protected if its membership is composed exclusively of especially protected cooperatives. If it has both protected and specially protected members, it will enjoy both the tax advantages of a protected cooperative and further relief for the especially protected cooperative members (LRFC art. 35). In Navarre, however, the region's Cooperative Tax Regime Act (Law 9/1994 art. 90) does not require an exclusively specially protected membership in order to be specially protected: it is sufficient for 70% of the member cooperatives to be of this type.[182]

5.6. COOPERATIVE GROUPS

A group is another form of business integration or concentration that allows different companies to set up a new company without giving up their separate legal identities.

In Spanish law, groups of companies are defined by articles 42 to 49 of the Code of Commerce, which rule on the presentation of their consolidated accounts.

---

181 Legal writers have questioned the exclusion of non-cooperative members from this distribution Alfonso, n. 164 above, p. 29). However, it must be borne in mind that the general rule for cooperatives is that after reimbursing the members' contributions, the residual assets are non-distributable. Rather than discriminating against non-cooperative members, this rule encourages integration among cooperatives.

182 P. Peris, 'Fiscalidad e integración cooperativa en las legislaciones estatal y autonómicas', in R. Chaves, G. Fajardo and R. Namorado (dir.), *Integración Empresarial Cooperativa*, CIRIEC, 2003, p. 66.

The Cooperatives Act of 1999 was the first to regulate cooperative groups. Its preamble states that this is necessary in order to boost business integration among companies of this type in view of the challenge of operating on increasingly globalised markets.

5.6.1. Regulating Cooperative Groups

Article 78 of Law 27/1999 regulates cooperative groups, which it defines as groups made up of various cooperatives,[183] of whatever class, with a head-of-group entity that exercises powers or issues instructions that are legally binding on the cooperatives in the group, so that unity of decision-making ensues within the scope of those powers. The head of group may or may not be a cooperative.[184]

Approval to join the group requires a resolution of the General Meeting of each of the cooperatives involved. The cooperative or company statutes of the head of group, or the group contract, must state the powers assigned to the head of group and the procedures for modifying them and for cooperatives to leave the group. The law allows modification, expansion or termination of the content of these documents to be delegated to the highest organ of the head of group. The law gives some examples of the powers that can be assigned to the head of group. They include decisions that lie within the exclusive domain of the cooperatives' General Meetings, such as modifying the cooperative statutes, adopting regulations, entering into association agreements or deciding new financial contributions. When the law regulates the exclusive powers of the General Meeting and states that they cannot be delegated, it makes an exception for cases in which they have been delegated to a cooperative group (LC, art. 21.3).

5.6.2. The Cooperative Group as a Coordinated Group

Until the 1999 Act was passed, legal writers agreed that cooperative groups could be set up under a unified management, but coordinated and born of consensus,

---

183 The possibility of setting up heterogeneous cooperative groups with non-cooperative company members has been barely mentioned by legal writers, although they have highlighted that in such a case it would be impossible to consolidate the accounts because the accounting and tax rules are different (A. Mateos, 'La consolidación contable en el ámbito cooperative', *CIRIEC – Revista de Economía Pública, Social y Cooperativa*, 2007, no. 58, p. 57). The rules for cooperatives adapt the accounts to their characteristics (Order EHA/3360/2010).

184 The Cooperatives Act of Catalonia allows other entities to join a cooperative group provided that the majority and the one heading the group are cooperatives (art. 125.1). As already noted, the national Cooperatives Act (LC) also allows mixed groups headed by a second-tier cooperative. The law of the Basque country also envisages this possibility (E. Gadea, 'Crisis e inter-cooperación: las cooperativas de segundo o ulterior grado como instrumento de colaboración empresarial', *Boletín de la Asociación Internacional de Derecho Cooperativo*, 2010, no. 44, p. 252).

not domination.[185] The need for members to participate in the cooperative activity (mutuality), democratic management, and the principle of autonomy that must preside over the functioning of the cooperative were not considered compatible with a subordinated group like those normally formed by capital-based companies.[186] However, some studies showed that recognition of multiple voting rights and the absence of effective limits could in some cases make it possible for a member of a cooperative to command over 50% of the voting rights.[187]

Today, the expansion of the subjective and objective sphere of second-tier cooperatives and, above all, the new possibilities afforded by cooperative groups raise doubts about whether it is possible for there to be cooperative groups in which the member cooperatives retain their autonomy. Even the requirement that integration cooperatives guarantee their members' freedom and autonomy (LGC, art. 150) has disappeared in the current Act. It is certainly true that resolutions of the General Meetings of the cooperatives involved are required to set up the group and regulate its operation (powers delegated, commitments undertaken, procedures for modification, etc.), as is characteristic of a coordinated group, but the law also allows the organisation that heads the group to acquire increasing autonomy and permits its highest organ to modify the resolutions initially adopted. This rule responds to a trend in legal opinion that calls for greater flexibility in the legislation so that cooperatives can use the same instruments that are available to capital-based companies, particularly those that enable the structure of the enterprise to grow.[188]

Faced with this dilemma, the present author shares Rosalía Alfonso's restrictive interpretation of the rule which respects the cooperative principles and prevents cooperatives in a group from becoming acquired companies.[189]

---

185 As an exception, subordinated groups of capital-based companies headed by a cooperative have been and are accepted.

186 J.M. Embid, 'Los grupos cooperativos', *CIRIEC – Revista Jurídica de Economía Social y Cooperativa*, 1995, no. 7, p. 226.

187 J. Duque and J.I. Ruiz, 'Los grupos en el ordenamiento jurídico. II. Grupos por subordinación integrados por entidades de economía social', *Grupos empresariales de la Economía Social en España. CIRIEC*, 1999, p. 186.

188 A. Celaya, 'Estructura y problemática jurídica de la Corporación MCC', *Anuario de Estudios Cooperativos*, Universidad de Deusto, 1992, p. 127; Embid, n. 186 above, p. 231; Vargas, n. 174 above, p. 174; and J. Juliá, G. Garcia and E. Meliá, 'La globalización y los modelos de crecimiento de los grupos cooperativos. Las cooperativas agroalimentarias en España y la Unión Europea', *EKONOMIAZ. Revista Vasca de Economía*, 2012, no. 79, p. 109.

189 R. Alfonso, 'Grupos y alianzas de sociedades. Especial referencia al grupo cooperativo y a la cooperativa de segundo grado', in J. Pulgar and C. Vargas (dir.) *Cooperativas agrarias y Sociedades agrarias de transformación*, Dykinson, Madrid, 2006, p. 742.

5.6.3. *Consolidated Accounts of Cooperative Groups*

Cooperative groups can present consolidated accounts but are not obliged to do so. Royal Decree 1159/2010 makes it obligatory for commercial companies to draw up consolidated annual accounts and management reports, consequently exempting cooperatives from this requirement. The Cooperatives Act of 1999 announced (in final provision 4) that the government would establish the cases in which cooperative groups would be obliged to draw up consolidated annual accounts and management reports. However, it has not done so to date. At present, consolidation of cooperative group accounts is not a legal requirement; it is available as an option making it possible for these groups to take advantage of the consolidated profit tax system. The rules for adapting these tax provisions to cooperative groups are set out in Royal Decree 1345/1992 and, for the Basque Country, in Provincial Laws (*Normas Forales*) 2/1997, 16/1997 and 9/1997.

5.7. INTER-COOPERATION AGREEMENTS

The other forms of economic cooperation mentioned in article 79 LC include 'inter-cooperative agreements', defined as agreements between cooperatives, in pursuit of their objectives, by virtue of which the cooperative and its members 'may effect supply operations, deliveries of products or services to the other cooperative signing the agreement,' and such events shall be considered cooperativised transactions.

Aside from the deficiencies of the rule,[190] the purpose of these agreements is to extend the cooperativised activities of a cooperative to the members of other cooperatives. This type of agreement is frequent between agri-food and consumer cooperatives.[191] It is expressly mentioned for housing cooperatives[192] but is possible in any type of cooperative. Cooperatives (whether or not of the same class) cooperate with each other to benefit their respective members. However, it would not seem necessary for the benefits to be made reciprocal if no such agreement has been made.[193]

---

190 Paz Canalejo, n. 174 above, pp. 171 and ff.

191 P.A. Romero Candau, 'De las cooperativas de segundo grado, grupo cooperativo y otras formas de colaboración económica', *Cooperativas. Comentarios a la Ley 27/1999, de 16 de julio*, Colegios Notariales de España, 2001, p. 572.

192 Article 89.3 LC states that the statutes of these cooperatives may envisage and regulate the assignment and exchange of the right to use and enjoyment of the dwelling or premises to or with members of other housing cooperatives.

193 Alfonso, n. 189 above, p. 767.

The law tries to encourage these transactions by stating that they will receive the same treatment as cooperative transactions with the cooperative's own members. In this situation, it is assumed that the cooperative providing the goods or services will not treat the members of the other cooperative as third parties but in the same way as its own members, applying the same terms and conditions of supply or service to both.

Moreover, since the law considers these transactions equivalent to cooperative transactions it may be deduced that they will not count as operations with third parties, which are subject to limitations, and that the profits they may generate will be taxed as surpluses, benefiting the cooperative that provides the goods or services.

A criticism expressed by some authors is that the law considers these transactions equivalent to cooperativised ones, but finally states that the results so generated shall be allotted to the cooperative's mandatory reserve, instead of treating them like cooperativised transactions and allowing the surpluses to be distributed among the members of the cooperative providing the goods or services. The present author does not agree that this is a contradiction,[194] or an anti-cooperative solution.[195] Equivalence with the cooperative's own members would imply that if the cooperative resolves to distribute the year's surpluses, the members of the other cooperative should be able to receive their respective part. However, this would not seem possible, or at least not easy. Nor would it be very 'cooperative' for the members of the cooperative supplying the good or service to appropriate the surpluses generated by the transactions with the other cooperative's members. This provision of the law would therefore appear to be the best solution. When the cooperative calculates the cost of the goods or service that it will be providing, if it wishes to treat the members of the other cooperative like its own, it will need to take into account that the final results cannot be passed on to the members of the other cooperative.

5.8. SPECIAL FEATURES OF INTER-COOPERATION IN THE CREDIT COOPERATIVE SECTOR

Credit cooperatives are governed by Law 13/1989 of 26 May and its pursuant regulations (Royal Decree 84/1993). When the state reserved the exclusive right to regulate the basis for credit and banking (art. 149.1.11° of the Spanish Constitution), it also reserved the exclusive right to regulate credit cooperatives (as it considers most of the rules covering these to be basic legislation).

Inter-cooperation in the credit cooperative sector presents special features which it is worth highlighting.

---

194 Alfonso, n. 189 above, p. 768.
195 Paz Canalejo, n. 174 above, p. 173.

First, all the credit cooperatives are members of the National Union of Credit Cooperatives (*Unión Nacional de Cooperativas de Crédito* – UNACC)[196] and almost all the rural banks (rural credit cooperatives), except for Cajamar and IparKutxa,[197] are also members of the Spanish Association of Rural Banks (*Asociación Española de Cajas Rurales* – AECR). Lastly, credit cooperatives, of their own volition, have remained separate from the organisations that represent the cooperatives and the social economy.

The history of the rural banks in Spain reflects successive efforts to integrate this sector while respecting their independence.[198] The very existence of AECR, founded in 1984, was promoted by the government for this purpose, following a period of crisis.[199] From 1990 onwards, AECR set up *Banco Cooperativo Español SA*, together with the German cooperative group DZ Bank, and other special purpose vehicles in the form of capital-based companies (RSI, the *Seguros RGA* insurance company), which provide services to all the rural banks in the group.

The founding members of AECR, and those that have joined it since, agree to adhere to its statutes, regulations and resolutions. One resolution was to respect the geographical demarcations of the other rural banks. When *Caja Rural de Almería* (now Cajamar) began its expansion and breached this undertaking, a complaint was made to the Competition Court (*Tribunal de Defensa de la Competencia* – TDC), claiming that the resolutions of what was known as the *Grupo Caja Rural* were incompatible with the competition rules. After examining the undertakings adopted by the associated banks, the TDC concluded (Ruling of 13 July 1998) that *Grupo Caja Rural* was not a group for the purposes of competition law because it did not have a single management, and consequently declared that the resolution in question restricted competition.[200] Thereafter, a succession of rural banks in different autonomous regions merged with Cajamar.[201]

---

196 UNACC currently represents all the credit cooperatives, but their coexistence is not peaceful. No member may hold more than 10% of the decision-making power in UNACC's organs. This limit has been challenged by Cajamar, which has warned that it will leave UNACC unless it obtains representation in proportion to its volume of business, which it calculates at 40% of the credit cooperative total. http://cincodias.com/cincodias/2014/07/01/mercados/1404242024_614465.html.

197 http://www.cajarural.com/web_grupo/ae_cajas_rurales/ae_caj_rur.htm.

198 Cf. R. Palomo, 'La banca cooperativa en Europa UNCC/AECC.1995' and J.R Sanchis, 'El crédito cooperativo en España', *CIRIEC*, 1997.

199 A. Rojo Fernandez-Rio, 'La crisis de las cajas rurales', *Revista de Derecho Bancario y Bursátil*, 1985, no. 17, pp. 7–68.

200 F. Gonzalez, 'Grupos paritarios de cooperativas de crédito y prácticas restrictivas de la competencia. A propósito del Grupo Caja Rural', *CIRIEC – Revista Jurídica*, 2000, no. 11, pp. 26.

201 https://www.grupocooperativocajamar.es/es/comun/informacion-corporativa/sobre-grupo-cooperativo-cajamar/.

5.9. PARTICULAR FEATURES OF INTER-COOPERATION IN THE AGRICULTURAL COOPERATIVE SECTOR

Agri-food cooperatives unite the owners of farming or forestry holdings to engage in all types of activities that aim to improve the use of their members' and of the cooperative's land, improve the situation of the agricultural population, and develop the rural world. Agricultural partnerships (*sociedad de transformación agraria* or SAT, literally 'agricultural transformation company'), irrigation communities (*comunidad de regantes*) and partnerships and commercial companies that have the same objects or complementary activities may also be members of these cooperatives (art. 93 LC).

This sector is another in which the government, particularly the Ministry of Agriculture, has paid particular attention to integration. Annually, assistance 'to promote agricultural associationism' is made available to create larger business structures, facilitating inter-regional cooperation and economies of network.[202] Its beneficiaries are agricultural cooperatives formed by agricultural production SMEs, second-tier cooperatives, cooperative groups and agricultural partnerships (SATs), as well as other bodies provided that over 50% of their capital is owned by these cooperatives, groups or partnerships. It mainly subsidises integration-related expenses (studies, audits, technical assistance, formation of the organisation, etc.).

As well as these subsidies, Law 13/2013 was recently passed to encourage integration among cooperatives and other agri-food associative entities (*entidad asociativa de carácter agroalimentario* – EAA). Cooperatives, second-tier cooperatives, cooperative groups, agricultural partnerships (SAT), agricultural producer organisations (agricultural OPs) with legal entity recognised by the Common Agricultural Policy, and partnerships or commercial companies, provided that over 50% of their capital is owned by cooperatives, OPs or SATs, are all considered EAAs (art. 1).

This law aims to combat the fragmentation of the agricultural sector by implementing measures to encourage the integration and strengthening of cooperative and associative marketing groups. It promotes mergers and integration into cooperative groups headed by a body that gives instructions that the group is obliged to obey. The body that they are encouraged to set up is called a 'priority agri-food associative entity' (*entidad asociativa agroalimentaria prioritaria* or EAP). EAPs enjoy a variety of advantages and subsidies. Existing or new organisations that meet certain requirements can apply to be classed as EAPs: they must be EAAs of greater than regional scope; they must market in common the entire production of all their affiliated organisations and of the producer

[202] The selection process rules were adopted by Order APA/180/2008 and now by RD 1009/2015 of 6 November.

members of these; they must achieve certain levels of sales set by the regulations (RD 550/2014); their statutes or internal rules must state that the producers are obliged to deliver their entire production to be marketed in common; and the same rules 'must envisage the necessary provisions to guarantee democratic control of their functioning and decisions by their member producers and to prevent one or more of their members from occupying a dominant position ' (art. 3).

Complementing the above law, the first State Plan for Associative Integration (*Plan Estatal de Integración Asociativa*) was approved on 20 January 2014. It includes a number of measures that aim to reduce the number of cooperatives and increase their size by means of mergers that form new organisations, take-overs by existing organisations or the growth of existing organisations through adding new members.

5.10. OTHER BUSINESS INTEGRATION AND DISAGGREGATION TOOLS USED BY COOPERATIVES

Cooperatives can engage in other types of integration provided for in law such as mergers, or downgrading of second-tier cooperatives, and also in disaggregation processes such as splitting up and divestiture.

5.10.1. Mergers between Cooperatives and Heterogeneous Mergers

Spanish law has always allowed cooperatives to merge. The law provides both for mergers that form a new cooperative (amalgamation) and for those in which one cooperative takes over another (acquisition). The minimum requirements are dissolution of the merged cooperative(s) and the transfer of assets and members to the new or acquiring cooperative. The legal system for cooperatives provides that the merger agreement must be approved by a qualified majority and entered into the Register of Cooperatives. Members who disagree may leave the cooperative and creditors have the right to oppose the merger. The non-distributable funds become part of the non-distributable funds of the resulting cooperative.

Since Spain joined the European Union and the Third Council Directive on company mergers (78/855/EEC) was transposed into national law, some novelties have been introduced into cooperative law, such as heterogeneous (special or mixed) mergers, in other words, mergers between cooperatives and other forms of organisation. These were first envisaged for credit cooperatives (RD 84/1993) and insurance cooperatives (Private Insurance Act 30/1995),[203]

[203] This measure was criticised by authors as violating the principle of legality (M.J. Vañó, *Fusión heterogénea y cesión global en el sector bancario*, Tirant lo Blanch, Valencia, 2001, p. 115).

and shortly afterwards were allowed between some cooperatives and similar social economy organisations (labour companies and agricultural partnerships).

Heterogeneous mergers were not allowed as a general rule until the Cooperatives Act of 1999,[204] which in article 67 LC, under the title of 'Special Merger', provided that cooperatives might merge with partnerships or commercial companies of any class provided that no law or regulation forbids such a merger. In these mergers, the rules of the Cooperatives Act concerning adoption of the agreement and the rights of members and creditors apply to the cooperatives involved. The non-distributable funds are allocated as provided for in the event of winding up the cooperative (promoting cooperativism). The regional legislation varies and every possibility can be found, from regions that only allow mergers between cooperatives (Navarra, Madrid and the Balearic Islands) to those that copy the national Act or even allow free allocation of 50% of the mandatory reserve fund (law of Andalusia, art. 75 and 78).

Unlike the system that applies to heterogeneous mergers between capital-based companies (*Ley de Modificaciones Estructurales* 3/2009), which does not recognise the member's right to leave the company despite recognising it in the case of company conversion, the cooperative legislation does guarantee this right, as mentioned above.

A number of heterogeneous mergers have taken place in the banking sector, where cooperatives have been absorbed by banks and savings banks (*cajas de ahorros*). In these cases the cooperative members have been given shares in the bank or participation shares (subordinated debt) in the savings bank in exchange for their right to a share of the distributable equity of the cooperative.

5.10.2. Division of Cooperatives

The national Cooperatives Act also makes provision for cooperatives to split in article 68, which lays down certain specific rules and refers to the legal system governing mergers.

The division can be total or partial. In the first case (splitting up) the cooperative divides all its assets and its members into two or more parts and transfers these en masse (by universal succession) to newly-created cooperatives or to existing cooperatives that take them over. In these cases the cooperative that has split up is dissolved and extinguished without liquidation. In the second case (splitting off) the cooperative is not dissolved but divests itself of part of its assets and members, transferring them to an existing cooperative (which absorbs them) or to a new one. In these cases the law only allows cooperatives to

[204] Until then, Spanish jurisprudence had not acknowledged the possibility of such mergers even when the organisations involved were engaged in the same activity, since the nature and objects of the two are different (G. Fajardo, 'La fusión de cooperativas en la legislación española', *CIRIEC – Revista Jurídica*, 2006, no. 17, p. 82).

be involved. Heterogeneous division is not possible. Some authors criticise this situation.[205]

The division plans, signed by the directors of the cooperatives taking part, must contain detailed proposals about which assets and members constitute the part to be transferred. The law does not say anything about the distribution of non-distributable funds, nor have legal writings questioned it, but a reasonable interpretation would be that a proportionate share of these funds should be transferred to the corresponding funds of the acquiring cooperatives.

Division is not much used by cooperatives, with the exception of credit cooperatives. Historically, it was used to spin off rural banks from agricultural cooperatives when exclusivity became a requirement for credit institutions. Subsequently, some agricultural cooperatives have spun off their credit sections to set up new rural banks, or have transferred this part of their assets and members to other rural banks.

Cooperative legislation in Spain does not require the part that is divided off to constitute an economic unit, unlike the rules for capital-based companies (Law 3/2009, art. 70-1). The latter have been criticised by legal writers, who have proposed that the concept of 'economic unit' should at least be interpreted flexibly.[206]

5.10.3. Downgrading Second-Tier Cooperatives

Degradación (literally 'degradation', 'breaking down', 'demotion' or 'downgrading') takes place when a second-tier cooperative becomes a first-tier cooperative, taking over the assets and members of its member cooperatives. This is a process which does happen in practice, largely when the second-tier cooperative has absorbed the business activities of its members and operates directly with the members of the latter as third parties. This phenomenon is mentioned in the Cooperatives Act's provisions for second-tier cooperatives, as article 77.5 states that these can 'convert to first-tier cooperatives, taking over their member cooperatives according to the procedure set out in the present law'. This rule has rightly been criticised by authors[207] as no procedure is actually laid down. It is not a conversion because the legal form remains the same, and nor is it clearly a

---

205 F.J. Leon Sanz, *El acuerdo de transformación de una sociedad anónima*, Monograph RdS No. 16. Aranzadi, Navarra, 2001, p. 47; and A.J. Macías Ruano, 'Consideraciones críticas sobre la fusión, escisión y transformación en la Ley 27/1999 de 16 de julio de cooperativas', *REVESCO*, 2002, no. 78, p. 69.

206 F. Vicent, *Introducción al Derecho Mercantil*, Vol. I, 23rd ed., Tirant lo Blanch, Valencia, 2012, p. 1029.

207 A. Cuenca, 'Las cooperativas de segundo grado en la Ley 27/1999, de 16 de julio, de cooperativas', *CIRIEC - Revista Jurídica*, 2000, no. 11, p. 113; and Paz Canalejo, n. 174 above, p. 190.

takeover (*fusión por absorción*) because the member cooperatives do not always cease to exist.[208]

However, it certainly constitutes a structural modification of the cooperative, and the law therefore demands certain guarantees, for instance that the member cooperatives and the members of these that disagree with the 'conversion' and 'takeover' resolutions may leave the cooperative.

The process will require the resolution to be adopted by a qualified majority of the General Meetings of all the cooperatives involved. The second-tier cooperative has to approve its downgrading and its takeover of the members and assets of the cooperatives to be amalgamated. The General Meetings of the first-tier cooperatives have to approve the transfer of their members and assets to the amalgamating cooperative and, if applicable, their own extinction. These procedures have mainly been used when restructuring the rural banks.

5.11. CONCLUSIONS

Spanish law promotes inter-cooperation. Not only does it offer cooperatives different ways to cooperate, both to defend their political interests (cooperative associationism) and to improve their economic situation (inter-cooperation agreements, second-tier cooperatives, cooperative groups); it also sets out a number of measures to encourage these processes.

Additionally, integration mechanisms that encourage business growth have been made available to cooperatives in recent years, such as groups of companies, subsidiary companies and heterogeneous mergers. Under pressure from major cooperatives and the organisations representing cooperatives (often controlled by the former), the Cooperatives Act has broadened the subjective and functional scope of second-tier cooperatives and has allowed cooperatives that are members of a cooperative group to delegate any power whatsoever, including those of the General Meeting which are considered non-delegable, to the company heading the group, whether or not it is a cooperative.

These measures call into question some of the identifying features of cooperatives, such as autonomy and democratic control.

The agricultural and credit sectors are those that have made most use of these growth structures, although their strategies differ. On the one hand, integration among agricultural cooperatives is based on mergers and cooperative groups of cooperative or similar organisations, and it must ensure democratic control by the members and avoid domination by one or more of them. On the other hand, integration among credit cooperatives, particularly rural banks, has followed two models to date. One model is a subordinated group headed by

208 Alfonso, n. 164 above, p. 30.

a PLC (BCSC) but clearly dominated by a single cooperative (Cajamar), while the other is a coordinated group clustered around the Spanish Association of Rural Banks (*Asociación Española de Cajas Rurales* – AECR), which respects the autonomy of its member cooperatives and, rather than controlling them, has focused on offering them all the services that they may need to pursue their objects, including the services of a bank, the *Banco Cooperativo Español* (BCE). It should be mentioned that democratic control is not guaranteed in the credit cooperatives because the law allows their voting rights to be apportioned in proportion to the members' capital contributions.

A further feature of integration among the credit cooperatives is the lack of autonomy in relation to government: in the end, it is the Ministry of the Economy and the Treasury and the Bank of Spain that decide how and why the rural banks should amalgamate or whether they should be converted into banks, as was done with the savings banks. Given this interference, the silence of the organisations representing the credit cooperatives is surprising.

CHAPTER 12
UNITED KINGDOM

Ian Snaith

1. DEFINITION AND OBJECTIVES OF COOPERATIVES

1.1. INTRODUCTION

In the UK, a body wishing to function as a cooperative is free to use any legal form it chooses. That includes registering under the Companies Act 2006 or the Limited Liability Partnerships Act 2000 or operating as a partnership under the Partnership Act 1890, subject to restrictions on the use of the word 'cooperative'.

However, the Co-operative and Community Benefit Societies Act 2014 (CCBSA 2014) provides a legal structure specifically designed for cooperatives. Credit unions, a form of savings and loan cooperative, must register under the 2014 Act as adapted by the Credit Unions Act 1979 and are prohibited from otherwise registering under the CCBSA 2014. Similarly, an organisation using any other legal structure (including the European Cooperative Society (SCE) form) is prohibited from using the words 'credit union' as part of its name (ss. 1–3 Credit Unions Act 1979). Like other financial services businesses, credit unions are also subject to regulation by the Financial Conduct Authority (FCA) and the Prudential Regulatory Authority (PRA) as authorised deposit takers under the Financial Services and Markets Act 2000. For that reason, this report makes no further reference to the law governing credit unions.

The FCA is responsible for cooperative and community benefit society registration – a function similar to that performed by the Registrar of Companies for companies registered under the Companies Act 2006.[1]

As is generally the case in UK business organisation law, the emphasis of the CCBSA 2014 is on providing default rules and so maximising the freedom of those using the legal structure to develop and apply their own rules. This means that subject to compliance with the FCA's view of the nature of a bona fide cooperative society, the governance structure, rights and duties of members, elements of the capital structure and rules about the return to members are all left to be dealt with by the rules of each society. This reflects the system also applicable to companies and partnerships in the UK.

1.2. DEFINITION OF A COOPERATIVE SOCIETY

Section 2 of the CCBSA 2014 lays down the conditions to be satisfied for a society to be registered as a cooperative society. It must be a society for carrying on any industry business or trade (including dealings of any description with

1 Further information about the FCA and its role as the registry for mutual societies can be found on its website at http://www.fca.org.uk/ and in the information that it publishes on that site and in print.

land) whether wholesale or retail, and it must show to the satisfaction of the FCA that it is a bona fide cooperative society. Since 1 August 2014 registration has been *as* a cooperative society.

The only other provision of the legislation relating to the meaning of the term 'cooperative society' is to be found in section 2(3) of the 2014 Act:

> In this section, the expression 'co-operative society' does not include a society which carries on, or intends to carry on, business with the object of making profits mainly for the payment of interest, dividends or bonuses on money invested or deposited with, or lent to, the society or any other person.

Otherwise, the matter is left entirely to the FCA as the registering authority.

In November 2015 the FCA published its long-awaited *Finalised Guidance 15/12, Guidance on the FCA's registration function under the Co-operative and Community Benefit Societies Act 2014* (hereafter 'FCA Guidance 2015'). This chapter sets out how the FCA's statutory discretion under the CCBSA 2014 is exercised.[2]

The FCA approach follows the logic of the legislation which requires a cooperative society to be a bona fide cooperative as a condition of its initial and continued registration – CCBSA 2014, section 2(1). FCA Guidance 2015 notes the absence of a full definition of that phrase in the CCBSA 2014 and begins its analysis with the exclusion of certain societies from that category by section 2(3) of CCBSA 2014.

The FCA accepts that section 2(3) does not prevent a bona fide cooperative from paying interest or dividend on money invested in, deposited with, or lent to it or to another person. A problem arises only if those activities are the main purpose or objective of the society's business: FCA Guidance 2015, para. 4.5. Compliance with section 2(3) is an ongoing requirement, and the FCA maintains arrangements so that it can decide whether a cooperative society is complying. It is at this juncture in the FCA Guidance 2015 that the FCA lists points on which compliance is monitored.

However, the first and last of those points for monitoring apply to the overall bona fide cooperative requirement and not just to assessing compliance with section 2(3) of CCBSA 2014.

Compliance is assessed:

- on any application to register a society when the proposed rules and the information provided on the application form are used;
- on any application to change the society's rules when all information available to the FCA is used;

[2] http://www.fca.org.uk/your-fca/documents/finalised-guidance/fg15-12.

- when a society publishes information suggesting that its main object is to make profits to pay interest on shares when all information available to the FCA will be used to assess whether section 2(3) has been breached;
- at any time while a society is trading (and so filing accounts with the FCA annually), the FCA may analyse its accounts to assess compliance with section 2(3) by comparing the surplus distributed to members in proportion to their transactions with the amount of interest, dividend of bonuses that the society pays on shares or other investments in light of the amount paid by comparable investor-owned businesses;
- those financial indicators are used together with an analysis of the society's relationship with its members to decide whether the society is an association of persons united mainly to meet their common economic social and cultural needs or an association of capital with the main purpose of generating financial returns (see FCA Guidance 2015, para. 4.8).

The last bullet point above goes to the core of the application of the ICA Statement in defining a cooperative and applies it alongside section 2(3) of CCBSA 2014 to ensure that registered cooperative societies meet the bona fide cooperative requirement. The FCA indicates that the process of assessing compliance with section 2(3) will be carried out on a case-by-case basis and will usually involve discussions with the society. The same principle will apply to the process of assessing whether or not a society complies more generally with the bona fide cooperative requirement.

On the more general question of defining a bona fide cooperative, the FCA states:

> We generally consider something to be a *bona fide* cooperative society where it is an autonomous association of persons united voluntarily to meet their common economic, social and cultural needs and aspirations through a jointly owned and democratically controlled enterprise.[3]

This approach applies the definition of a cooperative set out by the International Co-operative Alliance's (ICA) 1995 Statement on Cooperative identity, values and principles, and the International Labour Organization's (ILO) 2002 Recommendation 193 on the Promotion of Cooperatives.[4]

The FCA takes the position that the definition sets out the minimum features of a bona fide cooperative. However, it also accepts that practising the values set out in the ICA Statement, through the principles quoted therein, is

3 FCA Guidance 2015, para. 4.10.

4 See respectively http://ica.coop/en/whats-co-op/cooperative-identity-values-principles and http://www.ilo.org/dyn/normlex/en/fp=NORMLEXPUB:12100:0::NO::P12100_ILO_CODE:R193.

another indication that the registration conditions for a cooperative society are met.[5]

Referring to the ICA Principles, set out in full in paragraph 4.10 of FCA Guidance 2015, the FCA accepts that it can verify a cooperative society's compliance with the first four Principles (voluntary and open membership, democratic member control, member economic participation, and autonomy and independence) through the society's rules and governance arrangements together with its statements of intent about how it will operate.

Equally, the FCA accepts that it will not necessarily be able to verify compliance with Principles 5–7 – education, training and information, cooperation among cooperatives, and concern for the community. Nonetheless, it will treat evidence of compliance with those principles as a positive indicator when assessing whether the society is a bona fide cooperative. That approach is reinforced by the FCA's commitment, in applying its guidance, to taking account of the diverse nature of cooperative enterprise. The associative characteristics of a particular cooperative and the variation in relationships between members (as co-owners and users) and the cooperative will be considered. That will be different as between workers' cooperatives, consumer cooperatives and producer cooperatives and, in each case, as between primary cooperatives and secondary or tertiary cooperatives with cooperatives or their federations as members.[6]

Paragraph 4.16 of FCA Guidance 2015 acknowledges the flexibility in the ICA Principles and the fact that other indicators may point to a society's bona fide cooperative status. This provides an appropriately open-textured approach to applying the ICA guidelines to societies which meet the minimum requirement of the definition of a cooperative. In doing so, it protects the identity of cooperatives by aligning with the ICA and ILO definitions widely accepted throughout the world, while both acknowledging the diversity of the Cooperative Movement and leaving room for the application of the cooperative structure to new and as yet unforeseen circumstances.

In particular, the acknowledgment that the practice of cooperative values through Principle 7 (Concern for Community) leaves the door open for cooperatives with an altruistic purpose to benefit groups other than their own members as long as they meet the minimum core definition set out in para. 4.10 of FCA Guidance 2015. That allows for the Italian-style social cooperative or 'general interest cooperative' provided that the enterprise is jointly owned, democratically controlled by members united voluntarily to meet their common economic social and cultural needs. When added to the acknowledgment in para. 4.15 of multi-stakeholder cooperatives with, for example, employees, customers and suppliers as membership categories, this illustrates the value of flexibility.

---

5 FCA Guidance 2015, para. 4.12.

6 FCA Guidance 2015, paras. 4.14 and 4.15.

Apart from the need to establish that a society meets the bona fide cooperative requirement on first registration, it is necessary that it continues to do so. The FCA has power to cancel the registration of a society for failure to adhere to section 2 of CCBSA 2014.

When an application is made to register a cooperative, a copy of its rules is submitted to the FCA. That copy is checked to ensure that the rules do not violate cooperative principles so as to cast doubt on whether the society is a bona fide cooperative. That process is repeated whenever any application is made to register an amendment to the society's rules and until the amendment is registered it has no legal effect. This system ensures that very considerable freedom is permitted to cooperatives to organise themselves as they choose, so long as the society's rules contain the provisions required by section 14 of CCBSA 2014 and are consistent with the society's status as a bona fide cooperative.

The legislation does not prescribe the content of the society's constitution even in respect of matters such as governance, share capital, distribution of surplus, or members' voting rights. The question of whether particular provisions of the society's rules are to be permitted is always decided on the basis of whether or not those provisions are consistent with cooperative principles as applied by the FCA. However, the use of model rules provided in advance by sponsoring organisations is encouraged by the availability of a very substantially reduced registration fee if such rules are used.

The use of the word 'cooperative' in the name of a business registered as a company or a limited liability partnership (LLP) requires the approval of the Secretary of State for Business Innovation and Skills. In practice, this allows the Registrar of Companies to apply the test used by the FCA for the registration of a cooperative society before a company or LLP registration is permitted with the word 'cooperative' in the name. The same obligation is imposed on anyone using the word in the name of an unregistered partnership established by agreement between individuals without registration under the Partnership Act 1890.[7]

1.3. COOPERATIVE SOCIAL OBJECT: DEFINITION, CONTENT, LEGAL EFFECTS

A number of points about the development of the UK legislation assist in understanding the UK regime. The division of what were, until 2014, called 'industrial and provident societies' into cooperatives and societies for the benefit of the community was first introduced by the Prevention of Fraud (Investments)

---

7 Companies Act 2006, sections 55(1) and 1194(1) and the Company, Limited Liability Partnership and Business Names (Sensitive Words and Expressions) Regulations 2014 SI 2014/3140, schedule 1.

Act 1939 to counteract the fraudulent use of the society form to evade the prospectus requirements of the Companies Acts. Before that, no reference to, or definition of cooperatives, was to be found in the legislation.[8] However, the Co-operative and Community Benefit Societies Act 2014 has reinforced that division by requiring registration as one or the other and adopted that terminology as the title of the UK legislation, partly to address the obscurity of the 'industrial and provident society' label.

The FCA's adoption in 2015 of the ICA definition of a cooperative emphasises the need for a common interest or interests among the members and the need to run the business for mutual benefit rather than profits on capital investments. Members' benefit is to arise from their participation in the business as suppliers, customers or employees rather than as holders of capital. The full inclusion in the FCA Guidance 2015 of the ICA Values and Principles and the willingness to use compliance with them as indicators that a society is a bona fide cooperative as a supplement to the ICA definition further underlines the importance of these features.

1.3.1. The Interest of Members: Modes of Pursuing it

The concepts of community of interest among members and the conduct of business for mutual benefit are central to the registration process for cooperatives in the UK. It is important to note that the societies governed by the legislation must now be registered either as bona fide cooperatives or as societies established for the benefit of the community. Only those 'pre-commencement' societies registered before 1 August 2014 are free to meet either requirement. The distinction generally made between the two is that cooperatives operate primarily for the benefit of their members while community benefit societies operate in the interests of people other than their members who constitute the community that they serve.

FCA Guidance 2015 on the registration of community benefit societies draws a clear distinction between the two different types of society. Under section 2(2)(a)(ii) of CCBSA 2014, the registration requirement for community benefit societies is that:

> the business of the society is being, or is intended to be, conducted for the benefit of the community.

The FCA interprets 'community benefit' as referring to the community at large so that, if a society serves the needs of a defined community that should not

8 See I. Snaith, 'What Is an Industrial and Provident Society?', *Journal of Co-operative Studies*, 2001, vol. 34, pp. 37–42.

inhibit the benefit to the 'community at large'. This represents a change from the position taken in previous consultation documents, which tended to emphasise service of a particular community.

However, the FCA rejected any attempt to apply the Government 'social enterprise definition' so that only the 'primary benefit' from the society need be social. The FCA views the registration requirement for a community benefit society as being that the conduct of the business should be 'entirely' and not merely 'primarily' for the benefit of the community.[9]

The FCA position is also that, while a community benefit society can be wholly charitable or benevolent, it need not meet those descriptions providing the business is conducted for the benefit of the community.[10]

However, the conduct of its business, including any joint ventures or other commercial ventures must be based on furthering the community benefit purpose.[11]

All profits made by a community benefit society must be used for the benefit of the community by either being ploughed back into the business or otherwise used for community benefit (including philanthropic or charitable activity). They cannot be distributed to members as such.[12] However, FCA Guidance 2015, para. 5.14 permits the payment of interest on community benefit society shares within the limits set out in FCA Guidance 2015, paras. 6.22 to 6.28.

Similarly, all assets and the proceeds of any asset sale must be used for community benefit. No distribution to members should be permitted on solvent dissolution, conversion or amalgamation of the society – even if no statutory asset lock is in place.[13]

The contrast between cooperative societies and community benefit societies is particularly clear when the issue of membership is considered. Both types of society must have members who hold shares because this is the only registration and formation mechanism recognised by CCBSA 2014. However, the FCA takes the view that a community benefit society should not exist to provide benefits which are contingent on membership.

It also follows from the FCA's logic that community benefit societies should operate on the basis of one member/one vote to avoid particular members being given greater rights, unless a different arrangement can be justified as helping the society to fulfil its purpose of benefiting the community.[14]

Cooperatives will not generally be able to register as community benefit societies.[15] This is justified by the argument that the CCBSA 2014 brings about

---

9 FCA Guidance 2015, para. 5.6 and see FCA Summary of Feedback, pp.13–14.
10 FCA Guidance 2015, paras. 5.4 and 5.5.
11 FCA Guidance 2015, para. 5.7.
12 FCA Guidance 2015, paras. 5.12 and 5.13
13 FCA Guidance 2015, paras. 5.15–5.17.
14 FCA Guidance 2015, paras. 5.10 and 5.11.
15 FCA Guidance 2015, paras. 5.8 and 5.9.

the complete separation of registration between the two types of society. There is no provision for conversion from one to the other. This indicates that the status of being a cooperative society and of being a community benefit society are mutually exclusive. However, the FCA acknowledges that the ICA Principle of benefit of the community is one of the features of a cooperative society and that a multi-stakeholder governance structure is possible for a cooperative.

To summarise the distinction between cooperative societies and community benefit societies, a housing association registered as a community benefit society may predominantly benefit the community of its tenants and potential tenants but that benefit must not inhibit the wider community benefit of providing social housing. By contrast, a housing cooperative is established for the purpose of benefiting its tenant members by operating in line with the ICA definition of a cooperative. The housing cooperative has no obligation to benefit any other group as a condition of registration as long as it operates according to the ICA definition, but its rules could commit it, while operating as a member-controlled cooperative, to concern for its local community as an application of ICA Principle 7 (concern for the community).

As the FCA puts it in its response to the consultation on the 2015 Guidance:

> We acknowledge that many co-operative societies also choose to benefit the community; and that many community benefit societies have active and engaged memberships who control the society democratically. However, a community benefit society must fundamentally exist entirely for the benefit of the community, not for benefits that depend on membership. Our view is that the purposes of a co-operative society and a community benefit society are fundamentally different. (*FCA Summary of Feedback*, p 14.)

1.3.2. Cooperative Advantage and Ways to Assign it to Members

1.3.2.1. Provision and Regulation of Patronage Refunds

Section 2(3) of CCBSA 2014 makes clear that a cooperative society must not carry on 'business with the object of making profits mainly for the payment of interest, dividends or bonuses on money invested or deposited'.

1.3.2.2. Concept/Legal Nature of Patronage Refunds and Distinction from Dividends (as Remuneration of the Capital Provided by Members)

Confusingly, it is the practice of many UK cooperatives to refer to the patronage refund as a 'dividend' while specifying that it is a 'dividend on purchases' in the case of a consumer cooperative. This term has been used from the earliest days of the UK cooperative movement in the mid-nineteenth century.

However, it is clear from both section 2(3) of CCBSA 2014 and FCA Guidance 2015 that distributions to members must be mainly based on their transactions with the society and should not be linked to the level of shareholding. The term 'patronage refund' is little known in the UK. The commonest term is 'dividend'.

FCA Guidance 2015 acknowledges that cooperative societies can pay interest on shares but only if the society can afford to do so after account has been taken of other liabilities and building reserves. Share interest should not be used to distribute surplus or profits or as a substitute for dividend in the sense of a patronage refund.[16]

The FCA points out that the use a cooperative society makes of interest on shares can indicate whether it is complying with its condition for registration. The society must not exist mainly to pay interest on money invested, and surplus distribution to members (if any) should be by a dividend on transactions with the society under ICA Principle 3.[17]

This issue is dealt with more fully in section 3. However, it is worth noting here that the legislation and the current FCA Guidance accept the payment of 'interest' on capital in a cooperative.

FCA Guidance 2015, then helpfully lists a number of positive factors about interest rates indicating that a cooperative society is likely to be complying with its registration condition if:

- primarily inviting people to become members of the society, along with any accompanying request for capital (additional to the minimum required for membership) from the prospective member;
- the maximum rate of interest paid on shares is declared in advance of the period for which it is intended to be paid, whether in its rules or elsewhere;
- the declared maximum rate of interest is the lowest rate sufficient to obtain the necessary funds from members who are committed to furthering the society's objects;
- in the event the society cannot afford to pay the declared maximum rate of interest, interest payments are reduced, or no interest is paid at all, without compensation in subsequent years;
- societies can justify a decision to pay interest at a particular rate, and be able to demonstrate the basis for that decision. (FCA Guidance 2015, para. 6.25).

This approach emphasises that shares represent risk capital. Hence the interest stated in the rules or the terms of a share issue (often fixed in rules by reference to a bank minimum lending rate) is a maximum figure. That distinguishes

16 FCA Guidance 2015, paras. 6.22 and 6.23.
17 FCA Guidance 2015, para. 6.22.

'interest' on shares from the contractual interest payable on loan capital. Less share interest will be paid if the amount available after debts and liabilities have been met and a contribution to reserves set aside does not permit payment at the maximum rate.

In this sense, the interest on shares is a 'distribution' of profits available for the purpose – just like the dividend on transactions that may be paid to members as consumers, workers or suppliers.

The interest is not, however, a distribution of surplus that fluctuates upwards above the maximum set either in the particular year or by paying compensation in later years. This reflects the cooperative concept of de-emphasising capital and limiting its reward and means that cooperative shares are not equity in the sense of an entitlement to a potentially unlimited return from ongoing profits or, indeed, entitlement to all surplus remaining on solvent dissolution.

This reflects the ICA Principle and deals with the difficulty raised by the use in previous guidance of the words 'a rate necessary to obtain and retain enough capital to run the business'. Those words could be interpreted to mean a market rate and even to extend to a rate related to profits. That created a danger of undermining the central cooperative idea of limiting the return on capital. Those words have now been modified to read 'the lowest rate sufficient to obtain the necessary funds from members who are committed to furthering the society's objects.'

The approach in most model rules over the years has been to set a maximum possible rate for both loan and share capital related to the rate set by the central bank on the basis that it should reflect the rate paid on bank deposits.

1.3.2.3. Right to Patronage Refunds?

It is clear from FCA Guidance 2015 and from CCBSA 2014 that the question of entitlement to a patronage refund is left to the society's own rules. The rules usually provide for a decision on the basis of a recommendation from the board of directors confirmed by a decision of the general meeting of members. The rules will often prevent the general meeting from deciding on a larger distribution than the board recommends but may well permit it to approve a lower amount than is recommended.

Once the decision has been made in accordance with the rules, members may well have a legally enforceable right to their refund. Before that point they will have no legal claim to a refund.

It is open to societies to provide no patronage refund or distribution to members but to build reserves or provide facilities for the use of members. This can be done either by making no provision for distributions to members in the rules or by choosing not to make any although the rules permit them.

1.4. COOPERATIVE SOCIAL OBJECT AND COOPERATIVE MEMBERSHIP (AND NON-USER, INVESTOR, MEMBERS)

For cooperatives, 2006 saw the liberalisation of FSA policy on the use of 'investor shares' for non-user investor members. Paragraphs 6.31 and 6.32 of FCA Guidance 2015 formulate FCA policy on these shares more succinctly than the extract from the 2006 FSA statement.

The relevant passages now read:

> 6.31 Generally co-operative societies offer membership to people who can use their services (whether as workers, producers or consumers). However, a co-operative society may sometimes need to raise capital from people who cannot or do not use the society's services. We describe these members as 'non-user investor members' – people who have only an investment relationship with the society.
>
> 6.32 While offering membership to non-user investor members gives a co-operative society access to capital, it also brings risks to its ability to comply with its condition for registration. The way capital is accessed must not compromise the society's compliance with the condition for registration. The following factors are indicators that the society is complying with its condition for registration as a bona fide co-operative society:
>
> - The rules of a society which wants to raise capital from non-user investor members expressly provide for non-user investor shares, and the terms attached to these shares are clearly stated
> - The voting rights of non-user investor shareholders are restricted by the rules of the society. The society's rules prevent this category of shareholders voting on a motion to convert the co-operative to a company. Societies can, however, include a power to elect one or more non-user investor share representatives to the board
> - Ultimate control of the society remains with members other than non-user investor members at all times. Non-user investor members do not together have voting rights that when combined would result in user-members losing control of the society.

This wording does not appear to change the substance of the 2006 FSA policy note. The 2006 change was uncontroversial among those consulted by the FSA as it addressed the need of cooperatives to raise capital.

However, this possibility for raising more capital may be of considerably more use and interest since the statutory limit on holdings by members other than cooperative or community benefit societies has been removed for non-withdrawable shares in societies.[18]

[18] CCBSA 2014, section 24.

1.5. COOPERATIVE ACTIVITY WITH MEMBERS: REGULATION

For most cooperatives, there is no particular regulation of transactions or other activities with members. Consumer cooperative members have the same rights against the cooperative from which they buy goods as any consumer would have against a retail business with which they made a contract. Similarly, the employee members of a worker cooperative have contracts of employment with the society which is their employer. Their rights under employment law are unaffected by their dual status as members of the cooperative. In both of these cases and in any other case in which a member makes a contract of purchase, sale or employment with their cooperative the fact that the society is registered and so has corporate personality permits contractual relationships between members and the cooperative society itself to be governed by the normal rules of contract law without regard to the membership of one party in the other.

In a case in which the nature of the business is such that particular legislative provisions apply between the parties, the usual regulatory provisions will apply if the legislation makes no different provision. One example of the exclusion of cooperatives from the usual regulatory provisions is the position of fully mutual housing cooperatives registered under CCBSA 2014. Such societies are excluded from provisions giving most social tenants (whose landlords are housing associations registered as community benefit societies or local authorities) security of tenure. For fully mutual cooperative society tenant-members the relationship is governed by the rules of the cooperative, the tenancy agreement, and the underlying case law.[19] A recent Supreme Court case confirms this absence of statutory regulation and indicates that the tenant-member's rights depend on the interpretation of the agreement between the cooperative and the tenant on the basis of its express terms, the context in which it was made, and the interaction of the agreement with the established case law on landlord and tenant.[20]

In another particular example, credit unions are regulated under the Financial Services and Markets Act 2000 as financial services organisations although they are subject to particular rules which may differ from those applicable to banks. That, however, is mainly due to the modest scale of credit union businesses and the limited range of activities that they are permitted to undertake, rather than to the particular nature of these societies as financial cooperatives.[21]

---

19 Housing Act 1985, section 80.

20 *Berrisford v Mexfield Housing Co-operative Limited* [2011] UKSC 52.

21 See Financial Conduct Authority, Credit Unions New Sourcebook (CREDS) at https://www.handbook.fca.org.uk/handbook/CREDS/1/1.html and Prudential Regulation Authority Credit Union Rulebook at http://www.prarulebook.co.uk/rulebook/Content/Part/320139/05-02-2016.

1.6. ACTIVITY WITH NON-MEMBERS

For tax purposes, a separate set of rules apply to a society seeking to argue that its distribution of surplus to members means that it has no profits for Corporation Tax purposes. To be allowed to do that, the society must be involved in 'mutual trading'. That means that the contributors to and participants in a surplus must be identical, the surplus must go back to contributors, surplus contributions must be returned and the members must control the common fund. A body will not pass the tests for mutual trading if its legal framework does not include these rules.[22] Most consumer cooperative societies will not meet these conditions because they trade with non-members as well as members. That means that they pay corporation tax on their profits.

Even where trading is not mutual, 'dividends' on purchases received by a trader from a cooperative society should be regarded as discounts and taken into account for tax purposes to the extent to which those purchases qualify for a tax deduction or allowance and 'dividends' on sales made by a trader to or through cooperative societies (for example, egg packing stations and auction societies) should be treated as additions to the sale proceeds and, therefore, as trading receipts.[23]

This separate treatment of the question of the nature of a cooperative for registration purposes and for tax makes the issue of trading only with members relatively unimportant as part of a cooperative definition in the UK. In addition, UK consumer cooperatives have long traded with non-members to a very considerable extent. The perception is that if all customers are able to become members and there are no artificial restrictions on membership, the cooperative principles are met. In that situation, profits from trade can be distributed to members despite the fact that a considerable proportion of the trade was with non-members.

There would, however, presumably come a point at which the FCA would decide that a very large proportion of trade with non-members called the society's status as a bona fide cooperative into question.

1.7. INDIRECT MUTUALITY (IN COOPERATIVE GROUPS)

This question is dealt with more fully in section 8.10. The basic UK position is that the legislation makes little explicit provision for the formation of groups by

---

22 HMRC, BIM24100 – Mutual trading: essential requirements, http://www.hmrc.gov.uk/manuals/bimmanual/BIM24100.htm.

23 *Pope v Beaumont* [1941] 24 TC 78 and HMRC, BIM24560 – Mutual trading: distributions: dividends from a co-operative society, http://www.hmrc.gov.uk/manuals/bimmanual/BIM24560.htm.

and from cooperative societies. However, section 3 of CCBSA 2014 lays down that a registered society is a corporate body. As such it is free to hold shares or otherwise be a member of any other society or company. Thus, one society can be a member of another and section 24(2) of CCBSA 2014 permits one registered society to hold an unlimited number of withdrawable shares in another while limiting the holding of other persons whether human beings or corporate bodies. In addition, the CCBSA 2014 provisions on accounting requirements for societies provide explicitly for group accounts to be kept by groups of societies or groups of societies and companies. Sections 100–102 of that Act define the expression subsidiary for that purpose in the context of one society being a subsidiary of another and of any other kind of corporate body (including a company) being a subsidiary of a society. This is a clear acknowledgment of the legality of groups of cooperatives and of mixed groups in which other types of corporate body are subsidiaries of cooperatives.

On the question of how a society's position as a subsidiary or a holding society can be reconciled with the definition of a cooperative, a starting point is section 2(2)(b) of CCBSA 2014 which allows a society to be registered with only two (rather than three) members if all its members are other registered societies.

FCA Guidance 2015 acknowledges that a cooperative society that is a subsidiary of another cooperative society must itself meet the registration requirement by being a bona fide cooperative. However, in examining this, the FCA will take the nature of the parent-subsidiary relationship into account. If the subsidiary's purpose is to meet the common economic, social and cultural needs and aspirations of the subsidiary's parent, the parent society's own members, the subsidiary's other member(s), and their members (if any), issues about open membership and autonomy will not present an obstacle even if membership is limited to a maximum of two members.[24]

However, where the parent of the cooperative society is not itself a cooperative society, this may be more difficult if the subsidiary's parent entity and other members exist 'only to fulfil economic need'.[25] This is the flip side of the FCA's willingness to look at the whole context of the group of which both parent and subsidiary are part. FCA Guidance 2015 also points out that the rules of the subsidiary must comply with the CCBSA 2014 and the FCA Guidance 2015 in the same way as those of any other society and cannot, for example, breach statutory thresholds by giving the parent extra votes on a conversion decision. Similarly, the way a cooperative parent society runs its subsidiary society must not compromise the parent society's compliance with CCBSA 2014.[26]

---

24 FCA Guidance 2015, para. 4.17.

25 FCA Guidance 2015, para. 4.18.

26 FCA Guidance 2015, paras. 4.19 and 4.20.

That last point may indicate the need for some element of control of the subsidiary by the members of the parent society through its board. As the Co-operatives UK, *Corporate Governance Code for Consumer Societies*, November 2013 points out under section C *The Role of The Board*:

> 35. The board should ensure that it has appropriate means of controlling and receiving information on any subsidiaries or related businesses ... 36. A report of the performance of subsidiaries and related businesses should be set out in the annual report.

1.8. COOPERATIVES WITH DIFFERENT/PARTICULAR SOCIAL OBJECT (AND SOCIAL COOPERATIVES)

Although the distinction between societies registered as bona fide cooperatives and those registered as community benefit societies is focused on the contrast between the objective of mutual member benefit in cooperatives and more altruistic objectives in other societies, a society can be structured as a cooperative and pursue altruistic objectives by, for example, stipulating such objectives in its rules and preventing any surplus distribution to members as patronage refund.

However, only community benefit societies and Community Interest Companies can, without the use of trust devices, ensure that it is impossible for the value of their assets to be released for other purposes.[27] It is always possible for a large enough majority of the members of a cooperative society, by one or more rule amendments, conversion to a different business structure, or dissolution, to unlock value for the members.[28]

1.9. COOPERATIVE SOCIAL OBJECT AND GOVERNANCE ISSUES: REFERENCE TO SECTION 2 'COOPERATIVE GOVERNANCE'

Issues about the governance of cooperatives will be fully explored in section 5. However, it can be noted here that democratic control by the membership is one of the key characteristics used by the FCA to decide whether a society qualifies as a bona fide cooperative. That is done by applying the ICA definition of a cooperative and the ICA's second principle.[29] Governance issues are further

27 CCBSA 2014, section 29, Community Benefit Societies (Restriction on Use of Assets) Regulations 2006 SI 2006/264 and Companies (Audit, Investigations and Community Enterprise) Act 2004, sections 26–56.

28 CCBSA 2014, sections 115–125.

29 FCA Guidance 2015, paras. 4.10–4.15.

elaborated by Co-operatives UK's Codes of Best Practice on Co-operative Governance for consumer, worker and agricultural cooperatives.[30]

2. COOPERATIVE GOVERNANCE

2.1. THE LEGAL CONTEXT OF COOPERATIVE GOVERNANCE

As indicated in section 1 of this chapter, the UK approach for cooperatives registered as or cooperative and community benefit societies is to leave most matters to the rules (statutes) of individual societies subject to the requirement that the society be and remain a bona fide cooperative as a condition of registration. This approach provides the theme for the topic of governance, subject only to a few exceptions.

2.1.1. Cooperative Governance and Cooperative Identity

This section deals with the link between the democratic control element of the cooperative definition and national rules about governance. The ICA defines a cooperative as 'a jointly-owned and democratically-controlled enterprise' based on values that include 'self-help, self-responsibility, democracy, equality, equity and solidarity'. The ICA Principle of Democratic Member Control lays down that:

> Co-operatives are democratic organisations controlled by their members, who actively participate in setting their policies and making decisions. Men and women serving as elected representatives are accountable to the membership. In primary co-operatives members have equal voting rights (one member, one vote) and co-operatives at other levels are also organised in a democratic manner.[31]

Similarly, the SCE regulation refers to the principle of 'democratic structure and control' as a defining feature of co-operatives.[32]

In UK law, the Co-operative and Community Benefit Societies Act 2014 (CCBSA 2014) requires a society to be a bona fide cooperative as a condition of registration under the legislation.

The FCA applies that test by requiring that cooperatives meet the ICA definition, including the requirement of democratic control. They also adopt the

30 http://www.uk.coop/developing-co-ops/grow-your-co-op/codes-governance/corporate-governance-code-consumer-co-operatives, http://www.uk.coop/resources/worker-co-operative-code and http://www.saos.coop/wp-content/uploads/2014/02/Agricultural-Code-Feb14-Final.pdf.

31 http://ica.coop/en/whats-co-op/co-operative-identity-values-principles.

32 Preamble, para. 7 of SCE Regulation 1435/2003.

ICA values and principles as the other key indicators that a society meets the legal requirement that it be a bona fide cooperative.[33] That imports the principle of democratic control quoted in section 2.1.1.

The ICA definition and principle are applied as an administrative matter by the FCA on the registration of a new society as a bona fide cooperative and on the registration of any amendment to the society's rules which is relevant to that requirement and the issue of member control. Initial registration as a cooperative society is conditional on the FCA being satisfied that the society is a bona fide cooperative and that its rules have provisions dealing with meetings and the election and removal of directors.[34] No amendment to a society's rules is effective until it has been registered with the FCA and any rule amendments must comply with the bona fide cooperative requirement.[35]

Thus in the UK compliance with this and other aspects of cooperative identity is dealt with as an administrative matter and not by the courts.

The ICA democratic control principle would normally require that the society's rules provide for some form of democratic election of the committee or board by the members and a similar process for their removal. Although the UK legislation does not explicitly require that decisions to amend the rules of the society should be made by the members in general meeting or should require any particular majority, a provision giving that function to the board or committee would probably be rejected by the FCA for failure to comply with the principle of democratic control of the society by members. A similar approach might be taken to any other society rules likely to inhibit democratic member control, including the number of unelected directors and the issue of non-member directors.

2.1.2. Cooperative Governance and UK Business Organisation Law

The UK legal culture generally leaves the detailed rules about the governance of business organisations to be decided by the articles of a registered company or the rules of a cooperative society (in each case, the equivalent of the statute of a business organisation under the Civil Law systems). That general principle is subject only to any provisions of the legislation governing the particular business structure requiring particular decisions to be made by either the general meeting or the board.[36]

Similarly, those setting up a business are usually free to choose any legal structure. As a result, a group wishing to function as a cooperative in the UK

33 FCA Guidance 2015, paras. 4.10–4.16.
34 CCBSA 2014, sections 2(2) and 14.
35 CCBSA 2014, section 16.
36 See section 2.1.3.

is free to use any legal form it chooses. That includes registering under the Companies Act 2006 or the Limited Liability Partnerships Act 2000 or operating as a partnership under the Partnership Act 1890. This is, however, subject to restrictions on the use of the word 'cooperative' in the name of a registered company or LLP or on carrying on business as an unregistered 1890 Act Partnership using the name.[37] The word 'cooperative' requires the permission of the Secretary of State for Business Innovation and Skills if it is to be used in the name of a registered company or LLP or if business is to be carried out using the name.[38]

CCBSA 2014 provides a legal structure specifically designed for cooperatives. Under that legislation, being a bona fide cooperative is a condition of both initial and continued registration as a cooperative society.[39]

Some of the contrasts between the legal rules to be found in the Companies Act 2006 and those laid down in CCBSA 2014 (a consolidating Act that did not change the substance of most of the legal rules) are due to the frequent and sometimes radical reforms applied to Company Law in the period since 1945 and the persistence of nineteenth-century provisions in the legislation governing societies. In the governance context, the Companies Act 2006 imposes mandatory rules requiring certain decisions to be made or approved by the general meeting of members more frequently than does the CCBSA 2014. This is particularly notable in the case of public limited companies with listed securities.

2.1.3. Where are Cooperative Governance Rules Found?

The principle of leaving the decision about the allocation of governance powers between the organs of a corporate body to those establishing the business structure is well established in the case law applicable to both companies registered under Companies Act 2006 and cooperative societies. The allocation

---

37 Companies Act 2006, sections 55(1) and 1194(1) and the Company, Limited Liability Partnership and Business Names (Sensitive Words and Expressions) Regulations 2014 SI 2014/3140, schedule 1.

38 Guidance on the Registrar of Companies' website indicates that only companies limited by guarantee are usually permitted to use the word 'co-operative' in their name and that more information will be needed before the use of the word will be permitted by any company – http://www.companyregistrations.co.uk/sensitive-name-issues.aspx. Information provided in 2009 by the Registrar of Companies in response to a Freedom of Information Act request from www.software.coop revealed that about 10% of the total of 1,342 companies using the word in their name had been registered between 2006 and 2009. This was felt by some to raise doubts about how carefully the use of the word was policed so as to limit its use to companies following Co-operative Principles, http://www.news.software.coop/whats-in-a-name-co-operative-in-names-at-companies-house/797/. Policing the rule for unregistered partnerships is presumably even more difficult.

39 CCBSA, sections 2(3) and 5.

of powers and functions between the general meeting of members and the board of a company or society is made by the constitution of the corporate body rather than being laid down in the legislation. Once the powers have been allocated, the members' meeting cannot usually make decisions in the areas allocated to the board.[40] The freedom to allocate powers in the constitution is subject only to any specific legislative provisions which allocate particular powers and, in the case of societies, to the power of the FCA to enforce the bona fide cooperative registration requirement.

Constraints on that freedom are found in the few explicit provisions of the legislation which require certain decisions to be made, or functions to be carried out, either by the members in general meeting or by the board of directors (or committee as it is called in the legislation). For example, certain fundamental structural changes to a society can be achieved only by following a procedure laid down in the legislation. Thus dissolution of the society, transfers of its engagements to another society or a company, the amalgamation of two societies and the conversion of a society into a company all require decisions by the members in general meeting with particular majorities and following specified procedures.[41] Similarly, the duty to ensure that proper accounts are kept is primarily imposed on the directors or committee members of the society but the appointment and removal of an auditor of the society's accounts is a matter for the general meeting of members.[42] Those sections when read with section 149 of CCBSA 2014 seem to indicate that a society should have a 'committee of management or other directing body'.

In the case of cooperatives registered as societies, the majority required to amend the society constitution is left by the legislation to be laid down in the society constitution itself, although there must be some provision for amendment.[43] A cooperative registered as a company under the Companies Act 2006 must use a special resolution requiring a 75% majority of those voting in person or by proxy or a higher majority laid down in the company's articles.[44]

2.2. THE ROLE OF THE MEMBERS

The ICA requires active participation by members in setting the cooperative's policies and making decisions plus accountability by the elected representatives to the membership. The SCE Regulation echoes this requirement (see section 2.1.1). In general, UK Law leaves this issue to be dealt with in each

40 Automatic Self Cleansing Filter Syndicate Co v Cunninghame [1906] 2 Ch 34 CA.
41 CCBSA 2014, sections 109–114.
42 CCBSA 2014, sections 75, 83 and 93 to 96.
43 CCBSA 2014, sections 14(5) and 16.
44 Companies Act 2006 sections 21–27 and 283.

society's rules (statutes) subject to the bona fide cooperative requirement laid down in CCBSA 2014, which is implemented by administrative decision.

2.2.1. *The Division of Powers Among the Organs of the Cooperative*

In the case of societies, because the law is older than the companies legislation, more is left to be determined by the rules. On the other hand, a society must satisfy the FCA, as registrar, that it is a bona fide cooperative and that will, as noted above, involve an application of principles broadly based on the ICA Principle of democratic control by the members.

By contrast in most civil law, and some common law, jurisdictions, the powers of each organ will be specified comprehensively in the cooperative law as it would be in the Company Law.

This part of the chapter concentrates on the powers and role of the members' meeting while section 2.2.3, deals with the powers of a society's board or committee.

The implications of the ICA Principle on this question seem to be that the organ directly representing members (members' general meeting or at least a delegate meeting) should have a major role in setting policy and making decisions. The latter point may indicate that at least certain major decisions should be reserved to the members rather than being allocated to the board. As noted below, the UK system for the division of powers between the society's organs leaves this to a particular society's rules (statutes), and many of the requirements about the involvement of members are left to the non-binding corporate governance codes published by the Co-operative Movement rather than being the subject of legally binding rules or principles.[45]

2.2.2. *Member Voting Rights: One Member/One Vote or Variations from it*

The ICA states that: 'in primary co-operatives members have equal voting rights (one member/one vote) and co-operatives at other levels are also organised in a democratic manner'.[46] While SCE's complex provisions are that, in general, each member has one vote.[47]

In the UK, the FCA Guidance 2015, paras. 4.10–4.13, and the ICA Definition and principle 2 on democratic control of cooperatives quoted in those paragraphs make it clear that one member/one vote is a fundamental requirement for cooperatives. Para. 4.13 of FCA Guidance 2015 states that the FCA will examine compliance with the democratic control principle by considering society rules and rule amendments.

---

45 See section 2.3.2.

46 See section 2.1.1.

47 SCE Regulation, art, 59(1).

In the case of non-user investor members, FCA Guidance 2015 preserves overall FCA discretion to assess whether the introduction of such members threatens the status of the society as a bona fide cooperative but provides, in para. 6.32, that:

> While offering membership to non-user investor members gives a co-operative society access to capital, it also brings risks to its ability to comply with its condition for registration. The way capital is accessed must not compromise the society's compliance with the condition for registration. The following factors are indicators that the society is complying with its condition for registration as a bona fide co-operative society:
>
> - The rules of a society which wants to raise capital from non-user investor members expressly provide for non-user investor shares, and the terms attached to these shares are clearly stated.
> - The voting rights of non-user investor shareholders are restricted by the rules of the society. The society's rules prevent this category of shareholders voting on a motion to convert the co-operative to a company. Societies can, however, include a power to elect one or more non-user investor share representatives to the board.
> - Ultimate control of the society remains with members other than non-user investor members at all times. Non-user investor members do not together have voting rights that when combined would result in user-members losing control of the society.

In the case of large societies spread over a wide geographical area, it may be necessary for decision-making to be divided between a number of different levels of council or committee, each elected by the body below it. Members will elect those delegates who are to represent them and, indeed, there may be further indirect election from that body. The rules, or regulations made under them, will define the powers, role and function of each level of delegate meeting as well as setting out their relationship with the board of the society – see section 2.3.2 for a discussion of the example of the UK Co-operative Group.

2.2.3. Mechanisms for Member Control: Meetings, Elections etc.

The ICA emphasises member control and refers to active participation by members in setting policies and making decisions as well as the accountability of elected representatives to the members.

In the UK, the FCA only lays down the general principle set out in section 2.2.2) but it will scrutinise rules and amendments to them before registration in respect of:

> The method of holding meetings, the scale and right of voting, and the method of making, altering or rescinding rules.

This enables the FCA to judge whether the society conforms to the principle of member control, but it does not lay down particular detailed rules. To illustrate the reality of how societies work, this section now considers common practices among UK cooperative societies.

In addition, there are some particular provisions in the CCBSA 2014 about meetings which are dealt with in section 2.2.3.1, section 2.2.3.2 attempts to summarise common approaches in the rules of UK cooperatives.

2.2.3.1. Provisions of the Legislation as to Meetings

The CCBSA 2014 does not lay down any general rules as to the types of meeting that a society might call, how often they should be called, the notice needed for meetings or resolutions, or the majority required for particular resolutions.

Its provisions indicate, however, that a society's rules should provide for at least one annual meeting at which audited accounts can be presented and that the rules should deal with the calling of the meetings needed for particular decisions such as the alteration of the rules. On certain matters, such as a transfer of engagements or the amalgamation of the society, the Act lays down specific requirements. More fundamentally, the FCA would refuse to register rules which did not provide for sufficient meetings to allow for democratic control. The society would not then be a bona fide cooperative or meet the other requirement of section 2(2) of CCBSA 2014.

Section 149 of CCBSA 2014 provides for meetings to be delegate meetings if the rules of a society permit it. This would apply to a society which had other societies as its members, for example a secondary cooperative, or to a very large society.

CCBSA 2014 lays down requirements about meetings for certain particular situations:

(a) Sections 109–114 of CCBSA 2014 require a 'special resolution' and lay down rules about procedures and majorities for:
   (i) the amalgamation of two societies;
   (ii) a transfer of engagements from one society to another; and
   (iii) the conversion of a society into a company.

(b) When procedures laid down in the Insolvency Act 1986 are to be followed to wind up a society under section 123 of CCBSA 2014, special meetings with particular periods of notice and majorities laid down by that Act or the Companies Act 2006 are needed.

(c) The FCA has power under sections 106 and 107 of CCBSA 2014 to call a meeting if one tenth of a society's members (or 100 members if there are more than 1,000 members) apply to them. The FCA can direct when and where such a meeting is to be held and what is to be discussed and decided there. The meeting can appoint its own chair regardless of the provisions of the society's rules and has all the powers of a meeting called under those rules. Applicants who ask the FCA to convene a meeting should give reasons for their application to show the FCA that it is not malicious, and the FCA may require them to give security for the costs of the meeting. Notice of the application must be given to the society in the way laid down by the FCA.

(d) The accounts of a society must be audited, if the society cannot or does not opt to disapply those requirements under section 84 of CCBSA 2014. Section 82 of CCBSA 2014 regulates the publication of the revenue account and balance sheet whether or not the society has opted out of a full audit and regardless of whether it is required to obtain an accountant's report. This implies that the accounts should be presented to a meeting of the society. If auditors are to be replaced, a special procedure must be followed. Auditors have a right to attend a society's general meeting and to be heard on matters which concern them as auditors. Reporting accountants appointed for a year in which the society has disapplied the audit requirement but has a turnover in excess of £90,000, have special rights of audience at society general meetings in respect of their report or other matters relevant to their functions.[48]

2.2.3.2. Common Provisions of Society Rules about Meetings

(a) Types of Meeting

Rules will usually define two classes of meeting: an annual general and a special or extraordinary general meeting. This is an example of a provision which, under the Companies Act 2006, is laid down in the legislation but which for societies is left to the rules (statutes) of each society.

The annual general meeting will be required to receive the accounts, balance sheet and auditors' report and to consider a report by the board or committee. It will elect the committee or board, or at least the part of it retiring that year, if that is not done by ballot of the members. The rules will usually allow that meeting to deal with any other business specified on the notice calling it. The rules will often give the secretary or the board the responsibility for calling the annual meeting but they will specify a time for it within a limited period after the end of the accounting year. Some societies may require a regular six-monthly meeting to receive accounts and reports for the half year between annual meetings. It is

48 CCBSA 2014, sections 93–96.

unlikely that the FCA would allow the registration of rules which provided for general meetings to be held less often than once a year after the society was up and running.

Rules will usually provide for a special or extraordinary meeting to consider matters mentioned in the notice by which it was called. Such a meeting can usually be called either by the board of the society or by the requisition of a proportion of the total membership or a fixed number of members.

In addition to provisions as to annual and special general meetings, the rules of small societies concerned to retain a large measure of direct democratic control will require frequent meetings. This is particularly common in worker cooperatives.

In the case of all meetings, certain general questions will arise and should be dealt with by the rules of a society.

(b) Notice

The rules of a society will usually lay down periods of notice for calling meetings and for particular types of resolution. The amendment of the rules or the expulsion of a member may also be the subject of such provisions. They may require that notice be posted to individual members and the secretaries of corporate members. On the other hand, they may only require that it be prominently displayed in a place which members frequent such as the workplace for a worker cooperative, the stores of a consumer cooperative or the club notice board for a working men's club. The provisions of the rules about notice must be scrupulously followed. Even if the rules make no provision, failure to give adequate notice can still invalidate a meeting's decision.[49] The rules of many societies lay down that the business of a special general meeting is to be limited to that stated in the notice convening it.

(c) Quorum

The rules usually lay down a quorum for meetings. This can be a fixed number or a proportion of the membership. If this is not reached, the meeting cannot take place. To overcome this, many rules provide for an inquorate general meeting to be adjourned (perhaps for one week) and for the adjourned meeting to be able to transact business regardless of the numbers attending. Rules frequently lay down that a meeting which is quorate at the beginning cannot become incompetent because it later becomes inquorate. If the rules do not fix a quorum, the common law lays down two as the minimum number that can constitute a meeting.[50]

---

49 See *Young v Ladies' Imperial Club* [1920] 2 KB 532 and *MacLelland v National Union of Journalists* [1975] ICR 116.

50 *Sharp v Dawes* (1876) 2 QBD 26.

(d) The Chair

It will be necessary for someone to chair a meeting to ensure the efficient execution of business and to keep order. This is a matter for the rules. Many societies will have a president or chairperson elected by either the members or the committee to perform this task at both general meetings and committee or board meetings. If that person is not present at a meeting or is unwilling to take the chair, the rules may provide for a person elected vice-chair to step in. Otherwise they may specify that the job is to be done by any director present or by a member chosen by the meeting. Some rules will allow each meeting to choose its own chair, which is the position if the rules are silent on the question.

(e) Procedure

This is often determined by the standing orders of the society. The rules may give the board power to draft these latter. In some societies, the rules themselves set out the procedures to be followed. There are generally accepted conventions such as the requirement for a proposer and a seconder for resolutions and the order of speeches by proposer and seconder with the right of reply by the proposer after the debate. They will operate in the absence of any standing orders or provisions in the society's rules. The chair will make rulings on such matters as which speakers are to be heard and how long contributions should last. However, such rulings can be challenged, in which case a vote of the whole meeting is necessary to decide whether to uphold the chair's ruling. It is preferable to have provisions in the rules so that members are aware of them from the beginning without the need to consult another document. The size of a society's membership will determine how many detailed procedural rules are necessary.

(f) Voting

Voting procedures are often set out in some detail in the rules of societies. Voting will usually be by show of hands, but the rules may provide for a secret ballot of the members present. The normal principle for non-federal societies is one member/one vote. The rules should deal with the issue of whether members can appoint proxies to vote on their behalf and, if this is allowed, the procedure for authorising a proxy and notifying the society of their identity. The rules governing the representatives of corporate members should also be set out. The rules may state which of two or more joint members can vote (e.g. the first listed in the register). Rules will normally allow most decisions to be made by a simple majority of the total of those present and voting and those voting by proxy. However, the amendment of the rules or the expulsion of a member may be stated to need a special majority of, for example, two thirds or three quarters. CCBSA 2014 requires a special majority for a transfer of engagements, the amalgamation of societies, or the conversion of a society into a company.[51] The chair is normally given a casting vote by the rules.

If a society's rules are silent on the question of the right of members to vote through a proxy, members must attend and vote in person.[52] However, the common law permits a society's rules to provide for proxies. The legislation makes no specific provision allowing or prohibiting the practice, and as long as such rules do not limit or affect the right of members to participate in voting or decision-making, the FCA will not limit the society's freedom. A society's rules may expressly prohibit proxies, provide only for other members to be used as proxies, or limit the number of members a particular proxy may represent.

Although most rules provide for a majority of those voting, some may require a particular majority of those entitled to vote.

(g) Adjournment

Rules will often include a power to adjourn a meeting and limit the business of the adjourned meeting to that which was unfinished at the original meeting.

2.2.4. Dispute Resolution between Members and the Cooperative

CCBSA 2014 provides for the resolution of disputes between societies and their members. These provisions facilitate the use of arbitration – usually a cheaper, quicker and more private means of resolving disputes than resort to the courts. In addition, certain of the provisions of CCBSA 2014 allow for proceedings in the county court or magistrates court rather than the High Court.

2.2.4.1. The Parties

Section 137 of CCBSA 2014 provides machinery for the settlement of disputes. That machinery may be used when the party on one side of the dispute is a society or an officer of the society. This includes all committee or board members, the treasurer, the secretary, a manager and any employee except one appointed by the committee but it excludes the auditor of the society.[53]

The party on the other side must be:

(a) a member of the society; or
(b) a person aggrieved who has ceased to be a member within the previous six months; or

51 CCBSA 2014, sections 109–114.
52 *Harben v Phillips* (1883) 23 Ch D 14 CA.
53 CCBSA 2014, section 149.

(c) a person claiming through a member or such an aggrieved person; or
(d) a person claiming under the rules of the society.

A 'person aggrieved' is one who has suffered a legal loss or liability or who has been deprived of some right by the fault of another or made to bear some burden or detriment.[54] The courts have decided that an expelled member cannot use this heading even if the parties agree that he or she was a member within the six months required by the Act and although one might think that expulsion was a grievance.[55]

A person 'claiming under the rules' covers non-members or members whose disputes with the society are in some other capacity. Thus a holder of loan capital which is dealt with under the rules could fall into this category.[56] Similarly, someone refused membership under the rules might seek to challenge that decision by the use of this procedure.

2.2.4.2. The Dispute

Although section 137(1) of CCBSA 2014 provides that every dispute between the parties described above may be settled as provided in the rules, the machinery is meant to apply to disputes arising out of the rules of the society and the relationship between the member and the society. The test is whether the dispute affects a member as such in the sense that the rights being enforced are those derived from membership.

A dispute which concerns the validity of the rules themselves or the question of whether the society has acted beyond its powers cannot be dealt with by the arbitration process but must be resolved by the courts.[57]

2.2.4.3. Who Decides?

A dispute of the kind referred to in the Act can be decided by anyone named in the society's rules.[58] If a society's rules have the effect that the FCA or the PRA would have to decide disputes, section 137(3) of CCBSA 2014 lays down that the dispute will be decided by the county court in England or the sheriff in Scotland.

The exclusion of a right to arbitration by the FCA as registrar since 1992 means that the use of arbitration rather than a court to decide disputes depends on the rules allowing this. If they are silent, disputes will be decided by the courts.[59]

---

54 *Robinson v Currey* [1881] 7 QBD 465.
55 *Judson v Ellesmere Port Ex-Servicemen's Club* (1948) 2 KB 52 CA.
56 Per Somervell LJ in *Judson v Ellesmere Port Ex-Servicemen's Club* (1948) 2 KB 52, 60.
57 *McEllistrim v Ballymacelligot Co-operative Agricultural and Dairy Society* (1919) AC 548.
58 CCBSA 2014, section 137(1).
59 CCBSA 2014, sections 138–140.

2.2.4.4. Settlement Under the Rules

If the rules of a society provide a procedure for the settlement of disputes covered by these provisions then that procedure is to be followed. This is the most common method of dispute resolution for societies.

The rules of a society may provide for the election of arbitrators by the members. They may lay down that arbitrators are to be appointed by a sponsoring organisation covering the appropriate sector such as the Co-operatives UK or other bodies which provide model rules and central services for particular types of society. No one with an interest in the dispute – such as the officers of the society involved – may be appointed.

2.3. MANAGEMENT AND INTERNAL CONTROL

ICA applies the one member/one vote rule to the election of directors subject to other appropriate means for secondary or tertiary cooperatives. It requires accountability by elected officials.

The SCE Regulation provides, in some detail, for either a two-tier or a one-tier board system.[60]

The UK law leaves substantial freedom to cooperative societies to provide in their own statutes for their own board structure so long as directors are elected by the members and can be removed from office by them. Under the legislation, the rules of any registered cooperative are required to deal with:

> The appointment and removal of a committee, by whatever name, and of managers or other officers and their respective powers and remuneration.[61]

This enables the FCA to judge whether the society conforms to the principle of member control.

2.3.1. Powers of a Cooperative's Board or Boards: The UK Legislation and the Case Law

Few of the legal rules governing the committee or board of a society and its senior employees are to be found in CCBSA 2014. The other sources for those rules are the rule book of each particular society and the case law developed by the courts in the context of company directors. In the case of all employees, including senior managers, the terms of the contract of service will lay down

60 Council Regulation 2003/1435 of 22 July 2003 on the Statute for a European Cooperative Society [2003] OJ L 207 of 18.8.2003, articles 36–51.

61 CCBSA 2014, section 14(6).

certain duties, and others will be implied by the courts because the contract exists.

Some societies will describe their governing body as a committee. Others will refer to it as a board. The words used make no difference to the legal position of the organ or the individual directors or committee members. As noted below, some societies operate *de facto* two-tier systems or complex committee and delegate structures – see section 2.3.2.

The democratic control required of the constitution of a society usually takes the form of a division of powers between the general meeting of members, on the one hand, and the committee or board of directors on the other. Provided that the board is elected by the members, the system remains democratic. The size and diversity of some societies may require a range of different boards or committees dealing with either specialist subjects (e.g. a member relations committee in a consumer cooperative) or different geographical areas (e.g. regional boards from which a central board is elected). Many societies will have senior employees who perform a management role under the supervision of the board or committee. They can provide expertise and management skills. Traditionally, the boards of societies, unlike company boards, have usually been composed mainly of elected part-time non-executive members. Similarly, individual directors or committee members of most UK consumer cooperatives have had no management role in the society outside their position as directors or committee members. The boards of most companies, on the other hand, are full-time executive directors, but those with shares listed on the London Stock Exchange are required to have a substantial number of independent non-executive directors and to give certain roles, such as membership of the Audit Committee, to such board directors.[62]

Since the collapse of the UK Co-operative Bank and the major financial crisis of the Co-operative Group in 2013, changes to the Co-operative Group's constitution have moved it closer to the model used by company boards with a process of recruitment for executive and non-executive directors with commercial experience and expertise being undertaken by a board nomination committee and the society members having the role of endorsing or refusing to endorse the nominees put to them on the basis of one member/one vote across the whole society at an annual general meeting. The governance structure involves an allocation of powers among the members' general meeting, a members' council, and the board. The board consists of seven independent non-executive directors nominated by the board after a recommendation by its Nominations Committee and endorsed or rejected by a majority vote at the general meeting without a contested election. A minority of four directors are nominated by

62 See Financial Reporting Council, The UK Corporate Governance Code, at http://www.frc.org.uk/Our-Work/Publications/Corporate-Governance/UK-Corporate-Governance-Code-September-2012.aspx.

members and elected, sometimes in contested elections in which all members can vote. Two directors can be executive directors (the chief executive and one other). The member's council deals with 'cooperative' matters, and the board with the running of the business. Apart from the Co-operative Group Ltd, most UK consumer cooperatives use the traditional system of having an elected non-executive board on which full-time executives do not serve.

CCBSA 2014 lays down some of the functions of the board or committee. Sections 37–40 of the Act require it to deal with the property of members who have died or who are mentally incapable. Section 41 gives it power to decide the form and amount of any security to be provided by the society's officers if the society's rules make such provision. Section 53 empowers any two committee members to sign written contracts or other formal documents on behalf of the society. Otherwise the role of the committee or board is to be laid down in the society's rules.

The powers of the board or committee must be set out in the rules.[63] This is usually done by laying down that the board or committee will manage or conduct the business of the society. The rules often state that the board or committee will act in all things in the name of the society and on its behalf. Some rules will list particular functions, such as buying and selling goods or hiring and dismissing employees, but this may be said to be without prejudice to the more general power to manage the society's business.

It is often the practice for rules to follow the provisions commonly found in the articles of companies. This will give the board power to do anything which the society can do and which is not required by the law or other provisions of the rules to be done by the general meeting. This wide power may also be made subject to any direction given by the general meeting, but some special majority may be required by the rules for such a direction.

These powers are conferred on the board or committee as a body. Individual directors or committee members will be able to act only if they are authorised to do so by the board, but the rules will usually allow for such delegation of power to a sub-committee or individuals. Some rules will set out that the society is to have a chief executive officer and will lay down the powers of that person. They may also give particular powers to committees which are to perform particular functions such as a member relations committee in a consumer cooperative or a loans committee in a credit union. In that case the powers of those bodies derive from the rules and are defined by them. If there is no such provision, sub-committees or particular full-time officers will have the powers delegated to them by the board in accordance with the rule permitting such delegation.

The law allows the rules of a society to define the powers of the board or committee and the general meeting as they choose. Once that division of powers

63 CCBSA 2014, section 14(6).

is laid down in the rules, neither body can interfere in the exercise by the other of its own powers. This means that the power of members in general meeting to control the board or committee is limited to their right to amend the division of powers set out in the rules for the future, to remove directors or committee members in accordance with the rules' provisions as to that, to refuse to re-elect particular board or committee members when they reach the end of their term of office or, if the rules allow for it, to pass a special direction requiring the board to behave in a particular way in the future. What the general meeting may not do is to make a decision on a matter which is within the powers of the board or amend the rules (or give a direction) with retrospective effect.[64] Likewise, the board cannot decide on a question which the rules leave to the general meeting.

It is permissible for the secretary to refuse to accept a resolution for the agenda of the general meeting which instructs the board how to deal with a matter which the rules leave to them. However, a resolution which recommends a course of action to the board is permissible.[65]

Rules will commonly specify the role of the secretary of the society and give that officer responsibility for submitting annual returns, calling meetings when requested to do so, and maintaining records and minutes (including the register of officers and members). Most of the documents required by CCBSA 2014 to be submitted for registration purposes have to be signed by the secretary.[66]

The frequency of board meetings may be laid down by the rules, which often allow meetings to be called as required but specify a minimum number to be held each year. Rules may lay down basic procedural rules such as the quorum for board meetings, who is to chair them, whether there is a casting vote, and that decisions are to be by a majority of those voting. A certain number of directors or committee members may be empowered to call special board or committee meetings to discuss matters specified in the notice of the meeting given to the secretary. More detailed procedural rules as to the running of committee or board meetings may be contained in standing orders made by the committee or board under a power given in the society's rules.

The rules often lay down that decisions of the board or committee are not affected by defects in the appointment of the board or committee or any of its members.

---

64 *Automatic Self-Cleansing Filter Syndicate Company Ltd v Cunninghame* [1906] 2 Ch 34 lays down this rule in the context of companies. The same approach was applied to cooperative societies by the Scottish Court of Session case of *Alexander v Duddy* (1956) SC 24 and 1956 SLT 146 and, in England, by *Roper v Long Eaton Co-operative Society Ltd* (1952) Chief Registrar of Friendly Societies Report Part 3, page 3, an arbitration case decided before 1992 when the Registrar of Friendly Societies' arbitration role was removed.

65 *Ruddock v Watford Co-operative Society Ltd* (1956) Chief Registrar's Report Part 3, page 3.

66 See, for example, CCBSA 2014, section 3(1).

The directors of UK cooperative societies using the co-operative society form have duties developed and defined by judge-made law. They are outlined briefly here. The duties are owed to the registered cooperative society as a legal person and not to the members of the society as natural persons. As a result, they can only usually be enforced by the society itself. The duties may be listed as:[67]

(a) A duty to act in accordance with the society's constitution and only to exercise powers for the purposes for which they were conferred.[68]
(b) A duty to act bona fide in what they consider to be the interests of the society.[69]
(c) A duty to exercise independent judgment except where acting otherwise but either in a way authorised by the society's rules (statutes) or in accordance with an agreement entered into by the society which restricted the future exercise of discretion of directors.[70]
(d) A duty to exercise reasonable care, skill and diligence as measured by the standard of a reasonably diligent person with both the knowledge, skill and experience to be expected of a person carrying out that director's functions in relation to that society and the general skill, knowledge and experience that the director actually has.[71]
(e) A duty to avoid any situation in which he or she has or can have a direct or indirect interest that may possibly conflict with the interests of the society unless the matter concerned was authorised by the society or could not reasonably be regarded as likely to give rise to a conflict of interest.[72] This usually takes the form, under the rules of a society, of a duty to declare his or her interest in any proposed transaction or arrangement of the society.
(f) A duty not to accept benefits from third parties that are conferred by reason of being a director or doing or not doing anything as a director.[73]
(g) A duty not to misuse the society's information, profits or business opportunities for personal benefit or the benefit of anyone else.[74]
(h) A duty not to disclose confidential information that the director knows or ought to know is fairly and reasonably regarded as confidential.[75]

---

67 This list draws on sections 172-177 of the Companies Act 2006 which codified and, in some cases changed the duties applicable to directors of companies. Societies are still subject to the judge-made law which was codified by those sections and that is used and is cited here.
68 *Eclairs Group Ltd v JKX Oil & Gas PLC* [2015] UKSC 71.
69 *Re Smith v Fawcett Ltd* [1942] Ch 304.
70 *Dovey v Cory* [1901] AC 477.
71 *Re D'Jan of London Ltd* [1993] BCC 646.
72 *Aberdeen Railway Company v Blaikie* (1854) 1 Macq 461.
73 *Philip Towers v Premier Waste Management Ltd* [2011] EWCA Civ 923.
74 See, for example, *Regal (Hastings) Ltd v Gulliver* [1942] 1 All ER 178 and *Bhullar v Bhullar* [2003] 2 BCLC 241.
75 *Attorney General v Guardian Newspapers (No. 2)* [1990] 1 AC 109.

Breach of these duties entitles the society, as a legal person, to seek compensation for loss or the profits made by a director from his or her breach.

2.3.2. Board Functioning, Structure and Composition

The flexibility of the UK system allows the use of a wide range of governance arrangements according to the needs of the cooperative. That may vary with the size of the society and the feasibility of direct member participation. It may lead to delegate or indirect election systems in large societies and it allows *de facto* one- or two-tier board systems. In the case of larger and more complex societies, the 'agency' issue about the expertise and role of non-executive member-directors and the accountability of expert managers (whether they are board members or not) arises just as acutely as it does in investor owned companies.

In a cooperative with a small membership, for example some workers' cooperatives, the founders may choose to design a completely collective structure with all decisions made by meetings of all members.[76] This can be done by making all members also directors so that the requirement that the society must have a committee and officers is satisfied. A member who is removed from the board may be regarded as being expelled from the society.

Where worker cooperatives, whether structured as societies, companies or partnerships, choose to have separate organs for member decisions and day to day control or monitoring, the Code for Worker Co-operatives indicates a tendency to have a much greater role for the members' meeting than is the case for other societies, such as consumer cooperatives. The Code reflects their smaller membership, simpler structures, flatter management systems, and preference for direct democracy. It emphasises key principles, is extremely user friendly and advocates the availability of information to all worker members to facilitate participation in management. It also acknowledges the use of a wide range of legal structures by worker cooperatives which may use limited liability partnerships or companies instead of cooperative societies. Consumer cooperatives generally use the industrial and provident society structure.

By contrast, in complex cooperatives with a large membership, such as large consumer cooperatives, a system of indirect democracy was traditionally used. For example, in the Co-operative Group Ltd, before 2013, members at the base level elected area committee members. All the area committees in a region elected a regional board and also the membership of the central board of the cooperative society from their region. The number of board members from each region was reviewed from time to time so that the balance reflected the purchases of the consumer members in the different regions.[77]

---

76 See Co-operatives UK, *Code for Worker Co-operatives*, 2nd ed., 2012, http://www.uk.coop/sites/default/files/worker_co-operative_code_2nd_edition.pdf.

77 Co-operative Group Ltd Rules, November 2010, amended May 2012.

Since the collapse of the UK Co-operative Bank and the major financial crisis of the Co-operative Group in 2013, changes to the Co-operative Group's constitution have moved it closer to the model used by company boards with a process of recruitment for executive and non-executive directors with commercial experience and expertise being undertaken by a board nomination committee and the society members having the role of endorsing or refusing to endorse the nominees put to them on the basis of one member/one vote across the whole society at an annual general meeting. The governance structure involves an allocation of powers among the members' general meeting, a members' council, and the board. The board consists of seven independent non-executive directors nominated by the board after a recommendation by its Nominations Committee and endorsed or rejected by a majority vote at the general meeting without a contested election. A minority of four directors are nominated by members and elected, sometimes in contested elections in which all members can vote. Two directors can be executive directors (the Chief Executive and one other). The members' council deals with 'cooperative' matters and the board with the running of the business, but the council reports to members on board performance and plays a role in the process of nominating some of the non-executive directors.[78]

Apart from the Co-operative Group Ltd, most UK consumer cooperatives use the traditional system of having an elected non-executive board on which full-time executives do not serve.[79]

Generally, the culture of UK business organisations has involved having a single unitary board, and CCBSA 2014 might be thought to imply that a single committee rather than a two-tier structure is required. However, the flexibility of the UK system permits the use of either a unitary board of directors or a two-tier board system with a supervisory board and management board. Similarly, in the case of a unitary board, the question of whether only elected directors without full-time executive roles in the society serve or whether appointed executives are also board members is left to each society to decide as long as the FCA accepts that the society is still controlled by its members. In many UK cooperatives it is customary for the board to comprise solely elected 'non-executive' directors and for the executive managers to attend board meetings without being directors. However, issues have arisen about the need, in such a system, for co-opted or appointed independent directors to provide the expertise needed to hold the executives to account for their performance. This and similar issues have been addressed by the UK Co-operative Movement by the development of Codes of Conduct which

---

78 Co-operative Group Ltd Rules, May 2015, http://www.co-operative.coop/PageFiles/350358825/Co-operative-Group-Registered-Rules.pdf.

79 See for example, Rules of the Scottish Midland Co-operative Society, 26 June 2014, as amended 30 September 2014, rules 17–22 and 40–43, http://www.scotmid.coop/wp-content/uploads/2013/05/Download-our-Society-Rules.pdf.

have no legal force but provide guidance to societies as the Financial Reporting Council's Corporate Governance Code does for listed companies.[80]

The Code of Best Practice on Corporate Governance for Consumer Co-operatives issued by Co-operatives UK recommends that all societies should have just such a document allocating powers in that way.[81]

In the Code, the centrality of member control and participation and the role of the board in directing the society and holding senior managers to account is emphasised. One aspect of that is ensuring that the directors have, between them, the skills and ability necessary to do that. Issues such as succession planning, training and development programmes for directors, and the appraisal of the board are dealt with in that context. It is suggested that professional outside directors might be appointed in some cases to complement the skills and abilities of the elected directors. Good communications between the directors and the financial auditors are emphasised, and the use of an audit committee of the board to consider the society's Annual Report and Accounts and the views of the auditors as expressed in a management letter is a central feature of the Code. In addition, it is recommended that every society should have a list of matters reserved to the board for decision so that the decisions devolved to executive managers are limited.[82] The practice of defining decisions that must be referred to the board resembles the division of functions between a supervisory board and a management board, particularly when executives are not board members and meet separately between board meetings.

In terms of communication with members and the use of 'virtual' meetings, the rules of a society may, at common law, provide for meetings to take place through electronic communication so long as members can 'attend in person so as to debate and vote on matters'. That may be achieved through the use of modern technology which permits 'real time' communication so that the members can see and hear what is going on and contribute.[83] The *Byng* case which concerned a meeting required by the Companies Act, does not prevent society rules from allowing 'non-real time' decisions by, for example, the circulation of documents and information to members for decision, or holding elections by post or electronic means – as long as the decision in question is not required by the legislation to be made at a 'meeting', as is the case for decisions discussed about fundamental transformations of the society.[84]

---

80 https://www.frc.org.uk/Our-Work/Codes-Standards/Corporate-governance.aspx.

81 Recommendation B1.1, http://www.uk.coop/sites/default/files/corporate-governance-code-of-best-practice_0.pdf, and see Appendix 5 for details, http://www.uk.coop/sites/default/files/appendices-to-the-code-of-best-practice_0_0.pdf.

82 Co-operatives UK, *Corporate Governance the Code of Best Practice for consumer co-operatives*, 2013, provision 26 on p. 9, http://www.uk.coop/sites/default/files/uploads/attachments/governance_code_0.pdf.

83 *Byng v London Life Association Ltd* [1990] 1 Ch 170 at 183.

84 CCBSA 2014, sections 109–114.

CCBSA 2014 facilitates electronic communications where obligations about communication are laid down in the legislation. It provides for the inclusion of email addresses in registers of members and officers, where the member or officer provides that information; allows societies to provide members with a copy of a retiring auditor's representations about his or her proposed removal on a website as long as the member has agreed to receive communications in that way and has been told that the information is on the website and how to access it.[85]

2.3.3. Mechanisms for Board Election

In the UK, this process is subject to the approach discussed in section 2.2.3 about voting at meetings and the recommendations of the non-binding Codes of practice discussed in section 2.3.2.

2.4. INFORMATION RIGHTS OF MEMBERS AND TRANSPARENCY REQUIREMENTS

2.4.1. Transparency: Obligations to Inform and Rights to be Informed

To have effective control of their cooperative, members need information. Similarly, the board itself needs information from full-time managers or executives if it is to manage the business.

The ICA lists openness as one of the ethical values to which cooperatives subscribe and adequate information is necessary if members are to retain control of the society. The education of members, managers, elected representatives and employees so as to facilitate an effective contribution to the development of the cooperative is a specific cooperative principle. Informing the public about the nature and value of cooperation is also part of that principle.

In the UK, information rights are dealt with in the legislation mainly by provisions permitting the FCA as registrar to investigate a society. Provisions covering financial audits and the non-binding Codes of Practice are also relevant. Otherwise, the question of the members' right to information is a matter for the society's own rules.

2.4.1.1. FCA Inspections and Investigations of Cooperative Societies

The FCA can inspect the accounts and records of the society or launch a fuller inspection of its affairs. Section 34(8) of CCBSA 2014 allows the FCA or anyone

85 CCBSA 2014, sections 3, 11, 12, 30 and 96.

authorised by the FCA to inspect the society's register of members or officers. Such action will, however, provide little financial information.

Since 6 April 2014, the FCA has also enjoyed the same powers of inspection and investigation in respect of societies that the Department for Business Innovation and Skills exercises in respect of companies under the Companies Act 1985.[86] Under those powers, the FCA can obtain and share information about a society after starting an investigation on its own initiative. Its investigator can require the society or any other person to provide specified documents and information, subject only to protections for legal privilege and banking confidentiality. This is enforceable in the courts against a person who refuses to co-operate and the person investigating the society has power to enter and remain on premises without a court order.[87] That means that by serving notice in writing on a society or any current or former officer, the FCA can require them to produce any documents or accounts relating to the business of the society that it requires. The FCA can also require them to furnish such other information about the business as it considers necessary and to verify any of the information provided by statutory declaration.

Under section 432 of the Companies Act 1985, the FCA also has power to appoint one or more inspectors to report on the society's affairs if the FCA suspects any fraud in connection with the running of the society. Such an inspector has extensive powers to investigate and find evidence in the course of his or her investigation.[88]

The documents and information demanded or the appointment of the inspector(s) must be considered to be necessary by the FCA 'to maintain confidence in registered societies'.[89] Those powers replaced the narrower equivalent powers of the FCA under section 48 of the Industrial and Provident Societies Act 1965.[90] The purpose of these changes was to subject societies to regulatory powers equivalent to those applicable to companies.

2.4.1.2. The FCA's Appointment of an Accountant to Inspect the Books

The two other powers that are available to the FCA in this area are only exercisable on the application of members of the society. They continue the existing powers under the cooperative law itself and remain in CCBSA 2014. Under

[86] Co-operative and Community Benefit Societies and Credit Unions (Investigations) Regulations 2014 SI 2014/574.
[87] Companies Act 1985, sections 447, 448, 450, 451 and 453A.
[88] Co-operative and Community Benefit Societies and Credit Unions (Investigations) Regulations 2014 SI 2014/574, regulation 2.
[89] Co-operative and Community Benefit Societies and Credit Unions (Investigations) Regulations 2014 SI 2014/574, regulation 3.
[90] Co-operative and Community Benefit Societies and Credit Unions (Investigations) Regulations 2014 SI 2014/574, regulation 4.

section 105 of CCBSA 2014 an application by at least ten members (all of at least one year's standing) gives the FCA power, if it thinks fit, to appoint an accountant or actuary to inspect the books of the society and prepare a report on them.[91] The person appointed then has power to copy the society's books and accounts and take extracts from them at all reasonable hours.[92] Unlike inspectors appointed under the powers of the FCA under Companies Act 1985, they have no power to question officers of the society or require any other information if the society does not agree to provide it. The society and the applicants are both entitled to a copy of the report once it has been prepared.[93] The appointment of investigating accountants is unusual as the FCA has to require the members who make the application to deposit funds as security for the costs of inspection and must then ensure that the costs of the process are defrayed by the applicants, the society or its members or officers (present or past) in the proportions that he or she directs. The FCA is now likely to use its Companies Act 1985 powers in place of this section.

2.4.1.3. The Inspection of a Society's Affairs

Under section 106 of CCBSA 2014 the FCA, on an application by one tenth of the total membership of the society or, in the case of a society with more than 1,000 members 100 members, may appoint one or more inspectors to examine and report on the affairs of the society or call a special meeting of the society. The applicants must support their application with evidence to show good reason for seeking a meeting or an inspection and that they are not activated by malicious motives. All the expenses of the meeting or the examination are met by the society, the applicants, or the present or former members or officers of the society in the proportions that the FCA directs. The FCA may, but (in contrast to section 105(2) of CCBSA 2014) is not obliged to, require the applicants to give security for the costs of the proposed examination or meeting before acceding to the application.[94]

The scope of an examination under section 106 is more extensive than that of an inspection under section 105. The former extends to all the affairs of the society while the latter is limited to its books and accounts. This is reflected in the fact that a section 106 inspector is not only entitled to demand the production of all the books, accounts, securities and documents of the society but also has power to question on oath any members, officers, agents or servants of the society about its business.[95]

---

91 CCBSA 2014, section 105(1).
92 CCBSA 2014, section 105(5).
93 CCBSA 2014, section 105(6).
94 CCBSA 2014, section 106(3), (5), and (6).
95 CCBSA 2014, section 107(2).

If a meeting is to be called as a result of a section 107 application, it is for the FCA to give directions about the time and place of the meeting and its agenda. Such a meeting has all the powers of a meeting called under the rules of the society but will have the power to appoint its own chairman regardless of any rule to the contrary.[96]

2.4.2. Financial Audit and the Codes of Best Practice

Societies are required to keep accounts and produce revenue accounts and balance sheets, including group accounts if appropriate, which provide a true and fair view of the position of the society.[97] Those documents are filed with the FCA as registrar as part of the society's annual return and are publicly available from the mutual societies register.[98] Generally, accounts must be audited by an independent qualified auditor. However, exemptions apply to societies whose turnover and net assets fall below certain levels.[99]

Similarly, the Code of Best Practice for Consumer Co-operatives suggests how information should be provided by management of the society to the board and deals with relations between the board and the statutory auditors. These matters are considered more fully in the section on Cooperative Control.

2.4.3. Member Education

UK law permits but does not require this. That is because this co-operative principle is not regarded by the FCA as one that it can monitor or enforce.

2.5. ADMISSION AND EXPULSION OF MEMBERS

This is the first ICA Principle and is, in a sense, the basis of governance:

> Co-operatives are voluntary organisations, open to all persons able to use their services and willing to accept the responsibilities of membership, without gender, social, racial, political or religious discrimination.

It raises a governance question on how decisions are dealt with. The financial aspects of expulsion and admission are dealt with in section 3.

---

96 CCBSA 2014, section 107(4).
97 CCBSA 2014, sections 79–80.
98 CCBSA 2014, sections 143–146.
99 CCBSA 2014, sections 83–85.

Articles 14 and 15 of the SCE Regulation provide for the SCE's board (or management board in the two-tier system) to admit or expel members with an appeal to the general meeting against refusal of membership or expulsion.

In the UK, the principle is used in the FCA Guidance 2015 as a key characteristic of a cooperative. For many years a requirement that membership 'should not be restricted artificially to increase the value of the rights and interests of current members' was used as a test to apply the 'open door principle'. That formulation does not appear in the text of FCA Guidance 2015. However, it is in fact likely to be applied, and at the time of writing still appears in the Notes to the application form to register a society.[100]

However, the legislation also requires the society's rules to deal with 'the terms of admission of the members, including any society or company investing funds in the society' and the 'determination whether members may withdraw from the society and if so how …'.[101]

On this basis, the requirement for the rules of a UK society will be that they do not artificially restrict membership. On expulsion, the issue will be whether the cooperative followed the procedure laid down in its own rules in deciding the question. That will normally involve giving a fair hearing to the member on any question about their behaviour and whether a ground for expulsion has been proved. This may also involve the protection of any financial interest involved.

The possible use of arbitration or other relatively cheap and fast dispute resolution procedures in the lower courts to challenge a decision to refuse a person membership or to expel them from the society is opened up by sections 137–140 of the CCBSA 2014 – see section 2.2.4.1. However, the definition of the right being protected is a matter for the rules (statutes) of the particular society.

3. COOPERATIVE FINANCE

3.1. THE LEGAL CONTEXT OF COOPERATIVE FINANCIAL STRUCTURE

3.1.1. Cooperative Financial Structure and Cooperative Identity

3.1.1.1. The Conditions of Registration

As noted in the UK reports for PECOL sections 1 (identity) and 2 (governance), for cooperative societies registered under CCBSA 2014, identity is mainly dealt

100 FCA Notes on Society Registration Form, p. 5, https://drive.google.com/file/d/0B3k1mIyJumBSYzhmWVVYMDVGcEU/view?usp=sharing.

101 CCBSA 2014, section 14(4) and (11).

with by the administrative discretion of the FCA as registrar rather than by detailed legislative provision. The same applies to community benefit societies. The FCA seeks to ensure that each society meets, and continues to meet, the relevant condition of its registration – either being a bona fide cooperative or, that its business is being, or is intended to be, run for the 'benefit of the community'.[102] Since 1 August 2014 registration has been as one type of society or the other, and FCA Guidance 2015 sets out the FCA's approach to this.

The only specific statutory provision about the definitions is that a society that carries on business with the object of making profits mainly for the payment of interest, dividends or bonuses on money lent to, invested in, or deposited with, any person does not qualify as a bona fide cooperative.[103] This is relevant to the capital structure and surplus distribution rules governing cooperative societies.

For cooperatives set up using a business structure other than that of a cooperative society, similar criteria will be applied to decide whether it may use the word 'cooperative' as part of its registered name or business name.[104]

The link between the ICA Principles and other international indications of how cooperative capital should be organised is to be found in FCA Guidance 2015.

3.1.1.2. Interest on Shares and Surplus Distribution Rules for Cooperatives and Community Benefit Societies

FCA Guidance 2015 provides the following view on share offers for both cooperative societies and community benefit societies:

> 6.20 In general, the share capital of a society should not be more than the level needed to support its activities. If the society can fund its activities from reserves then it ought not to need to issue additional shares. However, if a society does need to raise capital to pursue its purpose, it may wish to seek additional share capital from its members.

On the link between the payment of interest on society shares and the society's status as a bona fide cooperative or as a community benefit society, FCA Guidance 2015 is worthy of quotation in full:

> 6.23 Generally speaking, interest on shares should only be paid where the society can afford to do so, having taken into account other liabilities and any contribution to the

102 CCBSA 2014, sections 2 and 6.

103 CCBSA 2014, section 2(3).

104 Companies Act 2006, sections 55(1) and 1194(1) and the Company, Limited Liability Partnership and Business Names (Sensitive Words and Expressions) Regulations 2014 SI 2014/3140, schedule 1.

society's reserves. Share interest should not be used as a means of profit or surplus distribution or as a substitute for dividends.

6.24 The way a society uses interest on shares can be an indicator of whether it is complying with its condition for registration because:

- in the case of a bona fide co-operative society:the society cannot exist mainly to pay interest on money invested and
- in accordance with ICA Principle 3, it would be an indicator that a society is a bona-fide co-operative where the distribution of surplus to members is in the form of a dividend based on a member's participation in the co-operative, rather than through payment of interest on shares
- in the case of a society conducting its business for the benefit of the community the society's funds must be used to further the community benefit

6.25 The factors below are indicators of where a society is likely to be complying with the conditions for registration:

- societies are primarily inviting people to become members of the society, along with any accompanying request for capital (additional to the minimum required for membership) from the prospective member
- the maximum rate of interest paid on shares is declared in advance of the period for which it is intended to be paid, whether in its rules or elsewhere
- the declared maximum rate of interest is the lowest rate sufficient to obtain the necessary funds from members who are committed to furthering the society's objects
- in the event the society cannot afford to pay the declared maximum rate of interest, interest payments are reduced, or no interest is paid at all, without compensation in subsequent years
- societies can justify a decision to pay interest at a particular rate, and be able to demonstrate the basis for that decision

6.26 The factors below are indicators of where a society is likely to be failing to comply with the conditions for registration:

- the society seeks to attract capital mainly by focusing on potential return on investment
- the declared maximum rate of interest is in excess of the lowest rate sufficient to obtain the necessary funds from members who are committing to further the society's objects
- a rate of interest greater than the declared maximum rate is paid to members where a society is more profitable than expected
- greater profits in one year are used to compensate members for reduced or no interest payments in previous less profitable years

6.27 We will consider these factors on a case by case basis. What is appropriate for one society may not be appropriate for another.

> 6.28 There are some instances where these factors are not appropriate, specifically in the case of non-user investor shares in co-operative societies, and shares in agricultural co-operatives. In these instances other indicators will suggest whether societies comply with the bona fide co-operative society condition for registration ...... For agricultural co-operatives, requirements in the rules around the use of share capital linked to members' participation in the business suggest compliance with the legislation.

This approach to the payment of interest on shares and to the distribution of surplus reflects the great importance now attached by the FCA to adherence to the ICA Statement of Co-operative Identity for cooperative societies and to the community benefit purpose for those societies. Paragraphs 6.27 and 6.28 indicate some flexibility about these matters but the main thrust of emphasising limited return on capital is clear.

For societies registered as community benefit societies (which may sometimes be general interest cooperatives in PECOL terms), the provisions on capital and surplus distribution are clear. FCA Guidance 2015 permits no distribution of surplus whatsoever and interest on shares must be paid at a limited rate:

> 6.33 Share terms, whether in community benefit society rules or a separate document, must be consistent with the society's purpose of community benefit.
>
> 6.34 We consider the following factors as indicators that the society is complying with its condition for registration:
>
> - Any surplus is used to benefit the community by reinvestment in the business, or by application to some external but related community benefit
> - Any retained reserves are committed to community benefit
> - The society's rules prohibit any distribution of assets to members unless sold at market value to those members
> - The society only pays interest set at the lowest rate sufficient to obtain the necessary funds from members committed to furthering the society's objects
> - On dissolution, society assets are either:
>   - transferred to one or more other bodies with similar objects, or
>   - used for similar charitable or benevolent purposes.

3.1.1.3. UK Registration Criteria and the PECOL Classification of Cooperatives: A Note

While the concepts of bona fide cooperative and community benefit society share some of the features of PECOL's division between mutual and general interest cooperatives, they are not identical.

There is no absolute FCA requirement that a community benefit society must be controlled by its members, and many are not subject to any meaningful democratic control. However, FCA Guidance 2015 expresses a strong preference for a one-member-one-vote system to apply to the governance of community benefit societies:

> 5.10 It is not usually appropriate for a community benefit society to give any particular group of members greater rights or benefits, because the society must be conducting its business for the benefit of the community. So, for example, we would expect to see community benefit societies run democratically on the basis of one-member-one-vote.
>
> 5.11 A community benefit society deviating from this principle would need to be able to satisfy us that the arrangement helps it fulfil its purpose of benefiting the community.

Conversely, a bona fide cooperative may choose never to distribute any surplus and have purely nominal amounts of share capital, e.g. £1 per member, as a condition of membership rather than a source of funds for its business. There is no explicit condition about the proportion of business that a bona fide cooperative must conduct with its own members.

The FCA no longer allows a community benefit society to describe itself as a cooperative or a cooperative to call itself a community benefit society. It argues that the separate registration of the two different types of society was intended by the legislature to make them mutually exclusive and no procedure was provided for conversion from one type of society to the other.[105] However, a registered cooperative society can pursue community benefit as part of its activities and may have an entrenched rule preventing distribution of any surplus to its members. As the FCA puts it in its response to the consultation on the Guidance:

> We acknowledge that many co-operative societies also choose to benefit the community; and that many community benefit societies have active and engaged memberships who control the society democratically. However, a community benefit society must fundamentally exist entirely for the benefit of the community, not for benefits that depend on membership. Our view is that the purposes of a co-operative society and a community benefit society are fundamentally different.[106]

The Community Interest Company (CIC) company structure allows for the dedication of assets to a general interest purpose.[107] If other company structures are used, it is possible to entrench the statutes to prevent change, but amendment by unanimous agreement of the company's members is always possible.[108]

---

105 FCA Guidance 2015, paras. 3.58, 3.59 Annex 1.
106 FCA Summary of Feedback, p. 14.
107 C(AICE)A 2004, sections 26–63.
108 CA 2006, sections 22(1) and (3).

3.1.2. Financial Structure of the Cooperative and National Law on Business Organisation

The financial structure of cooperatives is a matter largely left to the choice of each society or company through its own statutes,[109] subject to certain specific legislative and judge-made legal rules. This reflects the liberal approach of UK business organisation law as discussed in the UK reports on both identity and governance. For cooperatives wishing to register as cooperative societies or to use the word 'cooperative' as the name of a business using a different legal structure, FCA Guidance 2015 is the main restriction on their freedom to decide matters in their own statutes.

A feature which encourages many cooperatives to use the cooperative society structure is the availability of 'withdrawable shares'. This form of capital is the UK's version of variable capital, and it is not available if a company is used. Historically, it was used by members of the consumer cooperatives that dominated the UK cooperative scene as an account into which money could be placed and from which it could be withdrawn. Members' patronage refunds would be credited to their share account and frequently left there as savings.

A cooperative or community benefit society may have withdrawable share capital but may, alternatively or in addition, have transferable shares or shares with neither feature – which then operate as a form of membership fee.[110]

Like any other business, a cooperative, whatever business structure it uses, may borrow money on a long or short term basis and with or without providing security over assets. So long as a business is empowered by its statutes to borrow, the question of how that is done is a matter of contract between borrowers and lender. Similarly, retained earnings are a source of business capital open to any business and have traditionally been significant for UK cooperatives.

FCA Guidance 2015 lays down that the rights given to loan-stock holders or other lenders should not undermine the society's compliance with the registration conditions. It focuses on constitutional and financial rights as the main areas of concern in this respect – FCA Guidance 2015, para. 6.37.

In terms of constitutional rights, the FCA acknowledges the fact that creditors do not usually enjoy any constitutional rights in the society. If the loan stock or other lending instrument or agreement gives the creditor a right to appoint a member of the society's board, this must not compromise the society's compliance with the registration requirement by, for example, threatening

109 In this report the word 'statutes' is used to refer to the constitutional document which governs a particular business. The actual documents are: the articles of companies, the rules of cooperatives and community benefit societies, and the partnership agreement in an LLP or unincorporated partnership.

110 CCBSA 2015, section 14(9).

member control of a cooperative or the community benefit purpose of a community benefit society – FCA Guidance 2015, para. 6.38.

The financial terms of a loan security or agreement are a matter of contract between the society and the lender or creditor. The rate of interest is a commercial matter, but if loans 'or similar methods' are used to distribute profits, that may indicate that the society is not meeting its registration condition – FCA Guidance 2015, paras. 6.39–6.41. If debt securities are convertible into shares, the rights attached to the shares on conversion should comply with those parts of the guidance concerned with share capital – FCA Guidance 2015, para. 6.42.

3.1.3. *Where are Cooperative Financial Structure Rules Found?*

Most rules about the financial structure of UK cooperatives are laid down in the statutes of each cooperative. In the case of cooperatives using the cooperative society structure, little specific provision is found in legislation but the bona fide cooperative test always applies. For those operating as companies, the Companies Act 2006 lays down detailed rules about share capital, debentures and the source of any distributions to the members of the company.[111] For cooperatives and community benefit societies, the gap left by the absence of such detailed legislative provisions is filled by judge-made rules developed for companies before the Companies Acts were amended to contain such provisions. This chapter concentrates predominantly on cooperative and community benefit societies, although brief reference is made to the rules governing other business structures when appropriate.

The rules regarding accounting standards for cooperatives registered as cooperative or community benefit societies are based on the concept of accounts providing a 'true and fair view' of the position of the society.[112] For societies, there is little more by way of detailed legal provision about accounting treatment and the detail is a matter for the accounting standards applied by professional accountants. They generally apply 'International Financial Reporting Standards as adopted by the EU' as their financial reporting framework to meet the 'true and fair view' legal requirement.

The application of IFRS in the UK is through the standards set by the Financial Reporting Council known as UK Generally Accepted Accounting Principles (GAAP).[113] The interpretation applicable to whether cooperative shares can be classed as equity, International Reporting Standards Interpretation Committee (IFRIC) Update 2,[114] applies in the UK through the availability in the cooperative's statute of an unconditional right for the board to refuse redemption

---

111 CA 2006, Parts 17 and 19.

112 CCBSA 2014, section 75.

113 http://frc.org.uk/Our-Work/Codes-Standards/Accounting-and-Reporting-Policy/The-future-of-UK-GAAP.aspx.

114 See http://www.iasplus.com/en/standards/ifric/ifric2.

(withdrawal) of shares, and that standard is used to give the 'true and fair view' required by the legislation.

The UK tax system acknowledges the particular nature of cooperatives in two ways. One focuses on the cooperative and community benefit society legal structure. The other is concerned with the reality of *fully* mutual trading between the members, regardless of the precise legal structure involved.

Like companies, cooperative and community benefit societies are subject to corporation tax on annual 'profits'. However, for cooperative and community benefit societies, unlike companies, the interest paid on shares by the society is deducted in calculating the 'profit' or loss for this purpose. A cooperative society which carries on a trade can also deduct the full amount of any patronage refund on a member's transactions with the society, regardless of what proportion of their trade is with members. Such deductions are not available to cooperatives using other corporate forms.[115]

Under UK tax law, any business that is not making 'profits' because its trade with its members is fully mutual is exempt from any tax levied on 'profits'. This will usually be corporation tax. This principle is laid down in case law and applied by the tax authorities, who set out their approach in administrative guidelines.[116]

Unincorporated groups, companies and cooperative societies gain the mutual trading exemption provided that: the contributors to, and recipients of, any surplus are identical; all of the surplus goes back to contributors according to the amount of business they do with the body; on winding up, the amount distributed to contributors bears a reasonable relationship to their contribution; and the members control the common fund. The exemption only applies to trade with members and not to trade with non-members or gains such as income from property ownership or bank interest. No capital allowances are available for capital expenditure, and no tax relief is available for losses made in the mutual trading.[117]

3.2. COOPERATIVE SHARE CAPITAL

3.2.1. The Essential or Non-Essential Nature of Cooperative Share Capital

A cooperative registering under the CCBSA 2014 can only confer limited liability on its members on the basis of share capital. That is the measure of the limited

---

115 Corporation Tax Act 2009, sections 132 and 499.

116 *Ayrshire Employers' Mutual Insurance Association Ltd v Inland Revenue* [1946] SC HL 1, and HMRC, *Company Taxation Manual (CTM)*, 40950 to 4098, http://www.hmrc.gov.uk/manuals/ctmanual/CTM40950.htm.

117 See I. Snaith, 'United Kingdom', in D. Cracogna, A. Fici and H. Henry (eds.), *International Handbook of Co-operative Law*, Springer, Heidelberg, 2013, para. 35.11.

liability of the member.[118] However, the absence of any substantial minimum share capital holding requirement for either the cooperative society or a member means that shares of minimal value can be used as a token of membership rather than a source of capital.

If other structures are used, it is possible to have no share capital whatsoever. Under the Companies Act 2006, a company with the liability of its members limited by guarantee can be established but may not have share capital.[119]

The LLP structure registered under the LLPA 2000 provides a corporate body and limited liability for members in return for the public disclosure of financial information but does not have share capital of the kind found in cooperative or community benefit societies and companies.[120]

The absence of any substantial minimum share capital requirement for any legal structure other than a public limited company permits the use of a share as a non-returnable and non-transferable membership fee in a cooperative or community benefit society, a company, or a partnership.

The nature of share capital has been defined in case law as follows:

> A share is the interest of a shareholder in the company measured by a sum of money, for the purpose of liability in the first place, and of interest in the second, but also consisting of a series of mutual covenants entered into by all the shareholders inter se ...[121]

Shares are classed as a form of property (called a 'chose in action') which confers on the holder the rights and duties in or arising from the statutes of the corporate body in which the share is held. Those statutes operate as a contract between all the members *inter se* and between each member and the corporate body itself as a legal person.[122]

In a cooperative, that contract will reflect cooperative principles with limited return on capital and one-member-one-vote. Cooperative or community benefit society shares have features which distinguish them from company shares. As FCA Guidance 2015 puts it:

> 6.4 In our view there are some unique features of society shares:
>
> - their number can fluctuate significantly
> - they remain at par value (unless written down)
> - they do not automatically give the shareholder a share in the underlying value of the society
> - they cannot be held by the issuing society itself
> - they do not carry votes in proportion to the amount of shares held.

[118] CCBSA 2014, sections 3(3) and 124.

[119] CA 2006, sections 3, 5 and 16(1)–(3).

[120] LLPA 2000, section 1.

[121] *Borland's Trustee v Steel* [1901] Ch 279, 288.

[122] CCBSA 2014, section 15 and CA 2006, section 33.

3.2.2. *Assets as a Natural Element of the Cooperative*

The member's share is an interest in the corporate body which does not confer any direct rights over the corporate body's assets.[123] Under UK law the question of assets focuses on the nature of the cooperative as a corporate body. The cooperative society, community benefit society, LLP or company owns the assets and has the liabilities of the business undertaking. The only assets that the members own are any shares (or loan securities) that they hold in the society or company and their ownership stake under the LLP partnership agreement. They do not directly own or have rights over the assets of the corporate body by virtue of their membership of that body.[124] The accounting rules will govern how the corporate body's assets are described in accounts (see section 3.1.3).

Those principles apply to any business. Similarly, neither companies nor societies are generally required by law to have any reserves, but the statutes of the body may lay down such a requirement. Even for cooperatives, there is no legal requirement for indivisible reserves, but the society's rules may establish restrictions on distributions and reserves for education or other purposes.

In the case of a community benefit society registered or a company registered as a CIC, any distribution of surplus assets to members on dissolution and any distributions to members before that stage, by way of dividend on shares or interest on loans or otherwise, are regulated and limited.[125]

In the case of an unincorporated partnership operating as a cooperative, assets will be owned by the individuals or corporate bodies that have formed the partnership as 'tenants in common' and can be divided when the partnership is dissolved. The proportionate ownership and terms for dissolution and distribution of the assets will be governed by the contract made by the parties on forming the unincorporated partnership and, if it is to use the word 'cooperative' as part of its business name, must follow the requirements of FCA Guidance 2015 on the nature of a bona fide cooperative. In the absence of any contractual agreement (written spoken or by conduct) between the partners, the provisions of the Partnership Act 1890 will apply and all property of the partnership will be held equally by the partners.[126]

3.2.3. *Regulating Principles of Cooperative Share Capital*

The FCA requires that, in accordance with ICA Principle 3, members should receive only limited compensation (if any) on any capital which they subscribe

123 *Borland's Trustee v Steel* [1901] Ch 279.

124 *Short v Treasury Commissioners* [1948] 1 KB 116, 122, CA.

125 For societies, see FCA Guidance 2015, paras. 6.33 and 6.34 and for CIC's see the Community Interest Company Regulations 2005 SI 2005/1788, regulations 17–25.

126 PA 1890, section 24(1).

as a condition of membership and that interest on share and loan capital generally must be limited as described in section 3.1.1. When combined with the requirements that any distribution to members of a mutual cooperative should be by way of patronage refund and that members' voting rights should not be linked to their capital holding, this reflects the ICA Statement of Co-operative Identity Values and Principles.

The rules for general interest cooperatives depend on the legal structure used. In the case of a community benefit society, there should be no distribution to members at all on the dissolution of the society or from annual profits. The payment of interest on shares or member loans is permitted but must not be unlimited, as described in section 3.1.1. A CIC, on the other hand, is permitted to pay dividend on shares and interest on members' loans, within limits laid down by law.[127] A CIC is prohibited from transferring assets other than for full value other than to another 'asset locked' body.[128]

A significant issue affecting the UK rules on capital is the silence of the legislation applicable to cooperative and community benefit societies compared with the Companies Act 2006 on matters of capital maintenance.

Principle of Determination. The CCBSA 2014 requires the rules of societies to provide for:

- the terms of admission of members (which will include holding at least one share);
- the maximum limit on a member's shareholding in the society (at or lower than the maximum laid down by law);
- whether the shares or any of them are transferable or withdrawable; and
- either provision for the form of transfer and its registration with the consent of the committee or provision for mode of withdrawal and payment of the balance.[129]

Rules will in fact designate the unit of value of each share. The legislation is silent on their divisibility.

On the *Principle of Publicity*, the register of members of a cooperative or community benefit society will contain a record of the number of shares held by each member, but only the member can discover the value of his or her own share account.[130] However, the accounts prepared by the society, filed with the FCA each year, and displayed at the registered office will contain in the balance sheet the total value of the society's share capital on the date of the balance sheet, and

127 Community Interest Company Regulations 2005 SI 2005/1788, regulations 17–25.

128 Community Interest Company Regulations 2005 SI 2005/1788, paragraph 1 of each of schedules 1–3.

129 CCBSA, section 14.

130 CCBSA 2014, section 30.

that information is open to public inspection.[131] In the case of a company, similar rules apply but the whole register of members is usually publicly available.[132]

On the question addressed in UK law as 'maintenance of capital', the CCBSA 2014 is largely silent, and so the case law developed for companies before company legislation addressed it for companies almost certainly applies. For companies, those issues are now dealt with in Companies Act 2006. As a result, on the *Principle of Correspondence*, cooperative and community benefit societies are governed by case law rules.

Where cash is paid, the shares can be issued as 'partly paid' if the statutes of the society or company so permit. In that case, the unpaid balance must be paid when it is 'called up' by the directors. However, any amount credited as paid up on shares must actually have been paid to the company or society.[133] Where shares are issued in return for non-cash considerations such as goods, land, services, or a business undertaking, both societies and private companies are governed by case law rules which do not require prior independent expert valuation of the non-cash consideration. The valuation can only be questioned if dishonesty or negligence sufficient to invalidate any contract is established.[134] In the case of a PLC, the Companies Act 2006 requires an advance independent expert valuation report which is made available to company members and formally registered.[135]

3.2.4. *The Legal Minimum Cooperative Share Capital*

The only minimum capital requirement for any UK business structure is the requirement that a public limited company should have a minimum allotted share capital of £50,000.[136] Cooperatives are unlikely to use that legal form, so no minimum capital requirement will apply to them other than the need to have at least one share per member as a means of limiting liability which theoretically amounts to a minimum of £0.03p (£0.01p x 3). A cooperative that uses the company limited by guarantee structure is unable to have any share capital.[137]

3.2.5. *The Variability of Share Capital*

For cooperative and community benefit societies, the legislation limits holdings of WSC by any member other than another society to a maximum

131 CCBSA 2014, sections 81, 82, 89, 143 and 145.
132 CA 2006, sections 113–128.
133 CA 2006, section 580(1) for a company and *Ooregum Mining Co of India v Roper* [1892] AC 125 for societies.
134 *Re Wragg Ltd* [1897] 1 Ch 796.
135 CA 2006, sections 593–597.
136 CA 2006, section 762.
137 CA 2006, section 5.

of £100,000.[138] No such limit applies to other society shares. A society's rules may impose a lower maximum limit on holdings of withdrawable share capital and limits on holdings of other types of share. They can also limit the times at which withdrawal of share capital is possible, empower the board to suspend all withdrawals, or otherwise lay down conditions, such as a minimum notice period, for a withdrawal.

A cooperative or community benefit society using withdrawable share capital (WSC) is prohibited from engaging in the business of banking other than as a credit union.[139] Shares in a cooperative or community benefit society, not designated as withdrawable, cannot currently be redeemed or bought back by the society itself.[140] However, non-withdrawable shares can be made convertible into withdrawable shares by a society's rules so long as holdings always stay within the £100,000 limit. After conversion the shares can then be withdrawn.

Withdrawable share capital in cooperative and community benefit societies is exempt from anti-money laundering rules, financial promotion rules, and the regulatory requirements arising from deposit taking.[141]

3.2.6. The Functions of Share Capital

In the event of insolvency, the share capital of a cooperative, whether it uses a society or a company legal structure, serves as risk capital. Unless all debts, liabilities and costs of the insolvency procedure are paid off, the members as owners lose their capital. As a result, it represents a cushion for creditors and affects the credit rating of the cooperative on the markets.

In a winding up, past members of either a society or a company, whose membership ended within a year before the beginning of the insolvency procedure, are liable to contribute towards paying debts incurred while they were members up to the amount unpaid on any shares they held.[142] This rule applies to both companies and societies but impacts particularly on members holding WSC in a society because members who cash in withdrawable shares within a year before insolvency may have to pay back some or all of the amount withdrawn if the amount remaining in their share account is less than the nominal value of the shares they were issued.[143]

---

138 CCBSA 2014, section 24.

139 CCBSA 2014, section 67 and CUA 1979, section 4(1) and schedule 1, paragraph 8.

140 *Trevor v Whitworth* (1887) L.R. 12 App Cas 409.

141 Money Laundering Regulations 2007 SI 2007/2157, regulation 4(1)(a); Financial Promotion Rules 2005 SI 2005/1529, article 4 and schedule 1 paragraph 14; and Financial Services and Markets Act 2000 (Exemption) Order 2001 SI 2001/1201, article 4 and schedule 1 paragraph 24.

142 CCBSA 2014, section 124 and IA 1986, section 74.

143 *In Re United Service Share Purchase Society, Limited* [1909] 2 Ch. 526, 536 and see *In Re United Citizens Investment Trust, Limited* [1932] 1 Ch. 395 CA.

For a cooperative using a society or a company limited by shares, shareholding is the only means by which a person can become a member.[144] If a cooperative uses either a company limited by guarantee structure or a limited liability partnership there can be no share capital.[145]

Share capital in a society or a company limited by shares serves as the measure of, and limitation on, the member's liability for business debts.[146] In an LLP it is the agreement between the members and the LLP that defines the member's liability on a winding up of the LLP.[147]

The cooperative requirement which limits the return on capital and provides votes to members and not shares leads cooperatives to rely heavily on loan capital or retained profits.

Under the rules on accounting, share capital can only be regarded as 'equity' for the purpose of assessing the capital gearing of the cooperative if the board of the cooperative has the power to refuse to redeem it.[148]

The issue of the treatment of creditors is generally dealt with by the theory that it is for them to use the publicly available information to choose whether or not to contract with the corporate body and, once they have made the contract, their only protection is the order in which debts and share capital are paid out on insolvency.

3.3. MEMBER CONTRIBUTIONS TO CAPITAL

3.3.1. Obligation to Pay Up Capital

The amount of any minimum required holding is a matter for the statutes of the cooperative. The rules on payment on shares are addressed in section 3.2.3.

3.3.2. Types of Capital Contribution

Sources of capital for any business are loans, shares, or retained earnings. In terms of direct individual member contributions, they will only be shares or loans. As noted at section 3.2.5, shares in a society can be withdrawable or transferable. In a company, variable share capital is not possible. Section 1.2 explains the criteria used to determine whether an enterprise is a cooperative.

144 CCBSA 2014, sections 3 and 124 and CA 2006, sections 3 and 5.
145 CA 2006, sections 3(3) and 5(1), LLPA 2000, sections 1–4.
146 CCBSA 2014, section 124 and IA 1986, section 74.
147 Limited Liability Partnerships Regulations 2001/1090, regulation 5 and schedule 3.
148 IFRIC D8 on FRS25 (UK) IAS 32 of 30 June 2004, http://www.iasplus.com/en/standards/ifric/ifric2.

3.3.3. *Amount*

See section 3.2.3.

Depending on the nature of the cooperative, e.g. consumer, worker, or housing, the FCA may regard an excessive minimum capital requirement as an inhibition on open membership and refuse to register the rule imposing it. Otherwise, the matter of contributions is left to the statutes of the society or company.

3.3.4. *Payment*

This is a matter for the statutes of a cooperative, subject to the matters discussed in section 3.2.3.

3.3.5. *The Value of Member Contribution*

Section 15(2) of CCBSA 2014 requires an existing member's individual written agreement to any amendment to the rules of a cooperative or community benefit society which requires the member to increase his/her shareholding or otherwise increases his/her liability to contribute to the loan or share capital of the society.

That permission is in addition to the majority required under the statutes for any rule amendment – a matter left to the statutes of a cooperative or community benefit society and not laid down in the legislation. If a company is used, amendments to the articles generally require a majority of 75% of the votes cast or a higher majority laid down in the company's statutes.[149]

Otherwise, matters such as the conversion of reserves, or reduction of share capital by the allocation of losses, are left to the statutes or the terms of issue of the shares for a society, subject to the requirements of the FCA for a bona fide cooperative (see sections 1.1 and 1.2). In the case of a company limited by shares, detailed rules about the variation of capital by division or consolidation or the redemption or purchase by the company of its shares apply.[150]

3.3.6. *Compensation*

The amount of interest paid on shares, the distribution of profits, patronage refunds to members from any trading surplus, the existence and level of reserves and their potential use or distribution to members are not specifically governed by IPS legislation. Subject, as always, to the requirement that the FCA is satisfied that the rules are appropriate for a bona fide cooperative, this is left to the statutes of the cooperative.

---

149 CA 2006, sections 21–27 and 283.

150 CA 2006, sections 641–737.

As discussed in sections 3.1.1.2, 3.2.1 and 3.2.3, FCA Guidance 2015 lays down a number of guidelines used by the FCA about capital to assess whether the society is a bona fide cooperative.

The same criteria will apply to the use of the word 'cooperative' as part of a business or trading name by a company, partnership or individual.

If a company structure is used for a cooperative, specific statutory rules about the source of any distribution to shareholders will apply to ensure that only profits available for the purpose are used.[151]

Those specific statutory rules do not apply to societies, but it seems likely that the gap is filled by similar judge-made rules which were replaced by the above-mentioned Companies Act provisions. The statutory definition applicable to companies defines profits available for the purpose of distribution as:

> accumulated realised profits so far as not previously utilised by distribution or capitalisation, less its accumulated, realised losses, so far as not previously written off in a reduction or reorganisation of capital duly made.[152]

Although this definition may not reflect the legal provision strictly applicable to cooperative and community benefit societies, it is applied to them on the basis of accounting standards as discussed in section 6.1.3. The common law definition may permit a distribution without taking account of accumulated realised losses provided that the payment would not make the society insolvent.[153]

If a society has withdrawable shares, the FCA has taken the position that withdrawal should only be permitted when a very similar test is satisfied. Among indicators that a society is meeting the bona fide cooperative or community benefit conditions of registration, FCA Guidance 2015 cites a provision of the society's statutes that:

> only allows the withdrawal of shares if:
>
> - it has trading surpluses that match or exceed the value of shares involved; and
> - the directors believe the society can afford to pay its debts, taking into account:
> - all of its liabilities (including whether it will be able to pay its debts at the date of withdrawal and, for a year after that, any contingent or prospective liabilities) and
> - the society's situation at the date of the transaction.[154]

151 CA 2006, sections 829–853.

152 CA 2006, section 830(2).

153 *Ammonia Soda Co Ltd v Chamberlain* [1918] 1 Ch 266.

154 FCA Guidance 2015, para. 6.11.

3.3.7. *Redemption*

As indicated in section 3.2. this is subject to the statutes of the cooperative and the rules of common law or, for companies, the legislation.

3.3.8. *Transfer*

For cooperative and community benefit societies, section 14(9) of CCBSA 2014 on transferable shares indicates that committee approval is required for each *inter vivos* transfer. FCA Guidance 2014 has confirmed that the FCA sees this as a requirement in every case where a society share is to be transferred from one person to another so as to avoid the creation of a market in the shares and the possibility of capital gains.[155] The statutes may lay down more detailed procedures and formalities. For a company, there are no special rules for cooperatives using that structure, and the statutes of each company will generally state the procedures and rules.

Transfer *mortis causa* takes place under normal probate rules and in accordance with the will or intestacy of the holder of the shares, subject to any provisions laid down in the statutes of a society or company or the terms of issue of the shares. The property inherited on the death of the holder will be defined by the statutes or terms of issue which fix the rights attached to the shares and any limits on them. For cooperative and community benefit society shares, a parallel system for transfer *mortis causa* applies where the amounts held in the society are limited. This permits the member to record a 'nomination' with the IPS which indicates the recipient of the shares on the death of the member.[156]

3.3.9. *Political and Economic Rights Granted by Member Contributions to Share Capital*

In a society or a company limited by shares, membership depends on holding at least 1 share, but this is formalistic. The rights conferred by the statutes of the corporate body only apply to someone holding a share. A cooperative may use a Company Limited by Guarantee (CLG) or an LLP, so that membership will not depend on holding any share because the cooperative will be unable to have any share capital.[157]

---

155 FCA Guidance 2015, para. 6.14.

156 CCBSA 2014, sections 37–39.

157 CA 2006, sections 3(3) and 5(1), LLPA 2000, sections 14.

3.4. RESERVES

No obligation to create reserves exists in the UK. The issue is left to the statutes of the society or the company unless special regulatory rules such as those applicable to banks and insurance businesses apply.

3.5. MUTUALIST CAPITAL (MASA DE GESTIÓN ECONÓMICA)

No such concept exists as an obligatory rule in UK law. The cooperative society or other corporate body used by the cooperative for its legal structure is a legal person.[158]

It owns all property, and the members have whatever rights and duties are laid down in the statutes or the terms on which any shares were issued. If the cooperative's statutes require disinterested distribution, that denies individual members any rights to a surplus left on a solvent dissolution of the corporate body. The question of what property rights the society or company as a corporate body has over members' property is a matter of contractual agreement between members and the legal person of the society or company. For example, the corporate body could act as the agent of the members to sell members' property to others or as owner of property that the members transfer to it.

The key issue is whether members can change the statutes so as to permit distribution to individual members of any surplus. In the case of a cooperative society, they can always convert it into a company and then distribute if the appropriate majority uses the correct procedure.[159] As discussed in section 4.8.7 at footnote 27 above, a community benefit society can choose to impose an 'asset lock' on itself to avoid that possibility, and a company registered as a CIC is required to do so. Any company can entrench provisions of its statutes by making them impossible to change or requiring a special high majority for change (above the usual 75%). However, a unanimous decision of all the members can always amend the statutes.[160] In the case of a cooperative society or a community benefit society that has not chosen to apply an asset lock to itself, the statutes cannot exclude the power conferred by the legislation to convert it into a company or otherwise reorganise itself. However, it is possible to impose a high quorum in the statutes for the meeting that will make the decision.

In the case of a cooperative choosing not to use a corporate body, a trust mechanism would have to be employed to dedicate the assets to a particular purpose and to restrict the distribution of the assets among the members as partners in the business.

---

158 CCBSA 2014, section 3, CA 2006, section 16 and LLPA 2000, section 1(2).

159 CCBSA, sections 112–114.

160 CA 2006, section 22.

3.6. REVENUE FROM COOPERATIVE ECONOMIC ACTIVITY – HOW IT IS DETERMINED AND ALLOCATED

In the case of cooperatives using a cooperative or community benefit society structure, this question is determined by a combination of the statutes of the cooperative and the accounting rules. As always, the statutes are subject to the bona fide cooperative or community benefit tests on registration of the society or later amendment of the statutes (see section 1.1). If a company structure is used, Companies Act 2006 lays down detailed rules about what defines profits available for distribution. The equivalent common law rules applicable to societies are similar but not quite so strict.

3.7. FINANCING THROUGH RETAINED COOPERATIVE REFUND

The cooperative's statutes will determine whether and when any cooperative refund is payable to the members. They will usually confer power on the board of directors to recommend a level of distribution for approval or reduction (but not increase) by the general meeting. The use of retained profits as a source of funding is therefore a matter of choice for the board and members. However, in FCA Guidance 2015, the FCA recommends the use of this source of funding as preferable to the use of share capital.[161]

3.8. MEMBER CONTRIBUTIONS TO PURPOSES OTHER THAN SHARE AND MUTUALIST CAPITAL

This is a matter for the cooperative's statutes and the contractual arrangements between members and their cooperative. Membership fees are possible as are restrictions on withdrawal of WSC and the accumulation of reserves from retained profits. Member loans to the cooperative are allowed under freedom of contract but are subject to the FCA restrictions on returns discussed in section 3.1.1.2.

3.9. OTHER SOURCES OF FINANCE (INCLUDING INVESTOR MEMBERS)

In 2006, the FSA developed a policy on the admission of non-user investor members. It is based on the provisions of the SCE regulation. Currently, FCA

[161] FCA Guidance 2015, para. 6.20 quoted in section 4.1.1.2.

Guidance 2015 permits cooperatives to have non-user investor members who hold 'Investor Shares', subject to restrictions to protect the interests of user members. These include restricted voting rights for investor members, compliance with applicable regulatory requirements under FSMA 2000, and an overriding requirement that the society remains, in the FCA's view, a 'bona fide cooperative'.[162]

Broad possibilities for borrowing exist because a corporate body has full power to issue loan securities or bonds, to give security over its assets, and to enter into other contracts to receive credit or borrow money. The only restriction is on the level of return applied by FCA Guidance 2015 as discussed in section 1.3.2.2. In the case of a CIC, the return on loans is limited by legal rules enforced by the CIC Regulator (see section 3.2.2).

3.10. CREDIT SECTIONS IN THE FINANCING OF COOPERATIVES

As a corporate body the society or company is one legal entity, but subsidiary societies or companies are common – usually wholly owned. As part of democratic control, many consumer cooperatives will use a regional committee system to elect directors and oversee relations with members, but these arrangements are to be found in the statutes of each cooperative. I am not aware of any use of 'credit sections' as described in the guidance.

3.11. RELATIONS BETWEEN COOPERATIVES AND CREDIT COOPERATIVES

This is entirely a matter of the general law of contract and of the regulatory rules applicable to banks and to credit unions.

3.12. COOPERATIVE AND COOPERATOR LIABILITY

If registered as a corporate body, the cooperative's members will stand to lose only the amount of their share capital. However, as with other small businesses, creditors of smaller cooperatives may require personal contractual guarantees by members or directors of certain debts and liabilities of the corporate body as a condition of entering the contract with the cooperative. This is common for bank loans and liabilities under leases of land.

---

[162] FCA Guidance, paras. 6.31 and 6.32.

Any shares held by members are their property and so could be taken in the case of the insolvency of the member, but that would be subject to the terms on which the member holds them under the society or company statutes. All cooperative funds and assets are available to creditors in its insolvency, unless they have been placed on trust, in which case they can only be used for the benefit of the beneficiaries of the trust. That would be very unusual, and the existence of such an arrangement would be known to creditors before they contracted with the cooperative. As a result, they would be less likely to lend to it.

If a cooperative operates as an agent to make contracts on behalf of its members – again an unusual arrangement – then the member will be fully liable on the contract made and the society will not be liable. However, an explicit agency agreement would be required to achieve this effect, and it would never be presumed without evidence of such an agreement.

3.13. COOPERATIVE AUTONOMY

There are no special legal rules about relations between cooperatives and public authorities. Relations with non-user investor members will be governed by the statutes of the cooperative, which, for cooperative societies, will be subject to FCA Guidance 2015 (see section 1.4). FCA Guidance 2015 emphasises the need for cooperatives that are or have subsidiaries to meet the registration requirements.[163]

3.14. WINDING-UP AND LIQUIDATION

The insolvency rules applicable to the winding up and dissolution of cooperatives are broadly similar across all business structures and are to be found in the Insolvency Act 1986 as applied to cooperative and community benefit societies by section 123 of CCBSA 2014. They provide for a creditors' voluntary liquidation to begin by a members' resolution with control by creditors of the process, including the appointment of a qualified insolvency practitioner to act as liquidator.[164] Alternatively, the process can begin by court order (a compulsory winding up) on the application of a creditor, normally on the ground that the cooperative is insolvent either because it cannot pay its debts as they fall due or, less commonly, because its liabilities exceed its assets.[165] The process of liquidation then follows the pattern laid down in the Insolvency Act 1986 with the liquidator gathering

163 FCA Guidance 2015, paras. 4.18–4.20.
164 IA 1986, sections 84–90 and 97–106.
165 IA 1986, sections 122–160.

and realising all assets and distributing the proceeds to creditors in accordance with their legal rights – broadly, secured creditors first, then unsecured creditors but with a preferential position for employees in respect of unpaid wages and certain other employment law rights.

The anomaly that companies and partnerships could benefit from rescue procedures known as the administration procedure and a company voluntary arrangement (CVA), but cooperative or community benefit societies could not, has now been rectified.[166] As a result, since April 2014, those procedures have been available on almost identical terms both to cooperatives registered as societies and to those registered as companies. This permits a moratorium during which a qualified insolvency practitioner can continue the business protected from creditors' claims and prepare recommendations with a view to rescuing all or part of the business, making an arrangement with its creditors, or realising greater value for creditors in an subsequent liquidation. The administration procedure is the only redress for creditors with a floating charge over company or society assets which includes the right to appoint a receiver to realise their security.

By definition, in any case of insolvency a cooperative using any legal form will have no surplus to distribute to members as all assets will be used to pay creditors. Cooperative members are then in the same position as company shareholders in this respect, and cooperatives enjoy no special protection even if they would have applied a disinterested distribution to any remaining surplus. This is because all assets of the cooperative are subject to the claims of its creditors.

On the solvent dissolution of a cooperative, the destination of any surplus assets is governed by its statutes, and most cooperatives provide for transfer to other cooperatives, cooperative organisations or charities and other disinterested purposes. However, a distribution among the members on the basis of their transactions with the cooperative over a fixed period near the end of its life has been allowed in cooperative society rules and is used by some agricultural cooperative societies. There is some danger that, in the absence of any provision whatsoever in a cooperative society's statutes, the applicable rules about the destination of a surplus on solvent liquidation might lead to distribution according to shareholding since the applicable rules are to be found in the insolvency regime applicable to companies. As a result, the inclusion of an appropriate provision in cooperative society rules is particularly important.

Any member of either a society or a company can apply to court for a winding up order in respect of a solvent cooperative on the grounds that the court considers it just and equitable that it should be wound up.[167] However,

---

166 CCBSA 2014, section 118 and the Co-operative and Community Benefit Societies and Credit Unions (Arrangements, Reconstructions and Administration) Order 2014 SI 2014/229.

167 IA 1986, section 122(g).

courts are reluctant to grant this remedy if the business is functioning and are required to refuse the winding up if they believe that another remedy is available so that the member is behaving unreasonably in seeking to wind the company up.[168] As a result, this has never, as far as I am aware, been used in the case of a cooperative.

If a cooperative is registered as a company, a member may petition for a remedy if they prove in court that the company is being run in a way that is unfairly prejudicial to that member.[169] This remedy is not available in a cooperative or community benefit society, and it is normally a means for a minority to force a buy-out by the majority if the company statutes make no adequate provision for that and there is no market in the shares. The remedy is only normally granted where the applicant has suffered due to unlawful behaviour by the majority such as a serious breach of directors' duties causing them financial loss or where there is evidence of an understanding or agreement not reflected in the statutes which has been broken by the other members.[170] It seems that this remedy has never been applied to a cooperative using a company structure. It would only be worth suing in a case where the minority had a significant financial stake in the company.

Community benefit societies are permitted, on formation or by later rule amendment, to 'lock' the assets of the society in for the community benefit purpose for which the society was established. This restricts the possibility of converting the society into a company or even a cooperative society and closely controls the disposal of any assets on dissolution or during the life of the society.[171] This level of protection of assets dedicated to the purpose of community benefit is similar to the rules that govern any company registered as a CIC.

Such protection is not available to cooperative societies.[172] The legal protection of any surplus in mutuals and cooperatives and the application of the principle of 'disinterested distribution' on dissolution has been recommended by the 2012 Report of the Ownership Commission which examined issues surrounding business ownership across the UK economy and its effects.[173]

3.15. GENERAL INTEREST COOPERATIVES

See the treatment of community benefit societies and CIC's throughout this report and, in particular, section 1.8.

---

168 IA 1986, section 125(2).

169 CA 2006, section 994.

170 *O'Neill v Phillips* [1999] 1 WLR 1092.

171 CCBSA 2014, section 29 and The Community Benefit IPS's (Restriction on Use of Assets) Regulations 2006 SI 2006/264.

172 CCBSA 2014, section 29.

173 Recommendation 3 Ownership Commission, Plurality, Stewardship and Engagement, March 2012, MUTUO, London http://ownershipcomm.org/ Chapter 4 at pp. 76–94 and 96.

4. EXTERNAL CONTROL

4.1. INTRODUCTION

In the UK there are no specific legal rules about any audit other than the purely financial. I refer to this as a 'Legally Required Audit'.

However, the FCA as registrar of cooperative societies decides whether a society meets the requirement for registration as a bona fide cooperative. That can be investigated and monitored through information required by the FCA to confirm compliance with cooperative principles. That role is and always has been carried out when an application is made for the registration of the society or a rule amendment. The FCA can decide that a society no longer satisfies the registration requirement. This allows the FCA to monitor compliance with Co-operative Principles. I refer to that as 'Discretionary Regulatory Monitoring'.

Other aspects of the performance of a society as a cooperative can be monitored by or on behalf of the society and its members either by a federal cooperative body or by other people. I refer to this as 'Self-Regulation'.

The table below attempts to summarise which of these three processes applies to some key issues raised in the Guidelines for the external control of co-operatives:.

Legally Required Audit	**Discretionary Regulatory Monitoring**	**Self-Regulation (at choice of Cooperatives and Federations)**
Audit of Accounts and Balance Sheet	Initial Society Rules	Assessment of Commercial Performance beyond accounts
Registration of Annual Return	Rule Amendments	Audit of member-promotion
Publication of Annual Return	Annual Return Confirmation to FCA	Measure of Cooperative Performance
Small Society Exemptions	Powers of Investigation – Current and Proposed	Measure of Social and Ecological Effectiveness
Investigation Powers		Provisions of Society Rules to allow for scrutiny
Super Audit of Financial Auditors by Financial Reporting Council		
Training Independence and Qualification of Auditors		

This section is structured according to those three divisions and, within each part, seeks to explain the UK approach to the external control of co-operatives.

4.2. LEGALLY REQUIRED AUDIT

All references are to the Co-operative and Community Benefit Societies Act 2014 (CCBSA 2014).

4.2.1. Accounts

Registered societies must keep proper books of account giving a true and fair view of the state of the society's affairs and explaining its transactions. Societies are also required to maintain satisfactory systems of control of their books, cash holdings and receipts and payments.[174]

4.2.1.1. Minimum Standards

Societies must produce accounts to at least the minimum standards required by the legislation and their own rules. Briefly, that is a revenue account dealing with the affairs of the society as a whole or two or more revenue accounts covering the whole year which deal separately with different businesses of the society. These, together with any balance sheet, must give a true and fair view of the income and expenditure of the society and of its affairs at the date of the balance sheet.[175]

The principles set out in Financial Reporting Standards published by the Accounting Standards Board are generally relevant (but see also 'Group Accounts' below). Some societies are affiliated to sponsoring bodies or are regulated by other organisations which may issue accounting requirements more rigorous than those described above.

4.2.1.2. Publication and Display of Accounts

Every society must display its latest balance sheet in a conspicuous position at its registered office.[176]

In addition, a society must give a copy of its latest annual return, including the accounts and auditor's report, free of charge to any member or other person interested in its funds who asks for it. With the member's agreement, that can be done through the society's website.[177]

As a general rule, every published revenue account or balance sheet must be signed by the secretary and two members of the society committee and have been audited or subject to an accountant's report incorporated in the account or

174 CCBSA 2014, section 75.
175 CCBSA 2014, sections 79 and 80.
176 CCBSA 2014, section 81.
177 CCBSA 2014, section 90.

balance sheet. A society may publish an unaudited interim revenue account or balance sheet if it is published with the latest audited year-end revenue account or balance sheet and is marked in clearly and prominently with the words 'UNAUDITED REVENUE ACCOUNT' or, as the case may be, 'UNAUDITED BALANCE SHEET'.[178]

4.2.1.3. Date of Society's Financial Year-End

Generally, each year of account begins immediately after the previous one ended. However, societies can choose their own year-ends, subject to certain conditions:

- a newly registered society must have an accounting year of at least 6 months;
- no society's accounting year may extend beyond 18 months;
- notice to the FCA to change the year-end by extending a year of account cannot be given less than five years after the end of a year of account that was itself extended so as to change the year-end.

If the society does not choose a financial year-end, its financial year will automatically end on the last day of the month in which the anniversary of its registration falls.[179]

4.2.1.4. Group Accounts

Societies with one or more subsidiaries at the end of a year of account must produce audited group accounts for that year. They must give a true and fair view of the income, expenditure and state of affairs of the society and its subsidiaries and must be submitted to the FCA with the auditor's report in the annual return.[180]

The group information (for the society and its subsidiaries) can be presented alongside the society figures in one set of accounts or separately in a further booklet.

A parent society is exempt from the group accounts requirement if it is a wholly owned subsidiary of another corporate body.

Group accounts need not deal with a particular subsidiary if the FCA approves the parent society committee's opinion that to do so:

(a) is impracticable, or would be of no real value to the society's members, in view of the insignificant amounts involved; or

---

[178] CCBSA 2014, sections 82.
[179] CCBSA 2014, sections 77 and 78.
[180] CCBSA 2014, sections 98.

(b) would involve expense or delay out of proportion to the value to those members; or
(c) give a result that would be misleading, or harmful to the business of the society or any of its subsidiaries or
(d) is inappropriate because the business of the society and that of the subsidiary are so different that they cannot reasonably be treated as a single undertaking.

If one or more of those reasons cover all the subsidiaries no group accounts need be filed at all. An exemption, once granted, can be continued in later years for the subsidiaries it covers without further application if the auditors certify their agreement that the committee's opinion and the grounds for it have continued throughout the later year.[181]

The Accounting Standards Board has published Financial Reporting Standard Number 2 (FRS2) Accounting for Subsidiary Undertakings. Paragraphs 25 and 26 refer to the exclusion of subsidiary undertakings from the consolidated financial statement. These paragraphs in FRS2 do not override the provisions of the legislation. Paragraphs 19 and 61 of FRS 2 state that the FRS requirements should be complied with except where they are contrary to any statutory framework under which the undertakings report.

4.2.2. *Audit Requirements Exceptions and Other Reports*

Every society must appoint one or more qualified auditors in each year of account to audit its accounts and balance sheet for that year unless it is subject to an exception.[182]

4.2.2.1. The Audit

The auditors must report to the society on whether the year's revenue account and balance sheet, and any other accounts they examine, give a true and fair view of the society's affairs, otherwise comply with the legislation, and are in agreement with the books of account for the year. Auditors also give their opinion on whether proper books of account and control systems have been maintained. To prepare the report, the auditors have power to carry out any necessary investigation, access the society's books and other documents at any time, and to demand information and explanations from the society's officers. They can also attend and be heard at society general meetings and must be given all communications about the meeting that members receive.[183]

---

181 CCBSA 2014, section 99.
182 CCBSA 2014, section 83.
183 CCBSA 2014, section 87.

4.2.2.2. The Auditor

The term 'qualified auditor' means someone eligible for appointment as a statutory auditor under Part 42 of the Companies Act 2006.[184] They must be a member of a recognised supervisory body (which includes the Institute of Chartered Accountants in England and Wales and the Association of Chartered Certified Accountants) and eligible for appointment under the rules of that body.

The Financial Reporting Council is responsible for disciplining and overseeing auditors according to professional standards.[185] It is currently investigating the KPMG Audit in respect of the audit of the accounts of the Co-operative Bank PLC before it needed restructuring to avoid insolvency and collapse in 2013 and ceased to be controlled by the Co-operative Group, which now holds only 30% of its equity.[186]

The auditor must not be an employee or officer of the society or its holding or subsidiary society or an employee, employer or partner of a society employee or officer. They must not be prohibited under the Companies Act 2006 from being auditor of a subsidiary company of the society for such a lack of independence.[187]

Auditors are appointed and removed by the members' meeting, but no annual resolution is required to reappoint the same auditor from one year to the next. The removal or replacement of the existing auditor requires a resolution of which 28 days' notice is given to the members and the auditor. The auditor can make oral and written representations to the meeting considering the resolution.[188]

4.2.2.3. Small Society Exemption

A society with turnover and assets of less that £5,000 and fewer than 500 members may appoint two or more lay auditors instead, unless the FCA directs it to use qualified auditors for the current year of account.[189]

If the society's rules only permit a full professional audit, appropriate rule amendments must be registered with the FCA before the small society exemption can be used.

The following societies can never use the small society 'lay audit' exemption:

- Housing Associations registered with the Homes and Communities Agency, Welsh Ministers or The Scottish Housing Regulator;

---

184 CCBSA 2014, section 91.

185 See https://www.frc.org.uk/Our-Work/Conduct/Professional-discipline.aspx.

186 https://www.frc.org.uk/News-and-Events/FRC-Press/Press/2014/January/Investigation-announced-in-connection-with-KPMG-Au.aspx.

187 CCBSA 2014, section 92.

188 CCBSA 2014, sections 93–96.

189 CCBSA 2014, sections 83(2)–(4).

- a subsidiary of another society;
- a society with one or more subsidiaries (whether those subsidiaries are companies or societies);
- a society that has to prepare accounts under the Insurance Accounts Directive (Miscellaneous Insurance Undertakings) Regulations 1993.

Anyone can be a lay auditor if they are not an officer or employee of a society and are not a partner, or an employee or employer of, any society officer or employee. Societies use lay auditors so that people other than committee members check the accounts against the books.

A society must prepare fully audited accounts if the FCA serve notice requiring it to do so.

4.2.2.4. Opting Out of Full Audit Requirements

Less stringent requirements apply to some societies.

Under section 83 of CCBSA 2014, this is only open to societies:

- which meet certain financial thresholds;
- which are not in a category required to have a full audit;
- whose rules do not require a full audit; and
- whose members pass an opt-out resolution by the necessary majority.

Thresholds

Non-charity	Charity
Value of assets in aggregate at the end of the previous year of account less than £2.8m, and	Value of assets in aggregate at the end of the previous year of account less than £2.8m, and
Turnover for the previous year less than £5.6m	Turnover for the previous year less than £250k

(a) Societies Needing Full Professional Audit

Under section 83 of CCBSA 2014 a full professional audit is always required for a society which had a turnover in excess of £5,600,000 (£250,000 if charitable) or total assets in excess of £2,800,000 in the preceding year of account.

Any society that is, or at any time during the accounting period was, in one of the following categories cannot use this exemption:

- a Scottish registered social landlord;
- a subsidiary of another society;
- a society with one or more subsidiaries (whether those subsidiaries are companies or societies);

- a society that must prepare accounts under the Insurance Accounts Directive (Miscellaneous Insurance Undertakings) Regulations 1993; and
- a society which takes deposits requiring PRA regulation under the Financial Services and Markets Act 2000 – that does not include a deposit in the form of withdrawable share capital.
- a credit union

(b) Society Rules

The society's rules must allow an opt-out from a full audit. If the rules only permit a full professional audit, then the appropriate rule amendments must first be passed and registered with the FCA.

(c) Opt-Out Resolution

An audit opt out resolution must be passed at a general meeting where:

- less than 20% of the votes cast are against the resolution; and
- less than 10% of all members entitled to vote cast a vote against it.

If the resolution is not passed, the society must have a full professional audit.

The resolution only operates for one year of account. A resolution must be passed in each year of account that a society wishes to opt out of the full audit requirement

(d) The Report

Societies which have chosen to opt out of the requirement for a full audit must, if their turnover was greater than £90,000 in the year of account, appoint a qualified auditor to prepare a report on the accounts and balance sheet.

The accountant's report is less onerous than an auditor's report. It must state whether, in the opinion of the qualified auditor making the report:

- the revenue account or accounts, the other accounts (if any) to which the report relates, and the balance sheet are in agreement with the books of account kept by the society;
- on the basis of the information contained in the books of account, the statutory account comply with the requirements of the legislation; and
- the financial criteria allowing the production of a report instead of a full audit have been met.[190]

---

190 CCBSA 2014, section 85.

Where the relevant conditions are met, and the society produces unaudited accounts, the revenue account and balance sheet must still be signed by the secretary and two committee members of the society acting on behalf of the society's committee.

The accountant preparing the report has similar powers to those of an auditor to carry out any necessary investigation, to access the society's books and other documents at any time, and to demand information and explanations from the society's officers. They are also entitled to attend and be heard at society general meetings and to receive all communications about the meeting that members receive.[191]

4.2.2.5. FCA Power to Direct a Full Audit

The FCA can direct that a full audit take place in respect of any year in which a society used either the small society or the 'opt out resolution' possibilities outlined above. The FCA direction will require the society to appoint one or more qualified auditors to carry out a full audit of one or more years and, if an annual return has already been filed, to file a new one to reflect the full audit.[192]

4.2.3. Conclusions about Legally Required Audit

These legal rules reflect the general UK approach of leaving the monitoring of managers and executives to the members (or, in companies, shareholders) as owners of the enterprise. All of the above rules about accounts and auditing are aimed at providing information to the members to allow them to carry out that function. If they fail to do so, that is seen as their responsibility; and if the business fails, it will go into insolvency and they will lose the value of their stake in it. There is generally no role for the State to do more than that.

The trend to exempt smaller societies from full audit requirements extends to those with turnover of less than £5.6 million. However, members must agree with a minimum turnout requirement, and those with turnover of more than £90,000 are required to prepare a less stringent accountant's report. In addition, certain types of society such as housing associations (not cooperatives) and credit unions must always prepare full accounts and the FCA can always require full accounts even where a society has opted out (see section 4.2.2.5). Small companies have wider exemptions from any audit at all.

---

191 CCBSA 2014, section 88.
192 CCBSA 2014, section 86.

4.3. DISCRETIONARY REGULATORY MONITORING

4.3.1. Legal Basis

Because cooperatives are registered only on the basis of being cooperatives and their registration can be cancelled if they are no longer cooperatives, the FCA checks whether the organisation is a cooperative.

The basis of registration as an industrial and provident society (IPS) before 1 August 2014 was that the society was either a bona fide cooperative or a community benefit society – section 1(2) IPSA 1965. A society only needed to be one or the other under that provision and it registered *as* an IPS.

Since 1 August 2014 registration has been *as either* a cooperative or a community benefit society, and a society must meet the requirements for the category in which it is registered.[193] The requirement for a cooperative is to be a bona fide cooperative. A community benefit society must conduct business for the benefit of the community.

In both cases, the FCA must be satisfied that the registration requirement is met. The FCA also has power to cancel the registration of a society that no longer meets the appropriate registration condition. Until 1st August 2014, cancellation was possible only if the society met neither registration requirement.[194] For societies registered after that date, failure to meet the particular condition which allowed the society to be registered as a cooperative or as a community benefit society is the basis of any cancellation of registration.[195]

This is an administrative discretion, and the way in which the FCA exercises it is largely a matter for them, subject only to broad Administrative Law requirements.

4.3.2. Checking Society Statutes for Compliance

On initial registration, the FCA will look at the rules of the proposed society and assess whether they meet its requirements for registration (see section 4.1.1).[196]

On each occasion on which a rule amendment is passed by the society's members, it must be submitted for registration with the FCA to be valid and will only be registered if it is consistent with the registration requirements.[197]

Those requirements represent a form of monitoring of cooperative practice but are very minimal. They only involve considering the rules (i.e. statutes) of the society.

193 CCBSA 2014, section 2.
194 Industrial and Provident Societies Act 1965, section 16(1)(c)(ii).
195 CCBSA 2014, section 5(5).
196 CCBSA 2014, section 2.
197 CCBSA 2014, section 16(1).

4.3.3. *A New Approach*

Until 2014, the approach of the registration authority to other forms of scrutiny of whether societies operate as a cooperative was variable. The Registrar of Friendly Societies (the authority until 2001) did occasionally respond to complaints from members by threatening to cancel registration but that was quite unusual. From 2001 when the Financial Services Authority took over the function, any such intervention became even less usual and that has continued to now.

In 2012 the FCA took over the registration function. As part of the legal changes to facilitate that, a new duty was imposed on that Authority as follows:

> The FCA must maintain arrangements designed to enable it to determine whether persons are complying with requirements imposed on them by or under. ... the legislation relating to mutual societies.[198]

FCA Guidance 2015 notes the absence of a full definition of that phrase in the CCBSA 2014 begins its analysis with the exclusion of certain societies from that category by section 2(3) of CCBSA 2014 which provides:

> co-operative society' does not include a society that carries on, or intends to carry on, business with the object of making profits mainly for the payment of interest, dividends or bonuses on money invested or deposited with, or lent to, the society or any other person.

In FCA Guidance 2015 the FCA states:

> 2.4 When a society applies to us for registration we assess whether it meets one of the conditions for registration. If a society applies to register as a co-operative society then the condition it must meet is that it is a bona fide co-operative society. If a society applies to register as a community benefit society then the condition it must meet is that it is conducting its business for the benefit of the community.

The FCA Guidance 2015 of the FCA lists other points at which compliance is monitored:

- on any application to register a society when the proposed rules and the information provided on the application form are used;
- on any application to change the society's rules when all information available to the FCA is used;

198 The Financial Services Act 2012 (Mutual Societies) Order 2013 SI 2013/496, article 2(a), schedule 1, paragraph 5(1).

- when a society publishes information suggesting that its main object is to make profits to pay interest on shares when all information available to the FCA will be used to assess whether section 2(3) has been breached;
- at any time while a society is trading (and so filing accounts with the FCA annually) the FCA may analyse its accounts to assess compliance with section 2(3) by comparing the surplus distributed to members in proportion to their transactions with the amount of interest, dividend of bonuses the society pays on shares or other investments in the light of the amount paid by comparable investor owned businesses;
- those financial indicators are used together with an analysis of the society's relationship with its members to decide whether the society is an association of persons united mainly to meet their common economic social and cultural needs or an association of capital with the main purpose of generating financial returns.[199]

The last bullet point goes to the core of the application of the ICA Statement in defining a cooperative and applies it alongside section 2(3) of CCBSA 2014 to ensure that the cooperative societies that are registered meet the bona fide cooperative requirement. The FCA indicates that the process of assessing compliance with section 2(3) will be carried out on a case by case basis and will usually involve discussions with the society. The same principle will apply to the process of assessing whether or not a society complies more generally with the bona fide cooperative requirement.

The assessment of whether a society is a bona fide cooperative is carried out wholly on the basis of the ICA Statement of Co-operative Identity, Values and Principles.[200]

This represents a new 'hands on' approach by the FCA and implies a form of annual reporting on continued adherence to Co-operative Principles.

4.3.4. Legal Powers of the Registration Authority

The legislation has always provided some powers for the registering authority to investigate societies or appoint others to do so. From 1 August 2014, those powers were substantially increased and updated and the need for member initiative to trigger the use of the power was reduced.

4.3.4.1. Members' Rights to Information

The UK system emphasises the availability of information to members and those dealing with corporate bodies such as cooperatives, and other requirements

199 FCA Guidance 2015, para. 4.8.
200 FCA Guidance 2015, para. 4.10–4.16.

complement that emphasis. Members and others are entitled to a copy of the annual return and accounts.[201] Documents and information are also available from the public records.

In addition, society members, and anyone else with an interest in society funds, can insist on inspecting the society's register of members, usually at the society registered office. Societies must provide access to that register, apart from details of the financial stake of other people, at all reasonable hours in line with society rules about times and methods of access.[202]

The FCA have a number of powers under CCBSA 2014 and The Co-operative and Community Benefit Societies and Credit Unions (Investigations) Regulations 2014 SI 2014/574 which apply the provisions of Part 14 of the Companies Act 1985 to societies. That provides the FCA with powers equivalent to those exercised by the Department of Business Innovation and Skills (BIS) in respect of companies registered under the Companies Act 2006.

In FCA Guidance 2015, the FCA states:

> 9.2 If we believe a society is not complying with its requirements under the Act, we can, subject to statutory requirements:
>
> - require the society to give us information and documents
> - require the society to have its accounts audited by a qualified auditor
> - appoint an inspector to inspect the society
> - suspend or cancel a society's registration
> - prosecute societies, which can result in a fine from the court
>
> 9.3 These are the powers given to us by the Act. Before we use them we will usually try to discuss our concerns with the society to resolve things without having to use our powers. However, we have, and will, use our powers where appropriate. We publish a list of prosecutions and cancellations.
>
> 9.4 Where applicable, we will use our powers to the extent necessary to maintain confidence in the society legal form.

It is clear from that the above quotation that these powers will be used mainly to assist the FCA to decide whether the society meets the registration requirements.

4.3.4.2. FCA Power to Require Documents and Information

Under section 447 of the Companies Act 1985, as it applies to societies, the FCA can direct a society to produce documents or information.

It can also authorise an investigator to exercise that power on their behalf and that person has power to enter and remain on premises used for the society's

201 CCBSA 2014, section 90.

202 CCBSA 2014, sections 103 and 104.

business to assist them in obtaining documents or information. It is an offence for anyone to destroy, mutilate or falsify documents relating to the society's affairs or to knowingly provide false information when those powers are used. The investigator may be either a member of FCA staff or someone hired specially to do the work.[203]

That power replaced the FCA's weaker and more limited powers under section 48 of the IPSA 1965, which was not consolidated in the CCBSA 2014.

4.3.4.3. FCA Ordered Inspection of Books by Accountant or Actuary at Members' Request

The FCA can appoint an accountant or actuary to report on the society's books. That power needs a request by at least 10 society members who deposit money with the FCA as security for the cost of the process.

At the end of the inspection, the FCA can order the costs to be paid by the applicants, the society, or present or former members or officers. To prepare his/her report, the inspector can make copies of the society's books at any reasonable time but cannot formally question people under oath.[204]

4.3.4.4. FCA Ordered Inspector's Investigation or Society Special Meeting at Members' Request

The FCA can appoint an inspector to look into the society's affairs and report to it or call a special meeting of society members. At least 10% of a society's members, or 100 members if that is a smaller number, must make a request supported by evidence that there are good reasons to do so, and that the request is not malicious. Notice of the request must be given to the society. Before the FCA acts on the request, it may require the applicants to give security for the cost of the inspector's work or of calling the meeting. At the end of the process, costs will have to be met by the applicants, the society, or present or former society members or officers as the FCA directs.[205]

An inspector appointed under that provision has power to see the society's books, accounts or other documents and to question society officers, members and employees on oath about the business. The FCA decides the time, place and agenda of any special meeting that they call and the meeting has all the powers of a members' meeting under the society's rules and can appoint its own chair.[206]

---

203 Companies Act 1985, sections 448 and 453A.
204 CCBSA 2014, section 105.
205 CCBSA 2014, section 106.
206 CCBSA 2014, section 107.

4.3.4.5. Inspections and Investigations Under the Companies Act 1985

From 6 April 2014, secondary legislation has placed societies in the same position as companies in respect of inspections and investigations under Part 14 of Companies Act 1985.[207] This involves substantial new powers for the FCA.

Where it appears to the FCA that a society's affairs are being or have been conducted:

- with intent to defraud creditors;
- for any other fraudulent or unlawful purpose;
- in a manner unfairly prejudicial to any of its members; or
- without giving members information they might reasonably expect

it can appoint inspectors with extensive powers to obtain documents and question people under oath. Obstruction of the work of the inspectors can be treated as contempt of court.[208]

The inspectors investigate the society's affairs and report to the FCA, which can choose whether or not to publish the report.

These powers deal with general business misconduct by societies rather than matters specifically concerned with the registration requirements for cooperatives and community benefit societies.

The provisions of Part 14 of the Companies Act 1985 concerned with investigations of company ownership do not apply to societies because issues about control are not linked with holdings of society shares.[209]

4.3.5. Conclusions about Legally Required Audit

The inclusion of these provisions is tenuous because they do not amount to very extensive controls or an audit in the usual sense of the word. However, they are the only external legally-based mechanisms that deal with the operation of a society as a cooperative. They only apply to those cooperatives registered as industrial and provident societies (from 1 August 2014 as cooperative societies).

A cooperative registered as a company or using one of the partnership business structures available in the UK will not be subject to scrutiny about whether it meets Co-operative Principles, although general investigation powers about fraud apply to companies and limited liability partnerships. The failure of BIS to date to take any steps to stop the use by the Co-operative Bank PLC of

---

[207] The Co-operative and Community Benefit Societies and Credit Unions (Investigations) Regulations 2014 SI 2014/574.

[208] Companies Act 1985, sections 442 and 443.

[209] The Co-operative and Community Benefit Societies and Credit Unions (Investigations) Regulations 2014 SI 2014/574, regulation 2.

the name 'cooperative' when it is owned 70% by stock exchange investors and less than 30% by the Co-operative Group is evidence of the weakness of the provisions applicable in those cases.[210]

4.4. SELF-REGULATION

It is open to cooperatives under their own rules or, more commonly, by decision of their directors to establish their own ways of monitoring their operation as a cooperative over and above the minimum legal requirements. This paper refers to this as 'self-regulation' as it is a practice not required by law and not even imposed by the exercise of administrative discretion on the part of the FCA to enforce the registration conditions for cooperatives.

The development of performance indicators to achieve this has long been encouraged and facilitated by Co-operatives UK as the federal body of UK cooperatives.[211] The most recent document setting out their approach to financial, non-financial performance and sustainability indicators in the context of integrated reporting is Co-operatives UK, *Simply Performance, A Guide to Creating Member Value*.

It indicates that Co-operatives UK, when referring to financial, non-financial and sustainability impacts for this purpose, means the ways that a cooperative creates member value in terms of:

- sharing profits (financial), e.g. distributing dividends or retained income to keep prices low;
- member ownership and control (non-financial) e.g. number of members and customer satisfaction;
- wider social and environmental successes (sustainability) e.g. staff engagement, supplier care, community development or reducing consumption of natural resources.[212]

The measurement of performance across these three areas is seen as driving value creation rather than just compliance. Co-operatives UK argues that this should lead to reporting that goes beyond the legally required minimum, and that a desire to demonstrate how cooperative principles run through the business so as to avoid 'tokenism' or 'green washing' leads to the measurement of performance.[213]

---

210 See http://www.iansnaith.com/?p=670 for a full legal analysis and comment on that issue.

211 See Co-operatives UK, *Simply Performance, A Guide to Creating Member Value*, 2013 ('Simply Performance'), http://www.uk.coop/resources/simply-performance.

212 Simply Performance, p. 5.

213 Simply Performance, p. 6.

The alignment of strategy, management and reporting and the production of a single integrated report is advocated in the Co-operatives UK *Simply Performance* This will involve leadership setting out a cooperative vision, establishing governance and cross-departmental and co-worker action plans, decisions about priorities and the selection of cooperative indicators. Performance data will then be collected and analysed before being subjected to external verification and being fed back into the process of setting the cooperative vision for that particular cooperative.[214]

The document then summarises a short list of key indicators in each area.[215] Key financial indicators are the change in annual turnover from year to year, the return on capital employed, and the net profit distributed to members.[216] The short list of non-financial indicators includes the number of members, the satisfaction rate in member surveys, amount of trade with members as a proportion of sales or income, and the satisfaction rate in customer or user surveys.[217]

In each case, specific data is used to report these matters in figures so that some comparison can be made between one cooperative and another and between a cooperative and another type of business. The Guidance tries to provide flexibility to suit all types of cooperative, but this inevitably limits the possibility of uniform application and comparisons.

This is not a development based on any legal requirement; rather, it is an attempt to comply with both the letter and the spirit of the Co-operative Principles. It gives members and others a basis to assess how far a particular cooperative is operating in accordance with a cooperative ethos. It amounts to a development of good practice and an attempt to promulgate it.

The focus on providing members and others with clear information in statistical form reflects the approach of the legal rules to financial accounting and is therefore comparable with other systems of cooperative audit.

5. COOPERATION AMONG COOPERATIVES

5.1. COOPERATIVE INTEGRATION IN UK LAW

As noted in previous UK national reports for PECOL and elsewhere,[218] the issue of cooperative identity in UK Law is largely a matter of administrative discretion

214 Simply Performance, pp. 12–16.

215 See Simply Performance, Chapters 4, 5 and 6 in full for the long list of indicators for each of the three areas and remarks on how they might be applied.

216 Simply Performance, p. 20.

217 Simply Performance, pp. 24–25.

218 See Snaith, n. 117 above, pp. 735–757; and I. Snaith, *Handbook of Cooperative and Community Benefit Society Law*, Jordan Publishing, Bristol, 2014, pp. 62–65.

for cooperatives registered under the Co-operative and Community Benefit Societies Act 2014. That Act consolidated the previous primary legislation. The most significant change was the introduction from 1 August 2014 of a requirement to register a society under that Act as either a cooperative or a community benefit society, rather than registering a society on the basis of fitting one of those two categories.[219] However, the role of the FCA as registrar of societies remains and the approach of allowing substantial freedom to society statutes (or 'rules' as they are called) to make their own arrangements continues, subject to the overriding requirement that, in the case of a cooperative, the society meets the registration requirement of cooperative identity on and after registration. The freedom to use any of a number of different business structures for a cooperative also remains but this report deals mainly with cooperatives registered as societies.[220]

In this part of the report, the framework provided by legislation and FCA Guidance are considered first and the statutes (rules) of the major secondary cooperative society as an example of economic integration and of the dominant UK are then used to indicate the concrete structures developed within that framework.

5.2. INTER-COOPERATION UNDER CCBSA 2014

While no separate registration status is set out for either horizontal or vertical inter-cooperation, whether economic or socio-political, CCBSA 2014 permits the creation of both types of structure within its general framework. A cooperative society can be registered with only two members rather than the usual three if both members are other societies.[221] The registration must be as a cooperative society if the purpose is to serve its own member societies rather than to benefit a non-member community. For any society, whether primary or secondary cooperative or community benefit society, registration must be 'for carrying on any industry, business or trade (including dealings of any kind with land)'.[222] This requires a fairly wide definition to accommodate the role of a trade association or promotional association. However, Co-operatives UK and, before it, the Co-operative Union, have been registered on that basis by successive registrars.

[219] CCBSA 2014, section 2(1) which implements and replaces the Co-operative and Community Benefit Societies and Credit Unions Act 2010, section 1.

[220] See Snaith, n. 218 above, Chapter 1 for a discussion of different structures in this context.

[221] CCBSA 2014, section2(2)(b).

[222] CCBSA 2014, section 2(1).

5.2.1. Membership and Shares

The CCBSA 2014 explicitly acknowledges that a corporate body of any kind, such as another society or a company, can be a member of a society and hold shares in it. Societies are also empowered to invest in the shares or in the security of other registered societies and enjoy the same limited liability for business debts as other society members.[223] Where another society is a member, specific provision is made for the secretary and two committee members to sign documents on its behalf, and there is no limit on the value of the shares that can be held by the member society, even if they are withdrawable.[224] The limit on the value of the withdrawable shares held by one society in another was specifically removed in 1867 to facilitate the development of the nascent Co-operative Wholesale Society Ltd as a secondary cooperative with the economic objective of collective purchasing on behalf of primary consumer cooperatives.[225] Those provisions apply to both primary and secondary cooperatives, whether vertical or horizontal, regardless of whether their objectives are economic or socio-political.

The prohibition[226] on any society, other than a registered credit union, operating a banking business if it has withdrawable share capital applies to both primary and secondary societies. The registration of credit unions under CCBSA 2014 is governed by the Credit Unions Act 1979 (CUA 1979)[227] which, unlike CCBSA 2014, acknowledges the different role of socio-political support cooperatives formed by credit unions by permitting the use of the words 'credit union' in the name of any person or association which has the written permission of the FCA to use the name even if they do not actually operate in the financial services business by lending to their members. The FCA will normally only give that permission to associations or groups of credit unions.

Under CUA 1979, a credit union is not permitted to be a subsidiary of any other corporate body or to have any other corporate body as its subsidiary. Although a credit union may have corporate members, those members are not permitted to have more than 25% of the voting rights in a credit union.[228]

223 CCBSA 2014, sections 27, 32 and 124.

224 CCBSA 2014, sections 33 and 24(2).

225 See Snaith, n. 218 above, p. 35; J.F. Wilson, A. Webster and R. Vorberg-Rugh, *Building Cooperation*, OUP, Oxford, 2013, p. 51; and A. Bonner, *British Co-operation*, Co-operative Union Ltd, Manchester, 1970, pp. 72–75.

226 CCBSA 2014, section 4(1).

227 CCBSA 2014, section 2(4) and Credit Unions Act 1979 section 1(1).

228 CUA 1979, sections 5A and 26.

5.2.2. *Role of Society Rules*

The CCBSA 2014 requirement that any registered society must have rules that contain provisions on the matters listed in section 14 of CCBSA 2014[229] applies to both primary and secondary cooperatives. The listed provisions allow for the registration of societies with other societies, companies or individuals as members, and they give scope for a range of governance, share capital, profit distribution and membership arrangements which can accommodate secondary cooperatives and associations of cooperatives for either economic or socio-political purposes.[230] However, as is the case with primary cooperatives, the administrative discretion of the FCA about whether or not a society is a bona fide cooperative governs the content of those rules.[231]

In section 5.3, the latest Guidance from FCA is used to flesh out its approach to this question, and in section 5.4 the rules of the two major secondary cooperatives in the UK, The Co-operative Group Ltd and Co-operatives UK Ltd, are used to illustrate how the flexibility provided by the legal rules is used.

5.2.3. *Agricultural Loan Cooperatives*

Section 22 of CCBSA 2014 specifically refers to secondary cooperatives in the context of agricultural and horticultural societies. It provides that societies consisting mainly of organisations of agricultural or horticultural producers or of persons engaged in forestry, like primary societies of that kind, can be registered to lend to their members without security if the society's object is to do so. That provision was introduced in 1961 to facilitate the use of primary and secondary cooperatives to finance the businesses of their farmer members.[232]

5.2.4. *Undistributable Reserves*

An obstacle to the full development of undistributable reserves by cooperative societies using the CCBSA 2014 legal regime is their inability to adopt an 'asset lock' which imposes a strict limit on the uses that can be made of assets. That device is only available to societies registered as community benefit societies or by the use of CIC's. Other legal devices such as trusts can be used to achieve the same result, but the inability of societies registered as cooperatives to use the device provided in CCBSA 2014 makes the achievement of a watertight

---

229 CCBSA 2014, section 2(2)(c).

230 See, in particular, CCBSA 2014, section 14, paras. 4 'Membership', 5 'Meetings, voting and changes to rules', 6 'Committees and officers', 7 'Maximum shareholding', 8 'Borrowing powers, etc.', 9 'Shares', and 12 'Application of profits'.

231 CCBSA 2014, section 2(2)(a).

232 Industrial and Provident Societies Act 1961, section 2.

dedication of a cooperative's assets to particular purposes more difficult and expensive to achieve than is the case for a community benefit society registered under the same regime or for a CIC used with cooperative democratic control built into its constitution.[233]

5.2.5. *Group Accounts*

The most detailed treatment of secondary cooperatives and groups is to be found in the provisions on Group Accounts. A society which has one or more subsidiaries at the end of a year of account must ensure that group accounts are prepared for that year.[234] The group accounts must give a true and fair view of the state of affairs and income and expenditure of the group as whole so far as the members of the society are concerned.[235]

To decide whether a society has a subsidiary, CCBSA, s100 lays down tests applicable to companies and other societies which are to be used to decide whether, in each case, the body is a subsidiary. In the case of a company, it will be deemed to be a subsidiary of a society if the society either is a member of the company and controls the composition of its board or holds more than half of the nominal value of the company's equity share capital.[236]

Slightly different rules apply to decide whether a society has another society as a subsidiary. The first test is that the society is a member of the other society and controls the composition of its committee.[237] The other test is one of control of the votes to which members are entitled under its rules. If a majority of votes can be cast by another society, then the society is a subsidiary of that society. In a secondary cooperative in which the one person, one vote principle does not apply, it is possible for another society to hold control in that way.[238]

5.2.6. *Reorganisation*

CCBSA 2014 provides for the reorganisation of societies and permits inter-cooperation by merger. That is a highly integrated form of inter cooperation and requires the agreement of the members of at least one of the societies by special majority. When two or more societies amalgamate, they create an amalgamated, or merged, society in which the historical identities of each are consolidated. The register of each society is updated to show that the amalgamation has taken

---

233 CCBSA 2014, section 29 and the Community Benefit Societies (Restriction on Use of Assets) Regulations 2006 SI 2006/264.
234 CCBSA 2014, section 98(1) and (2).
235 CCBSA 2014, section 98(3).
236 CCBSA 2014, section 100(1).
237 CCBSA 2014, section 101(1)(a).
238 CCBSA 2014, section 101(1)(b).

place. A similar result can be achieved by one society transferring all its assets and liabilities to another society by following the 'transfer of engagements' procedure. Both procedures require the same majorities and procedures but, when engagements are transferred, the transferring society needs to apply to be struck off the register after the full transfer of assets and liabilities and the transferor society remains in existence.

For an amalgamation, each society passes a special resolution as defined in the CCBSA 2014.[239] The result of this is that the property of each of the amalgamating societies becomes vested in the amalgamated society without the need for any form of conveyance other than that contained in the special resolution. It is possible to achieve this with or without any dissolution or division of the funds of all or any of the societies. In effect, the amalgamated society steps into the shoes of the amalgamating societies as if it had always been there. The assets and liabilities of the merging entities vest in the amalgamated society without the need for any conveyancing of land held or without the need to novate or assign contracts.

The effective date of amalgamation is, ordinarily, the date of the registration of the last of the resolutions received by the FCA from the amalgamating societies and not a date fixed by the societies if that date is earlier.[240] However, arrangements can usually be made with the FCA if a special date for the adoption of the resolutions is required for accountancy or other purposes. When the last special resolution is registered, the FCA will issue an acknowledgment of registration of the amalgamated society.

An amalgamation of societies does not prejudice the rights of creditors of the societies amalgamating.[241] This preserves in full their rights to security, their priority, and their right to sue for debts. In the unlikely event that the amalgamation involves any distribution of assets or cash payment to members, they may seek to protect themselves by using any security that they have.

When one society transfers its engagements to another, the transferor society usually loses its separate legal existence but the transferee society continues unchanged. This is achieved by a special resolution of the transferring society to transfer its engagements to the other registered society, which undertakes to fulfil them.[242] If, and to the extent that, the resolution approves the transfer of the whole or part of the transferring society's assets to the transferee society, it vests those assets in the transferee without any other conveyance or transfer.[243] It is usual for all assets to be transferred.

239 CCBSA 2014, section 109.
240 CCBSA 2014, section 111(7).
241 CCBSA 2014, section 109(5).
242 CCBSA 2014, section 110.
243 CCBSA 2014, section 110(2).

The registration of the transferor society is then cancelled at its own request, after it certifies to the FCA that all its assets have been transferred to those entitled to them.[244] The dissolution of the transferring society is not strictly necessary, but partial transfers are unusual because agreeing exactly which assets to transfer is complex and expensive. The CCBSA 2014 only refers to a partial transfer of assets but seems to contemplate a transfer of all engagements.[245]

'Engagements' means 'business undertakings' and includes all liabilities to and rights against both members and third parties. The transfer of property appears to be optional as CCBSA 2014 permits property transfers to be approved in the resolution and provides that if that is done, property vests in the transferee society.[246] The agreement of the transferee society to the transfer of engagements and its agreement to fulfil them is necessary as a precondition to passing a valid resolution as only 'any other registered society which may undertake to fulfil those engagements' can be a transferee.[247]

The meaning of a 'transfer of engagements' is important. The powers of the board are defined in the rules of most societies so as to enable it to exercise any power of the society. This enables the board to sell the assets of the society or any businesses owned by it (with both assets and liabilities). However, CCSBA 2014 lays down statutory rules and procedures requiring a special majority of the members and two general meetings to decide on a 'transfer of engagements' either to another society or a company. The power to do so therefore cannot be exercised by the board alone, whatever society rules may say.

Even in the case of a transfer of engagements by, or an amalgamation of, a society involving another society, members must agree by a two thirds majority of those voting and so are protected from change without their direct consent. Where such a decision (or a conversion of legal form) involves a company, it requires a special majority of a 75% majority of those voting and a 50% turnout.[248] The sale of a large proportion of the society's assets by decision of the board is not subject to a vote by members at all. This gives the definition of a 'transfer of engagements' its importance.

The statutory provision on transfers of engagements makes the transfer of obligations or liabilities a central part of the concept.

If greater member control is required, this can be achieved in society rules which are free to allocate powers and functions between the board and the general meeting so as to require member consent for acquisitions or disposals of a certain size or type. Similarly, there is no statutory requirement for the transferee society to gain member approval for the transfer unless the rules

244 CCBSA 2014, section 5(2) Condition A and section 126.
245 Compare CCBSA 2014, section 110(1) with section 110(2).
246 CCBSA 2014, section 110(2).
247 CCBSA 2014, section 110(1).
248 CCBSA 2014, section 113(2)

provide for that. However, in practice, rule amendments are often needed as part of the transaction, and this effectively gives members a vote on the question, normally with a special majority needed to pass the amendments. Unwise business acquisitions can be just as lethal as disposals for inadequate value.

The Co-operatives UK Corporate Governance Code contains the following paragraph on transfers of engagements:

> A board considering a transfer of engagements to another co-operative must satisfy itself that members' interests are safeguarded in transfer of engagements negotiations, and it must provide members with all the information they need to make an informed choice as to whether or not to approve the transfer.[249]

This provides a benchmark for the conduct of these transactions. The Code also recommends that societies proposing acquisitions, disposals or other transactions involving 25% or more of the society's members' funds should report to members at a consultative meeting, and it suggests that cooperative societies may wish to go further and invite member approval before such transactions go ahead.[250]

A cooperative society which became nothing more than a vehicle for holding shares in a company to which it had sold its business as its sole activity could hardly be said to be 'carrying on any industry, business or trade' so as to be registrable under section 2(1) of CCBSA 2014. This would certainly be the case if the society held less than a controlling interest in one company as its sole asset. If it held a controlling interest, it could be argued that it was carrying on business through that subsidiary company.

The effective date of the transfer is the date of registration of the special resolution by the FCA.[251]

5.3. FCA GUIDANCE AND INTERCOOPERATION

Paragraph 4.4 of FCA Guidance 2015 outlines the key requirements for registration as a cooperative. These 'are partially aligned to' the ICA Principles and are set out in full in Appendix 1 to the FCA Guidance. Accordingly, they require one member/one vote for primary cooperatives but accept that in secondary cooperatives it may be fairer to base voting on trade between societies. They also accept that member votes may be weighted in a way different from one member/one vote in multi-stakeholder or hybrid cooperatives with

---

249 Co-operatives UK, *Corporate Governance Code for Consumer Co-operative Societies*, November 2013 (CUK Code 2013), para. 23 on p. 8.

250 Ibid. para. 24 on p. 8.

251 CCBSA 2014, section 111(7).

different classes of member. However, the aim of any departure from the one member/one vote principle must be the protection of non-investor member rights, and measures that link votes to the amount held in shares will not be accepted. In addition, paragraph 4.5. provides that 'subsidiaries wholly owned by a co-operative parent should still remain fully committed to the co-operative values and principles'. Paragraph 4.6 adds the qualification that a society will; not 'generally' be considered a cooperative if most of its goods or services are sold or delivered to non-members, its business benefits non-members and more than 25% of the members are simply investors and have no other relationship with the society.

5.4. THE MAIN EXAMPLES OF UK INTER-COOPERATION

5.4.1. Cooperatives UK

As the successor organisation to the Co-operative Union, Co-operatives UK is the trade association and campaigning organisation of the UK cooperative movement. It includes, cooperatives of all types and federations and associations of cooperatives, as well as cooperative development organisations among its membership. As a result, its rules provide an example of inter-cooperation under the law for those purposes.[252]

Rule 2 sets out the purpose of the organisation:

> The purpose of the Society is to be a successful co-operative enterprise providing support for the creation and maintenance of businesses and enterprises which:
>
> reflect the aspirations of the founders of the Society to the creation of a Co-operative Commonwealth; and
>
> are founded upon principles of social justice and democratic control, such as the International Co-operative Alliance ('ICA') Statement on the Co-operative Identity, the Co-operative Principles published from time to time by the ICA or the principles of common ownership contained in the Industrial Common Ownership Act 1976.

Its objects include spreading knowledge about, and promoting the values and principles of, cooperation; supporting the growth and development of enterprises based on principles of social justice and democratic control; representing its membership at a national level and with the European and international cooperative movements; promoting the interests of its members and the principles of social justice and democratic control at all levels of

[252] Co-operatives UK Rulebook 2013, http://www.uk.coop/sites/default/files/uploads/attachments/rule_book_2_1.pdf last visited 24.04.16.

government including local, regional, national and European; strengthening and enlarging the cooperative movement; and fostering a sense of shared ownership and interdependence amongst its members.[253]

Membership is open to bodies corporate (which includes societies, companies and LLPs), firms and organisations on the basis that they support that purpose and cooperative principles and practice. Member groupings for voting purposes include: consumer cooperatives; worker-owned cooperatives; enterprise-owned cooperatives (including consortia, agricultural and secondary cooperatives); mixed ownership cooperatives such as multi-stakeholder cooperatives; mutuals; cooperative development bodies; federations and associations representing sectoral cooperative or mutual interests; and, even more broadly, associate members.[254] The governance rights of worker and consumer cooperatives and cooperative development bodies in the Co-operative UK Rules can only be changed by a general meeting resolution or referendum, but the rights of other categories of member are fixed by the board from time to time.[255]

Each member holds only one non-withdrawable and non-transferable share of 25p and must pay an annual subscription based on their trade with the society and the scale of their business. Subscription levels are fixed by the board according to the categories of member.[256] Membership sections are established to form the basis of meetings, voting rights, and the election of directors. Every member has one vote by virtue of their membership plus extra votes in proportion to their subscriptions (calculated twice yearly), with a cap of 40% of total votes.[257]

The Co-operatives UK board consists of at least 32 members appointed in various numbers (fixed in the rules) by different categories of member and according to the size of the larger consumer cooperatives. The Co-operative Group appoints six, the two next largest consumer cooperatives appoint one each, and other consumer cooperatives appoint four between them. Two represent worker cooperatives. Mixed ownership cooperatives, enterprise owned cooperatives, non-retail consumer cooperatives, members that are federations, and cooperative development bodies have one director each. That division of board places is reviewed every four years, but any proposed change must be agreed, like other rule amendments, by the society general meeting by a two thirds majority based on the sections' weighted voting rights.[258]

Profits are not distributed to members but held in a reserve fund for the pursuit of the purposes of the society.[259] On dissolution, any surplus is passed

---

253 Co-operatives UK Rulebook 2013, rule 3.
254 Ibid. rules 6 and 7.
255 Ibid. rule 8.
256 Ibid. rules 12 and 13.
257 Ibid. rule 26.
258 Ibid. rule 28.
259 Ibid. rule 56.

to a cooperative which pursues the same objectives and purpose or to a member society with a similar rule preventing surplus distribution to its own members, in each case chosen by the members in general meeting.[260]

5.4.2. *The Co-operative Group*

The Co-operative Group is the successor organisation to the Co-operative Wholesale Societies of England and Scotland and from the middle of the twentieth society increasingly developed as a primary consumer cooperative with individual members. As a result, is has developed a hybrid structure with individual consumer members and other independent cooperatives as members.[261] Since October 2014 the Co-operative Group has had a completely new governance system, and its revised rules implement that. However, the new rules still reflect the hybrid nature of the Group as consisting of both individual members and corporate members.[262]

The purpose of the Group is 'to serve its Members by carrying on business as a co-operative for the benefit of its Members in accordance with the Values and Principles' and in accordance with any agreed expression of purpose recommended by the board and council from time to time and approved by ordinary resolution of the members' meeting.[263] Its objects and powers are to operate businesses 'in accordance with its purpose'.[264] The governance structure involves an allocation of powers between the members' general meeting, a council and the board. The board consists of seven independent non-executive directors nominated by the board after a recommendation by its Nominations Committee and endorsed or rejected by a majority vote at the general meeting without a contested election. A minority of four directors are nominated by members and elected in contested elections in which all members can vote. Two directors can be executive directors (the Chief Executive and one other).

In the election process, individual members who meet a minimum purchasing qualification have one vote each across the whole society but collectively hold a proportion of votes determined by the trade of individual members as a whole as a proportion of total trade. Independent society members each have a number of votes depending on their trade with the society. That same voting process applies in society general meetings and in referenda about

---

260 Ibid. rule 76.

261 See Wilson, Webster and Vorberg-Rugh, n. 225 above, for a thorough and up-to-date analysis of the development of the Group.

262 Rules of Co-operative Group Ltd, May 2015, http://www.co-operative.coop/PageFiles/350358825/Co-operative-Group-Registered-Rules.pdf.

263 Ibid. rule 5.

264 Ibid. rules 6 and 7.

resolutions and policy issues. Members not present at a members' meeting can vote by appointing a voting representative and instructing that person how to vote on each resolution to be considered at the meeting.[265]

The independent society members are entitled to fill 20% of the seats on the senate of the council. The council and senate operate as guardians of members' interests by vetoing certain rule changes and particularly any attempt to demutualise the society, reporting annually to the members on the society and the board's performance in upholding values and principles, and determining eligibility for membership. It also has extensive rights to hold the board to account by insisting on information, reporting to members on whether or not directors should be re-elected, being consulted by the board, and seeking to influence its decisions. It also engages in consulting members and representing the society. The purpose of these bodies is to provide members with recommendations and information to help them in exercising their democratic control of the society and to influence board policy and decisions by the power to report to members on board performance and whether or not particular directors should be re-elected.

[265] Ibid. rules 38–40.

ABOUT THE AUTHORS

Gemma Fajardo graduated in Law, earned her PhD in 1992 with the thesis *Economic Management of Cooperatives. Member Responsibility* and currently is a lecturer in Commercial Law at the University of Valencia. She is in charge of the field of law at CIRIEC-Spain (Centre for Research on the Social and Cooperative Economy) and has been co-editor of its Social Economy Law Journal, since 1990. She is a founding member of IUDESCOOP (the University Institute of Research into the Social and Cooperative Economy) and Director of his Master in Social Economy. Her research work has centred on the legal and economic system regarding cooperatives, labour companies, social business, on comparative law and European harmonisation of cooperative legislation. She took part in drafting the Cooperative Acts of the autonomous regions of Valencia and Madrid, has published many books and articles and has given lectures and a number of graduate and PhD courses in Spain, Europe and Latin America.

Antonio Fici is a Professor of Private Law at the Department of Law of the University of Molise in Italy. His main fields of research include Contract Law, Cooperative Law, and the Law of Nonprofit and Social Enterprises, with respect to which he has published four books, four edited books (including the *International Handbook of Cooperative Law*, Springer, 2013), and more than 100 articles and chapters in journals and books. He is a member of the Cooperative Law Committee of the International Cooperative Alliance, of the EMES Research Network, of the International Association of Cooperative Law, of the European Corporate Governance Institute, of the Society of European Contract Law, and Senior Research Fellow at EURICSE. He is a member of the Reviewers Committee of 'Giustizia Civile', of the Reviewers Committee of *Boletín de la Asociación Internacional de Derecho Cooperativo*, of the Scientific Committee of *CIRIEC-España, Revista jurídica de economía social y cooperativa*, of the Editorial Board of the *Journal of Entrepreneurial and Organizational Diversity*, and of the Scientific Committee of 'Impresa sociale'. He currently advises the Italian Ministry of Labour and Social Affairs on the law of reform of the Third Sector.

Hagen Henrÿ is Adjunct Professor of Comparative Law at the University of Helsinki and Research Director at the Ruralia Institute of that university. He has published on development questions, land law, comparative law and cooperative law and has been a frequent contributor to seminars and conferences in many countries over many years. He is member of several scientific associations and of editorial boards of scientific journals. He worked at the Universities of Geneva and Saarbrücken for six years and as legal advisor to the German Federal Minister of Economy for eight years. Thereafter, he consulted on cooperative policy and legislation in some 55 countries for governmental as well as non-governmental, national, regional and international organisations for 13 years. Before joining the University of Helsinki he was Chief of the Cooperative Branch of the International Labour Office (ILO) from 2007 to early 2011. He is the Chairman of the International Cooperative Alliance Co-operative Law Committee. The focus of his research and work is: cooperative law and policy, and legal aspects of new forms of public/private/civil society organisations/ enterprises capable of regenerating social justice as an integral aspect of the legal concept of sustainable development.

David Hiez was lecturer in private law at the University of Lille 2 (France) until 2006. After classical training in civil law and legal theory, he completed his PhD under the direction of Professor Philippe Jestaz (Université Paris 12), defended on the concept of patrimony in civil law (published by LGDJ) in 2000. He is currently Professor of Civil Law at the University of Luxembourg, where he served as Director of Academic Bachelor in Law and Director of the Research Unit. His research focuses on the areas of social economy law, European contract law and African law. He is member of the editorial board of the *International Journal of Social Economy*, a founding member of the Study Group on European Cooperative Law, and a member of the International Social Contract Law Group. He has recently published, in collaboration with A. Kenmogne (ed.), *Le droit des coopératives OHADA* (Presses universitaires d'Aix-Marseille, 2017); and *Coopératives* (Dalloz, 2017).

Deolinda Meira is Adjunct Professor of Commercial Law at the Oporto Accounting and Business School, of the Polytechnic Institute of Oporto, in Portugal. Her current work focuses on the legal framework of cooperative and social economy, which has been the subject of several scientific communications, monographs, book chapters, and articles. She is a co-editor of the Journal *CES* (*Cooperativism and Social Economy*) published by the University of Vigo, Spain. She is also a member of the scientific committee of the *CIRIEC-España – Revista jurídica de economía publica, social y cooperativa*, of the *Boletín de la Asociación Internacional de Derecho Cooperativo* and of the *Revista Jurídica Luso-Brasileira*. She evaluates scientific papers in peer-reviewed journals. She also engages in consulting activities and participates in projects about the legal framework of cooperatives and other entities of social economy. She was member of the Committee for the Revision of the Portuguese Cooperative Code (revision introduced by Law No. 119/2015, of 31 August), created within the CNES (National Council for the Social Economy).

Hans-H. Münkner 1962–1963: Training as co-operative adviser for developing countries. 1963–1972: Research fellow and lecturer at Marburg University, Institute for Co-operation in Developing Countries (ICDC). Doctorate in Law 1970. From 1972: Professor for law of business organisations and co-operative theory, Marburg University. 1992–2000: Director of ICDC. Areas of research: Development of self-help organisations, co-operative legislation and land law. Since 1992 patron and since 2009 Fellow of Plunkett Foundation, Oxford, 1990–1995 member of reference groups of the ICA on co-operative values and co-operative principles. 2000, retired from active service at Marburg University. 2000–2010 member of the Faculté Européenne des Sciences du Foncier, Strasbourg. Consultant of ILO, FAO, UNIDO, UNDAD, USAID, GTZ, etc. on revision of co-operative development policy and co-operative legislation in Europe, Africa, Asia and South Pacific. Author of numerous books and articles on development, policy and law of co-operatives, land law, poverty alleviation and alternative forms of economy. Latest publications: 2nd revised editions of *Our Co-op, idea – mission – achievements* (LIT, 2015), *Co-operative Principles and Co-operative Law* (LIT, 2015) and *Ten Lectures on Co-operative Law* (LIT, 2016).

Ian Snaith retired from his role as senior lecturer at Leicester University in 2009. He has researched and written extensively on UK and European cooperative law for more than 35 years and currently works as a solicitor through UK law firm DWF LLP. Ian has participated in many collaborative projects on cooperative law of which the PECOL was the most recent and the most comprehensive. A new and fully updated of the 2014 edition of Ian's UK text, *Handbook of Co-operative and Community Benefit Society Law* was published in September 2014 and an updating supplement to the book was published in April 2016.

www.ingramcontent.com/pod-product-compliance
Ingram Content Group UK Ltd.
Pitfield, Milton Keynes, MK11 3LW, UK
UKHW051917100926
8556IPUK00021B/1228

9 781780 684277